American National Security

American National Security

Policy and Process

Fourth Edition

AMOS A. JORDAN
WILLIAM J. TAYLOR, JR.
LAWRENCE J. KORB

The Johns Hopkins University Press
Baltimore and London

Published 1981. Fourth Edition 1993
Printed in the United States of America on acid-free paper

The Johns Hopkins University Press
2715 North Charles Street
Baltimore, Maryland 21218-4319
The Johns Hopkins Press Ltd., London

Library of Congress Cataloging-in-Publication Data

Jordan, Amos A.
American national security : policy and process / Amos A. Jordan, William J. Taylor, Jr., Lawrence J. Korb. — 4th ed.
p. cm.
Includes bibliographical references and index.
ISBN 0-8018-4569-6 (alk. paper).–
ISBN 0-8018-4570-X (pbk. : alk. paper)
1. United States—National security. I. Taylor, William J. (William Jesse), 1933– . II. Korb, Lawrence J., 1939– . III. Title.
UA23.J66 1993
355'.033073—dc20 92–35161
CIP

A catalog record for this book is available from the British Library.

Contents

Foreword

I have always thought that the expression "a crossroads in history" tends to be slightly misleading. It conjures the image of four roads, clearly marked and identified, meeting in a geometrically perfect cross, where the choice of direction leaves little doubt. Unfortunately, sea changes in history are never that clearly defined, but are marked by disorientation and confusion. As Vaclav Havel, the former President of Czechoslovakia, observed in his address to a Joint Session of Congress in February 1990, events in the world are moving so rapidly that "we have literally no time even to be astonished."

The rapid pace of change which has marked the past few years are indeed extraordinary. The end of the cold war and the disintegration of the Soviet Union has removed the greatest military threat to Western security. Unfortunately, the demise of this threat does not mean that the world is now left without dangers.

Many statesmen have commented upon the nationalistic—in many cases, tribalistic—passions which have been released by the end of cold war hostility. No longer constrained by competing superpowers striving for stability within their spheres of influence, ethnic civil wars have erupted in the Balkans, the Horn of Africa, and the Caucasus and threaten to spread across Central Asia.

The end of the cold war has also challenged alliances, once the foundation of the American strategy of containment. With the disappearance of the common enemy, America's relations with other nations worldwide are undergoing significant change as the purposes and structures of these relationships are reconsidered, by all parties, in the light of post–cold war politics.

Even the very "currencies" of power have changed. Although military strength will remain an essential instrument of American foreign policy, it has lost the dominant role that it held throughout the cold war. Its primary successor is the increasing importance of economic leverage. Some suggest that "geoeconomics" is replacing geopolitics as the principal construct of international relations. In an age of growing international economic interdependence, in which billions of dollars are transferred electronically in a fraction of a second and transnational corporations defy traditional concepts of nationality and citizenship, the strength and resilience of national economies will continue to have increasing influence in international decision-making.

Perhaps equally important are what some describe as the "soft" currencies of power—culture, ideology, and the ability to use international institutions—which allow a nation to "lead" or encourage rather than coerce others. Dwight Eisenhower once defined leadership as "the ability to get others to do something you want done because they want to do it." More often than not, this approach to leadership requires persuasion rather than coercion. With the world arena no longer divided into two camps, diplomatic relations are likely to be much more fluid, placing a higher premium on such factors. In fact, the victory of the coalition forces in the Persian Gulf was as much the consequence of such "soft" factors as American persuasion and moral leadership as it was of American military technology and expertise.

With the end of the cold war, America can retire the logic which informed and guided our strategy for the past four decades. The Containment Strategy, adopted in 1947, provided a brilliant prism for balancing ends and means—identifying which strengths to reinforce, which alliances to form, and which priorities to emphasize. Now, as General Colin Powell, Chairman of the Joint Chiefs of Staff, noted in 1992 "the real threat is the unknown, the uncertain."

Thus one of the greatest challenges in the new era is to formulate a new grand strategy to replace containment. In so doing, we must strike the proper mix of competitive and cooperative strategies. We must take account of the fact that in this new era America often will find itself cooperating with a nation on the political plane while competing fiercely on the economic plane.

Such is clearly the case, for example, in America's alliances with NATO, Europe, Japan, and Korea. We have entered an age of tensions between unilateralism and multilateralism in both international economic and political–military relations. In the economic arena interdependence is a fact, but there is great tension between two simultaneous trends: one toward regional trading blocs, such as the European Community and the North American Free Trade Agreement; the other, reflected by the GATT process, toward global free trade.

There are similar tensions between the impulse to use the military instrument of power unilaterally and the benefits of first seeking a collective approach. Since the end of the cold war, American forces have participated in both a unilateral operation (Operation Just Cause in Panama) and a grand coalition (Operation Desert Storm). Policymakers will have to determine that fine balance of when to avoid direct involvement in a crisis, when to act in concert with our allies, and when our interests mandate that we act alone. That, in turn, will require our tailoring our policies to fit the unique circumstances of regional contingencies.

The formulation of a comprehensive strategy in such a new and complex environment is not a simple task. Nonetheless, a new strategy that recognizes the dramatic changes that have occurred in international relations is absolutely essential for the future well-being of the United States. In this significantly revised fourth edition of *American National Security*, which captures the momentous changes of our times, Jordan, Taylor, and Korb have provided an invaluable aid for this essential task—one which deserves the close scrutiny of American policymakers.

THE HONORABLE SAM NUNN,
UNITED STATES SENATE

Preface

The genesis of this book was the idea from the late Dr. Frank N. Trager, who observed in 1972 that there was a crying need for a textbook on U.S. national security. His forecast was that, after the trauma of Vietnam was behind us, there would be renewed interest among the nation's faculties and youth in the study of national and international security. He was, of course, proven correct. He suggested to two of his friends on the West Point faculty, Amos A. Jordan and William J. Taylor, Jr., that they undertake the task of writing a textbook. At the time, there were many books on particular aspects of U.S. defense policy and several edited compendia of articles. By their very nature, however, none of them could serve adequately the needs of students at most colleges, universities, and professional military schools to gain a basic understanding of the policies and processes involved in American national security. By the end of the decade, nothing had been published that changed the early estimate of the situation.

In 1972, Jordan and Taylor completed a detailed outline of 160 pages and drafted the first few chapters. Thereafter, major changes in assignments and responsibilities denied these two the long periods of consistent research and careful attention that a sound textbook requires. Over the intervening years, as the project's completion was delayed, a number of people listed as ''Associates'' in the first edition contributed significantly to research and writing, as chapters were drafted and redrafted to serve as material for the instruction of West Point cadets and also to capture changes in the international system and the development of new dimensions in international security.

Finally, in 1980 the principal authors carved out the major block of time needed for a complete rewriting and updating of the manuscript. This effort was assisted by several people in the Department of Social Sciences, U.S. Military

Academy, who read, critiqued, and worked in last-minute research. Their contributions are acknowledged in that first edition. The penultimate draft was critiqued carefully and most helpfully by one of America's leading soldier-statesmen, the late General Maxwell D. Taylor, to whom we are deeply indebted for writing the foreword to the first and second editions. Various chapters were reviewed and critiqued by several distinguished scholars and practitioners—George Carver, Chester Crocker, William T. R. Fox, Lieutenant General Robert G. Gard, Jr., Alexander Haig, James Schlesinger, Lieutenant General DeWitt C. Smith, and Admiral Stansfield Turner, among others.

The first edition was very well received. Feedback to the authors and to the Johns Hopkins University Press was most positive; so were the published reviews of the book.

As Jordan and Taylor approached the second edition, they solicited written comments from many professors who had used the book in the classroom as well as from their own students in national security courses both taught at the Georgetown University School of Foreign Service. They asked for appraisals of strengths and weaknesses and sought guidance on additions or deletions. In general, the response indicated that the book should stay with its basic approach, updating only as necessary. That advice was followed. The second edition met with the same success as the first. *American National Security* became the standard national security text in the United States and was widely translated for use abroad.

As the time approached in 1986 for work on a third revised edition, the authors turned to their long-time colleague, Lawrence J. Korb, then dean of the Graduate School of Public and International Affairs at the University of Pittsburgh, who accepted the responsibility for sharing in authorship. Published in 1989, the third edition was soon overtaken by the dramatic events of 1989 to 1991. From the falling of the Berlin Wall to the Persian Gulf war, to the collapse of the Soviet Union, these events necessitated a major redrafting of previous editions. Thus in 1991, Jordan, Korb, and Taylor began the formidable task of completely rewriting this fourth revised edition to reflect the new realities of the post–cold war world and their implications for U.S. national security policy.

We have long believed in the utility of political cartoons to convey fundamental ideas and have used cartoons in all previous editions. We were very much impressed by the ability of one political cartoonist in particular, Renan Lurie, to understand trends and forecast events in a unique way. He has been a contributor to all previous editions, and for this fourth edition, involving the most significant revisions since 1983, our respected friend granted us permission to select from a wide variety of his most recent creations.

We three coauthors are also indebted to our colleagues at CSIS and Brookings who worked with us on this latest edition. Jason Schroedl managed the revision process and contributed substantially. Brian Bank, Kate Bullinger, Ben Ederington, Eric Greenwald, Stan Humphries, Kacey Knick, Paul Konovalov, Jason Lewis, Bill Murphy, Mike Palaschak, Marlene Perritte, Amy Samsel, Leonid Torti, Debbie Wengel, and Jess Zimmerman all provided invaluable research support and devoted long hours to this project. Special expertise was solicited in reviews of several chapters; thanks go to Maria Alongi (''Europe''), Jim Blackwell (''The Middle East''), John Blodgett (''International Forces and Peacekeeping''), Greg Grant (''Low Intensity Conflict''), Mike Mazarr (''Limited War'' and ''Nuclear Strategy''), Shawn McCormick (''Sub-Saharan Africa''), Jim McDonald (''Latin America''), Brad Roberts (''Conflict and Arms Control''), and Don Snider (''National Security Perspectives for the 1990s''). Finally, we want to acknowledge the inspiration and support of our wives—Polly Jordan, Louise Taylor, and Lane Stone—who have shared our commitment to education in the field of national security affairs.

Abbreviations

ABM antiballistic missile
ALBM air-launched ballistic missile
ALCM air-launched cruise missile
ANZUS Australia, New Zealand, U.S. (treaty)
ASAT antisatellite
ASEAN Association of Southeast Asian Nations
ASW antisubmarine warfare
AVF all-volunteer force
AWACS airborne warning and control system
BMD ballistic missile defense
BN battlefield nuclear weapons
C^3 command, control, and communications
CD civil defense
CENTO Central Treaty Organization
CIA Central Intelligence Agency
CINC commander in chief
CMEA Council of Mutual Economic Assistance
DCI Director of Central Intelligence
DG Defense Guidance
DIA Defense Intelligence Agency
DMA demilitarized zone (between North and South Korea)
DOD Department of Defense
DPRC Defense Policy Review Committee
D.P.R.K. Democratic People's Republic of Korea (North Korea)
DRB Defense Resources Board

D.R.V.	Democratic Republic of Vietnam (North Vietnam)
EC	European Economic Community
EFA	European fighter aircraft
FBS	forward-based systems
FEBA	forward edge of the battle area
FOFA	follow-on-forces attack
FY	fiscal year
FYDP	Five-Year Defense Program
GAO	Government Accounting Office
GLCM	ground-launched cruise missile
GNP	gross national product
HUMINT	human intelligence
ICBM	intercontinental ballistic missile
IG	Interdepartmental Group
INF	intermediate-range nuclear forces
IRBM	intermediate-range ballistic missile
IRG	Interdepartmental Region Group
JCS	Joint Chiefs of Staff
JPAM	Joint Program Assessment Memorandum
JSOP	Joint Strategic Objectives Plan
JSPD	Joint Strategic Planning Document
LDC	less developed country
LNO	limited nuclear option
LTB	Limited Test Ban (treaty)
MAD	mutual assured destruction
MARV	maneuverable reentry vehicle
MBFR	mutual and balanced force reduction
MFN	most favored nation
MIRV	multiple, independently targetable reentry vehicle
MLRS	multiple-launched rocket system
MRBM	medium-range ballistic missile
MRV	multiple reentry vehicle
NATO	North Atlantic Treaty Organization
NORAD	North American Air Defense Command
NPT	Non-Proliferation Treaty
NSA	National Security Agency
NSC	National Security Council
NSPG	National Security Planning Group
NSDD	National Security Decision Directive
NTM	national technical means
NVA	North Vietnamese army
OAS	Organization of American States
OAU	Organization of African Unity
OECD	Organization of Economic Cooperation and Development
OMB	Office of Management and Budget

ONUC Organization des Nations Unies dans le Congo (UN Organization in the Congo)
OPEC Organization of Petroleum Exporting Countries
OSD Office of the Secretary of Defense
OTA Office of Technology Assessment
PA&E Program Analysis and Evaluation
PD Presidential Directive
PGMs precision-guided munitions
POM Program Objective Memoranda
PPBS Planning, Programming, Budgeting System
PRC Policy Review Committee
P.R.C. People's Republic of China
R&D research and development
R.O.K. Republic of Korea (South Korea)
RV reentry vehicle
R.V.N. Republic of Vietnam (South Vietnam)
SAC Strategic Air Command
SALT Strategic Arms Limitation Talks
SAM surface-to-air missile
SCC Special Coordination Committee
SDI Strategic Defense Initiative
SEATO Southeast Asia Treaty Organization
SIG Senior Interdepartmental Group
SIOP Single Integrated Operational Plan
SLBM sea-launched ballistic missile
SLCM sea-launched cruise missile
SSBN fleet nuclear ballistic missile submarine
SSN fleet nuclear attack submarine
START Strategic Arms Reduction Talks
TOW tube-launched, optically tracked, wire-guided missile
UMT universal military training
UNFICYP United Nations Force in Cyprus
WEU Western European Union
WTO Warsaw Treaty Organization
WWMCCS World-Wide Military Command and Control System

1

National Security Policy: What Is It, and How Have Americans Approached It?

1

National Security: The International Setting

National Security is a marvelously elastic term that has been stretched at times to cover a multitude of different issues and activities. Reminiscent of Dr. Samuel Johnson's definition of patriotism as "the last refuge of scoundrels," national security has sometimes even been invoked to justify or conceal illegal acts, as happened with the infamous Watergate scandal. But the term has come into such broad usage since World War II that, like a boomerang, we cannot throw it away. Clearly, it signifies protection of the nation's people and territories against physical assault and, in that narrow sense, is roughly equivalent to the traditionally used term *defense*. National security, however, has a more extensive meaning than protection from physical harm; it also implies protection, through a variety of means, of vital economic and political interests, the loss of which could threaten the fundamental values and vitality of the state.

Helmut Schmidt, former chancellor of the Federal Republic of Germany, was among the first leaders to note this broader meaning of national security by observing in 1977 that the decade coming to a close—which had included the oil crisis, monetary instability, worldwide inflation and unemployment, and other ills—had revealed, in his terms, a new "economic dimension" of national security. "By this," he said, "I mean the necessity to safeguard free trade access to energy supplies and to raw materials, and the need for a monetary system which will help us to reach those targets."[1] The chancellor stressed that this new dimension was an addition to, not a replacement for, the more traditional elements of security, such as military balances and arms control.

More than two decades later, Schmidt's broadening of the concept of security to include key international economic factors is now widely accepted. Indeed, foreign policy elements and national security are now seen to overlap broadly. A generation ago this concept was not widely recognized; one might then have depicted the relationship between foreign policy and national security policy as two slightly overlapping, but largely tangential, spheres (Fig.1. 1., *left*). One sphere was concerned generally with international, political, economic, scientific, cultural, and legal relationships, and the other sphere focused primarily on specific features of defense policy and the domestic politics of military forces and budgets. The area of overlap between the two resided largely in alliance politics and coercive diplomacy. Since World War II—especially during the period toward the end of the cold war—the two spheres of foreign policy and national security have drawn closer together (Fig. 1. 1, *right*), as strategic arms limitation talks began, political measures to contain East–West competition were launched, and international trade and finance and multinational business became increasingly "linked" with international politics. The suddenness with which the 1973 oil embargo impelled "interdependence" into the consciousness of political leaders and academicians alike, the breadth of the international debt crisis of the 1980s, and the upheaval in Eastern Europe have further pushed together the spheres of foreign policy and national security policy.

As noted, there also are important domestic aspects of national security policy, such as defense budgets and personnel policies. Domestic support, political and psychological as well as material, is the bedrock on which any national security policy is built. It is easy to drift from that self-evident statement, however, into a view that dissent from a whole variety of policies poses a threat to national security and hence must be suppressed. A chronic source of presidential difficulties with the Congress and, sometimes, the nation at large is the tendency to use the concept of national security very broadly, invoking it as a cloak to cover various controversial actions.

Despite such unwarranted domestic extensions of the term, national security does have important domestic elements. These will be discussed primarily in Part II, which examines the process and actors involved in national security decision-

FIG. 1.1 Relationship Between Foreign Policy and National Security Policy.

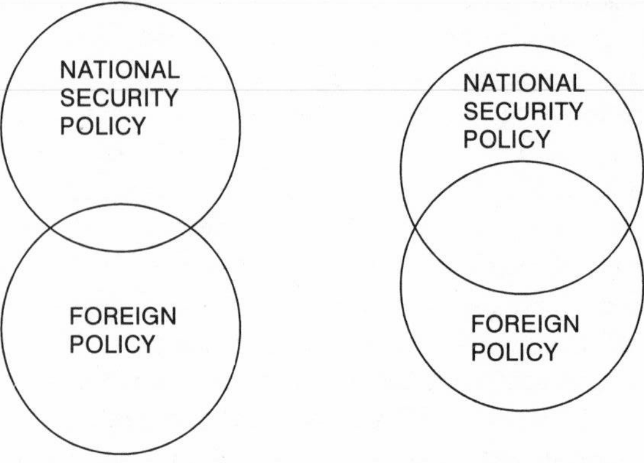

making. In the remainder of this chapter and the rest of Part I, we will deal essentially with the international dimensions of national security policy.

Theory and International Politics. If theory were money, political scientists would be among the wealthiest people on earth—and not among the nouveau riche. Theorizing about politics and power has abounded ever since the first person found reality too complex to grasp in its entirety and experience too limited to explain everything that happened. Members of every society from the hollows of caves to the halls of the White House have had to act upon occasion with a sinking feeling of uncertainty as to where chosen courses of action will lead. Yet they must act on that most basic of theories, namely, that effects do have causes and that changing the latter will necessarily modify the former. It is from this starting point that empirical theory has grown to its present immense proportions in all fields, national security policy included.

The number of political theories dealing with national security and international politics is so large that it is essential to divide them into broad categories. Stanley Hoffmann suggests a dichotomous arrangement between systems *theory* and *philosophical history*.[2] In the former classification he places theories that are suggested by regularities and patterns in international relations which lead inductively to testable generalizations. This category of theory, closely attuned to empirical methods of seeking to identify relationships between causes and effects, is also variously known as the *empirical* or *behavioral* approach.

In philosophical history, Professor Hoffmann places the "grand design" thinkers who, in seeking to unify large masses of historical data, have identified a principal cause or causes of international behavior. This group tends toward greater use of deductive reasoning, and it should come as no surprise that it includes the major ideologues of past and present. This category of theory is also known as the *classical* or *traditional* school.

A third group of growing influence, not identified by Professor Hoffmann, is in the minds of its adherents a synthesis of the best of both. In this company, called the *post-behavioralist* or *contemporary* school, are found those theorists who feel that the wisdom of the traditionalists is often basically valid, though incomplete and needing refinement. To rectify these shortcomings they turn to the methodology of the empirical school, employing its statistical formulations to verify and complete the work of earlier thinkers. In doing so, the post-behavioralists hope to discover both new applications and undetected limitations of established theory.

The most successful theories, measured in terms of acceptability and endurance, are those that best reflect reality. But since reality is different in the faces it presents to people in various times and places, it is no surprise that different theories have coexisted over the years. Furthermore, theories tend to be expressed in broad terms subject to wide interpretation, allowing for applications of a given theory in widely differing ways, some never imagined by the originator.

Theories centered on power—its acquisition, management, use, and balance—have a particularly wide following. Among proponents of various schools, the late Hans Morgenthau, the primary apostle of the "power approach" to politics, is generally considered part of that tradition.[3] Yet Morton Kaplan, a noted behavioralist, also used power as the basis for his various systems models, which identify the configurations that the distribution of power can produce in the international system.[4]

Other schools dealing with the general field evade simple classification. There are *man-milieu* theories, which exalt the role of environment in international relations; there are also theories broadly labeled as utopianist, economic, integrationist, decision-making, bargaining, gaming—and more.[5] The breadth of political reality is more than enough to furnish endless speculative frontiers.

Thus it is essential to simplify, to bring the bewildering into comprehensible pieces. This is the first purpose of theory. It is not enough, however, merely to simplify, for people engaged in politics, academia, and business demand more in order to achieve their purposes. As a second goal, then, theory must also help explain reality, demonstrating and clarifying the relationships that occur regularly enough to be identified as norms. This leads to the third and final purpose of theory, namely, to predict.[6]

It becomes clear, then, that the use of theory is fundamental to the subject of national security policy for two reasons. First, students and citizens need help in understanding; there is more happening in one minute in the world than can be grasped directly by anyone in a lifetime. Second, political leaders and elites must comprehend the reality in which they function; they, too, whether they realize it or not, rely upon theory to provide the basis upon which to act. The leaders are handicapped, in one sense, beyond the public or the academic analysts, for they must act within the limits set by their tenure in office, by their security in positions of power, and by events generated by others throughout the international system. Theory in their hands becomes the basis for the reality in which all of us live.

One can easily see how the theories of Locke and Jefferson have consequences for hundreds of millions of people, effects that are vastly different from those that flow from the theories of Marx and Lenin. The political results are even more awesome when societies guided by such widely differing theories find themselves technically competent to destroy the planet they share.

The Practice of Theory. None of the many international relations or national security theories thus far developed has seen totally consistent application. Moreover, experience dictates continuous revision and refinement of preconceived ideas, as circumstances arise that defy full understanding under existing theories. This experience then becomes the grist for new theory, as well as a critique of the old. The upheavals in the Soviet empire and then the collapse of the Soviet Union itself—events hardly predicted by any body of theorists—will undoubtedly give rise in time to new theories.

The generation that grew up shortly after World War II developed in an international system described by Western analysts as principally *bipolar*. That is to say, the political world was widely seen as divided for all practical purposes into two opposing camps, each camp centered upon one of the superpowers. This simplistic view had great attraction as long as both the United States and the Soviet Union were perceived as being unchallengeable, except by each other—with most of the other major and minor nation-states compelled to seek the protection of one of the giants against the designs of the other.

Reality, however, never was that simple. A considerable number of states, a group that grew over time, chose to go their own way as the "nonaligned" movement. The Soviet camp, where Russia's allies were getting "protective custody" as well as "protection," was never quite so solid as Secretary of State John Foster Dulles, for one, saw it to be.[7] Neither was the Western camp so solid as the exponents of the bipolar theory indicated. Dissent among even our principal European allies existed from the early postwar days. The French were adamantly opposed, first, to the formation of the Federal Republic of Germany and, later, to its rearmament. Britain, which never really recovered from the losses of World War I and the Great Depression, was often unable or unwilling after World War II to support American initiatives outside Europe if they detracted from efforts to hold the crumbling British Empire together.

The "orderliness" suggested by the bipolar theory could have been achieved only through virtual subjugation of all other states by the respective superpowers. But great as their strength has been in some respects, neither has possessed sufficient power to achieve and maintain over time such control—and the United States was unwilling to use, unrestrainedly, its power for such an end. The result has been that some autonomy always existed for the lesser states, and for the Western allies a great deal.

During the later 1940s and the 1950s, Yugoslavia and the People's Republic of China demonstrated by their breakaway actions the limits of Soviet power. With this cracking of the Soviet monolith, the further development of the nonaligned states, and the growth of economic strength and political self-confidence among U.S. allies, the bipolar era began fading during the course of the later 1950s and 1960s.

If changing circumstances have outdated and exposed the inapplicability of the bipolar theory, what has replaced it? Some theorists have suggested that the international system has returned to the earlier *balance of power* system wherein not two, but several, great powers compete for the realization of their respective goals. In this pattern, the several major actors, generally three to five, depending upon which theorists are consulted, vie back and forth, forming and reforming alliances to protect themselves against the hegemony of any one or group of the others. Historically, to make such a system work, there has had to be an exceptionally flexible major party willing to shift sides as necessary in order to preserve the balance. The "theory" springs straight from the experience of eighteenth- and nineteenth-century Europe, in which England played the swing role. As a political system, the balance of power arrangement broke down in the early twentieth century when England abandoned the balancing role and Europe moved toward bipolarity between Entente and Triple Alliance powers.

The balance of power design never was truly a world system, since it was largely played out in Europe by what were the major powers of the time. For a number of reasons, it is inapplicable to the modern world. Henry Kissinger has suggested that a contemporary version would include five members, the United States, the U.S.S.R., Japan, Western Europe, and China, (and perhaps India), but he has neglected the fact that there is as yet no Western Europe in a political or security sense; moreover, his formulation ignores the pervasiveness of ideologies in the current sense, which interfere with the free movement of potential balancers.[8] Also, the technology of modern weapons of mass destruction has allowed some states, specifically the United States and the former U.S.S.R., to deter attack upon themselves with or without allies.

The evident inapplicability of earlier theories has caused many analysts to speculate that the political world of today is neither bipolar nor balance of power in character but is instead "multipolar."[9] According to this view, several states are so powerful that they can largely ensure their own survival and independence without the aid of allies and are checked in their adventurism only by caution engendered by the presence of other great or superpowers with whom they must avoid general war or risk utter destruction.

Charles Krauthammer has suggested that, with the collapse of the Soviet Union and the American success in marshalling an international coalition to prosecute the Gulf war, world politics can be described as *unipolar hegemony*.[10] Although it is true that, in a purely military sense, biopolarity may be said to have given way to unipolarity, the United States is hardly in a hegemonic position. The diffusion of the other nonmilitary elements of power—particularly of economic strength—throughout the international system refutes this concept.

Joseph Nye has described a more complex international system as an alternative to various polarity theories, namely, *multilevel interdependence*. In this model,

> the distribution of power in world politics has become like a layer cake. The top military layer is largely unipolar, for there is no other military power comparable to the United States. The economic middle layer is tripolar [U.S., Japan, and Western Europe] and has been for two decades. The bottom layer of transnational interdependence shows a diffusion of power.[11]

In several respects, this is a heuristic approach, but its very complexity and the fact that some states are found at more than one level limits its utility.

All these various views of the world rely upon some estimation of the distribution of power among the several major political actors of the world. Each view has insights to offer, to a point; each tends to mislead when its proponents attempt universal application. The reality is that the varying levels of autonomy among states, their unequal abilities to influence events around them, and the different and changing priorities of the larger powers dictate that many members of the international community must find their own formulas for survival. This means that, in some regions of the world, reality more closely approximates the balance of power design, such as in Africa. In other places, bipolarity fits better. Central Europe was until the end of the 1980s one such bipolar region, albeit much looser on the Western side than on the Eastern. In a few cases, for example, India, Japan, and China, multipolarity is approximated, for on some issues and in some ways they stand apart from most others and can be checked in their policies only by a select few. Finally, there are some situations or cases in which none of the "power models" helps explain reality.

The Meaning of National Power. A considerable part of the disagreement among analysts of the international scene rests upon the absence of a universally accepted definition of power and the means by which to calculate it. This lack stems in large part from the fact that *power is dynamic*. New instruments of power have appeared continuously over the centuries, and new applications of old forms are always being found. Even the seemingly most backward societies can achieve surprising results under the guidance of strong political leadership, willing and able to engender sacrifice and a sense of purpose among its people. The rapid conquest of the Near East, North Africa, and part of Europe by the relatively few adherents of Islam in the seventh and eighth centuries is a classic case. Thus, too, the Soviet Union was able to rebound within a few years from its near destruction at the hands of Hitler to become the most formidable military and political opponent of the United States. Similarly, West Germany and Japan were resurrected from the ashes of defeat—in Germany's case twice in thirty years—to acquire major economic and political status.

What then is power? In the simplest terms, it is the ability to get others to do something they would not do of their own volition. All too often there is a tendency to think of power solely in coercive terms. Certainly, the ability to inflict physical violence upon an adversary represents an important type of power, but it should be recognized as just one of several and not necessarily the most appropriate or sensible form in many situations. Persuasion, based on common interests and values, and bargaining ability rooted in the possession of some desirable attribute or commodity (oil, perhaps?) and threats are also important forms of power.

Power can be viewed and appraised in several ways. Since it is based upon capabilities, power has certain objective characteristics. But *it also has a highly subjective element*, for the reputation for having and being willing to use power is sufficient to achieve results in many cases, without really applying it. Hobbes rightly wrote, "Power is what people think it is until tested."

Power is also essentially relative in character, for its utility depends in part on comparing it with whatever opposes it[12]; when this comparison is made explicit, the resulting calculus is often called *net power*. Further, *power is highly situational;* what may generate power in one set of circumstances may not in another. Such intangibles as the political and technical skills of the key actors, national will and solidarity on the issue, the nature of the issue in question, and the purposes being sought, all condition the power a state can bring into play in a given situation.

If power is dynamic, subjective, relative, and situational, as well as objective in character, can it usefully be defined at all? Despite the caveats and difficulties, the answer is "yes." Particularly if we focus on its objective characteristics (which are, more accurately, measures of "strength" and may or may not yield influence, as already noted) and qualify it appropriately for time and circumstances, we can say at least a few things useful about power.

In *Foundations of National Power,* Harold and Margaret Sprout provided an early approximation of the answer to the question, What is national power?[13] They suggested a crude equation: power is equal to human resources, plus physical habitat, plus foodstuffs and raw materials, plus tools and skills, plus organization, plus morale and political behavior, plus external conditions and circumstances.

In a subsequent article for the *Journal of Conflict Resolution*, Clifford German added his own arithmetical refinements to the Sprout theory.[14] He suggested that the factors should be weighted—admittedly in arbitrary fashion—before summing. His components of national power were land area, population, national economy, and military power; however, he weighted each of these so as to take into account qualitative factors. Thus, he adjusted actual land area in order to account for population density and for communications facilities; raw population was compressed, then stretched, to take into account age distribution, morale, productivity, and so on. To these square miles and heads per square mile was added a third figure—largely constructed out of industrial production data on steel, coal, oil, and the like—to account for economic strength. If the nation acquired nuclear weapons, everything up to this point was doubled. Finally, a multiple of the country's military personnel was added and a grand total obtained.

A similar, but more sophisticated, approach to "world power assessment" by Ray Cline used essentially the same quantitative factors as Sprout and German, weighted and manipulated more ingeniously.[15] Cline's approach improved upon the earlier efforts by multiplying the sum of various quantitative measures by a qualitatively defined factor compounded of "strategic purpose" and "national will." The resulting product, "perceived power," was again expressed as a number—apparently hard and suitable for comparative use but in reality as ambiguous and subjective as the numerous judgments that went into its compilation.

As a final example of this approach, the communist formulation of power, associated with the doctrine of the "*correlation of forces,*" deserves special attention. This Leninist concept contains the notion that a nation's "force" consists not only of its political, economic, and military strengths but also of the cohesion and loyalty of its people and the will and strategic vision of its leaders. *In contrast to the other formulations we have examined, this one is intended to have direct operational consequences: A true Marxist-Leninist is obliged to try to exploit every favorable balance or "correlation of forces."*

It is apparent from all the foregoing formulas that assessing national power is an art, not a science, and that any specific assessment will be open to a variety of challenges. National security analysts in and out of public office are inescapably faced with the task of identifying a moving and ill-defined target and of counting that which has often yet to be accurately measured. Still, policymakers in Washington and the rest of the world must act, however scant and unreliable their information may be.

Practical Assessments of Power. When decision-makers actually set out to assess power they invariably do so in specific contexts; that is, they engage not in some general, theoretical exercise but in a specific, situational analysis: *who* is involved, over *what issue, where, why,* and *when.*

Taking each of these questions in turn, the *who* element is crucial. Not only are all states not equal in the quantity of resources over which they exercise dominion, but the quality of resources also differs among societies, even if the nations are roughly equal on the basis of quantitative data. This is where the intangibles mentioned earlier hold sway. Health, education, motivation, and other factors all confound attempts to establish reliable equivalency ratios across national boundaries. Hence, Nazi Germany, while occupying most of the European continent and assaulting the British at home and in North Africa, still came close to crushing the Soviet Union. In fact, the Russians themselves had been sent reeling by the "weak" Finns only a few years earlier. Even today, Israel manages to more than hold its own against adversaries many times its size. The conclusion is that while no government can make something from nothing, clearly some can and do make much more with equal or lesser amounts of similar resources.

Making the most of available resources entails having organizational and managerial talents that enhance efficient operation, technical and scientific skills that maximize the use of resources and generate substitutes for resources in short supply, and, perhaps most important, leadership that is able to call up and orchestrate the other elements by instilling in its people the willingness to struggle and carry on, even in the face of imminent disaster.

This leads to the second element of situational analysis, namely, the *issue*. Its significance lies largely in the support or lack thereof given to national leaders over a particular matter. All governments depend upon at least the passive support of their citizens in order to function, and none can expect to endure once it has lost that minimum loyalty embodied in the term *legitimacy*. As long as a government satisfies the minimum expectations of the politically active or potentially active members of its society, there is little chance of internal upheaval.[16]

Mobilizing resources to apply to national security tasks requires more than passive support, however, it invariably necessitates some degree of sacrifice and active involvement. For some issues, such support may be difficult to muster; others have almost an electrifying effect upon a nation's consciousness, eliciting enormous willingness to sacrifice. The attack on Pearl Harbor in 1941 had such an effect upon the American people. The morass of Vietnam elicited no such support, even at the outset, and gradually generated quite the opposite. Between these extremes of support and dissent lie most national security policy issues faced by decision-makers. Under such circumstances, the leaders must themselves build support for those tasks they believe important—or resign themselves to impotence.

The third situational feature of power to be examined is geographic—*where events take place*. All states are capable of making some sort of splash somewhere in the pool of world politics, normally in their own immediate areas. Some countries, of course, make a more pronounced splash than others and, through ripples moving outward from the center, make their presence felt throughout a larger portion of the pool. No matter how large a given splash may be, its effects tend to dissipate with distance from the source. This latter phenomenon can be termed *the limited projectability of power*. The ability to apply resources at a distance sufficient to overcome resistance generated by those closer to the conflict area has always characterized great powers; it continues to provide a useful test by which to appraise claimants to that status. The states wealthiest in terms of the currency of power not only make the largest waves but are able to make them felt at great distances, regardless of countercurrents generated in opposition. Thus, certain actors and groups of national actors can be plaçed, *at specific points in time*, in a rough rank order of ability to influence, or power. (The phenomenon of proxy states, which will be discussed in Chapter 2, complicates the issue, but we shall ignore that for now.)

This introduces the final situational feature of power, namely, *time*. The interplay of leaders' ambitions and creativity, changes in resource base, the momentum of technology, and the public response to challenge all work to effect a continual redistribution of global power over the years. Empires acquired to the great satisfaction of their builders have overtaxed the abilities of their successors to maintain them, resulting not only in the loss of domain but in the collapse of the founding unit as well. The Soviet Union's demise makes this point dramatically, but both ancient and modern empires illustrate this phenomenon. Similarly, the piecemeal application of resources to what appears at each step a short-term goal may ultimately produce a long-term drain that adversely affects areas of national life not originally thought vulnerable by the planners. The effects of the Vietnam experience on the American economy, morale, and national will are indicative. Seldom in history—short of military catastrophe—has a power shift occurred more rapidly and decisively than in the decade after 1965, during which the United States slipped from world predominance to shaky parity with the Soviet Union, or than in the half decade after 1987, when the Soviet empire and state imploded.

Application of Power. Power for its own sake can be likened to money in the hands of a miser; it may delight its owner but is of little consequence to the world, since it is applied to no useful purpose. The American experience between the two world wars in many ways resembles such a situation. In profound isolation, the United States forfeited the initiative in world affairs to other states, principally to the traditional European powers and Japan. The reputation of the United States as a significant military power, established in the Spanish–American War and World War I, plus the geographic advantage of the oceans, served to protect the nation and its interest during this period. But reputation is a fleeting thing, especially for great powers that are identified in their own time with the existing world order. Steamship and bomber technology partially overcame the barrier of the oceans, while a foreign policy of isolationism eroded the American military reputation. Pearl Harbor and four very expensive years of war were the result of ignoring the relevance and uses of power.

All international actors, be they states, alliances, international organizations, or any of several other types of institutions that transcend national boundaries, have control over certain resources that provide them a power base. The power available to each participant will be applied by each in its own way to advance or maintain its purposes and goals; and, in the absence of a universal willingness to compromise on all issues, conflict between and among these actors is inevitable. Thus power and the will to use it become the prerequisite for success, even survival. This is the essence of power politics.

The purpose of power is to overcome resistance in an effort to bring about or secure a preferred order of things. When the resistance is generated by other human beings, the purpose of power is to persuade those others to accept the designs or preferences in question or to destroy their ability to offer continued resistance. Reserving to themselves the right to judge what type of application is appropriate in each case, national decision-makers use the power at their disposal in order to achieve the national (or personal) goals they have chosen to pursue. Depending upon the importance attached to the goal, the capabilities available to the respective protagonists, the skills they possess in applying those capabilities, the vulnerabilities each has in other areas upon which the opposition may capitalize, and the history of conflict behavior between them, the techniques of persuasion take either of two principal forms: rewards or punishments.

Rewards themselves are of two types: the presentation of some positive benefit in exchange for the desired reaction or the willingness to forgo some negative behavior in exchange for compliance. Threats in this context are considered part of the reward approach to persuasion for the simple reason that unless and until the threatening actor delivers on its threat, no actual harm has occurred. Either type of reward will work as long as all parties concerned feel they are getting something worthy of the exchange or are minimizing their losses in a situation where all the alternatives appear worse.

History is replete with examples of both types of rewards, and both are demonstrated by contemporary events. The 1978 treaty between the United States and Panama over the canal, for example, shows elements of both. Panama regained sovereignty over the Canal Zone through the treaty, while the United States avoided the disruption of shipping which would have resulted if the implicit threats of Panamanian nationalist violence against continued American control had been made good.

When nations in a dispute decide to carry out a threat, or initiate negative action without prior threat, they are seeking to persuade through punishment or coercion. Clearly, such persuasion works only if the actor being punished can avert its predicament by compliance. Therefore, the threatened punishment and timing and point of application must be chosen carefully in order to achieve the desired effect. To punish indiscriminately not only squanders resources, driving up costs, but also may be counterproductive in that it antagonizes and sharpens resistance by forcing a change in the perception of stakes.

Of the several schools of theory mentioned earlier, that which calls itself the *realist* school is more concerned in its central assumptions with the nature and use of power than the others. It is an old and traditional line of thought which lists many notable contributors: Machiavelli, Hamilton, Napoleon, Bismarck, Lenin, Morgenthau, and Kissinger, among others. Interestingly enough, many of these theorists were also holders of considerable power in their own day. What ties them together, across time and distance, are shared perceptions of the role of power in politics. From their thoughts and behavior the following "realpolitik" postulates can be drawn.[17]

1. Power is amoral, lacking in distinction between right and wrong. It can serve good or bad ends. Each actor, insofar as it is able, sits as judge in its own case.
2. The overriding common goal of all nations is self-preservation. All other goals and ambitions are contingent upon survival.
3. Each actor is ultimately responsible for its own survival. Pledges, promises, and good will notwithstanding, no actor can surrender its fate to another and remain even a theoretical equal.
4. Applied power (or the evident ability and willingness to apply power) is the chief determinant in relations among nations. Unwillingness to act invites others to take command of a situation.[18]

Naturally, if one accepts these precepts as true, one becomes predisposed to act in certain ways: first, because it is assumed to be the correct way to behave and, second, because it is expected that other actors will behave that way. Readiness to come halfway or more than halfway, the realists contend with a good amount of historical support, will always be construed as weakness to be exploited by those ready and able to do so.

Alternative Approaches to National Security. Since power is widely distributed among the world's many actors and is of limited projectability, none of the participants is entirely self-sufficient; none is perfectly capable of fully satisfying its perceived national security needs. Therefore, at one time or another, all have found it necessary to resort to one of several devices or approaches to compensate for national inadequacies. Principal among these are collective security, alliances and coalitions, and international law.

Collective Security. Collective security arrangements on a global basis, as embodied in the League of Nations and the United Nations, advance the hope that peace can be preserved if all states are prepared to unite in opposition to aggression. Under such an approach, an attack upon one member is taken as an attack upon all, with the expectation that such a united opposition would deter any would-be aggressor. In order for the concept to work, however, this design must have the unconditional support of all or virtually all the major power holders in the system, and this, in turn, is contingent upon their satisfaction with the status quo—or their agreement on its replacement. This never has been, nor is it now, the case. The result is that collective security in any universal sense does not now exist, nor does it seem likely to come to exist, given the sovereign state system and the inequalities within it. This does not mean, however, that all attempts at security cooperation are doomed at their inception; indeed, the multinational cooperation evidenced in ousting the Iraqis from Kuwait during the Gulf war suggests that in a post–cold war era there is some prospect that international security cooperation can grow.

As interdependence takes shape in its multiple political, economic, and other forms, national leaders are increasingly recognizing that closer cooperation is mandatory for both the economic welfare and the national security of their polities. Industrialized nations recognize their dependence upon the raw materials of the developing nations; for their part, developing nations recognize the need to import the technologies of the developed nations. All nations recognize the importance of a stable international monetary system, which depends in large part upon multilateral cooperation and restraint. International sharing of the resources of the high seas and multilateral efforts to meet worldwide environmental pollution have also become important targets. These mutual interests hold the promise not only of adding significantly to international political stability but also of reinforcing the bases for collective security. Both interdependence and collective security are discussed in some detail in subsequent chapters.

Alliances and Coalitions. Because global approaches have thus far failed to find the universal consensus needed to support them, most states have found it necessary to seek the help and cooperation of one actor or a few others in satisfying their security needs. The principal reason is, of course, that the cooperative approach is a practical, useful one. Alliances and coalitions come to exist for very specific and defined purposes, which permit their few members to pursue a wide variety of other interests without disturbing the basis for the arrangement. Thus, strains between the participants are less likely to occur than in a collective security pact, where all are supposedly allied in the preservation of an order that inevitably favors some more than others.

Alliances, in the first instance, are designed to increase a state's power through the potential call on allied strength. But they can serve a number of other related purposes as well. Preserving an ally's internal security by providing it material and moral support legitimized by the alliance may be a key goal, especially if the alliance involves nations with relatively unstable regimes; of course, such a purpose can backfire rapidly if the government is toppled.

Using the formal and informal ties of the alliance to restrain allies' behavior is common; it is practiced by both the larger, more powerful actors and the weaker, subordinate actors in an alliance. In this respect, the access the alliance provides to an ally's internal political processes and institutions may be important to other members of the alliance.

The buttressing of a particular aspect of international order and the strengthening of the consistency of behavior among its members may be a critical function of an alliance (the Soviet intervention in Czechoslovakia in 1968 is an extreme example). Predictable, regulated patterns of interactions based on the alliance structures reduce sources of friction and conflict. Furthermore, alliances usually provide some form of institution which facilitates contacts and communication among its members. Clearly, alliances are complex phenomena that do many things and that may encompass many differing objectives of their members.

International Law. This third major approach to coping with national security problems is often dismissed as being without real effect in regulating the affairs of nations. This erroneous view can be attributed in part to a failure to understand the development and purpose of law. Law exists not only to improve the distribution of justice but also to make life predictable by providing all who live under the law with a code of expectations regarding the behavior of others in the system. In more developed societies, if that code is violated, the wronged party can seek redress through authorities whose chief function is to enforce the rules. This is *mature* law.

There is another type, called *primitive* law, which derives its name from primitive societies that have not yet developed centralized administrative procedures including law enforcement structures. Within such a system, the members accept certain practices as customary among themselves and thereby achieve the benefit of predictability. Certain things are done under certain circumstances because they have always been done that way, or because they were agreed upon in advance by the parties concerned. In the event, however, that the custom is broken or the agreement ignored by a member of such a society, the aggrieved party has no police officer or court upon which to call for satisfaction. The only recourse is self-help—to enforce the rule oneself, to seek the help of others in doing so, or to gain compensation or revenge by reneging in some other area involving the wrongdoer.[19]

The outline of primitive law describes the level of development of international law, which is also unenforceable and made up of both *customary* and *treaty* elements. *The former are those norms of behavior that have general acceptance* among most states, while *the latter establish specific obligations and responsibilities* between and among those governments that agree to be bound by them. In neither case is the commitment inflexible, and states continue to violate both types as suits their needs. The decision to do so, however, is made with care, since the violator may find itself called upon to enforce its choice over the objections of others, which returns us to the topic of power.

The student of national security affairs must recognize these central distinctions between national law in developed societies and international law if he or she is to avoid the error of assuming pure anarchy in world affairs. International law has an important effect upon global politics because it provides the framework for most of the political traffic among states. The secret of its usefulness is not in forming rules that cannot be enforced but in achieving a consensus among states to observe certain practices because to do so is in their overall best interests.

All three of these approaches—collective security, alliances, and law—have been tried by states at one time or another, sometimes simultaneously, to meet their perceived security needs or as means to advance national goals. Each approach can count both successes and failures in avoiding armed conflict. One principal reason for this mixed record is that it is not generally peace but security that governments pursue in the conduct of their affairs—security to ensure survival and to realize the betterment of the societies they represent.

Change and Challenge. This brings us to the final theme of this introduction: major trends and issues that dominate the contemporary international political scene and powerfully influence the quest for national security. Some of these themes—nationalism, ideology, and equality—have been around a long time. Other trends, such as interdependence, are new or are new presentations of older concerns that have been magnified or accelerated by technology and rapid growth. We have grouped these trends into four "revolutions," both for the changes they have already occasioned and for the potential they have to affect further massive change.

Human Revolution. Largely as a result of the breakup of colonial empires and of increased communications after World War II, a human revolution has taken shape in the mobilization of hitherto passive masses, particularly in Asian and African states.[20] "Nationalism" in these countries was initially the political expression of an intense anticolonialism, which sought to rejuvenate traditional values and cultures suppressed by colonial powers. It also was, in some instances, the expression of an identity that came to being as an outgrowth of colonialism wherein the administration of the conqueror provided the first semblance of unity for diverse peoples. A major consequence of anticolonial nationalism was to shift the focus of the masses from traditional loyalties involving family, tribe, and village to national government and to create expectations about that government.

Newly mobilized publics expected to share quickly the benefits so long enjoyed by their colonial masters. A new nation's government was therefore confronted with rather extreme alternatives: (1) quickly close the gap between expectations and reality, (2) find a scapegoat for the gap, or (3) violently suppress dissent. Often elements of all three were and still are employed simultaneously.

Meeting expectations through economic development programs is fraught with many economic and political difficulties. Yet failure to close the expectation–reality gap or to provide hope that it will soon close can threaten the fledgling government with a new revolution or coup d'état. In an attempt to buy time or to assert control over additional resources, the new elites may choose the scapegoat route.

Scapegoats may be domestic or foreign, but it is not uncommon to find both being utilized. The Nazi regime did quite well with antisemitism at home and international communism abroad in explaining away the plight of the German people prior to 1939. Stalin was plagued by capitalists, saboteurs, and counter-revolutionaries in need of shooting, and Idi Amin was surrounded by white, Asian, and tribal traitors who failed to appreciate all he did for Uganda. But whichever scapegoat is used, the primary preoccupation is to satisfy popular expectations and quell dissent. The principal focus is inward.[21]

The forceful suppression of dissent as well as the use of the more subtle techniques of censorship and propagandizing have become standard practices in many states, old and newly emerging. Overburdened with massive social problems and hindered in finding remedies by insufficient managerial and material resources, new rulers are often tempted to resort to coercion with a fine disregard for those "human rights" that helped fire the nationalist revolutions. Repression requires organized force in the form of armies and auxiliaries. That same military structure also provides defense against regional enemies and serves as an important national symbol for a regime still struggling to establish its identity and legitimacy. For all these reasons, the newly emerging states have shown an enormous appetite for weapons.[22] For their own purposes, ranging from political competition to balance-of-payments problems, the industrial suppliers have been prepared to feed that hunger. The result is that the world has never been so well armed as it is today.

Nor is the human revolution played out. As the population of the planet continues to climb, expectations seem to grow even faster; as material resources become more strained and costly, the legitimacy of even longstanding regimes will be tested. Disadvantaged elements in mature states also are increasingly demanding a larger share of resources and more voice in their distribution. Increasingly, peoples of all types of states, including the most authoritarian ones, are insisting on political participation and a measure of personal freedom. The bloody repression of Chinese demands for a more democratic order that occurred in Tiananmen Square on June 4, 1989, has only temporarily quelled that particular instance of "people power." Inability of governments to cope and violent fragmentation may be the wave of the future.[23] The quality of political leadership will be the deciding factor.

Ideological Revolution. Ideological cleavages within and between societies die hard. In the case of East–West confrontation, the intensity had abated in the 1970s and early 1980s from the level of the late 1940s and the 1950s—but it persisted until the Gorbachev reforms. As nuclear arsenals grew, and particularly after the Cuban Missile Crisis of 1962, leaders in both the United States and the Soviet Union saw catastrophic dangers in the deterioration of ideological competition into military confrontation. Moreover, it became apparent to all in the

1960s that ideological allies could disagree in terms of the traditional political concerns of national governments. Thus, China, in conflict with Russia over mutual borders and over leadership of the Third World, could refer to the "revisionism" of the Soviet "paper tiger," and the Soviets could refer to China's "irresponsible" conduct in foreign affairs. By the same process, France could withdraw from NATO military coordination, asserting that the only meaningful defense was truly national defense.

Both the Soviet Union and the United States learned that claims of ideological allies often raised unwanted responsibilities and sometimes generated greater costs than benefits. Finally, both the Soviet Union and the United States became increasingly aware of the advantages of cooperation in various fields. The Soviet Union needed the technology and agricultural surplus of the West and appeared to be willing to make limited concessions for them. The United States, caught between the tremendous cost of high military preparedness and expensive domestic programs, sought East–West détente as a means of reducing both the dangers of military confrontation and large military expenditures. All these forces of compromise, propelled by the deep internal stresses in the U.S.S.R., led to a marked lessening of the ideological element of East–West relations, ending in the Gorbachev reforms and the Soviet Union's dissolution.

Further tempering ideological divisions including the East–West cleavage was the birth of what might be called "functional ideologies," which are shared by increasing numbers of people around the world and which respect no state boundaries—though they are clearly more important in the West than they are in the East. Functional ideologies are founded in the widespread perception of common problems facing all people, regardless of nationality. Examples of such mass perceptions that have tended to have the driving force of ideology from the late 1960s on are the antiwar movements in most of the Western democracies and the environmentalist movement to bridle national and international pollution.

In addition to these varying stages of East–West tension have been the ideological cleavages between the less developed, "have-not" nations of the Southern Hemisphere and the industrialized "have" countries of the Northern Hemisphere. While there has been no common ideology with sufficient force to unite the nations of the South, most of them share a common background (and hatred) of colonial exploitation of human and material resources. By and large, these states are major suppliers of resources vital to production in the industrialized nations of the North and, therefore, theoretically have a power base from which to press demands. The success of OPEC with oil and Brazil with coffee have inspired other attempts at cartelizing resources for the purpose of gaining economic and political advantage—thus far unsuccessfully. The purposes of the international commodity organizations that have been formed have been, for the most part, to facilitate the exchange of technical and scientific data, the expansion of trade, and most recently production and pricing arrangements. This development could yet give new economic power to producers ("scarcity politics"), but that seems doubtful. In any case, this threat to industrial consumers has to a degree been offset by the current tendency for such associations to include both producers as reliable sources of materials and consumers as reliable markets for resource exports.[24]

The major new ideological divide is neither East–West nor North–South but of an entirely different character—of nationalism or, more accurately, ethnicity. The 1991–1992 bloodletting in Yugoslavia is but one dramatic example of the tendency of national or subnational groups, based on race, language, and culture, to insist on self-determination and complete freedom of action—often at the expense of others. In the contemporary world these claims can be explosive. As Nye has pointed out,

> Less than ten percent of the 170 states in today's world are ethnically homogeneous. Only half have one ethnic group that accounts for as much as 75 percent of their population. Most of the republics of the former Soviet Union have significant minorities and many have disputed borders. Africa is a continent of a thousand ethnic and linguistic peoples squeezed within and across some forty-odd states. Once such states are called into question, it is difficult to see where the process ends.[25]

Technological Revolution. Technological development carries with it forces for both international stability and instability. Which impact occurs at any point in time will depend upon the ability of people to assimilate the products of technology and to adjust to the changes it generates. Assimilation has been increasingly difficult, for the rate of technological development staggers the imagination. One astute observer at the beginning of the 1970s noted the astonishing pace of change, as follows:

> In the brief lifetime of protesting youth today, we have had four major epochs—the atomic age, the computer age, the space age, and the bioengineering age, or DNA age. Each of them is as significant as the Bronze Age, the Iron Age, the Renaissance, or the Industrial Revolution, and all have been telescoped into the postwar years.[26]

The communications and transportation revolutions have made it possible to contact any part of the world in minutes and to travel to any part of the world in hours. The arena of diplomacy has quickly and dramatically been collapsed. Political decisions can be communicated instantaneously from heads of state to resident ambassadors (reducing their discretion), as well as between heads of state.

Political differences among states can be sharpened more quickly; so, too, can mutual interests. Yet, the ability to communicate decisions more quickly tends to reduce the time available for making decisions. "Muddling through," or letting difficult situations resolve themselves over time, becomes a less and less viable course.

Communications and transportation also have had a significant impact upon political mobilization of the masses. Increased contacts with the developed nations, through the news media and the travels of students and businessmen, have in particular helped shape the political and economic expectations of the masses in the developing nations. The communications revolution is systematically transcending the traditional boundaries between and within societies and in so doing is providing new and sophisticated techniques for propaganda and psychological warfare. The continuing advances in information technologies also present a continuing potent challenge to the closed systems of totalitarian and authoritatian governments.

In the short space of forty years, technology has yielded the nuclear means of destroying in a matter of hours civilizations that have evolved from the beginning of time. Yet nuclear energy will probably play a role in the solution of one of industrial society's most critical problems—finding alternatives to the dwindling supplies of fossil fuels, energy sources that increasingly pollute the world environment. The growing danger of proliferation of nuclear weapons compounds the problem of finding ways to use the power of the atom constructively.

The total impact of the post–World War II technological revolution cannot yet be assessed, but it is clear that the revolution has both simplified and complicated international politics. Technology creates an awareness of existing problems and leads to a complex of new problems, but it also provides capabilities to solve many of these problems. It can both exacerbate and ameliorate the problems of international cooperation.

The impact of technology has put social institutions everywhere in a state of flux. Part of the American experience with the technological revolution was summarized in 1973 by an American scholar.

> Fewer decisions of social policy seemed to be Whether or Not, as more became decisions of How Fast-and-When. Was it possible even to slow the pace, to hold back the momentum—of packaging, of automobile production, of communications, of image-making, of university expansion, of highway construction, of population growth?
>
> This new climate of negative decision, this new unfreedom of omnipotence was confirmed by forces outside the industrial machinery. For the atomic bomb along with space adventure and a thousand lesser daily demonstrations—the automobile and the airplane, radio and television, computer technology and automation, or the myriad products of Research and Development—were showing that the "advance" of science and technology, whether guided or vagrant, would control the daily lives of Americans. Not legislation or the wisdom of statesmen but something else determined the future. And of all things on earth the growth of knowledge remained still the most spontaneous and unpredictable.[27]

The real challenge of technology for the international political system is not more technological progress but finding politically acceptable means of harnessing technological progress to serve the common interest of humanity.

Institutional Revolution. By definition, "international politics" refers to the political relations among "nations" (or synonymously, "nation-states" or "states"). In describing the contemporary setting of international politics, we have referred primarily to the principal actors, that is, states, in the international system. Yet since World War II there have appeared so many new "actors" to be taken into consideration in the political system that one can refer to an "institutional revolution." These other actors are international organizations and transnational organizations.

International organizations can be categorized as *universal* or *regional*. Universal international organizations are described by the nature of the matters falling within their purview.[28] Those organizations with general competence to consider all aspects of the international system have been few, that is, the League of Nations and the U.N. Those with competence to deal with specific functions are many, represented by the so-called specialized agencies (e.g., the International Monetary Fund and the International Civil Aviation Organization), which have emerged as the international community's functional response to the social, technical, economic, and humanitarian requirements of modern interrelated societies.

Regional international organizations have grown as a response to communities of interest smaller than the scope of any world community of interest. Regional actors can be categorized as general or specialized. Three regional organizations with general competence to consider a broad range of matters are the European Community, the Organization of American States, and the Organization of African Unity. Specialized regional organizations have a narrower focus on economic, social, or technical matters. Examples are the Organization of Economic Cooperation and Development, made up of nineteen European states plus Australia, New Zealand, Canada, the United States, Japan, and the Association of South East Asian Nations (ASEAN).

International organizations had their greatest growth at the end of World War II, but they continue to proliferate. Their founding was and is based upon agreement among sovereign national actors, arising from shared or traded interests. This base constitutes an inherent limitation on the effectiveness of both general and specialized international organizations, especially the former. With rare exceptions, nation-states will not diminish their sovereignty by relinquishing decisions on important national interests to any "higher" authority. The European Community may pose such an exception during the course of the 1990s, but there are countercurrents of nationalism that could upset the collective boat as it steers through the economic, financial, and political straits ahead.

A relatively new addition to the international system is the *transnational* organization. It is, in both organization and function, very different from international organizations. Several important contrasts distinguish the two systems.

- International organizations are based upon shared interests among nations; a transnational organization has its own interests in many nations, which may or may not be closely related to particular national interests.
- Nations operate in international organizations; transnational organizations operate within and across nations.
- International organizations recognize explicitly the principle of nationality; transnational organizations seek to ignore it.

- International organizations are internationally managed; transnational organizations may be managed nationally, internationally, privately, or governmentally.[29]

Examples of transnational organizations are the Universal Postal Union, the Chase Manhattan Bank, the Ford Foundation, the General Motors Corporation, the International Television Satellite Corporation, and the Catholic church. These organizations are transnational in the sense that each is a centrally directed organization with large-scale operations in the territory of two or more nation-states.

Transnationalism could become even more significant for world politics in the future as both nationalism and internationalism encounter barriers. True, nationalism has shaped world order as we now know it, but interdependence is increasingly undercutting that base. Internationalism, after World War II, was seen by the framers of the U.N. charter as the great hope for a future peaceful world order; but the charter contains the limitation of dependence on consensus among sovereign nation-states with their own particular interests. Transnationalism on the other hand is based upon the interests of the transnational organization, which are virtually the same in any nation-state where the organization conducts its operations. It is conceivable that, within various fields, transnational organizations could grow so large and so important to the economies of nation-states that many states will acquire a major interest in the preservation and prosperity of the organization. Already, some of the world's largest multinational corporations, such as General Motors, produce more goods than most of the world's national economies.[30] Technology has provided the communications and transportation capability for transnational organizations to treat markets and production across national boundaries as if they were parts of a whole.

The future of the international system, whether toward a "new world order" or to a "new world disorder" or to something in between, is an open question.

Discussion Questions

1. What technological changes have "politicized" vast numbers of human beings in the past century?

2. What historical and geographical factors, unique to the United States, have contributed to its political development and to its image in international politics?

3. What is national power? Why were the United States and the Soviet Union referred to as "superpowers"? What are the indicators of "great power" status? Can you quantify national power? How?

4. Is it correct to say that a nation is a "great power" on one issue but not with respect to another issue? Why? Can you give illustrations?

5. What factors determine or influence the effective use of a nation's national power? What contributes to the effective use of power?

6. What is an alliance? To what alliances is the United States tied today? Why do nations align?

7. What is the role of international law in enhancing national security? How does

international law differ from national law? Who makes international laws? Give examples of international laws.

8. What impact have the human revolution, ideological revolution, technological revolution, and institutional revolution made on the international system? What are the indicators of each revolution?

9. What is "balance of power" politics? Can you provide examples of balance of power in action?

10. Does the emergence of economic interdependence indicate a probable shift to greater efforts toward collective security or does it signify increased efforts toward individual national security?

Recommended Reading

Allison, Graham T., and Treverton, Gregory F., eds. *Rethinking American Security: Beyond Cold War to New Regional Order*. New York: Norton, 1992.

Axelrod, Robert, and Keohane, Robert. "Achieving Cooperation under Anarchy." *World Politics* 38 (October 1985).

Dougherty, James E., and Pfaltzgraff, Robert L., Jr. *Contending Theories of International Relations,* 3rd ed. New York: Harper & Row, 1990.

Dulles, John Foster. *War or Peace*. New York: Macmillan, 1950.

Ferrell, Robert. *American Diplomacy: A History*. New York: Norton, 1975.

Gilpin, Robert. *War and Change in International Politics*. Cambridge: Cambridge University Press, 1981.

Gulick, Edward V. *Europe's Classical Balance of Power*. New York: Norton, 1955.

Jervis, Robert. *Perception and Misperception in International Politics*. Princeton, N.J.: Princeton University Press, 1976.

Kennedy, Paul M. *The Rise and Fall of the Great Powers: Economic Change and Military Conflict from 1500 to 2000*. New York: Random House, 1987.

Keohane, Robert, ed. *Neorealism and Its Critics*. New York: Columbia University Press, 1986.

Keohane, Robert O. *After Hegemony: Cooperation and Discord in the World Political Economy*. Princeton, N.J.: Princeton University Press, 1984.

Kissinger, Henry A. *American Foreign Policy*. 3d ed. New York: Norton, 1977.

Knorr, Klaus. *Military Power and Potential*. Lexington, Mass.: Heath, 1970.

Morganthau, Hans J. *Politics among Nations: The Struggle for Power and Peace*. 6th ed., New York: Knopf, 1985.

Waltz, Kenneth. *Theory of International Politics*. Reading, Mass.: Addison-Wesley, 1979.

2

Military Power and the Role of Force in the Post–Cold War Era

Chapter 1 portrayed international politics in large part as a struggle for power to protect or advance national interests and ideologies. National power was viewed as the general capability of a state to influence the behavior of others. Among the traditional elements of national power—geography, national resources, industrial capacity, population, military strength, national character, and political cohesion—military strength was cited as the most obvious, yet one of the most difficult to estimate accurately.

Military strength has as its basic rationale the contribution to a state's national security and the attainment of national foreign policy objectives. Practically every major sovereign polity has sought such strength. Indeed, until Japan chose to be the exception to the general rule by minimizing its military forces after World War II, the significance of a nation on the world scene had tended to be correlated directly with its armed strength.

> No "great power" in the present or past has failed to maintain a large military establishment and those states which aspire to great power status allocate a large portion of their resources to developing an impressive military machine.[1]

Yet this link between armed forces and state purposes is not the only explanation for building military forces. A military establishment has always been one of the trappings of "sovereignty," and heads of state feel compelled to maintain one as a status symbol. For some of the smaller developing nations, maintenance of a military establishment to influence external political relations appears to be purely a case of irrational allocation of scarce resources that could otherwise be devoted to internal development. In other less developed countries, however, the military has been instrumental in preserving internal political order and in fostering economic development.[2] Though interesting and not to be underestimated, these latter purposes—status, policing, and economic ends—are peripheral to our enquiry, namely, to elucidate the appropriate role of military force in national security in the post–cold war era.

The Nature of Military Power. As suggested in Chapter 1, it is a fundamental error to refer to military power in the abstract. To observe that the United States is the most militarily powerful nation in the world means that, contrasted with every other nation, the United States has the strongest military forces. Even given that additional precision, however, the statement tends to mislead; there are specific objectives, in certain situations, at certain times and places, that the United States might be powerless to achieve, despite its possession of great military strength.

As is the case with the abstraction *national power*, the term *military power* has little significance until it is understood in a specific context and is filtered through precise analysis. There are two quite different ways to assess the military problem posed by an adversary: analyze the adversary's capabilities or its intentions. The latter course is often taken by those who believe that potential adversaries "have no aggressive intentions" or who have strong reasons for wishing to cut defense budgets and forces. Certainly, if there are but a few, relatively minor, differences of interests with a potential opponent, intentions analysis is an enticing (though dangerous) way to proceed. A more cautious (and more expensive) way is to consider what the other side is capable of doing. There are two reasons for this. First, intentions can change for the worse for a variety of reasons and in a relatively short time. Second, one side may change its intentions for the worse if it senses opportunities opened up by the other side having underestimated it—for example, having taken the easier, cheaper road of assessing its intentions.

Both civilian and military agencies within the National Security Council structure are continually involved in military capability analysis and in providing the supporting data and estimates on the military forces of other states. But a military capability analysis, like a theater ticket, is useful at one time and at one place only. This is so because, as in the case of national power discussed in Chapter 1, the factors involved are dynamic—susceptible to constant, and sometimes dramatic, change. Further, factors are *situational*, varying not only with the given time period but also with the particularities of situation and geography. Finally, all factors considered in capability analysis are *relative* to other states' capacities to employ military means directed to the same objective or related objectives.

A classic example of the dynamic, situational, and relative nature of military capability is found in the Korean War. At the outbreak of that war in the summer of 1950, the United States enjoyed a virtual monopoly of nuclear weapons. One would think that American military capability was almost unlimited. If two atomic bombs dropped on Hiroshima and Nagasaki could end World War II with such finality, why not a repeat performance in Korea? First, the two cases were drastically different. By 1945 the United States had defeated all other enemies except Japan. In 1950, however, the Soviet Union was becoming an increasingly threatening cold war enemy. It maintained powerful conventional forces and had its own fledgling atomic force. In fact, the U.S. Joint Chiefs of Staff felt that the Korean War might well be a Soviet diversion and that America needed to save its small arsenal of nuclear weapons for the main Soviet attack in Europe. Second, nuclear weapons were not particularly appropriate for the Korean War, where the targets inside North Korea were essentially bridges and troop concentrations rather than cities like Nagasaki. Leveling Chinese cities after China's "volunteers" intervened massively would have raised the specter of all-out war with the People's Republic of China and perhaps with the Soviet Union as well. Third, America's allies, especially the British, and substantial numbers of Americans as well were strongly opposed to the use of nuclear weapons.[3] Obviously, the United States did not have in 1950 the same freedom to use nuclear weapons that it had in 1945; military capability had changed significantly because the overall situation had changed fundamentally.

Capability analysis is complex, requiring multivariate analysis. However, the following factors, illustrated at a high level of generalization, must normally be considered.

1. *Force size/structure*—How large are the relevant military establishments in terms of forces-in-being and trained reserves? How many people under arms are at the disposal of the various services (e.g., army, navy, air force, marines), in how many active and reserve units are they deployed, and how are the units structured and equipped?
2. *Weapons systems*—How many weapons systems of what types are at the disposal of the opposing forces? What is the potential of these weapons in terms of range, accuracy, lethality, survivability, and reliability?
3. *Mobility*—What are the locations of units and weapons systems? How quickly and by what means could they be moved to strategically and tactically important locations? How much airlift and sealift are available for overseas operations?
4. *Logistics (supply)*—Given the fact that military units can carry only so much equipment with them and must be resupplied if they are to remain in action for more than a few days, how efficient are systems of resupply?
5. *Strategic and tactical doctrines*—What are the nature and the quality of the doctrines of force deployment and military engagement that fundamentally control the employment of military units?
6. *Training*—What is the level of training of both forces-in-being and reserve units? How proficient are soldiers in employing their weapons under varying conditions? How skilled are forces in combined operations?
7. *Military leadership*—How effective are the officers and noncommissioned officers in the chain of command through which orders are issued and carried out?
8. *Morale*—A function of many variables and absolutely vital to success in combat, what are the levels of unit morale? Of fighting spirit? Especially

important for the armed forces of democratic nations, what would be the level of popular support for the employment of force in various contexts?

9. *Industry*—What is the industrial capacity of a given nation to produce military equipment of the types and in the amounts likely to be required for sustained, long-term combat? How quickly can the nation switch from production of civilian goods to war materiel?
10. *Technology*—What is the level of technological capability of existing weapons systems and command, control, and communications (C^3) systems? What is the status of technology of weapons and C^3 systems at various stages of progress in a nation's military research, development, test, and evaluation processes?
11. *Intelligence*—How effective are technical and human intelligence-gathering means? What is the level of competence in analyzing raw intelligence data and producing estimates useful to decision-makers?
12. *Popular will*—How prepared would the population be to sustain the domestic deprivations (conscription, rationing of various types, etc.) that would result from sustained, large-scale wartime activities?
13. *National leadership*—What are the levels of resolve and skill of a nation's leaders in managing a conventional war effort against the backdrop of nuclear deterrence?
14. *Alliance*—What is the status of alliances that can change opposing force ratios significantly? What is the quality of alliance commitments under various conditions, in terms of military units, weapons systems, bases, and supplies likely to be made available?

"Answers" to such questions establish the factors to be weighed and blended to produce a judgment of military capability. The analysis process is and must be continuous, for there is insufficient time available in crisis situations to gather anew all the data required for analysis.

No single judgment resulting from analyses such as just outlined can be made of how much "capability" a state needs—except, obviously, enough to achieve its policy objectives. The more useful product of such capability analysis is a series of cost/risk calculations, which, coupled with a political assessment of an adversary's intentions, can then form the basis for decisions about the preparation and use of the military instrument. Most major policy choices confronting decision-makers involve certain "costs"—material and nonmaterial, domestic and international—arising from the impacts of those choices. "Risk," in terms of the probabilities of success or failure, is also inherent in major policy decisions. Military capability analysis aids the policymaker in judging what costs and risks are acceptable relative to the values of the objective sought. The more important the objective, the higher the costs and risks the policymaker will be willing to judge "acceptable."

Uses of Military Force in the Post–Cold War Era. Assuming that conflict will continue to mark international life, a vital question for national security policy is, What are the most suitable means for pursuing or controlling conflict, and How should those means be used? The military instrument is only one such means, albeit the most violent and potentially conclusive of all.

Historically, military force has been employed for both the aggrandizement of interests and the defense of interests, although the distinction between the two has sometimes been more rhetorical than real. The nation-state system as we have known it is postulated on the ultimate right and capacity of states to resort to military force.

> The legitimacy of force as an instrument of foreign policy, although often denounced by philosophers, historians, and reformers, has rarely been questioned by those responsible for foreign policy decisions of their nations.[4]

By one means or another, military force has also been a technique for the resolution of disputes. But, given the possibilities of conflict escalation, the range of situations in which disputes can be "resolved" by the use of military force has been narrowed by the technology of the nuclear age.

What, then, can be said about the range of contemporary uses of military force? One can envision seven categories of "use," none of which are mutually exclusive. First, both nuclear and conventional military force can be employed in a *deterrent* role. Deterrence is not an invention of the nuclear era. The objective of deterrence has always been to prevent others from initiating an action that threatens a particular interest. Most people would agree that strategic deterrence functions at the nuclear level by threatening retaliation so severe as to discourage any rational government leadership from initiating a large-scale nuclear attack. According to some analysts, although far less probable, strategic nuclear weapons also serve to deter conventional attack by convincing an adversary that the costs and risks of potential escalation attendant to an attack would be higher than the object is worth. The same contention is sometimes advanced for tactical nuclear weapons.

Second, military force can be employed in a *compellent* role, that is, to compel an adversary to stop a course of action already undertaken.[5] The means of compulsion is the direct application of military force. The objective of compulsion is to hurt the adversary to the degree that it determines that further pursuit of its course of action would incur increasing costs incommensurate with any possible gain. If the application of force is tuned too finely, however, as was apparently the case with the gradual application of U.S. force in Vietnam, then the adversary may be able to take countermeasures that will mitigate the harm and avert compulsion.

Third, military force can be employed in an *acquisitive* role to seize territory or resources of others for exploitation or to use them for bargaining purposes. In view of the escalatory dangers, great powers may choose not to use their own forces but to employ the conventional military forces of a proxy in an acquisitive role, pursuing interests related to those of proxy states. (Of course, proxies can be used in a number of these military roles.)

Fourth, military force can be employed for *intervention* by one state in the internal affairs of another when a change in the other state's government or policy is deemed threatening to important national interests. The intervention might have as its purpose to stabilize a preferred regime against rebels or insurgents or to overthrow a hostile regime.

Fifth, military force can be used in a *counterintervention* role, to prevent success of another state's intervention considered contrary to important interests.

Sixth, military force may be employed by small groups of states in *collective actions* under authority granted by the United Nations or regional international organizations.

Finally, military force always serves as a *backdrop for diplomacy*. Louis XIV called military force "the last argument of kings" and so inscribed his cannons. The situations in which military force remains a final arbiter have been somewhat circumscribed in the nuclear era, at least in relations among nuclear powers and their allies. Accordingly, the employment of "gunboat diplomacy," the diplomatic use of force as a coercive instrument, has dwindled in frequency. Still, the opposing potentials of military force do serve to limit and regulate claims among states with competing interests.[6]

Constraints on the Military Instrument. The threat of resort to military force appears generally to have diminished in several ways in international politics. The deterrent value of nuclear weapons has already been cited, but many analysts would argue that, except for deterrence and prestige value, nuclear weapons are and should be unusable for other purposes, including diplomacy.[7] Thus, a threat by the United States to use nuclear weapons against a small, developing nation that expropriated U.S. property would not be received as credible. Neither, *as long as the United States—as the world's single military superpower—has massive nuclear forces and its national will and alliance structures remain strong*, would a military threat by any nation against an ally of the United States tend to be credible.

Constraints on the use of nonnuclear military forces also appear to be growing.

The use of military force historically has been a "prerogative power," reserved for the decisions of sovereigns. Beginning with the rise of European mass nationalist movements in the Napoleonic era, however, the power bases of heads of state have rested increasingly upon the support of the populace from which come the personnel and resources of mass warfare. Prior to the nineteenth century, battlefields were usually relatively restricted, for the most part touching only the lives of those directly involved in combat. The virtually total wars of the nineteenth and twentieth centuries—that is, the Napoleonic wars, the American Civil War, and the two world wars—changed this situation, bringing the carnage and anguish of war into the lives and homes of whole populations.

The communications and information revolutions have increasingly led to widespread revulsion (in democracies, at least) against the use of military force as a diplomatic tool. World opinion (or, more accurately, the opinion of the Western great powers) has for some time articulated its abhorrence of unrestricted warfare, codifying "laws of war" and turning to definitions of "just war," which had long been the province of theologians and philosophers. The League of Nations and United Nations both attempted to frame distinctions between legitimate and illegitimate uses of military force. Although problems of agreed definition still plague international law, "aggression" is outlawed and the use of military force for defense against aggression is "just."

Behind the development of international law concerning the use of military force has been an uneven and still weak—but growing—international moral consensus against virtually all international violence. The impact of such a consensus, and the world opinion that reflects it, upon the governments and foreign policies of nation-states has long been a controversial issue among students of international politics. Certainly, there is no unitary "world opinion" in the abstract, but there may be a near consensus among world leaders on specific international issues.

Recent history offers several examples of the changed international atmosphere in regard to the uses of American military force. In 1984 the Sandinista government charged the United States before the International Court of Justice with a breach of international law in the covert CIA mining of Nicaraguan Pacific Coast harbors. The international attention to this case (and sympathy in some quarters for the Sandinista cause) increased domestic pressures in the United States to strictly limit such paramilitary activities in the future. In the cases of brief, low-cost/low-risk commitment of regular U.S. combat forces, such as the April 1986 air strikes against Libya's capital and the October 1983 action in Grenada, the United States was again largely isolated within the international community in its assessment of the efficacy (and necessity) of military intervention.

In day-to-day diplomacy, an international consensus against an act of military aggression usually tends to represent more sound than fury. However, the longer-term impact may be quite different. As Klaus Knorr has pointed out:

> If a state flagrantly flouts an internationally sanctioned restraint on military aggression, it may, in the event of success, gain the object of aggression and in addition perhaps

> inspire increased respect for its military prowess; but it may also tarnish its non-military reputation and provoke attitudes of suspicion and hostility that, over the longer run if not immediately, will become organized politically, and perhaps militarily as well. This amounts to saying that the respect a nation enjoys—respect for acting properly, with sensitivity to internationally widespread moral standards, and with sobriety and restraint in resorting to military power—is a precious asset in foreign affairs. It is an asset that assists in holding and gaining allies, and generally in promoting a favorable reception for its diplomatic initiatives.[8]

The Bush Administration had internalized these factors in advance of the 1991 Desert Storm offensive against the Iraqi invasion of Kuwait and built a U.N. consensus to support the action, even before taking the case before the U.S. Congress for what resulted in *the* longest-standing foreign policy debate in U.S. history.

One might argue that the widely respected status of West Germany and Japan today disproves the thesis of adverse long-term effects of aggression. Yet it should be recalled that Germany and Japan are watched especially carefully by neighboring states, that Japan has rejected all but self-defense forces since World War II, and that neither state now has—nor is likely to acquire—a military nuclear capability at its discretion.[9]

Although international opinion clearly does not invariably deter the use of military force, as the 1979 Soviet invasion of Afghanistan, the 1982 Falklands War, and the 1989 U.S. invasion of Panama showed, there is another route through which world opinion can have a significant impact upon a state's choices regarding the use of military force. The communications revolution has made it possible, especially in the case of the democracies, for world opinion to have an impact upon the domestic opinion of a state contemplating or taking military action. What world opinion cannot accomplish by direct impact upon the leadership of a democratic state it may be able to effect indirectly by influencing public attitudes and national legislatures. Foreign opposition and criticism, for instance, had considerable impact upon American public attitudes during the U.S. involvement in Vietnam from 1965 to 1975. In turn, domestic public concern regarding "unrestricted" use of military force in that conflict resulted in the War Powers Act passed by the American Congress in 1973.

To the extent that opinion can influence decisions about the resort to military force, a new and complicating phenomenon has emerged in international politics.[10] This phenomenon, it should be noted, has little counterpart in strongly authoritarian or totalitarian states; Soviet military adventures in Africa and Afghanistan into the late 1970s and 1980s, and the Chinese and Vietnamese attacks upon their neighbors in the same period, do not seem to have encountered such indirect checks. But the subsequent withdrawal of Soviet troops from Afghanistan in 1989 appears to be at least partially a result of this form of check as President Gorbachev's "new thinking" began to erode the bases of Communist totalitarianism.

In addition to fear of escalation and public opinion, there is a third important constraint on the role of military force in diplomacy, namely, the high monetary costs associated with the military instrument. This problem is especially difficult for the more industrialized nations with advanced weapons. Technological sophistication has driven up the costs of weapons systems enormously. Costs associated with personnel requirements have also skyrocketed in the industrial democracies. Even after the breakup of the Warsaw Pact and disappearance of the Soviet military threat, defense budget outlays for the United States were $278 billion for fiscal year 1992, less than five percent of the American gross national product (GNP) but larger than the total GNPs of four of its NATO allies—Greece, Norway, Turkey, and Portugal—combined. The high costs of maintaining large standing military forces will be debated seriously in the United States in the 1990s as perceived threats to American national security change and as economic factors gain prominence in the calculus of international power.

Maintenance of a large military establishment and especially its use in war involve not only domestic expenditures but also payment for military-related goods and services to other countries. The costs of maintaining overseas forces have risen dramatically and, despite "Buy American" campaigns, "tied foreign aid" (the recipient must expend in the country providing the aid), defense "offset payments" by allies, and other measures, U.S. payments deficits reached crisis proportions in the early 1990s as Americans bought far more from abroad than they sold. Deficits generated by the military have added somewhat to the other massive strains on the dollar, thereby contributing to exchange rate instability and attendant political difficulties.[11]

Widespread attention to the high costs of the military instrument varies with the international climate. In recent years, the growing orientation of the industrial democracies toward the welfare-state psychology has refocused public attention on such costs.[12] In the United States, however, public sentiment began to swing back from favoring butter and toward guns by the final years of the Carter presidency; this swing supported the massive Reagan military build-up of the early 1980s. But the strength of this sentiment was not sustainable, given widely reported examples of waste and mismanagement in the Department of Defense, increasing federal deficits, and a slowdown in the growth of social spending. In the early 1990s, the American military establishment faced the prospect of very deep reductions in its budgets for years to come.

Alliances and Military Power. The numerous American alliances, treaties of guarantee, and military base agreements around the world constitute a complex alliance structure that is cumulatively a response to the various perceived threats to U.S. foreign policy objectives that have arisen since World War II. In 1947 the United States signed the Rio Pact, breaking a 150-year tradition of nonentanglement. The NATO alliance was concluded in 1949 as a direct result of the growing Soviet threat in Europe. With the outbreak of the Korean War (1950), the United States began adding Asian allies. In relatively quick order the following alliances were formed: U.S.–Japan (1951), U.S.–Philippines (1951), Australia–New Zealand–U.S. (ANZUS, 1951), U.S.–Korea (1953), Southeast Asia Treaty

Organization (SEATO, 1954), and U.S.–Republic of China (1954), followed by limited participation in the Central Treaty Organization (CENTO, 1956). Further bilateral defense treaties were signed with Iran, Pakistan, and Turkey in 1959. The United States added military base rights agreements with Spain and Thailand. In support of these alliances, the United States has dispersed military aid of billions of dollars to some sixty countries around the world and has deployed hundreds of thousands of U.S. service members overseas.

Why Do Nations Join Alliances? An alliance is a contract that like all other contracts, bestows rights and advantages but also places obligations and restrictions on the contracting parties. Unlike contracts in domestic law, however, nations have no higher authority to which to appeal when there is a breach of contract. The primary consideration of national leaders contemplating an alliance is that the benefits of the prospective alliance outweigh the loss of flexibility incurred in becoming dependent upon acts of omission or commission by other nations in the alliance. In this regard, Hans Morgenthau writes, "A nation will shun alliances if it believes that it is strong enough to hold its own unaided or that the burden of commitment resulting from an alliance is likely to outweigh the advantages to be expected."[13]

Faced with an international system best described as "semiorganized anarchy," nations seek various forms of cooperative behavior designed to generate strength and reduce risk. They pursue their national security in a selective manner in an attempt to produce the type and degree of international order that best ensures their own interests. Since power tends to be the common denominator in international politics, "the question as to whose values or ends will prevail . . . is determined finally by the relative power positions of the [opposing] parties."[14]

Three motives for alliances spring from this focus on power. First, a nation may join or create an alliance in order to aggregate the capabilities necessary to achieve a foreign policy goal (i.e., a nation's own means are insufficient for its ends). Second, a nation may enter into an alliance or entente to secure favorable treatment in the future; in short, nations selectively join alliances to gain coldly calculated advantages in the pursuit of future national goals.[15] Third, a nation may join an alliance to reduce the costs of securing its objective; that is, a nation, seeking multiple objectives, may not want to commit all or an undue part of its capabilities to any one specific end. Pursuing these motives, a nation will tend to judge cautiously in measuring the capabilities of nations that oppose its goals, acting to acquire more capabilities than may be objectively necessary.

As a variant of the third cost reduction motive, nations may join an alliance or use the structure of an existing alliance for reasons of defense economy. The situation of the NATO alliance in 1992 was instructive. With continuing weapons proliferation and the growth of indigenous defense industries around the globe, it was inevitable that allied governments should continue to desire a technological edge capable of adequately countering the threats inherent in a highly uncertain global security environment. Program affordability and cost saving were the watch words on both sides of the Atlantic as priorities shifted in the post–Cold War environment; thus the prospect of sharing the costs and benefits of technological advances became more attractive.

Such sharing makes sense for three reasons. First, the demand for increased technological sophistication in new defense systems is forcing development costs ever upward. Second, technology diffusion means that sometimes cost-effective solutions to a government requirement can be found only if industry can choose an international partner with whom to share the increased risks of development and production. Theoretically, all would benefit from greater flexibility to pursue cooperative industrial relationships, not only nationally or regionally, but also across the Atlantic. Third, common technology in common weapons systems means greater alliance interoperability and logistical flexibility.

In general, alliance defense industrial cooperation cannot only spread the costs of development but also can provide economies of scale in production. Uniquely, the transatlantic dimension offers governments and industry in the Atlantic Alliance cooperative opportunities that combine increasing technological parity with a record of successful industry partnerships at the subcontractor and licensed production levels and a mutual security treaty that can overcome fears of interdependency.[16]

Practically, however, there are strong pressures in the opposite direction as government officials and industry leaders on each side of the Atlantic express fears concerning the transfer and proliferation of sensitive military and commercial technologies and as they seek competitive advantage in Third World markets. A celebrated case in 1992 was the potential sale of seventy-two U.S. F15 fighters to Saudi Arabia. Without the F15 sale, McDonnell Douglas Corporation, the largest defense manufacturer in America, would be put in financial jeopardy and 40,000 jobs could be lost. British Aerospace waited anxiously to see whether American politics would prevent the sale, opening a major opportunity to sell its Tornado fighters. Alternatively, the sale, estimated at $5 billion, could provide European access to Saudi capital, breathing new life into a European consortium to produce a highly sophisticated European Fighter Aircraft (EFA).

Chapter 1 and thusfar Chapter 2 treat the concept of power as a function of a nation's capabilities and its willingness to use them, concluding that power is the ability to influence other political actors so as to shape the structure and processes within the international system in a manner favorable to a particular nation. The increased power that an alliance gives its individual member nations can of course be used for a variety of specific purposes, including deterrence or actual war-making. Robert Randle stresses this latter purpose.

> Certainly war is a major incentive for alliance formation, because war poses more starkly the threat to the single state's existence, inducing its policy makers to seek the cooperation of other states that feel threatened so that they may share resources for prosecuting the war against the common enemy. The pervasive and fundamental purpose of wartime alliances is the security of the component states or factions; survival of each partner is the key motivation.[17]

Robert Osgood noted that alliances may, in addition to increasing power, serve the functions of preserving the internal security of members, restraining allies, or creating a degree of international order.[18] Preserving internal security may emerge as the primary purpose of alliances in the future as nations seek to confront the increasing threats of international drug trafficking, terrorism, cross border refugee flows, and weapons proliferation.

Preserving an ally's internal security by providing it material and moral support legitimized by the alliance may be a key goal, especially if the alliance involves nations with relatively unstable regimes; of course, such a purpose can backfire rapidly if the government is toppled.

Using the formal and informal ties of the alliance to restrain allies' behavior is common; it is practiced by both the larger, more powerful actors and the weaker, subordinate actors in an alliance. In this respect, the access the alliance provides to an ally's internal political processes and institutions may be particularly important.

Predictable, regulated patterns of interactions based on the alliance structures reduce sources of friction and conflict, providing an element of international order. Furthermore, alliances usually provide some form of institution which facilitates contacts and communication among its members. Also, it may be that stabilizing economic reactions through alliances—securing access to oil and raw materials, for instance—will become a pattern in the future for creating a degree of international order.

Types of Military Force Employment. Analyses of military doctrine and strategy have proliferated since World War II. Many factors account for the rapid growth of literature on the employment of military force: the cold war's focus on the military threat of communism; widespread psychological involvement in the balance of terror; lack of faith in the U.N. capability to prevent wars; concern over the extent to which military preparedness establishes claims on scarce national resources; continued development of the welfare ethic; the rise of pacifism; and the information revolution. There is no easy route to comprehension of this plethora of conceptual treatments of the roles of military force. However, as a preliminary categorization of the types of military force employment, we can speak of deterrence, nuclear war, general conventional war, guerrilla (or unconventional) war, political bargaining and, more recently, U.N. peacekeeping and peace-making.

Deterrence. As noted earlier in this chapter, deterrence has a number of definitions. As used here, it means the ability "to hinder or prevent action by fear of consequences, or by difficulty, risk, unpleasantness, etc."[19] Deterrence is, therefore, at base a psychological phenomenon; its object is to master the expectations and fears of one's actual or potential opponents. Yet deterrence must rest on *hard capability*—the clear, demonstrable ability to do what is threatened if the necessity arises. Deterrence also rests on will, namely, the threatener's will to carry out the threat. Further, the success of a deterrent strategy

> depends on the deterrer's ability to convince his adversary that an attempt to gain his objective would cost more than it is worth, and that the cost to the deterrer of applying the deterrent would be less than conceding the objective.[20]

Deterrence assumes a rational, informed opponent. An irrational (or ill-informed) opponent who will accept destruction or disproportionate loss as a consequence of a selected course of action cannot be deterred. Accidents, by definition consciously unintended, cannot be "deterred." The deterrent role of any weapons system must always be considered in relation to the states, alliances, or groups that are to be deterred and precisely what action is to be deterred. For example, a threat of massive nuclear retaliation could hardly deter a terrorist group from planting bombs on aircraft.

Strategic nuclear deterrence essentially rests on the concept of "assured destruction" of the adversary, preventing that adversary from launching its strategic nuclear weapons for fear of an unacceptable level of devastation in return through nuclear retaliation. (In Chapter 11 a more demanding form of strategic deterrence is also discussed, namely, counterforce strategy.) For assured destruction deterrence, the United States has long employed three strategic nuclear systems, that is, the triad of intercontinental ballistic missiles (ICBMs), ballistic missile submarines, and bomber aircraft; the concept has been that at least one of the three systems would survive and deliver devastation no matter what.

Tactical nuclear deterrence is theoretically possible as well. There are two quite different ways in which the deployment of tactical nuclear weapons could deter aggressors from the use of either conventional forces or weapons of mass destruction, that is, nuclear, biological, or chemical weapons. First, such deployments could help convince the aggressor that its battlefield costs would be too high. This approach assumes that tactical nuclear weapons could be used effectively.

According to a second line of reasoning, the very presence of tactical nuclear weapons would force an aggressor to calculate that *any* use of nuclear weapons would likely escalate to strategic nuclear war. This approach to deterrence is the converse of the first in that it denies the "tactical" utility of low-yield nuclear weapons for battlefield fighting.[21]

Conventional (nonnuclear) force deterrence is possible between nonnuclear states where one state or alliance of states holds "sufficient" military capability to convince would-be attackers that costs would be greater than benefits. Conventional force deployments may also serve in the spectrum of capabilities required for deterrence between nuclear powers by providing "flexible response" (the ability to respond appropriately at nonnuclear as well as nuclear levels). In the aftermath of the cold war and the U.S.–Soviet nuclear standoff, nuclear weapons have declined in importance and conventional deterrence will be increasingly important.

Successful deterrence is virtually impossible to identify; so much depends on how one evaluates adversary intentions. Assessments can easily take the form of post hoc conclusions based on single-factor analysis. In addition, it should be noted that military force designed to deter military action does not necessarily deter aggression in the economic or political fields.[22] Because of the possibility of catastrophe inherent in nuclear deterrence, it is commonly believed to be easier to achieve than conventional deterrence.

Nuclear War. Nuclear war may be fought because deterrence breaks down and the parties involved believe no other viable option exists but employment of nuclear force. It may also occur by accident or, improbable as it may seem in view of past nuclear stability, by deliberate design. Finally, nuclear war may also arise out of escalation of conventional hostilities between nuclear powers or their allies.

Studies on escalation in warfare invariably draw distinctions among the types and yields of weapons employed and the types of targets attacked. The difference between the use of conventional weapons and the use of nuclear weapons is often referred to as *firebreak*, signifying a highly significant qualitative difference in levels of warfare. Some analysts argue that there is also a significant firebreak separating the use of tactical and strategic nuclear weapons and that tactical nuclear weapons can, as a consequence, be employed in "quasi-conventional" combat without undue risk of escalation to strategic levels. Others even argue that a number of firebreaks exist at various rungs of a tall ladder of nuclear escalation, suggesting further that "deescalation" is as possible as escalation and that deterrence can work at various rungs in the ladder.[23]

Certainly, it is possible to identify theoretical distinctions among major classes of nuclear warfare, including all-out or selective "strategic" attacks on "counterforce" targets (military installations and major force deployments) or "countervalue" targets (cities and industrial centers), as well as tactical, selective use of low-yield nuclear weapons on the battlefield or its approaches for tactical military targets.[24] However neat these distinctions may be in theory, most analysts suspect that any dividing lines would become blurred quickly in the reactions of military commanders and strategic decision-makers to the first use of nuclear weapons on any scale. (Further attention to these and other distinctions is given in Chapter 11, "Nuclear Strategy.") In the rapid tempo of crisis situations involving nuclear warfare, neat scenarios are not likely to be played out precisely as planned. Thus, many analysts conclude with former secretary of defense Robert McNamara that the use of one nuclear weapon in the field will likely lead to the use of any and all nuclear weapons.[25]

General Conventional War. The two world wars are commonly regarded as general conventional wars in which the resources of coalitions of belligerent nations were mobilized on a massive scale in a war fought for "victory" over the enemy.[26] In both wars one could measure progress toward victory by observing the geographical movement of battlelines established by mass military formations and by destruction or capture of enemy units. Victory was realized by advancing on the enemy's capital and by forcing a capitulation, sealed by a formal exchange of signatures on a document of surrender.

It is widely held that the advent of the nuclear balance of terror has precluded general conventional war along the lines of World War II.[27] Of course, general conventional war is still possible among small nonnuclear states fighting for objectives not centrally involving important interests of the nuclear powers; the Iran–Iraq war of 1980–1988 is one example. Some theorists would argue that conventional war can occur even among the nuclear states, inasmuch as nuclear deterrence is firm under the doctrine of ''mutual assured destruction'' (MAD), whereby the nuclear states in effect tacitly agreed they could not protect themselves against each other. Since no rational head of state would invite nuclear self-destruction by first use of strategic nuclear weapons, this argument goes, traditional military strategy and tactics remain applicable even among nuclear opponents. There are practical problems with this thesis, which has never been tested in the nuclear era. Carried to its logical conclusion, it obviates the traditional notion of victory.

Limited War. A limited war is one in which at least one side fights with only limited resources for limited objectives. Limited war

> reflects an attempt to *affect* the opponent's will, not *crush* it, to make the conditions to be imposed seem more attractive than continued resistance, to strive for specific goals and not for complete annihilation.[28]

While familiar to historians, the concept of limited war thus defined is relatively new to most Americans, for it marks a significant departure from traditional American approaches to war discussed in Chapter 3. Although the Korean conflict (1950–1954) was fought as a limited war, it was not the wellspring of limited war doctrines. In fact, Secretary of State Dulles's formulation of ''massive retaliation'' with nuclear weapons—designed to deter future limited wars such as the Korean War—was still widely viewed as a viable policy in the mid 1950s.[29]

Contemporary limited war doctrines were essentially the product of Western fears of nuclear war growing out of cold war hostilities, Soviet development of a thermonuclear capability in the 1950s, Russian sputniks, bomber and missile ''gaps,'' and the balance of terror. Obviously, alternatives to massive retaliation had to be found when the consequence of nuclear retaliation to nonnuclear threats was the likely destruction of oneself. Moreover, massive retaliation seemed particularly inappropriate to containing the threat of communist subversion in the form of so-called wars of national liberation in the Third World.

The most innovative period for limited-war doctrines was from the mid 1950s to the mid 1960s. During those years, several distinct scenarios were considered possible by various analysts.

- Limited tactical nuclear war
- Use of conventional forces to enforce ''pauses'' during crises and to raise the threshold between conventional and nuclear war (thus reinforcing strategic deterrence)

- Combinations of conventional and tactical nuclear forces as reprisals and demonstrations for political bargaining purposes
- Limited conventional force application for the purpose of compelling an enemy to desist in a course of action
- Counterinsurgency warfare

The American military involvement in Vietnam was influenced in its early years largely by various doctrines of counterinsurgency warfare (see Chapter 13). After the U.S. troop build-up in 1965, these doctrines were supplemented by limited war and controlled escalation doctrines in the application of conventional military force. Difficult though they were to convey, important intrinsic U.S. objectives—principally the security of an independent, noncommunist government in South Vietnam—were rather clear and limited at the conflict's outset, in contrast to North Vietnam's apparently unlimited objectives in the South. Except with hindsight, few could have estimated the intensity and impact of the restraints limiting American strategy, tactics, and resources. As limits on U.S. means grew—from mounting casualties, escalating monetary costs, concern about direct Chinese involvement, and international and domestic public sentiment against the war—U.S. objectives became still more limited, settling for the acceptability of any kind of government in South Vietnam as long as it was freely elected and free of North Vietnamese military aggression.

The outcome of the American experience with limited war in Southeast Asia has been stated succinctly. "The war is over, the cost enormous, and the side which the United States backed lost." Perhaps few conclusive lessons concerning the general utility of limited war can be drawn, but it was clear that for Americans the utility of that approach to warfare was very low indeed throughout the 1970s and 1980s. Indeed, the strategy, tactics, and force superiority that the United States brought to the Gulf war battlefields for a quick, decisive victory were in large part a consequence of lessons learned in Vietnam. Nevertheless, limited war remains an alternative in U.S. national security policy—albeit an approach fraught with various problems (see Chapter 12).[30]

Guerrilla, or Unconventional, War. The word *guerrilla* comes from the Spanish term "little war." Although on the low end of the spectrum of violence, guerrilla warfare has been a powerful instrument in shaping history. Governments may employ it against their enemies, but populations may use it against their governments as well. A recent addition to the spectrum of "unconventional" warfare is the development of state-supported terrorism. Terrorist violence today transcends territorial boundaries and traditional conflicts among nation-states. Terrorism spawned by ideological, religious, or political fanaticism has been manipulated internationally by Libya, Syria, Iran, North Korea, and other regimes as a tool of national policy. The response to this threat has been one of the greatest challenges facing the West.

For a further discussion of this subject, see Chapter 13.

Political Bargaining. The most common employment of military force in history has been as an instrument of political action. The possibility that force might be employed in a given situation introduces a powerful element into the calculus of diplomacy and has done so since mankind began to record either diplomacy or war. In the New Testament we read, "What king, going to make war against another king, sitteth not down first, and consulteth whether he be able. . . . Or else, while the other is yet a great way off, he sendeth an embassage and desireth conditions of peace."[31]

Britain's fleet gave that state a powerful voice at virtually every nineteenth century council table, yet its fleet did not fight a major engagement during the entire century between the battles of Trafalgar and Jutland. Naval forces have been a major diplomatic instrument for the United States as well. President Jefferson began the tradition of American "gunboat diplomacy" along the Barbary Coast. Theodore Roosevelt polished the instrument and used it broadly during his presidency. Successive presidents have similarly found the presence of a naval squadron a persuasive indicator of American readiness to take action—military in character, if necessary—in troubled situations.

One analysis of the use of military force found that in the period May 1975 to December 1982 there were 44 instances of the use of American military forces for political purposes. In 70 percent of these instances, naval forces were involved.[32] But navies, which have the advantages of mobility and flexibility, also have weaknesses: first, they can be just as easily withdrawn as inserted, giving rise to questions about the constancy of the intentions behind their employment. Second, there are a variety of instances in which a naval force is not readily applicable, even though it may have some symbolic value. This latter limitation of naval power was clearly demonstrated when the United States employed ineffective offshore naval support of the Western peacekeeping effort in Beirut, following the tragic October 1983 attack by terrorists on the American marine garrison.

It is noteworthy that during the period from 1975 to 1982, the analysis just cited found that ground forces were utilized in 87 percent of the significant, or "major," U.S. applications of military force, and that half of these deployments involved a battalion or more of troops.[33] But the failure of the U.S. deployment of marines in war-torn Beirut in 1983 suggests a vital caution: Without clear and realistic military objectives, the employment of U.S. ground forces can vitiate the very effectiveness of the military instrument sought by policymakers, threaten foreign policy objectives, and erode confidence in U.S. capabilities.

The U.S. use of military force to back up diplomacy, ranging from sending fleets or deploying significant military units (on the scale of Lebanon in 1958) to alerting strategic nuclear forces (as in the Yom Kippur War's terminal phases in 1973 when the Soviets threatened intervention) has become less frequent after reaching a high point in the decade from the mid 1950s to the mid 1960s. And, as the above-cited study indicates, American use of force in the recent past has most often been used to assure friends rather than to compel enemies.[34] This experience was again demonstrated in late 1987 when the United States decided to escort reflagged Kuwait tankers in the Persian Gulf. One reason for this decision was to assure the moderate Arab states that the United States had not tilted toward Iran.

In part, this trend away from gunboat diplomacy was undoubtedly due to U.S. disillusionment with military power, which followed the conclusion of the Vietnam hostilities; in part, it may also have been that American policymakers came to believe that there was less value in demonstrations and shows of force in the modern era. This perception of lessened value may, in turn, have been partially due to enhanced Soviet ability to "counterdemonstrate" and to increased sophistication of possible targets who discern American reluctance actually to use the force behind the demonstration. The character of the uses of military force by the United States in the 1980s represented as much pragmatic modern restraints on military instrument as a cautiously renewed American willingness to employ it.

In 1985, Secretary of Defense Casper Weinberger asserted that the use of military power abroad should be weighed against the lessons to be drawn from the post–World War II period; he presented six major tests to be applied before employing U.S. combat forces:

1. The United States should not commit forces to combat overseas unless the particular engagement or occasion is deemed vital to our national interest or that of our allies. . . .
2. If we decide it is necessary to put combat troops into a given situation, we should do so wholeheartedly and with the clear intention of winning. If we are unwilling to commit the forces or resources necessary to achieve our objectives, we should not commit them at all. Of course, if the particular situation requires only limited force to win our objectives, then we should not hesitate to commit forces sized accordingly. . . .
3. If we do decide to commit forces to combat overseas, we should have clearly defined political and military objectives. And we should know precisely how our forces can accomplish those clearly defined objectives. And we should have and send the forces needed to do just that. . . .
4. The relationship between our objectives and the forces we have committed—their size, composition and disposition—must be continually reassessed and adjusted if necessary. Conditions and objectives invariably change during the course of a conflict. When they do change, then our combat requirements must also change. . . .
5. Before the United States commits combat forces abroad, there must be some reasonable assurance we will have the support of the American people and their elected representatives in Congress.* This support cannot be achieved unless we are candid in making clear the threats we face; the support cannot be sustained without continuing and close consultation. . . .
6. The commitment of U.S. forces to combat should be a last resort.[35]

---

*In response to Weinberger's statement that a domestic consensus must be reached before the use of U.S. forces, James Schlesinger remarked in February 1985 that "Given the circumstances, that is indeed a demanding requirement. Were it to be rigorously implemented, it would virtually assure other powers that they can count on *not* facing American forces."

The Persian Gulf war of 1990–1991 involved the first real application of the new U.S. military strategy for dealing with regional contingencies (see Chapter 4). For a variety of reasons, deterrence of Iraq's Saddam Hussein failed, and the war became a "compellent" action to force Iraq's withdrawal from Kuwait. Congressional debate in the months between August 1990 and January 12, 1991, considered various options, including economic embargo, but given U.N. Security Council authorization to use military force and the military and financial contributions of coalition partners, the Congress reluctantly (passed by only five votes in the Senate) gave President Bush the authority to use "all means necessary" to force Iraq out of Kuwait. On January 16, 1991, the United States–led coalition began a major air campaign followed by a breathtaking 100-hour ground campaign which resulted in Iraqi surrender.[36]

Although it will be years before final judgments can be made, the Persian Gulf war provided grounds for several early general observations about American military power and the role of force in the post–cold war era.

- The war was in many ways unique. The enemy, terrain, and many other features would be different in different regions of the world.
- Deterrence theory needs to be reexamined. Adequate signals either were not sent or were not perceived by Saddam Hussein.
- The United States is both politically and logistically dependent on its friends and allies.
- High technology has led to a revolution in warfare—in weapons, command and control systems, intelligence, and many other areas.
- Only a highly trained, professional military capable of employing high-technology systems under appropriate strategy and in concert with allies will continue to win wars.
- The new regional military strategy which replaces containment will be no less difficult to implement given a challenging array of new political, military and economic uncertainties in the post–cold war world.
- There is an overwhelming need for a balanced, sustainable defense investment strategy, given the economic constraints that lie ahead.[37]

In addition to their role as active instruments of political action, military forces also serve as a backdrop for diplomacy merely by being there and being capable of deployment. An arms control negotiator's ability to achieve a satisfactory agreement, for instance, will likely depend significantly on there being suitable forces in the background; so, too, will the ability of a diplomat attempting to persuade an adversary to neutralize an area or issue in contention. Hans Morgenthau has reminded us that military strength is a prime element in prestige, which is itself a political multiplier of power.

> Besides the practices of diplomacy, the policy of prestige uses military demonstrations as means to achieve its purpose. Since military strength is the obvious measure of a nation's power, its demonstration serves to impress the others with that nation's power. Military representatives of foreign nations are, for instance, invited to peacetime army

> and navy maneuvers, not in order to let them in on military secrets, but to impress them and their governments with the military preparedness of the particular nation.[38]

Of course, the uses of armed forces as potential instruments do not solve underlying problems. In the short run they may avert a reverse and temporarily secure an advantage, but they cannot indefinitely substitute for other policy instruments. In an earlier, groundbreaking study of the use of force, Barry Blechman and Stephen Kaplan observed that

> the demonstrative use of the armed forces for political objectives is a useful step to shore up a situation sufficiently so that more extreme adverse consequences can be avoided, so that domestic and international pressures for more forceful and perhaps counter-productive actions can be avoided, and so that time can be gained for sounder policies that can deal adequately with the realities of the situation to be formulated and implemented.
>
> To reach this conclusion about the *effectiveness* of armed forces as a political instrument is not to reach any judgment about the wisdom of using the armed forces for these purposes. That question is a more difficult one, one which can only be answered in the context of the specific choices—and the various costs and benefits associated with each choice—facing decision-makers at the time.[39]

Military Doctrine in Transition. Barring the millennium, military forces will continue to be an instrument of sovereign states, and the central question for policymakers will continue to be: How does one manage the employment of military force to achieve national security objectives in the most effective, efficient way? Several distinct problems in military doctrine bear on this question and require solution or at least clarification.

First, a crucial problem remains of determining the appropriate roles of nuclear weapons in an era of continued heavy nuclear armaments and likely proliferation. Rational calculations have ruled out total war between nuclear powers as an instrument of national policy, but such a war could result from miscalculation or accident, to which deterrence is not applicable. Proliferation of nuclear weapons will make the situation worse, and the list of nations capable of acquiring nuclear weapons in the not too distant future has grown to more than a dozen today[40] (see Chapter 22).

Second, the doctrinal problem surrounding the utility of tactical nuclear weapons needs urgent clarification. Although there may be some deterrent value in maintaining ambiguities and uncertainties between opponents, there appears to be little such value among allies. NATO strategy has long contemplated the use of tactical nuclear weapons, although the conditions and modes in which they might be used have remained vague. Even with precisely defined criteria and scenarios for use, so repugnant has the specter of nuclear weapons employment become that it is difficult to envision a situation in which an American president would be the first to initiate the use of tactical nuclear weapons. Moreover, it is difficult to imagine a nuclear battlefield so controlled that the distinction between tactical and strategic nuclear forces would hold in the heat and turmoil of conflict. Yet in the early 1990s, tactical nuclear weapons continue to form an important part of the spectrum of deterrence, ensuring that conventional forces and strategic nuclear forces are securely linked or "coupled" in such a way that the adversary cannot hope to prevail at any one level of violence.

It was in this overall context and in an effort to gain assurances rapidly that tactical nuclear weapons in the hands of the republics of the former Soviet Union could be controlled that President Bush unilaterally took the initiative in September 1991 to withdraw worldwide all U.S. forward-deployed tactical nuclear weapons.

A third major problem with the role of military force in the future resides in the inherent ambiguities of limited war. Limits on war's objectives must be related to the nature of the interests to be pursued. Resort to military force in the post–cold war era, in which nuclear weapons continue to abound, carries with it so many dangers that the interests to be served should be particularly clear, strong, and specific. Although interests are difficult enough to identify, specific objectives in particular circumstances present an even more difficult problem. National interests tend to change slowly; specific objectives are situational. Objectives are shaped by both what is desirable and what is feasible in given situations. Determination of the militarily feasible must be the result of careful capability analysis that determines the limits of resources and adjusts the objectives thereto.

Discussion Questions

1. Under what conditions would you expect the mass media to be a factor in limiting or expanding the role of the military in conflict resolution?

2. How important is the reality of "assured destruction" if one side in a political conflict does not consider the concept valid?

3. What is "flexible response"? Is conventional (nonnuclear) force a deterrent between nuclear states? Under what conditions?

4. Under what conditions could the use of military force be limited to general conventional war between states possessing a nuclear capability?

5. What makes modern nuclear deterrence different from pre-1945 conventional (nonnuclear) deterrence?

6. What problems for nuclear deterrence does the proliferation of nuclear weapons create?

7. What nonmilitary factors must be considered when estimating a state's "national power"?

8. What are the dangers associated with employing military forces in a "compellent" role? What nonmilitary factors of national power can be employed in a compellent role?

9. What kinds of economic costs are associated with maintaining military power in developing Third World and advanced industrialized nations? Are there economic advantages?

10. Does a credible military force make some nations "more sovereign" than others? If so, why?

11. What are the realities of military conflict that challenge the concept of "firebreak"?

12. Why are "intentions" a dangerous guide to use when assessing the military problem that an adversary poses?

13. Did the advent of nuclear weapons mark a watershed in the decision-making process used to authorize military force to resolve disputes?

14. What are the principle motivations for nations to join alliances?

Recommended Reading

Betts, Richard K. *Nuclear Blackmail and Nuclear Balance*. Washington, D.C.: Brookings Institution, 1987.

Blackwell, James. *Thunder in the Desert: The Strategy and Tactics of the Persian Gulf War*. New York: Bantam Books, 1991.

Blechman, Barry M., and Kaplan, Stephen S. *Force without War: U.S. Armed Forces as a Political Instrument*. Washington, D.C.: Brookings Institution, 1978.

Garthoff, Raymond. *Detente and Confrontation: American-Soviet Relations from Nixon to Reagan*. Washington, D.C.: Brookings Institution, 1987.

Glaser, Charles L. *Analyzing Strategic Nuclear Policy*. Princeton, N.J.: Princeton University Press, 1990.

Kapstein, Ethan Barnaby. *The Political Economy of National Security*. New York: McGraw-Hill, 1992.

Krepinevich, Andrew F. *The Army and Vietnam*. Baltimore: Johns Hopkins University Press, 1988.

Kruzel, Joseph, ed. *American Defense Annual: 1991–1992*. New York: Lexington Books, 1992.

Mueller, John. *Retreat from Doomsday: The Obsolescence of Major War*. New York: Basic Books, 1989.

Tucker, Robert W., and Hendrickson, David. *The Imperial Temptation: The New World Order and America's Purpose*. New York: Council on Foreign Relations Press, 1992.

3

Traditional American Approaches to National Security

Generalizations about distinctly American approaches to national security matters should be advanced with the same caution warranted by all large generalizations. Not all Americans at all times are of the same mind. Americans tend to differ among themselves on policy issues along lines of age groups, sex, region, party, social class, education level, etc. Even during times when the nation has been committed to war, various citizens have been dedicated to pacifism. Invariably, some people have felt that the United States was committed to war for the wrong cause—or for the right cause at the wrong time, or for the right cause at the right time in the wrong place. At times of low defense budgets, some citizens have argued for greater armament; high defense budgets always have their antagonists.

Nevertheless, there are central themes in the American cultural tradition that repeatedly recur, providing patterns of thought and action in national security matters. Short of war, for instance, Americans have traditionally focused much of their energy on the pursuit of private interests and consequently have viewed national security as secondary, if they thought of it at all. On the other hand, once conscious of a threat, American attitudes have tended to shift quickly and dramatically. Gabriel Almond has suggested that such American attitudes are affected by two variables.

1. Changes in the domestic and foreign political-economic situation involving the presence or absence of threat in varying degrees.
2. The character and predispositions of the population.[1]

It is to this latter variable that we now turn, briefly examining certain tendencies of thought and action arising out of American experience and its historic context. We shall later examine the first variable at length.

Public Opinion and National Security Policy. As in most democracies, American public opinion on various aspects of national security policy has historically been important; it has always been to some degree a constraint on policymakers. de Tocqueville, writing in 1835, observed that a democratic system of government is by nature incapable of formulating and implementing a coherent foreign policy.

> Foreign politics demand scarcely any of those qualities which a democracy possesses; and they require on the contrary, the perfect use of almost all of those faculties in which it is deficient. . . . a democracy is unable to regulate the details of an important undertaking, to persevere in a design, and to work out its execution in the presence of serious obstacles. It cannot combine measures with secrecy, and it will not await their consequences with patience. . . . democracies . . . obey the impulse of passion rather than the suggestions of prudence and . . . abandon a mature design for the gratification of a monetary caprice.[2]

de Tocqueville, along with others who take a so-called realist position, essentially argued that the realm of foreign policy-making should be reserved for a small group of highly educated and competent elites who would discharge their duties secretly, efficiently, and effectively. In this view, there is no room in the policy-making arena for the uninformed and unsophisticated mass public.

Walter Lippmann felt that de Tocqueville's view of the dangers of the public role in national security policy-making became increasingly relevant with the passage of years.

> The people have imposed a veto upon the judgments of the informed and responsible officials. They have compelled the governments, which usually knew what would have been wiser, was necessary, or was more expedient, to be too late with too little, or too long with too much, too pacifist in peace and too bellicose in war, too neutralist or appeasing in negotiation or too intransigent. Mass opinion has acquired mounting power in this century. It has shown itself to be a dangerous master of decisions when the stakes are life and death.[3]

de Tocqueville, Lippmann and others, then, have seen the involvement of the American public in foreign affairs as dysfunctional, and some support can be offered for that position.

There are, of course, arguments to be made contrary to the realists and in favor of public involvement in national security and foreign policy decisions. When public opinion makes an impact upon international policies it has certain strengths. For one thing, public debates tend to clarify major issues. For another, if the public's view impinges on the process, the resulting policy is more likely to be in keeping with current national purposes.[4] Third, if the public's involvement has been steady, there is apt to be more continuing support for the sacrifices for which the policies call.

Clearly, there are many arguments that can be made for greater or lesser public involvement in foreign affairs, and those mentioned above are only representative. The classic liberal argument that grows out of the normative view that citizen opinions *should* influence all affairs—that all policy *should* reflect the beliefs of the people, or at least the majority of the people—could also be offered. On the other hand, realist propositions can be advanced, maintaining that foreign and security policy is so important that it deserves the control of the most informed; that mass opinion is often too slow to crystallize; that public discussion can provide other governments premature information concerning U.S. national security policy.[5]

Whatever the position taken on the desirable depth of public involvement, it is clear that any U.S. security policy requiring national sacrifices must be founded, in large part, upon basic public values. Indeed, inasmuch as values are often imprecise, diverse, and subject to change, part of the job of the policymaker is to clarify, interpret, synthesize, and articulate them as they bear on particular foreign and national security issues and problems. Further, the diversity of values impinging upon the process of policy formulation often requires the policymaker to reconcile competing values in relation to a particular aspect of national security. He or she may have to compromise, accept some values and reject others, or find some other reconciling device. The necessity of formulating policy on a foundation of implicit or explicit value choices cannot, however, be avoided.[6]

One time-tested means of generating consensus is to couch policy in terms that command a broad value base within American society, that is, in terms describing values so cherished by the polity that they are virtually beyond challenge; or, at least, such that it would appear almost "un-American" to challenge them. This practice is generally recognized by policymakers as desirable, on occasion politically necessary. Woodrow Wilson's call for morality in international politics and Jimmy Carter's stress on human rights were intended to have just such rallying effect.

During the Truman, Eisenhower, and Kennedy years the executive branch was able to exercise a great deal of influence on public opinion. Public information organizations within the departments and agencies concerned with foreign and national security policies were able to use the media to articulate the administration's viewpoint while sometimes withholding information that would tend to support opposing views. During this period, members of Congress generally deferred to the executive branch, for it was widely believed that Congress lacked the expertise necessary for challenging foreign and national security policy decisions.[7]

Most Americans look to the president for leadership in foreign affairs, particularly when the issues involve national security. Historically, this has meant that the president has had wide scope for initiative when working in the field of foreign relations. Cognizant of this, Lyndon Johnson told Eric Sevareid, "I can arouse a great mass of people with a very simple kind of appeal. I can wrap the flag around this policy, and use patriotism as a club to silence the critics."[8] However, the link between policy and mass values must be credible.

The Johnson approach appeared to work fairly well until about 1968, by which time the administration's "credibility gap" had grown to serious proportions over the war in Vietnam. By then the news media had begun to focus on the inconsistencies or inadequacies of U.S. policy in Vietnam, giving wide publicity in particular to the February 1968 reexamination of the Gulf of Tonkin incidents by the Senate Committee on Foreign Relations. Those hearings appeared to convince many that the Johnson administration had hoodwinked Congress and, therefore, the American people into the Gulf of Tonkin Resolution, which had been cited repeatedly by the president as proof of public support for his Vietnam policy.*

American presidents had been under attack before by the various media, but the 1968 attacks against Johnson were particularly strong; in effect, an American president and his administration, already suspect for news management, were implicitly labeled "frauds"—and only a few months before elections. Something truly serious happened: A major policy, inextricably linking American national security and foreign policy interests, apparently no longer commanded a broad national consensus. In political terms, this was a presidential disaster. On the evening of March 31, 1968, President Johnson announced on television that he would not run for reelection.

To some, the president's announcement meant recognition that U.S. policy in Vietnam, as articulated and executed by the Johnson administration, had failed. To others, the speech announced "the collapse of the messianic conception of the American role in the world."[9] Whatever conclusions one might draw from that dramatic event, it is clear that the public's role and interest in American national security policy took a dramatic turn in the spring of 1968. Not only was this true in the obvious case of Vietnam but also in other aspects of national security policy.

A change of administrations did not reduce the credibility gap. Indeed, it appeared to many that under President Nixon the link between American values and policy was becoming even more tenuous. The number of antiwar demonstrators and organizations increased, and on October 15, 1969, in various cities throughout the United States, more than one million people demonstrated against the Vietnam War.[10] These demonstrations tended to arouse the fear that continuing the war would rend the fabric of American society. They also seriously eroded the United States' credibility in the diplomatic effort to end the war on less than disastrous terms.

During the same period, the general American attitude regarding involvement abroad was undergoing fundamental change. The public—or at least a significant

*By every careful measurement, Hanoi's famous "Tet offensive" during the same period—while surprising in its scope and ferocity—was a military disaster for North Vietnam and its Vietcong allies and infrastructure in South Vietnam; the attackers' losses far exceeded their military gains. Yet the media reported Tet as a terrible defeat for the Americans and their allies, transforming a series of major tactical defeats of the Northern forces into a strategic psychological victory for Hanoi.

part of it—was becoming more vocal, critical, and discriminating with respect to foreign commitments; its mood seemed to vacillate between "noninterventionism and selective interventionism."[11]

This change of mood, combined with Watergate and other problems on the domestic front, resulted in growing public and congressional disenchantment with presidential leadership and in erosion of the influence of the office of the presidency in national security affairs.[12] Major legislation, such as the War Powers Act of 1973 and the Budget Reform Act of 1974, shifted the executive-legislative balance sharply away from the executive branch. The trend toward greater congressional assertiveness continued throughout the 1980s. This was manifested in the House passage of a nuclear freeze resolution in early 1983; the Boland amendments of 1982 and 1984, which prohibited military support to the contras in Nicaragua, and legislation reorganizing the Department of Defense in 1986. The impact of these changes is analyzed in Chapters 5 and 6.

Primacy of Domestic Affairs. As noted earlier, until recent decades American concern with distant events and matters of security was extremely limited. Geographic position provides a partial explanation of this lack of interest. Ocean barriers and great distances from likely sources of invasion made physical security a matter to be taken for granted. The fact that British sea power was committed to preserving the status quo in North America for most of the nineteenth century was further reason for complacency over security from foreign threats. Early security interests were essentially domestic—family or community security from hostile Indians, or from British troops supported by other Americans during the Revolution. The War of 1812 was relatively short, and much of the important action was at sea.

Most of the American historical experience occurred during the century of unprecedented and prolonged world peace from the Congress of Vienna in 1815 to the outbreak of World War I in 1914. (For Americans, of course, there was the bloody domestic experience of the Civil War, midway in that period, and there were other conflicts in the world as well; but, relatively speaking, the international scene was unprecedentedly peaceful.) Despite several minor variations, there were no general wars between great powers during the century. One exception was the Crimean War (1853–1856), which pitted Russian forces against the allied armies of England, France, Turkey, and Sardinia. There was also a pair of bilateral wars between great powers, namely, the Franco-Prussian (1870–1871) and the Russo-Japanese (1904–1905) wars. Though few Americans gave much thought to the exceptional nature of this good fortune, the extended period of peace allowed Americans to focus almost exclusively on things close to home—continental expansion and, secondarily, consolidation of American hemispheric interests (for example, those expressed in the Monroe Doctrine).

The idea that the American continent belonged by right to those who could colonize it was typically expressed by the Virginia planter Lewis Burwell, who wrote to the board of trade in London in 1751.

> That, notwithstanding the Grants of the kings of England, France or Spain, the Property of these uninhabited parts of the world must be founded upon prior Occupancy according to the Law of Nature; and it is the Seating & Cultivating the soil and not the bare travelling through a territory that constitutes Right; and it will be highly for the interest of the Crown (sic) to encourage the Seating of the Lands (sic) Westward as soon as possible to prevent the French.[13]

The founding fathers conceived the new nation as an expanding empire. Benjamin Franklin advocated westward expansion on the basis that it was necessary for the growing colonial population, which would double itself every quarter century.[14] Thomas Jefferson placed no hemispheric limits to American expansion in writing to James Monroe in 1801.

> However our present interests may restrain us within our limits, it is impossible not to look forward to distant times, when our rapid multiplication will expand it beyond those limits, and cover the whole northern if not the southern continent, with people, speaking the same language, governed in similar forms, and by similar laws.[15]

The Louisiana Purchase of 1803 secured the heartland of the American continent and became the basis of further claims for westward expansion to be pressed against Spain's holdings in Texas and New Mexico. The ''All Mexico'' movement swept the United States further westward in the 1840s and into the Mexican War of 1846.

America's lack of concern about external threats to its security during this period was reflected in the size of the military establishment. The naval fleet was almost nonexistent, and regular army strength, with the exception of the Civil War, averaged about 10,000, varying between 8,220 in 1817 and 47,867 in 1898.[16] The principal tasks of the army were to provide security for western settlements and to furnish engineering assistance for railroad expansion.

The Spanish–American War began a period of expansion into the Caribbean and the Pacific and marked a shift in the foreign policy involvement of the United States. The size of the army almost doubled from 1898 to 1901 as the United States, almost without knowing it, emerged from the ''Splendid Little War'' as a great power with a limited imperialist position in both the Pacific and the Caribbean. However, these holdings were unrelated to the impulse that drew the United States into World War I. Violation of American neutral rights, especially the sinking of the *Lusitania* by German submarines in 1915 and revelation of German plots in Mexico, finally ended a great debate over America's involvement in a European war. The United States entered the ''War to End All Wars'' as an ''associated power'' of the Allies.

Following World War I, America again tried to turn its back on the world outside the Western Hemisphere, rejecting President Wilson's hope for the League of Nations, pushing for disarmament in the Washington and Geneva Naval Conferences of 1922 and 1927, and renouncing war ''as an instrument of national policy'' in the Kellogg-Briand Pact of 1928.[17] Americans focused on a return to ''normalcy,'' that is, getting on with domestic concerns.

The Great Depression in 1929 and the early 1930s ensured that public attention would remain riveted on domestic problems. Meanwhile, the United States sought to legislate itself out of foreign political entanglements through the Neutrality Acts Of 1935, 1936, and 1937, which barred sales or shipments of munitions to belligerent nations. A popular "lesson" derived from World War I was that the United States had been unwittingly dragged into that war by the deceit and trickery of European diplomats and the "merchants of death" who provided the instruments of war to these diplomats. "Never again!"

Dissociation and Depreciation of Power and Diplomacy. "Normalcy" has traditionally meant more to Americans than merely the primacy of domestic affairs. It has also implied that peace or tranquillity in international relations is the normal condition of world order. This is not surprising when we recall that until recently most of the American experience has been peaceful. There is another important reason for the view that order is the norm. The American political heritage has been strongly influenced by the philosophy of the Age of Enlightenment and particularly by the Englishman John Locke, whose basic precepts were well known to the founders of the United States and were important in both the American Revolution and in the framing of the Constitution.[18] Locke expounded a natural rights doctrine, which conceived the state of nature as a condition of peace, mutual assistance, and preservation. He posited the ability of humans to arrive at a conception of "the right" through innate humanity, leading to trust in the rationality, even goodness, of human beings. Rational people would not want war and, hence, nations (viewed as the geographic personifications of humans) could and should resolve their differences through discussion and compromise.

Americans tended to ignore the contrary views of an earlier English philosopher, Thomas Hobbes, who wrote in *Leviathan* that in the state of nature a person's life is "solitary, poor, nasty, brutish, and short."[19] How do states naturally behave?

> In all times, kings and persons of sovereign authority, because of their independence are in continued jealousies, and in the state and posture of gladiators; having their weapons pointing, and their eyes fixed on one another; that is, their forts, garrisons, guns upon the frontiers of their kingdoms; and continual spies upon their neighbors; which is a posture of war.[20]

In the traditional American view, diplomacy should represent a process of ironing out differences through discussion, with eventual agreement based on rational accommodation of reasonable interests.[21] Power, in relation to diplomacy, was largely irrelevant, at best, and immoral, at worst. Given the many widely publicized idealistic attempts to eliminate the struggle for power from the international arena,[22] this public perception is hardly surprising.

Diplomacy was also depreciated in many American minds because of diplomats' longstanding reputation in the Western world for deviousness, duplicity, and secrecy. As noted, both during and after World War I, the opinion was widely held that the secret dealings of European diplomats were largely responsible for that war.[23] Deeply committed to this view, President Wilson was largely instrumental in the development of a new diplomatic procedure for "registering" and publishing treaties. "Open convenants, openly arrived at" became his credo. But the principles of open methods "almost wrecked diplomacy on the shoals of impotence. Taken literally (and it often was), negotiation must then be public."[24] Little wonder that politicians have subsequently laced formal instruments of agreement and their public statements with platitudes, whenever possible, leaving important details to secret exchanges. President Carter's promises to return to open diplomacy proved short-lived as he encountered the realities of power politics.

Utopianism. The great ideals of Christianity and the philosophy of the Enlightenment imbedded in the Western political heritage have affected not only American values and goals but also the means Americans typically embrace for attaining national goals. Humanity's presumed innate goodness and natural preference for peace have tended to condition the American approach to issues of national security.

The standards by which Americans have judged the world have been constructed quite naturally out of their own experience. By the early twentieth century, the United States had become not only a great power but also a relatively satiated power enjoying phenomenal economic growth and social harmony. In overall terms, America had become a status quo power, its people essentially satisfied with life as they knew it, holding their condition of peace and harmony at home as the ideal for all rational people everywhere. They believed in the virtues of democracy and took it for granted that the fruits of democracy should represent meaningful goals to all people throughout the world.[25]

Given this experience and the important role of religion in the origins of the republic, it was only natural that the American people early developed a sense of mission that was idealistic, messianic, and hopeful of divine favor for national aspirations.[26] From Cotton Mather (1663–1728) forward, Americans have tended to borrow Biblical metaphor and to view their country "as a city upon a hill," as a beacon for all to see and emulate. In the 1840s in an article on the Mexican War, Albert Gallatin provided a classic statement of the prevailing sense of mission.

> Your mission is to improve the state of the world, to be the "model republic" to show that men are capable of governing themselves, and that the simple and natural form of government is that which also confers most happiness on all, is productive of the greatest development of the intellectual faculties, above all, that which is attended by the highest standard of private and political virtue and morality.[27]

The sense of mission arose again in the 1880s, this time to check the baser rationales of American imperialism. It held back outright imperialist designs in Hawaii until 1898 and in the Caribbean until its defenders, the old-school Republicans in the Senate and Thomas B. Reed in the House, were overcome by the patriotic fervor of the Spanish–American War in 1898. This messianism reappeared in 1917 as a national sense of responsibility to save democracy in

Europe. Woodrow Wilson became its champion in taking the lead after the war in forming the League of Nations. It gave short-lived impetus to the "Good Neighbor Policy" in Latin America in the 1930s and helped give birth to the concept and realization of the United Nations and the Marshall Plan after World War II. Such idealism appeared again as one of the motivating factors for continuing American foreign aid to the less developed countries throughout the 1950s and 1960s.

Even during the times when the sense of mission was undercut by the forces of realism or imperialism, the leaders of such forces clothed their designs in terms of American ideals. They knew that the American self-image was a powerful block to any program expressed in terms of power or materialism.

For most of the twentieth century many Americans have been preoccupied with a long series of projects for shaping a better international system—after the wars, for returning the world to the natural order of peace and harmony—resting their hopes on various formal legal codes and international institutions. True to tradition, the popular perception of the proper American role in shaping the international order during this period has often been one of leadership by example, rather than by major participation in cooperative international projects. Many people have continued to think that the sheer weight of the American example would exert a decisive influence upon the rest of the world.[28] As will be pointed out later, this traditional utopianism has increasingly given way in recent decades to the realization that, while they are vital, ideals and examples by themselves are not enough.

Aversion to Violence. The Judeo-Christian gospel, which has been central in forming American values, teaches "Thou shalt not kill," and the liberal culture of Western civilization has applied that ideal to people in the collective entities called "nations." The Enlightenment philosophy of secular perfectionism further strengthened this belief, emphasizing that violence is not only morally wrong but irrational and unnatural. (Somehow, systematic violence against the hapless American Indians who stood in the way of the nation's manifest continental destiny lay outside this moral consensus; there, might made right.) Reflecting deeply ingrained views, Americans have been unwilling to consider war as anything other than a scourge. It kills, maims, and separates family and friends. Too, war and preparedness for war interrupt the routine cycle of self-directed materialism and prosperity.[29]

In these lights, war and peace are viewed as polar opposites. The resort to war or threats of violence between nations are seen as breaking down the normal, peaceful course of international affairs. With such a set of perceptions, it is not surprising that most Americans have had great difficulty accepting the dictum of von Clausewitz: "War is merely the continuation of policy by other means."[30] War cannot be an instrument, in a typical American view, for it is a pathological aberration.

As a related point, peace has been viewed as the responsibility of civilian policymakers and diplomats, while war, which should be used only when diplomacy failed, was the province of the military. This dichotomy led to the further notion that the military should have no peacetime function in policymaking. The military function was to be limited to two tasks:

1. To guard the (continental) security of the United States.
2. To fight—and win—a war at the command of the civilian authorities.[31]

Consequently, policies for the raising, deploying, and employing of military forces were generally created in a vacuum. Until American intervention in World War II, such military policies were formulated largely without a knowledge of relevant political objectives or consequences, and political decisions were reached without professional military advice about military capabilities.[32]

Traditionally, the American approach to war has leaned on several simple propositions. First, the United States should participate only in a "just war"—a "war fought either in self-defense or in collective defense against an armed attack."[33] The "unjust war" is any war fought for any other reason. Second, as noted above with the reaction to von Clausewitz, war should be banished as an instrument of national policy. Third, however, war is justified as an instrument of collective defense against armed aggression. Among other things, these propositions obviously rule out preventive or preemptive war (to strike an opponent first who clearly is making preparations to attack you).[34] President Truman made the point explicit. "We do not believe in aggressive or preventive war. Such war is the weapon of dictators, not of free democratic societies."[35]

Tied to the traditional devotion to the status quo in the international order, as noted previously, the American aversion to violence has also tended to deny the legitimacy of violent revolution against governments-in-being. Somehow, Americans have been inclined to forget that our own founders were steeped in the Lockean philosophy, which recognized the legitimacy of "the right to rebel" and that the United States was itself born of revolution.

Unwisdom of Standing Military Forces. Given the traditional view, which sees no necessary connection between diplomacy and armed might and which abhors violence, it is not surprising that until recently Americans have only in exceptional periods accorded much importance to the military. The central impulse has not merely been a distrust of large standing armies as a threat to the Republic (although this issue has been stressed periodically) but also a blind faith, a view born in the colonial period, that a citizen military force of "unprofessional soldiers" would always be sufficient to defend the nation.

> The militia system itself, with its axiom that every man was a trained and ready-armed soldier who would instantly spring to the defense of his country, encouraged the belief—which often proved a dangerous illusion—that the community was always prepared for its peril. In a country inhabited by "Minute Men" why keep a standing army?
>
> The long-standing American myth of a constantly prepared citizenry helps explain why Americans have always been so ready to demobilize their forces. Again, and

> again, our popular army has laid down its arms with dizzying speed, only to disperse into a precarious peace.[36]

George Washington was aware of the reality and discussed it in a circular of October 18, 1790.

> I am religiously persuaded that the duration of the war, and the greatest part of the Misfortunes, and perplexities we have hitherto experienced, are chiefly to be attributed to temporary enlistments. . . . A moderate, compact force, on a permanent establishment capable of acquiring the discipline essential to military operations, would have been able to make head against the Enemy, without comparison better than the throngs of Militia, which have been at certain periods not in the field, but on their way to, and from the field.[37]

The myth has persisted, however, acquiring reinforcement in the ability of the United States successfully to call its "militia" to arms to fight victorious wars against foreign foes in 1812, 1846, 1898, 1917, and 1941.

Peacetime conscription has always been a notoriously "un-American" idea. It was used late in the Civil War and again in World Wars I and II. The first peacetime conscription law was passed in September 1940 over substantial congressional opposition and the "Keep America Out of War" movement led by the veteran socialist Norman Thomas. Following World War II, in August 1945, President Truman asked Congress for a peacetime draft for an indefinite period to replace overseas veterans. At that juncture, the issue of peacetime conscription was intimately tied to proposals for Universal Military Training (UMT). In the end, UMT was defeated in Congress, but in June 1948 a two-year peacetime conscription bill was passed and was steadily renewed by Congress each year until 1972.[38] Thus, willingness to support conscripted standing forces in "peacetime" (i.e., absence of "declared" wars) represents only about 7 percent of the American historical experience!

Except in crisis, Americans traditionally have wished that the minimum essential military establishment would "go away" to its posts and camps to do whatever the military has to do—but with minimum diversion of public attention and funds. This wish has been very much a part of American liberal ideology, the dominant corpus of beliefs in the United States. Those who identify with this view tend to argue that the civil–military relationship should be one in which civilians make all but the most narrow, technical decisions, that military spending is essentially nonproductive, and, as suggested above, that the citizen–soldier is capable of donning a military uniform and defending the nation during times of crisis.

Once a crisis has passed, as indicated earlier, Americans have traditionally stumbled all over themselves in an attempt to demobilize as soon as possible. The rush to "bring the boys back home" after World War II was a dramatic example of this. In a matter of less than two years, the United States demobilized almost eleven million soldiers, sailors, and airmen, leaving a scattered residual force of about 10 percent of its wartime strength to safeguard the victories in Europe and Asia. A further excellent illustration of this was the hasty deactivation of the Continental Army in 1784:

> Resolved, that the commanding officer be and he is thereby directed to discharge the troops now in the service of the United States, except twenty-five privates to guard the stores at Fort Pitt, and fifty-five to guard the stores at West Point and other magazines, with a proportionate number of officers; no officer to remain in service above the rank of captain.[39]

The Crusading Spirit. Since it rejects the notion of war as an extension of politics, the United States cannot logically use the military instrument "to restore a balance of power" or "to protect economic interests abroad," or for any other mundane purpose. Instead, America goes to war as a last resort and in the name of moral principles—"to make the world safe for democracy," or "to end all wars." America gives its sons, daughters, and treasure only when forced and only in righteous indignation or outrage.

> Democracy fights in anger—it fights for the very reason that it was forced to go to war. It fights to punish the power that was rash enough and hostile enough to provoke it—to teach that power a lesson it will not forget, to prevent the thing from happening again[40]

Anger is sometimes further fueled by presumably God-given causes. Outraged by the "sinking of the *Maine*," the United States went to war in 1898 for retaliation but also for the stated purpose of liberating Cuba from Spanish tyranny, annexing the Philippines in the process—"to educate the Filipinos, and uplift and civilize them, and by God's grace do the very best we could by them, as our fellowmen for whom Christ also died."[41]

Although aversion to violence has been relatively consistent as one of America's best characteristics, the crusading spirit has itself sometimes been a catalyst for violence, showing that our worst qualities have sometimes been the other face of our best. Yet Americans do not have a tradition of glorifying violence per se. The problem has always been the relationship of ends to means. A cause noble enough justifies violent means. In fact, the sufficiency of some past causes has been a matter of considerable debate among American historians and philosophers.

The crusading spirit considers war essentially in terms of good versus evil. To engender public support for war—to get the public to sustain the privation thereof—policymakers are often driven "to draw pictures in black and white, to exaggerate differences with one's adversaries and solidarity with one's friends."[42] This has obvious benefits for the war effort, but the problem is that it is very hard to turn off the public's emotions once they have been aroused. If the president mobilizes support for specific military interventions abroad, for example, he may find later options restricted or foreclosed by the emotional stakes and simplified expectations of the public.

It becomes difficult to fight a war for limited objectives when the process of limitation involves negotiating with the ultimate evil represented by the enemy. "Total victory," or "unconditional surrender," once they have been advocated by policymakers, tend to become driving goals, and progress toward such goals must be demonstrated. But protracted war with limited objectives tends to obscure "victory." Highly competitive by nature, Americans do not relish tie games.[43] They want to win "big"—and early.

Impatience. The crusading spirit is marked by impatience and irritation with time-consuming complexity. Americans believe that, with a little common sense and know-how, things can be done in a hurry.[44] Neither protracted, limited war nor costly, sustained programs for military preparedness fit this temper. The initial public reaction to the need to occupy Germany following World War II was disillusionment; after all, the war was over. Stalemate at Korea's 38th parallel evoked a similar public reaction in the 1950s. (It is noteworthy, however, that despite the cost and difficulties, America's patience was rallied by its leaders to stay the course in both instances.)

Impatience, as one of several variables of mood, combined with the aversion to violence, is highly likely to produce public outcry for cessation of American involvement in a prolonged conflict demanding self-sacrifice unrelated to any clear vision of overriding national interest. Such was the case in the Vietnam War from 1966 to 1973.

On the other hand, impatience may mix with the American proclivity for retreat into domestic affairs to yield boredom with or aversion to national security affairs. Thus, although most would agree that the greatest direct military threat to the security of the United States is in the nuclear realm, Americans often seem to have been "forgetting about the unthinkable."[45] Despite occasional peaks of public attention to nuclear-related issues—in 1949 (after the first Soviet atomic test), in 1953–1954 (after the first Soviet hydrogen bomb tests), in 1958 (crises in Berlin, Lebanon, and Quemoy), in 1961–1963 (crisis in Berlin, the Cuban Missile Crisis, and the nuclear test ban), and in 1981–1983 (the deployment of American Pershing missiles in Europe and the nuclear freeze)—the American public seemed relatively uninterested, except in the special context of arms control.

Civil defense provides an example; the programs emphasized during the late 1950s and during the administration of John F. Kennedy held little interest for Americans by the latter 1960s and 1970s. By then, the virtual demise of public interest in civil defense was epitomized by the condition of fallout shelters—empty water barrels and missing or inoperable radiation monitoring equipment.[46] This situation developed in spite of the fact that numerous careful studies demonstrated that modest civil defense measures could save literally tens of millions of lives. Though there are several possible explanations for this phenomenon, opinion surveys of the late 1960s shed some light.

> While there has not been a significant decline of perception of the threat of nuclear war, there has been a very significant increase in concern about the magnitude and acuteness of national priorities and a relative retrenchment from international concerns and commitments by our people and government.[47]

The development of the mutual assured destruction doctrine of deterrence (see Chapter 11) also undercut the rationale for civil defense.[48] By 1992, with the cold war over and the Soviet Union in disintegration, Americans simply did not want to think about the fact that the republics of the former Soviet Union possessed sufficient offensive nuclear weapons to destroy the United States many times over.

Old Traditions and New Realities. The experience of World War II and the birth of the cold war in its aftermath transformed some important aspects of American approaches to national security. Reluctantly at first, Americans came to accept the role of the United States as a world power with worldwide responsibilities. The specter of communism as a challenge to the freedom of peoples everywhere and the advent of Soviet nuclear capability destroyed Americans' traditional sense of continental security and induced them to look to security matters well beyond their shores.

Traditional faith in the rationality of people was reexpressed through the United Nations. Yet other agreements—military alliances—hedged the bet on rationality as far as communists were concerned. In part, too, American utopianism was revived in the altruism of rebuilding a shattered Europe through the Marshall Plan and in the impulse to share the blessings of economic development worldwide through a massive program of foreign assistance. But, although partially rooted in utopianism and the familiar sense of mission, these initiatives also reflected a pragmatic view that the threat of communism could be stopped on two levels: (1) direct Soviet military threats could be deterred by confronting them with military forces deployed worldwide and backed by strategic nuclear forces; and (2) communist subversion could be stopped through foreign aid designed to "stabilize" allies and less developed nations worldwide. U.S. policy, thus, became one of "containing" communism through military and economic countermeasures.

Not only did the aversion to a peacetime standing army weaken after World War II, as noted earlier, but so did the tendency to isolate the military from decisions about war and peace. General George Marshall began the process during the war when he created the War Department's Special Planning Division (SPD) and charged it with postwar planning. The SPD established direct liaison with the Department of State, the Bureau of the Budget, and the War Production Board, and its members made regular appearances before congressional committees to provide information and gain congressional approval of major postwar proposals, for example, unification of the services and Universal Military Training (UMT). The National Security Act of 1947 further signaled a conceptual overhaul in the American approach to national security; military views became an inherent part of overall defense policy and planning. A new organization, the National Security Council, was established by the act to determine at the highest level of government the relationships between national objectives and military policy, in peacetime and in war—and in the zone of ambiguity.

The traditional primacy of domestic affairs remained—reinforced after the 1960s by a lingering "Vietnam syndrome"—but anticommunism and Soviet actions, especially after the December 1979 invasion of Afghanistan, drove

Americans to devote an increasingly substantial share of the nation's wealth to defense and foreign aid programs. The Reagan military buildup of 1980 to 1988 added $1 trillion to the defense program planned by the Carter administration. Americans demonstrated their resolve to use limited military force in Grenada (1983) and in Panama (1989) to protect U.S. security interests.[49]

By 1989 it had become increasingly clear that Soviet communism and its support for wars of national liberation in the Third World were coming to an end. Demand for large reductions in defense spending grew, intensified by an increasingly sluggish U.S. economy. By August 1990 when Saddam Hussein invaded Kuwait, U.S. security planners were free to enter operation Desert Shield and to conduct a collective limited war (Operation Desert Storm) under U.N. mandate without real concern that Soviet armed forces would intervene to support Iraq. The putsch of August 1991 that ended Gorbachev's regime and fragmented the Soviet Union spelled the end of the cold war and left the United States in the position as the world's sole superpower.

With the demise of the Soviet threat worldwide, Americans began in the late 1980s to cut back defense spending rapidly and to refocus on domestic priorities. But this did not mean that Americans were prepared to enter a new phase of isolationism. To the contrary, the concept of a "new world order" emerged which implied that—after other appropriate methods failed—the United States was prepared to use military force to stop outright aggression, to counter terrorism and drug trafficking, and to prevent the development and spread of weapons of mass destruction. But there is an important qualification; by over four to one, Americans want the U.N., not the United States, to take the lead in defending international security.[50] In addition to having coalition partners share the risks of military action, Americans want them to share the costs.

As the United States moves toward the twenty-first century, national security policymakers will have to continue to take into account American traditional values and attitudes, even as they try to adapt the nation's policies to new realities. To acquire a consensus supporting the use of military force, balance of power or preponderance of power rationales may no longer suffice as they did in the cold war years after World War II.

Discussion Questions

1. How would you describe the "American national character"? Would all agree with your description? What influences one's description of "national character"?

2. What is public opinion? How important is it today in national security policy formulation in the United States? How can it be determined?

3. How does public opinion both enhance and inhibit an effective American national security policy?

4. What is the difference between the Lockean and Hobbesian philosophies, and what impact have they had on typical American views? How have these philosophies had an impact on American national security policy? In your opinion, which philosophy has dominated American national security in the past? Which dominates it in the present?

5. If "war is abhorrent to Americans," how can you explain the fact that the United States has been involved in numerous wars and maintains a large military establishment?

6. How would you describe the historical role of the military in peacetime national security policy? How has it changed?

7. To what extent do traditional values now constrain American national security decision-makers?

8. How will movement toward a new world order be affected by the traditional American approach to national security?

Recommended Reading

Almond, Gabriel A. *The American People and Foreign Policy*. 2d ed. New York: Praeger, 1977.

Calleo, David P. *NATO Reconstruction or Dissolution?*. Washington, D.C.: The Paul Nitze School for Advanced International Studies, Foreign Policy Institute, 1992.

Foot, Rosemary. *The Wrong War: American Policy and the Dimensions of the Korean Conflict, 1950–1953*. Ithaca, N.Y.: Cornell University Press, 1985.

Gaddis, John L. *Strategies of Containment*. New York: Oxford University Press, 1981.

Gelb, Leslie H., and Betts, Richard K. *The Irony of Vietnam: The System Worked*. Washington, D.C.: Brookings Institution, 1979.

Huntington, Samuel P. *The Soldier and the State*. Cambridge, Mass.: Harvard University Press, Belknap Press, 1957.

Jonas, Manfred. *Isolationism in America, 1935–1941*. Ithaca, N.Y.: Cornell University Press, 1966.

Kennan, George F. *American Diplomacy, 1900–1950*. Chicago: University of Chicago Press, 1951.

Kissinger, Henry. *Nuclear Weapons and Foreign Policy*. New York: Harper, 1957.

Kober, Stanley. "Idealpolitik." *Foreign Policy* 79 (1990) pp. 3–24.

Merk, Frederick. *Manifest Destiny and Mission in American History*. New York: Knopf, 1963.

Osgood, Robert E. *Limited War: The Challenge to American Strategy*. Chicago: University of Chicago Press, 1957.

———. *NATO: The Entangling Alliance*. Chicago: University of Chicago Press, 1962.

Rearden, Steven S. *The Evolution of American Strategic Doctrine: Paul M. Nitze and the Soviet Challenge*. Boulder, Colo.: Westview Press, 1984.

Russett, Bruce. *Controlling the Sword: The Democratic Governance of National Security*. Cambridge, Mass.: Harvard University Press, 1990.

Tucker, Robert W. *The Just War: A Study in Contemporary American Doctrine*. 2d ed. Baltimore: Johns Hopkins University Press, 1979.

Tucker, Robert W. and David C. Henrickson. *The Imperial Temptation: The New World Order and America's Purpose*. New York: Council on Foreign Relations Press, 1992.

Weigley, Russell F. *The American Way of War*. New York: Macmillan, 1973.

4

The Evolution of American National Security Policy

National security strategy and military structure are shaped by the interactions of a number of influences, many of which defy precise identification. However, there are three principal categories of variables through which the evolution of strategic policy and military structure can largely be traced. They are international political and military developments, domestic priorities, and technological advancements.

International Political and Military Developments. The international environment is an important and constantly changing influence on U.S. policy. U.S. strategy is largely a response to perceived threats to American interests and objectives that exist in the international arena. As Walter Lippmann suggested, a nation is secure to the extent to which it is not in danger of having to sacrifice core values, such as national independence or territorial integrity, if it wishes to avoid war and is able, if challenged, to maintain those values by victory in such a war.[1] The perception of international threats to U.S. core values and interests is thus the base for the formulation and execution of national security policy.

A major factor in establishing the international environment is the presence or absence of alliances. The defense efforts of friendly and allied states help to define U.S. security problems and to condition the type and size of American effort required. American capability to pursue national security objectives is augmented or diminished by both quantitative and qualitative consideration of U.S. alliances vis-à-vis the alliance arrangements of potential opponents. It is also conditioned, of course, by the impact of unaligned nations or other third parties, including international and transnational organizations.

Domestic Politics. A nation's security policy is also heavily influenced by domestic politics. At a minimum, the internal environment determines the amount of effort that a society will devote to foreign and defense policy.[2] In the United States, the impact of domestic politics is seen most heavily in the budgetary process, but it is also felt in such areas as manpower policy (for example, the draft). Manpower strengths, weapons systems, strategic mobility, and other resources available for national security purposes are necessarily defined and tailored by defense budgets. Defense budgets and programs may not determine strategy, but national security options are heavily conditioned by the nature and extent of the resources available. Regardless of the type of regime, domestic goals have a great impact on the development of a nation's security policy and its allocation of resources.

Technological Change. Technology is a major variable in the interaction of influences that determine security policy. What is "possible" in American national security is in considerable part determined by the technological capabilities of both the United States and its adversaries. The impact of technological advances upon traditional security concerns and calculations is enormous. One need only look at the carnage of World War I to see the results of policy not keeping pace with technology. A century of relative peace in Europe had left military strategies largely as they were at the time of the Congress of Vienna, yet there had been a century of unparalleled technological advancement between 1815 and 1914. The military strategies of 1914 simply were not adequate for the proper employment of existing technological capabilities, and the stalemate that developed along the Western front was due in large part to the inability to adapt military strategy and tactics to the new realities of war imposed by those capabilities.

Today the security of the United States and its allies remains founded partly upon the strength and invulnerability of U.S. strategic nuclear weapons.[3] The extent to which a potential adversary is deterred from threatening the security interests of the United States is shaped in part by the perception of American capability and willingness to employ its vast nuclear armory. Rapid technological advancements, whether in the proliferation of offensive nuclear capabilities or in the development of systems of strategic defense, that affect this perceived quality of deterrence will powerfully influence the formulation of national defense policy. In the wake of the impressive allied victory in the 1991 Gulf war, a victory marked by the dramatic technological superiority of the allied forces, there is little doubt that nonnuclear technological advances, such as "smart weapons," can also have great effects on national security.

Strategy and Structure. National security policies or strategies are for the most part "implemented" by military force structures. Since international relations and domestic politics are intertwined, national security policy (which comprises both strategic and structural policies) exists in two worlds; any major decision about it influences and is influenced by both international and domestic politics. Strategic decisions are made largely in response to perceived threats in the international environment; they deal primarily with commitments, deployment and employment of military forces, and the readiness and development of military capabilities. Structural decisions are made mostly in terms of domestic politics and deal primarily with budget and force decisions on defense personnel, materiel, and organization.[4] The two types of decisions interact at all levels. Strategic decisions ''determine'' the force structures required to implement them, yet the resources made available through structural decisions limit the extent to which strategic decisions can be made. Indeed, ongoing programs that exist as the result of structural decisions have a dynamic of their own in shaping policy.

Containment Policy: Mobilization or Deterrence Strategy?

The United States traditionally has relied on a national security policy of mobilizing to meet threats rather than constantly maintaining adequate forces. Historically, America's geographic location, both the people and policymakers believed, would prevent direct attack on the United States, while recognition of impending hostilities abroad would give it sufficient time in a crisis to convert its industrial and manpower potential into operational military strength. Yet the realities of the international arena following World War II presented a threat for which the United States would have to be constantly ready. The security of the United States would depend on its ability to deter war by presenting a posture of military preparedness. The early postwar years then, were marked by a fundamental tension between the traditional strategy of mobilization and the new strategy of deterrence.

The Return to Normalcy, 1945–1946. The end of World War II saw the United States emerge as the most powerful nation on earth. Its homeland was untouched by war, and its enormous industrial potential had produced war material not only for its own armies and navies but for those of its allies as well. The collapse of Germany and Japan meant total victory and led to visions of a prolonged period of peace implemented through the collective security machinery of the embryonic United Nations. Technologically, the United States was also in an unchallengeable position. American development of the atomic bomb was probably the most important single event to affect postwar international relations.[5]

With victory came enormous public and congressional pressure for the United States to demobilize its armies and bring the troops home. This pressure led to one of the most rapid demobilizations in history. On V-J Day the army had 8,020,000 soldiers, but by July 1946, less than a year after the end of the war, it was down to less than a quarter of that, to 1,889,690.[6] In the two years from 1945 to 1947, the United States allowed its overall armed forces to decline from a wartime peak of 12 million soldiers to a low of 1.4 million.[7] This massive disarmament occurred despite the fact that the wartime alliance between the United States and the Soviet Union was being replaced by rapidly increasing tension. American policymakers, confronted with what they perceived to be aggressive Soviet intentions in Eastern Europe, Greece, Turkey, Iran, and the Far East, came to agree on the need for a tougher line with the Soviets. In 1947, George Kennan developed and expressed the concept of containment.

> The main element of any United States policy toward the Soviet Union must be that of a long-term, patient but firm and vigilant containment of Russian expansive tendencies.[8]

Acceptance of the policy of containment laid the foundation for the theoretical framework of American strategic policy for the next four decades. Opposition to communist expansion became *the* fundamental principle of American foreign policy. Although there were to be disagreements over the means to achieve this policy, there was little disagreement on the end itself. The United States, public and leaders alike, came to agree upon the policy of containment; that policy led in turn to the development of the strategy of deterrence.

Conflict between the New Strategy and the Old Military Structure. Successful implementation of the policy of containment required ready forces sufficient to deny the Soviets the ability to expand their empire. For this purpose mobilization potential was clearly less useful than forces-in-being. In December 1947, Secretary of Defense Forrestal listed the "four outstanding military facts of the world" as: (1) the predominance of Russian land power in Europe and Asia, (2) the predominance of American sea power, (3) U.S. exclusive possession of the atomic bomb, and (4) American superior production capacity.[9]

In a sense, the problem confronting President Truman was how to checkmate the first military fact with the latter three. Put differently, the problem for containment was twofold: (1) inadequacy of conventional ground and air units and (2) doctrinal inadequacy concerning strategic use of a tiny atomic arsenal. The United States could threaten the Soviet homeland with atomic attack if Soviet armies marched into Western Europe, but the atom bomb was of little help in such other defense tasks as preserving the integrity of Iran, deterring attack on Korea, or suppressing guerrillas in Greece.[10] Conventional ground and air power seemed essential for these latter tasks, yet the U.S. force structure was weakest in precisely those respects.

Continued Reliance on Mobilization. Implementing the policy of containment therefore raised the difficult problem of how to deal with narrow domestic political constraints on the size of the military effort. Overriding a presidential veto, Congress passed a general income tax reduction bill in early 1948, thereby limiting the revenue available for domestic and military expenditures. In spite of the president's requests, no substantial tax increases were approved until after the outbreak of the Korean War. Since President Truman was determined to balance the budget, the administration imposed a ceiling on military expenditures consonant with the reduced resources available. To compound the difficulty, the "remainder" approach to defense spending was developed, whereby funds available for security expenditures were calculated by estimating general revenues, subtracting funds earmarked for domestic programs, foreign aid, and interest, and devoting the remainder to defense spending. From fiscal year (FY) 1947 to FY 1950, security expenditures were virtually static at $14.4, $11.7, $12.9, and $13.0 billion, respectively.[11] Domestic political priorities ensured that there would be inadequate monies for the forces-in-being believed needed to contain Soviet power; by default, reliance on mobilization continued.

A second constraint on the successful implementation of the policy of containment was the doctrinal orientation of the military. American military thinking was preoccupied not so much with the development of strategy and forces-in-being to deter or fight limited wars but rather with preparations to mobilize forces to win a major war if one should occur.[12] The army continued to insist that World War III would be similar to the war it had just prosecuted so successfully. In his final report as chief of staff, General Eisenhower urged more extensive preparation for the total mobilization that would be required in the future.[13] "Armed forces and the nature of war, if war comes in the next few years," declared the chief army planner, Brig. Gen. George A. Lincoln, in 1947, "will in general be similar initially to the closing phases of World War II."[14]

Although the air force and the navy felt the weapons of World War II were obsolete and began to push for new strategic systems, in the immediate postwar years the concept of deterrence by forces-in-being had little place in military planning.[15] Effectively, the goals of each of the armed services had been set prior to the end of World War II, and since there was no unified budgetary process, each set of goals was based on the parochial conceptions of the roles and missions of the separate services. As Samuel Huntington summarizes, "The two great constraints of effective military planning, the doctrinal heritage from the past and the pressure of domestic needs, combined to produce a serious gap between military policy and foreign policy."[16]

The Truman Doctrine. On March 12, 1947, President Truman appeared before a joint session of Congress and outlined what he felt was the necessary U.S. response to communist pressure in Greece and Turkey. The president maintained, in what came to be known as the Truman Doctrine, that the United States must help other nations to maintain their political institutions and national integrity when threatened by aggressive attempts to overthrow them and to institute totalitarian regimes. This was no more than a frank recognition, Truman declared, that totalitarian systems imposed their will on free people, by direct or indirect aggression, and undermined the foundations of international peace and hence the security of the United States.[17]

The Truman Doctrine represented a marked departure from the U.S. tradition of minimal peacetime involvement in international affairs. The doctrine set forth themes justifying American foreign involvements and initiated military and economic aid programs to nations resisting communist aggression. The justification it contained for American intervention in foreign lands was used repeatedly by subsequent administrations.[18]

The Marshall Plan. The Marshall Plan, a massive economic aid program launched in 1948 and implemented through the Organization for European Economic Cooperation formed for that purpose, was designed to help restore the war-shattered economies of Europe. American leaders believed that the ability of Europe to resist communist aggression was dependent on its rapid economic recovery.[19] The Marshall Plan, taken in conjunction with the Truman Doctrine, marked the emergence of the United States as a world power bent on establishing stability in the international community and willing to expend major resources and adopt an activist role in seeing that U.S. interests abroad were maintained.

An accumulation of events in 1948 and 1949 solidified the U.S. view of the communist threat. The forced communization of Czechoslovakia and the blockade of surface access routes to West Berlin, both occurring in 1948, intensified Western perceptions of the Soviet Union as an overtly hostile nation. In 1949, two even more dramatic events affected the formulation of U.S. security strategy. In August, the U.S.S.R. exploded its first nuclear device. The U.S. monopoly on atomic weapons had been broken years sooner than anticipated by U.S. planners. In late 1949, the Communist Chinese completed the conquest of the mainland, creating the appearance of a monolithic communist adversary stretching from Central Europe across the length of the Asian continent.

NSC 68 and Its Implications. The disturbing events of 1948–1949 highlighted the inadequacies of the U.S. military posture. Awareness of these shortcomings led to the first serious attempt to reconcile strategy with structure, that is, to balance the strategy of containment with a force capability designed to implement the tenets of the strategy. A joint State–Defense Department committee was instructed "to make an over-all review and reassessment of American foreign and defense policy."[20] The report, delivered to the National Security Council on April 1, 1950, and labeled NSC 68, advocated "an immediate and large scale build up in our military and general strength and that of our allies with the intention of righting the power balance and in hope that through means other than all-out war we could induce a change in the nature of the Soviet system."[21] NSC 68 called for a substantial increase in defense expenditures, warning that the United States must be capable of dealing with piecemeal aggression and subversion, with both limited and all-out war. The problem was how to sell a substantial increase in the defense budget without an imminent threat in an administration committed to a policy of economy and balanced budgets. The problem was solved on June 25, 1950, by North Korea's blatant invasion of South Korea, overrunning the U.N. observers on the border.

War and Rearmament. The invasion of South Korea provided the immediate crisis that generated public support for vastly increased defense spending. Expenditures for national security programs rose from $13.0 billion for FY 1950 to $22.3 billion in FY 1951, $44.0 billion in FY 1952, and $50.4 billion in FY 1953.[22]

There were important differences of opinion within informed American circles concerning Soviet intentions in Korea. Some felt the attack by the Soviets' North Korean satellite was part of a general plan for expansion, while others saw it as a feint designed to divert resources from Western Europe.[23] Whatever the initial view, Communist Chinese entry into the war in late 1950 solidified the perception of an aggressive, monolithic communist threat to the Free World.

The outbreak of the war found the United States with an extremely limited conventional capability, with a corresponding loss of life, both military and civilian. The resulting rearmament effort was pulled by three competing, but complementary, purposes: (1) immediate prosecution of the Korean War, (2) creation of a mobilization base for the long term, and (3) development of active forces to balance Soviet strength and to deter further Soviet aggression.[24] In short, the war in Korea made rearmament possible, but rearmament was not directed solely at the problem of fighting the war; forces were also being developed for worldwide deterrence purposes. As Huntington described it, "Competitive and yet equally relevant, mobilization and deterrence marched shoulder to shoulder through the Korean War rearmament effort."[25]

NATO: The Institutionalization of Containment. Soviet political pressure on its neighbors to the west and south and the existence of very large Soviet conventional forces, the first of Secretary Forrestal's "four outstanding military facts of the world," caused widespread and increasing concern about the security of Western Europe. As a consequence, for the first time in history, the United States deemed it necessary to enter into peacetime military alliance with foreign states and to deploy its major forces on the territory of its allies in the absence of armed conflict. The North Atlantic Treaty was signed in April 1949. The twelve signatories agreed to keep the peace among themselves and to resist aggression jointly. An attack on one would be considered an attack on all. Europe became America's first line of defense; the North Atlantic Treaty Organization (NATO) was the expression of the American effort to contain communism by military means.

In February 1952, the Lisbon Conference set a 1954 goal of ninety NATO divisions (half active, half reserve) as necessary for conventional defense of Europe. It quickly became obvious that the goal would not be met as European members of NATO, less fearful of Soviet aggression after two years of war in Korea had failed to spread to Europe, began to reduce military budgets, cut terms of service for draftees, and stretch out arms procurements. In December 1952, the North Atlantic Council approved a drastic reduction in Lisbon force goals, and NATO came to rely in very large measure on the tactical and strategic nuclear weapons of the United States to deter Soviet aggression.

Conflicting Priorities. As the Korean War developed into a stalemate, it became evident that the war had not, as some had feared, marked the beginning of a general Soviet assault on the West. With continuing casualties and costs, and without a clear perception of an imminent Soviet threat, the American public became increasingly sour on the war in Korea. Public resentment over increasing military spending rose, and by 1952 the Truman administration made a marked shift toward domestic priorities. With the incoming (early 1953) Eisenhower administration's so-called New Look, the basic strategy of the United States explicitly shifted from mobilization to deterrence. By 1954 it was accepted by U.S. policymakers and the public that the international communist threat to American and European security was real and immediate, and that the United States no longer enjoyed the geographic protection that historically had afforded the time required for mobilization of military personnel and other resources. Acceptance of the strategy of deterrence and the necessity for forces-in-being to implement it reflected an acknowledgment of the realities of international and technological affairs.

Massive Retaliation and the New Look

Domestic Priorities and Strategic Reassessment. President Eisenhower regarded the threat to U.S. security as dual—military and economic. The military threat posed by the communist powers was obvious, but Eisenhower also believed that continued high levels of defense spending by the United States threatened the stability of the economy and was, therefore, also a significant long-term threat. The New Look was an effort to reconcile the conflicting priorities of economic growth and major military programs. Further, since the dual threat was a continuing one, the proper balance between domestic and military expenditures would have to be maintained for an extended period.

Upon taking office President Eisenhower was determined to reduce military expenditures and balance the federal budget. He had campaigned on a peace and economy platform and was committed to a tax reduction and spending cuts in order to reduce the Truman budget deficit. Proposed cuts in military spending were opposed by the Joint Chiefs of Staff (JCS), who maintained that any reduction in expenditures would endanger national security. An impasse developed between the administration and a JCS committed to a substantial military build-up directed to a future "year of maximum danger" (about 1956–1958), the time at which Soviet military capabilities would reach their highest strength relative to those of the West. The old JCS was replaced, and in May 1953 the new joint chiefs assumed the task (even before they took office) of wrestling with the difficult problems of strategic reassessment at which their predecessors had balked.

The National Security Council Planning Board, in a study labeled NSC 162, made an effort to define future national security policy in the broadest sense. The paper recommended the continuation of the policy of containment but with greater reliance on nuclear weapons and strategic air power and an expansion of capabilities to defend the continental United States from air attack.

The JCS had also begun its reassessment. The Sequoia study (named after the secretary of the navy's yacht, upon which the final discussions had been held) recommended further development of U.S. air defenses and strategic retaliatory forces, withdrawal of some American forces from overseas, creation of a mobile strategic reserve, reliance upon Allied forces for their own local defense buttressed by U.S. air and sea power, and strengthening of U.S. reserve forces.[26]

The Strategic Impact of Technology. In essence, technology provided the means by which Eisenhower escaped from the strategy versus structure box. American technological and numerical superiority in nuclear weapons systems provided a strategic option that, if pursued, made possible achievement of domestic goals. Technology, in the form of strategic nuclear air power and tactical nuclear weapons, permitted the blend of seemingly incompatible political goals, that is, a foreign policy of worldwide containment and a domestic policy focused on driving down military expenditures.

New Look Programs. The Eisenhower New Look strategy made a number of assumptions about the international environment. It assumed that there would be no significant increase in international tensions and no significant change in the relationship between U.S. and Soviet power. Massive retaliation was to be the major deterrent; conventional ground forces were to be reduced, continental air defense capabilities were to be expanded. The key aspect of the New Look was the decision to place very high reliance upon nuclear weapons.[27] Strategic air power became the mainstay of the U.S. deterrent posture, and tactical nuclear weapons were to be used to replace the reduced levels of conventional forces in forward defense areas.

The critical strategic change of the New Look was expressed by Secretary of State Dulles on January 12, 1954, and in the subsequent decision by the North Atlantic Council to deploy tactical nuclear weapons in Western Europe and to authorize the NATO authorities to base military planning on the assumption that nuclear weapons would be used in the event of hostilities. Although there were a number of interpretations of just what massive retaliation entailed, Secretary Dulles stated, "There is no local defense which alone will contain the mighty land power of the Communist world. Local defenses must be reinforced by the further deterrent of massive retaliation power."[28] Therefore, Dulles stated, the president had made the basic decision "to depend primarily upon a great capacity to retaliate instantly and by means and at places of our own choosing."[29] In sum, America's military capabilities were to hinge on nuclear weapons to meet even those military contingencies threatening less than general war.

Extending Containment. Extending the American military alliance system beyond NATO (and the earlier Organization of American States) became an integral part of containment strategy. Prior to the adoption of an explicit strategy of massive retaliation in 1954, the United States had already begun a process of expanding defense commitments worldwide with the goal of containing communism. One principal lesson of the Korean War, as perceived by U.S. policymakers in the 1950s, was the judgment that American disengagement and equivocation had tempted the communists to invade. The conclusion was that America's commitment to defend important friendly territories adjacent to communist countries must be made specific, and the most obvious way to do so was through military alliances.

The network of alliances began to form soon after the outbreak of hostilities in Korea. In 1951 the United States negotiated a security treaty with Japan, guaranteeing the defense of Japan and granting the United States land, sea, and air bases on the Japanese home islands. A similar mutual defense treaty was signed with the Philippines as well. Also in 1951 the United States signed with Australia and New Zealand the ANZUS treaty, pledging U.S. support for the security of those two nations. In 1953, following the armistice, Korea and the United States signed a security pact pledging consultation in the event of armed attack and establishing the disposition of land, sea, and air forces in and around the Republic of Korea. In 1954 the United States signed a treaty with Nationalist China which called for joint consultation in the event of danger of armed attack and specified the disposition of American forces on Taiwan and the Pescadores.

The Southeast Asia Treaty Organization (SEATO), of which Australia, France, New Zealand, Pakistan, the Philippines, Thailand, the United Kingdom, and the United States were members, was established in 1954. The SEATO Treaty provided that each member would "act to meet the common danger" in the event of hostilities in the treaty area. In addition to the formal alignment with SEATO, the United States was also sending millions of dollars in military aid to Indochina to help finance the French war with the Viet Minh. In 1954, as the French position in Vietnam became tenuous, the French government requested the commitment of American troops but was refused by President Eisenhower.

The Central Treaty Organization (CENTO), which the United States supported but did not formally join, was an American- and British-sponsored alliance to prevent Soviet communism from moving southward; the organization linked Britain, Turkey, Iran, and Pakistan. Additionally, the United States signed bilateral agreements with Pakistan and Iran.

Given the presumption that American nuclear weapons could and would serve to deter both large and small aggressions, and given the policy of a balanced budget and the widespread concern in the United States about communist aggression, it appeared to make sense in the 1950s to strengthen governments on the periphery of the communist bloc by

- Pledging the support of the United States to prevent or stop aggression, especially if communist-inspired
- Providing military assistance to strengthen the defense capabilities of governments bordering the communist bloc
- Providing economic and/or military assistance to preserve or help create

political and economic stability for governments that allied themselves with the anticommunist cause

- Training and supporting foreign troops in their own country as less expensive than maintaining American troops abroad
- Establishing basing rights as the quid pro quo of assistance

In short, the United States included the Asian rimlands in its ring of containment and, attempting to preclude another Korea, sought to knit the states of the region into a network of military alliances under American leadership.

The New New Look, 1956. In 1954, when the policy of massive retaliation was established, the United States possessed the ability to destroy the military forces of the U.S.S.R. with little likelihood of serious retaliatory damage in return. By 1956, however, this was no longer clearly so. Major Soviet catch-up efforts and technological innovations had led to an arms spiral; in an astonishingly short time, mutual vulnerability to nuclear devastation had apparently become a fact.[30] A ''balance of terror'' stemming from the rapid growth of Soviet strategic nuclear power had undermined the New Look's two key assumptions: that the earlier ratio of Soviet-to-American nuclear power would not be radically altered and that U.S. nuclear retaliatory forces would deter both large and small aggressions.

Even at the outset, the doctrine of massive retaliation had been criticized by such analysts as M.I.T.'s William Kaufmann and Harvard's Henry Kissinger, who argued that the threat of massive nuclear retaliation was not effective in deterring local, ambiguous wars because it was not believable. There exists a threshold of conflict, they argued, below which it is not credible to threaten to use strategic nuclear forces. Given the balance of terror, the insurgencies taking place in developing nations around the world fell below that threshold. Nonstrategic forces would be needed to deal effectively with such relatively low-level conflicts.

The administration began to look for a strategy that permitted greater flexibility. The resulting ''New New Look'' was an attempt to develop a new approach to deterrence by adjusting existing programs but without increasing military expenditures. The dominant characteristics of the New New Look included: (1) continuing efforts to stabilize military spending; (2) downgrading of mobilization, readiness, and reserve forces; (3) acceptance of strategic retaliatory capability sufficient, but only sufficient, to deter a direct attack on American territory or equally vital interests; and (4) grudging recognition of the need to build and maintain capabilities for limited war.[31]

It should be noted that the New New Look emphasized tactical nuclear weapons as a credile means of waging limited war. Indeed, one of the major distinctions of the new approach was the direct mating of tactical nuclear weapons with the strategy of limited war.[32] Writing in the October 1957 *Foreign Affairs*, Secretary Dulles explained that ''in the future it may . . . be feasible to place less reliance upon deterrence of vast retaliatory power'' because the ''nations which are around the Sino-Soviet perimeter can possess an effective defense [through tactical nuclear warfare] against fullscale conventional attack.''[33]

New New Look programs were shaped by the twin pressures of Soviet and American technological achievement and an American economy that was plagued by what was, at the time, a unique combination of continuing recession and inflation. Largely as a result of inflation, defense costs were rising. Confronted with a choice between increasing the national debt or reducing military spending, the Eisenhower administration chose the latter. Spending in FY 1958 was $39 billion; in FY 1959 and FY 1960, $41.2 billion; and in FY 1961, $43.2 billion (these are in current year, *not* constant dollar terms). In constant dollar terms, military spending was less in 1960 than it had been in any year since 1951.[34]

The final years of the Eisenhower presidency saw a number of international and technological pressures brought to bear on U.S. national security policy. In August 1957 the Soviets announced the successful test of an intercontinental ballistic missile (ICBM). In October of that year the Soviets launched the first artificial satellite, sputnik, causing an intense reexamination of U.S. strategic programs and demands for increased military expenditures. The Gaither Committee, appointed early in 1957 by President Eisenhower to study a fallout shelter program for the United States, presented its report shortly after the launching of sputnik. Defining its mandate very broadly, the committee recommended a substantial increase in the defense budget, aimed primarily at improving the U.S. strategic posture.[35] Although the committee's recommendations were largely rejected, the discussion of strategic capabilities which it evoked helped provoke the ''missile-gap'' controversy, which became an issue in the 1960 presidential campaign.

Flexible Response, 1960–1968

The Necessity for Change. As the new decade began, changes in both the external environment and technology dictated a serious reappraisal of military strategy. The growth of Soviet thermonuclear capabilities cast increasing doubt on the wisdom and credibility of a retaliation threat. The missile-gap controversy raised questions about the adequacy of U.S. nuclear force levels. Western awareness of the increasingly bitter dispute between China and the Soviet Union aggravated the problems of deterrence, for China came to be viewed as a power center and a threat in its own right.

Changes in weapons technology and force structure also made a reexamination of U.S. policy imperative. Overreliance on tactical nuclear weapons, particularly in Europe, was increasingly viewed as dangerous for two reasons. First, in view of the relatively weakened U.S. strategic position, deterrence could well fail; and, if it did, escalation to all-out nuclear war would be hard to check because there is no discernible ''firebreak'' between tactical and strategic nuclear weapons. Second, should a crisis arise, shortages of conventional forces appeared to place decision-makers in the dilemma of choosing between nuclear retaliation and inaction.

Turbulence in the developing countries of the world also demonstrated the shortcomings of U.S. retaliation strategy. Insurgencies spread in Asia, Africa, and Latin America, dramatically highlighting the inapplicability of nuclear weapons. Communist nations gave their support to "wars of national liberation," and Soviet military and economic assistance was extended to a number of regions. Massive retaliation was inadequate to deal with these complexities, and nuclear technology made general war too costly to both sides. Clearly, a new policy was called for, and the incoming Kennedy administration wasted little time in framing one.

The Search for Options. The search for policy options began at the outset of the Kennedy administration. The budget ceiling approach to defense policy-making was abandoned, and budget constraints on Secretary of Defense Robert McNamara were lifted by the president. The budget ceiling approach had not proven an effective means of rationally structuring the U.S. defense program. In effect, service missions were determined independently, monies were allocated on a "fair shares" basis, and programs were developed with little regard for what the other services were doing. National strategies and priorities were supposedly set forth in an agreed National Security Council document called the Basic National Security Policy (BNSP). However, the BNSP was a vague compromise document that provided little real guidance on how defense dollars should be spent. General Maxwell Taylor summarized the document's weaknesses:

> It was so broad in nature and general in language as to provide limited guidance in practical application. In the course of its development, the sharp issues in national defense which confront our leaders have been blurred in conference and in negotiation. The final text thus permits many different interpretations. . . . The Basic National Security Policy document means all things to all people and settles nothing.[36]

Given the vague nature of the guidance that they received, the services had a great deal of latitude to develop their own programs. McNamara, when he came into office, was appalled.

> The Army planning, for example, was based, largely, on a long war of attrition, while the Air Force planning was based, largely, on a short war of nuclear bombardment. Consequently, the Army was stating a requirement for stocking months of fighting supplies against the event of a sizeable [*sic*] conventional conflict while the Air Force stock requirements for such a war had to be measured in days, and not very many days at that.[37]

Strategic programs were developed independently by each service. For example, navy briefings to Secretary McNamara in 1961 on the number of Polaris missile submarines required never mentioned the existence of the U.S. Air Force or any of its strategic retaliatory forces. When the air force made analyses of how many Minuteman missiles were required, it assumed that no more Polaris submarines would be authorized than whatever the existing number happened to be.[38]

McNamara was determined to centralize and control the development of U.S. military forces. He received two instructions from the president: "Develop the force structure necessary to our military requirements without regard to arbitrary or predetermined budget ceilings. And secondly, having determined that force structure, procure it at the lowest possible cost."[39]

Before the formal elaboration of a new U.S. strategy, McNamara applied a number of "quick fixes" to the U.S. force structure. He accelerated the procurement schedule for the submarine-launched ballistic missile (the Polaris), doubled the production capacity for Minuteman ICBMs, and placed one-half of the bombers of the Strategic Air Command (SAC) on a quick-reaction alert.[40] Improvements began immediately in airlift and sealift capabilities, and the size of the army, marine corps, and tactical air forces was expanded.[41] McNamara's purpose was to increase U.S. combat strength measurably and quickly while developing a new strategy for the use of U.S. military force.

The Development of Flexible Response. Kennedy and McNamara were determined to tailor U.S. military capabilities to meet any threat with an appropriate force. The strategy of flexible response was developed to give the president the capability to respond effectively with any level of force, nuclear or conventional, to an adversary challenge.

Flexible response within the strategic nuclear posture provided policymakers a number of options for retaliatory policy. Massive (spasm) retaliation, limited nuclear countervalue (i.e., city) attacks, and counterforce strikes theoretically were all feasible war-fighting—and therefore credible deterrent—strategies. The development of submarine-launched ballistic missiles (SLBMs) such as Polaris enabled the United States to procure a relatively secure retaliatory force, and antiballistic missile (ABM) defenses were reaching the point of technological feasibility. The Kennedy and, later, Johnson administrations increased the U.S. strategic inventory dramatically, developing the capability to inflict "unacceptable damage" on the Soviet Union after absorbing a surprise Soviet first strike.* In fact, the United States developed an overwhelming strategic advantage over the Soviet Union, an imbalance that was not threatened until the end of the decade.

It was in the area of conventional forces that the doctrine of flexible response differed most dramatically from that of massive retaliation. If the United States

---

*What constituted unacceptable damage to an adversary could not be measured precisely. However, the planning figure accepted by U.S. authorities was 25 to 33 percent of Soviet population and about 75 percent of Soviet industrial capacity. This judgment was influenced primarily by the demographics of Soviet population distribution and by the rapidly diminishing marginal returns beyond a certain level of retaliatory attack. For a more complete explanation of assured destruction criteria, see Alain C. Entheven and K. Wayne Smith, *How Much Is Enough?* (New York: Harper & Row, 1964), p. 207.

were to respond with an appropriate level of force to a wide variety of challenges, its conventional forces would most likely be the ones used. Neglected under the policy of massive retaliation, these force capabilities had to be improved and modernized. The army increased from twelve to sixteen divisions, the navy surface fleet was enlarged, and the reserves and National Guard were revitalized. Counterinsurgency forces were enlarged greatly in order to deal with low-intensity conflicts. In general, the conventional capabilities of the United States were enlarged and improved to the point at which it was asserted (wrongly) that the United States could achieve a "two-and-a-half" war posture, that is, be capable of fighting simultaneously a large-scale war in Europe, another sizable conflict somewhere else in the world, and a small-scale local threat as well.

U.S. efforts to introduce flexible response doctrine into NATO strategy initially encountered Allied resistance. Any shift to even early reliance on nonnuclear forces was certain to cause uneasiness among the European members of the alliance, who feared erosion of the nuclear deterrent. Whereas the Eisenhower administration had asserted that such weapons might well be used, by the end of the Johnson administration the United States was reluctant even to contemplate the use of nuclear weapons in limited wars.

Conventional Forces and Intervention. Improvements in conventional capabilities were not matched by the development of any clear doctrine governing intervention and the application of force. In his inaugural address John Kennedy had made his famous pledge: "Let every nation know, whether it wishes us well or ill, we shall pay any price, bear any burden, meet any hardship, support any friend or oppose any foe to assure the survival and the success of liberty." Such an open-ended commitment was of course unrealistic, for it did not provide any useful guidance for deciding when the use of force was in the national interest and when it was not. In mid 1965 the United States deployed ground combat troops to the Republic of Vietnam and also intervened in a civil upheaval in the Dominican Republic. As the Vietnam involvement lengthened and deepened, popular dissatisfaction grew, and domestic dissent and economic pressure began to play a significant role in the formulation of U.S. strategy. By FY 1968, defense spending had climbed to $78 billion, $20 billion of which represented the direct cost of the war in Vietnam.[42] The incoming Nixon administration was faced with the prospect of stalemate on the nuclear level and an unpopular, costly war on the conventional level.

Realistic Deterrence, 1969–1976

As pointed out in some detail in Chapter 3, by 1969 fundamental national consensus on the nature of U.S. national security policy had seriously weakened. The prolonged and seemingly unsuccessful U.S. intervention in Vietnam called into question the ability of the United States to deal with insurgencies around the world, and the nature of the strategic balance dictated a reassessment of American defense policy. The policy of containment, practically unchallenged since its inception shortly after World War II, came under increasingly critical scrutiny, for it no longer seemed to reflect a realistic appraisal of the international situation.

Reassessment of the Threat. Changes in both the strategic and the conventional environment dictated a reassessment of U.S. military policy. By 1968 the Soviet Union had achieved rough nuclear parity with the United States. Both sides had acquired secure second-strike capabilities, whereby each was capable of inflicting unacceptable damage on its opponent even after an enemy first strike. Since neither side could "win" by striking first, there was no pressure in a crisis for the side that might perceive itself to be inferior to launch a preemptive strike. Given the size and nature of their nuclear forces, both the United States and the Soviet Union seemed to realize that it was in their best interests to limit the possibility of confrontation. From such reasoning, at least on the U.S. side, came the concept of détente and its associated Strategic Arms Limitation Talks (SALT).

There was also a perceived need for reevaluation of the role of U.S. conventional forces. The war in Vietnam demonstrated the inapplicability of a limited-war doctrine in a revolutionary situation, and public and congressional disenchantment with military and other foreign embroilments dictated a rethinking of where and how U.S. conventional forces might be used. Other constraints also had an impact on U.S. military policy. The position of the dollar in the world economy was deteriorating as wartime inflation proceeded; social and economic problems in the United States continued to demand priority for domestic spending. Under these pressures, defense outlays as a percentage of GNP fell from 9.4 in FY 1968 to 5.9 in FY 1975. In FY 1964, the last pre–Vietnam War budget, defense spending represented 41.8 percent of the federal budget. Roughly a decade later, for FY 1975, defense expenditures accounted for 27.1 percent of federal outlays.[43] The defense spending decline was not just relative—but also absolute—when measured in constant dollars.

Strategic Sufficiency. Given the Soviet Union's nuclear power and its demonstrated ability and willingness to respond to improvements in American strategic forces, the Nixon administration concluded that nuclear superiority was impossible to maintain.[44] Any attempt to do so would only result in a reescalation of the arms race, with little increase in security for either side. Nevertheless, Nixon was unwilling to allow the Soviet Union to achieve a position of nuclear predominance. Strategic planning for U.S. forces thus focused on a new doctrine called "strategic sufficiency." The doctrine of sufficiency, reflecting a recognition that nuclear parity is the best one can achieve, includes a number of precepts:

- *Assured destruction*—To ensure the reliability of U.S. forces to inflict unacceptable damage on an opponent, a retaliatory capability was (and is) maintained in three separate and independent offensive systems—land-based ICBMs, SLBMs, and manned bombers—each capable of inflicting unacceptable levels of damage on the enemy through destruction of a major fraction of its population and economy.[45]

- *Flexible nuclear options*—The structuring of U.S. strategic forces was designed to ensure that they could respond in a variety of ways to various military contingencies. The development of extremely accurate warheads gave the president the capability for alternative strategic responses. He could choose a counterforce strike to destroy Soviet land-based missiles or other military targets, large or small, rather than retaliate against population centers. Flexibility of forces and targets allowed the president to tailor U.S. strategic response to the nature of the provocation. (On the other hand, opponents of counterforce capabilities argued that the extremely accurate warheads needed for flexible options might be perceived as a first-strike threat to Soviet retaliatory capabilities, thereby destabilizing the nuclear balance.)
- *Crisis stability*—Soviet knowledge that the United States could respond in a variety of ways rather than having to choose between massive retaliation and inaction was expected to stabilize relations by reducing Soviet willingness to stage a less than all-out attack.[46] Further, large U.S. invulnerable retaliatory capabilities contributed to stability because the Soviets recognized there was no rational advantage to shooting first; accordingly, temptation for a preemptive strike in a crisis was eliminated.
- *Perceived equality*—The final criterion of strategic sufficiency was that a rough balance should exist between the strategic capabilities of the United States and the Soviet Union. The importance of maintaining a balance resided in the perceptions of the superpowers and their allies. If politically attuned people perceived that there was an advantage to numerical superiority, then there was. Thus, although numerical comparisons were misleading, a rough balance was necessary in order to prevent coercion or intimidation of the United States or its allies.

Conventional Force Policy. The proliferation of newly independent states during the 1960s and the decline in the cohesiveness of the Western and communist alliances undermined the traditional vision of a bipolar world power structure. The limited applicability of the use of force, dramatically demonstrated by the inability of American intervention in Indochina to prevent the communist takeover there, also necessitated a reevaluation of U.S. policy and the implications of U.S. alliance commitments. In 1974 the Nixon administration's appraisal of conventional war policy reaffirmed one traditional commitment and modified another.

The U.S. commitment to NATO was reaffirmed and strengthened following U.S. withdrawal from Vietnam. Although the overall size of the U.S. Army was reduced by 50 percent, American NATO forces—which had been stripped of personnel and equipment during the Vietnam War—were strengthened and reequipped. Additionally, the United States abandoned the so-called two-and-a-half war strategy and began to maintain forces based on a one-and-a-half war strategy, that is, a large war in Europe or Asia, but not both, and a minor contingency somewhere else. (In reality, the change was not that dramatic, for, despite declaratory policy, the United States had earlier never even approached the kinds and levels of forces needed for two and a half wars.) The NATO commitment became the primary planning contingency for structuring U.S. conventional forces, and the conventional war-fighting capabilities of U.S. NATO forces were improved.

A major reappraisal of U.S. policy was also made concerning the feasibility of deterring or fighting local conflicts and insurgencies in developing countries. The resulting policy, known variously as the Guam Doctrine or the Nixon Doctrine, concluded that the United States would no longer automatically intervene against externally supported insurgencies. The Nixon Doctrine could be expressed as three essential principles: self-help, primary regional responsibility, and residual U.S. responsibility.[47]

The principle of self-help dictated that the country being threatened must take responsibility for its own security. In the event of conventional attack, the country under attack must provide the first line of defense. In the case of insurgency, the local government must bear the full load of combat operations. Further, in the case of insurgency, the United States would expect the local government to initiate vigorous programs of economic and political development.[48] Experience had taught that military action alone is generally not capable of dealing successfully with an insurgency but must be accompanied by political and social programs.

Regional responsibility meant that the United States expected neighboring countries to work together to eliminate or deal with the causes of instability in their areas. Regional cooperation, it was believed, would enable the countries concerned to prevent the emergence of insurgency better and to develop both politically and economically. If military operations were required to deal with an insurgency and outside forces were needed, the United States expected that they would be provided, at least in part, by the neighbors of the country under attack.[49]

The principle of residual U.S. responsibility indicated that the United States would not conduct programs that the nations should undertake themselves, but would provide appropriate military assistance. The United States would maintain a minimum presence in friendly, threatened developing areas but would intervene only if vital American interests were threatened. President Ford, and subsequently President Carter, endorsed the policy of stringently limited U.S. involvement as the basis for U.S. action in dealing with insurgencies in the developing nations of the world.

Strategic Reassessment, 1977–1981

As customarily occurs with the advent of a new administration, President Carter initiated a reappraisal of U.S. national security policy when he came to office in January 1977. Such reappraisal was clearly warranted, for much had changed.

The traditional consensus supporting the American policy of containment had been shattered by the U.S. involvement in Vietnam. The failure of U.S. policy there had led critics to question the application of U.S. power anywhere. Further, the steady strengthening of the Soviet Union's strategic retaliatory systems had underscored the momentum of the strategic arms race and the importance, therefore, of moving forward with arms control. The reestablishment of the U.S.–Chinese dialogue in 1972 had reversed a longstanding policy of treating the People's Republic of China (P.R.C.) as a prime danger to U.S. security interests, also contributing to the questioning of traditional American security strategies.

"Détente," whereby relations between the superpowers would ostensibly be marked by a lessening of tension and hostility, even as competition between them continued—which had been a central theme of the Nixon administration's foreign and defense policy—had proven to be a shaky pillar; the U.S.S.R. had apparently interpreted it as mere American acknowledgment of the new power balance and a license to expand its influence and activities in hitherto Western areas of predominant influence.

Although the earlier SALT negotiations (SALT I), culminating in the Strategic Arms Limitation Agreement of 1972 and the Vladivostok Accord of 1974 (tentatively limiting strategic arms still further), institutionalized the policy of détente at one level, they seemed only to encourage Soviet expansionism at other levels. Accordingly, the policy of détente—at least as originally conceived—had increasingly become viewed in the United States as ineffective. Americans were less than happy with a policy that seemed incapable of checking adventurism in the noncommunist world by the U.S.S.R. and its allies and proxies.

The proliferation of newly independent countries in the preceding three decades and their increasing demands for a more just and equitable international economic and political order had also changed the international security environment. American strategy could no longer be based solely on conceptions of East–West rivalry, a competition deemed largely irrelevant by many of the developing areas of the world.

Domestically, the United States had also changed dramatically. The wars in Korea and Vietnam seemed to illustrate the reduced utility of military force, feeding renewed skepticism about defense spending and worldwide military deployments. The recession of 1974–1975 reemphasized domestic priorities and raised further questions about the extent to which resources should be channeled into increasingly expensive defense programs. Presidential candidate Carter emphasized his intent to reduce military spending in favor of domestic programs. Despite the increasing evidence of a continuing, massive Soviet military build-up, there was sufficient uncertainty about the facts to permit both presidential candidates to downplay the specter of future Soviet pressure and adventurism.

Technology also had, to some extent, restructured the security environment in which the United States lived. Continued technological advancements such as multiple, independently targetable reentry vehicles (MIRVs) for nuclear weapons, cruise missiles, and antisatellite capabilities threatened to upset perceptions of nuclear stability. Improvements in conventional weapons such as TV-guided bombs and laser-guided artillery shells had enhanced military capabilities with less than fully understood consequences for the stability of conventional force balances. History suggests that, because of their speed and extent, these various technological advances had not been adequately coupled with an appreciation of their strategic and political implications.[50]

In consequence of the dynamic factors cited in the preceding paragraphs and in light of its own comprehensive assessment of the comparative strengths of the United States and the Soviet Union, the Carter administration set forth the main lines of its strategy in a series of announcements and policy initiatives during the course of 1977. It reaffirmed the importance of maintaining a balance in strategic nuclear forces, choosing the label of "essential equivalence." It continued to rely upon the doctrine of "mutually assured destruction" but seemed to back away from any concept of even limited counterforce capabilities or any plans for so-called limited nuclear options with which the Nixon administration had tinkered. Also in the context of essential equivalence, the Carter administration picked up the lagging SALT II talks and pressed them vigorously. The subsequent treaty signed by President Carter and General Secretary Brezhnev in Vienna in 1979, though never ratified by the U.S. Senate, continued to define the upper limits of essential equivalence into the 1980s.

With regard to Europe, the Carter administration underscored the key role of NATO and reaffirmed the existing "forward strategy." Recognizing the mounting Soviet defense build-up in Central Europe, the United States persuaded the other NATO governments to commit to increasing real defense contributions to the alliance by 3 percent a year. This so-called Long-Range Defense Program was designed both to remedy near-term weaknesses such as inadequate ammunition stocks and to increase the overall readiness of NATO forces over a more extended period.

The overall concept of having forces sufficient simultaneously to fight a major war in Europe and a smaller war elsewhere—the one-and-a-half war strategy of the Nixon administration—was endorsed as the guiding principle behind the size and character of the defense forces. Special attention was focused on the Persian Gulf as the possible site of the one-half war. Although measures to create the kind of force projection capability required for an area such as the Persian Gulf were slow in getting under way, the administration at least staked out a declaratory policy that accorded the region higher and more explicit priority than given it earlier.

In a bid to stabilize the power balance in Asia and to create a more satisfactory framework for U.S.–Soviet relations, the administration proceeded with the normalization of American relations with the People's Republic of China. Formal recognition of the P.R.C. was accomplished in early 1979, immediately preceding the visit to the United States by Vice-Premier Deng Xiaoping. Also, following up the president's campaign promises, the administration began preparations to withdraw American ground forces from the Republic of Korea. Congressional opposition, however, forced the administration to reverse its course in the matter.

In terms of overall national security policy, the decade of the 1970s ended on a somewhat surprising note. The Soviet Union's invasion of Afghanistan in 1979 and its impressive and continuing defense build-up, combined with its gains in a number of regions—generally propelled by Soviet arms and advisers and sometimes by Cuban proxies—had so alarmed large sectors of the public and the Congress that a stronger defense policy and larger spending were being pressed on a reluctant president. President Carter's final defense budget (FY 1981) and five-year defense plan were marked by substantial increases.

Redressing the Military Balance and the Reagan Doctrine, 1981–1988

America entered the 1980s with a new administration committed to strengthening U.S. power, to resisting further Soviet-supported communist expansion, and to leaving Marxism-Leninism on "the ash heap of history." From 1981 to 1984, the U.S. defense budget was tripled—the largest peacetime military build-up in U.S. history. The United States moved rapidly to deploy a new-generation triad of strategic systems, to expand the U.S. naval fleet toward 600 ships, and to modernize U.S. conventional land and air forces. Perhaps the most dramatic development in U.S. national security policy came in March 1983 with the President's Strategic Defense Initiative (SDI), his call to develop a system to defend against ballistic missile attack that would make nuclear weapons obsolete. Such a development could radically alter the forms of military confrontation for the future. It was apparently this prospect which helped convince the Soviets of the futility of further military competition.[51]

In the area of East–West competition in the developing world, the Reagan administration returned, if cautiously, to a more activist policy of selective American support for noncommunist insurgencies against Soviet-supported communist regimes. This policy, generally known as the Reagan Doctrine, enjoyed several successes—most notably in contributing to the Soviet Union's decision to withdraw its support for the Marxist government in Angola and to withdraw forces from the Afghanistan quagmire in 1989. In Central America, support for the anticommunist contras led to free elections and the demise of the Sandinista government in Nicaragua and set the stage for eventual settlement of the communist-backed insurgency in El Salvador. U.S. military intervention also stopped the threat of a communist-supported takeover in Grenada.

The emergence of Mikhail Gorbachev in 1985 presented the opportunity for beginning a new dialogue in the midst of confrontation. The Reagan administration's strategy of deferring major efforts at arms control until it was in a position to negotiate from strength began to pay off in a series of Soviet concessions which eventually led to the Intermediate Nuclear Forces (INF) Treaty of 1987. With the subsequent dramatic changes in Eastern Europe and the breakup of the Warsaw Pact, other negotiations yielded the Conventional Forces in Europe (CFE) Treaty of 1990 and the Strategic Arms Reduction Treaty (START) of 1991.

Gorbachev's policies of "glasnost" (openness) and "perestroika" (restructuring) and the sheer force of his personality that led to the end of the cold war and the Soviet empire and ultimately the demise of the Soviet Union. By the end of the 1980s it had become clear that the Soviet economy was in dire straits, and equally clear that Gorbachev's attempts at economic reform and military restructuring were bitter medicine that many Soviet hardliners found especially difficult to swallow. By 1989 the cold war was over. The United States and its allies had effectively contained the Soviet Union for 40 years. After an aborted putsch in Moscow in August 1991 the old Soviet Union was finished, although the future of its 15 republics remains in doubt.

Toward a New World Order: Into the 1990s

Military threats to U.S. vital interests remain as Saddam Hussein's attack on Kuwait so vividly illustrated in August 1990. But two fundamental changes have occurred that will drive U.S. national security policy for the remainder of the 1990s. The first is the major change in military threats to U.S. interests. The second is the mounting set of economic problems confronting the United States. By 1991, the U.S. cumulative national debt had nearly reached the $4 trillion mark; annual federal budget deficits exceeded $400 billion, and the annual trade deficit was $77 billion.

As usual with most new administrations, the Bush National Security Council staff began a national security strategy review in the spring of 1989, but events were moving so fast that publication of its annual report "The National Security Strategy of the United States" was delayed in both 1990 and 1991. Both reports were subject to considerable criticism for their lack of precise guidance. Yet, their 1991 report did point to fundamental changes.

> More than preceding reports this one attempted to broaden the definition of national security. In purely military terms, it proclaimed regional conflict as the organizing principle for American military forces, and suggested that new terms of reference for nuclear deterrence would shortly be needed. Politically, it attempted to turn the compass on arms control from east–west to north–south for a much expanded discussion of policy to retard proliferation. Even more than the previous reports, the document attempted to communicate the idea that American economic well-being was included in the definition of national security, even though discussions of specific programs to improve competitiveness or to combat trade and budget deficits were generally lacking.[52]

Reflecting the new realities, Secretary of Defense Cheney and JCS Chairman Powell appeared before the Senate budget committee in January 1991, during the Gulf war, to propose an FY 1992 Defense budget with a multi-year 25 percent reduction in American forces from 1990 levels. By 1995, those cuts would reduce active-duty Army divisions from 18 to 12, the air force from 36 fighter wing equivalents to 26, the navy from 546 ships to 451, and reserve forces and Department of Defense civilian employees by over 200,000 each. The FY 1992 budget was based also on plans to cancel 100 weapons programs and to close or

realign over 200 bases and facilities worldwide. In the words of Secretary Cheney:

> These cuts would reduce the U.S. military to its lowest end strength since before the Korean War; they would cut our share of the Federal budget, once as high as 57 percent, to 18 percent, the lowest level in 40 years. The defense budget would fall by 1997 to 3.4 percent of GNP, by far the lowest level since before Pearl Harbor.[53]

The new military strategy guiding this "defense build-down" reflected the shift from containing the spread of communism and deterring Soviet aggression to a more variegated, flexible strategy. The major elements were

- Strategic deterrence and defense requiring a reliable warning system, modern nuclear forces, the capability and flexibility to support a spectrum of response options and a defensive system for protection against limited strikes.
- Forward but reduced presence of U.S. conventional land, sea, and air forces at a high level of readiness in regions vital to U.S. national interests; in this context, alliance strengthening as well.
- Capability for response to regional crises which could arise on very short notice involving U.S. forces unilaterally or as part of a multilateral effort.
- A force reconstitution capability against major military threats based on longer warning time and involving the formation, training, and fielding of new fighting units, mobilization of previously trained manpower, and activation of the U.S. defense industrial base which would maintain the capability for technological superiority.[54]

The Bush administration was determined that the United States not repeat the folly that followed previous wars of letting U.S. military capabilities plummet and American will be questioned. And in 1992, as the FY 1993 defense budget was being debated on Capitol Hill, it appeared that the Congress largely agreed—for the time being. But, as the recession of 1990–1992 wore on and problems of the domestic economy mounted, it appeared likely that the U.S. defense budget would resume its steep glide downward after the presidential election of 1992.

Discussion Questions

1. What international and technological impacts caused the United States to abandon its longstanding reliance on a policy of mobilization? How does a strategy based on deterrence differ from one based on mobilization?

2. What impact did the rapid demobilization of U.S. forces following World War II have on the formulation of American security policy?

3. The policy of containment was based on the perception of an aggressive, monolithic communist bloc of nations. What events of the late 1940s and early 1950s caused the U.S. to so view the nature of the communist threat? What impact did such an assessment have on established U.S. political and military policies?

4. In the early 1960s the United States adopted a strategic policy of "flexible response." What changes in technology and the international environment led to this change?

5. How do domestic considerations make foreign and security policies different than they would be on the basis of international and strategic considerations alone?

6. Has the development of nuclear stability encouraged political multipolarity? If the traditional uses of military power have become less feasible, what new forms of pressure have emerged?

7. Many analysts of national security policy allege that the distribution of nuclear power is at most a minor determinant of the outcome of political disputes. What impact have nuclear weapons had on the ability of the United States (or the former Soviet Union) to influence international affairs? Has nuclear "superiority" ever been a meaningful determinant of the outcome of a dispute in the post–World War II era?

8. How have technological innovations affected the evolution of U.S. security policy since the end of World War II? To what extent can it be said that technology determines strategy?

9. Should technological advances in weapons systems be integrated into the U.S. inventory as rapidly as they become available? Would doing otherwise risk technological obsolescence and military inferiority?

Recommended Reading

Allison, Graham, and Treverton, Gregory F., eds. *Rethinking America's Security: Beyond Cold War to New World Order*. New York: W.W. Norton, 1992.

Aspen Strategy Group, *Facing the Future: American Strategy in the 1990s*. Lanham, Md.: Aspen Institute for Humanistic Studies, 1991.

Dougherty, James E., and Pfaltzgraff, Robert L., Jr. *American Foreign Policy: FDR to Reagan*. New York: Harper & Row, 1986.

Huntington, Samuel P. *The Common Defense*. New York: Columbia University Press, 1961.

Kahan, Jerome. *Security in the Nuclear Age*. Washington, D.C.: Brookings Institution, 1975.

Kennan, George. *American Diplomacy*. Chicago: University of Chicago Press, 1963.

Kissinger, Henry A. *American Foreign Policy*. 3d ed. New York: Norton, 1977.

LeFeber, Walter. *America, Russia, and the Cold War*. New York: Knopf, 1985.

Lippmann, Walter. *U.S. Foreign Policy: Shield of the Republic*. Boston: Little, Brown, 1943.

Osgood, Robert. *Ideals and Self-Interest in America's Foreign Relations*. Chicago: University of Chicago Press, 1953.

Tucker, Robert. *The Purposes of American Power*. New York: Praeger, 1981.

II

National Security Policy: Actors and Processes

5

Presidential Leadership and the Executive Branch in National Security

''The direction of war implies the direction of the common strength; and the power of directing and employing the common strength forms a usual and essential part in the definition of the executive authority.''[1] With these words, Alexander Hamilton described the crucial role of the president in national security affairs. An appreciation of this vital role was shared by all the founders of the United States, but it was counterbalanced by their determination to avoid investing in the American president the ''sole prerogative of making war and peace''[2] exercised by the British monarch. As a result, the Constitution created a system in which the president and the Congress were given complementary, at times naturally conflicting, roles in the national security process.

Under the Constitution, the president is the commander in chief of the army and navy, but he has nothing to command unless Congress uses the power it possesses to raise and support armies and to support and maintain a navy. In addition, Congress is empowered to make rules for the governance and regulation of those forces. The president has the authority to make treaties and to appoint ambassadors and other public ministers as well as members of his national security team, like the secretaries of state and defense, the director of Central Intelligence and chairman of the Joint Chiefs of Staff. Each of these actions, however, is subject to the ''advice and consent'' of the Senate, a prerogative that the Senate is exercising with increasing frequency. For example, in 1989 the Senate rejected President Bush's nomination of former Senator John Tower to become Secretary of Defense.

The president is responsible to ensure that the laws are faithfully executed, and he has been vested with the ''executive power'' to this end. It is Congress, however, that is responsible to ''make all laws which shall be necessary and proper for carrying into execution the foregoing powers vested by this Constitution in the Government of the United States." The Constitution has given the president substantial authority and initiative in foreign affairs. However, having given the president important powers to make and execute national security policy, the founders were deliberate in their grant to Congress of the power to declare war. As a consequence of these built-in dynamic tensions, the Constitution has presented to each president and Congress an "invitation to struggle for the privilege of directing American foreign policy."[3]

A History of Increasing Presidential Prerogative. The outlines of the national security process provided by the Constitution were quickly elaborated by the actual conduct of public affairs. In 1793, George Washington asserted the prerogative of the president to act unilaterally in time of foreign crisis by issuing, without congressional consultation, a neutrality proclamation in the renewed Franco-British war.

Succeeding administrations continued to struggle with questions of presidential versus congressional prerogative. In 1812, President Madison was unsuccessful in restraining congressional "war hawks," who helped precipitate war with England. On the other hand, in 1846 it was President Polk who presented Congress with a *fait accompli* by placing American troops along the Rio Grande. The resulting clash of arms quickly led to a declaration of war.

Presidential prerogative in foreign affairs, claimed first by Washington and embellished by his successors, was a generally established concept at the time of the Lincoln administration. Lincoln greatly expanded the potential range of presidential action by invoking the notion of a "war power" as a derivative of the commander in chief clause of the Constitution. The growth of presidential power in the Civil War foreshadowed the relationship between national emergency and executive power. Time and again, the law of national self-preservation was seen to justify placing extravagant power in the hands of the President.[4]

Prior to World War II, Franklin Roosevelt's carefully orchestrated policy of aiding Britain and her allies once again revealed the power of the president to establish national security policy on his own. Using executive agreements of dubious constitutionality to avoid confronting an uncertain and isolationist Congress, Roosevelt increasingly bound the United States to the Allied cause. With the attack on Pearl Harbor, the power of the executive further expanded to confront the crisis of global war.

With the termination of World War II, the anticipated climate of peace under the aegis of a powerful international organization did not materialize; instead, the postwar years ushered in a period of continuing confrontation—the cold war. An ideological conflict permeated the international environment, a war of nerves stretched particularly taut by the specter of atomic war. In these circumstances, too, crisis spurred the growth of executive prerogatives. President Truman led the United States into the Korean conflict in 1950 under the auspices of the United Nations without seeking a congressional declaration of war. Similarly, President Kennedy escalated the small (less than 1,000-man) military advisory effort in Vietnam, begun under Eisenhower, into a 16,000-man effort, which included not only advisers but helicopter transportation companies and other logistical elements.

Vietnam: An Apparent Turning Point. In the mid 1960s, presidential initiative in foreign affairs again brought the United States into an extended conflict in Asia. This time it was Vietnam; and along with the locale, the rules of the game had changed. The conventional linear warfare of Korea yielded to the amorphous combat of revolutionary warfare. As the war dragged on in Vietnam—and in the living rooms of America via television—the presidential prerogative in foreign affairs came under vigorous attack. The "imperial president" became the subject of congressional and popular opposition. Congressional opposition culminated in the passage of the War Powers Act, over President Nixon's veto, in July 1973 (see Chapter 6). This measure set a sixty-day limit on the president's power to wage undeclared war.[5]

The real impact of the War Powers Act, however, has thus far proved to be minimal. Each of Nixon's successors called the act unconstitutional, and in practice, it has so far turned out to be a "paper tiger." Congress essentially played no role in President Reagan's decisions to invade Grenada, place Marines in Lebanon in 1983, put mines in Nicaraguan harbors in 1984, bomb Libya in 1986, or escort reflagged Kuwaiti ships in the Persian Gulf, and engage in several battles with the Iranian Navy from mid 1987 through mid 1988. Nor did Congress play any meaningful part in President Bush's decisions to invade Panama in 1989 or to liberate Kuwait in 1991.

The inability of Congress to restrict the President's war-making powers was amply demonstrated during the Gulf war. After Iraq overran Kuwait in August 1990, President Bush decided to send American troops to Saudi Arabia to prevent Iraq from conquering that oil-rich desert kingdom. Nearly six months later, on January 8, 1991, President Bush finally requested legislative approval to undertake military actions. However, by that time the United Nations had already authorized military action and the United States had over 500,000 troops in the Arabian desert, about the same number as it deployed to Vietnam. President Bush's unilateral actions had brought the nation to a point where turning back was not a realistic option; that is, a Congress, even one controlled by an opposition party, could not reject the President's request without damaging U.S. credibility and image. Even after the Congress approved his request, President Bush, in a rare moment of candor, said, "I don't think I need it."[6] Although many members of Congress were upset about Bush's lack of consultation with them all during the fall and winter of 1990, the success of Operation Desert Storm muted any public criticisms about violating the War Powers Act.

The Gulf lesson was apparent. If the President is determined to use military force, the Congress can do little to stop him. If the military operation is successful, like Desert Storm, there will be few public complaints about abuse of executive power. If, however, the military conflict turns out poorly, like Vietnam or Lebanon, there will be cries about presidential abuse of power. In placing troops in the Arabian desert in 1990, President Bush acted more like President Polk than Lyndon Johnson, who gradually escalated military force against Vietnam in a futile effort to break the will of North Vietnam and the Viet Cong.

The President and National Security. The president as chief of state personifies the United States in its dealings with the world. Through his constitutional powers to appoint and receive ambassadors, the president is placed at the focal point of diplomatic activity. As commander in chief, he is positioned at the apex of a large and elaborate security apparatus. In addition to these constitutional and organizational factors, the congruence of continual crisis and expanded presidential power have operated to build a national contingency system around the president. With the increasing involvement of the United States in world affairs, and the proliferation of weapons of mass destruction, an atmosphere of constant danger has translated many aspects of this contingency system into standard operating procedures.

Technology, too, has assisted the growth of presidential prerogative. The stakes in crisis management have escalated with the proliferation of nuclear weapons. Questions of peace and war can now relate directly to the survival of the human race. As the stakes of international confrontation have increased, so also has the tempo of communication and response. The national security process has become saturated with information, and it is the executive who largely controls the channels of communication and the organizations capable of assimilating these data. The communication revolution has not only enhanced the executive's ability to receive information, it has also provided him with direct access to operations if he so chooses. For example, President Johnson was able to select bombing targets in Vietnam, President Carter to communicate directly with the on-scene commander in the aborted Iranian hostage rescue mission of 1980, and President Bush to discuss the timing of the allied cease fire with General Schwarzkopf in the Gulf war in March 1991.

The external environment has thus generated forces encouraging recent presidents to be activists. This, however, should not be construed as implying that until recently the presidency has merely been the benign beneficiary of history. In fact, vigorous presidents have always reached out to grasp the levers of government. Beginning especially with FDR, presidential initiative has grown significantly in generating legislation and promulgating the federal budget. Congress, in this regard, examines presidential initiatives as much as, or more than, it generates its own.

The president plays multiple roles in the execution of the office. Not only is he chief of state, commander in chief of the armed forces, chief diplomat, principal initiator of legislation, and chief executor of the laws, but he also acts as party leader, national spokesperson, peacekeeper, manager of prosperity, and world leader.[7] None of these roles can neatly be isolated from the other, and the president must satisfy the particular demands of each as he confronts problems of national security. Moreover, in his various roles he must deal with a variety of entities, each with its own interests and viewpoints; these are shown in Figure 5.1.

Despite the complexity of these various responsibilities, three major functions in the conduct of national security can be identified: *resource allocation*, *policy*

FIG. 5.1 Relationship Between the President and the External Environment

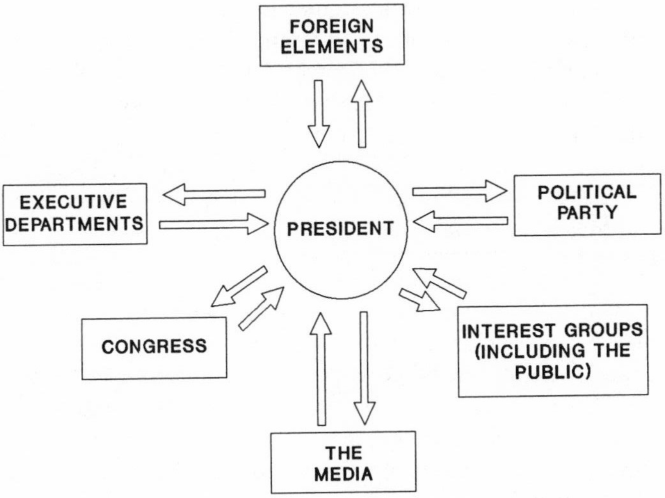

planning, and *coordination and monitoring of operations*.[8] The maintenance of national security is expensive, requiring a major commitment of resources each year in the president's budget, the main vehicle through which he communicates his ordering of the nation's priorities in resource use. The Office of Management and Budget (OMB), discussed briefly in subsequent pages, is the principal instrument that the president uses in this allocation function.

Policy planning involves the development of long-range designs, such as the Marshall Plan for the reconstruction of Europe after World War II, or the as-yet incomplete design for the "new world order" after the end of the cold war. It also includes less sweeping and shorter-term plans to advance U.S. interests and cope with emerging problems. The concept of the 600-ship navy in 1981, and the creation of the post–cold war base force in 1991, are examples of these types of plans. Inherent in this policy planning function is an intent to shape future events as well as to prepare policy planning for contingencies. Historically, the focus of such planning has shifted among (or been shared by) the Departments of State and Defense and the president's national security assistant, who heads the National Security Council staff. Unfortunately, this function, which is inherently a hard one conceptually and is invariably a difficult one to accomplish bureaucratically, has seldom been done well.

Coordination of operations requires overseeing the countless day-to-day foreign policy actions of government organizations and officials so that they remain consistent with and advance American policy. The associated monitoring function is designed to provide feedback to the executive branch to ensure that appropriate actions are being taken in light of policy guidance and to apprise it of changing conditions or assumptions, or new data. In practice, the president has leaned on the Department of State and/or his national security assistant for the coordination and monitoring task.

The Institutionalized Presidency and National Security Affairs. The complexity, scope, and magnitude of these functions have given rise to the institutionalized presidency. The president, as an individual, has been augmented by staffs acting in his name. This institutionalized presidency, together with certain executive departments, forms the principal means of developing, directing, and coordinating national security. The key elements of this collective executive are the White House Office, the National Security Council and staff, the State Department, the Department of Defense, the Central Intelligence Agency, and the Office of Management and Budget (see Fig. 5.2).

The White House Office. According to George Reedy, former press secretary to Lyndon Johnson, "the life of the White House is the life of a court."[9] Extending the analogy, the White House staff members can be seen as the president's courtiers. They are the personal and political assistants to the president. Without outside constituencies, they owe their status and position wholly to him. Accordingly, the organization and use of the White House staff is the function of a president's personal style.

In recent history, Franklin D. Roosevelt operated probably the most chaotic of staffs, but the chaos was purposeful. "F.D.R. intended his administrative assistants to be eyes and ears and manpower for him, with no fixed contacts, clients, or involvements of their own to interfere when he had to redeploy them."[10] There was overlapping of assignments, lack of coordination, and often frustration on the part of the staff, but these factors served FDR well, presenting him competing sources of information and analysis that enabled him to develop and maintain his personal options. This freewheeling approach was somewhat curtailed by the advent of World War II as sources of information became channeled through secrecy and censorship systems and the focus of efforts turned to the operational concerns of global war.[11]

President Eisenhower was at the opposite extreme. His staff was organized tightly around its chief of staff, initially Sherman Adams. With some exceptions, access to the president was through Adams, who was not reticent to ask if a meeting was really necessary. Responsibilities were clearly defined, and there was a military aura of hierarchy, neatness, and order.

In the 1960s, the Kennedy and Johnson administrations utilized a less formal staffing system, allowing a small staff concerned with national security more direct and frequent access to the president. Under Nixon (1969) and Carter (1977), the White House staff was again organized along more structured lines. Ronald Reagan (1981) adopted a looser, less structured model than his predecessors, while George Bush (1989) returned increased structure and hierarchy to the system.

In each of these administrations, from Eisenhower's forward, the position of special assistant to the president for national security affairs was a significant post (starting with Henry Kissinger in 1969, "special" was dropped from the title). In each case—and typical of relationships in the White House—the role of the assistant to the president for national security affairs was largely a function of the assistant's personal relationship with the president and how the president wished

FIG. 5.2 The Government of the United States

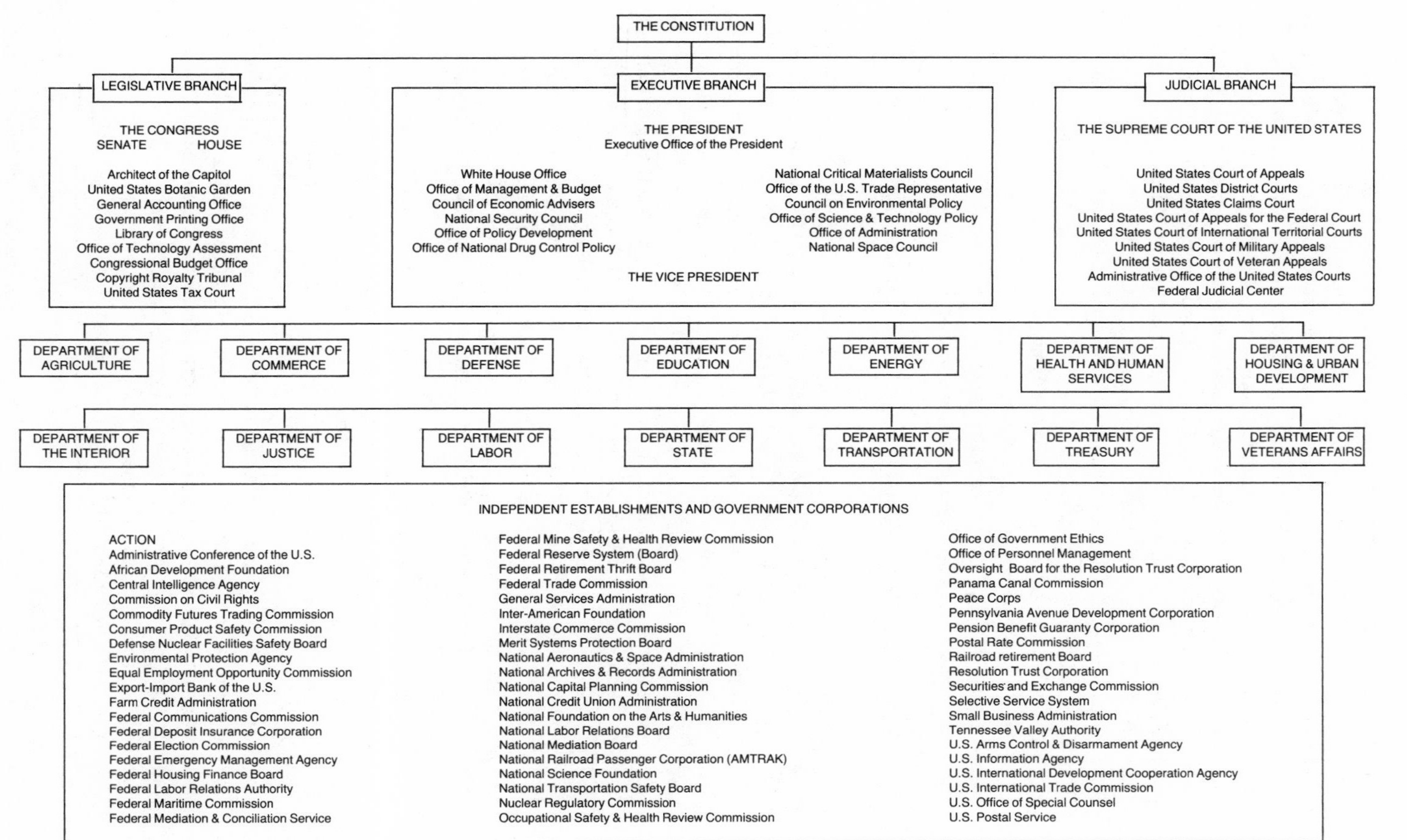

the office to be discharged. The role has also developed in conjunction with the evolution of the National Security Council staff, which the assistant heads.

Despite the similarities and differences in the functioning of the White House staff under different presidents, there have been some pronounced trends. The most obvious is growth. The entire Hoover presidency was staffed by three secretaries, a military and a naval aide, and twenty clerks. In contrast, the Bush White House contained in excess of five hundred people in 1989—both those ''hired'' and those ''on loan'' from other agencies and carried on those agencies' payrolls.[12] The growth in numbers is a symptom, and some would argue a cause, of a centralization of decision-making. In this regard, one should be mindful that centralization can cause a serious cleavage between policymakers and the instruments of policy. Another aspect of White House staff growth is the tendency for it to shield the president from the outside world. The life of the court can easily become one clouded by perceptions divorced from reality. Finally, as the National Security Council system has evolved and the position of the assistant directing its staff has strengthened, other White House office staffs have played an ever-diminishing role in national security matters.

National Security Council. The formalized coordination and policy planning functions of the presidency in national security matters are located in the National Security Council (NSC), created by the National Security Act of 1947. The NSC inherited many of the functions that had been earlier exercised by cabinet members in the State-War-Navy Coordinating Committee, itself an ad hoc product of World War II operations. As constituted in 1947, the NSC comprises the president, the vice-president, the secretary of state, the secretary of defense, and the director of the Office of Civil and Defense Mobilization (OCDM). The latter office has long since been abolished and its successor organizations are not represented in the NSC, so that there are only four statutory members. (Since the term ''NSC'' tends to be used loosely to mean the NSC staff rather than the council itself, there tends to be public confusion about the NSC's composition.) The director of the Central Intelligence Agency and the chairman of the Joint Chiefs of Staff serve as statutory advisors.[13*]

President Truman was instrumental in shaping the NSC to respond directly to the needs of the president rather than merely extending the interagency arrangements of the State-War-Navy Coordinating Committee. ''His adroit maneuvers scotched the scheme of those who wanted to assure defense domination of the National Security Council by housing it in the Pentagon . . . and by designating the Secretary of Defense as Chairman in the President's absence.''[14] In addition, the legislation that the Truman Administration shepherded through the Congress to become the 1947 National Security Act provided for a separate staff to support the NSC and did not rely, as was previously done, on staff contributed from involved agencies. In this manner, President Truman established the NSC as responsive to the president rather than to competing executive departments.

*The functions of the OCDM were absorbed in the late 1960s by the director of the Office of Emergency Preparedness until 1974 when the latter office was abolished and replaced by the Federal Emergency Management Agency (FEMA).

With the advent of the Eisenhower administration, the NSC system was restructured to reflect both the style of the new president and his view of the world situation.[15] In keeping with his view of the importance of economic health to security, Eisenhower regularly invited his secretary of Treasury and director of the Bureau of the Budget to attend NSC meetings. He attempted to routinize and regularize the decision-making process in line with his experience with military models of decision-making and coordination. He used the NSC apparatus intensively in the belief that

> the secret of a sound, satisfactory decision made on an emergency basis has always been that the responsible official has been 'living with the problem' before it becomes acute. Failure to use, on a continuing basis, the NSC, or some similar advisory body, entails losing the capacity to make emergency decisions based on depth of understanding and perspective.[16]

Two important subelements of the NSC were created by Ike—one at the assistant secretary level (of the departments involved in the NSC) to conduct interagency planning and policy development, namely, the National Security Planning Board (NSPB), and the other at the undersecretary level to oversee and coordinate policy implementation, the Operations Coordinating Board (OCB). While admirably suited to help the president avoid mistakes, these bureaucratic camels were not often the source of innovative, clear-cut recommendations or guidance.

The passing of the torch from the Eisenhower to the Kennedy administration involved a distinct change in presidential outlook and operating style. In regard to the NSC, this was reflected in a dismantling of the NSPB and OCB structure and a move to a more ad hoc system. At the heart of the criticism of the Eisenhower system was the view that it impeded initiative and flexibility by subjecting proposals to overly formalized bureaucratic argument. Regarding the world as inherently dynamic, President Kennedy hoped to shape a national security system capable of coping with rapid change. In lieu of the previous interagency focus, Kennedy built a strong staff in the White House, under his special assistant for national security affairs, to assist him in drawing advice from and coordinating operations of the various agencies involved with national security.

Further, President Kennedy chose to immerse himself in the details of selected aspects of policy much more than his predecessor. The Bay of Pigs fiasco in April 1961, shortly after Kennedy took office, was a lesson he did not soon forget. He had relied on the experts and judgments of the preceding administration, and he remarked a year and a half later, "The advice of every member of the Executive Branch brought in to advise was unanimous—and the advice was wrong."[17] Partly as a result of the Bay of Pigs, the president relied increasingly on his national security assistant to provide policy options. The full NSC met less frequently and tended to consider long-term questions that had already been extensively explored by ad hoc task forces. These interagency task forces dealt with such specific problems of the early 1960s as Laos, Berlin, and the Nuclear Test Ban Treaty.

Although established to provide a coherent means of coping with the urgency of the atomic age, the formal NSC in practice was not the locus of crisis management. As demonstrated in the Cuban Missile Crisis, Kennedy relied instead on a specially selected "Executive Committee" to bear the burden of deliberation and policy development. Consisting of the president's most trusted advisers and unfettered by the statutory membership requirements of the NSC, it represented a continuation of the ad hoc approach to national security policymaking.

With the assassination of President Kennedy in November 1963, Lyndon Johnson was thrust into the presidency. Although a master of congressional politics, he had but limited experience in international affairs—apart from his knowledge about military affairs as they affected, and were affected by, Congress. This factor, coupled with his desire to bring a sense of continuity to his administration, resulted in few immediate changes to the Kennedy NSC system as a consequence of the transition. Central coordination and direction continued to be provided by the special assistant for national security affairs.[18]

The emergence of the Vietnam conflict in the mid 1960s became the central drama and tragedy of Johnson's foreign policy. Accepting the existing national security apparatus and, unlike Kennedy, lacking the inclination to go beyond his advisers to key points in the bureaucracy, Johnson narrowed the process of deliberation and decision to a few people. In July 1965, the decision to expand America's hitherto limited commitment reportedly rested on the advice of a handful of people. The NSC and the Congress were consulted only after the decision was made.[19] Other important national security decisions were made at the informal, largely unstructured discussions at the president's periodic "Tuesday lunches"—which generally included only the NSC members and some invited guests.

In March 1966, the Johnson administration decided to provide more structure to the NSC system. National Security Memorandum 341 established a permanent interdepartmental committee called the Senior Interdepartmental Group (SIG), headed by the undersecretary of state. Subordinate to the SIG, Interdepartmental Region Groups (IRGs) for each region of the world were created and chaired by regional assistant secretaries of state. In theory, policy planning and coordination of policy decisions would flow through these organizations and up to the NSC. In practice, Vietnam dominated presidential considerations, and Johnson was unwilling to employ his new system in dealing with Vietnam. As a consequence, the SIGs and the IRGs found themselves working largely on peripheral issues, while crucial decisions concerning Vietnam continued to be resolved by the president and a few advisers.

The Nixon administration departed from the largely ad hoc arrangements of the Kennedy–Johnson years and returned in 1969 to a centralized system more akin to President Eisenhower's but with borrowings from President Johnson. The national security machinery was placed firmly in the White House under the control of the president's security assistant, Dr. Henry Kissinger. Although believing in a comprehensive and formal approach, Dr. Kissinger attempted to avoid the dilution in content and the inflexibility generated by the extended consensus approach of the Eisenhower system. The focus of the new NSC staff effort was not to produce, as in Ike's case, an agreed recommendation for the president but to develop rigorously a set of carefully considered options for presidential choice.

Kissinger adapted the SIG-IRG arrangements of the Johnson administration by assigning issues to Interdepartmental Groups (IGs) similar to the earlier IRGs and chaired, as before, by assistant secretaries of state. The IGs were responsible for studying problems, formulating policy choices, and assessing the merits of various alternatives. A Senior Review Group (SRG) was constituted at the undersecretary level, chaired by Dr. Kissinger, to deal with IG recommendations. By this process, less important or uncontentious issues were decided at subordinate levels rather than being forwarded to the NSC. Although this approach allowed for the inclusion of the views of operating agencies, it lodged control squarely in the White House, where Nixon clearly wanted it.

The Nixon–Kissinger NSC structure was further complicated or "systematized" by the creation of various special groups subordinate to the NSC. For example, major issues centered on the Vietnam War were handled by a Vietnam Special Studies Group, while crisis planning was done by the Washington Special Actions Group (WASAG). This evolution represented a further strengthening of the hand of the assistant for national security affairs and the dominance of the NSC staff over the Department of State. It is noteworthy that, out of office, Dr. Kissinger has decried this trend, recommending that a president should make the secretary of state "his principal adviser and 'use' the national security adviser primarily as a senior administrator and coordinator to make certain that each significant point of view is heard."[20]

In broad outlines President Carter's initial approach was to "streamline" his NSC staff but to entrust it with the same basic functions and powers as the Nixon–Ford staff. A number of NSC committees of the earlier era (which were really separate entities in name only) were collapsed into three basic committees: the Policy Review Committee (PRC), the Special Coordination Committee (SCC), and the familiar, assistant secretary–level IGs.

The organizational arrangements of the NSC system in the Carter administration initially led to an increase in the secretary of state's power at the expense of the NSC adviser. Through his chairmanship of many of the substantive PRCs, Secretary of State Vance at first was able to shape many of the fundamental policies of the Carter administration in such areas as human rights policy and arms transfers. As the focus shifted from policy-making to implementation, the power of the NSC adviser, Zbigniew Brzezinski, increased accordingly. Under Brzezinski's direction, the SCC dealt with issues concerning arms control, covert actions, and crisis management. Management of the Iranian hostage crisis, which consumed much of the last year of the Carter presidency, was handled by Brzezinski and the NSC staff.

President Reagan came to office determined to downgrade the role of the NSC and the assistant to the president for national security affairs. His first adviser for NSC affairs, Richard Allen, did not even report directly to him, and the NSC management structure was returned to the pre-Eisenhower days. After Allen's departure from office, the NSC structure was largely restored to the form used by Carter; Allen's five successors (William Clark, Robert McFarlane, John Poindexter, Frank Carlucci, and Colin Powell) reported directly to President Reagan. However, up to the time of the misdirected, mismanaged Iran–Contra operation, neither the NSC nor the assistant played much of a role in formulating national security policy in the Reagan years. The secretaries of state and defense reigned supreme in their own areas of responsibility with only occasional involvement by the White House and the President.[21]

However, under President Bush the assistant and the NSC had been restored to power. Brent Scowcroft, Bush's NSC assistant who had held the post briefly under President Ford, made himself chairman of a "Principals Committee" at the cabinet level. His own deputy, first Robert Gates and then Jonathan Howe, was placed in charge of the senior subcabinet interagency forum, the Deputies Committee, which reviewed and monitored the work of the interagency process and made recommendations on the development and implementation of policy. The Deputies Committee consisted of cabinet deputies as well as the vice chairman of the JCS and deputy director of the CIA. The interdepartmental groups have been renamed the Policy Coordinating Committees (NSC/PCC). There were six regional and four functional Policy Coordinating Committees composed of assistant secretary–level representatives from the appropriate agencies (Fig. 5.3).

President Bush held very few formal NSC meetings, preferring to rely on the Principals and Deputies committees to formulate and implement long-range strategy. For example, in April 1989, it was the Deputies Committee that drafted the document that spelled out the Bush administration's policy toward Iraq. President Bush preferred to handle crisis situations in selected ad hoc groups or in one-on-one meetings. For example, the August 4, 1990, meeting at Camp David to review military options after the Iraqi invasion of Kuwait was attended by 12 people—the President, the Vice President, the Secretaries of State and Defense (the NSC members), the NSC assistant, the Chairman of the JCS and the DCI (the NSC advisers), the White House Chief of Staff and Spokesman, the military commanders, an under secretary of defense, and an NSC staff director. But in early October 1991, when President Bush was trying to decide whether to let the sanctions work or adapt an offensive strategy, he met in the oval office with the Secretary of Defense, the Chairman of the JCS, and the NSC assistant. Bush's NSC Committee system resembled that of the Nixon era in formality, while his own personal decision-making style resembled the informality of Kennedy. General Colin Powell, the Chairman of the JCS, has described Bush's NSC process as too relaxed, too convivial—with no beginning, middle, or end.[22] In the first week of his administration, President Clinton incorporated into the NSC the new White House National Economic Council chaired by Robert E. Rubin, special assistant and economic advisor to the president. This action gave the NSC a broader economic emphasis than ever before.

The Department of State. The Department of State, since its creation in 1789 under its first secretary, Thomas Jefferson, has been the customary operational arm of the U.S. government in the conduct of foreign affairs. The department performs two basic functions: it represents the interests of the United States and

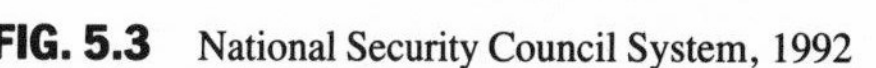

FIG. 5.3 National Security Council System, 1992

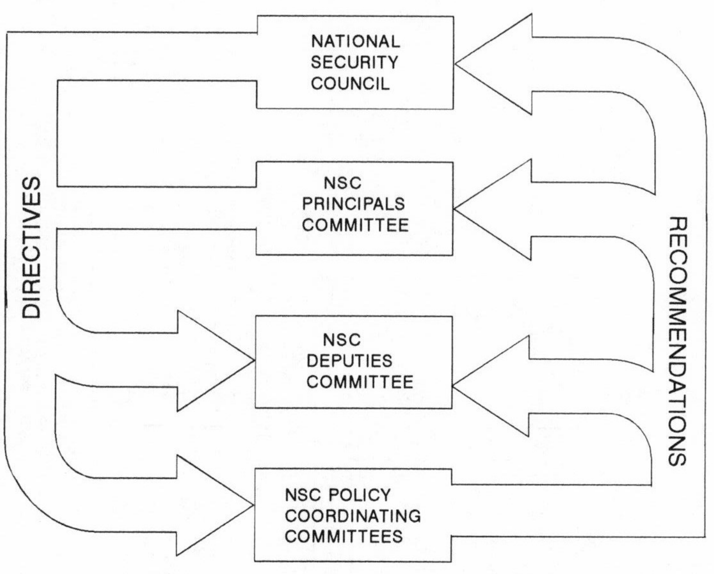

its citizens in relations with foreign countries, and it serves as a principal source of advice to the president on all aspects of foreign affairs—including national security policy (see Fig. 5.4).[23]

As a member of the cabinet, the secretary of state is traditionally the president's principal adviser on foreign policy, although this tradition has waned somewhat since the 1960s with the emergence of a succession of powerful presidential assistants for national security affairs. In all cases, the secretary's role is the result of his own talents, the personal relationship between him and the president, and the president's propensity to become directly involved in foreign policy-making. The more a president desires to become involved in foreign policy, the more difficult it is for the secretary of state to take initiatives and conduct his office. Since presidents normally anticipate their own policy-making tendencies in selecting secretaries, much of the criticism of a "weak" secretary of state should be directed at activist presidents. President Nixon's choice in 1969 of William Rogers as secretary of state and his systematic bypassing, even humiliation, of the secretary is an eloquent case in point.[24] On the other hand, presidents like Ronald Reagan, who wished to stay removed from the foreign policy process and downgrade the NSC, appointed strong secretaries of state like Alexander Haig, former White House chief of staff and NATO commander, and George Shultz, who had served in earlier administrations as secretary of labor, secretary of the treasury, and director of OMB before accepting the State post in 1983.

Finally, a president like George Bush, who wanted to focus heavily on certain areas of foreign policy, appoints a close friend and confidant, like James Baker, to handle the areas he is not focusing on. Thus, the President personally managed the Gulf war deployment and execution, while Baker followed up the victory by

FIG. 5.4 Department of State

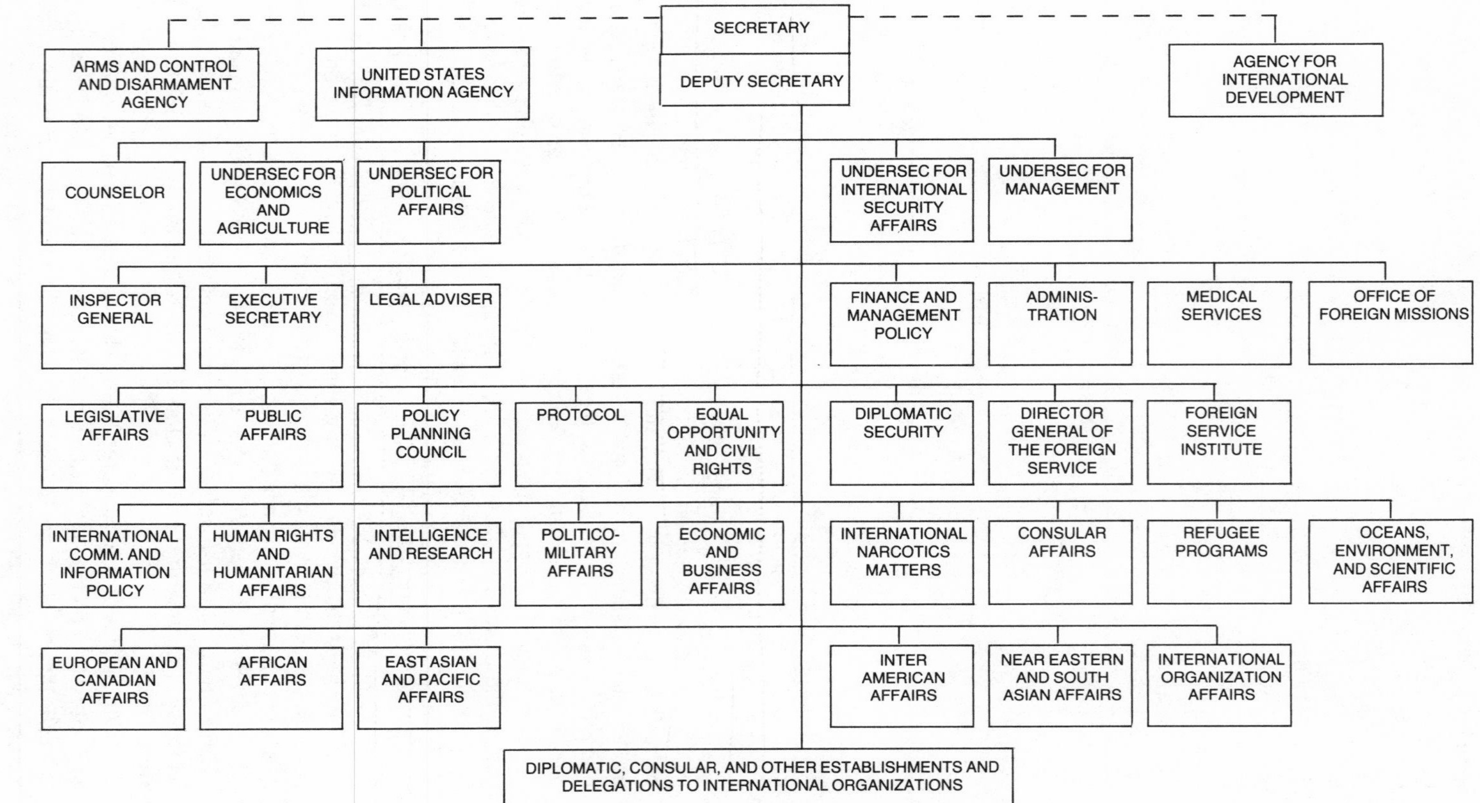

arranging a Mid-East peace conference in Madrid in 1991. President Bush in many ways was his own secretary of state, while Baker functioned as his deputy secretary of state.[25]

Presidential-secretarial dynamics aside, the secretary of state faces a complex task in managing the internal workings of his bureaucracy. The Department of State is broadly organized along two lines, geographic-regional responsibilities and functional responsibilities. Special "desks" within the regional bureaus monitor the more detailed actions and interactions of specific countries within the purview of a regional assistant secretary. An alternative view of international dynamics is provided by the functional areas, such as the Bureau of Intelligence and Research, Economic and Business Affairs, and Politico-Military Affairs. These functional bureaus present analysis that cuts across strictly geographic lines—and sometimes across analyses arising out of the regional desks as well.

The nature and structure of the department presents any secretary of state with a complex managerial and coordination problem. The "desk system" of organization in the department, in which deeply grounded experts on each country or functional problem funnel their analyses and recommendations to the various assistant secretaries, provides the needed expertise, but it can also generate parochial responses to policy problems, which in turn lead to striking contrasts in the nature of advice the secretary receives—Arabists versus Israeli experts, Russian versus Chinese analysts, etc. As a consequence, the secretary of state is often forced to sort out contradictory recommendations while shepherding a fragmented organization through the policy process. For those observers of public affairs who long for neat and "efficient" solutions to difficult problems (and who often think that the world is more malleable than it is), State is a source of constant frustration. Owing in part to the department's lack of a natural constituency within the United States, this frustration is often translated into vigorous and often mistaken widespread criticism of its role.[26]

Presidential displeasure with the Department of State seems to be a recurring and nonpartisan reaction. In general, presidential complaints about the State Department have centered around six "faults": (1) quality of staff work in terms of analysis; (2) slowness with which the State Department responds to requests and problems; (3) resistance to change and new approaches; (4) inadequacy in carrying out presidential decisions; (5) failure to lead in foreign affairs; and (6) the feeling that State does not have control of its own department.[27] These misgivings about the State Department—though in many cases exaggerated—have often led activist presidents, and activist secretaries like Dulles, Kissinger, and Baker, to bypass the institution and pursue largely individual initiatives in foreign affairs. For example, James Baker, who had served as the Undersecretary of Commerce, White House Chief of Staff, and Secretary of the Treasury before becoming George Bush's Secretary of State in 1989, was so contemptuous of the Department of State that he brought in a group of outsiders with relatively little foreign policy experience to most of the key positions and virtually ignored the career foreign service officers in the geographic and functional bureaus.

The appropriate employment of the Department of State in the national security process has long been a problem for presidents and secretaries. Periodic attempts have been made to harness the expertise in the context of policy planning, such as Secretary of State George Marshall's creation in 1947 of the Policy Planning Staff, with Ambassador George Kennan its head.[28] The Policy Planning Staff was designed to focus planning on current issues and to anticipate future contingencies. Yet that staff and its successor, the Policy Planning Council, have invariably fallen short of expectations. Mid- and long-range planning for a complex and untidy world is intrinsically difficult, and it requires exceptionally talented people who are sensitive to the purposes and limits of policy and who can draw clear linkages among policy realms and between policies and programs. Such talents, however, are always in short supply; and if the people who possess them are kept sufficiently close to genuine issues so that their planning is relevant to the real world, then they are constantly drawn into short-range, operational planning and policy advice. In short, if the planners are talented and their subject timely, they tend to be diverted; if they are not, they tend to be ignored. Thus, operational demands ("putting out fires") and the inherent tension between useful specificity and diplomatic generality have made the exercise of policy planning in the Department of State a perennial problem and have tended to shift the locus of policy planning—if any—to the NSC staff and the Department of Defense.

There is one area in which the Department of State has largely maintained its hegemony, namely, the daily conduct of American policy in foreign countries. The department's mandate to coordinate all American activities in foreign lands was reaffirmed by President Eisenhower in his (and subsequent presidents') endorsement of the "country team" concept. This approach places the American ambassador in charge of all American programs within the country to which he or she is accredited. (The mandate does not extend to American military forces in the field, though it does apply to military assistance teams and defense attachés.) The country team represents an important attempt to unify the implementation of American national security policy within each foreign country under the direction of the ambassador.[29] Succeeding administrations have continued to endorse this concept, but there is a continual tendency by departments, other than State, to fight it.

The Department of Defense. The Department of Defense (DOD) is the president's principal arm in the execution of national defense policy. Composed of the three military departments—army, navy, and air force—the Joint Chiefs of Staff (JCS) and the associated joint staff, a handful of operational commands (e.g., the Strategic Forces Command and the European Command), and numerous defense agencies with responsibility to provide services across the entire department (e.g., the Defense Intelligence Agency and the Defense Communications Agency), the department provides the military instrument essential to credible policies (see Fig. 5.5). Immediately after taking office as secretary of defense, former Representative Les Aspin restructured the Pentagon's policy-making apparatus. His action was aimed at directing more attention to new national security issues such as the promotion of democracy overseas and domestic economic renewal (see Fig. 5.6). As originally created in 1947, the position of the secretary of defense was that of a weak coordinator. In the course of a series of defense

FIG. 5.5 Department of Defense

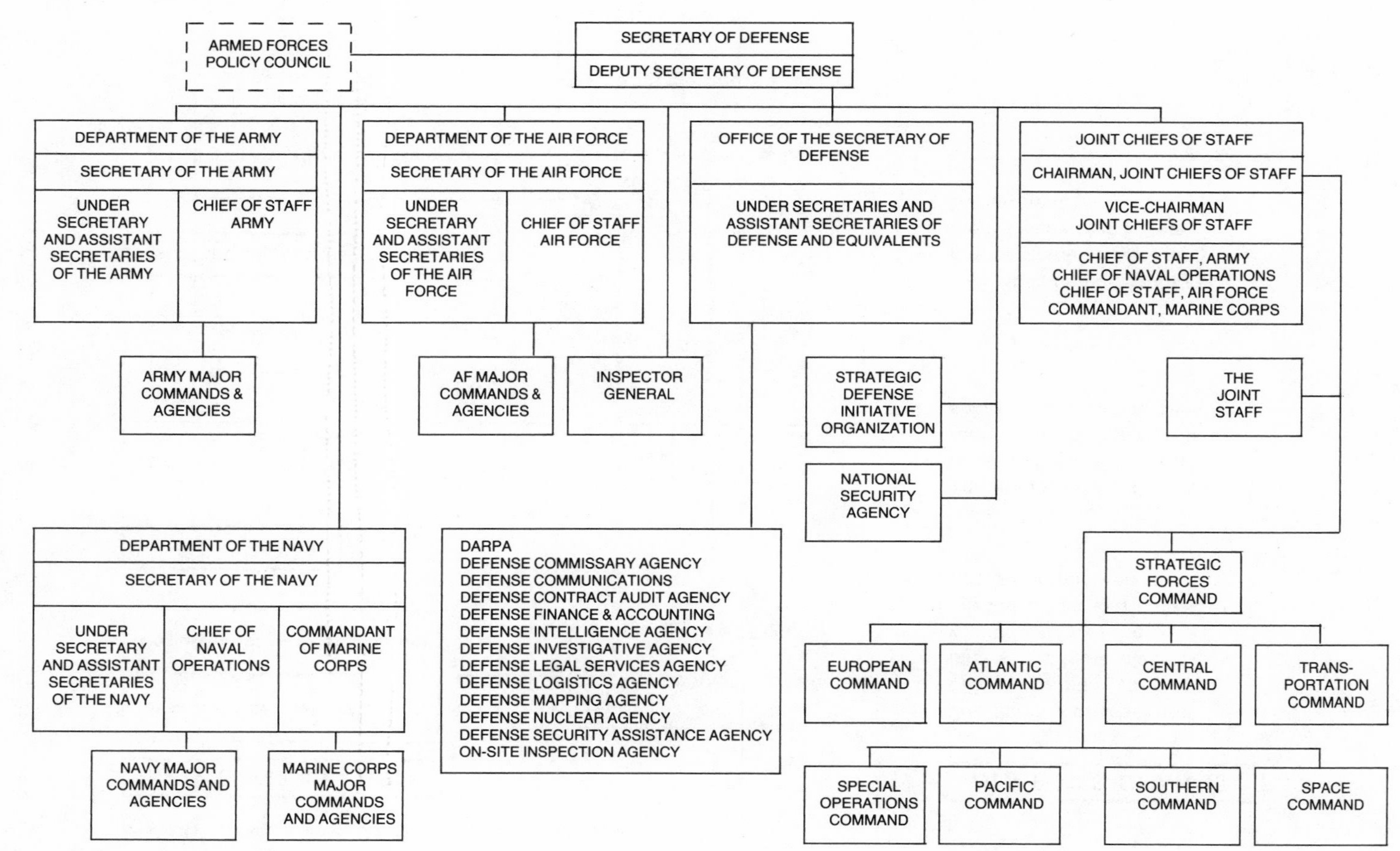

FIG. 5.6 Pentagon's New Organization in the Clinton Administration

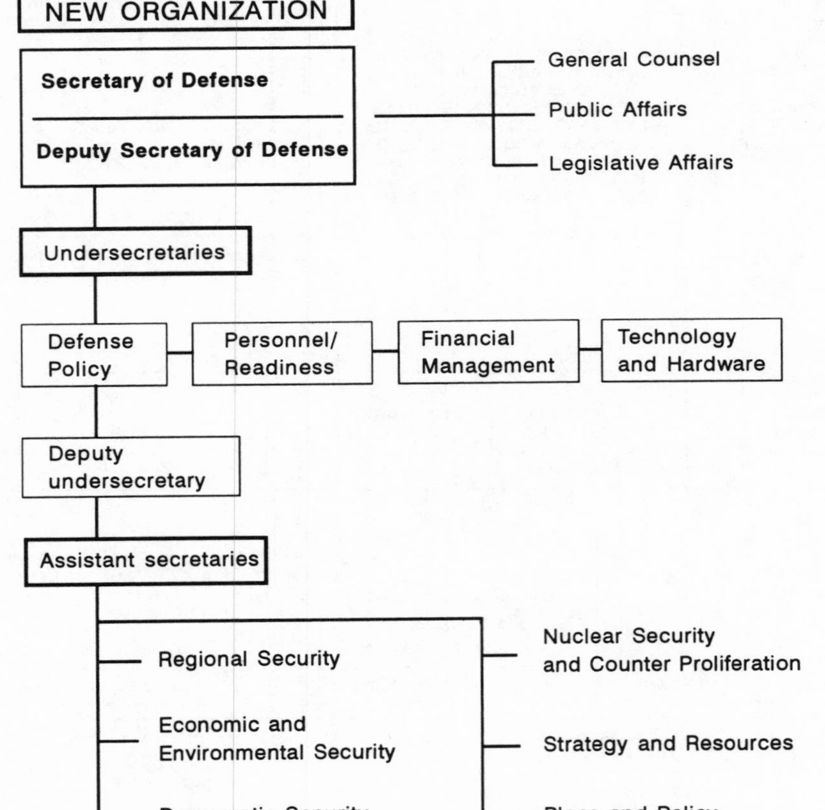

Source: The Washington Post, January 28, 1993.

reorganization acts, the latest of which was enacted in 1986, the secretary's role has been greatly strengthened and the department centralized in order to improve the efficiency and responsiveness of the military instrument. The essentials of the secretary's role, as they have evolved, have been described as follows.

> Foreign policy, military strategy, defense budgets and the choice of major weapons and forces are all closely related matters of basic national security policy and the principal task of the Secretary of Defense is personally to grasp the strategic issues and provide active leadership to develop a defense program that sensibly relates all these factors. In short, his main job is to shape the defense program in the national interest. In particular, it is his job to decide what forces are needed.[30]

During Robert McNamara's tenure as secretary (1961–1968), secretarial control was extended throughout the DOD by the application of systems analysis techniques to generate and justify military programs. The thrust of McNamara's approach was to steer the nature of debate in DOD on strategy and forces away from the intangibles of military judgment toward quantitative, management-oriented analyses in which civilian officials could dominate. Although the effects of the McNamara revolution have endured in considerable measure, subsequent secretaries have tended to turn more to military professionals in the department for expertise and advice. Indeed, during the tenure of Caspar Weinberger (1981–1988), the military professionals largely regained a position of preeminence in the department. (The role of the military in national security decision-making is treated at length in Chapter 7.)

The president exercises his constitutional authority as commander in chief of the armed forces directly through the secretary of defense and the chairman of the JCS to the commanders of the nine unified and specified commands. In effect, the secretary is the deputy commander in chief. In strict legal terms, the JCS as a body is not in the chain of command; in practice, defense secretaries often involve the chiefs, drawing on their professional advice on policy and operational means to implement directives from the president. Although the normal flow of advice from the chiefs normally goes up through the chairman and the secretary of defense, the 1986 Defense Reorganization Act explicitly gives the individual members of the JCS a statutory right to go directly to the president. This "end around" option was designed to assuage those opponents to reorganization who feared that independent military opinion would be stifled by a partisan secretary of defense or a dominant chairman.[31]

As the "hinge" between the highest civilian authorities and the uniformed military, the members of the JCS have two distinct roles in the DOD. In one, corporately, they are the senior military advisers to the president, the NSC, and the secretary of defense. In the other, individually, they are the chiefs of their respective services. As a corporate body, the JCS includes not only the army and air force chiefs of staff, the chief of naval operations, and the commandant of the Marine Corps but also the chairman and vice chairman of the JCS. The chairman or his deputy, the vice chairman, represents the JCS as a whole at meetings of the NSC and in other interagency forums.

The president not only leans on the JCS for military advice and operational plans but also for supporting opinion when he is undertaking politically controversial national security initiatives. Such support by uniformed leaders has often been a key element in developing a popular and congressional consensus. The U.S. political tempest in 1977 and 1978 over ratification of the Panama Canal Treaty was a striking example of the importance to the president of a JCS endorsement—so much so that JCS support of the president led some critics to attack the group's motives. Such critics saw the military's backing of the treaty as a concession to intense presidential pressure rather than a response to strategic considerations.[32] The JCS support in 1986 for President Reagan's decision to abrogate unilaterally the SALT II limits on offensive systems, and in 1990, for President Bush's decision to cut American force levels in Europe in half, brought similar complaints. Such complaints recall the remarks of General Ridgway concerning his tour of duty as army chief of staff (1953–1955): "The pressure brought upon me to make my military judgment conform to the views of higher authority was sometimes subtly, sometimes crudely applied."[33] Whether or not the debates over Panama and the abrogation of SALT II included such "pressure," they certainly highlighted the president's regard for the concurrence of his senior military advisers in critical foreign policy initiatives.

In view of the often heated political environment within which the JCS wrestles difficult problems of strategy, policy, and defense programs, it is hardly surprising that the decisions are often marked by "controversy, negotiations, and bargaining among officials and groups with different interests and perspectives."[34] A further discussion of the problems of the JCS recommendation process and interservice rivalry can be found in Chapter 8.

The Central Intelligence Agency. The Central Intelligence Agency (CIA) was established under the National Security Act of 1947 with responsibility for the overall coordination and integration of the intelligence efforts of various governmental groups engaged in national security matters. Its director was named an adviser to the NSC. The CIA inherited many functions of the wartime Office of Strategic Services, in the context of the cold war, including gathering and analyzing information and the conduct of covert operations.

Prior to America's entry into World War II, the gathering of intelligence was not institutionalized in any one agency but was incidental to the activities of several agencies, notably the State Department and the army and navy attachés. The climate of opinion was such that intelligence activities were looked down upon. Henry Stimson, as secretary of state in the Hoover administration, dismissed the "spying" business with the maxim that "gentlemen do not read other gentlemen's mail."[35] However, the ravages of global war and the threat of communism obscured the gentlemanly distinctions of an earlier age. Beginning in 1947, the CIA became a powerful force in the twilight battles of the cold war.

Through the 1950s and 1960s, the CIA played a major role and amassed considerable power within the government. As noted earlier, World War II and the cold war had demonstrated a strong need for a formal intelligence agency. As the dimensions and stakes of the cold war expanded, so did the CIA. Moreover, the agency enjoyed unusual autonomy. For thirty years, until 1977, the CIA was the only federal agency exempt from openly defending its budget and subjecting its policies and programs to the scrutiny of congressional oversight. Funds for the CIA were disguised in the defense budget, rendering any outside assessment of program effectiveness impossible.

The CIA's position was also strengthened by its primacy in intelligence gathering and analysis. Information is power, in government as elsewhere. As a result of long-term assignments to specific areas, in contrast to the approach of rotating personnel through differing assignments by other governmental organizations, the CIA's agents in the field, as well as its analysts at home, produced relatively high quality work.[36]

Since its inception, the CIA has been involved in a quite different and distinct role from mere intelligence production, namely, covert operations. In Iran in 1953 and in Guatemala in 1954, for example, the CIA sponsored coups that overthrew existing regimes. In the Bay of Pigs in 1961, the CIA was the agent of an unsuccessful attempt to remove Castro from power. Such episodes of clandestine warfare, combined with CIA activity in Chile during the overthrow of Allende and a few instances of improper actions by its personnel at home, convinced a number of critics that the CIA's scope and power should be curtailed. Elements in both the Congress and the public were prepared to sacrifice some of the agency's operational effectiveness in order to whittle down its power. The fact that the cold war was presumably replaced by détente and intervention by retrenchment in the early 1970s reinforced this tendency to downgrade and "domesticate" the CIA.

In due course it became apparent to many that downgrading of the CIA in the early 1970s went too far. When the Carter administration found itself caught off guard in 1979 by the seizure of the American embassy in Teheran and the Soviet invasion of Afghanistan, it belatedly began the process of revitalizing the CIA. Subsequently, during the Reagan administration, the CIA played a major role in American efforts to destabilize the Sandinista government in Nicaragua. These efforts, plus the agency's role in the Iran–Contra affair, again led to public and congressional criticism and a drop in public trust in the agency in the latter 1980s. By the early 1990s, the imposition of strict internal controls had again restored public confidence and agency morale.

The end of the cold war and the withering away of the Soviet Union has undermined one principal purpose of the CIA. In response, the agency has attempted to deal with the new environment by adjusting its mission. For example, in the early 1990s the CIA is attempting to intensify its economic intelligence activities, to coordinate U.S. and foreign intelligence on global terrorism, and to integrate intelligence and law enforcement activities against narcotics producers and drug traffickers. However, the agency is meeting considerable resistance in its efforts to shift its mission. Moreover, its inability to predict such major events as the collapse of the Soviet Union, the long survivability of the Soviet-backed Afghan regime, and the Iraqi invasion of Kuwait has again damaged its credibility. (Detailed attention is given to the role of intelligence in Chapter 7.)

Office of Management and Budget. Questions of strategy and national security have their dollars-and-cents counterparts. With his defense budget, the president structures the priorities of national defense. In the creation of this budget and in the daily oversight of executive operations, the Office of Management and Budget (OMB) plays a crucial role. As Theodore Sorensen remarked, "Any President, in short, must always be setting priorities and measuring costs. The official most often likely to loom largest in his thinking when he makes a key decision is not the Secretary of State or the Secretary of Defense but the Director of the Budget."[37] Indeed, in the early days of the Bush presidency, no individual was more influential in shaping his overall agenda than President Bush's director of OMB, Richard Darman.

As presidents have sought to extend their control over an expanding bureaucracy, OMB has become a most effective instrument of influence. OMB personnel establish, under presidential guidance, departmental budget obligations and spending ceilings within which departments must plan. Budgets from the departments, including the DOD, are routinely subjected to OMB review prior to presidential approval and submission to Congress to ensure that they are in accord with the president's priorities. This process helps restrain the special relationships that tend to proliferate between executive bureaus and congressional committees. In addition, as part of its management responsibilities, the OMB exercises a continuing oversight role over ongoing federal programs. This, too, enhances its position within the executive branch.[38]

The Nature of Presidential Power. Central to the Constitution's design was the concept that no institution should hold an unchallenged position of dominance in all aspects of the conduct of public affairs. This constitutional precept and the consequent governmental framework fundamentally shape the president's ability to influence the behavior of institutions, people, and the overall environment of governmental activity. Richard Neustadt has succinctly and insightfully described this system as one "not of separation of powers but of separated institutions sharing powers."[39] The president, as a result, sits in a position where many actors require his help in achieving their objectives. By the same token, the president is also dependent on other actors to accomplish his tasks. In the area of national security policy, this interactive process is clearly illustrated by the dynamic and historic tension between the president and Congress. This crucial dimension of the problem of national security policy leadership is addressed in the next chapter on the role of Congress.

In the context of our system of government, presidential power is, then, generally the power of persuasion. Teddy Roosevelt called the presidency a "bully pulpit"; his successor FDR said it was a "place of moral leadership." More prosaically, Neustadt noted that presidential power rests in the ability to induce others to "believe that what he [the president] wants of them is what their own appraisal of their own responsibilities requires them to do in their own interests, not his." At the heart of the process of persuasion is bargaining. As Neustadt emphasizes, "power is persuasion and persuasion becomes bargaining."[40]

All too often, the give and take of the bargaining system is obscured by the symbols of power and authority which surround the presidency. The president commands attention in the media by virtue of his office. He enjoys the prestige of being chief of state, as well as the head of government. He has at his disposal a wide spectrum of rewards and a significant number of penalties. These potential points of advantage in the bargaining process should not, however, be confused with presidential power, which, at bottom, involves the president's ability to wield these instruments so as to persuade other people that their own purposes are compatible with his and that cooperation with him advances their own interests.

The bargaining advantages accrued by a president come not only from his political acumen and persuasive skills but also from his ability to (1) develop and articulate an overall policy framework and strategy that give coherence to his actions, (2) choose able subordinates and weld them into an effective team, and (3) establish a pattern of successful leadership in important matters which will encourage those who are neutral to cooperate and provide support and those who would oppose or obstruct to await a more favorable time. Establishing a success pattern is, of course, partly a matter of good fortune (but, as Machiavelli has observed, a successful leader grasps good fortune and uses it); it is also a matter of readiness to sort out priorities and make hard decisions.

In his term in office, President Bush was spectacularly successful in the area of foreign policy. This success so frustrated his opponents that they criticized him, not for foreign policy failures, but for paying too much attention to foreign policy. His success was due largely to his foreign policy background (Ambassador to the United Nations, envoy to China, and Director of Central Intelligence), his personal contacts with world leaders (developed during his eight years as Vice President), and the ability and loyalty of his foreign policy team. In 1990 President Bush was able to assemble a coalition of some 30 states to join him in the fight to evict Saddam Hussein from Kuwait and obtain U.N. approval for the use of force, in effect presenting Congress and the American people with a *fait accompli*. Despite the misgivings of some of his advisers such as—reportedly—the Joint Chiefs' General Powell and Secretary of State Baker, who had misgivings about an apparent rush to war, he plunged ahead successfully. Bush's personal contacts also enabled him to assemble the Arab nations and Israel for a series of Middle East peace conferences beginning in Madrid in 1991, to get Chinese leaders to make sufficient concessions to keep most-favored-nation status, and to obtain trade concessions from Japan in 1992 during the recession that threatened his presidency.

The only person who truly can view an issue from a presidential perspective is the president; all others' views are colored by their own responsibilities. If he is to protect and advance his power, he cannot squander his time and influence. He must carefully weigh his choices so that they contribute to his influence on issues he deems crucial to the nation and to his administration. He must anticipate major issues early and seek out their crucial elements. When the matter is an important one, he cannot hesitate to invest his reputation and prestige, for they are important elements in the equation of power. Indeed, even the soundest policies and most adroit bargaining can be doomed if the president is suffering from a negative image—as evidenced by President Nixon's inability to lead the nation after the Watergate scandal.

On the other hand, reputation and prestige have acted as a buffer for many presidents in the face of controversy. The departure in 1987 of Caspar Weinberger as Secretary of Defense was widely viewed as a protest against President Reagan's softening of his attitude toward the threat of Soviet Communist expansionism. The political impact of Weinberger's action, even among the right wing of the Republican Party, was muted by Reagan's longstanding reputation as a virulent anticommunist, and Reagan was able to get the Senate to ratify the Intermediate Nuclear Forces Agreement (INF) in the spring of 1988.

Constraints on Presidential Power. The preceding discussion of presidential influence and leadership emphasized some of the counterbalancing forces that are inherent in the system. Although the president sits astride important action channels, his power is constantly challenged and tempered. The dynamic tension between the president and Congress is only the most dramatic of the checks on presidential action. Among the other important countervailing forces are public opinion, the impact of past policies and programs, the responsiveness of the executive bureaucracy, and the views, interests, and expected reactions of other nations.

Public Opinion. Effective presidential leadership can tolerate short-term reverses in public acceptance, but, over time, a president must have a favorable popular consensus behind his policies. The demise of LBJ's "Great Society" under the burden of the Vietnam War's unpopularity, the resignation of President Nixon in the wake of Watergate, and the inability of Ronald Reagan to set budget priorities and establish trade policies after the Iran–Contra scandal surfaced offer three striking examples of this phenomenon.

Since public opinion is a vital factor in maintaining and projecting presidential influence, it is also a subject for focused presidential attention. In discussing his approach to press relations, President Johnson revealed his view of the nature of the process.

> There's only one sure way of getting favorable stories from reporters and that is to keep their daily bread—the information, the stories, the plans, and the details they need for their work—in your own hands, so that you can give it out when and to whom you want. Even then nothing's guaranteed, but at least you've got a chance to bargain.[41]

In addition to underscoring the motif of bargaining as a means of presidential leadership, President Johnson's remarks are suggestive of the complex nature of public opinion formation. Public opinion is seldom a spontaneous expression of the "people's will." It is a reaction to selective information provided by institutions and individuals, often with contradictory purposes. Moreover, the public is frequently highly differentiated. The views of opinion leaders or the "attentive public" are often at variance with those of the mass public. Which ''public's'' opinion counts will differ with circumstances, but the president cannot long ignore the views of opinion leaders who control the mass media, particularly television, which provides the bulk of political information to most of the people.

In the realm of national security affairs, the president has a substantial initial advantage in the formation of public opinion. External crises have a cohesive effect on opinion. In addition, the executive frequently dominates the channels of information. This was vividly demonstrated in the Persian Gulf war in January and February of 1991. The President and his key advisers decided to manage the flow of information in such a way that the president and the military appeared flawless in their execution of Operation Desert Storm. Unlike Vietnam where reporters were allowed to roam freely throughout the country, reporters were confined to escorted pools and the Pentagon placed sharp restrictions on when and how they could talk to the troops. Two results were that President Bush's popularity and support for the war climbed dramatically. In the fall of 1990, less than half the population supported the war, and the President's approval rating was below 50 percent. On the eve of the war, support had risen to 62 percent, and once hostilities began, support for the war and the President climbed above 90 percent. This support remained high even after subsequent analysis showed that President Bush's policies and the military execution were far from flawless. It was subsequently revealed, for example, that the Bush administration furnished Iraq with limited intelligence information until the eve of the invasion of Kuwait, and that American weapons such as the Tomahawk cruise missile and Patriot air defense missile were successful less than 50 percent of the time.* The initial impression about the President's decisiveness and the military's success remained the predominant factor in shaping public opinion about the Persian Gulf war.[42]

Adverse opinion becomes crucial when it is expressed in the electoral process. In spite of growing dissension within the nation, President Johnson ''survived'' the Vietnam debate until Eugene McCarthy's near victory in the 1968 New Hampshire primary translated opinion into adverse votes. Similarly, President Carter's perceived weaknesses in dealing with the Soviet invasion of Afghanistan and the taking of American hostages at the Iranian embassy, coupled with his hesitance in rebuilding America's military strength, proved to be fatal to his reelection effort. To political leaders, including the president, the electoral process is the most forceful and attention-getting expression of popular opinion.

Public opinion provides a barometer of popular feeling. For a beleaguered president, however, the need is more often for a compass than a barometer. Public opinion polls report general reactions but seldom provide a president with adequate policy direction. Moreover, public opinion generally lags behind the problem. Roosevelt's struggle to awaken an indifferent or negative America to the dangers prior to World War II is a case in point. On the other hand, President Bush's popular decision in March 1991 to keep the Kurds in northern Iraq from

---

*It should be noted that the Patriot weapons were being used in a missile defense role rather than in the air defense role for which they were designed. Ballistic missiles, such as the Iraqi Scud, travel at much higher speeds than aircraft and thus the intercept speeds are of a much higher magnitude.

being slaughtered by Saddam Hussein is illustrative of the rare instances in which public opinion pointed out a correct course of action. Both interpreting public opinion and influencing it have proven to be difficult yet essential presidential arts.

Past Policies and Programs. As each president assumes office, the rhetoric of autumn campaigning takes on a different perspective in the cold January light. The responsibilities of the presidency, including the continuing programs and initiatives of a previous chief executive, now belong to the new officeholder. An example of this situation is the Bay of Pigs invasion in 1961. President Kennedy "inherited" from President Eisenhower a small army of Cubans poised in Guatemala for a do-or-die strike against the Castro regime. With planning in its final stages and with Eisenhower's previous endorsement, Kennedy pondered the decision to proceed with the assault. Some would have interpreted cancellation as an admission that Castro was too powerful and too popular to be overthrown; others would see cancellation as a sign of presidential weakness and a disavowal of the "free" Cubans.[43] On a practical level, Kennedy was confronted with the problem of disarming and disbanding a sizable and fanatical military force, should he opt for cancellation. He chose to let the Cubans strike but resisted recommendations that crucial and earlier planned air support be provided. The results were disastrous. The invaders were routed. Castro's prestige was enhanced, and the image of the United States was tarnished. Kennedy's mishandling of his dubious inheritance was a serious blow to his young administration.

Another example of the difficulties a new president faces when confronted with the commitments of his predecessor is President Carter's exclusion of the Palestine Liberation Organization (PLO) from the Middle East peace process. President Ford had asserted that the United States would not negotiate with or recognize the PLO until it recognized United Nations Resolution 242 and Israel's right to exist. Throughout his presidency, President Carter refused to negotiate with the PLO, but in 1987 on a Middle East peace mission as a private citizen he expressed his willingness to meet with representatives of the PLO. When asked why, as president, he did not change U.S. policy and establish a formal relationship with the PLO, Carter said, "The reason is straightforward and it remains relevant to this day. It stems from the necessity for preserving the honor of our nation and our credibility as a negotiating partner. . . . Even though the promise was made by my predecessor, I was duty bound to keep it."[44]

As the foregoing indicates, policy is not created *in vacuo*; rather, each new decision must be made within the context of already existing decisions and commitments. Notable among these accumulations are the budget decisions of previous administrations. This is especially true with regard to the development of weapons, for the military procurement process is characterized by long lead times. A new president is often unable to influence the types and amounts of weapons available to conduct military operations—availability which may shape overall strategy during his term of office. President Carter's decision in 1977 to forgo production of the B-1 bomber is noteworthy in part because it represented one of the few times a president has rejected an inherited major weapons system after it had completed development and was ready for production. An important element contributing to President Carter's decision was the fact that full-scale production had not yet begun. Although President Reagan subsequently resurrected the B-1 program, had Carter approved it the Air Force would have reached initial operating capability in 1982 rather than 1986.

Lack of Bureaucratic Responsiveness. Presidents often find their ability to execute or even influence national security policy diminished by their inevitable reliance on the executive bureaucracy for the implementation of policy decisions. During the 1962 Cuban Missile Crisis, for example, President Kennedy was chagrined to learn that Thor and Jupiter intermediate-range missiles located in Turkey had not been removed as he had ordered several months earlier. Undoubtedly, there were many reasons why the presidential directive failed to be implemented; in part, the lapse was due to a lack of enthusiasm for the policy on the part of those who were charged with seeing it through.[45]

The expansion of the executive bureaucracy has been in many respects a two-edged sword. Presidents derive from this expanded bureaucracy greater access to and control over information as well as the ability to develop and analyze a broader range of policy options. However, executive decisions are necessarily implemented through the bureaucracy, and its growth serves to widen the gap between policy-making at the top and implementation at the grassroots level. Within that gap the occasion often arises for presidential decisions to be delayed, amended, or even nullified.

While senior agency officials are generally appointed by the president, the federal bureaucracy is largely staffed at middle and lower levels by career civil servants who may not fully share the president's perspectives on national security affairs. Experienced bureaucrats often learn to influence the policy-making process by manipulating the number and range of policy alternatives circulated for consideration, by drafting implementing instructions that blunt the impact of a particular policy, or by delaying the implementation of a policy to the point that it becomes "overtaken by events." Oftentimes, bureaucratic "leaks" develop which alert the media, and thereby the public, to particularly controversial policies under consideration before they can be fully implemented. For example, in February 1991, a career official in the Department of Defense leaked a draft of a classified Pentagon planning document that stated that the principal goal of U.S. national security policy in the post–cold war period should be to thwart the emergence of a new rival to American military supremacy. The tone of the document caused such a storm of protest in the United States and in allied capitals that the document was completely rewritten and its tone changed dramatically.[46]

One need not always invoke such mischievous motives, however, to explain how the executive bureaucracy can act as a constraint on presidential power. In order to receive the careful analysis and consideration that they deserve, major policy initiatives are circulated, or "staffed," among the various agencies of the bureaucracy with an interest in the ultimate policy outcome. Again due to the increased size of the bureaucracy, this staff coordination can be a time-consuming process. Although clearly possessing the means to bypass much of this process, presidents who attempt to short-circuit the full consideration of policy initiatives do so at the risk of an incomplete or inaccurate understanding of the implications of their action. In short, presidents are often constrained in implementing major policies by the time required to study and analyze, as well as implement, such initiatives.

In many respects, the president's role in national security policy-making is the most fluid and least predictable of all the major actors' in the decision-making process. In both a constitutional and an institutional sense, the president is the focal point of the national security policy process. But more than most participants in that process, the president has wide latitude in defining his own role. Patterns of presidential involvement have varied according to the style and experience of various presidents. Always subject to important constraints, some presidents have chosen to become personally enmeshed in the details of policy-making and implementation. Others have chosen a more passive role while delegating broad responsibilities to their cabinet and other senior officials. Given the nature of presidential authority and power, however, even the most passive chief executives of recent decades have occupied a pivotal position in the national security process.

Interests of Other Nations. Both in traditional foreign policy matters and also in what might initially appear to be domestic matters—such as environmental issues—the president must take into account the views of other nations' leaders. As interdependence deepens in the years to come, this constraint on presidential freedom of action is likely to grow in importance. Examples of this factor can be deduced or found in Chapters 16 to 21, dealing with various regions of the world.

Discussion Questions

1. With respect to national security policy-making, how does the Constitution divide responsibility between the president and Congress?
2. How has the War Powers Act of July 1973 shaped presidential decision-making on the employment of U.S. military forces?
3. How have changes in technology had an impact on the scope of presidential prerogative in determining national security policy?
4. "The role of the National Security Council in the policy formulation process has not been static but has fluctuated, in almost cyclic fashion, according to the style and personal experience of various Presidents." Is this an accurate assessment of the historic function of the NSC? Explain.
5. The recent evolution of the national security policy-making process reflects a generally expanding role for the assistant to the president for national security affairs. What factors have contributed to this trend? Is this trend irreversible?
6. What factors have tended to blunt the role of the Department of State in the formation of national security policy?
7. What evolutionary changes in the role of the secretary of defense have occurred since 1947?
8. How might each of the key executive branch agencies concerned with national

security affairs contribute to the formulation and implementation of U.S. policy toward the Middle East? Which persons or agencies would you expect to be most influential in that process? Why?

9. What is the function of the Office of Management and Budget as it relates to the national security process?

10. What are the domestic constraints on presidential decision-making power? Which constraints, in your judgment, are most important?

11. How does President Bush's handling of the Persian Gulf war reflect both the power of the presidency and constraint on that power?

Recommended Reading

Allison, Graham. *Essence of Decision: Explaining the Cuban Missile Crisis*. Boston: Little, Brown, 1971.

——— and Treverton, Gregory. *Rethinking America's Security*. New York: Norton, 1991.

Cronin, Thomas E., and Greenberg, Sanford., eds. *The Presidential Advisory System*. New York: Harper & Row, 1969.

Destler, I.M. *Presidents, Bureaucrats, and Foreign Policy*. Princeton, N.J.: Princeton University Press, 1972.

Gottemoeller, Rose, ed. *Strategic Arms Control in the Post-START Era*. London: Brassey's, 1992.

Hilsman, Roger. *The Politics of Policy Making in Defense and Foreign Affairs*. New York: Harper & Row, 1971.

Hunter, Robert E. *Presidential Control of Foreign Policy*. New York: Praeger, 1982.

Hyland, William. *The Cold War—50 Years of Conflict*. New York: Random House, 1991.

Jordan, Amos A., ed. *Issues of National Security in the Seventies*. New York: Praeger, 1967.

Kissinger, Henry A. *The White House Years*. Boston: Little, Brown, 1979.

Lord, Carnes. *The Presidency and the Management of National Security*. New York: Free Press, 1988.

Lowi, Theodore J. *The Personal President: Power Invested, Promise Unfulfilled*. Ithaca, N.Y.: Cornell University Press, 1985.

Neustadt, Richard E. *Presidential Power*. New York: New American Library, 1960.

Report of the President's Special Review Board. Washington, D.C.: U.S. Government Printing Office, 1987 (Tower Commission).

Rossiter, Clinton. *The American Presidency*. New York: New American Library, 1960.

Schlesinger, Arthur M., Jr. *The Imperial Presidency*. Boston: Houghton Mifflin, 1973.

Smyrl, Marc E. *Conflict of Codetermination? Congress, the President and the Power to Make War*. Cambridge, Mass.: Ballinger, 1988.

Sorensen, Theodore C. *Decision Making in the White House*. New York: Columbia University Press, 1963.

Tucker, Robert, and Hendrickson, David. *The Imperial Temptation: New World Order and America's Purpose*. New York: Council on Foreign Relations, 1992.

6

The Impact of Congress on National Security Policy

Historic Alternation of Congressional Activism/Passivity. Few developments in the national security affairs arena have been so significant in the past three decades as the increasing assertion by Congress of a strong and continuing role, indeed, a full partnership, in the national security policy process. As noted in Chapter 5, the Constitution presents to the Congress and the president an "invitation to struggle for the privilege of directing foreign policy." In an earlier era, Congress declined the invitation, at least in that part of the foreign policy field known as national security, allowing the president to dominate the process. Since the latter 1960s, Congress has both challenged the president's preeminence across many of the important issues and has largely acquired the resources, information, and legal authority to do so on a comprehensive and continuing basis.

These comparatively recently asserted claims of Congress are soundly based in the Constitution's deliberate distribution of powers among the three branches of government. The dangers of concentrated power were still fresh in the Constitution's framers' minds from their break with the British crown. "The accumulation of all powers, legislative, executive, and judiciary, in the same hands, whether of one, a few, or many, and whether hereditary, self-appointed, or elective, may justly be pronounced the very definition of tyranny," as Madison put it in Federalist Paper No. 47. Or, as Justice Brandeis expressed it later, the purpose of the constitutional architects was "not to promote efficiency but to preclude the exercise of arbitrary power."[1]

Those selfsame architects were nonetheless conscious of the danger of too much dispersion of power. They had, after all, experienced government by committee during both the Revolutionary War and the Articles of Confederation period and the gross and dangerous inefficiencies to which those eras gave rise. "It is not surprising that an energetic John Adams complained that serving on ninety recorded committees busied him daily from 4:00 a.m. until 10:00 p.m. Within the Congress there developed an unbounded factionalism in which the competition between committees was settled by producing new committees to gain dominance over old ones."[2] (The fact that during the energy crisis of the late 1970s there were eighty-three committees and subcommittees in the House of Representatives alone with some claim to jurisdiction in energy matters and that 421 of the 435 House members belonged to one or more of these committees suggests that certain lessons have to be relearned periodically.[3]) Reflecting this experience of deliberative dalliance, the Constitution's framers gave certain key powers, namely those clearly requiring central direction, such as treaty-making and commanding the armed forces, to the executive; even so, the wary politicians made the former subject to legislative, that is, Senate, approval.

The bulk of the enumerated powers relating to national security were reserved for Congress. While there are no explicit "national security" powers in the Constitution, Congress is allocated the power to declare war, raise and support armies and the navy, make rules for the government and regulation of the forces, call the militia, and make all laws which shall be "necessary and proper" for carrying out these functions.[4] Additionally, the advice and consent of the Senate must be obtained for treaties and the appointment of ambassadors, ministers, and other key officers of the government.

As a consequence of this constitutional ambivalence, with some leaning toward congressional preeminence, there have been several periods in American history when Congress has clearly been predominant in national security matters. That the first of these occurred during Madison's presidency is not surprising, for Madison had been the leader of the House of Representatives in the 1790s and an ally of Jefferson in the fight against the executive. "As Corwin notes, their theory was 'that the right to determine the foreign policy of the United States devolves on Congress by virtue of its power to declare war and that the powers of the President in the diplomatic sphere are instrumental only, of no greater range of discretion than the determination of matters of fact.' "[5] Madison was so low-key in his dealings with Congress and the so-called war hawks therein that he permitted the legislators to drag him and the country into war at the end of 1811.

After the Civil War and the strong leadership of Lincoln, Congress again seized the reins, ushering in another generation of what the young scholar Woodrow Wilson called "congressional government." Not until the turn of the century and the deeper involvement in international affairs following the war with Spain did the president, in the person of Theodore Roosevelt, regain the initiative. Roosevelt's technique was to confront Congress with accomplished facts, as in Panama, or in sending the fleet around the world. Roosevelt noted the following in his autobiography.

> The head of the Senate Committee on Naval Affairs announced that the fleet should not and could not go because Congress would refuse to appropriate the money—he being from an Eastern seaboard State. However, I announced in response that I had enough

> money to take the fleet around to the Pacific anyhow, that the fleet would certainly go, and that if Congress did not choose to appropriate enough money to get the fleet back, why, it would stay in the Pacific. There was no further difficulty about the money.[6]

President Woodrow Wilson, drawing on his own earlier scholarly analysis of the evils of government by committee, also attempted to draw Congress in his wake. As long as World War I was in progress, this approach was reasonably successful, but Wilson's unilateral methods pulled him down in 1918–1920 as he attempted to negotiate peace and to bring the United States into the new League of Nations. Senate's defeat on the Versailles Treaty, incorporating both peace and the league, ushered in another period of congressional dominance in foreign and national security affairs—one that lasted until world war again forced the nation to close ranks behind the presidency.

The Japanese attack on Pearl Harbor in late 1941 welded Americans together as they had not been since 1918. There was some weakening of this solidarity after the war's end and, in particular, during the Korean War. Essentially, though, from the onset of the cold war in about 1948 until the mid 1960s there was such a strong national consensus on the main lines of national security policy that Congress went more or less quietly along with the executive branch on virtually every major national security issue. Lack of information, perception of danger, complexity of issues, need for solidarity—all were reasons, in addition to public consensus, why the Congress deferred to the executive. In many cases, indeed, it gave the president a blank check in advance in a series of resolutions authorizing him to act unilaterally, namely, on Formosa (1955), Cuba (1962), and the Gulf of Tonkin (1964). By the latter 1960s, however, the public consensus had begun to dissolve under the strains of the Vietnam War, and Congress started the pendulum of executive–legislative powers swinging in the opposite direction. This swing toward the Congress lasted until the mid 1980s, when first President Reagan and then President Bush began to assert presidential prerogatives in national security policy. (Both of these comparatively recent swings will be discussed later in this chapter.)

Structural Explanations of Congressional Role in National Security. Where as the president can—at least in theory and subject to the constraints cited in Chapter 5—move with dispatch and secrecy in the national security arena, the deliberative processes of Congress are slow and open—or, if not avowedly open, "leaky." Investigations, hearings, debate, resolution of differences between the two houses—all these take time. Hence, in both hot wars and cold, the public and the congress itself traditionally have expected the president to take the lead. The readiness of the public to follow a presidential lead in times of tension or danger was dramatically illustrated in late 1979 as, first, Iranian militants took American diplomats hostage and, second, the Soviet takeover of Afghanistan underscored the possibility of spreading Russian aggression; whereas only twenty percent of the American people approved of President Carter's handling of foreign affairs just before the crises cited, by January 1980, approval had risen to sixty percent.

Even President Reagan, who maintained a comparatively high level of personal popularity throughout his two terms in the White House, saw his approval rating increase markedly after he ordered the invasion of Grenada in 1983 and the air attack on Libya in 1986. Opinion polls showed an average gain of about 10 percentage points after each action. Finally, President Bush saw his popularity rating soar nearly 40 points after the U.S.-led coalition drove Iraq from Kuwait in forty-two days.

In part related to its slow and open processes, another reason for the secondary position of Congress has been the fractionalization of its power and influence. Congress works through committees, and this traditional organization of the legislature powerfully influences its behavior in national security affairs just as in other realms of foreign and domestic policy. The sheer number of legislators has long necessitated the division of Congress into smaller bodies to conduct hearings and debate complex policy issues. Legislation adopted by Congress is not, therefore, primarily the result of discussion by the full body but rather the consequence of tedious committee work. Although the estimated number varies with definitions, Congress now has some thirty committees and fifty subcommittees with upward of twenty thousand congressional staffers and members of congressional agencies involved in national security affairs oversight. As a result of this multiplicity, there is no focal point in Congress to bring disparate views together. Each committee tends to have a partial interest and partial view of the broad national security picture. Congress is unable to determine coherent national priorities—except implicitly, through the budget; the executive branch has furnished the only focal point in the government. (''And where,'' columnist George Will has asked, ''in any public square in the world have you ever seen a war monument erected to a committee?'')

The ways legislators have traditionally tended to define their roles and responsibilities is a third factor in explaining how Congress handles national security. Basically, members have been concerned with subjects that impinge directly on their reelection and on their influence within their respective houses of Congress.[7] In general, members of Congress do not consider questions of military policy in terms of their implications for strategic objectives or goals. Instead, they have focused on constituency-related issues such as spending that aids their districts, National Guard Armories, or the ''minutiae of line items'' which have popular appeal, such as the high prices paid by the Department of Defense for hammers and toilet seats.[8] As former Senate Armed Services Committee chairman Barry Goldwater observed, ''The budget process distorts the nature of congressional oversight by focusing primarily on the question of how much before we answer the key questions of what for, why, and how well.''[9] ''Thus, congressional committees considering the annual defense budget have traditionally examined with some care defense *structure,* that is, financial, personnel, materiel, and organizational matters. Yet, while they explore the details of the defense budgets in these areas, they seldom question the *strategy* from which the structural requirements flow. When an individual member does try to question the strategy of a particular budget, he or she is normally overwhelmed by colleagues concerned about constituency issues. Throughout 1992, Congressman Les Aspin, Chairman of the House Armed Services Committee, tried to get his colleagues to focus on building a post–cold war force structure from the bottom up. Most of his colleagues were more concerned with the jobs that would be lost if weapon systems like the B-2 bomber and Seawolf submarine were canceled and bases or armories in their districts were closed.

Recognizing the importance of committees in the legislative process, congressmen tend to seek membership on committees that offer the most control over policy fields and resources important to their constituents. Because of the seniority system in Congress and one-party dominance in the South for many decades, an undue proportion of the chairmen of armed services and appropriation committees and subcommittees have been Southerners; it has been observed in this context that had Georgia been an island it would have long since sunk under the weight of the military bases emplaced there. This traditional focus by congressmen on "delivering the bacon" for the home district has been validated by studies showing that their constituents do indeed care more about such matters (and about intercession with federal agencies, providing information about federal programs, and similar service functions) than they do about the legislator's classic law-making activities.

Another reason offered in the past to explain secondary congressional roles in national security matters was lack of expertise and access to information. The committee system tended to generate some expertise in the armed services or appropriations committees; members of those committees generally became well versed in some aspect of their committees' work. Yet even those committee members seldom developed a full appreciation of all the full committee's concerns and often did not master national security policy issues under consideration elsewhere in the House or Senate. A given member of Congress might, for example, know a great deal about military personnel expenditures but relatively little about weapons procurement—let alone about strategy, mobilization, economic warfare, or other aspects of national security.

Given the increasing complexity and vast amounts of information relating to any major national security issue, the executive departments that controlled the information-producing and intelligence-gathering agencies had an advantage over Congress. The executive's affixing a security classification to weapons system capabilities or to strategic intelligence further restricted access to information necessary to formulate and evaluate alternative proposals. Indeed, one of the tactics used by the Department of Defense in the 1980s and early 1990s to deal with the increasing congressional scrutiny of its weapons systems requests was to increase the number of classified, or "black," programs in its annual budget request. According to congressional critics, the Pentagon's black programs soared in cost from $5 billion in 1981 to approximately $38 billion in 1990, almost a quarter of the entire investment budget.[10] (Chapter 8 treats in some detail the topic of congressional access to intelligence.)

Congress offsets executive branch advantages to some extent by using its power to hold hearings and conduct investigations, such as the widely publicized hearings on the Iran–Contra affair, which lasted throughout the spring and summer of 1987. In these hearings Congress brought executive branch witnesses before it to explain policies and programs and to explore various points of view. Such hearings about national security matters often allow interdepartmental or interservice rivalry to surface, giving legislators the opportunity to choose concepts or particular programs that they find personally appealing or in the interest of their constituents. In any case, hearings show not only that Congress can use its investigatory powers to acquire information needed to make strategic decisions but also that Congress with its powers of legislation and appropriation could be the place of final decision—even on matters of strategy.

We should note that congressional security decisions have traditionally been characterized by bargaining that includes matters not strictly germane to the strategic question being considered; that is, a senator might trade his or her support on a defense policy matter in exchange for reciprocal support on a domestic water resources project. Not surprisingly then, national security decision-making, as it has occurred in the Congress, both in strategic and structural terms, has been as much political as rational in nature. Only in times of major crisis, and sometimes not even then, have these traditional horsetrading ways been abandoned. An interesting example of the inapplicability of traditional political compromise methods to national security issues occurred when Congress addressed the annual requests of Presidents Reagan and Bush for military aid to the Nicaraguan contras. Liberals said that the United States should not provide aid to a band of thugs fighting against the legitimately installed Marxist government of Nicaragua. Conservatives said the United States had the right to aid the freedom fighters trying to bring down a Soviet client state in close proximity to U.S. borders. The legislature compromised by passing seven different versions of contra aid, each authorizing support for the contras but encumbering that aid with restrictions that varied from year to year and that contradicted congressional consent to the principle of support for the Nicaraguan resistance. In effect, Congress provided enough funds to keep the contras from going out of existence but not enough to allow them to achieve their objective of overthrowing the government.

Public Opinion. Congress is particularly sensitive to public opinion. The morning paper and the television news, the latest public opinion poll and the hometown press coverage of issues (and of their own activities) are scrutinized by legislators, especially by those who must seek public endorsement at the polls every two years. Constituent mail and other communications from important individuals and groups in his or her district or state receive priority attention by an experienced legislator and staff. If, therefore, a strong current of opinion is building "back home," the Congress will respond in Washington.

The impact of public opinion on Congress was visibly demonstrated during the testimony of one NSC staffer, marine Lieutenant Colonel Oliver North, during the Iran–Contra hearings of 1987. After the public opinion polls and congressional mail showed sympathy for North's predicament as the "loyal staffer following orders,'' many members of the investigating Select Committee praised him effusively, even though North admitted shredding documents and lying to Congress—conduct that would normally have enraged members. Ideally, congressional responsiveness to shifting public attitudes will be dampened by the individual legislator's own knowledge and convictions about the nation's security. In some cases this does indeed occur, but in many cases, the response to such shifts in public attitudes will be amplified by reelection calculations. Reflecting on this tendency of Congress to swing with, and often beyond, public moods, Will Rogers is said to have remarked that ''if you don't scare Congress, it goes fishing; if you do scare it, it goes crazy.'' Representative or not, this lack of constancy, what de Tocqueville called the inability of democracies to persist in a design, can prove dangerous under various circumstances.

Ascertaining what public opinion is on a given issue is not, of course, simple or easy; it does not generally arise spontaneously, as the morning mist. The media play a crucial role in generating public opinion, selecting from a glut of facts and ideas just what information to emphasize and deciding what type, amount, and intensity of coverage to give a particular issue. Television has become the principal source of national and international news and opinion for most Americans.

Unfortunately, not many important national security issues lend themselves to the twelve-second sound bite, video-drenched treatment typified by the evening news show. The consequence seems to be that while the public at large has more information than ever before, it may not be appreciably better informed about national security matters. Indeed, if there is a systemic press or television bias on some matter, as has been documented on various issues, then the public may actually be less well informed about many key issues than was the case in an earlier era.[11]

Whatever the gauge of public opinion or the authenticity of the claims of those who seek to speak for the public, there is no doubt that, in a democracy such as the United States, popular support is essential if expensive, perhaps risky, national security policies and programs are to be pursued. While both president and Congress subscribe to this observation, the frequency of congressional elections necessarily makes Congress the more sensitive institution.

Return to Congressional Activism. The broad public consensus on national security policy which began with Pearl Harbor melted in the latter 1960s in the flames of the Vietnam conflict. Some would date the beginning of the meltdown somewhat earlier, in 1965, when President Johnson, citing his authority as commander in chief and without congressional consultation, sent an intervention force of 22,000 into the Dominican Republic.[12] Bipartisanship, the notion that party politics should not extend to foreign policy or that ''politics ends at the water's edge,'' is sometimes also listed as a casualty of this period; actually it had been less than robust ever since the 1950s. Whereas bipartisan consensus formally expired in 1979, when the Senate Foreign Relations Committee followed the longstanding practice in other congressional committees by dividing its hitherto unified staff into majority and minority staffs, it had long been more rhetoric than reality. The facts are that politics overleaps water as readily as land and that presidents seek support wherever they can find it. As Representative Lee Hamilton, chairman of the House Foreign Affairs Committee, noted some years ago:

> A President with a large party majority has never been thereby in a strong position to bend Congress to his will on foreign policy; on the contrary, the ''great'' periods of executive leadership and congressional cooperation have come when the majorities (in terms of party labels) were narrow or nonexistent so that the two branches had to work together. . . . [I]t is almost a law of contemporary American politics that a Republican President with a majority is under great pressure from the extreme Right, while a Democratic President is under similar pressure from his liberal constituency. If a President finds—as both Gerald Ford and Jimmy Carter have recently found—that foreign problems rarely yield to extreme approaches, he needs the opposing party to neutralize his own zealots. Although the tradition of bipartisanship grew up in the time of cold war national consensus—and can itself be carried to extremes that stifle needed debate—the pragmatic reasons for cultivating support in foreign policy from both parties are extremely powerful.[13]

With the loss of societal consensus in the latter 1960s came a mounting flood of congressional challenges to executive dominance. It is important to realize that the causes for this return to activism were deep and strong.

> Reassertion of congressional involvement in the many dimensions of American security policy can only be understood in the foregoing context of the breakdown of policy consensus, the erosion of the notion of executive competence, the shock of widespread illegal activities, and the impetus each of these developments gave to the growth of congressional ability independently to create and criticize policy. At the same time, the reassertion must also be viewed in the broader context of constitutional flexibility and the historical pattern of shifting balances between executive and legislature.[14]

Congressional challenges to the president on the conflict in Southeast Asia, which had begun when Lyndon Johnson was president, escalated in 1969 when Richard Nixon assumed that office. Under Chairman Fulbright's stimulus, the Senate Foreign Relations Committee took the lead. Its new Subcommittee on Security Agreements and Commitments Abroad critically reviewed worldwide executive agreements and produced a National Commitments Resolution to the effect that presidential action alone cannot commit the United States to assist a foreign country. Subsequently, in 1972, in the so-called Case Act, the Congress dropped the other shoe, requiring the executive branch to transmit promptly to it the text of any international agreement other than a treaty to which the United States is a party; Congress would then decide whether to withhold funds, or whatever other action seemed appropriate if it did not approve.[15]

The power of the purse strings was also used vigorously by the Congress, from late 1969 on to the final, fateful denial of assistance to the Republic of Vietnam in early 1975, which contributed to the rapid demise of that nation. Repeated substantive amendments to money bills also succeeded in an unprecedented limiting of the commander in chief's role in conducting military operations by

U.S. forces in the field. By this new technique of so amending authorization or appropriation bills, the Congress gained the ability to restrict and channel day-to-day operations as well as to guide the grand strategy of the war. (Having succeeded with this technique, Senator Fulbright went on to institute for the first time an authorization bill for the Department of State, so that the same congressional role could be played in diplomacy as well.[16])

An example of another type of congressional initiative that has become common occurred first in 1974 when Turkey invaded Cyprus, using American arms. Throughout the subsequent crisis, President Ford continued the policy of arms sales to Turkey, although many members of Congress opposed the policy and to some the sale of arms appeared to violate the military assistance laws. These critics were encouraged when Secretary of State Kissinger, in response to a question by Senator Eagleton, virtually admitted that the sales violated existing laws. Thereupon the Senate passed a sense of the Senate resolution urging termination of the sales.[17]

Fortified with Kissinger's admission and the Senate resolution, both houses then proceeded to pass a bill to compel the president to cease shipments. President Ford twice vetoed such bills until a compromise was reached that permitted arms sales until December 1974. In that bill the Congress directed that no further arms sales to Turkey would be permitted after that date until and unless the president certified to Congress that substantial progress toward agreement had been made regarding Turkish forces in Cyprus.[18] In the summer of 1975, when the president, unable to certify progress, nevertheless again sought to raise the issue, the Congress refused to consider the matter. The resumption of arms sales to Turkey had become not a matter of executive preference within congressional appropriations but an issue of foreign policy and procedure, with Congress establishing the new rules of the game. The fact that a potent Greek-American lobby marshaled the congressional votes is also part of the story, providing a telling example of single-issue politics in the Congress and the country at large. It might be noted, too, that when Congress did resume arms sales to Turkey in 1978, it insisted that for every $10 in aid to Turkey, Greece receive $7, even though Turkey is five times the size of Greece.

Another example of the new participatory and activist role of Congress had been the increasing use of "legislative vetoes," which enabled Congress to nullify an action proposed by the executive branch. Presidents contended that such vetoes violated the constitutional separation of powers. Supporters claimed that the vetoes kept the government attuned to public sensitivities. In 1983, the Supreme Court finally decided this issue and in the landmark *Chadha* decision declared the legislative veto unconstitutional. However, as Justice White observed in his dissenting opinion, pressure for a greater congressional role in the policy process would not be diminished by the elimination of the legislative veto.

> It is an important if not indispensable political invention that allows the President and Congress to resolve major constitutional and policy differences, assures accountability of independent regulatory agencies, and preserves Congress' control over lawmaking. Perhaps there are other means of accommodation and accountability, but the increasing

> reliance of Congress upon the legislative veto suggests that the alternatives to which Congress must now turn are not entirely satisfactory.[19]

Indeed, the legislative veto was an important vehicle for ensuring congressional participation in the national security policy process.

One of the most significant examples of the use of the legislative veto in national security matters was the Nelson–Bingham Bill. In 1974, Senator Gaylord Nelson of Wisconsin and Representative Jonathan Bingham were able to convince their colleagues to amend the Foreign Assistance Act, so that whenever the U.S. government offered to sell any defense article or service above a certain value, the president, before issuing the letter of offer, was obligated to send both houses of Congress a detailed description of the sales terms and the weapons involved. This led to the passage of the 1976 Arms Control Act. As amended, this act means that all arms sales over $14 million can be blocked by Congress within thirty calendar days should a concurrent "veto" resolution be passed, unless the president certifies an emergency.

Until the *Chadha* decision nullified the legislative veto provision of the Act, no proposed arms sale was ever vetoed by Congress. According to Senator Joseph Biden, the very existence of the legislative veto ensured that "any administration would give careful consideration to the support or opposition a contemplated sale might encounter in Congress."[20] However, to avoid its loss of active control in the arena of arms transfers, Congress amended the Arms Export Control Act to allow congressional "veto" through the passage of a "joint resolution." Unlike the concurrent resolution, however, the president may veto the joint resolution. This means that in order for Congress to block an arms sale, the joint resolution of disapproval would need the support of at least two-thirds of both houses to survive the president's veto.

The reality of this loss of congressional control became apparent in 1986 when both houses of Congress disapproved, through joint resolution, an administration plan to sell AIM-9 Sidewinder air-to-air missiles to Saudi Arabia. President Reagan vetoed the resolution. The House overwhelmingly overrode the president's veto, while the Senate narrowly sustained it, thus giving the president the authority to proceed with the sale, which he did.

The fact that the sale was allowed by the approval of only one-sixth of the House of Representatives and one-third plus one in the Senate frustrated many members of the Congress.[21] Observers have correctly predicted that unless the executive "is aggressive in providing for congressional participation, the backlash against the Supreme Court decision is likely to result in even more restrictive laws."[22] Indeed, some members of Congress have proposed that arms sales initiated by the president be approved by a majority of both houses of Congress. This process would significantly increase the role of Congress at the expense of the president. This example provides useful insights into the increased pressure Congress exerts on the national security process. The pressure is likely to continue, especially in the traditional forms of authorization and appropriations control.

Congressional determination to trim the president's powers and to assert at least a coequal role in national security matters has been exercised with increasing frequency in recent years through the budgetary process. The fight with the Reagan administration over the MX missile serves as a good illustration. One of Ronald Reagan's first actions as president was the cancellation in January 1981 of Jimmy Carter's proposed deployment of 200 MX intercontinental missiles in multiple protective shelters in the Far West. For the next two years, the Reagan administration, committed to ICBM modernization, searched for an alternative basing mode for the MX. In late 1982, the president formally proposed basing the missiles in closely spaced silos on existing U.S. military reservations. In December of that year Congress rejected the so-called Dense Pack proposal and blocked MX procurement. Congress had thus taken command of one of the key programs in U.S. strategic force modernization.

To break the stalemate with Congress, the president appointed a Commission on U.S. Strategic Forces (the Scowcroft Commission) to consider the future of the U.S. triad. In 1983, the Scowcroft Commission recommended the deployment of 100 MX mobile multiple-warhead ICBMs for the 1990s. In the FY 1984 Defense Authorization Act, Congress approved the general outline of the Scowcroft plan but provided funds for only fifty MX missiles in fixed silos. The legislators demanded that a more survivable basing mode be developed for the second fifty missiles.

The first deployment of MX ICBMs in fixed silos took place in 1986. However, the Reagan administration's 1987 proposal that the second fifty be deployed in railway trains located at secure military garrisons encountered stiff resistance in the Democrat-controlled 100th Congress. With the end of the cold war and the dissolution of the Soviet Union, the Bush administration eventually decided that fifty MX missiles in fixed silos were sufficient.

A prime example of the changed role of Congress in national security matters is afforded by the War Powers Act. The hotly contested debates over U.S. policy in Vietnam and over the associated limits of presidential power culminated in November 1973 in the passage, over President Nixon's veto, of legislation designed to restrict the president's authority to involve the United States in armed conflict or in situations likely to involve such conflict. The language of the act explicitly requires the president to report to Congress, within forty-eight hours of their deployment, any commitment of troops to actual or imminent hostilities or any introduction of troops into the territory, air space, or waters of a foreign nation while they are equipped for combat. The act also requires the president to consult with Congress prior to so acting, though the nature of this consultation is not spelled out.

Further, the act requires the Congress to approve or disapprove the continued use of troops within sixty days of their commitment; if the president certifies that troop safety requires it, this can be stretched to ninety days. If Congress fails to authorize within the sixty to ninety days the continued use of the forces, the president must withdraw them.[23]

Although no one can predict whether Congress will be inclined to approve or disapprove various possible uses of force, the very unpredictability under this statute could weaken deterrence in some circumstances. President Nixon's veto message (given in vain) put the point thus: the resolution

> would seriously undermine this Nation's ability to act decisively and convincingly in times of international crisis. As a result, the confidence of our allies in our ability to assist them could be diminished and the respect of our adversaries for our deterrent posture could decline . . . further increasing the likelihood of miscalculation and war.[24]

Proponents of the resolution agree that it will inhibit the executive's willingness to use force but judge that constraint an asset, not a liability. In their view a more measured, careful decision about the use of force—with Congress playing the full role that they argue is envisaged in the Constitution—is precisely what the resolution is intended to bring about.

Between 1973 and 1991, there have been twenty-five instances to which the War Powers Act has applied since its passage. Congress has never used it to restrain a President from putting or keeping American soldiers in harm's way. Indeed, only once has Congress invoked, and has the president signed, language restricting in any way the war powers of the president. In October 1983, after 240 U.S. Marines were killed, Congress began to question the U.S. role in the multinational peacekeeping force in Lebanon. Although President Reagan had reported to Congress "consistent with the War Powers resolution," he had not acknowledged that the marines had been introduced "into hostilities or into situations where imminent involvement in hostilities is clearly indicated by the circumstances," which would automatically trigger the War Powers Act's sixty-day time limit. As the fighting around Beirut intensified, so did congressional resolve for adherence to the act. The president did not want his powers curtailed, nor did he want to set a precedent for compliance with the War Powers Act's provision. Reagan argued that any deadline on the U.S. presence in Lebanon would weaken the deterrent force of that presence and encourage attacks after the U.S. forces went home.[25]

In a major compromise, President Reagan agreed to sign a joint resolution to the Congress which declared the War Powers Act's time provision applicable but also authorized the marine presence in Lebanon for an additional eighteen months. After the complete withdrawal of U.S. troops from Lebanon in early 1984, administration officials, while not admitting failure of their Lebanon policy, "blamed Congress for interfering by using the War Powers Resolution and thus preventing the outcome that the president had desired."[26]

The War Powers Act met its severest test in January 1991, immediately before the launching of the Desert Storm offensive during the Persian Gulf war.[27] In November 1990, the United Nations had authorized the U.S.-led coalition to use all necessary means (including force) to expel Iraq from Kuwait if it did not withdraw by January 15, 1991. That same month President Bush had switched the U.S. force posture in the Gulf from one of defense (of Saudi Arabia) to offense, and he increased U.S. troop strength from 200,000 to over 500,000, including ten divisions of ground forces, ten tactical air wings, and six carrier battle groups. This force was too large to be rotated.

Many members of Congress, including Senator Sam Nunn, influential Chairman of the Senate Armed Services Committee, and the entire Democratic leadership, were unhappy with President Bush's "use it or lose it" offensive strategy. Nunn and the democratic leadership in the Congress favored giving U.N. sanctions more time to work and in December 1990 held hearings on the President's strategy. Most of his witnesses, including several retired members of the Joint Chiefs of Staff and veteran diplomats supported the sanction option.

The President did not think he needed congressional approval to begin hostilities because the United States was operating as a member of a U.N. coalition, and the United Nations had authorized force. Many House members disagreed, and fifty-six members brought suit against the President to prevent him from going to war without getting a declaration of war from the Congress. The court ruled that congressional approval is required if Congress desires to become involved, that is, if a majority of the Congress seeks relief from an infringement on its constitutional war declaration powers, then it may be entitled to receive it.

When the Congress reconvened in early January 1991, it was in a difficult position. If it ignored the issue, and the President launched a major war, the Congress would step back into its pre-Vietnam irrelevance. On the other hand, if the Congress took up the issue and voted not to support the president, it would be blamed for Saddam's not leaving Kuwait. In the end the Congress decided to vote on whether it should support the U.N. resolution. After three days of debate, the measure passed the House by 100 votes and the Senate by five. While the debate was impassioned and the vote close, especially in the Senate, the Congress had no real choice. The President had maneuvered them into a position in which a negative vote would have destroyed U.S. credibility or created a constitutional crisis. Moreover, because the war appeared to turn out so successfully, the Congress was eager to share in the glory, so none of its members was eager to raise publicly President Bush's apparent flaunting of the War Powers Act and of their interpretation of the Constitution.

Congress was not responsible for lack of a successful Lebanon policy or for a successful Gulf policy. Nonetheless, the Reagan administration was able to spread some blame for the failure of its Lebanon policy onto the Congress by letting it invoke the War Powers Act. Similarly, if the war in the Gulf had not gone well, President Bush might have argued that the congressional debate had sent the wrong signal to Iraq about American resolve. Rather than deterring the executive branch, the War Powers Act may have harmed the ability of Congress to control the President's use of military force.

Preparing the Congress for Its New Roles. As the Congress reached out for new roles and a greater share of power in national security matters in the 1970s and 1980s, it began concurrently to acquire the information and the means to underwrite its new activism. In case after case, it mandated that the executive branch evaluate existing programs or study newly identified problems and report these findings with recommendations for legislation to the Congress. For example, the DOD alone prepares over 400 studies and reports for the Congress—an increase in such activity of over 1,000 percent since 1970. In short, through its legislative power the Congress had begun to change the structure and extent of the information flow coming to it from the executive branch. At about the same time, it began to pry away from the executive data and reports from the intelligence community, as detailed in Chapter 8.

In order further to arm itself with relevant facts and analyses, the Congress created two new organizations, the Congressional Budget Office (1974) and the Office of Technology Assessment (1972), and strengthened two existing ones, the Congressional Research Service and the General Accounting Office (GAO). These institutions, with some six thousand employees, not only conduct studies, surveys, and audits (which include analyses of the efficiency, economy, and quality of various government activities) but also develop, and in some cases calculate the costs of, alternative strategies, programs, and budgets for the Congress.

The increased flow of information resulting from the foregoing initiatives, together with the mounting torrent of information from lobbyists, research organizations, special interest groups, etc., has taxed many legislators' ability to assimilate it. In order to assist in this regard, as well as for other reasons, Congress has vastly increased its own staff in recent years. From a total of 500 committee and 2,000 personal staffers in 1947, the number had grown to almost 20,000 committee and personal staff members by 1992.

This eightfold expansion in overall congressional staff has been fully reflected in the staff time spent on Capitol Hill on national security affairs. It has also had an explosive effect in the executive branch. Annually this congressional bureaucracy adjusts about 1500 line items in the defense authorization and appropriation bills, mandates that the Department of Defense take some 700 specific actions, and enacts over 200 general provisions into law. In addition it deluges the Department with about 600,000 telephone and written inquiries that demand responses—often in great detail.

Equally or more startling has been the impact of this dramatic growth of staff on the members of Congress themselves. Not just committee or subcommittee chairmen but the newest and most junior legislators have sufficient information on which to base judgments. Equally, however, it is true that fewer and fewer of them can assimilate or manage the vast new flow of data which has been added to their traditional concerns. Unable to cope with their workload, in large part because they have all the information and staff resources just cited, members of Congress are increasingly forced to cede power to their staffs, a bureaucracy they created to offset the power of the executive's bureaucracy! "Senators . . . are functioning more and more like the president . . . of a corporation, giving direction to policy and giving staff the responsibility for details."[28] Senator Goldwater once put the point more bluntly, "Staff runs Congress. . . . You get off an elevator to vote and you have to beat your way through fifty or sixty [staff members] standing around."[29]

Side by side with these crosscurrents has been another development that bears importantly on the ability of Congress to fulfill the larger national security affairs role it has demanded, namely, the increasing decentralization of power within Congress. Internal reform, beginning with the 94th Congress,

> undermined the hierarchy and the seniority system in the House, overthrew certain committee chairmen, and even invaded the jurisdictional lines of committees. Diplomacy by statute was not left to chairmen of standing committees. New members maintained an active caucus and at times built reputations for themselves by ignoring the leadership and having their names attached to amendments that changed foreign policy. Frequently a more junior senator or congressman with the right timing and the right coalition could upstage the leadership. In such a fluid structure new ad hoc coalitions were formed, which happened with the Greek lobby opposing Turkish aid. In an increasingly balkanized Congress, the leadership often became not leaders but followers, who either eventually executed the legislative wishes of the new coalition or, if they opposed them too much, jeopardized their chances of survival.[30]

Decentralization plus increased information encouraged individual legislators to invade hitherto sacrosanct committee preserves. The floor of each house was more frequently the scene of debate over defense bills as legislators were no longer willing to accept the work of the defense committees. Defense bills are routinely debated on the floor of each house for about 10 days and over 100 amendments are normally offered in each chamber. Twenty-five years ago, floor debate rarely lasted more than a few days and amendments never went above twenty.

Also coinciding with decentralization has been the decline of the political party in America generally and in Congress particularly. In the 1980s and early 1990s the Legislative Branch was frequently unable to marshall its forces effectively either to override Republican presidents (Reagan or Bush) or to support a Democratic one (Carter). On the Panama Canal Treaty vote, President Carter was dependent on Republican support to secure the needed majority. Despite the opposition of the Democratic leadership, Reagan was able to get Democratic support for his first-term defense build-up, and Bush received substantial Democratic support for his Persian Gulf war policies.

One special aspect of the decline of party influence worth noting is the rise of "special interests." Often cutting across the traditional political spectrum, these groups or factions tend to be organized around a single issue or interest—ethnic, economic, or social. Armed with modem communications, computerized mailing lists, and a singleness of purpose that contrasts with the complexity of other, more traditional political groups, these organizations have further fractionalized American politics. Whether the cause be pro-Israel, pro-Greece, antinuclear, or antidraft, the compromises and trade-offs that are the normal stuff of politics and party life are anathema to the special-interest lobbies.

The result of the various forces cited above has been a growing inability of Congress to function effectively at a time when it has insisted on at least a coequal role with the executive. Essentially, each of the 535 members is a separate power center with its own imperatives, loyalties, and resources.

Is the Power Pendulum Swinging Back? By the end of the 1970s, many Americans had begun to be concerned about the waning power and influence of the United States in the world. The 1979 seizure of American diplomats by Iranian revolutionaries, sanctioned by Iranian authorities and televised into American homes, brought widespread public reevaluation of the turbulent international arena and the importance of armed strength for dealing with it. The Soviet invasion of Afghanistan at the end of 1979 powerfully underscored these concerns. As a consequence, the traditional public rallying around a president in time of trouble began to reemerge with the advent of the 1980s. Sensitive as always to public opinion currents and aware that some of its zeal in correcting executive abuses of the past may have overshot the mark, Congress, too, began to close ranks with the president.

This trend was accelerated during the first Reagan administration. Yet even while facing the most popular president since Franklin Roosevelt, Congress showed no inclination to return to its passive posture of the 1950s. Congress went along with Reagan's plans to sell AWACS aircraft to Saudi Arabia and initially supported his requests to provide military aid to the Nicaraguan contras. However, it refused to allow the administration to sell the high-performance F-15 fighter aircraft to the Saudis or sophisticated air defense weapons to Jordan, and in 1984 it cut off aid to the Nicaraguan rebels. Likewise, Congress did not initially question the deployment of the marines to Beirut but as discussed above, later placed a time limit on their stay.

By 1985, President Reagan had become so frustrated with congressional involvement in Central American policy that he was moved to say, "We've got to get where we can run a foreign policy without a committee of 535 telling us what to do."[31] By 1987, the executive's Iran–Contra affair had so damaged its credibility and public standing that many outside of government had concluded that a committee of 535 telling the executive what to do was probably the lesser of two evils.

Events in the early 1990s demonstrated that while there are limits to congressional activism, particularly in using armed force, Congress will resist returning to passivism. As discussed above, President Bush invaded Panama in December 1989 and launched Operation Desert Storm in January 1990 with minimal congressional involvement and significant congressional opposition, much as Presidents Truman and Johnson sent American forces into Korea and Vietnam. But because the Panama and Gulf operations were so short and successful, Congress was reduced to the role of bystander.

On the other hand, Congress refused to sign a blank check when it came to formulating a post–cold war military strategy. In the summer of 1990 the Congress forced the Bush administration to agree to deeper-than-projected force structure reductions. Moreover, in the early 1990s the Congress limited the production of B-2s to twenty rather than seventy-five, forced the Bush administration to refocus the Strategic Defense Initiative (SDI) from a space to a ground-based system, and insisted on more emphasis on reserve forces.

Since the Congress is apparently unwilling to give up the increased sharing of power it largely carved out in the 1970s, is it prepared to change its internal organization and procedures to enable it to play a more fruitful partnership role? Many proposals have been recommended over the years to strengthen congressional capacity in national security affairs. Some recommendations, such as increasing staff and acquiring better access to information, have already been effectuated—or overshot. It is highly doubtful that further staff increases will improve congressional performance. Indeed, the size of congressional staffs has leveled off somewhat since 1980.

Nor does further information sharing seem likely to have a salutary effect. Members of Congress may, and many still do, complain that they are inadequately informed about national security matters, particularly in instances in which the executive branch has already launched on a course of action. But this problem will not be cured by further data flows, for the difficulty is essentially one of "outsiders" in a policy process feeling that they are inadequately abreast of situations. Only if policy formulation is *jointly* conducted will the legislators involved feel confident that they know what they need to know. Unless the constitutional separation of powers is thus diminished, with all the problems inherent in such a unified process, the president will continue to have superior access to information. This is inherently the case, for it is he who controls the bureaucracy that is essential to policy-making and execution; and it is that bureaucracy, by virtue of its responsibilities, that is the primary source of information.

If strengthening the ability of Congress to discharge a coequal role in policy formulation cannot proceed from further increasing staff or enhancing information flow, can it result from institutional reform within the Congress? Would, for example, the creation of a single committee in each house on national security or of a joint national security committee, bringing together the leadership from both houses, significantly improve the situation? If feasible, either of these steps would be a great leap forward in adding coherence to what is currently a badly fragmented process. It is not practical, however, for such committees or committee to be legislative in character, as are the existing armed services, foreign relations, appropriations, and intelligence committees in both houses. For one thing, the workload simply would be unmanageable for such umbrella committees with a legislative function; even the existing committees with only a fraction of the scope envisaged are overworked. Moreover, the existing committees would certainly not yield power to an upstart poaching in their terrain or seeking to supersede them. If the umbrella committee or committees were nonlegislative (as is the Joint Economic Committee, for instance), that is, with the power to hold hearings, conduct studies, and make recommendations but not to write legislation, then the workload would become manageable and the jurisdictional tangles avoidable. Unfortunately, the results from such a nonlegislative committee, while useful, would likely fall far short of hopes; the existing legislative committees would probably continue with minimal regard for the insights or recommendations of the umbrella group. This was demonstrated in 1985 when the newly designated Chairman of the House Armed Services Committee, Les Aspin, created a Policy Panel. During its first year of operation it held a few well-publicized hearings with the secretaries of state and defense appearing jointly to defend the Reagan administration's national security policy. But it had no real impact on the 1986 defense budget and never met again.

Further alignment of committee jurisdictions and certain changes in procedures, such as the holding of joint hearings on issues when jurisdictions overlap, would be helpful. Some further tailoring and refining of staff roles might also assist. Essentially, however, the search for "structural solutions" to the problem of making Congress a more effective partner in national security policy-making is not likely to resolve the existing difficulties. The tensions between the roles and powers of the two coordinate branches, while reducible, are inherent in the constitutional structure of the United States.

However, a coherent national security policy is certainly desirable, and one way to enhance this possibility is to provide for earlier congressional involvement in policy-making. Such involvement will itself produce difficulties and misunderstandings and is certainly not a panacea; yet it would help Congress to work more in tandem with the executive.

Across the board, continual consultation between the two branches is perhaps the most important facet of greater congressional involvement. Though generally given lip service (and sometimes required by legislation), consultation has all too often in the past been *pro forma*. The executive branch has almost invariably minimized congressional consultation because of the difficulties and delays it introduces in the policy process and the possible leaks that might attend continuous consultation on sensitive matters. As a result, "consultation" has largely consisted of informing Congress a few hours before an executive decision is implemented, as happened in 1989 when the United States invaded Panama and in 1990 when the Bush administration switched to an offensive posture in the Gulf.

Presidents are understandably reluctant to complicate their lives politically by the "shared participation and responsibilities" that the Murphy Commission called for between Congress and the executive.[32] Even when consultation on an issue has been continuous and detailed over a protracted period, such as on the START Treaty, the result may still be a stalemate.

Yet, the two branches should find better ways to work together in the national security arena, where the stakes are high and history can be unforgiving. Attitudinal changes are required on both sides. For the part of Congress, it needs to achieve broad agreement among its members that it cannot and should not try to exercise detailed control of policy or military operations—in short, to assume executive functions. For the part of the executive branch, it must accept the reality that the congressional diffidence and passivity of an earlier era will not return and that the executive's personal and institutional working relationships with Capitol Hill must be strengthened through early and continual consultation and cooperation.

Discussion Questions

1. What domestic and international factors contributed to a generally accepted "national consensus" on national security issues prior to the late 1960s?

2. What factors or characteristics of Congress have traditionally inhibited Congress from a more active role in national security policy-making?

3. How does "politics" have an impact on national security policy-making?

4. What are the constitutional powers of the president and Congress in the national security area?

5. What factors contributed to the loss of a national consensus in the latter 1960s on national security issues?

6. How will the end of the cold war affect the congressional role in national security affairs?

7. What is the War Powers Act? Has it enhanced the role of Congress in national security affairs? Has it inhibited the president in national security policy-making and execution?

8. How has the increase in information available to Congress and a growing staff to assist in analysis had an impact on the role of Congress in national security affairs?

9. How might Congress use the Congressional Budget Office and the General Accounting Office to influence national security policy-making?

10. Construct as strong as possible a case for a "Joint Congressional Committee on National Security Affairs" as a means of decisively strengthening the role of Congress in this area. Do you consider the case compelling? Why or why not?

Recommended Reading

Allison, Graham, and Szanton, Peter. *Remaking American Foreign Policy*. New York: Basic Books, 1976.

Blechman, Barry M. *The Politics of National Security: Congress and U.S. Defense Policy*. New York: Oxford University Press, 1990.

Crabb, Cecil. "Invitation to Struggle: Congress, the President and Foreign Policy." Washington, D.C.: Congressional Quarterly, 1989.

Cutler, Lloyd N. "To Form a Government." *Foreign Affairs* 59, no. 1 (1980): 126.

Fascell, Dante. "Congress and Arms Control." *Foreign Affairs* 65 (1987): 730.

Fenno, Richard F. *Congressmen in Committees*. Boston: Little, Brown, 1973.

Frye, Alton. *A Responsible Congress*. New York: McGraw-Hill, 1975.

Graves, Ernest, and Hildreth, Steven A., eds. *U.S. Security Assistance: The Political Process*. Lexington, Mass.: Lexington Books, 1985.

Hunter, Robert E., Berman, Wayne L., and Kennedy, John F., eds. *Making Government Work: From White House to Congress*. Washington, D.C.: Center for Strategic and International Studies, 1986.

Lehman, John. *Making War: The 200 Year Old Battle Between the President and Congress Over How America Goes to War*. New York: Charles Scribner, 1992.

Long, Franklin A., and Rathjens, George W., eds. *Arms, Defense Policy, and Arms Control*. New York: Norton, 1976.

Nye, Joseph, and Smith, Roger, eds. *After the Storm: Lessons from the Gulf War*. New York: Madison Books, 1992.

Russett, Bruce M. *Controlling the Sword: The Democratic Governance of National Security*. Cambridge, Mass.: Harvard University Press, 1990.

U.S. News and World Report. *Triumph Without Victory*. New York: Warner Books, 1992.

7

Intelligence and National Security

Intelligence: Definitions and Capabilities

Intelligence and Its Role in Policy Formulation. Intelligence in the simplest sense is knowledge about events, trends, and personalities that may affect the observer—or the country, institution, or military service for which the observer works—in some immediate or immediately foreseeable situation. Such information identifies, describes, and defines situations requiring or likely to require decisions.

Intelligence is more, however, than mere description. It is a product ''resulting from the collection, collation, evaluation, analysis, integration and interpretation of all collected information.''[1] Intelligence, then, is ''distilled knowledge'' created by people. Intelligence professionals attempt to envision possible or likely futures by analyzing and synthesizing the flow of current data, providing decision-makers with background projections against which to measure current policy and action alternatives. For example, in mid-July 1990, Walter Lang, the Defense Intelligence Agency's officer for the Middle East and South Asia, warned his skeptical superiors that his analysis of the movement of Iraqi forces and Saddam Hussein's personality profile made it clear that the Iraqi dictator intended to invade Kuwait—which he did in August.[2]

Professionals may also suggest action alternatives to policymakers and provide a basis for intelligent choice among them. An example of this direct policy use of an intelligence product is furnished by the specific request by Secretary Kissinger to the CIA shortly after the 1973 Middle East war ''to examine all aspects of possible Sinai withdrawal lines on the basis of political, military, geographic, and ethnic considerations. Eight alternative lines were prepared for the Sinai, a number of which Secretary of State Kissinger used in mediating the negotiations between Egypt and Israel."[3]

Essentially, then, the U.S. intelligence effort is composed of information-gathering and information-analyzing activities in support of the process of policy formulation. Functionally, the activities involve collecting information, processing it, assessing its meaning, relating it to policy issues, and disseminating the resulting intelligence to officials who may use it to form or adjust national security policies. These activities comprise what is known as "positive intelligence." Related but separate intelligence capabilities are covert action and counterintelligence, both of which, while not primarily concerned with the gathering or analyzing of information, have traditionally been integral to the overall intelligence effort.

Though the ability to make informed decisions is especially important in an interdependent and nuclear-armed world, it is not a new concern of national leadership. Intelligence is an inherent function, whether performed well or ill, of every state; the governing authority must provide itself with intelligence in order to be effective and to protect itself. The framers of the Constitution knew about, and valued, the intelligence function of government. They foresaw, in Alexander Hamilton's words, that "accurate and comprehensive knowledge of foreign politics" would inevitably be required in the management of America's external relations.[4] And they knew that *secret* intelligence, managed prudently, would be a useful—and indeed necessary—capability for the infant republic.[5] More than two hundred years later, national security policymakers in the more mature American republic still recognize their reliance on, and indebtedness to, accurate information about the external world.[6] While the best information cannot guarantee sound policy in a complex and dangerous world, policy made without intelligence support, or with inadequate support, can succeed only by accident.

The Policy Implementation or Covert Action Role. The intelligence community also provides policymakers an "action" capability to assist in some types of policy implementation. Especially during the cold war era, American leadership conceived of and used the intelligence agencies as means of affecting or influencing events abroad in accordance with U.S. foreign policy goals. Among these implementing actions have been such activities as subsidization of foreign newspapers and political parties, arming of guerrilla forces, and logistical or paramilitary support for foreign military organizations or operations. *Covert action*, as this function came to be known, has been the subject of much recent controversy both within and outside of the intelligence community. Any treatment of the community's national security contribution must, therefore, take note of this particular capability. It has been a significant foreign policy tool and will continue to provide national policymakers a carefully regulated alternative for carrying out selected policy decisions by means not within the purview or capability of other agencies. For example, in 1991 President Bush reportedly authorized the CIA to develop plans, including covert action, to block the proliferation of weapons of mass destruction in the Third World.[7]

There is a danger that unduly focusing on the covert action aspect of the broader intelligence scene can generate control mechanisms and create a climate, at home and abroad, of opinion prejudicial to the overall intelligence mission. Another danger lies in the fact that "covert action" is a very imprecise, elastic term. It covers everything from having lunch with a foreign journalist in order to encourage him or her to write an editorial that may well have been written anyway to running elaborate, large-scale paramilitary operations over a time span measured in years. It is therefore hard to discuss this concept in a rational, meaningful way—especially in a public forum. In any such discussion, strong feelings about certain specific, limited types of covert action almost inevitably spread to, and becloud consideration of, other kinds of activity included under this far-too-encompassing label.

Though clandestine activities abroad have long been a part of statecraft, only since the late 1970s have the mechanisms by which they are conducted and controlled come under close public scrutiny in America. By the early 1990s it was safe to say that in no other country in the world did clandestine activities receive such a high degree of public examination as in the United States. When Congress created the CIA in 1947 to perform certain intelligence coordination functions, it directed the agency also to undertake "such other functions and duties related to intelligence affecting the national security as the National Security Council may from time to time direct." Since then, NSC directives have given the CIA authority to conduct covert operations abroad consistent with American and military policies.[8] As part of the public and congressional scrutiny of these operations, legislation (principally the Hughes–Ryan Amendment) was enacted in 1974 that required the CIA to report any planned action to the appropriate committees of Congress "in a timely manner."

By the early 1980s, following general public dissatisfaction over the inability to extricate American hostages from Iran during the Carter administration, the covert action function had regained a sense of vitality. The trend toward a more fully developed covert action capability was short-lived, however, as the consensus that had been building in support of covert action was severely weakened by the highly publicized 1985–1986 Iran–Contra affair. As a result of this episode, new legislation was enacted and signed by President Bush in the summer of 1991. Under this new law the president must give written approval of any covert action undertaken by any component of the U.S. government and must notify Congress in a timely fashion. In addition, the president must notify Congress when third countries or private citizens are to be used or take part in covert activity in any significant way.[9]

Although covert operations survive in theory as an important vehicle for foreign policy implementation in special cases, even after Iran–Contra, there is a real question about their future practicality under existing constraints (which make it extremely difficult to achieve the degree of secrecy essential to the successful execution of such operations; as a recent example, in 1992 it was reported in the press that the Bush administration had allocated $40 million to the CIA to help overthrow Iraqi leader, Saddam Hussein from power[10]). Policymakers still place some value on this capability, but its role will likely be minor, at best, for at least several years to come.

The Role of Counterintelligence. The intelligence community also provides a defensive effort to policymakers. Known as *counterintelligence*, or CI, this effort attempts to deny real or potential adversaries the ability to collect information that can be directed against the United States. Counterintelligence is one of the least understood, and least appreciated, functions of the intelligence community. It has been defined as

> the national effort to prevent foreign intelligence services and foreign-controlled political movements (which are often supported by intelligence services) from infiltrating our institutions and establishing the potential to engage in espionage, subversion, terrorism, and sabotage. Counterintelligence involves investigations and surveillance activities to detect and neutralize the foreign intelligence presence, the collation of information about foreign intelligence services and the initiation of operations to penetrate, disrupt, deceive, and manipulate these services . . . to our advantage.[11]

In the wake of the cold war, with foreign intelligence agencies in many cases focused on acquiring classified technological data and business and economic secrets, the definition of CI apparently needs to be broadened somewhat to include frustration of foreign efforts to acquire sensitive information of all kinds.

Like covert action, counterintelligence operations often lead to controversy. There is general public distrust of intelligence activities conducted *within* the United States, yet this is precisely where counterintelligence officers must operate. The problem here is not that domestic counterintelligence operations often violate the liberties of U.S. citizens (although arguably this has occurred), but that the *potential* exists for such violations.

A Conceptual Look at Players, Products, and Processes. For purposes of their work, intelligence professionals divide the national security establishment into two categories: those who produce intelligence, and those who consume or use it. Producers comprise agencies involved in collecting, analyzing, and disseminating intelligence. The results of their efforts—intelligence products—range from nearly real-time current intelligence reports to longer-term, forward-looking reports which are fully coordinated by all concerned agencies at the national level. Current intelligence products are normally essentially reportorial in style and often (though not invariably) relatively short on analysis. Longer-term documents, on the other hand, are generally wide-ranging, in-depth studies that frequently attempt to project analysis several years into the future.

Consumers of intelligence include the national leadership and their advisers in the policy-making departments/agencies, plus analysts who are (in other capacities) technically part of the intelligence community itself. They "consume" information and analyses as foundations for decision-making or as the bases for decision-making advice. Beyond their role as users of products, however, these consumers also perform an important initiating and directing function in the overall intelligence effort, since it is to meet their needs that the intelligence community exists and continues to operate.

The intelligence community takes its initial bearings and guidance from its mission to support national security decision-making. That responsibility in itself provides continuing direction for the intelligence production effort. In addition to the overall orientation and momentum imparted by that mission, however, particular policy-making problems generally result in the identification of specialized information needs. These needs, when passed from consumers to producers as tasks, activate a production process that can be conceptualized and described in the four successive stages shown in Fig. 7.1.[12]

The first stage begins with announcement or deduction of consumers' specific information needs or their continuing interests. Intelligence managers review those statements, and if ongoing production efforts or the existing data base cannot satisfy the requests, the statements are approved as requirements and levied or "tasked" upon agencies having the requisite operational capability. Depending on the original declaration of needs/interests, the requirements may be continuing or long-term, or they may generate only one-time projects.

FIG. 7.1 The Intelligence Production Process: A Model

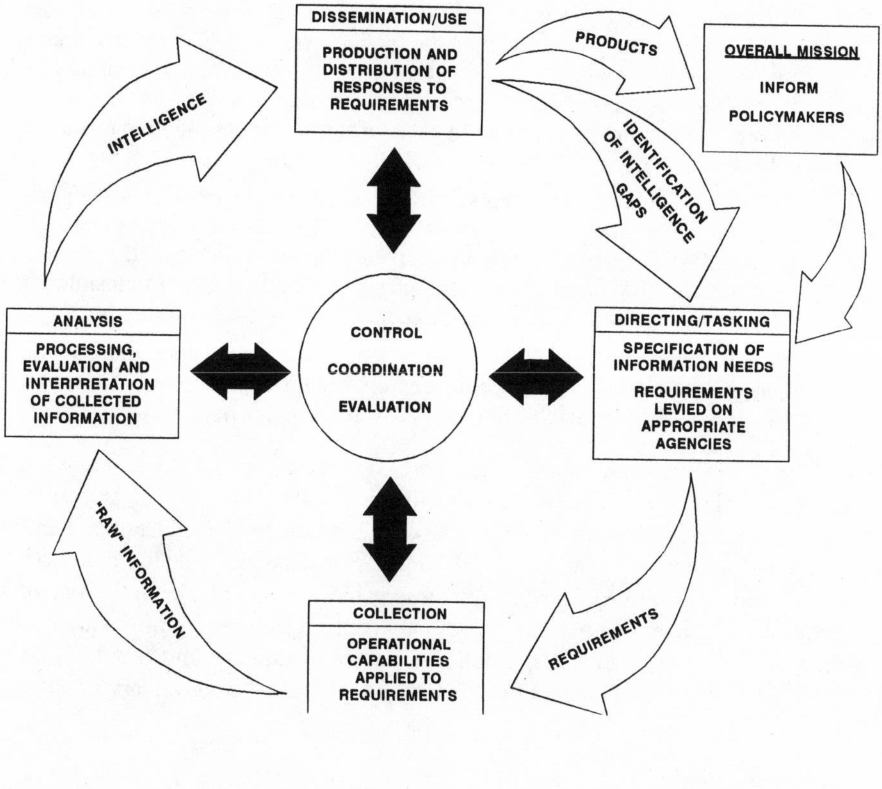

In the second stage, information is collected. Available techniques of collection include:

- *Gathering of ''open'' material*—such as news media (including broadcast) reports and popular literature. A very large part of the relevant data on most issues comes from such unglamorous open sources.
- *Human intelligence*—the cultivation of human sources, both open and clandestine, who have access to the information needed. Though this ''HUMINT'' technique has been much discussed and dramatized recently, and though it was the preeminent collection technique during much of the cold war, it has been overshadowed in recent years by collection systems that use advanced technologies—particularly the systems mentioned below. It is estimated that HUMINT receives only about one-eighth of all the resources devoted to intelligence collection.[13] However, any statistical ratios—such as the one just cited—can be misleading. Technological collection systems (such as imagery satellites) are unrivaled for generating a solid base of evidentiary data on which to base an assessment of another nation's *capabilities*, particularly in relation to those of one's own country. But even if objectively accurate, *X*'s assessment of *Y*'s capabilities may well *not* be the assessment made by *Y*'s leadership. Nonetheless, whether or not they be objectively accurate, it is the assessment and judgments of *Y*'s leadership (not *X*'s) which will shape *Y*'s policy determinations and decisions. Human sources are the best, often the only, sources that can provide reliable information on what another country's leadership thinks about its capability (relative or absolute) or believes it to be. Furthermore, humans are the best sources of reliable information on the *intentions* or *moods* of other humans (such as another country's leaders). Consequently, the importance of human sources in filling critical information gaps is not reflected by any statistical ratio of the amount of total intelligence resources devoted to human source collection.
- *Signals intelligence*—interception and analysis of electronic communications and other electronic emissions (e.g., missile and satellite telemetry). This ''SIGINT'' capability requires very large sums of money and manpower resources. The National Security Agency (NSA), which is responsible for this means, represents a major resource in the intelligence community.[14]
- *Imagery intelligence* (IMINT)—collection efforts using photography and related imagery-producing techniques from satellites and aircraft (known by the national security establishment as ''overhead platforms'').

These three techniques are often described as complementary sources—complementary in the sense that they facilitate cross-checking of data gained by any one means and also in the sense that each has unique capabilities that helps offset the limitations of others. To illustrate: reconnaissance satellite collectors can provide detailed information on observable and countable indicators of military strength or deployment; signal intelligence can provide information on the structure, movements, and planned activities of military units; and human intelligence can help policymakers understand what kind of adversary opposes them, and what an adversary may be thinking or planning. When fully coordinated, these three collection systems are synergistic.

Impressive as these collection systems may seem, they may not be used at all if information already on hand is sufficient to respond to a given intelligence requirement. Particularly in the case of signal intelligence, the volume of collected information is such that vast quantities are stored immediately after collection, without further processing. Review of that data base may itself yield enough information to satisfy production needs. In such cases, the second stage in the operational model, that is, the collection of fresh "raw" data, will be bypassed.

In the model's third stage, analysts process raw information into intelligence by evaluating it for reliability and interpreting it to determine its meaning and significance. This is the stage in which processing (e.g., translation, photo interpretation, indexing) occurs as well as analysis. It is also the stage that most critics identify as the weakest link in the overall process and one that characteristically receives less than an adequate share of total resources.

In the fourth stage, intelligence products are given to the original requestors and to any other interested agencies. If the original information needs are not thereby satisfied, or if new questions emerge, consumers may generate additional intelligence requirements, activating the production process once again. The process is a continuous one, with many requirements in various phases of the cycle at all times.

The schematic model sketched above, though illustrative, should not be given an overly literal or rigid interpretation. In the real world, things simply are not so tidy. Indeed, real-life intelligence activity involves a degree of human interaction among all who are involved in the total intelligence process that cannot be reduced to a simple schematic diagram. Consumers, to cite but one example, seldom take the time to articulate even their major continuing interests with a precision sufficient to drive the whole collection and analytic phases of the cycle. As a result, intelligence managers themselves will frequently generate information needs and requirements, providing consumers with intelligence they "need" but cannot or do not specifically request.

The Intelligence Community

Some knowledgeable observers might contend that the term "intelligence community" overstates the degree of cohesiveness in the American intelligence establishment. The community concept embodies an intent to get disparate entities working together in sufficient harmony to meet both national and departmental intelligence needs without excessively duplicated efforts. The four major intelligence entities are the CIA; those of the Department of Defense, including the Defense Intelligence Agency (DIA), the new Central Imagery Office (CIO), and the service intelligence components of the army, navy, and air force; the Bureau of Intelligence and Research of the Department of State (engaged solely in analysis); and the National Security Agency (NSA). Although part of the Defense Department, the NSA should be discussed separately both because of its size and primary (national) responsibility in the field of signal intelligence. The CIA, by legislation-enshrined design, is precisely what its name says: "central" in the sense of nondepartmental, and vested with analysis, collection, and other responsibilities.

Diverse and inherently competitive in nature, the community presents a formidable management challenge. It was to meet this challenge that the National Security Act of 1947 established, by statute, the position of director of central intelligence (DCI) and made its incumbent, concurrently, the head of the CIA, which that act also brought into being. (Although the title "Director of CIA" often is and has been used, even on the letterhead of some DCIs, technically there is no such position in the federal government.) The DCI's position has been progressively strengthened in the community since the 1947 act, and the CIA, as an institution, has clearly had a leading role in the intelligence effort. However, managing and coordinating the community's effort as a whole has produced continual difficulties. With the end of the cold war, the chairmen of the House and Senate Intelligence Committees drafted legislation, which among other things, was intended to strengthen the DCI. Robert Gates, who became DCI in November 1991, moved faster than the Congress, however, and in early 1992 instituted (with express presidential approval) a number of reforms and initiatives that made the intelligence committees' efforts largely moot.[15]

Current Structure and Missions. In the present organizational structure (Fig. 7.2), the National Security Council (NSC) is the highest executive branch entity (other than the president himself) providing direction to the national intelligence effort. The NSC announces national foreign intelligence objectives and priorities, which are then translated into specific guidance for the intelligence community. It reviews all proposals for "special activities" (i.e., covert actions), making recommendations on each to the president. It also assesses proposals for sensitive intelligence collection operations and has cognizance of counterintelligence activities. Theoretically, the NSC also evaluates the quality of the intelligence product. It is important to note that most of these missions are, in fact, accomplished by the NSC staff acting under the direction of the assistant to the president for national security affairs or one of the NSC subgroups (see Chapter 10). The National Security Council itself seldom provides specific direction to the intelligence effort. If both the NSC staff and the CIA become involved in foreign policy formulation and operations (as was the case in the Iran–Contra affair), the intelligence dimension of the relationship is likely to be distorted.

Below the NSC, the intelligence community is composed of the offices/agencies that follow.

Director of Central Intelligence. The DCI is appointed by the president (and confirmed by the Senate), acts as his principal adviser on intelligence matters,

FIG. 7.2

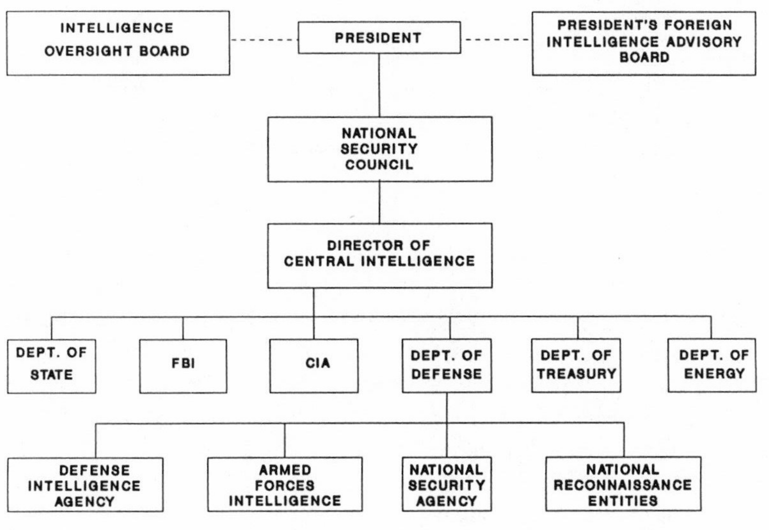

Source: Adapted from U.S. President, Executive Order 12333, ''United States Intelligence Activities,'' *Federal Register* 46, no. 235 (December 8, 1981): 59941.

and holds the position of the U.S. government's senior intelligence officer. As the focal point of management efforts in the community, the DCI's office naturally has far-reaching authority. As with all close presidential advisers, however, the DCI's real influence and effectiveness depend largely upon the working relationship with the president. Frequently, the DCI has not been an intelligence professional but has been chosen because of the president's special confidence in the candidate.*

Every DCI has been faced with the complex managerial problem posed by holding concurrent positions as the head of the entire U.S. intelligence community and the administrative head of the CIA (the only element of that community over which a DCI has direct command authority). Various DCIs have solved this problem in different ways. During his brief but important tenure as DCI in the spring of 1973, James R. Schlesinger created the ''Intelligence Community Staff'' to assist him in discharging his community responsibilities, particularly those involving community budgets and resource allocation. This staff, which had been retained by Schlesinger's successors until the Gates reforms, has been replaced by a ''Community Management Staff,'' which will have responsibility for assisting the DCI in both his budget-resource allocation tasks and his program coordination needs.

---

*Of the thirteen DCIs appointed between 1947 and 1991, four have been military, and four of the nine civilians have been intelligence professionals.

President Bush, when he was DCI in the mid 1970s, created the National Foreign Intelligence Council to coordinate the analytical activities of the intelligence community. This council, which Director Gates' reforms strengthened considerably, provides the entire intelligence community with an independent analytical and estimative capability. It is this Council that prepares National Intelligence Estimates (NIEs) using all the community's resources, including Team A–Team B working groups and nongovernmental experts.

Central Intelligence Agency. The CIA collects information abroad and has "executive agency" responsibility for human source collection, including foreign counterintelligence. As a part of the Gates reforms, in 1992 the Agency created a National Human Tasking Center, managed by the Deputy Director for Operations, that provides an integrated, interagency mechanism to coordinate HUMINT tasking. It produces intelligence through participation in the national intelligence estimate (NIE) process, through preparation of special research projects, and through generation of current intelligence products. It is the only agency within the community authorized to conduct covert activities, although the president could direct other agencies to be involved. And, though its operations are conducted almost entirely outside the United States, it can be involved in counterintelligence activities at home in support of the FBI, as well as in certain limited domestic activities that support overseas collection operations.

Department of State. Diplomatic reporting is, of course, a valuable information-gathering resource. Representatives of the State Department stationed overseas report to Washington on developments relevant to U.S. foreign policy, including information about foreign political, sociological, economic, and scientific trends or events. For the rest of the community as well as for the secretary of state, the department, through its Intelligence and Research bureau, generates intelligence products pertinent to U.S. foreign policy. The secretary of state works closely with the DCI, and the State Department with the CIA, in a continuing endeavor to ensure that intelligence activities are both useful to and cognizant of American foreign policy.

Department of the Treasury. The DOT overtly collects and produces intelligence related to U.S. foreign economic policy, and it also is responsible for the Secret Service. The role of the DOT in intelligence is growing in importance in a world of "geoeconomics," where the economic instruments of power are gaining in importance (see Chapter 14).

Department of Defense. The DOD collects and produces foreign military and military-related intelligence. Its attachés and other military officers abroad are an important source of information feeding into the overall collection effort. DOD agencies normally considered members of the intelligence community include:

- *Defense Intelligence Agency*—DIA, whose director is headquartered in the Pentagon, produces military and military-related intelligence for the Defense Department. It also provides military input for national intelligence products (such as the NIEs) and supervises the work of all military attachés abroad.
- *National Security Agency* (NSA)—The community's signal intelligence operating arm and the largest member of the community, NSA also has a wealth of computer-assisted analytical expertise and a huge data base with which to support the national intelligence effort. From its headquarters at Fort Meade, Maryland, it controls numerous "listening posts" at strategic locations throughout the world that can eavesdrop on (and break codes in) virtually any electronic communication.
- *National Reconnaissance Office* (NRO)—Although the reconnaissance collectors are under the DOD, they serve requirements generated by the entire national security establishment. These assets include satellites in strategic reconnaissance programs—the so-called national technical means of collection—such as those capable of verifying compliance with treaties on arms control or nonproliferation, or providing timely battlefield intelligence during hostilities like the Persian Gulf war.
- *Central Imagery Office* (CIO)—This new office or agency is charged with interpreting imagery collected by the NRO vehicles and other collectors and furnishing these to the intelligence community as a whole.
- *Intelligence and counterintelligence elements of the armed forces*—Each of the services has intelligence and counterintelligence capabilities at both strategic and tactical levels. These serve the information needs of military commanders in a manner analogous to the national intelligence operational model discussed earlier.

Department of Energy. The DOE participates with the State Department in overt collection of information on foreign energy matters, particularly nuclear energy, and it also produces such intelligence as the secretary of energy may need to discharge the duties of the office.

Federal Bureau of Investigation. Although primarily a domestic investigative and law enforcement agency, the FBI has extensive domestic counterintelligence and security responsibilities. Additionally, it may, at the request of the DCI, become involved in counterintelligence activities conducted outside the United States. The FBI also maintains legal attachés in a number of foreign embassies, both for liaison with foreign law enforcement agencies and to aid the U.S. counterintelligence effort.

Drug Enforcement Administration. The DEA, also under the supervision of the attorney general, collects and produces intelligence on foreign and domestic aspects of narcotics trafficking. It may also participate with the State Department in overt collection of general foreign political, economic, and agricultural information relating to its narcotics mission.

Executive Branch Oversight of the Community. In the early and mid 1970s, sensationalized allegations of intelligence community "abuses" generated considerable concern, both within and outside government. As a result specific "watchdog" procedures to preclude unauthorized activities were instituted, and intelligence supervisory responsibilities at the national level were clarified. The President's Intelligence Oversight Board (PIOB), a three-member panel of private citizens appointed by the president, was created in 1976 to review and report to the president on the intelligence community's internal procedures and operational activities. When serious questions of legality were involved, PIOB was to report such questionable activities to the attorney general or, in exceptional cases, directly to the president. Within the intelligence community itself, inspectors general and general counsels were specifically made responsible to report to the PIOB on all potential breaches of the law by their agencies. The attorney general, in addition to acting upon reports forwarded from PIOB, was charged with establishing or approving operational procedures to ensure that intelligence community activities are conducted in accordance with law. Further, he was to ensure that such procedures protect the constitutional rights of individuals who may be affected.

Another different type of "watchdog" group is the President's Foreign Intelligence Advisory Board (PFIAB). Established in 1956 by President Eisenhower as the President's Board of Consultants, PFIAB has had an on-again, off-again existence since the 1960s. Dissolved by President Kennedy, then revived by him, then again dissolved by President Carter, PFIAB was reconstituted in 1981 by President Reagan. President Bush kept the Board but downsized it from sixteen to six members; his appointees had strong backgrounds in intelligence and science and technologies, in contrast to the earlier heterogeneous Board of President Reagan. PFIAB has no line authority; but since it reviews all intelligence activities with a special responsibility for the quality of products and management, and since it reports to the president at least semiannually, it has an important role. These formalized executive branch checks are matched by congressional oversight processes, discussed below.

The Intelligence Problem: Correcting Abuses

Public Perceptions of Abuses. During the 1970s, American intelligence agencies were subjected to intense public scrutiny in an unprecedented, open debate about their activities. It was exceedingly difficult, however, for most Americans to isolate and analyze pertinent issues. The veil of secrecy surrounding intelligence operations, combined with official reticence about them, limited authoritative information to a few partial, often biased descriptions of intelligence community structure, purposes, and activities. Attentive segments of the public had to rely on impressions conveyed by largely unanswered charges in news media coverage. Spectacular allegations generated limited explanations or denials, stories improved with every retelling, and inquiries into intelligence activities were often treated as a kind of exorcism of governmental demons.

In the absence of agreed-upon facts and conclusions, an unsettling public realization grew that America had an important, but as yet undefined, intelligence "problem." Moreover, most of this occurred in the wake of Vietnam and Watergate, when the earlier national security policy consensus had crumbled and Americans were asking themselves hard questions about their government and the nation's ideals, purposes, and directions. Since these public perceptions provided the backdrop for the official actions taken later to investigate, restructure, and control the intelligence community, it is important to understand the dimensions and general content of the underlying public concern.

Overall, two major themes of criticism appeared: objection to intelligence activities (information-gathering and some aspects of covert action) conducted *within* the United States; and objection to certain activities allegedly conducted, or even contemplated, *abroad*. In a series of "exposés," embittered or disillusioned former intelligence operatives and others sketched sometimes broad and sometimes detailed descriptions of intelligence agency activities and purposes to which they objected.[16] Apart from the exinsiders, various outsiders published protests based upon officially released government documents that were used to illustrate "runaway official intrusiveness."[17] At other times, serious, professional critiques were offered that may have had more effect within the executive branch and in Congress than in the public debate.[18]

Activities at Home. The 1970s attacks on domestic information-gathering focused on the CIA and the FBI, although a precedent had been set several years earlier by criticism and subsequent curtailment of the army's intelligence role in civil disturbance coverage during the 1960s. There was particular sensitivity over domestic operations because, unlike most foreign collection situations, the constitutional rights of Americans were directly involved. Examination of FBI operations went beyond the bureau's information collection activities to its now-infamous program of clandestine activity, called COINTELPRO, from "counterintelligence program." Widespread indignation was aroused and fear was expressed that the FBI might become a political agency instead of a police agency. COINTELPRO was designed to disrupt certain dissident groups—the Communist Party (U.S.), the Socialist Workers Party, the Ku Klux Klan, the Black Panthers, and various other extreme left and/or white or black hate groups—and to discredit their leaders. Dating back to the late 1950s, these FBI disruptive activities clearly went beyond the law in many instances, and the program was terminated in 1971 by the attorney general.[19]

CIA activities at home were attacked, too, as unwarranted extensions of the agency's *foreign* intelligence charter. Special interest was attracted by allegations of clandestine domestic surveillance operations (including wire-taps, "break-ins," and mail intercepts) whose targets included national political figures, training in clandestine techniques for domestic police officers, and involvement in the academic world through subsidies and research contracts.

While there was no direct challenge to the foreign collection mission itself, there was a drumfire of criticism about supportive activities within the United

States which had not been a matter of public knowledge in the past. The public's curiosity was fired, for instance, by charges that CIA programs were aimed against innocent foreign students and other visitors to the United States and that the Agency had programs targeted on Americans traveling abroad.[20] Although the more lurid and exaggerated of these disclosures were later deflated, they helped create a sense that American intelligence itself was on trial.

Activities Abroad. With regard to overseas activities by the intelligence agencies, it was CIA covert action that drew the most criticism. Alleged assassination plots, in particular, were reported as evidence of government betrayal of basic American ideals.[21] Other covert activities abroad were criticized as supportive of repressive, undemocratic regimes or movements. These activities included funding of parties and other groups that were anticommunist, propaganda schemes, and support for guerrilla forces opposing foreign governments.[22] While these and other similar activities were particular targets, responsible commentators took pains to note the distinction between such operations and the foreign collection effort; the latter (with its own clandestine methodology) was generally treated as a useful, if overdone, capability.[23]

Outrage in some quarters about such domestic and foreign intelligence activities drew strength from initial impressions that the intelligence agencies, especially the CIA, had been operating in large measure on their own.[24] Abuses were thought to have resulted largely from the runaway, uncontrolled initiative of the agencies, many of whose activities were not sufficiently supervised (perhaps were even unknown) at high levels. We will return to these "rogue elephant" charges later.

Modes of Controlling Intelligence. The "intelligence problem" is in part an aspect of the larger phenomenon discussed in earlier chapters, namely, the continuing competition between the president and the Congress over national security policy. At the heart of the problem is the question of inherent presidential powers—powers asserted by or assumed to accrue to the president by virtue of his responsibilities rather than by virtue of any explicit constitutional or statutory mandate. Since there is, in fact, no explicit provision in the Constitution for the control of intelligence, authority for it must be inferred from provisions for the national defense and foreign affairs functions that intelligence serves. Inasmuch as the Congress shares power with the president in these functions, its claim in the 1970s to comparable authority in the field of intelligence was hard for the executive branch to counter, particularly in the overall political climate then prevailing.

In some respects, as the confrontation between the two branches for policy control took place in the intelligence context, it resembled nothing so much as a siege by the Congress against an increasingly encircled executive. Only under great pressure have presidents permitted entry by others into the intelligence preserve.

Legislative Perspectives and Actions. For the Congress, the intelligence community presents a special opportunity as well as a problem of oversight designed to preclude violations of the law or abuses of individual rights. If congressional participation in foreign policy formulation and control is to be significant, Congress must have access to information. Members of Congress particularly interested in influencing national security have therefore seized the opportunity presented by disputes over the community's actions to gain access to intelligence products. Others have exploited the opportunity to participate in controlling official U.S. activities abroad—particularly the covert action tool of foreign policy implementation.

It is only recently, however, that Congress has exerted its "oversight" capability. From the enactment of the National Security Act of 1947 until the end of the Vietnam War, there existed a consensus on Capitol Hill which acknowledged the president's control of the intelligence community. By the early 1970s, however, that consensus had been eroded by the unfolding Watergate scandal and allegations concerning CIA involvement in Chilean presidential elections. Responding to these developments, Congress in 1974 passed the Hughes–Ryan Amendment, which required that the president, prior to the expenditure of CIA funds for noncollection activities in foreign countries, had to issue a "finding" that declared the activity in question to be "important to the national security" of the United States. This finding was to be reported to the House Foreign Affairs and Senate Foreign Relations committees.[25] Subsequently both the House and the Senate launched investigations into alleged CIA misconduct.

Although the respective committees operated concurrently, the Senate committee (known as the Church Committee after its chairman, Senator Frank Church) took the lead. Its investigatory charter was broad and open-ended, instructing the committee to measure intelligence activities against standards of both legality and propriety. It issued an interim report in November 1975, after the committee had listened to more than one hundred witnesses, and decided that the United States had been implicated in several political assassination plots. While the evidence was admittedly ambiguous in places and fell short of proving that murderous activities had been planned as a matter of national purpose, the committee felt it had nevertheless identified a problem worth addressing immediately: operational authorization procedures within the intelligence community seemed so deliberately compartmented and secretive that a plan to kill a foreign leader could have been generated without explicit presidential approval.

Much of the public debate on this matter, however, missed an important point. The president had been deliberately "insulated" from formal involvement in covert action decisions, not to keep him ignorant of them but to "distance" him enough from them so that he could credibly take the public line that the chief of state was not involved. Most of the rest of the world understood and accepted this posture as being useful, even though it might be widely recognized, in any particular case, as a convenient fiction. (President Eisenhower's public acknowledgment in 1959 that Gary Powers's U-2 had in fact been overflying the Soviet

Union for espionage purposes created such a furor abroad precisely because that was the sort of thing no chief of state ever publicly acknowledges.)

Since the committee was particularly concerned with overly compartmented planning procedures and inadequate approval mechanisms, the interim report argued for clear and open specification of the locus within the executive branch of responsibility for approval of covert action operations. The committee also believed that, as a governing proposition, "traditional American notions of fair play" should control all American activities internationally, even with respect to nations whose ideals, standards, and practices are less than generously disposed toward our own.

The committee's final report echoed that concern for adherence to "fair play" ideals. The committee clearly believed that the looseness of operational rules and discretion had sometimes led to intelligence operations resembling those of our totalitarian competitors. Remedies suggested by the committee included clear legislative delineation of the scope of permissible activities (via a statutory charter for the intelligence community) and better procedures for supervising intelligence agency operations (including more and better congressional oversight).[26]

After completion of those investigations, Congress had before it two self-imposed tasks; to put its oversight machinery in order, and to pass legislative charters announcing authorizations and restrictions for the intelligence community.

To meet the first point, the Senate quickly established an oversight committee: the Select Committee on Intelligence. A companion committee was eventually established in the House of Representatives, but again the Senate committee took the lead. After a year, the Senate committee issued a brief report confirming the existence of an oversight procedure worked out with the executive and explaining its mechanics.[27] The report also stated the committee's belief that the intelligence agencies were by then (in 1977) well controlled and that national security interests justified retention and exercise of their properly supervised capabilities. The committee also stated its intent to serve congressional and constitutional interests in the following ways:

1. *Obtain information relevant to foreign policy decisions*—The committee was instructed by the Senate to

   > provide informed and timely intelligence necessary for the executive and legislative branches to make sound decisions affecting the security and vital interests of the nation.[28]

   This task was clearly intended to diminish the significant information advantage of the executive in foreign affairs which had been recognized early in our constitutional history. Access to intelligence products became a matter of institutional right, with a view to supporting informed decisions by Congress.

2. *Use the budget process as a control mechanism*—During the committee's first year, it helped prepare legislation specifically authorizing appropriations for all aspects of intelligence, including a project-by-project review

of covert action. This review procedure was a major step beyond the "blind" approvals of the past, when intelligence monies were hidden throughout the budget, and opened the way for far more congressional influence than had been felt before in the intelligence arena.

3. *Control by investigation*—In its first year, the Senate committee investigated one hundred allegations of improprieties. The role of Congress as an institutional inquisitor is a well-established one, and the committee cited it as an especially valuable means of discharging congressional oversight responsibilities.
4. *Review of covert operations proposals*—The oversight procedure established in conjunction with the executive branch gave the Senate committee what amounted to an approval role in covert action operations. Once the president approves a proposal, the committee is informed. Should the committee feel that pursuit of a covert action would not be in the best interests of the country, its procedures provide for taking the issue to the Senate in closed session. The rules even envisioned disclosure of facts concerning the operation if confrontation over its advisability persisted.

Work on a statutory charter for the intelligence community proved more difficult than the provision of oversight. Congress is, of course, well aware of the advisability of making its intelligence role a matter of law, not of executive condescension or bargaining. To that end, the Senate Intelligence Committee drafted a charter that included a requirement that the DCI serve Congress as well as the president in intelligence production. The proposal also attempted to solidify the operational oversight procedure in statute, establishing specific operational restrictions as a matter of public law.[29]

The Senate committee disagreed over whether the statutory charter should contain any explicit recognition of the president's powers. Although the Ford administration insisted on due recognition of presidential authority, the Carter administration did not.[30] Strong differences in views about the appropriate nature and detailed content of intelligence charters, plus changing perceptions in some quarters about the wisdom of "hobbling" the intelligence community, resulted in protracted delay. Finally, in the spring of 1980, a last attempt to pass a charter for the intelligence community failed. In its place a wholly different bill, repealing the Hughes–Ryan Amendment, was passed. This bill, known as the Intelligence Oversight Act of 1980, reduced the number of committees that needed to be informed of covert action activities to two, but required that they be fully and currently informed of all significant activities, including "intelligence failures."[31] As noted above, this act was amended in 1991 to define covert activities, to require written approval in advance by the President of any covert activity by any federal agency, and to require that the House and Senate intelligence committees be informed of the activities as they proceed.[32]

But the Carter perspective prevailed in other legislation. An early proposal on electronic surveillance—a core issue of presidential prerogative—was signed into law in 1978 as the Foreign Intelligence Surveillance Act after much work by the Senate Intelligence Committee. The Act requires judicial warrants for all electronic surveillance for foreign intelligence or counterintelligence purposes in the United States when communications of "United States persons" *might* be intercepted. Not only did the president thereby submit to congressional rule-making in a field long held to be within his protected national security sanctuary, but he also submitted to a system of judicial review, to be conducted by the Foreign Intelligence Surveillance Act Court, of specific operational proposals. President Carter, in his public statement at the signing of the bill, merely observed that the statute introduced clarity where before there was contention.[33]

Legislators, however, were clear that restraining the president and sharing powers were at stake in the struggle over control of intelligence. When President Carter signed the key document setting forth the intelligence community's roles, missions, and restrictions—Executive Order 12036—Senator Bayh framed the remaining issues as follows:

> This is the first time in history that the Congress has had this kind of cooperation with the Executive Branch. This is the second step, I would like to remind those who are here, in which you our President have undertaken a landmark initiative. We met in the Rose Garden in the spring where for the first time in history you were willing to waive your inherent authority to get involved in electronic surveillance.
>
> As we move forward with the charters, I think it is important to understand that this is critical.[34]

Judicial Perspectives and Actions. Concern about unilateral presidential power in intelligence matters has found expression not only in the Congress but also in the courts. Judicial decisions have had significant impact upon certain intelligence capabilities long left largely within the province of executive branch discretion. And they continue to influence self-corrective actions undertaken within the community.

Courtroom challenges to domestic and foreign activities of intelligence agencies have been largely focused on protecting individual rights from unwarranted government intrusion, in particular, on certain investigative activities undertaken in the name of "national security." Under traditionally recognized rules, such activities—for example, wiretapping—were to a large extent exempted from restrictions applicable to the same techniques when used in criminal investigations. Despite challenges, federal courts long adhered to the principle, announced in *Olmstead v. United States* (1928),[35] that government wiretapping did not raise constitutional issues. In 1967, two Supreme Court decisions revised that rule, holding that electronic surveillance was a search and seizure within the meaning of the Fourth Amendment and that in criminal proceedings the fruits of domestic electronic surveillance activities would be inadmissible if the probable cause and warrant requirements of the Constitution had not been satisfied.[36] It is significant, however, that these decisions were criminal cases, and two justices took pains to point out in their opinions that national security or intelligence cases might produce different rulings. Subsequently, courts hearing national security cases scrutinized domestic investigative activities closely but still recognized special interests that might justify "intrusive" government action in many national security, or foreign intelligence, cases.[37]

In 1974, intelligence activities conducted abroad were brought to judicial attention in a dispute over alleged invasion of constitutional rights of Americans overseas. In a federal district court ruling, it was stated that electronic surveillance of Americans overseas, if it occurred as there alleged, must be subjected to the domestic rules of the Fourth Amendment, even though the actual surveillance may have been conducted, after U.S. request, by foreign authorities under foreign law.[38] In short, the intelligence community in the course of the 1970s came to face a judiciary that was of the same mind as the legislature—that is, no longer prepared to accept national security rationales as sufficient to confer absolute protection for the exercise of executive powers in intelligence matters, either at home or abroad.

Executive Branch Perspectives and Actions. In January 1975, in response to mounting criticism of the CIA, President Ford established a blue ribbon panel headed by Vice President Rockefeller to investigate charges that the agency's activities within the United States had exceeded its statutory authority. The commission ultimately found the great majority of CIA domestic activities unobjectionable, in essence ratifying the thrust of existing operational rules. It did, however, make specific recommendations in several areas.

The commission urged amendment of the CIA's statutory charter to make it clear that the agency's domestic activities must be related to foreign intelligence. The commission also recommended revitalization of both executive and legislative oversight. For the Congress, the commission recommended establishment of a Joint Committee on Intelligence to supervise the CIA in a disciplined fashion from outside the intelligence community. And within the executive branch, the commission was concerned with checks against misuse of the CIA by the president and others, as well as with clarifying the agency's operational rules.

Executive Order 11905, issued by President Ford in February 1976 in response to congressional criticism and the Rockefeller Commission's recommendations, was in effect a new charter for the intelligence community. It clarified the functions, roles, and restrictions of the community, listing the intelligence responsibilities of all community members.[39] It forbade involvement in political assassination plots. And it stated clear prohibitions and restrictions applicable to operational activities, especially insofar as those activities might impinge on the constitutional rights of Americans.

Under President Carter, the executive position regarding the intelligence community was subtly, but significantly, revised. Standards for control of intelligence activities were frequently framed in terms of propriety as well as legality. The President himself told his DCI that intelligence activities must be conducted not only in accordance with law but also in accordance with "American values."

In addition to whatever operational limitations the notion of propriety brought, the Carter administration's view of legality also altered both the structure and the process of the intelligence community's effort. In particular, the attorney general was given an important role in reviewing clandestine operational proposals. If he believes any proposed activities violate the rights of Americans, he could recommend disapproval directly to the president.

President Reagan's Executive Order 12333 provided a new charter for the community, reflecting his administration's concern for reinvigorating intelligence capability to deal with a wide array of national security threats. The role of the attorney general in the intelligence community was appreciably diminished, and intelligence activity was enhanced not restrained. Because of the climate created by Reagan's executive order and because of his inattention to the activities of his influential and strong-minded DCI, William Casey, President Reagan lost control of the intelligence community. This led to a number of excesses such as mining Nicaraguan waters without informing Congress and the Iran–Contra scandal. These led in turn to congressional investigations, a call for more restrictions on the CIA, and the appointment of a highly respected, nonpolitical outsider, William Webster, to preside over the CIA.

Throughout his four years in office, ending in 1991, Webster kept the Agency on a short leash. Moreover, with the end of the cold war, many argued that the United States should either abolish or fundamentally alter the mission of the CIA. Given the wide recognition in Congress and throughout the executive branch of the essentiality of sound intelligence, there is no prospect of disbanding the agency. Senator David Boren, Chairman of the Senate Select Committee on Intelligence, put the point clearly, "as the world becomes multipolar, more complex and no longer understandable through the prism of Soviet competition, more intelligence—not less—will be needed."[40] But by the early 1990s it was clear to both ends of Pennsylvania Avenue that reforms were needed to adapt the agency's and the community's missions and to improve the post–cold war structure. On behalf of the executive branch, Director Gates took the initiative in a series of measures in April 1992, as noted earlier. Congress will likely not be far behind.

The Continuing Problem of Quality

The quality of the intelligence community's product has been of concern to intelligence professionals and policymakers alike. In the late 1980s and early 1990s, the record of the intelligence community seemed particularly poor. It predicted that the Soviet-backed regime in Afghanistan would fail within weeks of the Soviet withdrawal (it lasted five years); it failed to predict the speed of the collapse of the Soviet Union and the Soviet empire; and it failed to give adequate warning to the Bush administration in 1990 of Iraq's aggressive intentions and clear preparations for the invasion of Kuwait.

Tasking. One of the more durable problems of quality and relevance concerns the policymakers' own roles in the intelligence process. As noted earlier, the intelligence effort derives both focus and impetus from consumers' declarations of interest. The effort suffers if consumers grow complacent, or if they become too involved in the day-to-day maintenance or defense of policy to generate intelligence requirements. If policymakers do not periodically seek data and analyses, for example, of North Korean efforts to build nuclear weapons, the topic will slide into low-priority status as more pressing matters come to absorb the time and attention of intelligence officials. That just such a process occurred in early 1992, generating a flap over the sudden discovery that North Korea might be close to developing a bomb, is reasonably clear.

Experienced intelligence officials are agreed that one of the most striking and persistent deficiencies affecting intelligence production is the "inadequacy of guidance by policymakers as to their needs."[41] This deficiency is related, in turn, to the difficulties in performing policy planning, discussed in Chapter 5; in both cases, the main problem is officials' reluctance to devote attention on a continuing, priority basis to tomorrow's issues as well as to today's.

At this point, the question of resource allocation comes very much into play. There is an inevitable and continuing "dynamic tension" between the instinctive preferences of intelligence managers and those of policy-level officials, particularly those who set or approve budgets. Intelligence managers would like to keep all bases permanently covered in order to meet any emergent need, interest, or desire of policy-level intelligence consumers. Policy-level officials, especially those with budget and resource management responsibilities, naturally want the weight of effort devoted to their current concerns. However, the redirection and/or retargeting of intelligence efforts is not a simple process. It requires long lead times, often measured in years or even decades, to build a core of analysts trained and experienced in a given, formerly low-priority, area or to develop a reliable pool of human source collectors with meaningful access to significant information on particular issues.

A more subtle—but nonetheless insidious—problem can arise when consumers *do* energize the production system but primarily to find support for existing or preferred policy. If thus directed, intelligence can become a dangerous instrument. A natural tension between intelligence and policy

> should be taken for granted; there would be reason for alarm if it were absent. This is so because if intelligence does its job well, i.e., with as much objectivity as possible, it will present a picture of the external world more intractable and less responsive to our view of our just interests than policy-makers would have it; the latter, and especially political leaders, prefer lesser costs and simpler solutions than generally are possible. A good intelligence organization will frequently be a messenger bearing bad news.[42]

It has been argued both that intelligence and policy should have an arms-length relationship and that they should be closely related. Both arguments are sound; both relationships should hold: there must be both a functional separation—to avoid intelligence's becoming a pliant team player—and continuous two-way dialogue so that intelligence will know what is needed and policy will be adequately informed.

Policymakers can, of course, discourage intelligence producers by simply ignoring analyses they do not believe or do not want to believe. Intolerance of, or indifference to, unwanted views inevitably reduces the quality of the intelligence product. No one wishes to talk to, or write analyses for, a blank wall. That, in fact, was in part what happened to our intelligence effort in Iraq before the Gulf war, according to a report compiled by the House Government Operations Committee.[43] Inevitably, too, policymakers will tend to ignore advice, whatever its source, if it is too fuzzy or delphic to be useful. Persian Gulf Commander General Schwarzkopf noted in his report to Congress that the analyses from intelligence agencies were so "caveated, footnoted, and watered down that we [the forces] would still be sitting over there if we were dependent on that analysis."[44]

Alternatively, policymakers will ignore advice if it is internally inconsistent or key analysts disagree. One way to meet this problem was cited for the Commission on the Organization of the Government for the Conduct of Foreign Policy:

> It was the intelligence community's judgment, expressed with some dissenting views in National Intelligence Estimates (NIEs), that the Soviets were not testing a MIRV in 1969. Analysts in DOD, with access to the same information, believed that they were. The President's NSC staff could not tell from reading the NIE what the basis for the disagreement was. They were reluctant to choose the DCI's view over that of Pentagon officials simply on the grounds that DOD analysts had a vested interest in believing the worst about the Soviet threat. They wanted to know the basis for the two views.
>
> Dr. Kissinger convened a MIRV panel composed of experts from State, CIA, DIA, and OSD (chosen, incidentally, for their expertise and not for their rank or status). After a series of lengthy meetings and much drafting and redrafting, the MIRV Panel produced an excellent report that precisely and in detail described the evidence, the areas of agreement about its implications, and the points of disagreement. (A similar but much more extensive process took place concerning the U.S. capability to verify arms control agreements.)
>
> What was valuable to policy makers was the thorough and precise analysis that the community in the end provided. Yet, despite the success of this and similar analyses, it always seemed to be unreasonably difficult to get the community to produce them. If the community sets as its objective the production of analysis that is thorough, objective, and well presented, the President and his key aides cannot help but rely on it, ask for more, and invite its purveyors to be close at hand in time of need.[45]

Collection. Quality can also be limited by problems with collection techniques. Reports from human sources are only as reliable and insightful as the sources themselves. Collectors cannot depend only, or often even primarily, on official sources; U.S. failure to anticipate the fact that Saddam Hussein would invade Kuwait in August 1990 was apparently due to just such dependence. Signals intelligence is vulnerable too, for fabricated transmissions and false trails can be and are broadcast. And overhead reconnaissance, despite remarkable advances in technology, cannot see everything, as General Schwarzkopf discovered in the Gulf war when he was trying to find mobile Scud missiles.

Those limitations, and others, can result in collection of too little information or, more likely, of too little information of real value. Equally important, however, inadequately conceived, controlled, and coordinated collection can result in just the opposite: an unmanageable, all-source glut that obscures and defies analysis. Thoughtful members of the intelligence community are particularly concerned about this surfeit and the related problem that "collection tends to guide production."

Analysis. Even when the collection effort is well focused and properly managed, analysis remains a most difficult task in the intelligence cycle. The stage in which raw information is collated, assessed, related, integrated, and made understandable is the critical link between the intelligence manager and the decision-maker. When a policymaker will read only a segment of the intelligence reports available to him, both the analytical quality and brevity of those reports may well determine the success or failure of enacted policy. The analysts' aim cannot be to predict the future; their data are generally too fragmentary and questionable to make prophecy a sensible enterprise. Rather, they hope to discern trends, assign probabilities to various outcomes, and illuminate the choices available to policymakers.

One of the more intractable problems for the intelligence community—indeed, for any bureaucracy—is bias. When creating intelligence, the analyst must act as a funnel, condensing and interpreting large amounts of raw information into a succinct intelligence report or briefing. In this process, the analyst's personal knowledge, experience, and observations will impact upon the final product. A good analyst will utilize these skills objectively, denying the potential for personal or organizational gain based on the conclusions reached. A serious problem, however, results when analysts attempt to create or defend unwarranted conclusions that benefit their particular organization or institution. *Institutional bias* is the term that describes such attempts to "cook the books." *As a hypothetical example* of this phenomenon, it is not that difficult to envision elements within the DIA, a part of the Department of Defense, inflating the strength of North Korean forces, lending support to the budget proposals put forward by the secretary of defense.

Even the CIA, an organization with no institutional client and one that is assumed to serve the national interest evenhandedly, has bias problems. One such problem concerns an analyst's attributing his or her value systems and thought processes to his or her analytical subject, an action akin to the psychological concept of *projection*. In 1990 CIA analysts believed that Iraq would not invade Kuwait because such a move would be irrational. In these instances, analytical conclusions were based on standards of "rational" behavior created and applied by Americans, standards that missed a critical observation: Nowhere is it written that one's subject will act logically or rationally by one own's standards of logic or rationality. An analyst's conclusions must be based on what the subject is likely to do; if a subject is likely to act "irrationally," then that is what an analyst should report. It should be noted that these problems are generic to all intelligence organizations. Even Mossad, the crack Israeli intelligence service, misread Egypt's intentions until late on the eve of the attack against Israel in 1973.

A final form of bias concerns *subcultures* within intelligence organizations. Problems occur when intelligence analysts are loath to challenge (or it might not occur to them to challenge) the "party line," that is, the theme advocated by the dominant subculture within the organization. During the 1960s, for example, it became established wisdom in the CIA, as it was elsewhere in the government, that the Soviet Union was seeking strategic parity with the United States. When evidence showed that the Soviets were heading for nuclear superiority, the analysts simply discounted the evidence, suggesting that the Soviets were leveling off as the United States had already done.[46]

Similarly, and apparently for much the same reasons, the agency developed certain approaches to estimating the production costs and logistical backup for Soviet combat materiel and forces, approaches that it consistently applied in costing Soviet military forces during the 1960s and early 1970s. This method was maintained despite indications that it resulted in understating Soviet defense spending, until defector information overturned the approach in the mid 1970s. Also, the agency's approach to gauging improvements in Soviet strategic forces resulted in underestimation, until the famous Team A/B exercise of 1976; at that point, the agency's leadership was persuaded to provide the same basic data to two competitive teams of analysts—one of which was largely staffed by non-agency experts. The nonagency team concluded that the Soviet Union was, and for many years had been, doing a great deal more than the agency had believed up to that point; upon cross-checking assumptions, methods, and conclusions, senior policy-making officials concluded that the outsiders were a good deal closer to the truth than the insiders were and had been. Such sobering exercises lend weight to the argument against centralizing all collection and analysis activities; a certain amount of competition and duplication can provide a healthy cross-check against blind spots and biases.

It is well to remember, however, that no amount of brilliant effort or cross-checking can produce infallible results. The Church Committee report put this point well:

> Clearly what is needed is a realistic understanding by both producers and consumers about the limits of intelligence: what it can and cannot do. As a former senior analyst explained to the Select Committee, what intelligence *can* do is to follow the behavior of foreign leaders and groups over a long period of time in order to get a sense of the parameters within which their policies move. American policymakers are then not likely to be greatly surprised by foreign behavior even though intelligence analysts might not be able to predict precise intentions at any given moment with respect to a given situation. Nor can analysts be expected to predict human events when often the actors themselves do not know in advance what they will do. As the Schlesinger Report said: "In a world of perfect information, there would be no uncertainties about the present and future intentions, capabilities, and activities of foreign powers. Information, however, is bound to be imperfect for the most part. Consequently, the intelligence community can at best reduce the uncertainties and construct plausible hypotheses about these factors on the basis of what continues to be partial and often conflicting

evidence.'' To expect more may be to court disappointment. Despite this recognition on the part of many policymakers, if analysis is not correct, there is often the charge of an ''intelligence failure.'' Good intelligence or accurate predictions cannot insure against bad policy, in any case.[47]

Intelligence for the Future

After its near emasculation in the 1970s, the intelligence community entered the 1980s as a constrained and carefully supervised entity. Nevertheless, there was a growing trend, grounded in part in general frustration over events in Iran and Afghanistan at the close of the 1970s, toward greater acceptance of covert activities. Indeed, the intelligence community as a whole was a beneficiary of the public consensus for a strong foreign policy which helped elect Ronald Reagan in 1980. After years of hand-wringing over alleged abuses committed by the various intelligence agencies, it appeared that the nation had come to realize that only a full-service intelligence community could adequately respond to the Soviet challenge. This is not to say, however, that the intelligence community was given free rein; by the start of the decade the community realized that it essentially had two masters—the legislative branch as well as the executive branch. Covert activities were to be conducted carefully on a limited and delineated basis.

Unfortunately, that growing support for the community was squandered by involving it in an operation as politically unwise and volatile as the arms-for-hostages deal with Iran in 1985–1986—and its offspring, the diversion of profits to the Nicaraguan contras. The fact that a politically powerful and activist DCI, William Casey, bypassed his own organization's procedures and checks when he engaged it in questionable covert activities did not alleviate the problem. Additionally, by bypassing much of the intelligence bureaucracy, that operation engendered great hostility and division among intelligence professionals.

The challenges faced by the intelligence community in the 1990s will be markedly more difficult than those that existed during the cold war. With the collapse of the only other military superpower, many observers think that, rather than gathering intelligence on ''nonexistent'' military threats, the intelligence community should switch its emphasis to gathering economic intelligence for the coming economic war with Japan and the European Community. Still others believe that after the cold war and the dissolution of the spheres of influence of the great powers, the intelligence community must be strengthened to keep track of the chaos that appears to be erupting around the globe.

In November 1991, President Bush issued National Security Directive No. 29 to address this question of direction. The directive dealt with intelligence requirements until the year 2005 and noted an urgent need for a top-to-bottom examination of the mission, role, and priorities of the intelligence community. As a result of this directive, DCI Gates, identified five main concerns for the community in the future: (1) political and economic development in the Commonwealth of Independent States, including proliferation of weapons of mass destruction and control of nuclear weapons; (2) the spread of nuclear, chemical, and biological weapons and ballistic missiles worldwide; (3) narcotics and terrorism; (4) financial and trade issues and technological developments that could adversely affect the United States; and (5) new issues such as threats to the environment, natural resources, and health.[48]

Whatever its structure and functions, one thing is clear: the intelligence community will be held accountable to both the president and Congress. Without cooperation with and from both branches, American intelligence will not be able to conduct covert action operations and will find it increasingly difficult to manage liaison with foreign intelligence services and gain or simply maintain human sources intelligence—functions that are essential to the creation of timely intelligence.

Discussion Questions

1. What is "intelligence," and what contributions does the "intelligence community" make to the national security decision-making process?
2. What agencies/organizations compose the American "intelligence community," and what are their roles/missions?
3. What information-gathering techniques are used by the intelligence community? What are their respective capabilities and limitations?
4. How is collected information turned into intelligence responsive to the information needs of policymakers?
5. What issues are raised in America by the intelligence community's information-gathering function and by its "covert action" function?
6. What is your view of the intelligence community's covert action operations? Should we engage in them? Why or why not? If we should, what constraints should apply to them? What are permissible targets of such operations (e.g., terrorists)?
7. What has been the role of the federal judiciary with respect to intelligence community operations and capabilities?
8. What has been the role of Congress in control or oversight of the intelligence community?
9. How has the executive branch responded to issues raised concerning intelligence operations at home and abroad?
10. What additional or different measure would you recommend for control of intelligence operations or products, or for governmental interaction regarding the intelligence community?
11. Over the years, the news media have provided great amounts of public information concerning intelligence failures. Why is there so little information available on successful intelligence operations?
12. How can bias have an impact upon analysis? Explain the differences and similarities between institutional bias, projection, and subcultural interaction.
13. What changes, if any, should be made to the intelligence community now that the cold war has ended?

Recommended Reading

Barnds, William J. "Intelligence and Foreign Policy: Dilemmas of Democracy." *Foreign Affairs* 47, no. 2 (1969).

Breckinridge, Scott D. *The CIA and the U.S. Intelligence System*. Boulder: Westview Press, 1986.

Berkowitz, Bruce D., and Goodman, Allan E. *Strategic Intelligence for American National Security*. Princeton, N.J.: Princeton University Press, 1989.

Cline, Ray S. "The Future of U. S. Foreign Intelligence Operations." In *The United States in the 1980s*, ed. Peter Duignan and Alvin Rabushka. Stanford, Calif.: Hoover Institution Press, 1980.

Emerson, Thomas. "Control of Government Intelligence Agencies: The American Experience." *Political Science Quarterly* 53 (July-September 1982).

Fain, Tyrus G., ed. *The Intelligence Community*. Public Document Series. New York: Bowker, 1977.

Godson, Roy, series ed. *Intelligence Requirements for the 1980s*. vol. 1, *Elements of Intelligence*, rev. ed., 1983; vol. 2, *Analysis and Estimates*, 1980; vol. 3, *Counterintelligence*, 1980; vol. 4, *Covert Action*, 1981; vol. 5, *Clandestine Collection*, 1982; vol. 6, *Domestic Intelligence*, 1986; vol. 7, *Intelligence and Policy*, 1986. Volumes 1 through 5 were published by the National Strategy Information Center, Washington, D.C.; volumes 6 and 7 by Lexington Books, Lexington, Mass.

Lowenthal, Mark M. *U.S. Intelligence*. New York: Praeger, 1984.

Oseth, John M. "Regulating U.S. Intelligence Operations, 1974–1982: A Study in Politics of the National Interest." Ph.D. diss., Columbia University, 1983.

Powers, Thomas. *The Man Who Kept the Secrets: Richard Helms and the CIA*. New York: Knopf, 1987.

Sciolino, Elaine. *The Outlaw State: Saddam Hussein's Quest for Power and the Gulf Crisis*. New York: Wiley, 1991.

Turner, Stansfield, and Thibault, George. "Intelligence: The Right Rules." *Foreign Policy*, no. 48 (1982).

U.S. Congress. Senate. Select Committee to Study Governmental Operations with Respect to Intelligence Activities. *Final Report*. 94th Cong., 2d sess., 1976.

Weiner, Tim. *The Blank Check: The Pentagon's Black Budget*. New York: Warner Books, 1990.

Woodward, Bob. *The Commanders*. New York: Simon & Schuster, 1991.

8

The Role of the Military in the National Security Policy Process

Historic Noninfluence. Prior to World War II, it was only in exceptional cases—those directly linked to wartime circumstances—that the military significantly influenced the formulation of national policy. General Winfield Scott, commander in Mexico in 1846, established occupation policies as he conquered. Again, during the Civil War, the influence of the commanding general of the army upon the secretary of war, the president, and the Congress was great, especially in the latter years of Grant's ascendancy. Perhaps the most direct instance of military policy-making in that conflict occurred with the reestablishment of state and local governments in the South; the programs instituted by military commanders for such governance were underwritten as national policy by President Lincoln in 1863.

Military influence in policy formulation also was evident during the occupation of the Philippines immediately after the Spanish–American War. During World War I, General Pershing was given wide discretion in dealing directly with Allies and in establishing requirements on the national government at home. Shortly after World War I, both Generals March and Pershing proposed plans to Congress for maintaining an army substantially stronger than the pre–World War I establishment. These plans were at least seriously considered before being rejected.[1]

The scattered examples above typify the generally accepted rule, prior to World War II, that the military should play a role in the formulation of national security policy only when the duress of war made the armed forces responsible for executing such policy. The general absence of any major threats to the nation's existence, apart from the Civil War, left the military services with only the routine problems of continental defense, internal development (especially of rivers and railroads), protection of trade, contingency planning, and passive support of a largely isolationist foreign policy. Neither the structure of government nor the essentiality of military missions compelled sustained involvement of the military in national policy.

World War II and Its Immediate Aftermath. World War II and the immediate postwar years marked a total break with the past. The imminence of war in the late 1930s had generated new structural arrangements designed to bring military advice into the process of policy formulation. In April 1938, on the suggestion of Secretary of State Cordell Hull and with President Franklin Roosevelt's approval, a Standing Liaison Committee had been established by the State, War, and Navy departments to deal with military and political planning in the Western Hemisphere. The Standing Liaison Committee was discontinued in 1943, having fallen into disuse during the great military operations of World War II. However, the need for interdepartmental coordination of political-military affairs led to the establishment of the State-War-Navy Coordinating Committee (SWNCC) in late 1944. Consisting of ranking civilian officials from each department and supported by a system of interdepartmental subcommittees, including senior military participants, the SWNCC marked the beginning of institutionalized military influence at the highest levels of the national security policy formulation apparatus.

In a parallel development—largely to present a more unified American position to the allies during the war—the uniformed chiefs of the army, navy, and army air forces began to meet with increasing frequency after Pearl Harbor as the Joint Chiefs of Staff (JCS). Although the JCS's authority and responsibilities were never legislatively approved during the war, its position was recognized and, through Admiral Leahy, chief of staff to the president, it maintained direct liaison with President Roosevelt.[2] The influence of Admiral King and General Marshall was particularly important concerning strategic operations.

Military influence during the war extended beyond political-military planning for victory over the Axis powers. Given the comparative weakness of the Department of State and its divorce from day-to-day military operations (and given the doctrine of "total victory"), the services played the leading role in developing war termination and postwar occupation policies. On a host of issues, ranging from zonal boundaries in occupied Germany to postwar policies in the Far East, the military requirements for war termination and logistic support in occupied areas determined broader postwar policies. Indeed, the key political question of whether Berlin was to be taken by the U.S. Army was not decided in Washington but left to the discretion of the military commander in the field.[3] In occupied areas, including Berlin, officials of the military government made the crucial decisions. The question of the number and ideological composition of the political parties permitted to develop in postwar, allied-occupied Germany was, for instance, determined by senior War Department officials.[4]* In part, this

*The long-range strategic planning for the period when normalcy was expected to return (three years) was developed and coordinated by the War Department Special Planning Division.

imbalance of influence was inevitable, deriving from the necessities of war and the importance of logistic support and security in areas behind the combat line.

Military influence in all areas of national security policy formulation, however, also derived in part from superior organization and resources. Especially effective was the Operations Division (OPD) of the War Department's general staff, which formed the core of wartime and immediate postwar political-military planning for the U.S. effort.[5] Also noteworthy was the Civil Affairs Division of the army's general staff, which, by its direct access to theater commanders, insulated many of the policies of military government of occupied areas from State Department influence.[6] Finally, the War Department senior civilian and military leadership played a major role, in large part by default. Secretary of State Hull opted out of political-military planning even before American direct involvement in World War II. During the war he devoted a large part of his own and his department's energy and talents to planning the fledgling United Nations Organization.*

When America demobilized after the war, the lessons of political-military coordination were retained. The many joint and interdepartmental committees and advisory groups were first brought into a formalized plan for civil-military coordination in the National Security Act of 1947.[7] In addition to establishing the National Security Council, as discussed briefly in Chapter 5, the act created a "national security establishment," consisting of the three service departments (army, navy, and air force) linked together by a series of joint committees and coordinated by the three services' chiefs, sitting as the JCS. The chiefs were formally recognized and provided with a secretariat and a joint staff. The position of chairman was added to the JCS in 1949. Though given the power to preside and coordinate, he was restricted to only three assistants and was forbidden to appoint a military staff separate from the joint staff, which served the chiefs as a whole.[8]

The 1947 National Security Act was explicitly designed to ensure military-civil coordination and balance. In the immediate postwar years, the civilian elements had already begun to reassert their traditional roles in foreign policy. State Department leadership in postwar European recovery, symbolized by the Marshall Plan, and the central role of that department in the overall postwar political and economic structure of planning shifted the initiative in policymaking away from the military establishment. Not only did the military's advantage in organizational terms shrink sharply, but so did its vast resources. Military appropriations dropped sharply and army strength contracted from over eight million personnel on V-J Day to less than two million a year later.[9] At the same time, rapid changes in military technology meant that the vehicles and aircraft accumulated during the war already were obsolescent. It remained for events abroad to restore both policy influence and military capabilities to the armed services.

---

*Military officers, however, both active and retired, continued to have a major, if not dominant, influence on the substance of early postwar security policy, for example, Secretary of State George C. Marshall and General Lucius Clay.

The Impact of the Cold War and Korea. By 1949, the Communist party's victory in China's civil war, Soviet initiatives in Greece, the Middle East, Berlin, and Eastern Europe, and the Soviet acquisition of nuclear weapons had prompted a series of Western countermeasures, which together constituted the policy of "containment" discussed in Chapter 4. In turn, recognition of the urgent necessity for allied cooperation led to the provision of large amounts of U.S. military assistance to friendly states, a policy confirmed by the Mutual Defense Assistance Act of 1949 spelling out a major, continuing American role in providing materiel and advice to allies.[10] Military influence was also drawn on in constructing the NATO alliance and in securing allied agreement to the rearmament and participation of Germany in the build-up of NATO.[11] Military proconsuls such as Douglas MacArthur in Japan and Lucius Clay in Germany, as well as distinguished World War II leaders such as Marshall, Eisenhower, and Bradley, continued to serve in positions of high responsibility and great influence.

With the beginning of the Korean War in the summer of 1950, a major shift in resources again took place. In a period of four years (1950–1954), the national defense share of the Gross National Product rose from 5.2 percent to 13.5 percent and expenditures increased from $13.0 billion in FY 1950 to $50.4 billion in FY 1953.[12] If the hostilities in Korea again expanded the military's role in the formulation and execution of policy, however, they also complicated it. One of the first messages of the Korean War was that the World War II concept of autonomy for the theater commander in the prosecution of war was to be curtailed significantly. General MacArthur's relief from command in the Far East by President Truman was the result of a long series of attempts by MacArthur to shape U.S. policy in his theater independent of events in Europe or of national policy.[13]* In a time when expectation of war in Europe was high, the view of a local commander could no longer be followed without regard for worldwide ramifications of local actions. It was a lesson to be repeated in future incidents involving the use of American power.

Restraint on the theater commander did not signal his return to solely military concerns, however. After the accordion-like battles of the first phase of the Korean War gave way to a static war of attrition, the military was given the mission—with appropriate guidance—to conduct diplomatic negotiations for ending the war and to conduct combat operations so as to create conditions favorable for a settlement.[14] Although military planners were accustomed to dealing with broad questions of strategy involving political and military considerations, the new responsibilities for political negotiations further deepened military involvement in national policy-making.

As the nation moved through the uncharted waters of limited war, military leaders were forced to examine political and military objectives strikingly different from the "unconditional surrender" and "total victory" formulations

---

*Early in the conflict the JCS had been restrained from excessive interference with MacArthur by his great personal prestige and by the tradition of a theater commander's autonomy. By early 1951, however, the JCS had begun to question sharply MacArthur's estimates and objectives. There seems little doubt that the JCS, in fact, was completely supportive of the president's decision.

of World War II. They also had to adjust to fighting a war unsupported by a total national mobilization. While the doctrines for limited war had to be developed, at the cost of considerable casualties and frustration, one result of the process was a new pattern of cooperation between the Departments of State and Defense.

During the time that the Korean War focused attention on northeast Asia, events elsewhere were also shaping the military's role in the policy process, both domestic and foreign. Rearmament during the Korean War affected American defense posture worldwide—in Germany as well as Korea. The message conveyed by the initial defeats of the small U.S. units in Korea was that forces that could be mobilized were no substitute for forces-in-being. Reserve forces, even if well trained and equipped, could not be activated and deployed rapidly enough to serve as a deterrent or to provide effective protection should deterrence fail. As detailed in Chapter 4, the "mobilization" approach to defense strategy was replaced after the Korean conflict by the more expensive but less risky concept of deterrence through forces-in-being. Although defense spending declined again under Eisenhower from its Korean War levels, during the cold war it never subsided to its "mobilization" nadir of the late 1940s.[15]

Interservice Rivalry and the Continuing Evolution of Military Influence. The enlarged military establishment after Korea and the increased projection of military influence abroad did not reflect a monolithic front of military influence at home. Strong interservice rivalries tended to weaken the military's voice within the national security establishment. Paradoxically, these rivalries were generated by attempts to achieve better interservice coordination as well as to reduce defense spending.

Post–World War II recognition of the need for better coordination of the services was first manifested in the Legislative Reorganization Act of 1946, which consolidated the old Military Affairs and Naval committees in Congress into the Armed Services Committee. No longer would the services submit separate budgets to Congress. The unified approach to defense budgeting was furthered by the National Security Act of 1947, which gave the newly designated secretary of defense responsibility for supervising the budgeting process. Both actions ensured that the services would compete for slices of the same budgetary pie—a gain for one service would be a loss for another. The results were intense rivalries, command shake-ups, resignations, and a host of strategic disagreements evolving from the fundamental competition for resources—all amplified by the media.

Such rivalry had certain advantages, of course. The conflict of ideas and doctrines protected against unanimous error. Moreover, potential conflict between civil and military institutions was deflected into competition among military groups. Since the resolution of these basic conflicts required civilian judgment, civilian control was enhanced. Not only were civilian political leaders able to find military support for almost any plausible strategy they might propose, but also they were given a convenient political dodge: interservice rivalry provided "a whipping boy upon whom to blame deficiencies in the military establishment for which (just possibly) they (political leaders) conceivably might be held responsible.''[16]

Yet the deficiencies of these rivalries were just as obvious. Cost-effective management of the Department of Defense proved inordinately difficult, with the uniformed services sometimes appealing departmental—or even presidential—decisions to congressional allies and winning support. The JCS was seldom able to agree upon an overall defense program within budgetary ceilings. Confidence in the efficacy of military judgment, so high in the early years after World War II, tended to be eroded by the spectacle of public disagreement and dissension.* More serious were fears that the defense organization was simply ineffective, relying on logrolling and compromise, with neither effective planning nor real control by anyone.[17]

Efforts at Defense Department reorganization after 1947 were aimed at increasing civilian control over the military, while reducing the harmful tendencies to allocate resources and to develop policies on a bargaining for shares-of-the-pie basis. In the 1949 reorganization, the service secretaries were removed from the cabinet, the size of the joint staff was increased, and a chairman was added to the JCS. In 1953, service autonomy was reduced still further by giving the chairman of the JCS responsibility for the joint staff and by increasing the number of assistant secretaries of defense.

Controversy over weapons systems procurement and service missions prompted still further efforts toward centralization of control. In 1958, the National Security Act was again amended to give the secretary of defense greater authority, more influence in strategic planning, and greater control over the JCS. The military departments were further downgraded administratively, and the functions of the services were revised to exclude control over major operational commands such as the Strategic Air Command, the Alaskan Command, and the European Command. Under the new provisions, these commands were to be controlled directly by the secretary of defense.

The reforms of the 1950s gave the secretary of defense the legal power to expand greatly his control of the department and the services. The tools of cost accounting and systems analysis developed under Secretary of Defense McNamara in the 1960s made this control a reality. Supported by a host of young, talented, civilian ''whiz kids,'' McNamara used the new techniques to preempt military influence in both procurement and strategy (see Chapter 9). In part, this greater centralization was a logical outcome of the development of new budgetary techniques; but more fundamentally, it grew out of the persistent service disagreements, extension of civilian staff, and increased demand for civilian control over the military.

---

*Among the more inflammatory comments noted by one analyst were the following: an Army Air Corps general asked, ''Why should we have a Navy at all? There are no enemies for it to fight except apparently the Army Air Corps''; an air force general called the marines ''a small, bitched-up Army talking Navy Lingo,'' quoted in Huntington, *The Common Defense*, p. 369. Also see Lawrence J. Korb, *The Joint Chiefs of Staff: The First Twenty-five Years* (Bloomington: Indiana University Press, 1976), p. 11.

However necessary for both strategic and economic reasons, centralization posed a severe dilemma for the military, and especially for the JCS. Unanimous agreements among the chiefs could usually be obtained only by compromises, which were often unsupportable by systems analysis. Split decisions, however, were even worse—they placed the locus of final decisions on military matters squarely in civilian hands. A fundamental dilemma rose from the dual responsibilities of the chiefs described earlier—corporately for defense as a whole and individually for the roles and missions and capabilities of their respective services.

The personal loyalties of the individual chiefs to their services were, of course, sometimes a factor in disagreements, but the continued rivalry reflected more fundamental imperatives of the military bureaucracies. Each service chief had a service staff to assist him in running his particular service. As noted earlier, the JCS as a whole was provided with a small joint staff to give assistance in the joint area. Not surprisingly, the advice of the service staffs was heavily colored by their respective service perspectives. In order to overcome service parochialism and provide unified staff work, the 1958 DOD reorganization directed the joint chiefs to concentrate on their joint responsibilities and to delegate running the services to their vice-chiefs. Furthermore, control of the joint staff was transferred from the JCS as a whole to the chairman of the JCS. The joint staff was increased in size to 400 positions, split evenly among the army, the air force, and the navy and marines.

In practice, these reforms did not solve the problem. Service members who rotated through the joint staff retained their service orientations. Additionally, every paper prepared by the joint staff had to be cleared by affected service staffs. In fact, each service chief was briefed for his JCS meetings not by the joint staff but by his service staff. Since the issues were often of critical importance to the competing interests of the services, compromise was frequently impossible at the lower working level. Nor could the more senior officers disregard this staffing process without seriously undercutting the authority and trust of their staffs. Not surprisingly, interservice rivalries continued despite logical reasons for ending, or at least attenuating, them.[18]

In 1986 Congress attempted once again to reduce interservice rivalry by passing legislation aimed at promoting "jointness" within the Department of Defense. The Defense Reorganization Act of 1986 had several key features, perhaps the foremost being to strengthen the authority of the chairman of the Joint Chiefs of Staff. The new law increased the chairman's authority in his role as the "principal military advisor to the President, the National Security Council, and the Secretary of Defense." He was no longer required to report only JCS positions but was given latitude to provide such advice as he deemed appropriate. A new position, vice-chairman, was created, the holder of which was expected to act in the larger interest. The authority of the commanders of the forces in the field was strengthened as well. In addition, the legislation created a "joint specialty" within the services' personnel systems and required the services to send a fair share of their most outstanding officers to both the joint staff (in

Washington) and the unified commands (in the field) and to ensure that these officers received a certain share of available promotions. This push for "jointness" and interservice cooperation was the underlying purpose of the 1986 act. Known as "Goldwater–Nichols," the names of the senator and representative who cosponsored the bill, the analysis and the policy recommendations underlying the bill were drawn from a study done by a Washington think tank, the Center for Strategic and International Studies (CSIS).

Military Influence in the Broader Policy-making Arena. Persistent interservice rivalry during the 1950s and 1960s did not prevent significant military roles in the wider policy arena. The increased size of the military after the Korean War left its imprint on the formulation and execution of national security policy. The commitment to relatively larger ready military forces and, after 1961, to forward defense and some form of the strategic doctrine of "flexible response" inevitably gave rise to an important role for military advice. During international political crises, presidents generally sought the counsel of experienced military commanders who understood political objectives in addition to strategic realities.

Continuing overseas defense commitments, such as NATO, also greatly furthered military involvement in policy-making. When General Eisenhower, first Supreme Allied Commander in Europe, reported to Congress on his mission in 1951, he stated clearly the nature of civil-military relations with regard to NATO:

> I spoke in every country to the Prime Minister and foreign minister at their request, and then I talked to the defense ministers and their chiefs of staff. There is no escaping the fact that when you take an area such as is involved in all Western Europe and talk about its defense, you are right in the midst of political questions, economic, industrial, as well as strictly military, and you couldn't possibly divorce your commander from contact with them.[19]

The worldwide alliances developed by Secretary of State John Foster Dulles in the 1950s and the extensive military supply and training missions that they generated projected U.S. military presence and influence beyond Western Europe. Associated with this network of bilateral and multilateral alliances were aid funds for "mutual security," to be administered by U.S. military advisory groups. Such military assistance made up more than half of all U.S. foreign aid between 1950 and 1968, with much of the economic aid also justified in terms of "national" security.[20]

Within the country team, as discussed briefly in Chapter 5, the head of the U.S. Military Assistance Advisory Group (MAAG) served as the chief adviser on military affairs to the U.S. ambassador. As such, he was a leading figure in the small group, including the local heads of the Agency for International Development (AID) and the U.S. Information Agency (USIA), who helped formulate and execute U.S. policy abroad. Indeed, the local MAAG chief often had the strongest voice in the ambassador's team, given the comparatively large resources that the Defense Department wielded. Not only did military personnel frequently outnumber State Department personnel assigned to a given overseas mission, but many of the competing bureaucracies, such as those of AID and USIA, were relatively weak in the field and in the Washington staffing necessary to support field operations.[21] Also, the extensive field operations of the MAAGs provided both timely information and access to important local decision-makers—further reasons for deference to military advice and policy influence.

By 1960, a little more than a decade after their inception, there were sixty-one U.S. MAAGs or comparable advisory missions comprising 15,000 U.S. and local nationals, with additional thousands of U.S. military and DOD civilian personnel in supporting positions.[22] As discussed in Chapter 2, military forces have often played an important role as instruments of diplomacy. Fleet movements, alerts, and troop dispositions express national concern in conjunction with diplomatic notes, UN statements, and presidential messages. In the 1950s and 1960s, the MAAGs, too, became such instruments—expressions of U.S. commitments and possible further U.S. involvement—giving them diplomatic as well as practical military utility.

During the 1960s, military influence on national policy also expanded within the structures that grew up around the National Security Council (NSC). As noted in Chapter 5, a number of new interagency advisory and decision-making committees were created in the 1960s to deal with national security issues. Interdepartmental Regional Groups (IRGs) and the Senior Interdepartmental Group (SIG) included military representatives from the JCS organization on an equal basis with those from the office of the secretary of defense, the Department of State, the CIA, the NSC staff, and other agencies.[23] As a result of their IRG/SIG participation and vigorous support from above, military officers were often influential in shaping policy in Washington as well as in the field.

The 1960s also saw a limited reemergence of the military elite in personal advisory roles. Given his military experience and prestige, President Eisenhower accepted little military advice. However, during the Kennedy years, retired officers, especially General Maxwell Taylor, who served as the military representative to the president, gained influence. After 1962, when Taylor became chairman of the JCS, he maintained a JCS liaison office in the White House. President Lyndon Johnson also relied on General Taylor, especially with regard to Vietnam War policies. Taylor's successor as chairman, General Earle Wheeler, often met informally with Presidents Johnson and Nixon and reported JCS views to the president independently of the secretary of defense's views.

During the 1960s, there was concern in many quarters about the extent of military influence on U.S. policies in Southeast Asia. It is true that, although dreading a land war in Asia, once the military established itself in substantial numbers in Vietnam in the early 1960s, it acquired the most extensive information, developed the most comprehensive staffing system, carried most of the burdens of counterinsurgency, and gained a more influential position in policy formulation than competing agencies such as AID or the State Department. Secretary McNamara, so effective in curtailing military influence within the DOD, became an early spokesman for military escalation in Vietnam. Secretary of State Dean Rusk let the initiative rest with the Defense Department. Thus, in effect he became a quiet supporter of Defense Department positions.

The final decisions on Vietnam, however, rested with the president. While military information, General Westmoreland's views, and JCS recommendations set the background for these decisions, President Lyndon Johnson often overruled his generals, particularly with respect to the heightened intensity and scope of operations that the armed forces felt were needed to terminate the war quickly and successfully. That the military significantly influenced national policy toward Vietnam throughout the period is incontrovertible; but that military influence was subordinated to civilian views is equally clear.[24]

For a variety of reasons, not the least of which was a military education system that produced large numbers of officers with advanced civilian university degrees, in the 1970s and 1980s military officers continued to be influential in policy matters. They participated significantly in various interdepartmental groups within the NSC system and on the NSC staff, where they examined a variety of issues. However, the proper role for the military became the focus of controversy following revelations that marine Lieutenant Colonel Oliver North had conducted covert operations from the NSC with the approval of Vice Admiral John Poindexter, the assistant to the president for national security affairs. Instead of developing and reviewing policy options, the NSC became involved in the implementation of foreign policy. The role of the uniformed military in these actions became a topic for debate in the aftermath of the Iran–Contra affair, as revelations about shipments of American arms to the regime in Iran, along with details about the diversion of funds received in exchange for the arms to the Nicaraguan contras, were explored in widely broadcast congressional hearings in the summer of 1987. Eventually it became widely realized that the involvement of North and Poindexter was an isolated incident. In late 1987, then Lieutenant General Colin Powell was named the national security adviser to President Reagan; his outstanding performance through the remainder of the Reagan administration in that position helped erase whatever stain North and Poindexter may have brought to the military profession.

The Military and Domestic Security. National concern for civil rights, emerging strongly during the latter 1950s, provided yet another political-military role for the services. In Little Rock in 1957, the governor of Arkansas mobilized the National Guard to block the desegregation of Central High School. President Eisenhower promptly federalized the guard, using it and regular army units to enforce court-ordered desegregation in the first use of troops for domestic purposes in the South since Reconstruction. Their success established a new pattern of army involvement in law enforcement: the final decision to involve the army would be made at the highest levels of government; commitment of troops would be delayed until all local means of dealing with the problem proved inadequate; local National Guard forces would be federalized and used to assist as soon as practicable; and the channel of authority would extend from the president and attorney general to the executive agent, the secretary of the army, and then to the commander directly involved. In all of this, a request for troops from the governor of the state, as had been customary earlier, was not needed. During the early 1960s, this general pattern of crisis response was repeated in Mississippi (1962) and in Alabama (1965) when local officials defied federal law.

By the mid 1960s, rising frustration in the ghettos of large cities precipitated other kinds of law and order problems. Riots in Watts (1965), Newark, Detroit, and Milwaukee (1967), and Rochester, Baltimore, and Washington (1968) required the National Guard and, in some cases, federal troops to preserve order; numerous lesser disorders also contributed to a rising public outcry against lawlessness. Governmental response to civil disorder was generally predictable; a slow and usually reluctant escalation in numbers of forces until order was established. No one professed to want federal troops committed except as the last resort. For mayors and governors, an appeal for federal help was an admission of their inability to govern. Federal officials recognized that to commit troops would be to assume responsibility for a situation already out of control, fraught with great risks to property, lives, and, some suggested, political reputations.[25]*

Military leaders, though loyal in executing orders, saw these domestic security missions as detracting from their requirement to be ready for possible commitment overseas. Moreover, civil disturbance control required a high state of training of a different variety than normal military missions. Too, troop commitment to domestic order carried the risk of considerable harm to life and property and associated risks of failure with possible public opposition. Nevertheless, the effectiveness of disciplined, properly trained army units in quelling civil disorders and in addressing the inadequacies of local law enforcement made the use of federal troops a feature of the era.

With increased U.S. involvement in Vietnam in the 1960s came disturbances of a more focused political nature. The 1967 march on the Pentagon, the attempt to disrupt the Democratic party's national convention of 1968 in Chicago, numerous marches on military bases and posts, and finally the dissidents' attempts to close off Washington, D.C., in 1971, left the army with an increasing role in civil disturbance control against an ill-defined but apparently identifiable sector of American youth. In the late 1960s, concerned by the lack of coordinated advance information on leaders, issues, and locales of disturbances, the army began to focus part of its intelligence assets on the tasks of identifying ringleaders and their plans. Young soldiers were assigned to infiltrate and monitor radical political groups, and many military installations developed a network of "coffee-

*For example, the decision to commit troops in Detroit was delayed over a period of two days while the Republican governor, a potential presidential candidate, negotiated with the Democratic president over the wording of the request for federal troops. For a detailed chronological account of the maneuverings, see Charles P. Stone, "The Lessons of Detroit, Summer 1967," in *Bayonets in the Street*, ed. Robert Higham (Lawrence: University of Kansas Press, 1969), pp. 185–89.

house informers.'' An effort was made to coordinate information thus acquired within the army and with other federal agencies. A central data bank was started at the U.S. Army Intelligence Center at Fort Holabird, though most of the information for the data bank was gathered from the press and published materials rather than by informers and undercover agents.

As public awareness of these army intelligence activities developed in 1970, there was an outcry against invasion of privacy and free speech. Congressional investigations probed the extent of army involvement in domestic intelligence gathering.[26] Faced with mounting public and media concern, Secretary of Defense Melvin Laird ordered the army to discontinue its collection and dissemination of domestic intelligence. Although the army still retained responsibility for carrying out civil disturbance control measures, the restrictions on data collection seemed to indicate that it would remain only in an executory, and not a policy advisory, role. In truth, the army had been pressured to expand its activity into an area peripheral to its main mission of national defense and inimical to its broad tradition of noninvolvement in politics. As the cessation of hostilities in Vietnam reduced the number of domestic disorders in the United States, the army appeared relieved to settle back into its traditional preparedness concerns. In fact, the military was not used again in domestic disturbances for another twenty years. In May 1992, 9,000 National Guard troops and 4,000 active-duty Army and Marine forces had to be sent to Los Angeles to deal with the worst peacetime riots in our nation's history.

In the 1980s the military was called upon to help solve another domestic security challenge—the widespread narcotics trade in the United States. Drug trafficking had become so extensive by the mid 1980s that the responsible agencies at the federal, state, and local levels could not manage the three major approaches to the narcotics problem: reducing the foreign supply, interdicting transport into the United States, and reducing the demand among our population. By the late 1980s the American public rated drug trafficking as the number one problem confronting the country. Under pressures from Congress, the DOD became increasingly involved in providing active-duty and reserve military forces to the drug interdiction mission. The military services, of course, had at their disposal vast quantities of ships, aircraft, and communications and surveillance equipment, in addition to a large manpower pool trained in some aspects of required operations which could enhance narcotics interdiction operations. During the late 1980s the military devoted increasing resources to such missions as surveillance (e.g., by airborne and ground radar systems) and communications (e.g., through long range, secure satellite communications terminals). In addition, increasing amounts of military equipment (e.g., fixed wing and rotary wing aircraft, ships, and trucks) and personnel to man them were dedicated to drug traffic interdiction as well as—in a minor way—to operations in Bolivia in 1986 to reduce the supply of narcotics. These DOD efforts in cooperation with civilian law enforcement agencies were undertaken within existing defense budgets at a time of declining defense spending.

However, despite these efforts and the creation of a cabinet level ''drug czar,'' drug use and related crimes showed little decline. Nonetheless, the Bush administration kept the DOD involved in combating drugs throughout Central and South America. By 1992 DOD personnel and equipment were deployed to Guatemala, the Dominican Republic, Jamaica, Colombia, and Peru for antidrug operations, and the DOD was spending $1.2 billion on this effort, about 10 percent of all federal counter-drug spending.

The Military and Congress. Having emerged from World War II with high prestige and faced by the developing cold war, the military found Congress generally responsive to its requests. Indeed, Congress was frequently more supportive of the budgetary and weapons procurement views of the military than were secretaries of defense and presidents. Only with the widespread public dissatisfaction during the Vietnam War did the Congress shift from two decades of relatively strong support for the military establishment.

In certain areas of military policy, some members of Congress had remained active and knowledgeable throughout the period of the cold war. Concerned with overall budgets, personnel, and procurement policies, Congress continually exercised its decision-making power in the field of military "structure," exercising considerable influence in questions of the organization of the military establishment, pay scales, conscription, training, service discipline, housing, and weapons system procurement. Congressional subcommittees developed considerable expertise in many of these issues, and policy initiatives from the executive branch often were altered substantially.

On strategic matters, however, such as defense policy, weapons system priorities, force deployments, and national strategy, Congress remained generally on the sidelines in the first two decades after World War II. In most cases, military programs and policies dealing with these matters were developed largely through the executive branch's decision-making apparatus. (The rare cases in which executive policy was overruled by the Congress were usually done on the basis of advice from the military!) After the Korean conflict, individual service strength ceilings were kept so high by the Congress, for example, that they tended to provide little restraint on the executive's plans. Reductions of military appropriations were never so great as to jeopardize a strategic program, and in many instances the Congress tried to prevent the administration from curtailing service sizes or activities.*

Congressional hearings and investigations were often forums for the presentation of the viewpoint of the professional military, as opposed to that of the administration. It is important to realize in this context that a U.S. military officer has an obligation to present his own professional views to the Congress when asked, not merely to repeat the president's or the secretary of defense's view.

---

*For example, between 1950 and 1958, Congress reduced military appropriations requests by only about 3 percent. See Huntington, *The Common Defense*, p. 134. Examples include the Marine Corps Act of 1952 and persistent congressional efforts in the late 1950s to prevent a reduction in the size of the army.

Military influence within Congress is often explained in terms of constituency politics—"pork barreling"— and there is a strong correlation between the defense-related payroll or weapons spending in a state and congressional voting practices.[27] U.S. Army Corps of Engineers civil works projects are viewed by some observers as critically important tools in maintaining military influence in Congress.[28]

In fact, however, a number of other basic reasons have existed for military influence in Congress. During the cold war, the American people and Congress felt genuinely threatened by hostile forces abroad. The resulting public consensus limited disputes over foreign and strategic policy. The lessons of 1939–1941, when Congress approved the draft by only one vote, were not forgotten. Not only was military expertise recognized and respected, but the Congress was loath to assume the burdens of developing military strategy. As suggested in Chapter 6, developing strategy was simply an inappropriate task for Congress in view of its own nature and interests and in light of the assets with which it could work.

As the national consensus on foreign policy broke down during the Vietnam War, however, disenchantment with the military arose in many congressional quarters. Military spending increased slowly during the Vietnam War, but it never reached the 13 percent of GNP achieved during the Korean War. (By 1969, in fact, it was only 8 percent, in contrast to the much higher shares in earlier conflicts.) Yet a majority of the public felt that military spending was too high.[29] Reflecting this shift in public opinion, Congress began to unearth cost overruns and performance shortfalls in military procurement. Elements in Congress fought with the military and the administration over a number of programs, such as the army's antiballistic missile (ABM) program and the air force's multiple, independently targetable reentry vehicle (MIRV) system.

Isolated incidents such as the My Lai massacre in Vietnam were painted as typical and magnified by some critics in the Congress in order to cast aspersions on military integrity, while the seemingly interminable war and the unanticipated ferocity of the Tet offensive of 1968 appeared to strike at the military's technical competence. Drugs and indiscipline within the forces, subjects that were easily exploited by unfriendly media, added to the tarnish. Although the military retained many of its friends in Congress, lack of public support and occasional but conspicuous lapses in military competence stimulated broadening congressional criticism.

Despite the accusations and the real shortcomings during the cold war, Congress did not, however, cripple the military by budgetary or force-level restraints. Nor did it mandate the withdrawal of American forces from Europe, despite strong efforts by Senate Majority Leader Mike Mansfield and like-minded colleagues. By 1974, the military as an institution appeared to have weathered the worst criticisms of the Vietnam and early post-Vietnam periods. Nevertheless, defense budget cuts led to a condition described by the Army Chief of Staff Edward C. Meyer as a "hollow army." Times were not good in the U.S. military establishment in the late 1970s.

The election of a "pro-defense" Ronald Reagan and a Republican-controlled

Senate in 1980 signaled a renewed public consensus to increase defense spending. Congressional willingness to fund most new weapons systems evaporated, however, under the federal budget strains of the mid 1980s. Horror stories about the outrageous prices the DOD paid for such mundane items as hammers ($435), wrenches ($9,600), toilet seats ($640), and coffee pots ($7,000), and major development setbacks, such as experienced with the army's Divisional Air Defense System (DIVAD) and Bradley Fighting Vehicle and the air force's B-1, rekindled intrusive congressional management of the U.S. military build-up.

Throughout the 1980s, Congress also challenged the Reagan administration's strategic planning and arms control policies, using the power of the budgetary process. Funding for MX missile production and research on the Strategic Defense Initiative was slashed by congressional opponents of the administration's arms control strategy. In addition, Congress regularly passed amendments to defense spending bills that cut off funds for systems tests that were deemed to violate the traditional interpretation of the 1972 ABM treaty.

With the end of the cold war, the decline of defense spending, and the debate over an appropriate U.S. role in the world, Congress has taken an increasingly assertive role in shaping strategy and force structure. Senator Sam Nunn, Chairman of the Senate Armed Services Committee, has taken the lead in developing overall defense strategy; in 1992 the House Armed Services Committee actually produced an alternative force structure developed from the "bottom up."

The Changing Role of the Joint Chiefs. As suggested in Chapter 5, the JCS plays a crucial role in the national security policy process, for it is the hinge between the most senior civilian leadership and the professional military. As noted earlier, it is charged with providing military advice to the secretary of defense, the Congress (when requested), the NSC, and the president. Consequently, the role the chiefs play in the policy process can change as the relations among these other actors fluctuate.

During the Eisenhower administration, the JCS was faced with a president determined to balance the budget and restrict military spending. The inability of the chiefs to agree on forces within prescribed budget limits meant that important decisions on the size and organization of forces were left entirely to the president and the secretary of defense. On occasion the chiefs responded to these decisions by criticizing administration policies in front of Congress. While these criticisms greatly irritated President Eisenhower, they had little effect on his policies.[30]

There was considerable tension between the military and Secretary of Defense McNamara during the Kennedy/Johnson years, in large part because of the secretary's management style and his introduction of systems analysis into the decision-making process. His management approach deprecated military advice and favored new quantitative methods rather than traditional threat analysis. Some of the military perceived McNamara's approach as an attack on their very professionalism as well as a threat to their roles in the policy process. The result of the secretary's new methods and of the continuing inability of the JCS to overcome service rivalries was that military influence was partially overshadowed by the work of the civilian-dominated Office of Systems Analysis in the Office of the Secretary of Defense.

President Kennedy's view of the JCS was soured at the outset of his administration by the Bay of Pigs fiasco. Although the operation was under the aegis of the CIA, not the military, the new president believed that the JCS and the other experts had provided him with bad advice. He tended to turn to his brilliant secretary of defense, who was prepared to cudgel the senior military leaders into new modes of analysis and new processes and organizational structures. Initially, President Johnson also relied heavily on the advice of Secretary of Defense McNamara. However, as time passed, the military staffs became fully conversant with systems analysis, and McNamara's relationship with the president began to erode as a result of the secretary's increasing disenchantment with the Vietnam War. As a consequence, the chiefs' influence grew as the president increasingly turned to them for advice.[31]

The chiefs' greater influence within the executive branch continued in the succeeding Nixon and Ford administrations. In particular, Nixon's secretary of defense, Melvin Laird, signaled the reduced role of systems analysis and civilian analysts by leaving the post of assistant secretary for systems analysis vacant for a year.[32] Furthermore, he introduced "participatory management" as his method of dealing with the JCS. Meetings between the JCS and the secretary of defense became explicit negotiating sessions in which bargaining and compromise took place. While the chief's views often failed to prevail, the JCS at least felt that it had significant input into the decisions of the executive branch. As noted previously, the late 1960s breakdown in the foreign policy consensus resulted in a Congress that was often hostile to the views of the military. In that period, when Secretary Laird was at the helm, the chiefs supported the administration's policy before Congress—not only because they had helped formulate it, but also because of the low probability of success in making their case before a deeply skeptical Congress had they failed with the executive branch.[33]

The relationship between the JCS and the other principal actors in the national security policy process changed again during the Carter administration. In particular, the chiefs' relative influence in the executive branch and with Congress reversed. In the executive branch, changes in the formal procedures of the defense budget process decreased the impact of the JCS: lack of policy guidance and tight time constraints on the chiefs' review of budget planning documents restricted their role in shaping the budget. Furthermore, the president made key policy decisions, such as the withdrawal of troops from Korea (subsequently suspended), without real JCS input.[34] By early 1980, the chiefs' concerns about budget adequacy and the diminished impact of their advice thereon resulted in their open and united opposition to the president on military spending levels.[35]

In contrast, by the end of the 1970s an increasing awareness of Soviet military potential among influential congressional elements had made Congress more receptive to military advice. The president's decision to cancel the B-1 bomber program was sustained by only three votes in Congress; it took a presidential veto to delete a nuclear aircraft carrier from the 1979 budget; and the president's decision not to produce the "enhanced radiation weapon" (neutron bomb) came under strong congressional fire. Furthermore, prominent members of Congress, such as Senators Sam Nunn and Henry Jackson, made persistent and intensifying demands for increases in defense spending.[36] In sum, when they disagreed with the president and chose to make this known to Congress, the chiefs got a more receptive hearing of their case than they had during the previous three administrations.

During the Reagan presidency, the relationship between the JCS and the other principal actors changed once more. Secretary of Defense Caspar Weinberger paid much more attention to the role of the uniformed military than to his own OSD staff. General John Vessey, who served as chairman of the JCS from 1982 to 1985, met almost daily with Secretary Weinberger and was normally successful in getting Weinberger to overrule decisions of the OSD staff when he chose to take his case to the secretary.

President Reagan also met separately at least once a month with the entire JCS to get their views. Indeed, it was at a meeting of the president and the JCS in February 1983 that the JCS laid the groundwork for what would become the Strategic Defense Initiative. The president's confidence in the military was demonstrated clearly in October 1983 when he and the secretary of defense turned over conduct of the invasion of Grenada to the JCS. The civilian leaders also adopted a "hands off" policy during the attack on Libya in 1986.

JCS influence remained high during the Bush administration. General Colin Powell, who was appointed Chairman of the JCS by President Bush in the fall of 1989, became part of the president's small inner circle of national security advisers. (The other members included the Secretaries of State and Defense, and the National Security Adviser.) Powell's relationship with President Bush deepened and intensified during the invasion of Panama in 1989 and the Persian Gulf crisis in 1990 and 1991. In both military operations, the president gave the chairman the forces he requested and, more importantly, allowed him and the chiefs to conduct the campaign with no presidential interference. So great was Powell's influence with Bush that he was able to persuade the president to get involved in the Kurdish and Shiite rebellions against Saddam Hussein, which followed the war. Powell was reportedly also instrumental in getting President Bush to stop the ground war after 100 hours.[37]

Whatever one's tentative judgment of how the JCS will develop, the chiefs' future roles will certainly not be static. The strong congressional support for the Goldwater–Nichols Defense Reorganization Act of 1986, following many months of intense debate, demonstrated the political will in both parties to strengthen the role of the JCS. Since the JCS remains the primary contact between the military and civilian leadership in the national security policy process, its role is bound to fluctuate with changes in civilian leadership and with the evolution of the military instrument.

Future Military Roles. As implied in the foregoing pages, the nature and extent of military influence in the formulation and execution of American foreign and defense policy varies with a number of factors. Among these have been—and will continue to be—the American public's perception of threats to U.S. and allied interests, the size and nature of the defense establishment, the military's own definition of its appropriate role, the extent of alliance ties and other overseas commitments, organizational structures and political forces in Washington, and the extent of public and congressional support for the military.

Between the end of the Korean War and the end of the cold war, active-duty military forces generally hovered between 2.0 and 2.5 million men (and, increasingly, women), though during the Korean and Vietnam conflicts force levels reached as high as 3.6 million. Organized reserve and National Guard strengths were smaller. In 1990, actual reserve force levels of all the services totaled 1.1 million, while the National Guard figure was 0.55 million. Additionally, it should be noted that approximately 1.0 to 1.5 million civilians were directly employed by the Department of Defense during most of the cold war period, with millions more people working for defense contractors as part of the overall civilian labor force.

The total of all the foregoing categories represented a share of the electorate with a large and continuing economic stake in national security policy.[38] If all those people were of one mind and tightly organized, the "defense establishment" could indeed have wielded significant political power. That they have not been unified, and hence have not represented a major power bloc regarding defense and foreign policy matters, did not alter the fact that their sheer size provides them the potential to influence public policy in the future. When, in his famous valedictory of 1960, President Eisenhower warned the nation against undue influence by the "military–industrial complex," he undoubtedly had in mind this potential.[39]

President Eisenhower's warning was probably intended to apply particularly to the business leaders who direct the major firms supplying defense articles and to the senior ranks of the professional military. But even if one so restricts his meaning, there is room for doubt that the idea of a military–industrial complex reflects reality. Certainly, air force generals and senators from states producing certain aircraft generally have a common interest in promoting air power. But, placed in the context of overall defense policy and limited budgets and faced with competition not only from navy sea power advocates but also from senators from other states also looking after other aircraft manufacturers, the agreed generalities tend to dissolve in the cauldron of pluralistic politics. The surge of prodefense opinion in the nation in the 1980s was not limited to industrial interests but was spread widely across regional, political, and economic strata. The decline in the late 1980s was similarly broad-based.

As has often been observed, the American military itself is far from monolithic in character or in outlook. One of the recurring differences within the profession since World War II has been over its appropriate role in the formulation and execution of national security policy. General Douglas MacArthur expressed one side of the argument in a 1962 address to the cadets at West Point as follows: "Your mission remains fixed, determined, inviolable—it is to win our wars. Everything else in your professional career is but corollary to this vital dedication.'' He went on to observe that the merits or demerits of our processes of government and of such issues as deficit financing, taxes, and personal liberties are ''not for your participation or for military solution.''[40]

General Matthew Ridgway, army chief of staff in 1955, had earlier expressed essentially the same traditional, ''military purist'' point of view:

> The military advisor should give his competent professional advice based on the military aspects of the programs referred to him, based on his fearless, honest, objective estimate of the national interest, and regardless of administration policy at any particular time. He should confine his advice to the essential military aspects.[41]

The *purist* case does not deny the complexity of national security issues; they are recognized to be a blend of economic, political, and military components but *as determined by civilian policymakers*. The professional officer is an expert in the military component. Experience and training prepares him to make judgments about how force can be utilized most effectively. In providing advice to policymakers, therefore, the professional officer should confine himself to the military considerations of a proposed policy. The officer is not competent, nor should he be asked, to provide economic or political judgments or assumptions in offering advice.

The alternate view, the *fusionist* approach, maintained that in the changed circumstances of national security policy in the post–World War II environment, there was no such thing as purely military considerations.[42] In a nuclear world in which the military consumes significant economic resources and in which the use of force may have tremendous political implications, both domestic and international, military decisions have economic and political consequences and vice versa. Therefore, in giving their advice, professional officers should incorporate political and economic considerations along with military factors.

By and large civilian leaders have tended to be fusionists; they have not wanted purely military advice. President Eisenhower, for instance, reflecting his experiences both in World War II and in NATO, implicitly instructed the joint chiefs to consider relevant political and economic factors in formulating their military positions. President Kennedy issued similar instructions. In 1962, speaking to West Point cadets, President Kennedy further expounded the fusionist thesis when, after stressing their future military command responsibilities, he added,

> The non-military problems which you will face will also be most demanding—diplomatic, political and economic. You will need to know and understand not only the foreign policy of the United States, but the foreign policy of all countries scattered around the world. You will need to understand the importance of military power and also the limits of military power. You will have an obligation to deter war as well as to fight it.[43]

Robert Lovett, former secretary of war and undersecretary of state, pinned JFK's advice as follows:

> The ability of the military expert to give wise advice and to get it listened to by policymaking officials depends in great measure on his possessing knowledge in key nonmilitary fields and in seeing issues in broad perspective. A military career officer must be highly skilled in his own profession, but he cannot afford to become trapped in narrow professionalism.[44]

Not all fusionists were civilians. Indeed, by the 1960s that view of military responsibilities had become influential in the profession. General Maxwell Taylor, chairman of the JCS, was an articulate believer that

> nothing is so likely to repel the civilian decision-makers as a military argument which omits obvious considerations which the President cannot omit. If the Chiefs are concerned only about the record, it may be all very well to try to abstract the military elements of a problem and to deal with them alone; but if they want to persuade a President, they had better look at the totality of his problem and try to give maximum help.[45]

Not only did many military leaders increasingly acknowledge the broader dimensions of their profession, but they also moved to incorporate those dimensions into military education and training programs. The new air force academy was launched in 1955 with a broader curriculum than its older army and navy counterparts. In turn, both the latter increased the proportion of nontechnical subjects in their curricula. Graduate schooling programs for promising young and midcareer officers at civilian universities began to flourish in the social sciences as well as the physical sciences and engineering. Senior professional schools, such as the war colleges, added study of the nonmilitary aspects of national security to their programs.[46]

The fusionist interpretation of the military's policy role has been something of a double-edged sword. Proponents who encourage military officers to incorporate civilian political perspectives into their policy role argue that such a tailoring of military advice will make it more influential, realistic, and relevant to the civilian authorities who set the nation's strategic goals. In this way, the military will gain increased access to the upper levels of the policy process.

For those who believe that the military has had too restricted a role in the national security policy process and that the conceptual gap between military means and strategic ends has resulted in questionable security goals or confused guidance to military leaders, fusionism is seen as a useful remedy.

An early critic of fusionism, Samuel P. Huntington,[47] warned that if the military "broadened" its professional world view in order to incorporate civilian-defined "political realities," it might gain access to the supreme levels of the policy process, but it would no longer speak on strategic matters from an adequately military perspective. Fusionism, he argued, makes the military an excessively civilianized institution that is overly responsive to the political interests (particularly those of a domestic character) of the government's civilian leaders. Given a political culture inimical to traditional military values and a constitutional structure that divides civilian control of the military between executive and legislative authorities, Huntington stated that military and political responsibilities risk being hopelessly intertwined in a confusing and debilitating manner.[48]

The country and the national security policy process would be better served, he suggests, by a military that cultivates its autonomous organizational values in a politically neutral, professional institution. Such a military profession would be allowed to separate itself from much of the society it serves and would be concerned primarily with developing and fine tuning its functional expertise as an instrument of war and deterrence. As such, Huntington's analysis is a variation of the "purist" view reinforced by a dose of cultural isolation.

In recent years, critics of fusionism have raised a new concern. The political and social principles of fusionism have so permeated the professional values and organizational patterns of the military establishment that now the military's instrumental purposes are in danger of being subordinated to its administrative role in the national security policy process.[49]

Historically, the military's operational function—its role as an instrument of war and deterrence—has determined its organizational priorities. Concern with such traditional matters as weapons development, the adaptation of tactics and forces, military logistics, unit morale, and the awful, risk-filled world of the battlefield has dominated the military's traditional character and organizational behavior. This focus on institutional requirements, specialized expertise, and functionally derived values has given the military a "professional ethos."[50]

According to contemporary critics of fusionism, this professional ethos and institutional autonomy has made the military an effective instrument of the policy process. As the military becomes increasingly sensitive to "political necessities" at the instrumental as well as the administrative level of the policy process, a new organizational pattern emerges. The bureaucratic character of the military becomes emphasized. Military officers gradually redefine their role and come to see themselves as managers of resources. Ultimately the military's instrumental role in the policy process becomes dominated by its administrative priorities. Five-year budgets, program objective memorandums, personnel management systems keyed to the individual's self-interest, "organizational effectiveness" techniques, like total quality management, negotiated decisions by committee, and quantifiable measures of progress become the driving variables.

Further, the critics say, as fusionism accelerates the convergence of military and civilian values throughout all levels of the policy process, the military instrument increasingly takes on the coloring and operational behavior of a large-scale governmental bureaucracy. The critics charge that dominant leadership styles change from the traditional "heroic warrior" model to the more prosaic "managerial-technical" model and that the military's senior leaders develop a new "political-bureaucratic" ethos that involves them more actively, but less effectively, in the policy process.

To critics of fusionism, this "convergence" between the military and its civilian masters has seriously impaired both the national security policy process and the military instrument. Edward N. Luttwak, an influential civilian strategist, has harshly cautioned that it is not the military's purpose to be "administratively efficient":

> The conflict between civilian efficiency and military effectiveness runs right down the organization. Conflict is different from civilian activity, and leadership in war is totally different from management. Our people are managers in uniform. Actually, the American armed forces are very efficient; they just aren't very effective.[51]

While such critics of fusionism clearly overstate their case, they have effectively drawn attention to an important dilemma. The military's political responsiveness to civilian authority and its functional expertise as an instrument of policy are complementary values—yet they are always in tension. Some circumscribed sphere of institutional autonomy within which the military can develop its professional ethos and organizational expertise may be necessary to ensure the military's functional effectiveness as an instrument of the national security policy process.

To sum up, during the cold war the profession gradually broadened its self-definition, going beyond the narrow track of the purist (which General MacArthur had proclaimed but did not follow in terms of his own career). Even so, the profession continued to focus on military skills, particularly in the process of rebuilding its forces and revising its doctrines after the Vietnam War. With the end of the cold war, the profession is likely to emphasize the purist approach even more. The size of the military–industrial complex will shrink dramatically. Unless some unforeseen military threat to U.S. interests arises, by 1995, the total force of active-duty and reserve military personnel will number less than 2.5 million; civilians employed by the DOD no more than 0.7 million, and defense industry workers less than 1.5 million, for a total complex of about 4.7 million, 50 percent below the 1990 level. In addition, the military component of national security policy will decline as the United States worries more about economic than military threats. This narrowing of its role is likely to produce a narrowing of its professional focus.

Locating the Military's Role in the Policy Process. By and large the American military's involvement in the national security policy process has (with rare exceptions) been restricted to instrumental and administrative roles. By tradition, functional expertise, and professional inclination, the military has long defined itself as a subordinate element in the policy process. "Grand strategy"—the first level of the policy process in which fundamental political goals are established—has been largely "off limits" to the military officer. It is a restriction the American military has internalized in both its professional values and its organizational purposes.

Even with the passage of the Defense Reorganization Act of 1986, the military's senior leadership does not get centrally involved with grand strategy. The act has enabled the chairman of the JCS and the Joint Staff to be more effective in designing the force structure to support the national strategy, but the chairman and his staff have not been given a role in establishing these fundamental political goals. Their primary contribution has been to design the post–cold war base force, not the U.S. role in the world in the post–cold war period.[52]

A close review of senior officers' schedules quickly reveals their priorities. Far more time, energy, staff, and imagination are dedicated to the mundane but essential tasks involved in running the armed services than are committed to strategic planning. Few military officers spend much effort on strategic-political matters, but many have mastered the byzantine intricacies of the planning, programming, and budgeting system (PPBS) that dominates the Pentagon's calendar. America's senior military officers know that in the U.S. government, programs and budgetary decisions tend to determine the military's strategic functions, not vice versa.

The virtual exclusion of the American military from the first or initiating level of the policy process appears ironic because the very concept of "grand strategy" has a strong military connotation. In Western culture, at least, significant advances in the development of the strategic thought are associated with great military names, for example, Frederick the Great, Napoleon, Clausewitz, and Moltke. Historically, military leaders who have made the most vital contributions to strategic thinking usually have had a large appetite for ultimate political power—the authority to choose their nation's strategic goals. Or they have represented a military elite that was a close partner of an authoritarian ruling class.

By contrast, in democracies, military officers are generally consigned to narrower political functions at the instrumental and administrative levels of the policy process. Thus, with few exceptions, the military establishment in a contemporary democracy does not have a major contribution to make at the most critical policy levels—the establishment of strategic goals.

In the United States, the military's leaders are not asked by their political superiors when and where to wage war. They are asked a far more restricted question: How can the military instrument be most effectively used at a particular time for a given strategic purpose? In 1983, the JCS was not asked *whether* this country should take up peacekeeping duties in Lebanon or evict the communists from Grenada but, rather, *how* to accomplish those missions. In 1989 and 1990, President Bush did not ask the JCS and the unified commanders *whether* to overthrow Noriega in Panama or evict Iraq from Kuwait, but only *how* to accomplish those objectives quickly and with a minimum of casualties.

An understanding of the military's role in the national security policy process must therefore begin with this fact clearly in mind—the American military lacks the charter, the inclination, and the opportunity to play a *primary* role in the establishment of strategic ends. Theirs is a secondary but still vital functional responsibility—an instrumental and administrative role—and sometimes, an advisory one as well. Nevertheless, the military can be influential, albeit in an indirect way, at the most senior levels.

> The potential impact of the chiefs' views on the public and the Congress can never be ignored by a president or a secretary of defense. On some issues, such as the amount of

> defense spending, their opinions may already be discounted; on others like the Vietnam War, their views ultimately become discredited. But the chiefs no doubt retain power to influence national decisions to some degree on some security issues, and to add legitimacy to one view or another.[53]

Largely restricted to an instrumental role in the policy process, the military officer takes a back seat to the "civilian strategists"—elected and appointed—who make the key decisions and set the direction on America's strategic goals. In recent years, a number of officers (e.g., Scowcroft, Haig, and Powell) have served in the White House or on the NSC staff as assistants to key decision-makers. They are the exceptions, however, who were usually selected for their personal qualities as talented, hard-working individuals who could be useful in an unobtrusive way. Only one officer, General Maxwell Taylor, was selected for such a position principally because of his reputation as a strategic thinker.[54]*

Perhaps the quality of America's strategic decisions has been weakened by the absence of a continuing, influential, and relevant military perspective at the highest levels of the policy process. In some respects it is odd that those most intimate with both the capability and the limitations of military force are usually consulted only after the strategic issue has been joined and the key decision on strategic ends has been made.

No doubt this restriction on the military's policy roles has stunted one important aspect of its professional development—the American military does not cultivate strategic thinkers. On the other hand, the military's very absence from the initiating level in the policy process has also insulated it from a dangerous appetite that has destabilized other political systems—a hunger for the power to determine the state's priorities and its security goals.

The decline in the size of the American defense establishment with the end of the cold war suggests that the military's impact on national security policy will decline. As American troop strength around the globe declines by more than half, and as the United States turns its attention toward its problems at home and economic problems abroad, the role of the military in our national life will inevitably be less significant. However, since the United States will still remain a world power deeply involved in the international political system, it is highly unlikely that the impact of the military will ever again be as insignificant as it was prior to Pearl Harbor.

Discussion Questions

1. What was the predominant role of the military leadership in the formulation of security policy prior to World War II? Why?

2. What was the significance of the basic provisions of the National Security Act of 1947? Of its subsequent amendments?

---

*The military establishment has not always welcomed such "tappings" of its ablest officers for temporary duty at the senior levels of the policy process. These officers were not expected, nor did they seek, to use their influence positions to represent, let alone advance, service or professional interests.

3. What international events in the late 1940s and early 1950s eventually resulted in the greater impact of military advice on security policy formulation?

4. What are the advantages and disadvantages of interservice rivalry?

5. How have the armed services modified their education and training programs to cope with the shifting requirements of participation in political-military planning? Have they been effective?

6. What have been the consequences of increased centralization of decision-making within the Department of Defense?

7. How has the American system of military alliances affected the influence of the military in the formulation and execution of security policy?

8. Does the "blame for the Vietnam fiasco" rest primarily with civilian or military elites?

9. What are the advantages and disadvantages of regular forces being involved in a domestic security role?

10. How effectively has Congress performed its oversight role of the military establishment since World War II?

11. Has the overall performance of the military services since World War II warranted the respect and confidence of the American public? Why or why not?

12. What will be the likely impact of the end of the cold war on the role of the military leadership in the formulation of security policy?

Recommended Reading

Allard, C. Kenneth. *Command, Control, and the Common Defense*. New Haven, Conn.: Yale University Press, 1990.

Betts, Richard. *Soldiers, Statesmen, and Cold War Crises*. Cambridge, Mass.: Harvard University Press, 1977.

Blackwell, James, and Blechman, Barry, eds. *Making Defense Reform Work*. Washington, D.C.: Brassey's, 1990.

Halloran, Richard. *To Arm a Nation*. New York: Macmillan, 1986.

Janowitz, Morris. *The Professional Soldier*. New York: Free Press, 1971.

Karsten, Peter, ed. *The Military in America: From the Colonial Period to the Present*. New York: Free Press, 1980.

Millis, Walter. *Arms and the State*. New York: Twentieth Century Fund, 1958.

Sapin, Burton M., and Snyder, Richard C. *The Role of the Military in American Foreign Policy*. Garden City, N.Y.: Doubleday, 1954.

Schwarz, Urs. *American Strategy: A New Perspective*. New York: Doubleday, 1966.

Taylor, Maxwell. *Swords and Plowshares*. New York: Norton, 1972.

U.S. Congress. House. *The Department of Defense Reorganization Act of 1986*. H.R. 3622. Public Law 99–433, approved October 1, 1986.

Weinberger, Caspar. *Fighting for Peace*. New York: Warner Books, 1990.

Wilson, George. *Super Carrier*. New York: Macmillan, 1986.

Woodward, Bob. *The Commanders*. New York: Simon & Schuster, 1991.

Yarmolinsky, Adam. *The Military Establishment*. New York: Perennial Library, 1973.

9

Defense Planning, Budgeting, and Management

One central problem of national security strategy is the limitation on the resources that can be allocated to meet security objectives. A nation's resources available—traditionally categorized by economists as land, labor, and capital—are valued by society because they can be used to produce a variety of outputs of goods and services that the society desires. When part of those resources is transferred to government in order to meet national security objectives, an "opportunity cost" is imposed on society—the lost opportunity of producing other goods and services with those resources to meet private consumption or other social goals. Even if the options open to society broaden over time as total available resources grow and as more efficient technology is developed, the question of how that expanded output will be shared among competing social claims remains.

The ultimate physical constraint on security expenditures is most directly related to the potential GNP—the dollar value of all the final goods and services that could be produced in the nation in a given year if all its resources were fully employed. Invariably, unemployment and/or excess productive capacity will cause actual output to fall below its potential level, but the potential level is useful in national security analysis, since all resources could be pressed to maximum use in an emergency. Of course, even in a crisis, the full potential GNP could not be tapped for security objectives, for essential civil consumption and services would have to be provided. Also, the division of resources to defense expenditures cannot be accomplished instantaneously or without considerable transitional costs.

Competing claims on the nation's total output are made by individuals for consumption, by firms for investment, and by local, state, and federal governments for a host of public programs—including national security. How should the proportion of total resources directed to national security objectives be determined? In theory, advocates of national security expenditures should demonstrate that the benefits to society of those national security expenditures exceed the benefits society would derive from equal expenditures on other government programs or private consumption and investment. In practice, however, the total federal budget and its division among different agencies are largely determined by prior decisions and external factors with little flexibility in the short run. As Charles Schultze, an individual who has served as both the Chairman of the President's Council of Economic Advisors and as Budget Director, has noted:

> Recent history, prior commitments, current political realities, relations with Congress, economic and social events beyond the control of budget makers—all play a role in limiting their ability to change radically the current shape of the budget. What they consider desirable must be tempered by what they consider feasible.[1]

Thus, in practice, the major determinants of the level of national security expenditures generally tend to be economic and political judgments of the opportunity costs in terms of competing government programs or private consumption or investment that must be reduced or can be expanded if security expenditures increase or decrease marginally.

While security expenditures are constrained by the limitation on the nation's resources in general, and by interdepartmental competition for those resources allocated to the federal government in particular, ideal security goals are essentially unlimited. Given this condition, one objective of defense policy must be to obtain the most security possible for each dollar of defense expenditure. But even if a system could be designed to achieve the greatest possible efficiency in the defense sector, it would still be impossible to meet all our ideal national security goals. Resource constraints translate ideal goals into less than ideal "objectives." National security objectives are therefore not absolutes but are defined by the process of evaluating the options that are available to meet security goals. The realistic options facing society are not bankruptcy with perfect security on the one hand or prosperity with a high risk of national security disaster on the other. Rather, society must confront the far more difficult question of how much expenditure for national security is enough and how great a risk it is willing to take with its national security in order to fund other government programs or to facilitate private consumption and investment.

As we examine the various approaches that have been used to reconcile security goals and expenditure constraints in the recent past, it will be helpful to focus on three key questions:

1. How is the federal government to determine how much of total government spending to allocate to security expenditures?
2. How should the Department of Defense (DOD) allocate the total amount to be spent on defense to its various subordinate agencies?
3. Are the two preceding questions independent issues to be resolved sequentially, or are they interrelated questions that must be handled jointly and simultaneously?

Evolution of Defense Budgeting, 1947–1960. Earlier chapters have traced the major organizational changes within the DOD since its birth in the National Security Act of 1947. Successive amendments and reorganizations in 1949, 1953, 1958, and 1986 combined to expand the potential for centralized control in the hands of the secretary of defense at the expense of the individual services and to enhance the power of the chairman of the JCS. These two objectives received special emphasis under the most recent legislative reform of the defense establishment, the Goldwater–Nichols Act of 1986. (Some of the changes instituted by this wide-ranging law will be discussed in the concluding section of this chapter.) Of course, the actual degree to which power was centralized at each juncture depended as much on individual personalities and management styles as on formal organization.

Under the 1947 act, the DOD—or, more accurately, the National Military Establishment—was to function as a confederation, not a unified department, presided over by a secretary of defense with carefully enumerated statutory powers. Yet the secretary had considerable influence—if he chose to exercise it. His primary source of power was political, derived from his direct link to the president and his influence over appointments, promotions, and dismissals. In addition, his control of a unified budget applicable to all defense activities and his mandate to provide general direction over all agencies in the defense establishment gave the secretary considerable leverage. Along with the structural reforms of the 1949 amendments, a whole new section of the law (Title IV) was added for the "promotion of economy and efficiency through establishment of uniform budgeting and fiscal procedures and organizations."[2]

As the process of centralizing control in the hands of the secretary of defense continued in the various reorganizations and as more undersecretaries and assistant secretaries of defense were appointed and unified (interservice) commands expanded, the services became subordinate administrative subdivisions of the department. With unified command commanders reporting directly to the secretary of defense through the JCS, the services were no longer operationally independent and indeed found themselves outside the key chain of command. Following the 1958 amendments, the secretary of defense had wide authority to consolidate, transfer, or abolish functions of the services—certainly a far cry from the confederation envisioned in 1947. The 1986 Reorganization Act reaffirmed these prerogatives of the secretary and gave him further control over the procurement process through the establishment of a procurement czar in his office—the undersecretary for acquisition.

While successive defense reorganizations brought the secretary of defense increasing authority, reform of the budgetary process proceeded more slowly and left him with inadequate tools for integrating strategic and budgetary decisions. Any budgetary process assists an organization in performing three essential functions—planning, management, and control. The planning process, which translates the goals of an organization into specific objectives, must provide some mechanism for adjusting objectives and resource allocations to total levels of expenditure. The management function involves the establishment and execution of projects or activities to meet the approved objectives, while the control process monitors the results of various activities measured against the objectives and ensures that expenditures fall within specified limits. Although any budgetary process encompasses all three of these functions, any specific system will tend to emphasize particular functions at the central decision-making level.

Of course, centralization is a relative concept, and the operative question concerns the level at which decisions on different issues will be made. An observer at the Pentagon is overwhelmed by the prospect of monitoring the myriad processes of defense planning, much less coordinating those activities and centralizing the decision-making processes. The building itself, which covers thirty-four acres and provides office space for about thirty thousand persons, cries out for decentralized management. Five concentric pentagonal corridors, or "rings," are joined by ten spoke-like main corridors, which emanate from a five-acre central court. The structure suggests its content. Independent army, navy, and air force staffs gather and analyze data with the full realization that information often means power in institutional battles, while a joint staff drawn from all the services attempts to coordinate interservice planning for the chairman of the JCS.

Within the joint staff, coordination takes the form of myriad pyramiding concurrences as "flimsy paper" first drafts are upgraded in a color-coded process through "buff" and "green" stages. An action officer is assigned to each issue and coordinates the first flimsy draft with other action officers on the joint staff and the services. When differences are resolved at this level, the draft is retyped on buff paper and is then coordinated with the joint staff agencies and more senior officers in the services. Dissenting views by any service or joint element either are resolved by a joint staff "planner" (usually a brigadier general) or are attached to the paper. The final staff report becomes a formal JCS green paper, which is presented to the JCS through its operations deputies.

Add to this process a collage of interservice agencies and DOD staffs, and it is easy to conjure up a relatively accurate picture of action officers passing in the night, en route to their next concurrence. The point is not that the process is ineffective—indeed, the action officer approach may be a reasonably efficient solution to the coordination problem—but rather that centralizing and enforcing decisions in such a far-flung bureaucracy can be a painful and perhaps empty enterprise. The potential for the services or agencies to abide by the letter rather than the spirit of an unpopular decision is vast. In addition, extracting information from the bureaucracy can be a difficult process even if there is complete cooperation; simply finding the office responsible for monitoring the needed data is hard enough, without then attempting to check and assemble the information in a desired format.

There can be no definitive answer to the question of how much to centralize. A consensus-building, decentralized structure is valuable in developing lower-level initiative and in generating institutional support for decisions, thereby ensuring implementation. On the other hand, a decentralized process is oriented toward the status quo; change, which requires a redistribution of institutional power, is sure to be slow in coming. Within the DOD, the management and control functions have traditionally tended to be decentralized, with the individual services or defense agencies establishing and monitoring activities to meet their perceived or assigned objectives. The planning function has been more centralized and has remained the primary concern of the secretary of defense. However, from 1947 to 1960, his ability to control even the planning process was restricted by insufficiently integrated service planning that did not relate operational requirements to budget realities.

In the aftermath of World War II, as national defense expenditures fell from $81.6 billion in 1945 to $13.1 billion in 1950, interservice competition for funds was intense. That competition was heightened by divergent views of the shape of future conflicts. While the army planned to fight future wars on the World War II model, the air force argued that ground force weapons were outmoded and planned for a conflict dominated by strategic air power, and the navy emphasized the need for a new fleet of supercarriers. Despite Secretary Forrestal's attempts to negotiate budget cuts with the JCS, it was impossible to bring their planning into line with new budget realities. Defense expenditure ceilings were independently determined as the residual of gross federal revenues minus required domestic expenditures and foreign aid programs. Hence, arbitrary defense ceilings for the next fiscal year were determined by what was judged to be economic and political feasibility. Plans for meeting security objectives were determined with little regard for budgetary restraints, and budgetary restraints were set with little or no regard for security objectives. It is not surprising that "Truman's Chiefs were developing plans predicated upon defending at the Rhine, while budgetary constraints did not even allow them to maintain a line of communication in the Mediterranean."[3]

Under President Truman, defense budget requests were scaled down to the budget ceiling by the Bureau of the Budget, and the chiefs were forced to negotiate service cuts or to appeal, often successfully, to Congress for additional funds. It is not surprising that this negotiating process produced budget shares that were approximately equal for each military department.

After Dwight Eisenhower was elected in 1952, the process changed somewhat in form but not in substance. The secretary of defense first established the budget and workforce ceilings for the department, based on economic and political feasibility, and then asked the JCS to allocate that total among the services and to establish force levels. The JCS was required to submit a unanimous recommendation within the ceiling. Through this approach, the secretary of defense could arbitrate service disputes and ensure that the financial ceilings were enforced. The JCS was left free to decide the key issues of strategy and force requirements—although, divorced as these issues were from implementing budgetary decisions, their impact was seldom if ever so great in practice as in theory. Each service had its own view of where future battlefields might be and how future wars should be fought. Each had its independent intelligence network and, hence, its own threat estimates. Each maintained its own supply system; indeed, by 1960, each had developed its own ballistic missile systems.

Under President Eisenhower, the National Security Council and its staff arms played a significant role in the defense decision process, replacing the Bureau of the Budget as the reviewing agency for defense expenditures. Although the NSC review was effective in limiting the level of defense spending, it was not very effective in controlling the composition of spending. Infrequent NSC statements of Basic National Security Policy provided some guidance for service expenditures, but the policy statements were largely based on institutional tradition and were vague enough to support any one of a number of defense postures.

Attempts were made to integrate service planning through the Joint Strategic Objectives Plan (JSOP), prepared by the joint staff, which contained estimates of the forces needed to carry out national strategy and to meet military objectives. Military requirements therein, however, were based largely on experience and intuitive judgments rarely related to costs; moreover, there was no mechanism to tie force requirements to budgetary ceilings, and, as a result, estimated costs of force requirements always greatly exceeded the budget ceiling. For these reasons, the JSOP had little real impact on defense budgeting.[4]

Even after the JSOP was introduced in 1955–1956, military planning remained essentially a collage of unilaterally developed service plans. Faced with tight budget ceilings and disagreement over roles and missions, each service acted to preserve its share of the budget. Research and development (R&D), procurement of new weapons systems, and expanding force structures were influential cards in budget negotiations. The services often sacrificed supply inventories and support equipment to obtain them. The "foot in the door" approach to R&D (i.e., beginning major programs with small initial expenditures) was possible for one simple reason: while planning was projected several years into the future, the budget was projected only one year ahead. The services learned quickly that a budget cut might be avoided if they threatened to reduce their most important functions first. As one might suspect from a process requiring the unanimous approval of all the services, service budget shares remained virtually constant from 1954 to 1961. However, the emphasis on strategic nuclear objectives kept the balance tilted toward the air force, which averaged 47 percent of defense expenditures, while the navy and marines obtained 29 percent and the army was forced to settle for 24 percent.[5]

Little attempt was made to integrate strategy and budgetary decisions in the planning process. Since requirements were derived without reference to costs, and the budget ceiling was derived without an analysis of requirements, the annual result was a confrontation between large, open-ended requirements and much smaller, arbitrary budget ceilings. Clearly, requirements had to give, but no basis existed for identifying and cutting those requirements that made the least contribution to security per dollar expended. The wide gap between the demands of the JCS and the budget restrictions imposed by the president put the secretary of defense in an impossible position. Cuts were inevitably arbitrary and resulted in an improperly allocated budget. More security could have been obtained for the ceiling expenditure if requirements had been properly related to costs in the planning phase.

The McNamara Revolution. Unlike most of his predecessors, Secretary of Defense Robert McNamara viewed his role as a leader in shaping defense policy rather than as a reviewer of service plans. Moreover, McNamara arrived at the Pentagon in 1961 with a strong presidential mandate to shift the nation's defense posture from one of massive retaliation to one of more flexible response. The shift required new emphasis on mobile general purpose forces while continuing to emphasize the importance of strategic nuclear delivery systems. The mandate was to be prepared to fight simultaneously major wars in Europe and Asia and a "brush-fire" war anywhere in the world—the two-and-a-half-war strategy. To accomplish these more ambitious objectives, something had to give; it was budget constraints. President Kennedy freed Secretary McNamara from specific budgetary ceilings and eliminated any review of the defense budget in the executive branch outside the DOD.

Thus, Robert McNamara came into office with strong presidential support and theoretically unlimited funds, eager to make sweeping changes in the planning and budgeting procedures used by the DOD. He was committed to playing an active role in shaping defense programs, particularly in determining force and weapons requirements. McNamara agreed with those who argued that the close relationships of foreign policy, military strategy, budget expenditures, and the choice of major weapons and force structures made it imperative that planning be coordinated in each of those areas. Since military experts had been allowed to determine security requirements without any independent review, McNamara reasoned that there was a possibility of bias, based on service orientation, institutional pressure, and prior experience. The record of the 1950s argued that traditional compromises usually brought pressure for more total spending in order to avoid reductions anywhere, and that such compromises often discriminated in favor of the traditional elements of the services and against support functions or less glamorous weapons programs. In his view, the secretary of defense needed to play an active role to ensure that all the relevant alternatives were considered, since the individual services might not be bureaucratically able to take the broad perspective needed. Finally, the revolution in technology threatened to render traditional military expertise less relevant in force planning. Since strategic nuclear war had never been fought, analysis would have to replace experience.

McNamara heeded the advice of numerous critics of defense budgeting practices in the 1950s who had observed that national planning required an evaluation of alternate methods of accomplishing security objectives on the basis of the comparative outputs and costs of each alternative.[6] For example, several strategic weapons systems—Minuteman missiles, strategic bombers, Polaris missile submarines—contributed to the objective of deterring nuclear attack by providing a second-strike capability, that is, the ability to retaliate effectively after an initial attack on the United States. In deciding how much of the defense budget to allocate to each of those strategic systems, the costs and effectiveness of each system should be considered simultaneously. This had been made virtually impossible, however, by the defense budget's arrayal of expenditures in terms of inputs—personnel, maintenance, and military construction—used by the services rather than of end products or missions. While forces and weapons were normally considered horizontally across services in the planning process, expenditures were portrayed vertically within each service by input category. The integration of military planning (the domain of the JCS) with budgeting (the domain of the civilian secretaries and comptroller organizations) required a link between mission objectives and expenditures.

The solution McNamara adopted was "program budgeting," by which all military forces and weapons systems are grouped into output-oriented programs according to their principal missions, even though missions cut across traditional service boundaries. Programs are divided into subprograms (e.g., army forces—divisions, brigades, combat support forces—under the subprogram of General Purpose Forces) and still further into program elements (e.g., army battalions). With expenditure data arrayed in the program format, a decision-maker can readily observe how funds are distributed over objective-related outputs and how those funds are allocated over different forces and weapons systems within each program. (For nearly two decades, program categories were used exclusively within the DOD for internal defense planning, while Congress continued to receive budget proposals under traditional budget categories [Table 9.1]. Beginning with the Reagan administration, however, a blend of traditional and program categories was utilized in the defense budget presentations to Congress.)

McNamara used the potential of "program" budgeting to establish the preeminence of the Office of the Secretary of Defense (OSD) in the national security policy-making process. The Planning, Programming, Budgeting System (PPBS) he instituted made it possible to link expenditures more closely to the national security objectives to which they were directed, to compare the relative value of various expenditures, and to enforce the resultant decisions on force structure and weapons procurement. The basic document of PPBS was and remains the Five-Year Defense Program (FYDP), which contains an eight-year projection of forces (based on estimates prepared by the JCS) and a five-year projection of costs and personnel requirements divided into mission-oriented programs. By

Table 9.1 Traditional Budget Categories and Program Classifications

Traditional Budget Categories	*Program Categories for Defense Planning*
Military Personnel	Strategic Forces
Retired Military Personnel	General Purpose Forces
Operation and Maintenance	Intelligence and Communications
Procurement	Airlift and Sealift
Research, Development, Test and Evaluation	Guard and Reserve Forces
Military Construction	Research and Development
Family Housing	Central Supply and Maintenance
Civil Defense	Training, Medical, and Other General Personnel Activity
Special Foreign Currency Program	Administration and Associated Activities
	Support of Other Nations

presenting five-year cost projections, the full-cost implications of program decisions are revealed more effectively than they were in former annual projections. The FYDP is updated annually as part of an iterative planning and programming cycle, as decisions are reached on expenditures within each program. The FYDP plays a central role in linking force and financial planning, providing an official set of planning assumptions, estimating total costs of program packages, and portraying a road map for defense planning over a five-year time span. Estimates of expenditures for the next fiscal year from the FYDP become the basis for service and DOD budget requests each fall.

The PPBS described thus far produces an array of force and financial data which facilitates an evaluation of alternative forces and weapons on the basis of their costs and contributions to security objectives. While it is perfectly consistent with either centralized or decentralized processes for evaluating the alternatives, from 1961 to 1968 McNamara used PPBS to centralize power within the OSD. Clearly, such centralization of power would be opposed by the services, but McNamara held strong cards: most importantly, he had the firm backing of President Kennedy and, subsequently, President Johnson. McNamara's philosophy of management and his personal style led to his active role in a centralized decision-making process and complemented his willingness to assume the political risks of centralized decisions on policy and the budget. The 1958 amendments to the National Security Act had provided the statutory authority for a strong, activist secretary of defense. The relative inactivity of the formal NSC machinery under Kennedy and Johnson and Secretary of State Rusk's cooperative approach provided a low-pressure area for an activist defense leader to exploit. Finally, McNamara's personal management and analytical skills and those of the key civilians working in his office gave him a clear advantage initially in dealing with the service staffs, other departments, and the Congress.

Charles J. Hitch, McNamara's first comptroller and an early proponent of program budgeting, was charged with producing a budget for the next fiscal year (1963) formulated in terms of major programs. Hitch was to implement the first FYDP within nine months. In April 1961, he established a small systems analysis section under Alain Enthoven, to give the secretary of defense independent staff assistance in reviewing JCS and service force and weapons proposals, in developing alternative proposals, and in integrating data on requirements, costs, and effectiveness. The systems analysis staff quickly became a focal point of controversy in the McNamara PPBS because it seized the initiative in evaluating competing programs on the basis of statistical analyses of costs and effectiveness. Civilian analysts, often young Ph.D.s with little military experience, dominated the office because Enthoven felt they had a degree of professional and intellectual independence which allowed them to be more objective in evaluating proposals of the different services. As the staff expanded, the status of the office increased, and, by 1965, Enthoven had become an assistant secretary of defense for systems analysis, a position which still exists as the assistant secretary for program analysis and evaluation (PA&E).

McNamara used his staff of analysts to define force and weapons issues that required study, to develop alternative proposals for dealing with the issues, to probe the services for relevant data, and to evaluate alternatives. While the secretary's analytical staff and the initiative gained by having the services comment on completed studies provided a strong centralizing influence on the decision process, several other factors worked to McNamara's advantage. Most of the key issues pertaining to weapons systems and force levels lent themselves to quantitative analysis, and many concerned nuclear strategy when actual experience was nonexistent. The historic split among service chiefs within the JCS, which produced the budget battles of the 1950s, persisted into the early 1960s, and the JCS was unable to present a united front to block McNamara's initiatives. JCS planning incorporated in the annual JSOP continued to be unconstrained by any fiscal guidance and continued to call for expenditures vastly in excess of the eventual budget. As a result, JCS planning remained an ineffective counter to McNamara's initiatives, and major resource allocation decisions were deferred until the last weeks of the budget review and then dominated by OSD analysis.

As noted, the essence of the PPBS lay in its division of weapons systems and forces into output-related programs, incorporation of cost and force projections for each program in an FYDP, and linking of the planning and budgeting processes. In the abstract, the PPBS provided an improved base of information for analyzing defense decisions and coordinating interrelated activities. In practice, it also provided a systematic method for focusing attention on key issues, organizing the sequence and participation in the decision process, and recording decisions. As it was applied from 1961 to 1968 under Secretary McNamara, with emphasis on quantitative analysis of alternatives, PPBS became a powerful tool for centralizing power in the hands of the secretary of defense. Before critiquing the PPBS as it was used under McNamara and tracing subsequent developments of the system (which continues to be in effect in the 1990s), it will be helpful to focus on the techniques of systems analysis which McNamara and his staff exploited so effectively.

Systems Analysis. Under Secretary McNamara, the systems analysis staff was instrumental in developing the assured destruction strategy for nuclear deterrence, pushing the expansion of army aviation and the airmobile concept, and deciding the fate of numerous weapons systems: the B-70 manned bomber (no), the Skybolt missile (no), the Poseidon missile (yes), the Minuteman III missile (yes), and the F-111 fighter (yes). The forte of the systems analysts was the application of then-relatively new statistical techniques, often assisted by computer processing of data, to evaluation of the costs and effectiveness of alternative weapons and forces—although most of the systems analysts preferred to explain their approach as applied common sense. Indeed, the basic idea of systems analysis is a straightforward application of the scientific method, although sophisticated techniques of data analysis are often used.

The six-step sequence of systems analysis is similar to that of any logical problem-solving process:

1. Determine the purpose or objective of the system.
2. List the feasible set of alternatives for dealing with it.
3. Evaluate the alternatives on the basis of cost and effectiveness.
4. Develop decision criteria for ranking the alternatives.
5. Check the sensitivity of ranking to assumptions and uncertainties.
6. Iterate the process, exploiting new information and insight.

After the purpose of the system is determined, all the feasible alternatives that would fulfill the system's objectives are identified and listed. This is perhaps the most crucial phase of the analysis.

> Much of the formal literature on analytical methods—particularly that on operations research—seems to suggest that formulating the problem, gathering data, and making assumptions are uninteresting preliminaries and that the action really starts when the mathematical model begins to calculate the optimum solution. But in most analyses of policy issues, the vast majority of the important effort is devoted to seeking and then asking the right questions, formulating the problem, gathering relevant data and determining their validity, and deciding on good assumptions. Rather than preliminaries, these items are in fact the heart of good systems analysis.[7]

Next, each of the alternatives is evaluated to determine all its relevant costs and its effectiveness in meeting the objectives of the system. This process often includes building an analytical model of the system, when real construction and testing of the system are not feasible, in order to evaluate costs and effectiveness over time and to test the implications of risk and uncertainty. The models of cost and effectiveness attempt to represent reality by isolating the factors that are most relevant to the problem under analysis.

After the costs and effectiveness of competing systems are determined, decision criteria are applied to rank the alternatives and aid the decision-maker in selecting the most acceptable alternative. The particular decision rule depends on the nature of the problem but is generally stated as finding the system, or combination of systems, that meets the objective at the least cost. An alternative rule is to find the system providing the most effectiveness at a given cost level, a criterion that is applicable when an absolute budget constraint is imposed. The sensitivity of the ultimate ranking of alternatives to changes in assumptions, or to changes in cost and effectiveness parameters, is evaluated to determine the key assumptions that influenced the ultimate decision. Finally, the whole process is repeated, exploiting the insights into the problem statement and new alternatives gained in the last iteration and refining the estimates of crucial parameters when possible.

A major contribution of this approach to defense issues is the broadening of perspective it requires. Various configurations of individual weapons or forces are viewed as part of a larger "system" for achieving national security objectives. Thus, the first step in analysis is to place a given problem in perspective. What national security objectives are at stake? What alternative approaches could be used to meet those objectives? What are the relevant costs and benefits of a particular method of meeting the objective, and how do they compare with the alternatives? This broad approach requires that the issues and alternatives be defined clearly and makes it possible to demonstrate how disagreements are related to different underlying assumptions. The objective of systems analysis is not to produce "the" answer but to demonstrate how the various answers depend on different assumptions and judgments. Ideally, this approach makes it possible for the high-level decision-maker to evaluate real alternatives and concentrate on the key parameters of a given problem, rather than being limited to a choice between a polished proposal and "straw-man" alternatives.

The "analysis" portion of systems analysis attempts to define issues and alternatives clearly and to provide the ground rules for constructive and convergent debate. The analytical tools employed vary widely with the specific nature of the problem. Numbers are usually used to replace adjectives for clarity in the analysis, and statistical techniques for evaluating hypotheses are often useful. Utilized properly, however, quantitative analysis should focus, rather than replace, reasoned judgment.

The great debate over the antiballistic missile (ABM) system in the 1960s and early 1970s provides some useful insight into the systems analysis technique. The ABM system clearly falls into the "strategic forces" program, but what particular security objective does it serve? Prior to 1963, the proposed Nike-Zeus ABM system was designed for area defense and deployment around urban centers. After 1963, its more complex offspring, the Nike-X, added to the long-range Zeus missile a faster, short-range "Sprint" missile for interception within the atmosphere. The modified system could be used to defend point targets, including the Minuteman missile force, but deployment of the Nike-X was initially rejected based on its alleged vulnerability to a sophisticated Soviet attack that could include decoys, large numbers of warheads, and attacks on vulnerable radar. In 1966, it became clear that the Soviet Union was tipping the strategic balance (1) by deploying an ABM system around Moscow, (2) by developing more sophisticated intercontinental ballistic missiles (ICBMs) with larger warheads, which threatened our missile force, and (3) by experimenting with a space bombardment system and a satellite interceptor. Deployment of an ABM system was nevertheless resisted by the Johnson administration because the capacity of the contemplated system to handle sophisticated attacks was still in question, and such deployment might be provocative and destabilizing—stimulating further deployment of offensive missiles by the Soviet Union. By 1967, however, the perceived Soviet threat could no longer be ignored, and there was increasing evidence that the People's Republic of China might have a limited ICBM capability sometime in the 1970s.

How should the United States respond? Several alternatives to the ABM were considered. If the objective were defined as protecting our Minuteman force to ensure that sufficient missiles would survive to inflict unacceptable damage on an attacking Soviet Union, deployment of the ABM might be justified. On the other hand, the same objective might be reached by "hardening" existing missile sites, that is, by reinforcing the concrete silos to absorb greater overpressure. Other alternatives, such as the dispersal of fixed missile silos and mobile land-based missiles, were also feasible. If the ultimate objective, however, was to deter Soviet attack, perhaps the correct response would not be to build ABMs or improve land-based missiles but to expand the Polaris missile force at sea or to improve the manned-bomber force, or both. After all, the major purpose of the triad deterrent, of maintaining three independent forces—ICBM Minuteman, Polaris submarine-launched ballistic missiles, and the manned-bomber force—was to inflict unacceptable losses on the enemy despite technological breakthroughs in any one area. This "assured destruction" capability was believed essential to deter a first strike by the Soviet Union.

By 1968, three alternative missions for the ABM were being actively considered as part of a deterrence system: (1) defend U.S. cities against a massive, sophisticated Soviet attack, (2) defend U.S. cities against future limited third-power attacks, and (3) defend Minuteman ICBMs. Preliminary analysis eliminated the first alternative as infeasible, given the likely Soviet response of expanded offensive deployments. A light deployment to defend the Minuteman force remained a possibility, and that option might also provide adequate defense from third-power attacks or accidental Soviet launches. Thus, the first step in systems analysis was to place the ABM issue in perspective and enumerate alternative systems that should be considered.

The second step was to evaluate the full system costs and effectiveness of each alternative. Considering only the hardened silo and ABM alternatives, how did the number of surviving Minuteman missiles vary with different levels of deployment and, hence, costs? To determine the relationship of costs to effectiveness (surviving Minuteman missiles), cost and effectiveness models were needed. Effectiveness was clearly related to assumptions as to (1) the nature of the enemy threat (number of missiles, missile accuracy, warhead number and size, deployment strategy, etc.) and (2) the performance characteristics of the ABM (probability and range of radar detection, probability and range of destroying an incoming missile, deployment strategy, etc.) or the hardened silo (overpressure withstood at varying thicknesses). Costs included future R&D, procurement, installation, and operating costs over the lifetime of the system.

Given the relationship between costs and effectiveness for each system, a decision criterion was needed to rank the alternatives. One such criterion might have been to find the system that ensured the survival of a desired number of Minuteman missiles at the least cost. Or, a given budget expenditure might have been stipulated and the systems ranked on the basis of the largest number of surviving missiles for that expenditure. Next the ranking could be tested for its sensitivity to the assumptions or system parameters. Suppose the number of attacking missiles were twice as large as expected, or their accuracy were greater, or procurement costs were understated, or our missile failed if radiation in the atmosphere were too great.

This information was certainly helpful to decision-makers. Indeed, the debate over the proposed deployment of the Sentinel system (the sequel to the Nike-X, which was to be deployed around urban centers) or its modified version, the

Safeguard (which was to provide point defense for the Minuteman) centered on estimates of technical performance and cost data. The real issue at stake, however, was the future direction and objective of our nuclear strategy vis-à-vis the Soviet Union and China. Was strategic nuclear superiority essential? Would parity suffice? Or was an assured destruction capability sufficient? How would the Soviet Union react to ABM deployment—by negotiation or by expansion of its offensive missile force? Mathematical models of costs and effectiveness could not address these bargaining alternatives, but systems analysis could be, and was, used to assist in evaluating feasible and efficient responses. Thus, the 1969 decision to deploy the Safeguard system around Minuteman bases, which passed the Senate by one vote, was based as much on estimates of Soviet response as on systems analysis of the costs and effectiveness of the ABM. Subsequent Strategic Arms Limitation Talks (SALT) resulted in no further ABM development. In this case, systems analysis helped focus the debate on alternative solutions and correctly emphasized the critical nature of assumptions about Soviet response.

The debate over defensive systems resurfaced after March 1983, when President Reagan publicly announced the Strategic Defense Initiative (SDI), which he hoped would make nuclear weapons obsolete. After the president's announcement, the DOD gathered together under one program the various research projects that had been in existence since the earlier ABM debate, placing much greater emphasis on the development of advanced technologies. While the approach of the SDI to defense against nuclear attack was very different from the original ABM concept, the nature of the controversy over the SDI was reminiscent of the ABM debate. Cost-effectiveness, one of the three criteria for deployment of defenses outlined by senior arms control adviser Paul Nitze in 1985, was again an issue of much contention. Because the technologies involved were frequently at an immature stage of development and the nature of the Soviet response was still critical, systems analysis was difficult to apply in this area. Moreover, former Secretary of Defense Caspar Weinberger, an enthusiastic supporter of early deployment of the SDI, explicitly rejected cost-effectiveness as a criterion. He argued that, given the potential benefits to the United States, cost should play no role in the decision. Congress was more impressed with the cost-effectiveness argument of Nitze than the position of Weinberger and kept the SDI in the laboratory.

In the early 1990s, with the collapse of the Soviet Union, and the use of Scud missiles by Iraq in the Gulf war, the Bush administration shifted the focus of the SDI to the more restricted mission of protection of the United States against limited or accidental attacks and lowered the estimated cost of deployment dramatically ($135 billion for a ground- and space-based system). While this new approach was supported by the chairmen of the Armed Services Committees, many in the Congress still wondered if it made sense to spend over $100 billion on a system that could be thwarted by a terrorist bringing in a nuclear bomb in a suitcase. Reportedly, the assistant secretary of defense for program analysis and evaluation also felt that the new plan would produce a technologically inferior system that would be unable to defend the country effectively even against a limited attack.[8]

The use of systems analysis is often confused with a misleading distinction between ''rational'' and ''political'' decision processes. PPBS in general and systems analysis in particular are often referred to as ''rational'' processes that stress objective evidence, presumably devoid of political judgment, in contrast to the more decentralized ''political'' bargaining processes that lean on subjective evaluations. There is no such thing, however, as a ''rational'' decision process in that sense—any analysis contains value judgments. The question in any particular case is, What weight is to be given to whose value judgments? One impact of PPBS has clearly been to make conflicts in value judgments more explicit and to permit decision-makers to weigh quantifiable evidence—over which there may also be considerable disagreement—against less quantifiable, often institutional, considerations. The decision on how many missiles to deploy on the original fleet ballistic missile submarine, the Polaris, illustrates this trade-off. Systems analysis suggested that, while any even number of missiles between four and forty-eight was technically feasible, thirty-two launching tubes would be the most cost-effective. However, submarine officer support was essential in gaining congressional approval of the system and in implementing the Polaris program. Since the submarine officers had a strong aversion to large submarines, especially large submarines with many six-foot-diameter hatches, the ultimate decision was to choose sixteen tubes.[9] To define such a decision as either ''rational'' or ''political'' would clearly oversimplify the process—it was both.

While the weight applied to judgments from various sources will certainly vary with the individuals operating the system, the systems analysis approach to the evaluation of alternatives does imply some centralization of decision authority, since alternatives could easily cut across institutional boundaries and institutions would tend to take advocacy positions in the analysis. The real impact on the distribution of authority, however, is more apt to be defined by the locus of analytical skill and by the pattern of initiating and responding to the studies within the organization. Under Secretary McNamara, systems analysis became synonymous with centralization because of the initial analytical advantages of his civilian staff and because his analysts took the initiative in raising issues, drafting studies over the secretary's signature, and requiring prompt service comment before final decisions. That process produced considerable controversy within and outside the defense establishment—controversy to which we now turn.

Critique of the McNamara PPBS and Evolving Revisions. Armed with a staff of mostly young civilian analysts—the ''whiz kids''—in the systems analysis office, Secretary McNamara used the PPBS to break through traditional service barriers. The rise in power of the OSD and the emphasis on quantifiable cost and effectiveness measures in the planning and budgeting processes were not wholly supported either by the services or by many members of the Congress.

The services generally opposed the secretary's reliance on civilian analysts with little or no military experience. It was widely held by military officers that attempts to quantify the effectiveness of weapons systems or forces prejudiced decisions against options that held nonquantifiable benefits and overweighed quantifiable factors in options in which only some or partial quantification was feasible. Further, many career military officers felt that systems analysis was pushed too far, that insufficient weight was being given to expert intuition and experience, and that too much import was given to abstract mathematical models. In many cases in which effectiveness was hard to quantify, they felt that too great an emphasis was placed on system costs, which were consistently underestimated. In short, uniformed officers viewed the civilian analysts as Oscar Wilde viewed the cynic who knew "the price of everything and the value of nothing"—and in the case of weapon systems like the F-111 fighter or the C-5A jet transport (or the A-12 bomber or the C-17 jet transport in the 1980s and 1990s), they apparently did not know the price all that well either.

The centralized approach of McNamara's PPBS also tended to deemphasize the value of bargaining and consensus in gaining the support of the bureaucracy. In an important critique of PPBS, Aaron Wildavsky argued that decision-makers should avoid being overburdened with details at any one time and should rely more on feedback information on whether or not subordinates had unduly been hurt by their actions. He further argued that a sequential, nonprogrammatic organizational approach had the advantage of fitting with political reality, since cost-benefit formulas often omitted political costs and benefits. He concluded that a partial adversary system had a better chance than program budgeting to arrive at reasonable decisions that took into account a multiplicity of internal and external political values.[10]

McNamara's approach encountered a mixed reception on Capitol Hill. Legislators were clearly impressed with the detail contained in the secretary's reports and perhaps even more impressed with his knowledge of those details. But frequently they lamented the difficult options with which they were presented. In 1967, at hearings on the PPBS, Senator Karl Mundt revealed his frustration:

> We used to face the question, "How much should we spend for a weapons system?" Defense had a united front and asked for a certain amount of money. Now we have to make decisions . . . on which defense system and techniques we should have. . . . It is in the wrong arena at our end of the Avenue, because we are not experts in defense, and we are not economists and the engineers. We are here trying to make overall policy and to do what we can to keep the budget relatively sound. It is very difficult if part of [the] team says you need B-52 bombers, otherwise in the early 70's you will have no bombers at all, and other officials say, "Don't worry about that, just let the B-52 bombers go, and don't put any money in." That shouldn't be the kind of decision we have to make.[11]

Similarly, many critics argued that the secretary was spending too much time on decisions that he should not have made. Centralization through systems analysis, they argued, ran the risk of distorting key issues. True, it did seem that it would be more cost-effective for each service to adopt a standardized belt buckle; but was that issue worthy of the secretary's scarce time, and were the potential savings worth the political cost? A small group of analysts could not hope to review all the options available to the secretary. Were they focusing on the right issues? Were they raising and exploring the complete set of feasible alternatives? Many argued that in a centralized decision process subordinates might not reveal all the relevant alternatives as they would in a more decentralized adversary process.

These criticisms have had significant impact on the evolution of PPBS in the post-McNamara period. The central concepts of the system have remained, but there has been a clear decentralization in the process of raising issues and analyzing alternatives. The result has been a modified system that provides for an expanded role by the NSC in evaluating security objectives, early fiscal guidance to the services to assist in making their planning more realistic in terms of budget limitations, and a shift in initiative for proposing changes and raising issues for debate away from the systems analysis group within the OSD and back toward the services and the JCS, with more participation by the unified and specified commanders (CINCs) in the entire process, and with an explicit limit on the number of issues that can be raised.

As noted earlier, under Secretary McNamara operational planning by the JCS had little impact on budget allocations, since planning was unconstrained by realistic budget limitations. Thus, the OSD played the dominant role in the process of updating the FYDP and adjusting requests for budget allocations down to a total consistent with federal fiscal policy. Under the PPBS followed since 1968, the FYDP remains the central document, but the process of reviewing alternatives and proposing issues for debate has been decentralized.

The relative power of the OSD, the services, and the JCS over the past twenty-five years has been largely a function of the management styles of McNamara's successors. In the Nixon–Ford years, under the aegis of Secretary Laird, power tilted toward the services and JCS. The Carter administration saw the return of a very strong secretary in Harold Brown, and a much greater programmatic role for the OSD. During the Reagan administration, Secretary of Defense Weinberger allowed the services and the JCS to achieve primacy in the process. In the Bush administration, Secretary of Defense Cheney took some power back from the individual services and divided it between the OSD and the JCS. Indeed, as a result of the Reorganization Act of 1986, in several regards the Joint Staff became more powerful than either the services or the OSD.

The defense budget process begins in October, some fourteen months before the budget is to be submitted, when the JCS completes the Joint Strategic Planning Document (JSPD).[12] This document, which broadly conforms to the resource levels projected by the secretary of defense, contains a strategic assessment and force structure requirements. Using the JSPD plus input from the NSC and OMB, the secretary of defense issues his Defense Guidance (DG) in late January. The 100 or so pages in the DG provide goals, objectives, and fiscal guidelines to the services and defense agencies in some fifteen areas. Before the DG is finalized, the JCS, the services, and the CINCs have an opportunity to make formal written comments on it. If any of these three groups does not have its concerns satisfied by means of its written comments, a meeting of the Defense Planning and Resources Board (DPRB) is convened.

The DPRB is chaired by the Deputy Secretary of Defense and has eight other permanent members: the chairman of the JCS, the under secretary of defense (Acquisition), the secretaries of the three military departments, the undersecretary of defense (Planning), the assistant secretary of defense (PA&E), and the DOD comptroller. Depending upon the agenda, additional officials such as the service chiefs, the CINCs, and other OSD officials can be asked to participate.

Throughout the first part of the calendar year, service planning continues to translate broad force structure decisions (outlined in the Joint Program Assessment Memorandum [JPAM] issued by the JCS) into more specific program objectives. The resultant Program Objective Memoranda (POM) released by each service and defense agency, beginning in May, for each major mission area and support activity, present the detailed program implications of the Joint Strategic Plan and defend deviations from that initial guidance. The net impact of this procedure is to place the initiative in raising issues for further debate with the services and the JCS. Since JCS recommendations are generally consistent with the fiscal guidance, its positions are less vulnerable to last-minute budget adjustments.

After a review of the POMs, PA&E promulgates a series of issue papers. These papers outline areas in which the POMs differ from the DG without an acceptable rationale. The issues can be raised by the OSD, the services, the JCS, or the CINCs. While PA&E is the final arbiter of which issues can be raised for the DPRB, it raises very few issues itself. Instead, it allocates many of the issues to each of the major parts of the OSD, the services, the JCS, and the CINCs.

During the summer, after the dozens of meetings of the DPRB, the deputy secretary issues Program Decision Memoranda for each budget area. These decisions are incorporated in the FYDP, and the plan's cost and force structure data for the next fiscal year become the basis for service budget proposals submitted to the OSD in early fall. Following a joint review of these proposals by the DPRB and the OMB, the consolidated defense budget is reviewed by the president and incorporated in his annual budget submission to Congress early in the new year.

Important to an understanding of the budgetary process within the DOD is appreciation for the fact that the process is inherently complex and driven by tight deadlines. It is probably accurate to say that there are relatively few officials within the DOD who comprehend the entire process in all its intricacy. Those officials who, by virtue of long experience with the annual cycle, understand the process and the techniques by which it can be manipulated find quickly that understanding often translates into political influence and organizational clout.

The Outlook for Defense Management. Returning to the three questions posed at the beginning of the chapter, it should now be clear that the allocation of scarce government resources to security expenditures as a whole should be closely related to the allocation of those resources within the DOD. Only by determining the maximum increment in security, which may be obtained from a given budget expenditure, and comparing that increment to the additional benefit that might be derived from alternative government expenditures can society choose efficiently between competing social objectives. Such an analysis, however, presupposes that the defense budget has been allocated internally to subordinate agencies to maximize the increment in security. The appropriate level of defense expenditures should therefore be linked to the maximum amount of added security which can be obtained for any given increment in the expenditure level. Hence, the optimal allocation of resources to security objectives and the proper allocation of funds within the DOD are interrelated questions that, conceptually at least, should be handled simultaneously rather than sequentially.

Under PPBS, the DOD has made some progress in relating the internal allocation of budget expenditures to security objectives. The highly centralized process of the McNamara era has been replaced with a more decentralized system of participatory management placing increased weight on institutional costs and service measures of effectiveness. The essential elements, however, of the system of comparing similar outputs across services within a program format and of providing open analysis of the costs and effectiveness of competing weapons or force structures remain.

The ability of the government to decide how much to spend on national security and to evaluate defense versus other types of expenditures, however, has lagged far behind. Program budgeting has been generally unsuccessful outside the DOD, and efforts in the early 1970s to coordinate security and economic priorities in a national security council structure were abandoned. The OMB, of course, reviews the budget submissions of the DOD, and the OMB's budget guidance does provide the initial judgment on the allocation of defense versus other expenditures. That budget guidance, however, has traditionally been strongly influenced by past expenditure patterns and by particular interests of the president. Indeed, within the executive branch's review of the DOD budget, the secretary of defense has generally been supported by the president. For example, in the fall of 1991, with the size of the federal deficit exploding and the Soviet Union collapsing, President Bush resisted pressure from the OMB and even many congressional Republicans to cut defense spending for FY 1993 below the level agreed to in the Budget Summit of 1990. The President accepted Secretary Cheney's argument that deeper cuts would jeopardize the integrity of the force.

To suggest that the level of defense expenditures is determined with little reference to competing nondefense programs is not to imply that defense expenditures are unconstrained. Rather, allocations for defense tend to be constrained by past levels of spending, by the desired level of total government spending based on economic conditions, and by changes in national security objectives or perceived threats. Thus, in the early 1970s the reaction to the war in Southeast Asia, concern with inflation, overtures to the People's Republic of China, an apparent era of détente with the Soviet Union, and the prospect of SALT and Mutual and Balanced Force Reduction negotiations all contributed to a period of declining real defense expenditures.

By the late 1970s a variety of factors led to a reversal of this downward trend.

Pepper . . . and Salt

"I don't have any cash on me, but here's a $19.95 paper clip."

From the Wall Street Journal—permission, Cartoon Features Syndicate.

The Soviet Union's invasion of Afghanistan, coupled with the generally more adventurist character of Soviet activities abroad, resulted in a worsening of East–West relations. In addition, it became increasingly clear that the military position of the United States relative to the Soviet Union had deteriorated significantly. The American public shared this concern, and by the decade's end had become much more receptive to higher defense spending. This general concern was translated into plans to upgrade both strategic and conventional forces, particularly naval forces for power projection. The last two defense budgets prepared by the Carter administration called for greater levels of spending, but it was the incoming Reagan administration that pursued the military build-up in earnest. Between 1980 and 1986 defense spending increased fifty-three percent in real terms, that is, after inflation, with the greatest percentage gains being in the categories of procurement and research and development. However, massive budgetary deficits, coupled with complaints of Pentagon mismanagement, brought an end to this climb in FY 1986 and led to a real decline in defense expenditures of fifteen percent by 1990. In the 1990s, the collapse of the Warsaw Pact, the dissolution of the Soviet Union, and the exploding federal deficit led to another twenty percent decline by 1993. Indeed had it not been for the recession which gripped the country in 1991 and 1992, defense spending would have been reduced further. The prospect of adding further workers to the unemployment lines kept Congress from following through on proposals to eliminate such weapons as the B-2 bomber, the Seawolf submarine, the V-22 tilt rotor plane, and the F-14 fighter, or to cut tens of thousands of selected reservists.

The early 1980s witnessed the promulgation of highly touted reforms of the defense establishment. Reports of waste and mismanagement in the Defense Department, as well as heavily publicized instances of contractor abuses, led both the president and Congress to take action. A significant factor in the greater attention paid to this area was the need to alleviate growing public concern over reports of waste and abuse. Such reports did much to weaken support for increased defense spending in the mid 1980s and led to the institution of a variety of changes, both organizational and procedural.

A number of the reforms instituted were based upon the recommendations of the presidentially appointed Blue Ribbon Commission on Defense Management (the Packard Commission), which submitted its final report in June 1986. The defense acquisition process received major attention in this report and in the Goldwater–Nichols Reorganization Act of 1986 as well. The latter represented the first large-scale legislative reform of the defense establishment in thirty years and incorporated numerous provisions designed to improve the planning, budgeting, and procurement processes in the Department of Defense.[13] The act's primary objective was to strengthen the institution of the Joint Chiefs of Staff, which was to play a much greater role in strategic and contingency planning, review of the services' budget proposals, and supply of military advice to the president. All of this was to take place under the enhanced leadership of the JCS chairman, now finally placed in full control of the joint staff and clearly the nation's preeminent military officer. As in previous defense reorganizations, a major goal was to overcome service separatism by means of increased centralization and coordination of service requirements and operations. This was pursued at the joint command level by granting the CINCs much greater control over their forces and increasing their involvement in the PPBS process. The CINCs were to have much more say in planning, as well as in weapons procurement and acquisition. A new "joint specialty" category of officers was created to improve interservice coordination and to help overcome the difficulties described earlier caused by traditional rivalries and dissension.

There is no doubt that these changes have in fact increased the power and importance of the Chairman of the JCS and the joint staff in the PPBS and acquisition processes. Indeed, the Base Force Structure, which became the foundation of the nation's post–cold war force structure, was produced by the JCS in 1990, and was vigorously defended by the chairman and vice-chairman before the Congress and the public in the early 1990s. Similarly, the vice-chairman of the JCS is the Chairman of the Joint Requirements Oversight Council (JROC), which establishes requirements for new weapon systems.

But, on the larger problem of the relationship between the defense budget and national strategy, there is still an inherent dilemma in any reasoned analysis of the case for particular weapons systems and force levels. Ideally, the decision process of PPBS is designed to translate national security goals into objectives, to define programs that meet those objectives, and to evaluate which weapons systems and force structures accomplish the objectives at the least cost in budgetary and political terms. There is, however, an inevitable feedback from forces-in-being which influences the perception of national interest. Having a capability to react to a particular threat makes it more likely that a response will be made and may tend to bias the evaluation of national objectives toward commitment of force. In discussing the case of the Fast Deployment Logistics (FDL) ships proposed by Secretary McNamara to provide a rapid response capability, Graham Allison noted that such a capability could increase the probability of force commitment in a crisis. He concluded that "creating some kinds of military capabilities does affect decisions about the use of force, and we must find ways of including this fact in choices about such weapons systems."[14]

Certainly there is a link between the development and the probability of using that capability. For that very reason, it is essential that our national security posture be continually modified in response to shifting security objectives and that defense decision-makers remain alert to institutional pressures that might prevent such adjustments. This is especially true in an era of dramatic change such as that of the 1990s, when most of the planning assumptions of the past 45 years have evaporated. The PPBS, despite its weaknesses, provides a valuable mechanism for raising those key issues and searching for solutions consistent with budgetary realities, if the secretary of defense uses it prudently.

Discussion Questions

1. What are the economic constraints on defense planning and budgeting?
2. How should the proportion of total resources directed to national security objectives be determined after the end of the cold war?
3. What factors limit the ability of Congress to shape the defense budget radically?
4. How and by whom are national security objectives defined?
5. How does the federal government determine how much of its resources to allocate to security?
6. How should the DOD allocate its resources?
7. What are the essential functions of the DOD?
8. What are the advantages and disadvantages of a centralized system of defense planning and budgeting?
9. What is meant by "the McNamara Revolution"? How was this approach to defense planning and budgeting different from previous arrangements? How did the "PPBS" approach work? What is the "six-step sequence" of systems analysis?
10. What is meant by the statement that "there is no such thing as a 'rational decision' process"? If defense planning and budgeting is not the process of "rational decisions," how would you describe the process?
11. How has defense planning and budgeting changed since the McNamara era?
12. Does the DPRB contribute to centralization or decentralization? How?

Recommended Reading

Allison, Graham T., and Treverton, Gregory. *Rethinking America's Security*. New York: Norton, 1992.

Cimbala, Stephen J., ed. *The Reagan Defense Program: An Interim Assessment*. Wilmington, Del.: Scholarly Resources, 1986.

Enthoven, Alain C., and Smith, K. Wayne. *How Much Is Enough?* New York: Harper & Row, 1971.

Fallows, James. *National Defense*. New York: Random House, 1981.

Guertner, Gary. *Deterrence and Defense in a Post-Nuclear World*. New York: St. Martin's Press, 1990.

Kaufman, William, and Steinbruner, John. *Decisions for Defense*. Washington, D.C.: Brookings Institution, 1986.

Kaufman, William, and Korb, Lawrence. *The 1990 Defense Budget*. Washington, D.C.: Brookings Institution, 1989.

Korb, Lawrence J. *The Joint Chiefs of Staff: The First Twenty-five Years*. Bloomington: Indiana University Press, 1976.

Kruzel, Joseph, ed. *American Defense Annual, 1991–1992*. Lexington, Mass.: Heath, 1991.

McNaugher, Thomas. *New Weapons, Old Politics: America's Military Procurement Muddle*. Washington, D.C.: Brookings Institution, 1989.

Pfaltzgraff, Robert. *New Directions in U.S. Defense Policy*. Newbury Park, Calif.: Sage, 1991.

Sapolsky, Harvey. *The Polaris System Development*. Cambridge, Mass.: Harvard University Press, 1973.

Taylor, Maxwell D. *The Uncertain Trumpet*. New York: Harper, 1959.

Wildavsky, Aaron. *The Politics of the Budgetary Process*. Boston: Little, Brown, 1964.

10

The National Security Decision-making Process: Putting the Pieces Together

Policy Rings. National security decision-making is in part complex and fascinating because of the two worlds it involves. As Samuel Huntington explains:

> One [world] is international politics, the world of balance of power, wars and alliances, the subtle and brutal uses of force and diplomacy to influence the behavior of other states. The other world is domestic politics, the world of interest groups, political parties, social classes with their conflicting interests and goals.[1]

National security affairs have an impact on and are influenced by both worlds, for national security involves the application of national resources to the international arena in an attempt to make the domestic society more secure.

Previous chapters have discussed the individual roles of the president, the Congress, the military, and the intelligence community in national security affairs. This chapter will address the overall decision-making process and attempt to show how these various roles are combined and how the people and organizations that fulfill them interact.

One way to characterize the national policy-making process is as a series of concentric circles.[2] At the center is the president, surrounded by his closest advisers. These are the people who, by virtue of position or personal relationship to the president, are involved in the national security issues that require presidential decision. The inner circle of advisers usually includes the Secretaries of State and Defense, the assistant for national security affairs, the Director of Central Intelligence, and, more recently in the Bush administration, the Chairman of the Joint Chiefs of Staff (JCS) and the White House Chief of Staff. The composition of this "inner circle" will of course depend somewhat upon the issue and upon the desires of a particular president. Closely associated with this innermost circle are the organizations of the executive office of the president and some members of the White House office. Executives of these organizations, such as the Council of Economic Advisers and the Office of Management and Budget, are members of the President's personal staff and among his most frequent advisers.

Beyond this circle lie the relevant departments of the executive branch and various independent agencies and commissions. Farther still from the center in this particular model is the congressional ring with the organizations of the legislative branch. Beyond them lies the public arena consisting of the media, interest groups, and the general public.

This concept of concentric rings in policy-making obviously focuses upon the president and the executive branch, placing Congress in a very much secondary role. Yet, as explained in preceding chapters, Congress generally plays an important and, in many cases, decisive role in national security affairs. Although it will be useful to pursue the concentric ring analogy for a moment, it should be recognized that in reality Congress occupies a ring in another plane from the executive branch circles.

The boundaries between the policy-making rings should not be viewed as impenetrable barriers. Individuals and even organizations can and do move from one ring to the other depending upon the issue. Most cabinet officers and their deputies and assistants—for example, from the Department of Commerce—are part of the third ring of bureaucracies. When they are invited to participate in the deliberations of the National Security Council (NSC) or its committees, say on a strategic trade issue, they become members of the second ring or even the innermost circle.

There is no one way in which national security decisions are made. Issues range from the relatively mundane, such as how many separate agencies require representation at a foreign embassy, to the more critical, such as the amount of aid to be given to the former Soviet Union. There are regularized processes for decision-making, but the issues themselves and the particular ways they arise often dictate the precise method by which they are addressed. Factors such as secrecy, immediacy, political sensitivity, and seriousness of impact tend to place decisions into either the "routine" or the "priority" category. Routine decisions generally involve more of the circles of policy-making, while priority decisions, especially those that require great secrecy and quick action, are often made in the inner one or two circles. An example of the routine would be a proposal for shaping the post–cold war defense force, which is formulated in the DOD, debated and reshaped in the inner circle, and sent to Congress, where it becomes part of the public arena for discussion. President Bush's decision to respond militarily to Iraq's invasion of Kuwait in 1990 is an example of a priority decision in which only a few members of the innermost circle were involved in decision-making.[3]

National Security Council System. Under normal circumstances, the NSC system is among the least publicized but most powerful units of the U.S.

government. As noted in Chapter 5, the NSC is at or near the center of the national security decision-making process within the executive branch and has become the focal point for most of the important decisions. Its comparatively low profile was abruptly ended midway through the Reagan administration's second term, however, by revelations of a series of controversial activities by the assistant to the president for national security affairs and members of the NSC staff. In a report to the president by the Special Review Board (the Tower Commission)[4] and in the hearings conducted by the Congress, the image emerged of an NSC system that had strayed far from its intended purpose and had far exceeded its legal mandate. It had become a government within a government.

Rather than serving as an integrator or honest broker for the president concerning the positions of various agencies, the NSC staff actually became a policy-making and policy-executing organization. It made policy concerning the transfer of arms to Iran without even informing some of the major players, that is, the State and Defense Departments; and, in regard to using proceeds from the arms sales to support the contras in Nicaragua, apparently without even informing the president. Similarly, rather than monitoring the actions taken by the executive departments in implementing the president's policy, the NSC staff

FIG. 10.1 Policy Rings

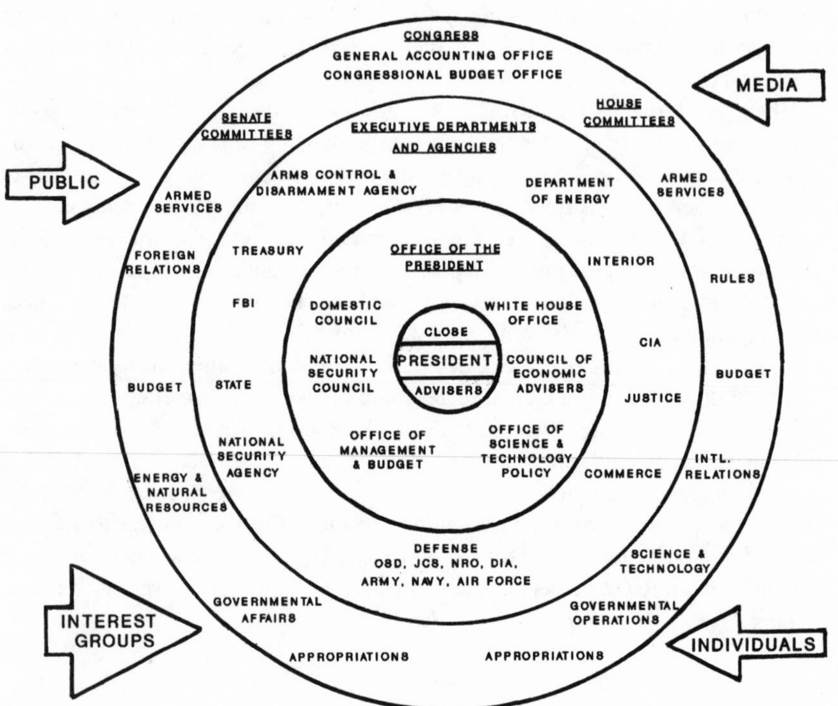

actually became a policy implementor on their own by setting up a dummy corporation to handle the arms transfers.

From every indication this stage in this NSC's evolution appears to have been an anomaly. Under Admiral Poindexter's successors, the NSC has returned to a more traditional operation. Frank Carlucci, Colin Powell, and Brent Scowcroft have ensured that the NSC staff has functioned as an integrator or honest broker and not a policy-making organization.[5]

The 1947 legislation establishing the NSC left substantial flexibility regarding its precise structure and function to individual presidents, allowing each to adjust the system as he saw fit. Thus, the titles and responsibilities of the various committees and groupings, as well as the stature accorded its head, have varied both between and within administrations. The Bush administration system presented here was established in early 1989 and remained essentially intact throughout the remainder of his presidency. And it is likely that a new president's NSC system will have a similar look. (See Chapter 5 for a discussion of the evolution of the NSC system.)

In the Bush administration, three NSC subgroups supported the NSC system: the NSC Principals Committee (NSC/PC), the NSC Deputies Committee (NSC/DC), and the NSC Policy Coordinating Committees (NSC/PCCs).[6] Members of the NSC/PC were the Secretaries of State and Defense, the Director of Central Intelligence (DCI), the Chairman of the JCS, and the Chief of Staff to the president. The Principals Committee was chaired by the Assistant to the President for National Security Affairs. The Deputies Committee was chaired by the Deputy Assistant to the President for National Security Affairs. Its members were the Undersecretary of Defense for Policy, the Undersecretary of State for Political Affairs, the Deputy DCI, and the Vice-Chairman of the JCS. On certain occasions Defense and State were represented by the deputy secretary rather than the undersecretary. The members of the NSC/PCCs included a representative at the assistant secretary level from each of the executive departments or agencies that had members on the NSC/DC. The Policy Coordinating Committees were chaired respectively by an individual at the assistant secretary level from Defense, State, Treasury, intelligence or the NSC, depending upon the subject.

The heart of the Bush administration's NSC system was the Deputies Committee. This group initiated studies on major policies and responded to requests for policy changes from the various executive departments and agencies. For example, in 1989, the Deputies Committee initiated a strategic review of U.S. national security policy and in 1992 responded to plans initiated by the Director of the Drug Enforcement Agency for escalating U.S. antidrug efforts in the Caribbean.

The policy objectives, options, and recommendations for the Deputies Committee are developed and coordinated by the Policy Coordinating Committees. If the deputies agree on an issue it goes directly to the president for promulgation as a National Security Directive (NSD). If the deputies cannot agree, the issue is usually sent to the Principals Committee for resolution. Extremely important or divisive issues, like military intervention in the Yugoslavian civil war go to the NSC itself for resolution. Crisis management is handled by the Deputies Committee.

Essentially the NSC system provides a forum for interagency consideration of policy issues. The committee structure brings together mid- to upper-level representatives of the different parts of government, paired with their counterparts from the NSC staff itself. A system of three- or four-person divisions within the NSC staff, grouped by geographic region or specific issue, uses the vast information resources available to the NSC in order to support the function of the PCCs. Among the hardest-working members of government, NSC staffers also may have a substantial impact on the policy process.

Because of its small size and access to information, the NSC machinery is well suited for dealing with crisis situations. It was used extensively after the Iraqi invasion of Kuwait on August 2, 1990. A well-briefed reporter's authoritative account of how the administration used the NSC appeared after the war.

> On August 3, after returning from Aspen, Scowcroft opened the regular 8 a.m. meeting of the National Security Council. Scowcroft had sought to chair the morning meeting the day before, but the President had jumped in and run things himself. By mutual agreement that would not happen this time. Perhaps it would be better, Scowcroft had urged the President the evening before, if he [Scowcroft] took the lead in the next morning's meeting. "In order to have a free debate," Scowcroft had told Bush, "let me make the argument. People will be more willing to criticize me than you." This way, Scowcroft suggested, Bush could sit back, having not shown his hand, and get the benefit of the other players' "unvarnished advice."
>
> Scowcroft began the meeting with a simple premise. As hard as it might be for the United States to respond to a crisis so far away, the invasion of Kuwait had to be considered unacceptable. All the participants in the meeting were familiar with an analytical paper on world oil reserves prepared by economists in the CIA's new Office of Resource, Technology, and Trade. The impact of Iraq's invasion of Kuwait, Scowcroft said, according to several people present, was bad news not just to the economy of the United States but to that of the world. Therefore, no matter how difficult it was, the United States would have to respond. And the only response that would guarantee results, Scowcroft said, was force. The President remained silent.
>
> Scowcroft opened up the discussion. Defense Secretary Cheney said that he agreed that a military response was required. General Powell seconded the sentiment. "My visualization was that we had to get something over there rapidly and get the American flag in the ground," he later said. "I was reasonably sure in my own mind that although Saddam Hussein was willing to go to war with Kuwait, and was quite prepared to go to war with any regional actors who wanted to get in the way, it certainly couldn't have been in his mind to go to war with the United States of America. And therefore we had to get the United States of America there. And we had to do it rapidly before he realized we weren't there—or how badly we weren't there."
>
> Powell was followed by Lawrence Eagleburger, Baker's Deputy Secretary of State. A career foreign-service officer, Eagleburger had risen higher than any professional diplomat in the State Department. Like Scowcroft, with whom he had worked in the blue-chip consultancy established by Henry Kissinger, Eagleburger wielded a kind of special influence. Over the course of his more than two decades in the foreign service and through a variety of postings overseas, Eagleburger had found himself in the thick

of hundreds of foreign-policy dilemmas. He was a man who some thought would favor quiet talk over wielding a big stick. But now he was urging a military option.

Finally the President spoke. He agreed with Scowcroft and Eagleburger on the need to use force. He was, aides said, becoming convinced that Saddam Hussein would not respect anything short of military action. The President mentioned his conversation with King Fahd the day before. The question was whether the Saudis would accept a sizable American military presence such as that called for by Plan 1002–90.

General Powell indicated that Schwarzkopf and General Kelly were working on an "options package" for the President. They would be ready to present it shortly. Bush said that the next day would be fine. He would be leaving for Camp David that afternoon. Powell, Cheney, and Schwarzkopf could all take the helicopter out to the presidential retreat in Maryland's Catoctin Mountains the following morning. For the President and his senior advisors, it would be a working weekend, the first of many.[7]

In preceding administrations, as well as the Bush administration, ad hoc study groups are sometimes attached to the NSC staff to analyze particular issues. Such groups may be placed under the directorship of an "outsider" in an attempt to get new insights and to divorce bureaucratic interests from the study.

The NSC staff has consisted in recent years of about forty professional analysts plus technical and clerical support. In the words of its 1980 head, Zbigniew Brzezinski, the staff exists to "assist the President in coordination and implementation of policy, provide a management arm on security questions, and be a think tank for assistance in development of a longer-term perspective on foreign policy."[8] Composed primarily of upper-level military and CIA officers and State Department personnel on temporary assignment, along with a few academics, and having unparalleled access to information, this staff screens, organizes, and often synthesizes most of the information on national security matters which the president sees.

Certain recurring issues, such as defense and intelligence budgets, arms control matters, and alliance relationships are routinely dealt with through the NSC system. Other matters, such as a reappraisal of U.S. policy toward a particular country or the consideration of a one-time issue, are inserted into the policy mill by a special process. This process normally begins with the identification of an issue by any agency in the executive branch. (Theoretically, it could also arise from a congressional initiative.) The agency might be seeking a clarification of policy, a reevaluation of existing policy, or a formulation of policy where none exists. If the policy is interdepartmental in its effects, which national security policy matters almost invariably are, the NSC is the appropriate mechanism to handle it. To introduce it into the NSC system, the agency or department will draft an Interagency Study and forward it to the NSC staff for consideration. That staff, in turn, reviews the draft and presents it, with recommendations, to the special assistant who discusses it with the president. If the president decides that the issue or policy requires NSC consideration or review, he so directs in a formal National Security Study Directive (NSSD).

Of course, the initiative for an Interagency Study need not come from the bottom up; indeed, the president or his assistant for national security affairs will frequently identify an issue for NSC consideration. An Interagency Study requires the agencies and departments that are, or would be, affected by the issue or policy to make recommendations for appropriate action. After reviewing the responses of the agencies, the Policy Coordinating Committee (PCC) formulates a draft interagency response and sends it to the Deputies Committee for further debate and consideration and if necessary to the Principals Committee or to the full NSC.[9]

After all this detailed committee and council consideration and debate a decision is made by the president (not the council itself, which is, again, a recommending body) and then is announced in the form of a National Security Directive (NSD) to the various agencies. The NSD prescribes the policies and actions the president wishes implemented and assigns responsibilities and allocates resources accordingly. (It should be noted that, although the foregoing descriptions and labels were those in effect in the Bush administration, with minor variations they describe the essence of the process which was also followed by the preceding five administrations.)

To give a further hypothetical example of the way the NSC process works, let us assume that the foreign minister of country *X* in Southeast Asia lets it be known to the American ambassador that, in view of troubled relations with a neighbor strongly supported by China, his country would like to discuss military cooperation, perhaps to include military assistance from the United States, joint U.S.–*X* military exercises, and U.S. base rights within *X*. Passed back through diplomatic channels, undoubtedly with accompanying views from the Ambassador, such a message would trigger preliminary discussions among Department of State, Defense, and NSC officials concerned with Southeast Asia, leading to an agreement that a PCC for East Asia should examine the matter.

At the subsequent PCC meeting will be assistant secretary–level officials from those same agencies, plus a representative from the CIA and perhaps one or two staff officers to back up each principal. The State Department will chair the meeting. From the DOD will be the assistant secretary for international security affairs or, more likely, his deputy for East Asia and Pacific affairs, plus a general from the joint staff—perhaps the three-star officer who is director of the joint staff for plans and policy or his deputy. State may well have representatives from its Politico-Military Affairs and Security Assistance offices, as well as the assistant secretary for East Asia and Pacific Affairs, who will be chairing the session.

After discussing the elements in the foreign minister's message and their bearing on U.S. interests, the participants turn to the bureaucratic problem: Who initiates the draft interagency study? What division of labor is called for in the memorandum? and What should the general content be? A joint drafting team from the State Department and the DOD is finally decided upon. After several days' or even weeks' work in the various departments and by the drafting team, a draft is developed, circulated for coordination, and forwarded to the deputy assistant to the president for national security.

Meanwhile, the secretary of state will have been informed of this potentially important development (as will the other cabinet-level officials) and he may choose to mention it to the president as an information item, noting that a draft study is being prepared. The assistant for national security will likely also take the information to the president. The president, if he approves of the initiative, will sign and issue an NSSD, or he will direct the assistant for national security affairs to issue it in his name.

The NSSD, which will be classified at least secret, will go to each of the agencies represented in the PCC and, since there will be budgetary implications, will also probably go to the Office of Management and Budget (OMB). (If so, the OMB will ask to be represented in the various study and drafting exercises necessary to respond to the NSSD.) Upon receipt of the NSSD, which will define rather precisely the nature of the problem to be reviewed and indicate which agency is to take the lead and which may indicate subtasks to be accomplished, each agency will designate appropriate officials to work on the study. At the CIA, the National Intelligence Estimate dealing with *X* will be reviewed, and a special updated and newly focused version of it may be issued. In the Pentagon, the joint staff and OSD's International Security Affairs (ISA) office will each begin work; they may at various junctures consolidate, or at least coordinate, their efforts. The joint staff will be calling on the military services for input as well as undertaking staff work on its own. The air force, for example, will be asked to set forth the type of joint air exercise which would be desirable, the kind of basing arrangement which might be useful, and the type of air force equipment which might be provided in any military assistance program.

In the Department of State (which we will assume is designated the lead agency) not only will the various concerned bureaus begin studying the problem and developing issues, but—at some juncture—the topic of allied involvement will also be addressed. When and how should the Japanese be briefed? What, if anything, should be asked of them? How will South Korea react? Can it play a constructive role, and how should its involvement be managed? What of China? What of ASEAN? State will also be responsible for informing the appropriate congressional committees and for maintaining communication with leading members of the Senate and House and their key aides as the study proceeds.

Without unduly drawing out this example, we can begin to sense the complexity of the decision process. As the NSSD process nears completion and the PCC, deputies, principals, and perhaps NSC meetings held, the president reaches a decision and issues an NSD. The underlying situation in *X* may change or other complicating factors arise. It is not surprising that the entire decision process generally takes many weeks, often months. Indeed, in a few cases, NSSDs finally expire with no NSD result. Conversely, there are also NSDs issued occasionally, without any underlying NSSD and study; in such instances, if the NSD is a substantive one, either time pressure or familiarity with the issue, or both, induced the president to go directly to an NSD without the intervening interagency work.

The Bureaucracy. The preceding description of the NSC system as a relatively neat and orderly procedure for national security decision-making is apt to convey an erroneous picture of clarity when in fact clarity often does not exist. The NSC serves as a coordinating and advisory body near the center of the policy-making process, but beyond it, in the next ring, lie much larger and more complex organizations. This is the ring of the bureaucracy—the so-called permanent government composed largely of career civil servants, Foreign Service officers, and the military who work in the many agencies involved in the daily conduct of national security policy. One need only glance at an organization chart of the State Department's 25,000 personnel or the DOD's 750,000 civilian personnel worldwide to realize that the NSC forms only the tip of a huge bureaucratic iceberg.

All of the departments, agencies, and offices in the bureaucratic ring participate to some degree in national security decision-making, for they are the ones conducting the daily business of national security. They develop most of the information and analyses that go into decision-making and, equally or more importantly, implement the decisions when they are finally made. Most of the input to NSC studies normally comes from these organizations. It is in this ring that weapons systems are conceived and compared, policy options are formulated, and many of the ordinary or "less important" decisions are made. Much of the budget process described in Chapter 9, for instance, is routinely conducted at this level of the policy process.

For the purposes of studying national security decision-making it is unnecessary to deal with each bureaucracy separately. However, they exhibit important common characteristics. Each of the organizations involved is distinct in that it has a defined mission that contributes to the overall national security goal. These organizational missions are continuing in nature; indeed, the perceived requirement to deal with recurring events or problems is the fundamental reason for establishing bureaucratic organizations.

While distinct, the missions of the organizations are usually stated in rather general or ambiguous terms with considerable latitude for interpretation. The air force, for example, is charged with the mission of "providing an Air Force that is capable, in conjunction with the other armed forces, of preserving the peace and security of the United States." Some organizational missions, such as those of each of the armed services, require development of large capabilities for policy implementation; others, for example, the DOD's Office of Program Analysis and Evaluation, require capabilities primarily for research, analysis, evaluation, and planning.*

Once created, organizations tend to take on a life of their own. They develop subunits to carry out portions of the mission, develop standard operating procedures, establish coordinating mechanisms, and recruit and train personnel. The organizations, although usually headed by a presidential political appointee, are

*The rational actor and bureaucratic politics models are not mutually exclusive perspectives on the decision process. As noted in Chapter 9, a rational decision process, such as systems analysis, still takes place with a political context. The bureaucratic politics model envisions "players in position" attempting to achieve goals and interests through political bargaining; each player's goals or objectives, however, may reflect at least an intuitive process of rational analysis.

staffed with career civil and military officials. As issues appear and disappear and as presidents come and go, these career officials of the organizations do not.[10] They owe their prospects for success and promotion to the organization and develop a sense of loyalty to it.

Typically, career officials are experts in some aspects of their organization's mission and have a relatively narrow organizational outlook, focusing upon the unique importance of their organization to the overall national security mission. In their view, national security can be improved primarily through improvements in their organization or agency. The essence of this organizational perspective is captured by Alain Enthoven's description of the "bomber general":

> Picture if you will, a man who has spent his entire adult life in the Air Force, flying bombers and leading bomber forces. Bombers are his professional commitment and his expertise. His chances for promotion, public recognition, and success, and those of the officers serving under him, are largely tied to the continued importance of bombers. He believes strongly in what he is doing, that is one of the main reasons he does it well.[11]

Each of the many organizations seeks to be "successful," but success for a government agency is not an easily defined or measured concept. Unlike their business counterparts, government organizations have no product that can be priced and sold for profit on an open market. A dollar measure can be applied to tanks and airplanes in terms of cost, but not to their final product—national security. Success tends to be measured indirectly, through surrogate means. For example, unable to give a viable definition of "victory" in the traditional sense during the Vietnam War, U.S. government organizations substituted such measures of progress as "body count," weapons captured, tons of bombs dropped, hamlets "secured," and so on. We know in retrospect that those numbers were all poor measures of American success. The true measure of success was achievement of or failure to meet the national objective—a self-determined government of Vietnam, free from communist coercion.

Another bureaucratic measure of organizational "success" is size; a successful organization is one that is growing, usually in terms of budget and personnel. Organizational growth implies increasing capabilities and greater importance in decision-making and implementation. Morale is tied to these measures of organizational success because career personnel perceive their own chances for influence, promotion, and "success" augmenting as the size of their agency increases. (Yet, most successful business managers would agree that organizational size must be geared to output measured in terms of quality and quantity of product, with a bottom line of profit margin. Hence, the objective in the private sector is the smallest and most efficient organizational size possible as a factor of profitability.) In the early 1990s, morale in the armed forces plummeted as the Department of Defense instituted a twenty-five percent reduction in the size of the military. Ironically, this cut was made possible because of the military's successful contribution to the national objective of winning the cold war against the Soviet Union, so that now U.S. interests could be protected with a smaller force.

Organizations seek autonomy; that is, they seek to be as independent as possible from higher authority and safe from threats to their missions and capabilities.

> Career officials of an organization believe that they are in a better position than others to determine what capabilities they should have and how they should best fulfill their mission. They attach very high priority to controlling their own resources so that these can be used to support the essence of the organization. They wish to be in a position to spend money allocated to them in the way they choose, to station their manpower as they choose, and to implement policy in their own fashion. They resist efforts by senior officials to get control of their activities.[12]

Organizations pursuing their own interests frequently come into conflict with one another on national security issues. An NSSD that directs an overall review of military force posture in Europe could be viewed by the army as a threat to the size of its forces there and by the air force as an opportunity to increase the relative role of air power. The State Department's Bureau of European Affairs may see any force reduction as a threat to good relations with European allies, while the Treasury Department might see a force reduction as a possible means to improve the U.S. balance of payments position vis-à-vis Europe. Each organization's response to an NSSD will be designed both to further the national interest and to protect the organization's interests. This quest for security of organizational interests provides a link between the inner and outer rings of the policy-making circles where organizations find support for their positions in the Congress, the media, among interest groups, or in the public at large.

Of course, organizations are not monoliths, and intraorganizational issues are sometimes played out in larger circles. Early in 1992, the Department of Defense geared up to protect its base force, that is, the force structure the Chairman of the JCS and the Secretary of Defense felt was necessary to protect American interests in the post–cold war era. This base force, which was about 75 percent of the size of the cold war force, was originally developed after the collapse of the Warsaw Pact but before the disintegration of the Soviet Union. It came under increasing attack in late 1991 after the breakup of the Soviet Union. The chairmen of both the House and Senate Armed Services Committees agreed that the base force was too large and that it should be reduced significantly. Within the Pentagon, the undersecretary of defense (policy) and the vice-chairman of the JCS developed force planning guidance built around six possible scenarios to justify the base force. In late February 1992, when the document was circulated within the government for comment, someone opposed to the base force and a large post–cold war military leaked it to the *New York Times*. Publication of the document caused such an outcry in the United States and around the world that both the president and the Pentagon repudiated it. The document was "toned down" before it was formally approved by the Secretary of Defense in May 1992, thus ensuring that the base force would not fully survive.[13]

In sum, the national security decision-making process relies on bureaucracies for such critical tasks as providing information; identifying issues; formulating, analyzing, and evaluating alternatives; making decisions (within certain parameters); and implementing policy. Even when the focus of decision-making is the innermost circle, organizations still provide major inputs and must be relied upon to implement the policy.

Bureaucratic Politics. Thus far the description of national security decision-making has focused upon the NSC system and the bureaucracies operative therein. Decisions are made by people, however, and understanding decision-making necessitates taking account of decision-makers themselves. Bureaucratic politics, as this kind of analysis is named, explains national security decisions as "political resultants,"

> resultants in the sense that what happens is not chosen as a solution to a problem but rather results from compromise, conflict, and confusion of officials with diverse interests and unequal influence; political in the sense that the activity from which decisions and actions emerge is best characterized as bargaining along regularized channels among individual members of the government.[14]

Many individuals who play a role in national security decisions have independent sources of power. As noted earlier, the president shares power with Congress and the Supreme Court and, in less formal terms, with his advisers and executive appointees. The secretary of defense, for instance, is an independent power in his own right as the head of a very large organization with a very large budget, the national spokesman on defense issues, and a prominent public figure. He normally enjoys support from some legislators and from interest groups and the public at large.

An individual official's stand on a particular security issue will be determined by many factors, among which are personal analysis of information available, experience, psychological mind-sets or images, organizational interests, the formal position he or she occupies (whether inside or outside government), and personal interests. For critical decisions—those on issues posing the greatest threat to national security—images play a powerful role in determining the stand an individual takes. These images are the consequences of education, views of the world, values, past experience, and perceptions of national security interests.[15] President Bush, when informed of the Iraqi invasion of Kuwait in 1990, undoubtedly thought of past disastrous experiences with aggression in Ethiopia, Manchuria, and Austria. The lesson of those experiences seemed to be that aggression must be met with force, and this played a key part in his decision to respond quickly and with force.[16] Similarly, President Bush's decision to provide the military with clear objectives and then let them conduct the war in the Gulf in 1991 was a reflection of his belief that President Johnson had wrongly micromanaged the war in Vietnam. Finally, the military's desire to confront Saddam with overwhelming force (10 divisions, 10 air wings, 6 aircraft carrier battle groups, and 100 ships) and to call up the selected reserves was a product of their belief that gradual escalation and lack of public involvement contributed to the debacle in Vietnam.

An understanding of the personal images, or *Weltanschauung*, of particular decision-makers may be sufficient to predict outcomes for particular critical decisions, but for more routine decisions other factors may dominate a decision-maker's mind. Of course, routine items form the bulk of national security decisions. Individuals whose stand on an issue coincide with, and can be reliably predicted from, their positions within organizations can be considered "organizational actors," to use Graham Allison's phrase. ("Where you stand depends on where you sit" is a useful guide.) It is through these actors that the organizational interests discussed earlier are expressed in the decision-making and decision-implementing processes.

Influence in decision-making depends on what might be called individual and position variables. Individual variables include education, the ability to write, speak, and reason effectively, physical "presence," financial status, and personal relationships with other key individuals. Position variables include position within the governmental hierarchy, access to important information, and command of resources. James Baker's participation in and influence on events during President Bush's Gulf policy in 1990 and 1991 can be attributed not just to his position (Secretary of State) but to his long-time personal relationship with President Bush, which dated back to Bush's tenure as a congressman from Texas in the 1970s. Lieutenant Colonel Oliver North's influence on American policy toward the contras in Nicaragua emerged largely from his personal dynamism. Conversely, the power of the JCS to influence the START debate can generally be attributed not to individual factors but to the positions of its members. They command information and resources and are the military advisers to the president, the secretary of defense, the National Security Council, and Congress. These multiple roles give them great influence with many key decision-makers and the legal ability to appeal to different individuals if their advice is not heeded by one. Henry Kissinger's great influence in the early Nixon administration was a function of both his personal attributes and his position as assistant for national security affairs.

A key factor in explaining any decision will be the particular individuals who play a role in the process. To influence a decision an individual must have access to the decision-making body or decision-making channels. Decision-making channels are usually established in standing operating procedures (SOPs), used by large organizations to regularize the multitude of transactions that occur daily and to routinize or allocate authority for individual decisions on each transaction.

The NSC system specifies particular channels for many of the important decisions in national security policy. The NSSD process described earlier prescribes the "action channel" for other issues, when a special procedure or channel is not specified. An NSSD is directed to specific departments and agencies, which in turn delegate the study to internal groups or individuals, thus structuring further the decision-making channel. The flow of the NSSD up and down the chain gives all relevant members direct access to the channel. Individuals sometimes seek to avoid (or to restructure) certain decision-making channels to minimize what they perceive to be adverse factors; that is, they seek to speed actions or deny access to their bureaucratic adversaries. The Defense Policy Review Committee (DPRC) of Nixon's NSC serves as an example. The DPRC, chaired by Kissinger, was established to review the annual defense budget and to keep it compatible with foreign policy objectives.[17] The secretary of defense, however, who viewed the DPRC as an encroachment upon his prerogatives by Kissinger, did not cooperate or attend, and the committee quietly expired.

Personal relations among individuals from different agencies can create "informal action channels" that cut across or bypass formal channels or allow an individual access to a decision channel from which he or she might otherwise be excluded. Such relations, which are widespread, are especially important and heavily used when crucial, time-sensitive decisions are being made. Unfortunately, these relations facilitate what is called the "end run," by which an individual bypasses checks in the regular channels and goes directly to the president or other senior officials in hopes of avoiding some perceived disadvantage flowing from the regularized process.

The less time available and the more secrecy and sensitivity involved in a decision, the fewer the number of those who have access to the decision-making channel. On one or more of these grounds, some decision-makers will seek to exclude from action channels those whose views might be detrimental to their interests. (Also, they may plead secrecy or sensitivity to hide positions that, if made known publicly, might be unpopular or embarrassing.) Conversely, others with an interest in the outcome of a decision, but excluded from it, may "leak" it to the press, thereby drawing attention to the issue and introducing new or additional pressures on decision-makers.

As discussed above, those who disagreed with the Pentagon justification for the base force leaked it to the media in early 1992, in effect forcing the Bush administration to repudiate the document. Similarly, career officials upset by the Bush administration's support of Iraq up to the eve of the invasion of Kuwait informed Congress in late 1991 that the president had signed an NSD in October 1989 (NSD 26) to encourage arms sales to Baghdad.[18] In mid 1992, other officials, upset that the Bush administration was not acting vigorously enough to prevent proliferation of weapons of mass destruction, let the press know that the president had authorized only $20 million a year for the CIA to support the effort.[19]

Open disagreement with superiors, in which an official places his or her career on the line, may be disruptive of hierarchical control of the bureaucracy, but it can serve the national interest by providing a means of appeal to upper decision levels or the public on major issues. By contrast, the increasingly widespread practice of secretly leaking classified information is disloyal and holds unmitigated dangers. Left unchecked, it can, for example, make the keeping of vital secrets impossible and create distrust and paralysis within the decision-making process.[20]

Decision Implementation. Once a decision is made—even by the president of the United States—the decision process does not end. The critical task of implementation remains. An NSD may specify policy and actions, but, basically, implementation resides in the hands of the organizations of the third ring. Between the president and the final implementers of his decisions lie many levels of hierarchical control. At each level, there is a danger that a policy decision will be misunderstood—inadvertently or advertently. At each level, the individual responsible must understand the decision and then translate it into more specific directives for his or her own subordinates. If one assumes ninety percent accuracy of transmittal at each level and ten levels between the president and the person "in the field," there is less than a 35 percent chance—mathematically—that the person in the field will be directed as the president intended.

Neither the president nor his staff has the capacity to specify actions in such detail as to leave no room for manipulation or misunderstanding, nor is great specificity always desirable, since it would waste the expertise in problem solving and implementation that resides at lower levels. As a result, presidents are frequently frustrated by what comes out at the other end of the process. Even that most skillful of presidents, Franklin Roosevelt, remarked:

> The Treasury is so large and far-flung and ingrained in its practices that I find it is almost impossible to get the action and results I want—even with Henry [Morgenthau] there. But the Treasury is not to be compared with the State Department. You should go through the experience of trying to get any changes in the thinking, policy, and action of the career diplomats and then you'd know what a real problem was. But the Treasury and the State Department put together are nothing compared with the Na-a-vy. The Admirals are really something to cope with—and I should know. To change anything in the Na-a-vy is like punching a feather bed. You punch it with your right and you punch it with your left until you are finally exhausted, and then you find the damn bed just as it was before you started punching.[21]

The cabinet officers and other heads of agencies are appointed by the president, but they are responsible, as well, to Congress, to their staffs, to their "clients," and to themselves. The president appoints them mindful of the constraints of party and, in most cases, the advice and consent of the Senate, hoping that they bring to their positions personal views that are compatible with his own. Over time, however, even compatible heads of agencies tend to view issues from the particular perspectives of the organizations they head and on which their ability to function depends. A president can, of course, remove a recalcitrant agency head from office. But this action tends to reflect unfavorably on the president's initial decision to select the individual, and it also tends to antagonize the supporters of the individual in Congress, among interest groups, and the public. Simultaneous decapitation of several departments, such as President Carter executed in the summer of 1979, is bound to call into question the president's leadership ability, as public and congressional opinion at the time showed.[22]

Even if the president is ready to fire laggards, he cannot override most objections by fiat. As Richard Neustadt has observed, "Underneath our images of presidents-in-boots, astride decisions, are the half-observed realities of Presidents-in-sneakers, stirrups in hand, trying to induce particular department heads or Congressmen or Senators, to climb aboard."[23]

The media, in the outer policy circle, can also be a major problem in policy implementation. As Henry Kissinger has observed, any bureaucracy worth its salt has a considerable capacity to delay, attenuate, and obstruct; even more trying, it can leak confidential information to the press in an effort to reverse or weaken a decision it does not like. This latter difficulty, which has grown to serious proportions in the past decade or so, caused President Johnson to advise Kissinger, "Read the columnists, and if they call a member of your staff thoughtful, dedicated, or any other friendly adjective, fire him immediately. He is your leaker."[24]

"Even when the President does devote his time and effort and the issue is critical, disobedience or mishandling (of a presidential order) can occur."[25] During the Cuban Missile Crisis, president Kennedy allegedly was led to believe that U.S. forces were not in contact with Soviet forces, whereas, in fact, the U.S. Navy was forcing Soviet submarines to the surface in the Caribbean. President Kennedy ordered the navy to move the blockade closer to Cuba; the navy did not initially comply. He ordered the government to avoid provocative intelligence operations during the crisis, yet an American U-2 strayed over the Soviet Union at the peak of the crisis. Air Force planes located on bases in the southeastern United States were ordered dispersed; a subsequent aerial photograph flight ordered by the president showed the planes still lined up, wing tip to wing tip.[26]

In order to reduce the probability of faulty implementation, a president must get deeply involved—and early on—in a crisis; he must clearly articulate what he wants done. And he must have a thorough grasp of the capabilities and organizational routines of the participating bureaucratic players. As the Iran–Contra affair demonstrated, a president who distances himself too much from the implementation of policy creates problems both for himself and for his policies. In 1985 and 1986 President Reagan certainly wanted to use arms sales to Iran as a means of freeing American hostages in Lebanon. He also desperately wanted to keep the contras alive as a viable fighting force, at a time when Congress, through the Boland Amendment, cut off appropriation of funds for the Nicaraguan rebels. Through an extraordinary delegation of presidential authority over implementation of these policies, Reagan was apparently unaware that the Iran arms deal was handled by a network of dummy corporations and overseas bank accounts in private hands—and that profits from the arms sales were diverted to the contras.

Deep presidential involvement in a particular issue has high opportunity costs. In an environment of cascading deadlines and complex problems, the president seldom has the luxury of detailed involvement, full articulation of his program, or thorough oversight. Should he choose to dedicate himself to a particular policy issue, other programs and policies will not stand still. They too clamor for attention and, lacking presidential direction, they are a potential source of difficulty. President Bush and his national security team were so absorbed with the collapse of the Warsaw Pact and the unification of Germany in the first half of 1990 that they paid scant attention to Saddam Hussein's bellicose speeches and troop movements toward Kuwait until it was too late to stop the invasion. Similarly, in 1991, the president became so preoccupied with the Gulf war and its aftermath, that he seemed to be caught unprepared by the coup in the Soviet Union and the demise of President Gorbachev.

Yet the responsibilities of his office are so comprehensive and demanding that the president must order his priorities and focus his attention rather than let his energies be diffused. Of course, he must be prepared to refocus his attention and follow through actions as priorities and situations change. It is small wonder that the implementation of a policy is often as difficult and frustrating to a president as the development of that policy in the first place.

Conclusion. Two trends are apparent in surveying national decision-making and the actors and processes therein, namely, increasing centralization and the recently greatly strengthened role of Congress. The trend toward centralized control in the executive branch has been under way almost continuously since the National Security Act of 1947. This trend, which has been driven by the increased complexity and dangers of the nuclear age, has been fueled by the communications revolution that has permitted far greater central direction of large organizations than was possible in the past. It has occurred both within the individual departments and agencies in the decision-making process and also in the overall process itself. In this latter context, the increasingly dominant role of the NSC staff and the assistant to the president who heads it reached its natural limit in the Reagan administration when the role of the NSC adviser and the NSC staff itself grew to previously unimagined heights. Because of President Reagan's loose managerial rein and his preoccupation with secrecy, the NSC adviser became both policymaker and implementor, excluding even the statutory members of the NSC from the policy-making and implementing process. The result was an unsound, and illegal, policy conducted by the wrong part of government. When the policy and the policy process were exposed, the Assistant for National Security Affairs, Admiral John Poindexter, resigned, the NSC staff was reorganized, and a large number of staff members were replaced. Poindexter's immediate successor, Frank Carlucci, a man with wide government experience, promised to return the NSC to its traditional role as "a staff arm to the president in helping him make the necessary decisions in the foreign policy-national security area."[27] Brent Scowcroft, Bush's NSC adviser, has kept the NSC in this traditional role.

The increased power of Congress in national security affairs, one of the most striking developments since the latter 1960s, presents an interesting counterpoint. Not only does the congressional role blunt and diffuse the power of the president and his centralized decision-making apparatus, but it also represents a sharp contrast to that power in that the Congress has itself increasingly become decentralized in its decision-making. As party strength has declined and the authority of the committee chairmen dwindled, single-interest groups have multiplied and individual legislators have become less inclined to follow the leadership of the party and congressional leaders and the president.

The juxtaposition of these two trends poses the unwelcome prospect that throughout the 1990s the president and the Congress will continue to be at odds and that neither will be prepared to give way, short of major national emergencies such as the Gulf war. Indeed, one of the reasons for the Iran–Contra affair may have been the juxtaposition of these trends. The president and his advisers saw the Boland Amendment of 1984, which cut off aid to the contras from executive branch agencies, as an unwarranted intrusion into the president's authority in the field of national security, and they therefore sought ways to negate its impact. One of these methods was to argue that the amendment did not apply to the president or anyone working directly for him, that is, the NSC staff.

Discussion Questions

1. Presidents and high-level appointees come and go, but the career civil servants, the military, and the Foreign Service officers stay. What impact would you expect this to have on national security policy?

2. The NSC professional staff has always been relatively small (30 to 60 people) and has been composed of many relatively junior people who lack high-level experience in government. What are the good or bad points of this?

3. It is sometimes argued that the constraints imposed upon a president by Congress, by the public, and by a slow-moving bureaucracy virtually preclude anything but incremental changes in national security policy. To what extent is this true?

4. If bureaucratic politics characterizes decision-making and is a bargaining process among varying interests, is there anything in the system that ensures that appropriate interests have a voice? Who or what determines the weight of the different interests? Does the DOD have too much weight in the bargaining?

5. One critique of the "bureaucratic politics" of national security decision-making is that it obscures the power of the president and undermines the assumptions of democratic politics by relieving high officials of responsibility. Is this true? Are there offsetting beneficial effects from bureaucratic politics in the national security decision-making process?

6. Democracy is largely defined by the requirement that the ruled be able to hold their rulers accountable for their decisions and actions. Does the existing national security decision-making machinery degrade accountability? Can you suggest ways to alleviate the problem, to the extent that it exists?

7. Congress is formally excluded from the executive branch *policy formulation* process. Would the system work more smoothly if Congress were included earlier in the policy formulation process? Given the inevitable tension between the legislative and executive branches, could such a system be made to work?

8. How can the problem of "leaks" be dealt with?

9. What are the lessons of the Iran–Contra affair for the national security decision-making process?

10. Does the end of the cold war imply the need for an overhaul of the NSC machinery?

Recommended Readings

Allison, Graham. *The Essence of Decision: Explaining the Cuban Missile Crisis*. Boston: Little, Brown, 1971.

Enthoven, Alain C., and Smith, K. Wayne. *How Much Is Enough?* New York: Harper & Row, 1971.

Fallows, James. *National Defense*. New York: Random House, 1981.

Haig, Alexander M. *Caveat: Realism, Reagan, and Foreign Policy*. New York: Macmillan, 1984.

Halperin, Morton H. *Bureaucratic Politics and Foreign Policy*. Washington, D.C.: Brookings Institution, 1974.

Hunter, Robert E. *Presidential Control of Foreign Policy: Management or Mishap?* CSIS Washington Papers no. 91. New York: Praeger, 1982.

Huntington, Samuel P. *The Common Defense*. New York: Columbia University Press, 1961.

Mann, Thomas, ed. *A Question of Balance: The President, Congress, and Foreign Policy*. Washington, D.C.: Brookings Institution, 1990.

Nash, Henry T. *American Foreign Policy: Response to a Sense of Threat*. Homewood, Ill.: Dorsey Press, 1973.

Report of the President's Special Review Board. Washington, D.C.: U.S. Government Printing Office, 1987 (Tower Commission).

Stubbing, Richard A. *The Defense Game*. New York: Harper & Row, 1986.

III

Issues of National Strategy

11

Nuclear Strategy

For forty years, nuclear strategy formed the backbone of Western defense policy. Unable to match the former Soviet Union's conventional strength, the United States and its North Atlantic Treaty Organization (NATO) and, to a lesser extent, Asian allies used the threat of nuclear escalation to help avert what they perceived to be a serious risk of Soviet adventurism. In support of this policy, the United States and its allies built tens of thousands of strategic and tactical nuclear weapons and deployed them in Europe, Korea, and at sea. The policy had its risks—indeed some believed that the nuclear arms race placed the very survival of the human race in jeopardy—but Western leaders thought the threat justified the risk.

By the early 1990s, everything had changed. The Soviet Union had collapsed, the cold war was over, and the West's need for nuclear deterrence had dramatically declined. One of the key questions of nuclear strategy became not how many new weapons are needed, but how few. Many nuclear strategists were beginning to question whether the weapons served peace at all, whether their purpose of rendering major war obsolete had been overtaken by events.

As with any such theoretical questions, it is impossible to know for sure. What is possible, however, is to examine the issues involved in nuclear strategy and the choices faced by nuclear policymakers today. This chapter will briefly survey the role played by nuclear weapons during the cold war, and will proceed to examine their place in U.S. national security policy in the 1990s and beyond.

Nuclear Strategy During the Cold War. During the cold war, the United States was the undisputed leader of the free world. It was the principal guardian of Western Europe, the Middle East, Northeast Asia, and other regions against communist incursions. Its nuclear arsenal was the linchpin of containment, providing military strength and deterrence that buttressed U.S. and NATO conventional strength and political unity. On many occasions the United States enunciated or became party to doctrines explicitly relying on the threat of nuclear war to achieve U.S. aims. The predictable result was the deployment of a vast U.S. nuclear arsenal—more than 12,000 strategic warheads, thousands of tactical weapons studded throughout Europe and the Far East, superaccurate counterforce weapons and the satellites and command systems to help guide them, heavy bombers to penetrate enemy airspace, and, today, the planned deployment of strategic defenses.

There are two basic theories on how to deter an opponent from starting a nuclear war. Both recognize that nuclear war is a wholly unlikely contingency. But the strength of deterrence might be tested in a crisis—such as the Cuban Missile Crisis of 1962 or the Suez Crisis of 1973—when tensions and emotions are running high.

''Assured destruction'' holds that, as long as each side is capable of responding in kind to a nuclear attack, the nuclear balance is relatively stable, because any aggressor would know that an attack would be suicidal. Assured destruction stresses the importance of a ''secure retaliatory force''—a nuclear force that can withstand an enemy attack and hit back. If successful on both sides, this strategy establishes a situation of mutually assured destruction (MAD), in which neither side can rationally start a war because both are vulnerable to retaliation. In assured destruction–type strategies retaliation is often in part aimed at civilian targets, such as cities and industries; in other words, it has some elements of a countervalue (i.e., anticity or antiindustry) targeting scheme. Assured destruction does not demand a nuclear arsenal capable of destroying enemy nuclear forces.

A ''counterforce'' or ''war-fighting'' nuclear strategy, on the other hand, is much more ambitious than assured destruction; it holds that in order to deter an opponent, whose leaders might believe a nuclear war could be fought and won, the United States must be able, not merely to retaliate, but to prevail over an opponent in a nuclear conflict. Such a strategy requires numerous big and accurate weapons capable of knocking out enemy nuclear forces, as opposed to a few bombs to drop on enemy industries or cities. Counterforce strikes could be aimed at either nuclear or nonnuclear targets, but it is most commonly associated with counternuclear strikes.

One common analogy for the nuclear age is of two people with guns pointed at one another's heads. In the context of that image, assured destruction would have each side merely watch and wait and promise to pull the trigger if the other side does. Counterforce advocates say such a mutual suicide pact may not be credible, and argue that each side must prepare to win a gun duel rather than merely fire back. The distinction is between deterrence by threatening punishment and deterrence by preparing to win a conflict.

The earliest nuclear war plans, partly because of the small number of bombs available and partly due to their perceived destructiveness, emphasized countervalue targeting of Soviet cities. President Harry Truman saw little value in nuclear weapons and placed most of his emphasis on arms control with such initiatives as the Baruch plan. The earliest targeting guides such as the 1945 plans "Totality" and "The Strategic Vulnerability of Russia to a Limited Air Attack" called merely for a couple of dozen or so bombs to be dropped on Soviet cities. Civilian control of nuclear weapons was absolute; it was not until 1948 that the military was allowed to formulate plans for the use of nuclear weapons, and even then President Truman retained personal control of them.[1]

Eventually, however, even Truman redoubled U.S. production of nuclear weapons and began admitting some military control.[2] And once given the right to formulate nuclear options, the new Strategic Air Command rushed headlong into plans to destroy Soviet war-making potential. To many military men, the notion of deterrence by threatening punishment made little sense; if hostilities were to come, the aim should be to win. The August 1949 Soviet test of an atomic bomb, by opening the possibility of Soviet nuclear strikes on the United States, lent new urgency to plans for attacking Soviet nuclear weapons. By 1956–1957 the Soviet Union was expected to possess up to 250 bombs; the stockpiles, production facilities, and bomber delivery vehicles became the chief targets of the U.S. nuclear force.[3]

Publicly, this trend was not evident. John Foster Dulles formally endorsed massive retaliation in 1954, and U.S. public statements still stressed a general retaliation against Soviet society. Yet already counterforce targeting had begun, and the list of target priorities would remain essentially unchanged to the present day. In the August 1950 Shakedown plan, first priority was given to "the destruction of known targets affecting the Soviet capacity to deliver atomic bombs."[4] The 1950–1952 Joint Chiefs of Staff plans BRAVO, DELTA, and ROMEO emphasized similar priorities; as Michael Nacht has recognized, "The principal targets were counterforce (military forces) and urban—industrial (factories), not civilian population centers."[5] By the late 1950s, the push to target the Soviet military was in full force, and Defense Secretary Thomas Gates spelled out the implications: "We are adjusting our power to a counterforce theory," he said. "We are not basing our requirements on just bombing Russia for retaliatory purposes."[6]

From the beginning, U.S. military planners sought two primary goals with counterforce strategies. One was damage limitation. By hitting Soviet nuclear assets, U.S. planners contended, the United States could prevent their being launched against its territory and thus limit damage to itself. While few official U.S. publications advocate it, damage limitation has long been an implicit U.S. goal. "The counterforce strategy," concludes Michael Intrilligator, "is one of damage limitation."[7]

A second rationale for counterforce was that credibility was essential in threatening nuclear escalation in Europe's defense. Early on, U.S. and NATO officials recognized that they would be unable to match Soviet conventional force levels in Europe, and they looked to nuclear weapons as the absolute deterrent.

But if the United States were to use nuclear weapons in response to a Soviet conventional invasion of Europe, it would have to have something to hit with those weapons, something that would not call down an immediate Soviet retaliation on U.S. cities. As Scott Sagan argues, "The extended deterrent commitment" therefore became, and remains, "an important driving force behind U.S. counterforce capabilities."[8] This so-called extended deterrence began as early as 1948, with the deployment of B-29 bombers to Germany, and emerged fully during the Eisenhower administration.

The people who target U.S. weapons have apparently never aimed all or nearly all of them at Soviet nuclear forces; the U.S. target mix, by all unclassified indications, contains a mix of counterforce and countervalue targets, and counterforce itself is divided between nuclear and nonnuclear aim points. Thus, Philip Bobbitt has commented that it is "unhelpful" to characterize U.S. nuclear war plans as either countervalue or counterforce "when every United States war plan has necessarily included important elements of both these target types."[9] Two other analysts concluded in a 1986 study that the Single Integrated Operational plan (SIOP) "to this day appears to be dominated by urban industrial targets."[10]

Over time, however, the trend has apparently been to include larger numbers of counterforce (specifically nuclear) targets and to give them higher priority than other targets. While U.S. targeting strategy was not based only on counterforce targets, its intent was deterrence by denial, and the key elements of such a strategy remained attacking enemy nuclear forces. In short, U.S. strategy was primarily, though not solely, counterforce in character.

The Kennedy administration and Defense Secretary Robert McNamara pursued this same strategy and did so in part by replacing the spasmodic attacks of massive retaliation with flexible strategies of counterforce targeting. The Kennedy administration's nuclear war plans supposedly emphasized multiple options and flexibility. The further reliance on counterforce also stemmed from a growing ability to find and destroy Soviet nuclear forces: The United States had nuclear superiority, and because it possessed enough weapons to allocate to Soviet nuclear forces and because of developments in satellite technology the U.S. military was able to locate and target Soviet forces better than it had in the past. Some have termed the resulting nuclear strategy "flexible counterforce."

Domestic and international public opinion, however, quickly forced the Kennedy administration to retreat from public statements on flexible options. Some observers in the United States viewed the counterforce strategy as suggestive of an intent to launch a first strike at the Soviet Union. As might be expected, Moscow condemned the doctrine as provocative and dangerous. Ironically, American allies expressed their doubts about a strategy that contemplated fighting limited nuclear wars to avoid a spasmodic launch in Europe's defense.

Between 1964 and 1966, then, U.S. public policy shifted back to a modified version of assured destruction. Importantly, however, the concept of damage limitation had been appended to that strategy, and actual war plans did not revert to massive retaliation—they changed little, retaining flexible options of nuclear employment.

Nixon administration policies built upon these notions of flexible employment. Again a distinction emerged between publicly stated strategies and actual ones: Public opposition to counterforce targeting strategies forced Nixon to adhere to a variant of assured destruction called "strategic sufficiency"—a more limited doctrine than war-fighting which aimed at some ambiguous notion of "enoughness" rather than superiority—but in fact his administration accelerated the trend toward counterforce. Kissinger's National Security Study Memorandum 3 (NSSM-3), requested the day after Nixon's inauguration in 1969, was partly designed, as he put it, to "kill assured destruction" and establish the need for limited nuclear options and escalation control. A series of Nixon directives, including National Security Decision Memorandum 242 (NSDM-242) of January 1974 and the first Nuclear Weapons Employment Policy guide (NEUWEP-1) of April 1974, reflected these goals. So did Nixon's decisions on nuclear weapons; counterforce strategies encouraged development of both the MIRV and ABM systems.

The Carter administration left untouched much of the basis of NSDM-242 and NEUWEP-1, which were reaffirmed in Carter's Presidential Directive 18 (PD-18) of August 1977. Carter pushed this trend forward in July 1979 with PD-59, which discussed a variety of scenarios for limited conflict. This approach argued more forcefully than ever for a third justification for counterforce: it was necessary, Carter strategists contended, to adopt a policy of simple deterrence.[11]

U.S. nuclear forces had always had as a primary mission the deterrence of Soviet attack, but now Carter's officials argued that an ability to *fight* a nuclear war was an integral aspect of deterrence. Hawkish Western Sovietologists had by the late 1970s solidified the case that Soviet military men believed that their combination of heavy ICBMs and an evolving strategic defense allowed them to fight and win a nuclear war against the United States. U.S. planners concluded that they must threaten Soviet leaders with death and defeat, not just destruction, to deter them adequately, and counterforce capabilities would promote those goals. This was not a novel argument (Henry Kissinger had concluded in the early 1970s that the Soviets did not believe in assured destruction), but Carter's officials placed renewed emphasis on it.

By 1983, when the Reagan administration instituted its nuclear war plan (the sixth version of the SIOP), publicly available information indicated that counterforce targets dominated U.S. retaliatory plans. As documented in numerous books and articles during the early 1980s, U.S. planning to fight and win a nuclear war (and as a result the U.S. emphasis on the counternuclear aspects of counterforce) reached a peak during the early Reagan years.[12] Many proponents of Reagan's Strategic Defense Initiative (SDI) made their case in a counterforce context, arguing that missile defenses were necessary to deny Soviet war aims. The consensus that the United States continues to pursue some form of counterforce targeting is complete. Some reports suggest that Bush administration strategists had at first favored an even greater effort in that direction.

The Roles of Nuclear Weapons after the Cold War. Much has changed, of course, since the mid 1980s. The cold war is over; the former Soviet military threat is of little concern. Theoretically, Russia still possesses the capability to destroy the United States in a matter of hours with its huge nuclear arsenal, but no one believes Russian leadership has the slightest desire to do so. Nuclear policies in the 1990s are being directed to dismantling nuclear forces, not building them up or making threats of their use more credible.

This change in context requires a complete reexamination of the role of nuclear weapons in U.S. national security policy. For what does the United States need a nuclear arsenal today? Any answer to this question must begin at the most fundamental level: the role of nuclear weapons in U.S. geostrategy.

In the end, all decisions on nuclear weapons, nuclear strategy, and nuclear arms control flow—or should flow—from a nation's view of the roles those weapons play in its foreign and defense policies. If national leaders burden their nuclear forces with broad and difficult missions, then those forces will probably need to be large, flexible, and deadly. Minimal roles for nuclear weapons, on the other hand, require only minimal forces in terms of both size and capabilities. And the roles of nuclear weapons are in turn a subset of the roles a given nation and its armed forces play in the world community. The international context that gave rise to cold war arsenals has crumbled along with the former Soviet Union. U.S. officials and academics are rethinking the roles nuclear weapons must play. Different observers have come to very disparate conclusions, in part because of differing views of the U.S. role in the post–cold war world.

For some, the U.S. world role has in fact not changed that much from the cold war. Believing that the United States remains at the helm of world politics and that, even after the Soviet collapse, the world remains a very dangerous place, such analysts see little alternative to an energetic U.S. foreign and defense policy. In their view Europe and Japan cannot be expected to guard the free world's interests, and the United States must retain an assertive, often unilateralist approach to world affairs. Such thinkers are skeptical of the promise offered by collective security; references to the "anarchic world system" are common, as are warnings of the danger that a nationalistic, revanchist Russia could rise from the ashes of the Soviet Union.

For these observers, nuclear weapons must continue to serve numerous roles in an assertive U.S. foreign and defense policy. A good example of such thinking in the early 1990s was a report prepared by a study group working for the Strategic Air Command designed to help guide policy on nuclear weapons within the Department of Defense. "This is a time of soaring hope," the report suggests. "It is also a time of great uncertainty and latent danger. Not only has history resumed the sense of national and ethnic rivalries which were overshadowed by the Cold War, but nuclear weapons remain a fact of life." And the United States must bear the primary burden of responding to these uncertainties: "America is the only modern state," its primary authors, Thomas Reed and Michael Wheeler, contend, "which derives its influence from a broad base of military, economic, and cultural power. As such, America exercises a unique leadership role that cannot be assumed by any other single nation in the foreseeable future."[13]

The report is typical of this school of thinking in its fear of a Russian military threat succeeding the Soviet one in the next century. Supporters of a prominent U.S. nuclear posture point to other risks as well—the proliferation of weapons of mass destruction, for example, will pose an increasing threat to the United States and its allies and interests. Many cautious analysts today point to the growing need for nuclear deterrence in the Third World, where aggressive regimes such as Iraq and North Korea are striving for nuclear, chemical, and biological arsenals of their own.

In order to help deter and, if necessary, defeat these threats, these thinkers urge the United States to deploy relatively large nuclear forces (roughly one-third to one-half the size of those maintained during the cold war) and to plan for them to be employed in a variety of circumstances. Most fundamental, of course, is deterrence of the one existing threat to the U.S. homeland—the former Soviet nuclear arsenal. Ambitious nuclear planners suggest that the means of deterrence have in fact changed little from the cold war, as we will see in subsequent discussions on nuclear strategy.

In stark contrast to the preceding, assertive vision of U.S. world leadership, another school of thinkers—proponents of minimum deterrence policies and small nuclear forces—view the end of the cold war as a promising time for the United States to give up its dominant role in world affairs and assume a more modest position. The general world view of most thinkers in this second school is either isolationist or distinctly multilateralist; most believe that the United States can and must cede some of its authority as leader of the free world to other states, notably Germany and Japan.

In large part the declining need for U.S. leadership is traceable to the lack of a major threat to world order. Unlike the first school, these modest nuclear strategists reject the notion that a resurgent Russia could become a major threat to the West any time soon. "While still possessing formidable inventories of nuclear and conventional weapons," write Carl Kaysen, Robert S. McNamara, and George W. Rathjens in the decade's first prototypical minimalist essay,

> the Soviet state shows no will to use its military power externally, and almost certainly lacks the political coherence to do so. An immediate external threat appears to be the only circumstance that would change that situation, and it is hard to see whence one would arise. Even the failure of perestroika and a retreat from glasnost led by a new military-authoritarian regime would not constitute the powerful, ideologically driven opponent supported by East European allies that the United States saw from 1945 through much of the last decade.[14]

The only role for nuclear weapons today, this second school of thinking concludes, is to deter a direct nuclear attack upon the United States. Given the absence of any nation hoping to launch such an attack, this task—commonly referred to as "simple" or "central" deterrence—is not very difficult. Most such thinkers call for a shift to some form of minimum or "finite" deterrence, and they are fond of pointing to estimates like the one that even a 100-megaton attack—roughly 150 to 200 total warheads given today's common yields—on nonnuclear military targets in the United States would kill between 11 and 29 million people and cause between 23 and 35 million total casualties.[15] Given the risk of such massive devastation, minimalists do not see the need for large nuclear forces or extensive doctrines.

Most of these more minimalistic nuclear thinkers did not shift to this system of beliefs because the cold war ended; they always denigrated the role of nuclear weapons in U.S. foreign and defense policy. Many had long argued for a reduced U.S. role in the world, in part because they believed that the Soviet Union, contrary to the dire warnings of cold warriors, never had much intention of marching West in any case. The task of preserving peace was further eased by the nature of the "nuclear revolution," as Robert Jervis phrased it: MAD was the inescapable fact of the nuclear age, minimalists contended; it made nuclear war unimaginably destructive and hence out of the question as a policy option; and any doctrines predicated on the need to win, or to threaten to win, a nuclear war were at best foolish and at worst dangerous.[16]

That this basic line of thinking is not new is demonstrated by a quote from Robert McNamara, a statement made in the midst of cold war hostility: "nuclear weapons serve no military purpose whatsoever," he wrote unequivocally. "They are totally useless—except to deter one's opponent from using them."[17] And in particular, such analysts would reject significant roles for U.S. nuclear weapons in the Third World, arguing that deterrence and retaliation can be performed by other weapons.

Shattering the Crystal Ball? There is a broader question that relates to any discussion of the role of nuclear weapons in international politics: Does the very existence of nuclear weapons prevent major war? If so, there may be a case for preserving their helpful effects by avoiding too deep reductions. A recent study on the Cuban Missile Crisis, for example, argues that

> [c]aution was the byword right from the discovery of the [Soviet] missiles. The fear generated by *nuclear* danger was obviously behind it. . . . Feared nuclear inadvertence was in that instance the fear of a process and an outcome that was abhorred by both sides, thus creating a *de facto* but powerful common enemy against which both sides must unite to keep the nuclear crystal ball from shattering.

Without the "fear of nuclear inadvertence," the author concludes, "it would have been almost impossible to have had a settlement of the Cuban missile crisis with only one death."[18]

But not everyone agrees, and thinking on this argument is not split evenly between the two schools summarized above. Some of each school admire the peace promoted by nuclear risk, while others reject the crystal ball effect as unhelpful or unnecessary.

It is of course impossible to prove whether nuclear weapons were or were not essential ingredients in keeping the peace during the long cold war. There are simply too many variables involved to explain the post-1945 era of nuclear peace with an "essential" factor. But it is equally impossible to prove the opposite—

that the cold war would have remained cold without the dampening effect of the mutual capability for annihilation. Perhaps luckily, the issue will not be tested for some time: most calculations suggest that a level of assured destruction can be achieved at about 300 to 600 warheads, and it may be decades before the United States, Russia, China, and other nuclear powers are willing to go that low. In the meantime, the progress of world politics is likely to decide whether or not nuclear weapons will be needed to help deter major war. One can only hope that the growth of democratic, stable nations will be matched by increasingly powerful world bodies capable of dispute resolution, crisis management, and, if necessary, defense against threats to the world order. In such a context, the "nuclear crystal ball" could safely be packed up and stored away.

Targeting Strategy. A key rung on the ladder of nuclear policy is targeting strategy. Once one decides what nuclear weapons must do, one can begin allocating them to potential targets located within a possible adversary's territory. During the cold war, this process was straightforward: U.S. targeteers filled their lists with thousands of Soviet (and some Chinese) nuclear weapons sites, leadership bunkers, military bases and industries, and general industrial targets. As indicated earlier, by all unclassified accounts, U.S. targeting policy has for years been a mix of counterforce (targeting Soviet nuclear weapons, leadership, and some conventional forces to suggest to the generals in the Kremlin that they might actually lose a nuclear war) and countervalue (shooting at industries and other urban-industrial targets at the core of Soviet society). Especially during the 1980s, the balance became tipped heavily in the favor of counterforce, which officials of the Reagan administration viewed as necessary to deter Moscow's presumed nuclear war–fighters.

More-ambitious nuclear planners of the maximalist school continue to argue, as they always have, for such counterforce capabilities and war-fighting plans. If such doctrines were necessary in the cold war to deter Soviet military leaders by "denying their war aims," threatening their leadership and silo reload capability,[19] then similar strategies would be useful to deter a possibly hostile Russia. Supporters of minimum deterrence, on the other hand, object strongly to counterforce targeting, arguing that it is in counterforce and war-fighting policies that the real dangers of the nuclear age reside.

In this case, there may be a compromise alternative: "counterpower" targeting, a doctrine which targets opposing *nonnuclear* military forces. A mix of analysts from both primary schools of thought on nuclear deterrence support this proposition. It offers a number of advantages over both counterforce and countervalue. Because it does not threaten either side's nuclear deterrent, it is not destabilizing like counterforce; yet, as a specifically countermilitary strategy, it avoids some of the moral and credibility-related drawbacks of countervalue policies. Nor does it require a vast number of warheads. A finite set of 300 to 500 conventional military targets, for example, would capture the great majority of any nation's air, naval, and ground-force bases, ports, equipment storage sites, and key military industries. Whether this targeting approach can be sold in either the United States or Russia is an open question.

Numbers. Once a targeting strategy is chosen, strategists can proceed to the next step in their overall policy: determining how many nuclear weapons they need. The cold war's most dangerous aspect, the competition in nuclear arms between the United States and Soviet Union reportedly resulted in strategic arsenals of about 11,000 strategic warheads for the Soviet Union and roughly 12,000 for the United States. The START Treaty and subsequent nuclear weapons initiatives will lower these numbers considerably: once START, the September/October 1991 and January 1992 U.S. and Russian arms initiatives, and the June 1992 Bush–Yeltsin agreement are fully implemented, each side will have between 3,000 and 3,500 strategic nuclear weapons.

More and more, the debate over nuclear strategy during the early 1990s is collapsing into a discussion of numbers. The question of how many warheads the United States requires to fulfill its national security objectives is viewed as a fundamental test of one's view of the roles and purposes of nuclear weapons. The numbers proposed range from a few dozen to 5,000 or more, a gap which is the logical consequence of different assumptions about the mission that nuclear weapons should have in the future.

Interestingly, prior to the June 1992 Bush–Yeltsin summit—which set a limit of 3,000 to 3,500 strategic warheads—there appeared to be a growing consensus that the United States and Russia could and should cut to roughly 3,000 very quickly. As long ago as 1988, a report from the Brookings Institution identified the 3,000 level as one that could be made stable with the right combination of force structure and East–West amity, and since that time numerous observers have come together to propose near-term cuts to that level. Hence we found this number (or slightly less) mentioned by almost all writers on nuclear strategy.

Distinctions between various schools of thinking emerge more clearly when the numbers question is shifted into a longer-term perspective. To support their global targeting policies, counterforce doctrines, and extended deterrence pledges, more-conservative analysts were generally uncomfortable going below 3,000 or so warheads for the foreseeable, and perhaps indefinite, future. Indeed, some recommended retaining a force more on the order of 4,000 to 5,000 warheads for at least several years. For them, 3,000 warheads is a place to get to and stop, unless and until there obtains a U.S.–Russian relationship on a par with U.S. ties to France or Japan and the anarchic international system is brought under some control.

Advocates of more liberal arms control, on the other hand, view cuts to 3,000 warheads or even less as mere way stations on the road to truly minimal deterrence and, eventually, complete disarmament. Those who advocate very small nuclear forces tend to view the deterrent effect of even a few dozen nuclear bombs as sufficient. Their thinking is neatly encapsulated by a famous 1969 quote, widely cited in the minimalist literature, from McGeorge Bundy. Bundy, less than seven years after his sobering experience as National Security Adviser during the Cuban Missile Crisis, suggested that there is

> an enormous gulf between what political leaders really think about nuclear weapons and what is assumed in complex calculations of relative ''advantage'' in simulated strategic warfare. Think-tank analysts can set levels of ''acceptable'' damage well up in the tens of millions of lives. They can assume that the loss of dozens of great cities is somehow a real choice for sane men. They are in an unreal world. In the real world of real political leaders—whether here or in the Soviet Union—a decision that would bring even one hydrogen bomb on one city of one's own country would be recognized in advance as a catastrophic blunder; ten bombs on ten cities would be a disaster beyond history; and a hundred bombs on a hundred cities are unthinkable.[20]

Similarly, Carl Kaysen, Robert McNamara, and George Rathjens reject concerns that going to and well below 3,000 warheads would be destabilizing; they have ''no quarrel'' with Herbert York's suggestion (based on his ongoing research into minimum deterrence) that ''somewhere in the neighborhood of 100 weapons might be about right for each side.''[21] Various Russian analysts have proposed minimal deterrent postures of a few hundred or so weapons.

A moderate nuclear posture might roughly split the difference between these two schools and propose, as the 1991 National Academy of Sciences report does, a medium-term reduction to perhaps 1,000 to 2,000 warheads.[22] To nonspecialists—a group that includes most foreign leaders who may be looking to the U.S. nuclear arsenal as a sign of U.S. strength and influence—there may be something magical about the number 1,000. It seems solid, robust, able to mark off U.S. and Russian arsenals from those of the middle nuclear powers (China, France, and Britain). In ten or twenty years, if the positive trends in world politics are borne out, further reductions might be possible; and indeed many of those proposing a 1,000-warhead balance hope it will constitute an additional step toward very small forces. Advocates of extremely deep cuts consider nuclear balances in this range to be ''finite'' rather than ''minimal'' deterrent forces, because ''they would still be far larger than the minimum required to maintain the U.S.–Soviet mutual nuclear hostage relationship.''[23]

What is so far missing from the literature on numbers is a cogent discussion of the potential *value* of deep cuts. Historically, the strongest arguments for arms control have been that it would reduce the risk of war and contribute to an overall improvement in U.S.–Soviet relations. With these goals largely achieved, many in government and academia see little reason, beyond relatively small budget savings, to cut strategic nuclear weapons below 3,000 or so. National Security Advisor Brent Scowcroft recognized the issue—and betrayed a note of skepticism—in an October 1988 conference. ''We are asked,'' he said, '' . . . to take the value of deep reductions pretty much on faith.'' Scowcroft said his point ''is not to say that we are necessarily wrong [to propose deep cuts], but that the arguments in favor of this course seem singularly unpersuasive. What are the rewards of deep cuts which would lead us to undergo the kinds of risks they may present?''[24] Others contend that running such risks is less necessary than ever when the risk of war is so low; if there is no chance of their being used, what threat do nuclear weapons pose? Charles Glaser has suggested that, in a world of East–West amity, "once the superpowers resolve their disputes and develop confidence that these problems will remain resolved, there would be essentially no need to disarm." Fundamental improvements in U.S.–Russian relations, he contends, "greatly reduce the importance of disarming."[25] If the case for deep cuts is to gain intellectual momentum, these questions must be answered.

Force Structure. The next step in formulating a nuclear policy is to determine what types of nuclear forces best serve deterrence. Although both Russia and the United States have relied, and continue to rely, on a strategic triad of nuclear forces, the makeup of those triads differs substantially. Russia, a traditional land power, emphasizes the land-based component of its triad, intercontinental ballistic missiles (ICBMs); the United States, primarily a maritime and air power, deploys the majority of its weapons on submarines and bombers. Both nations face important choices about the makeup of their deterrent forces in the future, including whether a diad would suffice.

Debates about force structure tend to fracture the various schools of thinking on nuclear strategy. Much depends on the choice of a targeting strategy, for which a force structure has to be designed. A counterforce policy requires hard-target capable systems; traditionally these were thought to be ICBMs, new and highly accurate sea-launched ballistic missiles (SLBMs), and penetrating bombers, though more recently some analysts have made a case for a slower, more stable counterforce based on bombers and cruise missiles.[26] A countervalue policy would require relatively little in the way of accuracy. A policy of counterpower retaliation might again split the difference, requiring more flexibility and accuracy than city-busting countervalue warheads but far less than full-blown war-fighting plans.

Objective analysis aside, however, it seems likely that many force structure decisions will be made for budgetary and political reasons. For its part, the United States appears to be headed toward primary reliance on its strategic missile submarines as the basis of its secure deterrent. Some analysts have advocated such a course; the United States is firmly committed to banning multiple-warhead ICBMs, a provision included in the June 1992 Washington Summit Agreement; and in his 1992 State of the Union address, President Bush announced the final cancellation of all U.S. mobile, land-based missile programs and the termination of the B-2 program after twenty planes had been purchased. Stemming from these decisions, current plans—which of course are subject to modification—would have the United States rely on a day-to-day basis almost entirely on its submarines as a survivable deterrent. It might retain 500 or so single-warhead versions of the Minuteman III missile in silos, though these would not be very survivable; and it would have a small strategic nuclear bomber fleet which would not be on alert except in periods of great tension.

Russia, on the other hand, will likely rely on a combination of submarines and mobile, land-based missiles. As of this writing Moscow had deployed well over

200 SS-25 single-warhead mobile missiles, and it might, like the United States, be able to reduce other ICBMs to single-warhead configuration and retain them. Meanwhile Russia's large and modern force of fleet nuclear ballistic missile submarines (SSBNs), including the *Typhoon* and *Delta* classes, will remain a large and survivable deterrent force.

Perhaps the major force structure decision faced by Washington and Moscow in the future has to do with strategic defenses, and here the debate shifts back onto familiar ground. Maximalists, pointing to the inherent instability of the world situation and the thousands of missiles still residing in the former Soviet Union, call for the deployment of at least a small defense—and preferably a larger one. Advocates of strategic defense make a different case than the one made during the cold war; their argument has shifted from deterring a premeditated strike by the Soviet Union to defending against a number of smaller but deadly threats—an accidental or unauthorized Russian missile launch, the risk of missile and nuclear-weapon proliferation in the developing world, and the like.

Minimalists respond that anything but the smallest defenses create instability, and argue that even systems like the administration's plan for Global Protection Against Limited Strikes (GPALS) "could begin to seriously erode first-strike stability."[27] And they suggest that defenses are unnecessary, because the new threats to which conservatives refer are either not a concern (Russian missile launches) or not likely to be manifested in the form of intercontinental missile attacks (Third World proliferation). Like other force structure issues, however,

"Could you lend me your architect?"

Reprinted with permission of Renan R. Lurie.

the debate over strategic defenses may well be settled by fiscal and political, rather than mission-oriented, realities.

A Declining Index of Power. There can be little doubt that the end of the cold war has reduced the profile of nuclear weapons in international politics, at least among the major powers. It remains to be seen whether this trend will continue. In particular, pressures from proliferation in the developing world, if it continues unchecked, could before long present U.S. nuclear planners with a host of new challenges. Such proliferation would almost certainly obstruct deep U.S.–Russian nuclear reductions, and might also create new requirements for weapons and strategies aimed at new proliferators. In short, as of the early 1990s nuclear weapons play a far less important role in international security affairs than they did during the cold war—but this could very well change.

Discussion Questions

1. What is the role of images and ideologies in strategic nuclear bargaining?
2. How can nuclear war best be deterred? What are the critical elements of deterrence?
3. How do alliances impact on bargaining strategy?
4. What are the characteristics of the different nuclear strategies? What strategy (strategies) has (have) been followed by the United States?
5. What is meant by *counterforce? countervalue? first-strike capability? second-strike capability? triad?*
6. What are the difficulties of differentiating strategic nuclear forces from tactical nuclear forces?
7. What are the two principal schools of thought on nuclear deterrence theory? What are the major differences between them?
8. What are the distinctions between "active" and "passive" defenses against nuclear weapons?
9. Is a strategic defensive strategy feasible?

Recommended Reading

Ball, Desmond, and Toth, Robert C. 1990. "Revising the SIOP: Taking War-Fighting to Dangerous Extremes." *International Security* 14 (Spring 1990): 65–92.

Bundy, McGeorge. "To Cap the Volcano." *Foreign Affairs* 48 (October 1969).

———. "Nuclear Weapons and the Gulf." *Foreign Affairs* 70 (Fall 1991).

Congressional Budget Office. *The START Treaty and Beyond*. Washington, D.C.: U.S. Government Printing Office (October 1991).

Coté, Owen. "The Trident and the Triad: Collecting the D-5 Dividend." *International Security* 16 (Fall 1991).

Dowler, Thomas W., and Howard, Joseph S. II. "Countering the Threat of the Well-Armed Tyrant: A Modest Proposal for Small Nuclear Weapons." *Strategic Review* 19 (Fall 1991).

Feiveson, Harold A. "Finite Deterrence." In *Nuclear Deterrence and Moral Restraint*, ed. Henry Shue. Cambridge: Cambridge University Press, 1989.

Feiveson, Harold A., and von Hippel, Frank N. "Beyond START: How to Make Much Deeper Cuts." *International Security* 15 (Summer 1990).

Glaser, Charles. *Analyzing Strategic Nuclear Policy*. Princeton, N.J.: Princeton University Press, 1990.

Heisbourg, François. "The British and French Nuclear Forces: Current Roles and New Challenges." *Survival* 33 (September–October 1991).

Iklé, Fred C. "Comrades in Arms: The Case for a Russian–American Defense Community." *The National Interest* no. 26 (1991–1992).

Kull, Steven. *Minds at War: Nuclear Reality and the Inner Conflicts of Defense Policymakers*. New York: Basic Books, 1988.

May, Michael M., Bing, George F., and Steinbruner, John D. *Strategic Arms Reductions*. Washington, D.C.: Brookings Institution, 1988.

Mazarr, Michael J. "Beyond Counterforce." *Comparative Strategy* 9 (April–June 1990).

Mueller, John. *Retreat from Doomsday: The Obsolescence of Major War*. New York: Basic Books, 1989.

Perkovich, George. "Counting the Costs of the Arms Race." *Foreign Policy* no. 85 (1991–1992).

Sagan, Scott D. *Moving Targets: Nuclear Strategy and National Security*. Princeton, N.J.: Princeton University Press, 1989.

Slocombe, Walter. "The Continued Need for Extended Deterrence." *The Washington Quarterly* 14 (Autumn 1991).

Von Hippel, Frank, and Sagdeev, Roald, eds. *Reversing the Arms Race*. New York: Gordon and Breach, 1990.

Wander, W. Thomas, Kirk, Elizabeth J., and Arnett, Eric H., eds. *Science and Security: Technology and Arms Control for the 1990s*. Washington, D.C.: American Association for the Advancement of Science, 1989.

12

Limited War

Since 1945, when the United States exploded the first atomic bomb, at least six and perhaps seven or eight other nations have acquired nuclear weapons. Yet no nuclear weapon has been fired belligerently since 1945. Instead, the nuclear powers have carefully limited their use of military force, occasionally at a considerable price in military and political frustration.

It might be supposed that such a condition was inevitable. In the face of unlimited risk, extreme prudence seems no more than reasonable. However, there are objectives for which states would risk physical destruction; at least, there are conditions they would risk war to avert. In 1962 the United States was prepared to risk nuclear war to force the removal of Soviet missiles from Cuba. In 1973 the Soviet Union appeared ready to risk war with the United States to prevent military defeat of Egypt by Israel. Apparently, even with nuclear weapons in the background, there *are* interests for which nations will fight despite the risks.

And once hostile actions are under way, even substantial risk itself cannot by itself guarantee restraint any more than the threat of punishment can by itself deter crime. This is all the more true because restraint during war carries with it a number of penalties for the state exercising it. At the very least, such restraint might provoke domestic dissatisfaction with the conduct of the war—the belief that lives and resources are being squandered ineffectively. Obviously, it may also lead to battlefield reverses. Furthermore, restraint or deliberate limitation may appear to strip war of the function of "settling matters once and for all"—a function traditionally attributed to it by most Americans.

Yet throughout history, nations have shown restraint, having attempted to limit war in scope or area. Indeed, most wars from the Peace of Westphalia

(1648) up until the beginning of the twentieth century were distinctly limited affairs, restricted to battlefield encounters between armies with the respective societies well removed from the conflicts. Even in this century, nations have attempted to limit the weapons used in war and its geographic reach. The advent of nuclear weapons only temporarily reversed this trend: Before long analysts both within and outside governments tried to establish new, possibly enforceable limitations—between conventional and nuclear war, for example, or between tactical and strategic nuclear war.

Theories of limited war have a mixed record. In certain cases, their application to a regional conflict has limited its expanse and destructiveness—as in Vietnam, where China and the Soviet Union avoided involvement and where no nuclear weapons of any sort were used. In others, such as NATO's theories of flexible response and limited nuclear warfare, notions of limited war may have failed catastrophically if put to the test. History makes one thing clear: Any attempt to limit war is a dangerous and uncertain business—a warning that is more true than ever now that the cold war has ended.

Limited War: A Historical Perspective

Limited war is hardly novel. Historically, few wars have resulted in the utter physical or political demise of a contending state. Rome's total destruction of Carthage occupies a special place in history in large part because it was so unusual an event, and indeed the term ''Carthaginian Peace'' is frequently used to describe the consequences of total war. In contrast, throughout much of Western history, the means, scope, objectives, and consequences of war were sharply curtailed by the limited military power of states and by their limited ability to project that power beyond their own borders. Together, such constraints tended to restrict both the objectives for which states went to war and their expectations about what might be achieved thereby.

Types of Limitation. The most obvious reason why war was limited was simple insufficiency to prosecute it to the utmost—a limitation of *means*. As the destruction of Carthage suggests, it is not strictly true that limited means forbade total war. Even with crude weapons annihilation was possible. But until modern technology began to produce weapons capable of wreaking massive destruction rapidly and at great distances, the prosecution of total war implied an immense expenditure of effort: the raising and equipping of large armies and fleets, their sustenance under difficult conditions and at great distances, and the consequent disruption of normal patterns of agriculture, industry, and commerce. Even when simple insufficiency of resources did not impose a physical limit on war, the political and economic difficulties of generating them usually did.

Just as material insufficiency tended to limit the intensity of war, so lack of mobility tended to limit its geographical *scope*. Once again, the limitation was not rigid, as the exploits of Alexander, Attila, and other famous conquerors attest. The difficulties of transporting and sustaining large bodies of troops far from the homeland nevertheless figured prominently in the strategic calculations of rulers.

The inability of preindustrial societies to support large armies in the field from distant bases of supply meant that food, fodder, and other materials had to be foraged as a campaign progressed. This provided a strong incentive to keep armies on the move so that fresh supplies could be drawn from the surrounding countryside.[1]

Conflicts like the Crusades, the American Revolution, and Napoleon's invasion of Russia that required one side to project its power across very large distances conferred a substantial advantage on the defender, an advantage that was frequently decisive. Even today, jet aircraft capable of transporting great numbers of personnel and amounts of materiel worldwide have not entirely eliminated the logistical difficulties of conducting a larger-scale, lengthy war far from home.[2]

The number of states likely to become involved also limited the scope of war. Most wars centered upon disputed borders, territorial claims, or matters of royal succession and preeminence and thus tended to concern only the principals. Occasionally, one contender or both would call upon allies for assistance, but even then the number of active belligerents was likely to remain small. Indeed, the record suggests that as the number of participants increased so did the duration and intensity of the war and the uncertainty of its outcome.[3]

Material weakness served to limit war directly, despite the contrary intentions of the embattled states. More often, however, weakness limited war prospectively by influencing strategic calculations of the belligerents, moderating the *objectives* for which they fought. This interaction of means and objectives was not necessarily explicit; the lucrative target offered by Marco Polo's Cathay could hardly have moved a European monarch, to whom China was as remote as the moon. Even when the means existed, however, the absolute destruction of the adversary was rarely contemplated. Quite aside from the expense of the task, there was usually little to be gained from a policy of annihilation. On the contrary, there was frequently something to be lost, for a defeated state could be exploited and thereby repay the costs of the war with interest.

In any case, even objectives carefully tailored to means did not guarantee accuracy of the war calculus, as the failure rate of wars of conquest attests. Leaders concerned with matters of war and diplomacy were accordingly inclined to be fairly conservative in their estimates of attainable objectives.

While objectives may be influenced by calculations of relative power, they are not necessarily determined by them. Political pressures on decision-makers also affect objectives. In turn, these pressures are a function of the domestic structures of states. As long as war and diplomacy were the duty and prerogative of aristocratic elites, who enjoyed wide latitude in making decisions and who often had more in common with each other than with their respective populace, war aims were limited with relative ease. Both interest and necessity argued for self restraint—first, because no ruler wished to challenge the legitimate basis of the authority by which all ruled; and second, because ruling elites were frequently reminded of the fragile nature of their domestic support. Such support could easily erode in the wake of successive defeats, with loss of prestige by the ruler and strain on the fabric of society.[4] Assassination or rebellion might be the price of too wasteful an expenditure of the society's resources. It is no coincidence that the two great political convulsions of modern Western history, the French and Russian revolutions, both followed the engagement of these states in unsuccessful, exhausting wars.[5]

Modern War: The Removal of Physical Limits

For all the reasons mentioned, most early wars were conducted with limited means in the pursuit of limited objectives, and thus produced limited consequences. Such limitation, however, often constituted a condition, not a policy, and it frequently reflected, as we have seen, less the preferences of belligerents than their weaknesses. Moreover, the weaknesses were mutual; if the winner's gains were limited, so also were the loser's costs. Modern students of limited war who approvingly quote Clausewitz's injunction that war must be governed by political objectives are apt to forget (as Clausewitz himself did not) that the surest way to achieve war aims is not to nibble at an opponent but to render it incapable of interfering. Most early politicians would have agreed with this view; the problem lay in securing the means to effect it.

By the late eighteenth century, the means were becoming available. The Industrial Revolution made possible a vast increase in the effective means of waging war—at the price, however, of mobilizing the productive, as well as the military, sector of society. The rise of nationalism and the evolution of competing national ideologies provided the incentive for such mobilization, and the nation-in-arms provided the mechanism. Sheer material weakness ceased to be an inevitable governor on the engine of war.

Nor could prudence control belligerence. The very requirement to mobilize public support on a national scale promoted a diffusion of political power from aristocratic elites to the middle classes, whose money and members would be required to fight. Such a shift had been foreshadowed in Great Britain, where the rulers' persistent need to generate taxes to support war had led directly to parliamentary checks on royal authority. The result was to limit the freedom of governing elites to frame war aims in accordance with *raisons d'état*. A war demanding the concerted efforts of the entire society could not easily be justified by arguments of diplomatic expedience. Such a war would require universal objectives grounded in high moral purpose—liberty, democracy, survival, universal justice. Inevitably, the opponent in such a contest must be cast in unequivocally hostile terms—a moral leper to be purged from the society of civilized states. Such a characterization invariably made it difficult to end a war by negotiation. Thus, precisely when the removal of physical limits on the use of force made the exercise of prudence essential, development of democratic universalism began to render it impossible.

Finally, in World War I, the link between means and ends came full circle. The period 1914 to 1918 saw the primacy of "mobilization warfare" in which entire societies and economies were engaged in the effort of war. Indeed, the productive forces of modern industrial economies outstripped the mobility of armies in the field, contributing to the terrible strategic stalemate that we have come to associate with the World War I battles of Verdun and the Somme. As the war consumed life and treasure on an unprecedented scale, even the original objectives of the contenders became obscured in the demand for a conclusion capable of justifying the sacrifices already made. Totality of destruction required totality of result. Means had come once again to dominate war—but now, not with the result of limiting it, but rather of preventing its limitation short of absolute victory or utter defeat.[6]

Limited War in the Cold War Era

Discussions of the phenomenon of limited war took on a special focus during the cold war. Most issues of limitation arose in connection with the possibility of a general East–West conflict, or of U.S.–Soviet or U.S.–Chinese geopolitical competition played out in the Third World. Even during the cold war, however, the tensions and dilemmas of limited war theory emerged to challenge leaders in Washington and Moscow.

The most powerful, and terrifying, discussions of limited war during the cold war dealt with its core symbols, nuclear weapons. By the time the United States dropped the first atomic bomb on Hiroshima in 1945, many observers speculated that total war had become the rule in conflicts, rather than the exception. Both previous world wars had been total, with the victorious nations occupying the territory of those defeated and, in some cases, imposing whole new systems of government upon them. At first nuclear weapons seemed to augur no change in that condition. A nuclear war would, it was speculated, end as the world wars had ended—with an unconditional surrender after an essentially military contest. Nuclear weapons might hasten the victory, but initially few observers expected them to transform the process by which victory would be achieved. Even as late as 1955, President Eisenhower could still assert with conviction, "Where these things [tactical nuclear weapons] are used on strictly military targets and for strictly military purposes, I can see no reason why they shouldn't be used as you would a bullet or anything else."[7]

The Korean War called into question this view of the unconditional utility of nuclear strength. The United States refrained from employing nuclear weapons despite its virtual monopoly. The war offered few lucrative targets that did not risk spreading it, and—in any case—U.S. decision-makers were loath to squander a still-limited nuclear stockpile on a conflict that many believed to be a Soviet feint. Restraint thus represented no essential contradiction of the general belief in the war-fighting function of the nuclear arsenal. On the contrary, one immediate consequence of U.S. frustration in Korea was renewed insistence in many quarters that the United States must be ready to employ nuclear weapons in any future war.[8]

As nuclear arsenals grew, however, and as increasingly sophisticated means of delivery were developed, more and more analysts began to realize that nuclear weapons were not just "larger bullets." They did not offer simply a quantum jump in the military power of the state that owned them. Instead, they transformed the very relationship of that power to foreign policy—partly because of the immense damage they could do, partly because of the speed with which they could do it, but partly too because of the *ease* with which they could do it. In the past, international coercion was difficult and time-consuming. Historically, to coerce another state—whether by aggression or in self-defense—a state had first to defeat (or threaten to defeat) its armies. Until then, one could not seriously threaten an opponent's civil society. Accordingly, civil damage was incidental to the progress of defeating hostile forces in the field, although in some circumstances it might contribute to that objective by weakening the opponent's industrial base.

Nuclear weapons stood this relationship on its head. One weapon could destroy a city in the flicker of an eyelash. It is highly significant that it could do so without first defeating the opponent's military forces, provided that a few aircraft or missiles could penetrate the enemy defense. In the future, a state might conceivably find itself in total ruins without having "lost" a single "battle"—in which case, of course, traditional notions of victory and defeat would cease to have meaning.[9]

At first, such a prospect—which essentially destroyed any hope for limitation in war, rendering all major conflict an enterprise of unprecedented totality—seemed tailor-made to the requirements of U.S. security. Caught between economic pressures at home and Soviet divisions abroad, and enjoying a virtual monopoly on nuclear strength,[10] some U.S. policymakers saw in nuclear weapons the ideal alternative to dangerous military weakness or disastrous inflation. During the Eisenhower administration, the United States turned explicitly to nuclear weapons as the ultimate threat to deter and, if necessary, defeat Soviet aggression. As explained in Chapter 4, this policy acquired its own terms—the "New Look" and "Massive Retaliation"—referring to doctrines in which the threat of immediate and total nuclear escalation made up for cutbacks in U.S. conventional forces. In Winston Churchill's famous phrase, "Safety would be the sturdy child of terror," U.S. leaders definitively rejected the notion of limited war in order to make the consequences of war more terrifying and thus to strengthen deterrence. In theory, this doctrine even applied to regional wars begun by Soviet or Chinese proxies.

This policy enjoyed its most important application in Europe. To deter the 200-odd Soviet divisions lined up menacingly opposite NATO, the United States and its allies deployed thousands of tactical nuclear weapons on the continent, hoping to create the impression that a war of limited means—a conventional war—was virtually impossible. NATO's wide range of nuclear weapons, from nuclear land mines to bombs dropped by aircraft to medium-range missiles, made it nearly impossible to define—and hence limit—nuclear war in Europe according to precise distinctions among weapons characteristics, the more so because the Soviet Union acknowledged no such limitation. At some point, theater nuclear war would merge imperceptibly with strategic nuclear war, which was just the threat for which NATO planners hoped. By creating a seamless progression of nuclear escalation from tactical to strategic weapons, they effectively outlawed the notion of limited nuclear war as well.

It was not long before the fundamental paradox of such a policy became apparent: nuclear weapons were *too* powerful. To threaten their employment in response to any but the most extreme aggression established an absurd disparity between provocation and response. Worse, a deterrent based on such a threat might not be credible to a potential aggressor. Sole dependence for deterrence on a threat of nuclear retaliation might well invite aggression.

Partly for these reasons, NATO doctrine shifted in the 1960s, once again admitting the possibility of limitation. Recognizing the dilemmas imposed by Massive Retaliation, the Kennedy administration attempted to institutionalize the notion of limited war, including limited nuclear war, with a new doctrine: Flexible Response. The United States would no longer threaten an immediate and total nuclear response to Soviet aggression, nor would it threaten absolute escalation from regional wars. Rather, the United States and its NATO allies would rely on a series of escalatory moves, each aimed at demonstrating resolve and halting a Soviet military advance or operation. The hope was to add credibility to the West's deterrent policies by increasing flexibility and providing more options.

Flexible Response carried its own complications. Washington's European allies, having grown comfortable with Massive Retaliation and the absolute firebreak it presumably established against Soviet aggression, had real concerns that a policy of greater flexibility would be interpreted by Moscow as one of less resolve. The practical effect of NATO Europe's reservations can be seen in the amount of time required to implement Flexible Response: After first being announced by U.S. Secretary of Defense McNamara in 1962, it was not until 1967 that it became official NATO doctrine.

Moreover, Flexible Response did not change the ultimate threat that NATO posed to the Soviet Union. If Soviet forces were on the verge of victory, the Western Alliance still reserved the possibility of escalating to nuclear use. While the new doctrine therefore added further possibilities for limited war in a European conflict, it did not in any way seek to guarantee such limitation. Indeed, such a guarantee would have run directly against the grain of U.S. security pledges to Europe, which, it was hoped, suggested to Moscow that in all likelihood no war could remain limited in scope, either in terms of the weapons used or the area involved.

Today, of course, Western Europe no longer relies on the ultimate threat of nuclear war to guarantee its security. The fragmentation of the Soviet Union and the decline of Russia's military might has reduced the need for the West to manipulate the notion of limited or unlimited war for deterrent effect. President George Bush's September 1991 tactical nuclear weapons initiative demonstrated the extent of official recognition of this shift: No longer did the West require ground-based U.S. tactical nuclear weapons, long the bedrock of NATO's escalation threats, to keep the peace. The notion of "limited" war therefore has a new meaning in Europe: Today the question is not whether the former Soviet Union could attack the West and avoid nuclear use or U.S. involvement, but whether any state in Europe's fluid and often conflicting mix of nationalities and sovereignties can attack another without the threat of a wider war.

Outside Europe, the challenges posed by limited war have not changed significantly. Despite all the U.S. posturing on Massive Retaliation and other doctrines, it turned out that the United States treated limited, regional wars during the cold war as restricted conflicts. The United States fought for thirteen years in Korea and Vietnam without ever using nuclear weapons; and after the chastening experience of China's intervention in Korea, the United States spent most of the Vietnam War working strenuously to avoid escalation to a conflict with North Vietnam's powerful sponsors in Moscow and Beijing. During these wars, a number of particularly vexing questions and issues confronted U.S. leaders, including:

- What were the U.S. *interests* at stake? Did we really belong in the conflict, or was it of marginal importance to U.S. national interests? In Korea, Vietnam, and many other cases during the cold war, the interest rested in the countries' symbolic importance as areas of U.S.–Soviet confrontation. With that confrontation over, or at least in hibernation, it will likely become more difficult to enunciate persuasive U.S. interests in regional conflicts.

- What *objectives* did the United States have in these wars? Total victory? The defeat of the other side's military force? In one case—Korea—total victory would probably have cost the United States a war with China; in Vietnam, a vague and narrow definition of objectives seriously hampered the conduct of the war.

- What were the most effective *means* for prosecuting these wars—were they primarily military, or did they have important nonmilitary aspects? One of the chief criticisms of U.S. limited-war doctrine during the cold war was that it focused myopically on military issues and ignored the social, political, and economic causes of instabilities and conflicts. In this context, is there a role for nuclear weapons, in either a deterrent or war-fighting capacity, for limited, regional war? To what extent are security assistance and regional arms control, which are both potentially important elements of deterrence and confidence-building, mutually exclusive?

- What are the *constraints* on U.S. operations in limited wars? In the past three decades or so, the most powerful constraint has been public opinion as reflected through and amplified by the media, and the Persian Gulf war of 1991 demonstrated that the speed and ubiquity of mass communications is already having a revolutionary effect on warfare.[11] Increasingly, however, constraints may also be military in nature—the limitations of our own forces (such as a lack of strategic lift or theater missile defense) combined with the strength of regional powers (strength abetted by the proliferation of nuclear, chemical, and biological weapons).

Limited War after the Cold War

Limited wars may come to dominate strategic thinking in the United States, as it has long done elsewhere. American military strategy in the early 1990s had already shifted decisively to a focus on limited, regional conflicts, rather than on total, global war with the former Soviet Union. U.S. political and military leaders have begun a broad-based revision of strategy. With the threat of Soviet expansion largely dissipated, the U.S. military is gradually adopting a strategy focused on regional contingencies.[12] This policy views the major threats to U.S. interests as arising, not primarily from a central threat, but from spirals of regional instability or from a number of aggressive regional hegemonists such as Iraq and North Korea.[13]

This new strategy involves a fundamental shift in emphasis, a sea change from the geostrategy and military doctrines of the cold war. "U.S. global strategy," one recent study noted,

> is evolving from a modified version of containment to a doctrine providing responses to lesser but worldwide contingencies. U.S. thinking will shift from a potential "one-and-a-half war" scenario, involving Europe and one other region, to the need to deal with up to two simultaneous contingencies in different regions. The larger of the two would be a conflict on the scale of a Middle Eastern or Korean war, involving up to two corps of U.S. ground forces and a corresponding level of air and naval commitments. A European commitment in the future may also fit into this large contingency....The smaller contingency in the "two contingency" strategy might be a variety of low-intensity conflict, such as rapid intervention on the scale of Grenada or Panama.[14]

The strategy would be in service of a U.S. defense policy emphasizing regional stability, in which the United States would play a key role—"not as a world policeman enforcing the hegemony of its own laws, but as a militiaman of sorts, called from a militarily relaxed posture to respond, in concert with its allies, to specific crises for limited periods of time."[15]

The Gulf war indeed represented a test case of these post–cold war concepts. In terms of its basic nature—representing as it did a shift in concern from the Soviet Union and its clients to a non-Soviet contingency—the war applied new strategic concepts which are becoming the foundations of U.S. military strategy.[16] It was a telling coincidence that President Bush formally announced the U.S. shift to a strategy focused on regional contingencies on August 2, 1990, even as Iraqi tanks were rolling into Kuwait.

What conflicts and crises might this new strategy confront? Subsequent chapters will provide a detailed analysis of regional issues confronting the United States in the 1990s and beyond. It is worthwhile, however, to review quickly some of the potential contingencies offered by international politics today. Such a review will make clear that there are numerous possibilities for new limited wars.

In the early 1990s, one major focus of friction is the Korean Peninsula. Although tentative steps have been made toward reunification, a great gulf exists in trust between North and South Korea. North Korea reportedly continues to pursue a nuclear weapons program, even though both Koreas have agreed to maintain a nuclear-free peninsula. Adding to the South's distrust, infiltration tunnels from North to South were discovered as early as the 1980s. North Korea is finding itself more isolated as the Soviet Union, its patron, has crumbled. It remains a pariah state and attracts international scorn by exporting ballistic missiles. Moreover, the numerically superior, heavily armed, and forward-deployed North Korean troops pose a constant danger of surprise attack. South Korea's concerns are deepened by the fact that Kim Il Sung is transferring power to his enigmatic son, Kim Jong Il, who is thought to be unstable, inexperienced, and even more bellicose than his father.

Similarly, China is facing a transition of power. Should the new leaders of China attempt by force or threat to regain control of Taiwan, the reverberations throughout the world would be severe, especially in Sino-American relations, which would likely be irreparably harmed. Japan and other Asian powers would be gravely concerned by such Chinese bellicosity, and there would be a serious impact on regional economic relations. Other potential flash points include disputes within regions of the former Soviet Union bordering China, the Japanese–Russian contest over the Kuriles, and tensions over multiple conflicting South China Sea territorial claims. The role of the United States as the sole superpower could well include some role in and responsibility to help settle one or more of these problems and then to underwrite the settlements.

In the developing world, violence associated with migration and political instability within nations such as Zaire and Somalia may intensify, and U.S. expeditionary forces might again be called upon to evacuate Western civilians. Other possible conflict scenarios might involve African or Asian states attempting to obtain, by force, access to strategic raw materials reserves located in neighboring countries.

In Central and South America, several Latin American countries remain vulnerable to revolutions and wars of insurgency. Economic stabilization plans requiring fiscal austerity and smaller public sectors, along with slow or no growth prospects, have fueled discontent and opposition to regimes in power. This fractious political and economic environment does not foster democratic reform and could explode.

U.S. military involvement in fighting the drug war in Latin America has been limited, yet many U.S. servicemen remain in the region and are potentially targets of radicals or extremists. A U.S. retaliatory response, such as that taken in Panama, is not a wholly unrealistic scenario.

The inevitable transition of power approaching in Cuba may also lead to upheaval. In the absence of Soviet aid, the Cuban economy has worsened. As one conceivable contingency, a foolish new leader might, as the end of the U.S. lease on Guantanamo Bay Naval Base approaches, provoke an international incident to firm up a shaky regime.

In Eurasia, the traditional focus of limited-war attention, the struggle for independence by ethnic enclaves within Russia could generate an armed response from a resurgent Russian imperialist center trying to maintain control. Cross-border ethnic identities and rivalries could spark interstate friction among successor republics of the former Soviet Union; the struggle for control of the resources of the former Soviet territory such as industries, raw materials, and armies would likely feed these rivalries. Ethnic struggles brewing or occurring in Yugoslavia, Albania, and Czechoslovakia could have spill-over affects in NATO and other nations. Migration could also be a destabilizing factor, as economically disadvantaged Easterners swarm into Western European states, drawing prejudice and turmoil in their wake. Should economic recovery fail to occur in these Eastern states, authoritarian regimes could quickly return, counter to U.S. interests.

The Middle East remains at odds over the question of Palestine. Moreover, in addition to the Arab versus Israeli conflict, there are Arab versus Arab, Arab versus Persian, Arab versus Kurd, and Sunni Muslim versus Shiite. In such a tinderbox, violence could quickly escalate, accelerated by an abundance of arms, collected during years of an economically damaging arms race. The United States, dependent on the oil of the region and committed to Israel's security, could well be drawn in as a participant, supplier, peacekeeper, or guarantor of a settlement.

Clearly, not all the limited conflict possibilities cited in preceding paragraphs, plus others in South or Southeast Asia, would involve the United States. But several of them certainly could, in one way or another.

Issues in Limited War

Responding to these various regional instabilities and conflicts will pose the same set of challenges raised by limited-war concerns that prevailed during the cold war. At issue will be U.S. interests, objectives, means, and constraints. Each of these four factors will affect the American approach to future wars.

In the most objective sense, the issue of limitation ought to be settled by the U.S. *interests* at stake. The more significant the interests, the more total the war would be, if necessary. World War II, in which two global powers threatened the United States directly, involved a much more complete U.S. response than the indirect regional challenges posed by North Korea and North Vietnam. The nature of U.S. interests involved will also affect the issue of limitation: in the Gulf war of 1991, for example, American interests in Saudi Arabian security and the preservation of friendly access to Gulf oil were deemed by the Bush administration to be vital—worth a major, if still limited, effort.

Yet the very fact that the full weight of U.S. opposition to Iraq was not employed against that country to an unambiguous outcome suggests that national interests will not provide a certain, objective guide to conflict limitation. Some wars can possess a symbolic or line-in-the-sand value which exceeds their direct import to the United States and may draw a level of U.S. commitment not warranted by the situation itself. A classic example of this type of war, many would argue, is Vietnam. In other instances, the United States may not intervene, or may intervene only halfheartedly, when quite serious interests are at stake but there are other ways and times to pursue them.

Problems of defining and pursuing interests had been magnified by the end of the cold war. No longer will international politics be viewed by the United States as a largely zero-sum game, in which every gain for Moscow is a loss for Washington. In the 1990s it will be more difficult to determine whether U.S. interests are at risk in the developing world, and what level of military action would be justified to protect them.

In terms of *objectives*, architects of U.S. limited or regional war strategies face a crippling confusion between the notions of limited and total war. Regional conflicts will threaten only limited U.S. interests and will likely demand only a limited military effort, but the damage done to the target country will often approach that characteristic of a more total war. The new security environment, with its focus on regional contingencies, lends itself to great confusion of political and military objectives, arising from the tension between a limited stake in the conflict response and the nature of war, which often must be unrestricted in intensity even if its objectives are finite. There is also the possibility that when decision-makers consider responses to a regional "contingency," national security policies—including the military strategy designed to address such events—might encourage them to rely too much on the short-term use of military power to solve what are at heart political, economic, or social problems. This possibility is probably enhanced by intense media coverage and domestic attitudes which bias policy toward rapid, decisive action.

Once a war has begun, however, the opposite presumption—of limited rather than total ends—might emerge, in the minds of both leaders and their publics. In the case of the 1990–1991 war with Iraq, the Bush administration from the outset denied that it sought the removal of Saddam Hussein from power; at the time these statements seemed appropriate to a war of limited ends. As it turned out, however, U.S. and coalition interests would have been better served by a more ambitious set of military and political goals *if* allied and public consensus had been possible. Ruling out total victory also complicated war termination: when the key postwar U.S. goal was "getting out quickly," other goals—such as encouraging a transition to a democratic Iraq under different rule or protecting the Kurds from Saddam's vengeance—fell by the wayside.

Once the basic objective of the war, evicting Iraqi troops from Kuwait, was accomplished, there was no clear path for the coalition to follow. Some advocated a tough policy, arguing that the coalition should finish its job and force Hussein from power; others warned of the dangers that a fragmented Iraq would produce, and urged restraint. In the end, restraint won out.

It is once again clear from this war that military objectives and national objectives will not always coincide. The latter are preeminent and are established by political leaders looking at the whole array of U.S. military, political, and economic interests. As we are often reminded, war is an extension of politics, and as wars draw to a close, political considerations will often become predominant and dictate the nature of the outcome. It is not at all obvious that the coalition military effort in the Gulf should have gone on even an hour longer than it did; by the end of the war, coalition air and ground forces were merely slaughtering Iraqis for what seemed to be no pressing military purpose. The coalition's strategy for the transition from war to peace after retaking Kuwait had not been decided, and this impeded winning victories in peacetime as great as those that had been won in war.

The *means* used to pursue limited war may also be changing as a result of the end of the cold war. The notion that all international conflicts have important social, economic, and political foundations and cannot be treated merely as military phenomena has gained general acceptance. In the Gulf war, for example, waging "limited regional war" involved far more than the purely military tasks of fighting air and ground battles; it entailed the diplomacy needed to assemble an international coalition with U.N. backing, the economic incentives offered to certain Arab states (such as Egypt), the embargo levied against Iraq, plus the response to the environmental hazards posed by Saddam's forces burning Kuwaiti oil wells. To the extent that coalition military actions were afterward thought to be incomplete, perhaps it was because they did not adequately encompass nonmilitary considerations—the political implications of the removal of Saddam Hussein from power, for example, or the issue of democracy within Kuwait, or the economic cleavages between Arab states.

Even in the realm of military operations, it appears in the early 1990s that there is increased room for limitation in means. Precision weapons, as used in the Gulf war, allow the United States to be far more discriminating than ever before in its application of force. While (as we will see) this limitation may turn out to be unreliable, the scale of destruction will likely be much lower than would have been produced by World War II–era technology. There are reports, moreover, that the Department of Defense is working hard to develop weapons and tactics for "nonlethal warfare," aimed at incapacitating the enemy and its equipment rather than at killing or destroying them.

In the realm of *constraints* on U.S. action, the most powerful one will likely be public opinion. One of the biggest challenges confronting President Bush in August 1990 when Iraq attacked its neighbor was an apparent lack of public support for military action. Polls showed little public enthusiasm for a war to oust Saddam Hussein from Kuwait. Worse, the Congress, particularly its Democratic leadership, balked at the idea of actually declaring war or in some other way authorizing President Bush to initiate a major conflict.

In the end, of course, these public and congressional doubts were overcome (though not by much) in the longest standing congressional foreign policy debate in U.S. history.[17] In part this was a result of a robust international consensus: Americans were apparently much more willing to accept the use of force if it were clear that the world community also did and agreed to stand side-by-side with U.S. forces in the war. One well-known lesson was relearned in the Gulf, namely, that involving friends and allies in any major U.S. military effort contributes to, and may even be a precondition for, acquiring domestic public support for that effort.

Somewhat surprisingly, President Bush's decision to call up major elements of the National Guard and Reserves also had a galvanizing effect on public opinion. Public support for the U.S. military deployment in the Gulf rose noticeably once the reserve call-ups were under way. In this sense the Defense Department's Total Force policy served its primary goal: After the Vietnam War, it was determined that in any future war the whole American public would have to be involved, and thus the military services (and particularly the Army) placed major support and combat elements into the National Guard and Reserves, creating a "Total Force."

One of the clear lessons of the Gulf war therefore relates to the means by which national leaders can create support for a U.S. military intervention. Such support will result from a sense of shared purpose and a perception of a common goal, perceived not only among the American people but a major part of the world community as well. In the Gulf war, U.S. leaders were fortunate because, early in the build-up, the goal was clear and simple—the expulsion of Iraq from Kuwait. In and of itself, however, that goal was apparently not persuasive to the American people at the moment Iraq's armies crossed the Kuwaiti border on August 2, 1990. It only became persuasive with the emergence of a broad sense of international, and subsequently national, commitment.

A corollary of this experience is that prewar public opinion surveys may tell very little about how the American people will react once a conflict is under way. For example, 1992 polls showed only about half the respondents in favor of U.S. military support to South Korea if it is attacked by the North. If, however, such an attack occurred, and if the American people were flooded with media images of South Korean people fleeing from Northern aggression, and if the United Nations quickly and unanimously condemned the invasion and began assembling a military response, and if U.S. National Guard and Reserve troops were called up and declared their pride in preparing to defend an ally—in short, if developments paralleled those of the Gulf war—then it seems highly likely that a large majority of Americans would support U.S. intervention on South Korea's behalf.

The extent of support for limited operations will depend, of course, on the conduct of the war and on how quickly it is over. If it is defined by a specific, powerful moment—the Japanese attack on Pearl Harbor, President Harry Truman's decision to defend South Korea, President Bush's pledge that Iraq's aggression would "not stand"—the outset of a war will often serve to galvanize public opinion behind the U.S. military effort. The risks inherent in war can create a unique expression of shared fate and common purpose. It may only be when the war is extended and the casualty lists are burgeoning that the citizenry is confronted with the brutal reality of war and begins to rethink its wisdom. This is certainly what occurred in Vietnam.

The Bush administration never faced this problem, because miraculously few U.S. personnel died in the Gulf war, which was over rapidly. But future U.S.

leaders, if they confront more difficult regional contingencies offering a prospect of longer wars and more casualties, will likely encounter more serious public opposition. In the "contingencies strategy," dealing as it does with regional as opposed to global threats, and dealing only with vital, or perhaps less than vital, overseas interests, rather than direct threats to the U.S. homeland, no set of interests is likely to seem terribly compelling to the public. The challenge of the contingencies strategy is, as the name implies, how to frame a contingent response in defense of important U.S. global interests when those interests do not involve national survival. If such interventions or wars are to be politically feasible, they will have to be of short duration and incur minimal casualties.

Partly because of this complexity, it is difficult to know for sure if the Gulf war invalidated the so-called Vietnam syndrome. The wars in Indochina and the Gulf were separated by more than time; they were completely different kinds of military campaigns. The Vietnam conflict was a counterinsurgency war, in large part fought not against standing armies in the field but against shadowy guerrillas, pervasive infiltrators, children terrorists—almost a whole people, but one that was seldom seen in the media until after a battle. In the Gulf, by contrast, the targets of U.S. military power were very explicit, and could be seen daily in the worldwide media—Iraqi tanks, trucks, air defense sites, military headquarters, bases, supporting civilian infrastructure, and the like.

Much of the Vietnam syndrome may therefore still be alive and flourishing. In the jungles of Indochina, the American people—and their military, as well—developed a sharp distaste for fighting guerrilla wars, not necessarily for all kinds of wars. This distaste likely remains, even after the Gulf victory. Comparisons with Vietnam could still be conjured up recently in opposition to a U.S. drug interdiction intervention into Colombia, for instance. Perhaps this is as it should be, because military intervention alone will seldom solve the social and economic problems that underlie most insurgencies. As we learned in Vietnam, other instruments of power are absolutely necessary, and even then they may be insufficient.

The issues of public opinion and public diplomacy are further complicated by the pervasiveness of information technologies in today's world. During the Gulf war, the Cable News Network (CNN) often broadcast stories in the United States before they were reported through military channels. Every American network covered the war in excruciating detail, abandoning virtually all other programming for the war's first few days. The requirements for effective public diplomacy are more demanding than ever; the Department of Defense may face a media that is at times better informed about the battlefield situation than the Department of Defense is. If public support is to be maintained, U.S. interventions must be swiftly decisive; and during such operations the government's ability to report accurately and correctly must be the equal of the world's media.[18]

The fragility of the physical infrastructure of modern economies can also constrain the application of force in regional wars. Iraqi infrastructure proved vulnerable to American military power to a surprising degree. An air campaign directed primarily at the Iraqi military forces crippled Iraqi communications, transportation, and civil services such as those that provide health care, water, and electricity. The full ramifications of such destruction, in the form of malnutrition, or disease, only later became fully evident. This result is particularly ironic, because precision weapons supposedly had created the option of conducting wars with far less civilian damage than was common in the past. But while collateral damage was minimized in some cases, the destructiveness of precision weapons was such that more damage was done to certain targets than anticipated.

The Gulf war may therefore have demonstrated an additional difficulty with U.S. contingency operations. U.S. military forces can use precision weapons and firepower restraint in an effort to reduce civilian deaths and suffering, but the inherent brittleness of economies may prevent them from achieving this goal. For moral and political reasons we can try to avoid more lasting damage than necessary to accomplish our military objectives, but the fragility of the adversary's economy may confound our ability to do that.

Discussion Questions

1. How might "limited war" be defined?
2. Is it possible to establish limits on a conflict involving the use of nuclear weapons?
3. In a time of international crisis, would domestic considerations likely constrain U.S. actions in regard to limited, regional conflicts?
4. What factor(s) would be most important for a successful strategy of limitation during war? Are these factors different for global and regional conflicts?
5. Why can it be said that revolutionary war knows no limits?
6. Were the Arab–Israeli wars of 1967 and 1973 limited wars? What about the Falklands conflict? The Persian Gulf war of 1991? Was the Iran–Iraq War limited or "total"? By what standard?

Recommended Reading

Betts, Richard. *Surprise Attack.* Washington, D.C.: Brookings Institution, 1981.

Dougherty, James E., and Pfaltzgraff, Robert L., Jr. *Contending Theories of International Relations.* New York: Harper & Row, 1981. See especially Chapter 8, "Microcosmic Theories of Violent Conflict: Revolution and War."

Huntington, Samuel P. *The Common Defense.* New York: Columbia University Press, 1974.

Jones, Rodney W. *Small Nuclear Forces and U.S. Security Policy: Threats and Potential Conflicts in South Asia.* Lexington, Mass.: Lexington Books, 1984.

Kaplan, Stephen S. *Diplomacy of Power.* Washington, D.C.: Brookings Institution, 1981.

Kissinger, Henry. *Nuclear Weapons and Foreign Policy.* New York: Norton, 1969.

Osgood, Robert E. *Limited War: The Challenge to American Strategy.* Chicago: University of Chicago Press, 1957.

Posen, Barry R. *Inadvertent Escalation: Conventional War and Nuclear Risks.* Ithaca, N.Y.: Cornell University Press, 1991.

Reynolds, Charles. *The Politics of War: A Study of the Rationality of Violence in Inter-State Relations.* New York: St. Martin's Press, 1989.

Scales, Robert H. *Firepower in Limited War*. Washington, D.C.: National Defense University Press, 1990.

Schelling, Thomas C. *A Strategy of Conflict*. New York: Oxford University Press, 1960.

Smoke, Richard. *War: Controlling Escalation*. Cambridge, Mass.: Harvard University Press, 1977.

Waltz, Kenneth. *Man, the State, and War*. New York: Columbia University Press, 1959.

13

From Low Intensity Conflict to Forward-Presence Operations

''Low intensity conflict'' (LIC) was the name the Reagan administration adopted in 1981 as an umbrella term for the various low-level Third World conflicts that had characterized much of the 1970s.[1] The perceived need for a new doctrine and strategic approach to address Third World conflicts stemmed from the recognition that America's principal foreign policy failures of the previous twenty years had been primarily in the Third World. Moreover, the Reagan administration was determined to ''draw the line'' against ''communist aggression'' in the Third World.[2] Thus, American arms, money, and in some cases military personnel were used to bolster friendly governments battling communist insurgencies and, in an ironic cold war role reversal, to support anticommunist insurgencies fighting to overthrow governments friendly to Moscow. A new term was needed to describe these counterinsurgency and proinsurgency activities—in large part interrelated by a common anticommunist thrust—that would indicate a fresh doctrine that absorbed the painful lessons of the Vietnam War and at the same time demonstrate a new and improved capability to deal with the complexity of Third World conflicts.

The 1980s generated a considerable body of literature, bureaucratic squabbling, and resources devoted to contemplating, planning, and waging low intensity conflict. Much bureaucratic blood was spilled in arguments over the definition of what actually constitutes a low-intensity conflict. The Joint Chiefs of Staff define the term as: ''Political military confrontation between contending states or groups, below conventional war and above the routine, peaceful competition among states.''[3] Under this rather broad and inadequate definition, the Pentagon has lumped nearly every outbreak of fighting since 1980. Everything from counterdrug operations in Peru and Bolivia to the 1989 invasion of Panama has been described as low intensity conflict. The military's in-house low intensity conflict think tank, the *Center for Low Intensity Conflict* (CLIC), even described Operation Desert Shield, the deployment to defend Saudi Arabia in 1990, as a low intensity conflict. As one analyst noted, however, it is difficult to conceive of "the largest military logistical feat in history as a low intensity conflict."[4]

The problem probably begins with the term itself. Few people were ever pleased with it, for the intensity of any conflict is a subjective determination. For the United States, conflict in distant locales such as El Salvador or Angola may appear to be low intensity, but for the individual soldier or military unit caught up in a firefight it is of rather high intensity. Moreover, actual combat need not be a necessary part of the definition, for even nation-building assistance and humanitarian assistance activities are included under the LIC rubric. The attempt to lump such disparate activities under a single bureaucratic heading creates confusion for those engaged in policy-making and resource and budget allocation.[5]

Because of this confusion, along with the strategic upheaval of the past few years, the 1990s will likely witness the disappearance of the term "low intensity conflict." The end of the cold war means that the Third World is no longer an East–West battleground and that the principal concepts included under low intensity conflict, namely, insurgency, counterinsurgency, and proinsurgency, have lost their primary strategic rationale for the United States. This is not to say that these forms of conflict have disappeared or will disappear, or that the United States will ignore their occurrence or outcome. Indeed, now that the cold war is over, Americans may have a vital interest in a particular preinsurgency or insurgency situation, but deciding for or against intervention will rest on other than East–West competition. In the Pentagon's own publications, low intensity conflict has been downgraded in importance. For example, a glance at the Department of Defense (DOD) 1990 edition of the *Annual Report to the President and the Congress* reveals that, "Low intensity conflict continues to be the most likely form of violence involving U.S. interests." In contrast, the 1992 version of the same report notes rather ambiguously that the collapse of the Soviet Union means "the United States should be able to counter low intensity conflict threats with greater selectivity."

The Pentagon's terminology is moving away from defining conflict intensity as it did during the 1980s, when conflicts were classified as either low, mid, or high intensity. The scenarios used in the 1991 Joint Chiefs of Staff *Joint Military Net Assessment* publication focus instead on peacetime engagements, contingencies, and global conflicts.

Less Military, More Political Conflict. The more political and lower-level operations that have also been included in the past as low intensity conflicts—such as nation-building assistance and peacekeeping—have not disappeared. A new term "forward-presence operations," has largely replaced "low intensity conflict" in the Pentagon's definition of those low-level military operations short of limited war but above the normal political and diplomatic process—with the list of missions remaining largely unchanged. According to the 1992 version of the DOD's *Annual Report to the President and the Congress*, forward-presence operations include "missions such as peacekeeping, disaster relief, nation building assistance, humanitarian assistance, military-to-military contacts, and security assistance."[6]

The new definition of forward-presence operations recognizes a strategic environment where, instead of—or along with—training host-nation militaries to combat antigovernment guerrillas, American advisers will be called upon to help strengthen institutions in the developing world and former communist bloc nations. Accordingly, the doctrines that guided American low intensity operations over the past decades are being supplemented by new doctrines, as yet inadequately defined, that recognize that the Soviet Union no longer lurks behind the turmoil in developing world states. American policy is moving away from the tendency of the past to think of the Third World in a bipolar context. The policy currently taking shape must be, at once, more tuned to a multipolar world and more sophisticated in its recognition of the country-specific demands of modernization and the complexities of institution building.

The new strategic concept of forward-presence operations acknowledges that the conflicts likely to characterize the "new world order" will often be of a more political than strictly military nature. The Pentagon anticipates these conflicts largely taking place in an environment of "peacetime engagement." Warfare has always been recognized by acute observers as a highly political act, in that armed conflict is designed to forward a state's or organization's political objectives. However, with the end of the cold war, the traditional norms of organized violence are undergoing a transformation such that previously military-dominated strategic concepts—mostly concerned with nuclear throw weights or the balance of opposing conventional forces in Central Europe—are giving way to strategic concepts with much more political and socioeconomic content.

The likely increasingly political nature of conflict implies that the traditional distinction between war and peace may become far less relevant. The same may also become true of the distinction between combatant and noncombatant. Indeed, civil society itself, once considered "noncombatant" or at least excluded from direct engagement, has evolved from being an acceptable field for military action, as in World Wars I and II, to the point that it often becomes the principal focus of armed conflict.

The Decline of Ideological Communism, the Resurgence of Other Animosities. The collapse of the former Soviet Union and its Eastern European empire has signalled the end of ideological communism as a rallying point for Third World revolutionaries. A tiny few, nominally communist insurgencies survive—in Peru and the Philippines for example—but they are pale shadows of an earlier threat. Massive economic failures throughout the communist world, as well as the collapse of the Soviet Union and its empire, when coupled with the desire for greater personal and political freedom among many who earlier subscribed to some form of Marxism, have resulted in the demise of ideological communism as a rallying point for aspiring revolutionaries.

But the decline in communist-driven internal conflict does not mean that the frequency of intrastate conflicts will diminish. Quite the contrary, their number can be expected to increase as a result of persistent animosities and lingering malaise in the Third World and the former communist world. Over the past decade—even with the thawing of the cold war—the frequency of intrastate conflict has only increased as societies have refocused hostility from an occupying power or government to various internal rivals. To the familiar social frustrations and political mobilization that accompany the process of modernization can be added ethnic and religious animosities, usually dating back centuries. Moreover, even if these latter ideological bases for internal conflict in the developing world are lacking or have disappeared, many of the underlying causes of instability—political, social, and economic problems—will remain.

As events in the former Soviet Union and in Eastern Europe illustrated in the early 1990s, the impetus to internal war is not limited to the Third World. In both those areas ethnic hostilities that have stayed latent under the pressure of Soviet armies are surging to the surface. The battles in Moldova and between Georgians and Ossetians epitomize the less than favorable results of the collapse of Soviet communism and are a disturbing harbinger of other potential conflicts in the region. A very real threat exists of a "proliferation of Yugoslavias," where hostilities among ethnic, religious, and nationalist factions produce casualties and chaos, with the further danger that surrounding states may become involved in the play of forces within the warring states.

The Central and Eastern European revolutions of 1989 sparked what is actually a second, and potentially much stronger, wave of modernization—of what can now be characterized as postcommunist modernization. The first wave was the rapid growth of new states throughout much of the Third World in the post–World War II era. The second wave of modernization currently under way in Eastern Europe and the former Soviet Union in many ways resembles the birth of nations in the postcolonial period, though clearly not at the same scale. The same dynamics which plagued new democracies in the Third World are evident in Eastern Europe, where the process of modernization generates powerful social and political forces which quickly overwhelm the old established institutions of government. As was the case during the 1950s, 1960s, and 1970s the same influences of ethnic nationalism, democratic aspiration, social mobility, and separatism are at play today. Former Secretary of Defense James Schlesinger has observed,

> It is doubtful that this country is prepared for the lengthy period of semi-chaos that must follow the breakdown of the previous structures of authority in the formerly communist states of Eastern Europe and the Soviet Union. . . . Most Americans are blind to the fragility of democratic institutions in unprepared soils.[7]

Revolutionary War. Following the great debate in the United States of the late 1960s and early 1970s over American involvement in Indochina, and the apparent consensus that emerged therefrom that there should be "no more

Vietnams,'' why a section on revolutionary war in a 1990s book on national security issues? The answer is twofold. First, there is no way of assessing where we now are without some appreciation of the immediate past—the United States, like many other states, has been involved in several revolutionary wars since 1945. Second, revolutionary war or a variant form of violent internal political change is likely to continue to be widespread in the future. Although some contemporary analysts dismiss internal or revolutionary war as a phenomenon of the cold war era, there are ample reasons to question such a hasty judgment. There is plenty of tinder about to ignite, even though the communists are not at hand to ignite or fan the flames with their ideology. Ethnicity and religion are alternative ideological bases on which revolutionary wars have occurred in the past and could well fill that role in the future.

Revolutionary war, as distinguished from other forms of political violence, such as the coup d'état, jacquerie, and mass rebellion, is largely a phenomenon of the twentieth century.[8] This is due to the higher frequency of such wars in this century, their broader geographic distribution, and the development of a body of theory spelling out the nature of revolutionary war and emphasizing it as a path to power. Moreover, two of the major world powers of this century, the Soviet Union and the People's Republic of China, specifically commended and endorsed revolutionary war as a legitimate political act. In the Soviet case, Premier Khrushchev's famous declaration in 1961 that the Soviet Union considered it its duty to support such ''wars of national liberation'' formalized what had been Soviet practice since the end of World War II.[9] Indeed, one of the original triggers of the cold war was the Soviet-supported communist insurgency in Greece from 1946 to 1948.

Some Defining Characteristics of Revolutionary War. *Revolutionary war* is organized violence, largely from within a state, with the political aim of overthrowing a government and restructuring the political, economic, and social order of the state. It is sometimes loosely called *internal war* or *insurgency* but actually is a larger concept than either of those alternatives. Revolutionary war, in its twentieth-century form, may be distinguished from other forms of conflict by several characteristics. It has an *organized, disciplined leadership*—the general staff of the revolution—usually in the form of an elite party. A charismatic figure frequently has a leadership role, such as did Mao Tse-tung Zedong in China, Ho Chi Minh in Vietnam, or Ahmed ben Bella in Algeria; such a figure permits revolutionary movements to manage the divisiveness that generally tends to mark them, particularly in their early stages.

The revolution's leaders follow (or say they follow) and proclaim a *popular ideology that is used to explain the past, present, and future* in ways supportive of the elite's goals. Where possible, the elite attempts to monopolize the appeal of nationalism, anticolonialism, or antiimperialism.

In order to develop, the revolution generally requires a *sanctuary* to serve as an administrative or logistical base. Such a sanctuary may be outside the national boundary, at least early on, but an internal sanctuary is usually created in due course, where the revolutionary leadership has near absolute security. This internal sanctuary also serves to support the claim of the revolutionary movement to legitimacy as an alternative to the regime, as well as to the particular government in power.

A sufficient *mass base* must be built to provide intelligence, material support, recruits, and external legitimacy. It should be noted that if the structure being attacked is sufficiently weak, the revolution may succeed so rapidly that popular support never becomes a true "mass base"; such was the case in Fidel Castro's takeover of Cuba.

Finally, the revolution must have the *military forces* to wage war; these usually will be a mix of local guerrillas, regional militia, and so-called regulars.[10] A measure of popular backing for these forces is essential for their success, crucially so in the early stages when they are most vulnerable to counterintelligence and suppression operations. Mao's dictum that the "people are water and the guerrillas, the fish" sums up the point.

Revolutionary wars are often further characterized in terms of stages or phases. One may speak of an initial or organizational stage, marked by covert political activity and propaganda. This is accompanied and followed by terrorist activity, designed to paralyze the regime and awe the populace, and by the initiation of guerrilla operations. Then comes a period of stepped-up guerrilla activity and initiation of conventional military activities. Finally, the revolutionary side becomes strong enough to meet and defeat the forces of the regime in major set-piece battles, leading to the defeat or collapse of the regime. Although each stage depends on revolutionary success in prior phases, it is entirely possible that several stages of the war will proceed simultaneously—for example, once the revolutionary forces have initiated conventional military activities, they are likely to continue their organizational, terroristic, and guerrilla activities as well.

Another version of phasing in revolutionary warfare refers to the strategic defensive, stalemate, and strategic offensive. Such characterizations are useful, but they may be misleading in their precision. In most revolutionary wars, there is a blurring of stages as both sides experiment and probe, succeed and fail. From an internal point of view, however, the phase/stage characterizations have great importance because decisions about phases may have significant impact on the strategies and tactics of both the regime and the revolution.[11]

In the struggle to overthrow the old order and to legitimize a new one, the matter in contention is not ultimately one of territorial advantage or destruction of armies, but, to use a hackneyed phrase, one of the "hearts and minds" of the people. The revolutionaries' point of strength or vulnerability lies in their populace base—what Clausewitz called their "centre of gravity."

Alexander had his center of gravity in his army, as had Gustavus Adolphus, Charles XII, and Frederick the Great, and the career of any one of them would soon have been brought to a close by the destruction of his fighting force: in states torn by internal dissensions, this center generally lies in the capital; in small states dependent on greater ones, it lies generally in the army of these allies; in a confederacy, it lies in the unity of interests; in a *national insurrection, in the person of the chief leader, and in public opinion*. Against these points the blow must be directed.[12] (Emphasis added.)

Revolutionary War Experience. Analysts are far from agreement on the theory of revolutionary war. It understates the case to say that the causes and conduct of revolutionary wars are diverse and particularized. Nevertheless, a brief review of six of the revolutionary war experiences since World War II provides several instructive lessons.

Greece. Greece was the scene of an unsuccessful revolutionary war in the immediate (1946–1948) aftermath of World War II. Communist-led guerrillas who had operated behind the German lines during the war contested the restoration of the monarchy. With British and then American support, the Greek government managed to hold on and make some progress in suppression. However, external events had a decisive impact on this war. The revolutionary forces were largely dependent upon the Soviet Union, Albania, and Yugoslavia for sanctuary, training, and equipment. When Yugoslavia, the key country, closed its border with Greece following Tito's break with the Soviet Union and the Cominform in 1948, the Greek revolution was suppressed quite rapidly.

Philippines. A very serious postindependence revolutionary war raged during the period 1948–1951 in the Philippines. The Huk (*Hukbalahap*, or People's Liberation Army)[13] launched a campaign that very nearly brought the Philippine government to its knees. The revolution was suppressed under the Secretary of National Defense Ramon Magsaysay (1950–1953), who later became president (1953–1957). However, Magsaysay's successors proved unwilling or unable to maintain the reforms and military momentum he built up, and small-scale revolutionary activities have continued to be a running sore. Cut off from the aid from abroad that it received earlier, primarily from China, the New People's Army successor to the Huks continues to fight a phase one-plus insurgency. Despite progress in democratization under President Aquino (1986–1992), the poverty, corruption, and population pressure that provide fertile ground for revolutionary warfare remain, and the Philippines could again become the scene of a large-scale revolutionary war during the 1990s. The situation is complicated by the presence of a large and defiant Moslem minority in the far south, requiring the government to divert attention and resources from Luzon and the central Philippines.

China. It is helpful to the revolutionary party if it can appeal to nationalist sentiment among the people. The Chinese Communist Party (CCP) exploited anti-Japanese and antiforeign sentiments quite successfully, both before and after 1945. Nevertheless, we should remember that the Chinese revolution was much more than a nationalist struggle against Japanese and Western dominance; it was also a genuine revolution against the Chinese political, economic, and social order. The CCP leadership of the Chinese revolution in its later stages sometimes overshadowed the true nature of this cataclysmic event, beginning in 1911 and ending only in 1949–1950.[14]

Vietnam. The wars in Indochina after 1946 provide the textbook case of revolutionary war that succeed despite incredibly difficult obstacles. Frustrated for nearly thirty years by the resistance of internal opponents, aided and encouraged first by France and then by the United States, the Vietnamese revolutionaries finally managed to unify all of Vietnam under their control in 1975. Building on the theories and practice of the Chinese revolutionaries, Ho Chi Minh and his Vietnamese colleagues succeeded—not once, but twice—in revolutionary warfare. From 1946 to 1954 they fought a successful, classical three-phase insurgency against the French colonial forces and their Vietnamese auxiliaries. From 1956 to 1975 they again struggled successfully, this time against the South Vietnamese forces and their American allies. Chapter 17, on East Asia, contains a further description and analyses of this conflict.

Algeria. An outstanding example of a successful anticolonial revolution (1954–1962), the Algerian case is a curious one. The revolutionary military forces were suppressed within Algeria, but the colonial power, France, decided that the price of maintaining its rule was too high over the long run and negotiated an agreement of independence *after the suppression*. The political will of France broke—as it had done earlier in Indochina.

Iran. The Iranian internal war in the late 1970s presented such contrasts to the earlier, classic cases of Algeria, China, and Vietnam that some observers might not classify it as a revolutionary war at all. Yet, the Iranian revolution fits the definition given earlier and exhibits (in variant forms) such wars' distinguishing characteristics. Several aspects of the Iranian revolution of 1978–1979 were new, most strikingly the facts that its ideological force was Islam, rather than the usual anticolonialism or nationalism (although there were important elements of these appeals as well) and that its leadership was clerical rather than secular.

From his sanctuaries—first in Iraq, then in France—the Ayatollah Khomeini rallied a wide coalition of interests opposed to the regime with the call that traditional religious values were being destroyed by the Shah's westernization program and by his corruption. Drawing on the tradition that the Shia form of Islam has long offered an alternative source of authority to Iran's secular rulers, Khomeini—while still safely in France—stimulated enormous public demonstrations in Teheran and Iran's other major cities, calling for the Shah's overthrow and installation of a new Islamic order.

The mullahs, relatively secure in their mosques and Moslem schools and seminaries from the Shah's secret police, formed the disciplined cadres and agents for the revolution. The Ayatollah and these clerical allies had their own military forces—the revolutionary militias—but it was not necessary for them to proceed through the terrorism–guerrilla–conventional warfare phases of classical revolutionary war in order to defeat the government's armed forces. Rather, the appeal of a new Islamic order, the massive and sustained nature of open public support, the disciplined leadership of the ayatollahs and mullahs, and the charismatic appeal of Khomeini combined to undermine the Shah's political and military base. The Shah's center of gravity disintegrated like a peasant's house in the all-too-frequent Iranian earthquakes.

Some Lessons from the Cases Cited. Although the foregoing examination of a few of the significant revolutionary wars since 1945 is sketchy, even from our limited sample it is possible to draw some important lessons. Some of these have already been mentioned, but it may be useful to restate them briefly.

First, though there have been variant patterns, successful revolutionary wars have rested on most or all of the elements listed earlier, namely, disciplined leadership, strong ideology, sanctuaries, mass base, and military forces. Of these factors, leadership and ideology are crucial; given them, the revolution can generally create the other elements.

Second, it is not necessary for revolutionaries to win a military victory in order to win a revolutionary war—although they have to be able to fight sufficiently to protect their key leaders and cadre and to inflict casualties on the government's forces. The case of Algeria is decisive on this point, as already suggested. In the end, revolutionary war becomes predominantly a matter of will and public opinion, as the example of the French in Indochina also attests. The American experience in Vietnam further illustrates the crucial role of public support.

Third, many revolutionaries are impatient. Obviously, they would prefer to have the revolution completed so that they could enjoy the fruits that they see as accompanying victory. The path to power through revolutionary war is not an easy one. To choose that route is to condemn oneself to years of difficult, bloody, and dangerous organizational activity and protracted conflict, the end of which is in doubt and the consequences of which may be dire.[15] Many cadre leave the revolution, convinced of its rightness and ultimate success but unwilling to endure. Existing regimes can use this weariness–impotence factor to wear out revolutionary opponents.

Fourth, in most cases the revolutionaries' struggle is an uphill one: established regimes are supported by inertia, by structures, by habit. Most people, most of the time, accept the legitimacy of an existing regime—even if they are dissatisfied with the way it works. Most states are conceded by their populace to have a monopoly over legitimate forms of violence—defense and the police power. Bureaucracies—civil, police, and military—can often be used by regimes to counter the revolutionary forces soon enough and with enough strength to suppress them. Moreover, in much of the world, people do not really see themselves as a part of a political process—they eke out a living under the current regime and do not see any real alternative.

Fifth, where revolutionary forces are heavily dependent on external support, withdrawal of such support can cause the balance to shift decisively to favor the regime. One such case is Greece, discussed earlier in this chapter. South Vietnam may have been another. During most of the 1960s, U.S. policy was based on an assumption that if North Vietnam withdrew support and direction of the revolutionary war in South Vietnam, the revolutionary movement would collapse or be successfully suppressed. This assumption may have been true, but it was never tested because the gradual, incremental pressures and penalties that the United States placed on North Vietnam did not compel it to desist.

Sixth, a threatened regime can preempt revolution by eliminating the conditions that provide fertile soil in which revolutionary wars are nurtured. As noted, President Magsaysay combined the successful use of this approach with skillful military tactics to suppress the Huks. In contrast, the Shah of Iran attempted too much, too fast, failing to build a broad popular consensus—thus providing openings for his revolutionary opponents.

Seventh, timing and phasing can be crucial. If the revolutionaries take to the streets or hills and jungles prematurely, the regime may nip the war in the bud. If they wait too long, the regime may grow stronger and change the objective conditions that once contributed to generating support for revolution. In ideological jargon, it is essential that the revolutionary leadership place itself always at the vanguard of revolution. If it ventures ahead of the vanguard, the leadership will fall into adventurism; behind, it will fall into mimicry. In the former case, suppression or liquidation will follow; in the latter, the revolutionary leadership will be swept aside as anachronistic.

The Struggle to "Institutionalize the Irregular." The American military's role in shaping the outcome of foreign internal conflicts has historically suffered from what J. Bowyer Bell describes as difficulty in "institutionalizing the irregular."[16] Even though, as Bell explains, since the 1950s the unconventional has occurred regularly, the military still resists familiarity with the concept of politically dominated internal warfare.[17] Along with the rest of American society, the American military has traditionally drawn a clear distinction between military and political affairs, and, as "an explicitly politico-military doctrine, counterinsurgency violated this distinction."[18] The fact that internal conflict is first and foremost a political conflict that often exists in a condition of neither war nor peace has made it exceedingly difficult for a military establishment to develop an effective doctrine to meet it.

Although the American military had provided training and logistical assistance to the Greek and Philippine governments in their successful efforts to counter revolutionary warfare early in the post–World War II period, it was not until the Kennedy administration (1961–1963) that the United States focused on Third World internal wars and the first attempts were made to institutionalize a distinctive approach to revolutionary warfare. The new president was so impressed by Premier Khrushchev's speech announcing the Soviet Union's support for "wars of national liberation" that he read excerpts from the speech at his first National Security Council (NSC) meeting.[19] Kennedy's determination to counter communist-inspired insurgency spurred academia and the military alike to attempt to draw a blueprint for dealing with the challenge of such conflict under the title of "counterinsurgency warfare."

Under the president's personal urging, the government for the first time stressed integrated policies of economic development, support for democratic institutions, and security. The army's Special Warfare Center at Fort Bragg, North Carolina, which was redesignated the John F. Kennedy Center for Special Warfare, broadened its curriculum to teach and train in counterinsurgency warfare. Every army school was required to add counterinsurgency to its syllabus.

It is doubtful that the administration could have chosen a more difficult locale than South Vietnam to apply the lessons it was attempting to teach. That country was characterized by a lack of national unity and identity, weak and divided leadership, a government with a tenuous claim to legitimacy, and a larger, more cohesive neighboring communist state determined to exterminate it. In retrospect, it may well be that, facing such odds, underwriting and shoring up a government in South Vietnam until it could stand on its own was simply not possible.

In Vietnam, moreover, the American military was unfamiliar with, unprepared for, and initially and for too long unwilling to adapt to its new mission of counterinsurgency warfare. Not understanding this kind of warfare, senior military leaders were far too optimistic in their estimates of how well the South Vietnamese (and later the American) forces were doing against the insurgents, the Viet Cong. Furthermore, they never accepted the idea that political efforts should be equal to or have greater priority than military operations. Preoccupied with the threat of a North Vietnamese invasion—understandably in view of the recent Korean War experience—the senior military rejected the slower, more patient approach which emphasized population protection over offensive military operations.[20] Perhaps that patient approach which had proven successful in the often cited example of Britain's successful counterinsurgency campaign in Malaya would not have worked in Vietnam, given the very great differences in the two situations, but it was never tried.

White House efforts to strengthen the country's capabilities for counterinsurgency ran up against U.S. armed forces that were reluctant to change their institutional missions and doctrines from those developed for the European theater—which, in turn, leaned on the conventional war lessons learned in World War II and Korea. As one example, the military's primary response to Kennedy's call for additional special units to wage counterinsurgency war was to create special operations forces more appropriate for operations behind enemy lines in support of a conventional conflict against the Soviets than for counterinsurgency in Vietnam.

From 1955, when its military assistance and advisory group (MAAG) to Vietnam took over responsibility from the French, until 1963 when Kennedy directed a major expansion in the advisory effort and provision of helicopters (with American pilots) to support the floundering South Vietnamese forces, the United States was singularly unsuccessful in its own counterinsurgency campaign and in training the South Vietnamese in theirs.

By 1965 the situation had deteriorated so badly that further modest help would clearly be insufficient; only the intervention of major U.S. forces could prevent the collapse of the South. In response, President Johnson authorized the dispatch of the first American ground combat units, which began arriving mid year. Once its combat units became fully engaged in Vietnam, the U.S. military could focus its own efforts on conventional war against larger guerrilla units and regular North Vietnamese army forces that were by then increasingly infiltrating the South.[21] The counterinsurgency war's central task of rural pacification, crucial to eventual victory or defeat, was essentially left to the South Vietnamese army and its associated local and regional militias. In theory, this was a logical division of labor, but in practice the South Vietnamese forces were not up to the challenge and the U.S. military's heavy firepower, high mobility, and search and destroy operations were of little help—and indeed were often counterproductive.[22]

Following the catastrophic conclusion of the Vietnam War, the United States failed to develop a coherent approach to addressing the challenge of Third World low-level conflict. The trauma caused by the war and its domestic U.S. reaction encouraged both civilians and the military to neglect reflection on and analysis of that conflict. Perhaps the principal lesson learned by the military was never again to use power incrementally, and by the civilians, never again to commit forces without the full understanding and support of the American people.

Theories developed prior to and during the war about countering insurgencies were put in the inactive files by the military and much of academia, while the American government continued to approach Third World conflict in an ad hoc manner. In effect, the military services turned again to their conventional war missions and expunged the experience of Vietnam from their memory. The units with the most experience in counterinsurgency warfare, the Special Forces, were cut back from a high point of 13,000 personnel in 1969 to 3,000 in 1980.[23] During the 1970s Special Forces training changed from a foreign area emphasis to the traditional mission in support of conventional forces in a general war scenario. Cuts in security assistance and in security assistance personnel also followed in the 1970s in the wake of Vietnam; many Americans, including a majority of the Congress, were not convinced that these were useful in LIC; rather, it was widely believed that such instruments might drag the country into another quagmire.

The Record of the 1980s: Continued Struggle. Early in the first term of the Reagan administration, key policymakers decided the best tools to "draw the line" against communist expansion in the Third World were, again, American advisers and military aid. American military advisers were dispatched or augmented throughout Central America, for instance, while money and military hardware went to anticommunist forces in Afghanistan, Nicaragua, and Angola. The outcomes of the anticommunist contests in El Salvador, Nicaragua, Angola, and Afghanistan were determined by the transformation of the strategic environment—that is, the weakening and then demise of Soviet communism—as well as by American policy. One positive result of the Reagan administration's activist policy in low intensity conflict situations was to force the U.S. military to confront this subject, which had mostly been ignored since the end of the Vietnam war. As one analyst put it, the 1980s "ushered in a new counterinsurgency era."[24] The military spent the early years of the decade developing a new doctrine of low intensity conflict that incorporated lessons of Vietnam. The United States found the test case for the application of this new doctrine in El Salvador, the most prolonged conflict involving the United States since Vietnam. Both military and government policymakers were determined to demonstrate in El Salvador the effectiveness of low intensity conflict doctrine in defeating communist guerrillas, facilitating economic development, and establishing legitimate democracy.[25]

However, ten years and $6 billion dollars later, America had failed to reach its goal of a clear victory for the Salvadoran regime. Although the fighting in El Salvador ended, the U.S.-backed Salvadoran government failed to defeat the communist guerrillas and, in the end, was forced to make numerous concessions that Washington had long opposed. Not surprisingly, the goals of economic development and democratization have yet to be realized. The enormous sums of money the United States poured into El Salvador during the 1980s did prevent the fall of the Salvadoran government to the guerrillas. Yet, the dependence of El Salvador's government on U.S. support undercut the regime's autonomy and hence weakened its legitimacy.[26] American aid also served to empower the military, which continues to dominate the political process.

Reflecting one of the problems in Vietnam, Americans overestimated their ability to shape the outcome of an intrastate conflict. The United States believed that in El Salvador it could transform what was a violent and unjust society into a more liberal and democratic one. American policymakers failed to consider that "human character, history, culture, and social structure are highly resistant to outside influence."[27] According to one assessment of America's low intensity conflict doctrine in El Salvador: "Those complex and ambitious tasks whose fulfillment we have regarded as essential to defeat insurgencies in foreign lands are not, it appears, within our power to accomplish."[28]

The experience of the American government and political process in foreign internal conflict indicates that the complexities of intrastate warfare, in which military, political, social, and economic factors are all combined, demand a strategy that thoroughly integrates all these factors. In this highly complex and highly politicized form of conflict the employment of military resources comprises only an element, albeit an essential one, in the overall strategy designed to bring about a political or societal change. Undoubtedly, the American military possesses the basic capabilities for functioning in low-level Third World conflict and is able to enhance those capabilities as necessary; but without a priority mission focus on LIC and a national strategy into which the military element is fitted, these capabilities will likely continue to be misdirected or wasted.

Transnational Narcotics Trafficking. Drug trafficking has surged to the forefront of national security policy concerns. Toward the end of the 1980s, the American public and policymakers alike realized that drug trafficking and drug abuse posed a fundamental threat to American security. Consequently, the Reagan administration declared a war on drugs and stepped up military involvement and funding for antidrug operations, along with increases in the budgets of other agencies countering drug trafficking and drug use. However, unilateral and bilateral efforts by the United States to contain an expanding drug trade have proven to be no match for the challenge.

Despite a $39 billion national investment in federal drug control programs since 1989, the creation of a "drug czar," stiffer prison sentences, and the invasion of Panama to choke off part of the flow, America's drug problem continues. The average price and purity of cocaine has remained relatively unchanged in the past ten years. Heroin is a less expensive and more potent drug than it was two decades ago, and the United States has become the world's second largest producer of marijuana. While there has been a modest decline in the consumption rate among casual users, consumption among frequent users (who consume an estimated 70 to 80 percent of all drugs) has changed little and has actually risen among some population groups. The most favorable interpretation of these grim statistics is that the problem would be a good deal worse were it not for recent U.S. counterdrug efforts. Such a view seems unlikely to counter the growing public disenchantment with the "war on drugs." Absent a clear direction and purpose, budget allocations for antidrug programs may well decline; but military involvement in such programs, still small in 1992, could grow as political leaders seek for low-cost solutions to the problem.[29]

The latest challenge posed by narcotics trafficking may now rest outside the United States, as more countries become involved in one capacity or another. Particularly ominous is the expansion of criminal networks and their connection to insurgency movements, the attendant corruption of political institutions, and the fueling of underground economies that is associated with the expansion of the drug trade. Collectively, these trends could threaten many of the world's new fragile democracies and undermine their fledgling market economies.

A leveling off of U.S. drug consumption, the breakdown of regulatory and social institutions within the former communist bloc, the growing integration of the international economy, and the desperate plight of many developing nations are leading to a transformation of the drug problem. The foregoing developments, along with record levels of global production, have created something of a global glut in heroin, cocaine, and marijuana, spurring trafficking organizations to expand their markets outside the Western Hemisphere. These organizations appear to be benefitting from the collapse of the command economies and the end of nearly a half-century of economic isolation in Eastern Europe and in the former Soviet Union. The resultant regulatory "no-man's land" has provided new opportunities for smuggling drugs and the laundering of profits. Also, the growing social alienation and disaffection, combined with the prospects of convertible currencies, are making the region's population irresistible targets for the marketing of drugs.

These developments in the former Soviet and East European scene come on the heels of recent trafficker efforts to create a broader West European market—efforts that have been helped when the member nations of the European Community carried through their decision to open their borders by the end of 1992. Open borders mean that, once illicit drugs manage to enter the community, their movement will be much more difficult to monitor and control.

In the developing world, demographic trends, the persistent problem of debt, lackluster commodities markets, and the recent global recession leave most governments with few resources and in many cases little incentive to fend off a growing economic dependency on the drug trade. Global free trade may receive a setback as states adopt restrictive regulatory measures to stem a perceived or actual rise in the drug market within their borders.

The one bright light in this dismal picture is that opportunities for international cooperation are increasing now that the cold war is over. Fundamental policy shifts in the republics of the former Soviet Union, Eastern Europe, and China, along with a growing sense of concern by Japan and the West Europeans, make cooperative international arrangements feasible for the first time since the early twentieth century opium conventions. Such arrangements will require a reassessment of the present U.S. national drug control strategy, with its emphasis on unilateral and bilateral law enforcement efforts. Traditional U.S. drug control initiatives will have to be subordinated to a strategy that recognizes the American problem as part of a collective challenge posed by worldwide drug production, trafficking, and consumption. Stirrings in the United Nations suggest that it may focus on this scourge in the course of the 1990s. One former U.N. senior official who headed many peacekeeping operations suggests that

> a multilateral surveillance system for drug interdiction could be developed on the basis of present experience. Joint patrolling and surveillance across land frontiers could be greatly improved by the creation of a specialized paramilitary force.[30]

Terrorism. Beginning with the October 1979 takeover of the American Embassy in Teheran, and the ensuing 444-day hostage crisis, Americans realized that international terrorism was no longer someone else's problem. During the early to mid 1980s international terrorism emerged as a significant threat to American interests and citizens overseas. As incidents increased, it became clear that this threat was one to which the U.S. government and its allies would have to devote more attention and resources. As the *Report of the Vice President's Task Force on Combatting Terrorism* observed in 1986, "during the past decade, terrorists have attacked U.S. officials or installations abroad approximately once every seventeen days."[31] The most significant of these was the 1983 suicide attack on the U.S. Marine Compound in Beirut, in which 241 Americans were killed.

The disastrous American intervention in Lebanon in 1982 provided strong evidence of the complexity and unconventional nature of terrorism. The military was pushed into a peacekeeping mission in Beirut by an administration with little understanding of Lebanon's complex and volatile environment. The American leadership failed to realize that direct American support for the Lebanese Army, including offshore bombardment by the 16-inch guns of the battleship New Jersey, prejudiced the Marines' ostensible peacekeeping image to the point of ineffectiveness. Moreover, military action cast the United States as an active participant in the conflict, causing American forces to become a target for rival factions, as evidenced by the bombing of the Marine barracks. No amount of training or preparation could have enabled the Marines to avoid the dangerous situation into which they were cast by political requirements.

The unprecedented high number of international terrorist incidents of the mid to late 1980s showed a decline by the early 1990s. The exact reasons for the decline are unknown, but several hypotheses have been suggested. One is that the 1986 air attacks on Libya carried out by the United States in retaliation for the bombing of a Berlin disco had somehow deterred terrorism; but the number of recorded international terrorist incidents did not begin to decline until 1989.

A second, more likely, hypothesis is that a decade of ever more violent terrorist attacks had compelled Western nations to step up their defenses against terrorism. This included increasing counterterrorist cooperation among governments, although there are as yet no ongoing procedures for pooling information on potential terrorist threats. Third, international organizations have assumed a more active role; for example, as a result of the 1988 Lockerbie and 1987 Korean Airline bombings, the U.N.'s International Civil Aviation Organization sponsored a convention in 1991 to better monitor the production and distribution of plastic explosives. This concluded with the signing of the "Convention on the Marking of Plastic Explosives for the Purpose of Detection" by all major nations producing such explosives.

The end of the cold war has also had a positive influence on combatting terrorism. Not only has the democratization of Eastern European states denied terrorist groups traditional sources of funding, weapons, and the havens behind which they could safely operate, but the involvement of previous totalitarian regimes has been revealed. Files maintained by the Eastern European security forces have permitted the identification and prosecution of suspected terrorists. One example was the dismantling of the Red Army Faction in Germany, which was possible only through analysis of the former East German secret police (Stasi) files and the assistance of former Stasi personnel. At the same time, however, the collapse of the Soviet Union raises the possibility of terrorist acquisition of nuclear technology.

At this point, it should be noted that Middle Eastern–affiliated terrorist activity has been declining.[32] Again, this trend should be seen partly as a result of the warming of East–West relations. Middle Eastern states, such as Syria and Iran, no longer confident of being able to play on U.S.–Soviet animosity, have been forced to reevaluate their relations with the United States, with whom they hope to improve economic ties. This was likely the prime motivating factor behind the 1991 release of the American hostages in Beirut by Iranian-supported groups such as the Islamic Jihad.

In the early 1990s terrorism directed against the United States by Asia and Latin America increased. Latin America not only had the highest number of terrorist attacks in 1990, but two thirds of all anti–United States incidents occurred in the region.[33] Narcoterrorism, a relatively new phenomenon that will likely increase in the 1990s, was a major contributing factor to this trend. Especially troubling is the interdependency of the drug industry and terrorism in South America. The Sendero Luminoso (Shining Path) group, which controls much of Peru's drug-producing regions, has used the narcotics trade as a primary funding source. Outside Latin America, narcotics-funded terrorist activity is also evident in Thailand, Afghanistan, and Laos.

As the political environment of the post–cold war era develops further, the influence of international terrorism on world politics in general and on American national security in particular remains unclear. The recent positive trends in Europe are likely to continue, although we could see increased nationalistic terrorism in the Eastern Europe and the former Soviet Union. In the Middle East, the situation is even vaguer. Although the first significant efforts to promote an Arab–Israeli settlement are under way as of 1992, continued anti-Israel terrorist incidents can be expected. An increase in terrorist activities in South America could well occur with a proliferation of narcotics trafficking.

New Directions. A predictable American response to any serious failure or disappointment has invariably been to tinker with organizational charts. It is not surprising, then, to find that in 1986, Congress mandated three steps to reorganize America's LIC capabilities. First, establishment of a unified service command for special operations called the Special Operations Command (SOCOM); second, creation of an office at the assistant secretary of defense level for special operations and LIC; third, the recommendation that a board be established at the National Security Council to discuss and formulate LIC policy. Nor has Congress been the only source of ideas for reordering the bureaucratic structure to support the prosecution of LIC. In 1989, the military's own Center for Low Intensity Conflict recommended the creation of subunified commanders at the theater command level to manage LIC challenges.[34]

Although the budget for special operations and LIC had increased by the early 1990s, it still remained less than one percent of the total DOD budget. As one analyst notes, "this budgetary insignificance deadens the prospect that special operations . . . will ever receive the serious, prolonged attention hoped for by congressional supporters."[35] The establishment of SOCOM itself initially met with opposition from the Service chiefs and various regional commanders. Despite the objections of Congress, the joint chiefs decreed that SOCOM be located in Florida, effectively removing the command from mainstream Washington activity and bureaucratic warfare. Moreover, the general commanding

SOCOM, is not responsible for LIC policy or prosecution but rather for the special operations forces culled from the different services.[36] The other regional commanders retain some LIC functions, thus dividing responsibility among disparate commands with often widely differing, regional specific objectives.

Two crucial questions that policymakers contemplating forward-presence operations will be forced to confront in the future are where the United States should intervene and with what resources. As a recent study argues: "the United States needs a new, more accurate triage mechanism, an analytical tool for assessing 'the realities of each case' lest blind application of the policies of the past once again commit us to an unwinnable war."[37] Without the alignments provided by the "stable" bipolar system, answering those two questions will become more complex.

Clearly, the demise of the East–West contest will limit U.S. involvement in Third World conflicts, for its interests in those areas can now be more narrowly defined. But too narrow a definition of interests can be dangerous, as the case of Secretary of State Dean Acheson's 1949 exclusion of South Korea from a list of America's vital interests demonstrates, an exclusion which may well have encouraged North Korea to invade in 1950—in turn providing a scenario that may have been imitated in Iraq's attack invasion of Kuwait in 1990. In a similar vein, a country such as Chad is hardly vital to U.S. national security; however, when threatened by Libya, Chad became a symbol of "American resolve to help protect countries from Qadafi's expansionist designs."[38] Thus, American arms and assistance were funneled to the Chadian military, helping them to deal Qadafi's Libyan forces a humiliating military defeat in 1987.

Assessments of where America's military forces should be involved in LIC and with what resources will in the future be made in the context of what the United Nations or other international bodies are doing or are willing to do. In low-level conflict and peacekeeping operations, we will need to look increasingly to our allies for assistance. The Persian Gulf war highlighted the fact that economic and political realities will prohibit the United States from undertaking major interventions alone; that same lesson may apply in the future to smaller, low intensity interventions. Our ability to contribute to peace in many situations may be facilitated by also working through regional organizations. In early 1992, NATO agreed, for the first time, to take part in peacekeeping operations outside of NATO country borders. Although American support for such operations will likely consist primarily of logistics and strategic lift assets, future American participation could extend to the actual deployment of American forces.

Perhaps the most important question to be answered before becoming involved in forward-presence operations in intrastate conflicts is whether and to what extent the United States can decisively influence a nation's political and societal course. As Michael Shafer contends: "For policymakers contemplating involvement the issue is not what threatened governments *ought* to do, but rather sober analysis of what they *can* do and what leverage the United States possesses to make them do it."[39] Though America has tried to bring about societal and political reform in Vietnam, El Salvador, and elsewhere, the record has not been encouraging. We have been able to help others buy time, but our capability to assist countries struggling for democracy or basic social change is limited. Local efforts that we can assist but not direct will essentially determine success or failure.

Discussion Questions

1. Describe the new strategic concept of forward-presence operations. Will this demand greater or lesser American intervention in foreign disputes?

2. Why can it be argued that modern industrial "total war" may have ended with the cold war? Do you agree or disagree with this position?

3. How will the decline of ideologically based communism affect world conflict? Will conflicts likely increase or decrease in number? Why?

4. Explain the American military's resistance to adapt to Third World counterinsurgency warfare. When did the United States first encounter this type of warfare? How did the United States respond?

5. Draw comparisons between America's involvement in Vietnam and its later involvement in El Salvador. Has America's low intensity conflict doctrine changed during the interim period?

6. What will determine U.S. involvement in future low-level intrastate conflicts now that the threat of global communism is gone?

7. Is Joseph Nye's characterization of the new international strategic system accurate? Will the American public support U.S. involvement with the world's "grey guys"? Discuss the case of Syria as ally in the 1991 Persian Gulf war.

8. Do you think the term "low intensity conflict" is an accurate one? Should it continue to be used as it has in the past? What would you use as a replacement?

Recommended Reading

Asprey, Robert, ed. *War in the Shadows: The Guerrilla in History*. 2 vols. Garden City, N.Y.: Doubleday, 1975.

Bacevich, Lt. Col. A. J., Hallums, Lt. Col. James, White, Lt. Col. Richard, Young, Lt. Col. Thomas. *American Military Policy in Small Wars: The Case of El Salvador*, for the Institute for Foreign Policy Analysis. Washington, D.C.: Pergamon-Brassey's International Defense Publishers, 1988.

Blaufarb, Douglas. *The Counterinsurgency Era: U.S. Doctrine and Performance, 1950 to the Present*. New York: The Free Press, 1977.

Brodie, Bernard. *War and Politics*. New York: MacMillan, 1973.

Clutterbuck, Richard. *The Long War: Counterinsurgency in the Third World*. New York: Penguin Books, 1976.

Cohen, Eliot A. "Distant Battles: Modern War in the Third World." *International Security* 10 (Spring 1986): 143–71.

Currey, Cecil B. *Edward Lansdale: The Unquiet American*. Boston: Houghton-Mifflin, 1988.

Drew, Col. Dennis. *Insurgency and Counterinsurgency: American Military Dilemmas and Doctrinal Proposals*. Maxwell Air Force Base, Ala.: Air University Press, March 1988.

Duncanson, Dennis J. *Government and Revolution in Vietnam*. New York: Oxford University Press, 1968.

Greentree, Todd R. *The United States and the Politics of Conflict in the Developing World: A Policy Study*, Report for the Foreign Service Institute, Center for the Study of Foreign Affairs, U.S. Department of State, Washington, D.C.: U.S. Government Printing Office, 1990.

Huntington, Samuel P., and Weiner, Myron, eds. *Understanding Political Development*. Boston: Little, Brown, 1987.

Joint Low Intensity Conflict Project. *Analytical Review of Low Intensity Conflict*. vol. 1. Fort Monroe, Va.: U.S. Army Training and Doctrine Command, 1986.

Klare, Michael, and Kornbluh, Peter, eds. *Low Intensity Warfare, Counterinsurgency, Proinsurgency and Antiterrorism in the Eighties*. New York: Random House, 1988.

Krepinevich, Andrew. *The Army and Vietnam*. Baltimore: Johns Hopkins University Press, 1986.

Kupperman, Robert, et al. *Low Intensity Conflict*. vols. 1 and 2. Fort Monroe, Va.: U.S. Army Training and Doctrine Command, 1983.

Lewy, Gunter. *America in Vietnam*. New York: Oxford University Press, 1978.

McClintock, Michael. *Instruments of Statecraft: U.S. Guerrilla Warfare, Counterinsurgency, and Counterterrorism, 1940–1990*. New York: Pantheon Books, 1992.

Odom, William E. *On Internal War: American and Soviet Approaches to Third World Clients and Insurgents*. Durham, N.C.: Duke University Press, 1992.

Palmer, Bruce. *The 25-Year War: America's Military Role in Vietnam*. New York: Simon & Schuster, 1984.

Paschall, Rod. "Low Intensity Conflict Doctrine: Who Needs It?" *Parameters* 15 (Autumn 1985).

Rikhye, Indar Jit. *Strengthening UN Peacekeeping: New Challenges and Proposals*. U. S. Institute for Peace, 1992.

Sarkesian, Sam, and Scully, William, eds. *U.S. Policy and Low Intensity Conflict*. London: Transaction Press, 1981.

Schultz, Richard H., Jr. "Low Intensity Conflict: Future Challenges and Lessons from the Reagan Years." *Survival* (July–August 1989).

Schwarz, Benjamin C. *American Counterinsurgency Doctrine and El Salvador*. Santa Monica, Calif.: Rand, 1992.

Shafer, Michael D. *Deadly Paradigms: The Failure of U.S. Counterinsurgency Policy*. Princeton, N.J.: Princeton University Press, 1988.

Tanham, G. K. *War Without Guns*. New York: Praeger, 1966.

Taylor, Maxwell. *Swords and Plowshares*. New York: Norton, 1972.

Thompson, Sir Robert. *Defeating Communist Insurgency: The Lessons of Malaya and Vietnam*. New York: Praeger, 1966.

14

Economic Challenges to National Security

Chapter 1 introduced the profound effects on the traditional international political system of the human, ideological, technological, and institutional revolutions since World War II. These revolutionary changes have been accompanied by an unprecedented period of world economic growth, driven in part by dramatic increases in economic interaction among nations. As the economies of the nations of the world have grown more complex, they also have become increasingly interdependent. Even excluding trade in services,* the total value of U.S. imports and exports exceeded $900 billion in 1991, about 16 percent of the gross national product (GNP). In Europe, where interdependence has a longer tradition, reliance upon trade is enormous. For example, almost 20 percent of the United Kingdom's GNP is in the form of exports; for Germany the figure is even higher, over 30 percent. And Japan, relatively isolated from the global economy until its post–World War II reconstruction, exports almost 11 percent of its GNP (now the second largest in the world).[1] Vital raw materials, energy, and food, as well as manufactured goods move in international commerce in staggering amounts. Global trade topped the $2 trillion mark for the first time in 1986 (Table 14.1), and reached $3 trillion in 1991.

The governments of many countries have assumed in the postwar period much greater responsibility for the economic performance of their societies. Political decision-makers have been answerable for traditional national security policy, but their increasing accountability for economic performance and growing economic interdependence have opened new relationships between national security and economic problems. Decisions made to advance national security objectives

---

*The services category, while substantial in value (approximately 30 percent of U.S. trade in recent years), has not been clearly defined by the U.S. government. Its value is estimated, but trade statistics used in this chapter refer only to the merchandise sector.

Table 14.1 World Trade, 1950–1991 (in Millions of $)

Year	*Exports*	*Imports*
1950	58,400	60,100
1955	87,000	91,900
1960	118,200	124,100
1965	170,300	179,500
1970	286,400	300,400
1975	811,600	826,700
1977	1,046,600	1,072,300
1979	1,537,000	1,567,500
1980	1,883,000	1,928,600
1981	1,851,300	1,909,700
1982	1,716,300	1,792,200
1983	1,666,300	1,736,000
1984	1,763,400	1,846,800
1985	1,782,900	1,879,000
1986	2,003,100	2,067,000
1987	2,355,300	2,418,400
1988	2,693,500	2,768,200
1989	2,906,600	3,005,100
1990	3,309,900	3,449,400
1991*	3,441,200	3,544,500

Source: International Monetary Fund, *International Financial Statistics, Yearbook 1991* (Washington, D.C.: IMF).
Note: Figures not adjusted for inflation.
*IMF, *Direction of Trade Statistics Yearbook,* 1992.

may adversely affect the accomplishment of economic goals, for example. Poor economic performance in itself may cause national security problems as unfulfilled expectations lead to political unrest or as budgetary pressures cause defense forces to shrink.

In a highly interdependent international system, a nation's stability can be powerfully affected by factors over which it has little control. Events in distant parts of the world, the policy choices of other governments, and the condition of the global economy as a whole all serve to complicate the situations confronting political decision-makers. These economic challenges can arise as a result of sudden dislocations in the system or because a confluence of factors has allowed long-term imbalances to develop. A severe reduction in the world oil supply is a dramatically clear example of the former that could produce devastating strains. The Iran–Iraq War, waged throughout the 1980s, resulted in attacks by both belligerents on oil tankers. This situation created an ever-present possibility of a drastic supply cutoff.

Although the United States has significantly reduced its dependence on Persian Gulf oil in the past decade, Japan and Western Europe remain heavily dependent on that area. For example, in 1990 Japan received about 70 percent of its oil from the Gulf, and sharp reduction or elimination of this source of oil would disrupt its economy, despite its stockpiling of oil reserves. This, along with the resultant competition for other sources of oil, would have severe consequences for the U.S. economy and its national security.

The danger to U.S. economic security posed by supply cutoffs is evident in the cases of a number of commodities, though not nearly so dramatically and drastically as in the case of oil. Of the twenty-four major nonfuel minerals needed by an industrial nation (aluminum, copper, iron, manganese, tin, zinc, etc.), the United States is substantially dependent on foreign sources for almost all of them; Japan and European nations are, again, even more import-dependent for these than are we (Table 14.2).[2]

In much of the past decade, an economic issue of great concern to national security was the mounting U.S. trade deficit, which during the 1980s had exceeded $160 billion per year. Between 1982 and 1986 the United States had grown from a net creditor nation with a surplus of over $140 billion to the world's largest debtor nation. At the end of 1991, America's cumulative net foreign debt was about $450 billion, greater than the amount owed by the next three largest debtor nations combined.

The causes of this deterioration are complex, but the effect is simple: a resurgence of protectionist sentiment in America. Critics of protectionist policies often recall the lesson of the worldwide depression of the 1930s, caused in large part by protectionism, in order to stave off a fresh wave of protectionist measures. But the American zeal for open markets and expanding trade that underpinned world economic growth for more than four decades after World War II had begun to flag by the end of the 1980s—even as interdependence continued to grow. Extensive and generally successful multinational negotiations have been conducted since that time to decrease trade barriers so that the protectionist trend may be reversed.

While increases in world trade and interdependence are not new, their explosive growth rate since World War II and their effects on the economic preeminence of the United States have been significant. At the end of World War II, the United States was the only major industrial nation whose economy had not suffered severe war damage. In 1945, the U.S. economy was relatively self-sufficient and far stronger than that of any other nation or group of nations. As the postwar "economic miracle" unfolded in Japan and Europe, trade among industrialized countries grew rapidly and many large industries, particularly in Western Europe and Japan, became increasingly export-oriented—in many cases heavily dependent on the American market. The rapid growth of industrial might in Europe and Japan began to shift the economic power balance away from the United States. During the 1970s and 1980s, the world witnessed a major increase in the economic performance of other East Asian nations, such as Singapore, Taiwan, and South Korea, as well. In the 1980s, these newly industrialized economies (NIEs) experienced real GNP increases annually of about 10 percent and by the 1990s are increasingly challenging Japan's dominant position in various economic sectors.

The giant American economy was not substantially dependent upon imports in

Table 14.2 U.S. Net Import Reliance through the Year 2000 for Selected Mineral Commodities

	Percentage of Total		
Material	*1984*	*1991 (est.)*	*2000 (est.)*
Antimony	54	57	94
Asbestos	75	95	90
Bauxite/alumina	96	100	93
Cadmium	56	54	69
Cesium	100	100	100
Chromium	82	80	100
Cobalt	95	82	71
Columbium	100	100	100
Copper	21	E	11
Corundum	100	100	100
Gold	16	NA	56
Gypsum	38	30	31
Iron ore	19	14	17
Lead	18	4	20
Lithium	E	E	E
Magnesium	E	15	18
Manganese	99	100	100
Mercury	60	W	100
Sheet mica	100	100	100
Molybdenum	E	E	E
Nickel	74	74	66
Phosphate rock	E	E	E
Platinum	91	88	100
Potash	74	67	67
Salt	10	11	11
Selenium	51	52	35
Silver	61	NA	64
Strontium	100	100	100
Sulfur	17	15	12
Talc	E	E	0
Tantalum	94	85	35
Tin	79	73	99
Tungsten	71	75	82
Vanadium	41	W	47
Zinc	67	30	58

Sources: Data from U.S. Department of the Interior, Bureau of Mines, *Mineral Commodity Summaries 1985 & 1992,* and *Mineral Facts and Problems,* 1980 ed. In Harold Bullis and James Mielke, *Strategic and Critical Materials* (Boulder, Colo.: Westview Press, 1985), p. 12.
E = net exporter; W = withheld to avoid disclosing company proprietary data; NA = not available.

the early postwar years (Table 14.3). Europe, Japan, and the developing world needed American markets for their exports more than we needed the products that those countries produced. By the 1970s, however, the U.S. economy had begun to develop significant dependence on less-developed countries (LDCs) for imports—mainly raw materials, of which oil was the most important. The Arab oil embargo of 1973–1974 indicated the degree of dependence of the U.S. economy on petroleum from the Middle East—a lesson underscored in early 1979 by the loss of Iranian exports. Inexpensive imported oil had, prior to 1973, helped fuel the rapid economic growth of the Western industrial economies. As these developed economies depleted their domestic reserves and increased their rates of energy consumption, the potential economic power of less-developed, oil-rich nations increased. The steep jumps in the price of imported oil in 1973–1974 and 1979–1980 reflected the shift in economic power away from the industrial nations and toward the oil exporters that had occurred—in large part because of the exhaustion of U.S. excess supply of oil.

Although the oil-induced power shift in the 1970s was highly visible and important, what is remarkable is the massive nature of that shift and the suddenness with which it occurred—both of which were at least partly the result of faulty American policies. This economic power shift, in turn, upset the traditional balance of political–military influence in the world and posed serious problems for U.S. national security in the late 1970s and 1980s.

U.S. international preeminence in the 1950s and 1960s rested on simultaneously strong economic, military, and political bases. When the economic and military legs began to weaken in the latter 1960s and early 1970s, it is not surprising that the whole national security stool became shaky. The United States

Table 14.3 U.S. Merchandise Trade and the Gross National Product

Year	*GNP (in Billions of $)*	*Exports*	*Imports*	*Exports plus Imports as Percentage of GNP*
1946	212.4	11.8	5.1	8.0
1950	288.3	10.2	9.1	6.7
1955	405.9	14.4	11.5	6.4
1960	515.3	20.5	15.2	6.9
1965	705.1	27.8	22.2	7.1
1970	1,015.5	44.5	40.9	8.4
1975	1,598.4	109.6	99.0	13.1
1980	2,732.0	225.1	247.5	17.3
1985	3,998.1	219.6	341.7	14.1
1986	4,206.1	217.3	387.1	14.4
1987	4,515.6	250.3	409.8	14.6
1988	4,873.7	320.3	447.3	15.7
1989	5,200.8	360.5	475.3	16.1
1990	5,463.0	393.6	495.3	16.0
1991	5,685.8	422.16	487.72	16.0

Sources: Economic Report of the President (Washington, D.C.: U.S. Government Printing Office, 1991), pp. 244, 266; Department of Commerce, Bureau of Economic Analysis, *Current Business,* March 1, 1987, p. 4; *International Financial Statistics,* August 1992, IMF, p. 538.

attempted to restore the military leg in the first half of the 1980s with a massive defense build-up that saw defense spending increase from $140 billion in 1980 to over $320 billion in 1991. However, by refusing to ask its populace to sacrifice to pay for this build-up (in fact, reducing taxes while building up!), the United States created massive budget and, in turn, trade deficits that eroded its economic position in the world and undermined support for a strong military at home.

This chapter examines international economic interdependence among the nations of the world and the contemporary problems for U.S. national security posed by the vulnerabilities inherent in such increased interdependence. The chapter will first survey the elements of international economics that have increased this interdependence, including international trade and capital flows, the international monetary system, and the adjustment mechanism for balance-of-payments disequilibria. In the latter half of the chapter, we relate these aspects of international economics to current U.S. national security issues.

The Elements of Interdependence

International Trade: Interdependence through Specialization. Before the Industrial Revolution, basically rural countries could be relatively self-sufficient. With industrialization, however, came large-scale production that required land, capital, labor, entrepreneurial talent, and raw materials, which often did not exist in sufficient quantities in one location to allow self-sufficiency. Thus, the need for increasing trade arose. Each trading partner could benefit by specializing in the production of the goods in which it enjoyed an advantage and by trading for other goods. Specialization, in turn, creates interdependence: when, for example, farmers in Great Britain gave up their crops and herds and went to work in factories producing textiles and machine tools, they had to depend on their American trading partners to produce food to be exchanged for their textiles and machine tools. Not only does increased trade among nations create interdependence at the national level, it also makes individuals within each country more dependent for their livelihoods and living standards upon economic developments abroad.

Trade raises real incomes in the countries that participate, because it results in a more efficient use of world resources. "More efficient" means that, with specialization and trade, a given amount of land, labor, and capital will produce more goods and services than would be possible if the same resources were used without specialization. If each country specializes in the production of goods in which it has comparative advantage and trades for other goods, it will be able to consume more goods and services than if it were to produce every good it used at home.

Comparative advantage theory requires that each country produce the goods that it produces relatively most efficiently, that is, with the smallest input of production resources in comparison with its trading partners, and that it trade for other goods at prices reflecting production costs. Each country will benefit from trade, *even if it can produce every good more efficiently than any other country.* If it uses its resources in the production of the goods it makes most efficiently in relation to its trading partners and exchanges those goods for other things it needs, the country's real income, that is, the goods and services available to its people, will be increased. Obviously, increased specialization and trade among nations is one of the primary means by which economic growth, generally measured as the rate of increase in the output of goods and services per capita, can occur.

As mentioned above, the post–World War II period has been one of unprecedented economic growth. From 1945 to 1978, for instance, the total of the GNPs of all the countries of the world, the gross world product (GWP), had increased more than three and one-half times in real terms (adjusted for inflation), while world trade volume (exports), similarly adjusted, had increased more than six times. When this rate of growth of world trade is compared with the record of the first forty-five years of this century, in which world export trade volume increased by only ten percent, the dramatic developments in postwar international trade seem the more remarkable.[3]

While most of the nations of the world have increased their participation in international commerce, the bulk of the postwar increase in world trade has been accounted for by rising trade among the industrialized countries. To the extent it is a function of rising international trade, then, interdependence among nations has grown most among these industrial economies. The depletion of petroleum reserves in developed countries and the rise in world oil use have, however, also made the industrial powers increasingly dependent on the oil-exporting LDCs. By 1990 roughly 15% of all world trade was in oil, dwarfing all categories of traded goods.

Table 14.4 shows the distribution of U.S. international trade by trading partner.

The large and relatively open American market has been an important source of export earnings for U.S. trading partners. Japan, in particular, but the NIEs as well have relied heavily on the United States as an outlet for their export-oriented economies. Table 14.5 shows the percentage of total commodity exports of various nations or groups that were sold in the U.S. market in 1985.

Obviously, policy changes or other economic developments in the United States that tend to restrict imports can have serious consequences for our trading partners. Similarly, if the United States were denied access to goods it imports, American living standards would fall because home-produced import substitutes, if indeed they could be produced, would cost more than the formerly imported goods. Since the maintenance and improvement of living standards are political imperatives, U.S. policymakers must always be concerned about developments that hinder or restrict international trade.

International Capital Flows. *Capital goods* are commodities that can be used to produce other goods. They are resources used in the production process, such as machines, buildings, and inventories. *International flow of capital* normally

Table 14.4 Percentage of Total U.S. Trade by Country/Group

	Exports						*Imports*					
Country/Group	*1973*	*1980*	*1982*	*1985*	*1989*	*1990*	*1973*	*1980*	*1982*	*1985*	*1989*	*1990*
Eastern Europe	3	2	2	2	2	1	1	1	1	1	1	1
LDCs	29	37	38	34	34	33	30	48	41	35	38	40
Japan	12	9	10	10	12	12	14	12	15	19	20	18
Canada	23	19	18	25	22	22	25	17	20	21	19	19
Western Europe and other developed countries	33	33	32	29	27	28	30	22	23	24	22	22

Sources: Adapted from *Economic Report of the President* (Washington, D.C.: U.S. Government Printing Office, 1982, 1987, 1991), pp. 349, 361.

Table 14.5 Percentage of Trading Partners' Total Exports Sold to the United States, 1991

Trading Partner	*Percentage of Total Exports*
Japan	30
Canada	74
Mexico	75
European Economic Community	7
Other industrial countries	6
Developing countries	22

Source: International Monetary Fund, *Direction of Trade Statistics, Yearbook 1992*.

refers to moving money from one country into investment in capital goods or financial assets (stocks, bonds, or short- and long-term loans) in another country. These capital flows comprise a second important part of international economic relations. Whereas trade involves movement of commodities, capital flows represent movement of one of the factors of production.[4]

Capital movements increase the resources available for production in a receiving country and expand world output by more efficiently allocating among nations one of the scarce factors of production, namely, capital. The flows accomplish this by moving capital from countries where it is plentiful—and therefore relatively cheap—to those where it is scarce and more expensive.

Capital flows can be categorized in a variety of ways. For simplicity, we begin by distinguishing *public* from *private* capital movements. Public capital flows are those implemented by national governments or international institutions such as the International Bank for Reconstruction and Development (IBRD)—also known as the World Bank—and the International Monetary Fund (IMF). Since World War II, public flows have been primarily designed to spur economic growth in LDCs through foreign aid or to assist countries in meeting their import bills. By contrast, private capital movements are motivated primarily by the promise of a higher return on investment abroad than in the capital-exporting country.

Many of the world's poorest nations do not offer sufficiently profitable opportunities for private investment, despite the scarcity and consequently high expense of capital, largely due to misguided policies or the woeful state of their economic infrastructure (ports, roads, education, etc.). Development of this infrastructure requires investment in "social overhead capital," the return on which is not easily captured by a private investor. One crucial role of public capital flows, then, is to help a country develop its infrastructure so that it can attract private capital through normal market incentives. For a variety of reasons, including their trade importance, as shown in Table 14.4,[5] the United States and the developed world cannot afford to neglect the LDCs and their social overhead capital and other public capital needs. Under these circumstances, foreign aid grants and loans assume major importance.

Private capital movements respond largely to differences in the available rates of return on investment that can be earned in different countries—with due attention to relative risks. Developed countries tend to be relatively capital abundant and may offer, therefore, a poorer return on investment than developing nations, whose capital supply is much smaller. Accordingly, private investment funds, seeking the highest rate of return, tend to flow, considering market forces alone, to the developing nations. These funds serve a vital purpose in the LDCs. Economic growth generally proceeds by continuing capital formation that gives each worker more tools with which to work, raising productivity and real income. Domestic capital formation requires that a portion of a nation's output not be consumed but be saved and invested in capital goods. Many of the poorer LDC populations exist so close to subsistence levels that nearly all available output is needed for consumption. Private capital flows are a way to meet this problem, transferring savings from the developed world to the LDCs, thereby facilitating economic growth.

While private flows are theoretically beneficial to both the investing and the receiving nation, it is clear that risks are incurred by both parties. Investors in the developed countries may lose their capital through expropriation, mishaps, or default, and the receiving nation may feel a loss of economic autonomy because the imported capital does not really belong to it and might be taken away or used in ways incompatible with its priorities or values. Clearly, then, the developed nations and the LDCs can engage in mutually beneficial investment projects only if they can meet each other's concerns and manage the problems of interdependence which inevitably arise.

Contrary to many Americans' impressions, the United States contributed only about 14 percent of world *public* capital flow in 1986. U.S. foreign aid as a percentage of GNP fell from 1.68% in 1950 to 0.17% in 1990—one of the lowest percentages in the developed world. Not only has U.S. public capital flow shrunk as a proportion of all public flows, but private capital flows from the United States, principally in the form of bank loans, have also decreased in recent years. Much of the petrodollar wealth deposited in banks here and abroad in the 1970s by the oil-exporting nations was recycled by banks as loans to developing Third World countries. But as these countries found it increasingly difficult to repay their loans, or even the interest, on schedule, banks have been less willing to provide new capital.

The capital flows discussed so far have been so-called long-term capital flows, that is, investments in financial assets whose duration or maturity is longer than one year. There is, however, another category of investment—short-term capital flows—which serves different purposes and creates another set of problems. Many short-term capital flows reflect the efforts of owners of liquid assets to maximize the return on the funds by shifting them into foreign markets paying higher rates of interest than are available at home. Tens of billions of dollars of such short-term funds slosh around in the international monetary system, far exceeding the amount required to finance international trade. Exchange rates are heavily influenced by these short-term capital movements because of their size and potential volatility.

The movement of large sums of short-term funds among countries causes inflows and outflows of bank reserves that form the monetary base in countries with fractional reserve banking systems. This expansion and contradiction of a country's monetary base can quickly affect its money supply, which, through its influence on interest rate structure, is an important determinant cf economic activity. Since these capital flows are often beyond the control of national economic policymakers, they can frustrate attempts to use traditional economic policy instruments to influence the domestic economy.

In terms of both trade and long- and short-range capital movements, policymakers in today's interdependent world find that they need to coordinate economic policies with their neighbors if they are to succeed in stabilizing their domestic economies. Since national circumstances and preferences differ, however, this coordination has not worked well in practice—despite the realization by nearly all nations of the need for increasing it. An interesting example involves the pleas of both the United States and the European nations with relatively weak economies in late 1976 and again in the 1980s and early 1990s for expansive economic policies in Japan and West Germany which would raise their demand for imports and hence help the exporters regain noninflationary growth. Neither nation, however, showed much interest in risking higher inflation at home to help its neighbors abroad.[6]

In the case of the United States, the Japanese and West Europeans responded by telling it to reduce its massive budget deficit in order to help restore international equilibrium. Meaningful policy coordination may be essential, but it is also very difficult to manage.

The International Monetary System. In the aftermath of World War II, the developed nations designed an international monetary system to prevent a recurrence of some of the more disastrous monetary developments in the interwar period. The new system, frequently referred to as the Bretton Woods system, provided for stable exchange rates linked to gold and created the IMF, an international organization intended to supervise the operation of the international monetary system and to assist countries with short-term balance-of-payments problems by loaning them foreign currencies. The overall system helped create a relatively long period of stable international monetary relations which, in turn, contributed to the dramatic expansion of international trade already cited. Exchange rates between currencies were stabilized by pegging the value of national currencies to gold or to a gold-pegged currency at predetermined par values. Under the system, countries were obliged to convert their currencies into gold, at par, on demand.

As the system evolved, the U.S. dollar rather than gold, became the key currency to which other countries tied their currency values. This development led to increasing use of the dollar, along with gold, as an international reserve asset. The United States provided liquidity (i.e., increasing dollar reserves) to the rest of the world by running balance-of-payments deficits, which were settled by exporting gold reserves or by generating dollar claims. As the volume of dollar claims (IOUs) held abroad rose far beyond the declining value of the U.S. gold reserve, confidence in the dollar began to weaken; it became obvious during the 1960s that the United States could not convert all the outstanding claims into gold; America could not continue to run substantial deficits without undermining the strength of the dollar and the entire financial system.

By 1971, a continuing deterioration of the U.S. trade balance had created a "dollar crisis," sending a massive outflow of short-term capital from the United States in search of stronger currencies. America finally suspended convertibility of dollars into gold in August 1971, effectively removing the anchor holding exchange rates in a stable pattern, undercutting the Bretton Woods system. The dollar began to "float," depreciating in value against many major currencies, its value determined by supply and demand in the foreign exchange market.[7]

The resulting continuing floating rate system has both pluses and minuses.[8] It can be argued that floating rates facilitate adjustments of international payments imbalances and, in the short run, insulate countries from economic disturbances generated abroad. On the other hand, the potentially extreme volatility of floating rates can be injurious to the expansion of international transactions because of the added risk of exchange rate losses. It is noteworthy that the European Common Market tried, in early 1979, to stabilize a major segment of the world system by creating a European Monetary System (EMS) to operate along with the overall floating rate system.

The EMS established an artificial unit of account, the European Currency Unit (ECU), based on the trade-weighted values of the currencies of the participating countries, which itself floats but in terms of which the individual national currencies are fixed—or, more accurately, float within a very narrow band.[9] Although the EMS has undoubtedly served a useful purpose, it has sometimes created or exacerbated problems as well. As pointed out below, in late 1992 it was under great strain, and several members had left it temporarily; monetary coordination is very difficult, particularly with disparate national economic conditions.

As students of introductory economics know, the primary functions of money are to serve as a medium of exchange and as a store of purchasing power. Economic history abounds with examples of the extreme disruption caused by the loss of the ability of a society's money to serve these functions. The well-remembered German hyperinflation of the 1920s was an instance in which an economic system's money lost its effectiveness as a medium of exchange because it was not an effective store of purchasing power. If the monetary system fails, trade collapses and living standards plummet. Given the growing dependence of American living standards on world trade, the stability of the U.S. dollar is, then, of direct concern to U.S. national security. It is also of great concern to all members of the international economic system that still depend in large degree on the health of the dollar and the American economy.

The instability of the dollar was repeatedly demonstrated during the decade of the 1980s. Between 1980 and 1985 the trade-weighted value of the dollar rose by 60 percent, causing a precipitous decline in U.S. exports and a large increase in debt; in that period the real value of U.S. exports dropped by about 25 percent and U.S. global accounts declined by $400 billion, threatening the stability of the international trading system. After an emergency meeting of the United States and its major trading partners in the spring of 1985, steps were taken to reduce the value of the dollar—the so-called Plaza Accords. By 1987, the trade-weighted value of the dollar had returned to its 1980 level, and the U.S. trade deficit had begun to shrink. Currency volatility has become a major factor blocking the freedom of action of both governments and multinational corporations.

The Settlement of International Accounts: The Balance of Payments. The international monetary system functions to adjust imbalances in the international balance of payments. (Since there is frequently confusion about the significance of these imbalances, a brief description of the working of the balance of payments may prove helpful.) A country's balance of payments measures the flow of transactions between it and the rest of the world. It is essential to realize that the balance of payments, a system of double-entry bookkeeping, must indeed always "balance." If American Widget Corporation sells a widget to France, that transaction results in a credit item in the U.S. balance of payments. When Americans buy Japanese-built Toyota automobiles or Sony television sets, a debit item is entered in the U.S. balance (and a credit in Japan's balance). Similarly, capital flows result in debit or credit items; a capital outflow, such as a loan from a U.S. bank to Mexico, results in an American debit item (it is treated as the import of an IOU from Mexico). A credit item is entered on the American balance sheet as Mexico repays the loan.

International payments are divided into several categories. Merchandise trade, services (such as shipping and tourism), income on investments made abroad, and government spending abroad are all included in the *current account*. Capital inflows, whether short- or long-term, public or private, are included in the *capital account*. A final category of international payments—gold and reserve assets movements—must make the debits and credits in the balance of payments equal. If, for example, a country has a deficit on both current and capital accounts, it must pay for these goods, services, and capital flows by making "accommodating" transfers of gold or reserves of foreign currency.

It is possible for a country to run a trade deficit, that is, import more than it exports, but in effect to pay for this deficit by maintaining a surplus on long-term capital account—that is, long-term borrowing or export of IOUs. In such cases, no accommodating transactions are required, and the balance of payments is said to be in equilibrium. However, if the long-term capital account surplus is not sufficient to balance the trade deficit, and short-term capital flows do not fill the gap, accommodating transactions are required. The country must transfer gold abroad or draw down its reserves of foreign currency to "balance" the balance of payments. Accommodating transactions are signs of disequilibrium because they cannot be maintained indefinitely; both the gold stock and foreign currency reserves are finite, and no country can expect foreigners to continue accepting long- or short-term claims. As indicated earlier, the collapse of the Bretton

Summit of Seven

Reprinted with permission of Renan R. Lurie.

Woods system and the devaluation of the U.S. dollar were largely the result of a prolonged and deep trade deficit situation in the United States.

Under floating exchange rates, the problem of disequilibrium can be met by changes in the exchange rate. A chronic excess of the value of debit items over the credit items for a country should result in excess demand for the currencies of its trading partners in order to pay for the amount that debits exceed credits. This excess demand in the foreign exchange market drives up the price of those foreign currencies or, as we say, depreciates the value of the domestic currency. Real-world conditions, however, do not allow exchange rates to move quite so freely in order to correct payment imbalances. *Depreciation* of a country's currency not only tends to promote its exports but it also makes imports more expensive and hence feeds domestic inflation. *Appreciation* makes a country's exports more expensive abroad, generally lowering demand for them, with adverse consequences in the country for employment and profits in export-oriented industries. These inflationary or employment implications frequently induce national decision-makers to intervene in the foreign exchange market to hold the value of their currency within acceptable limits. Such intervention against market forces can succeed, however, only within fairly narrow limits and for a relatively short period.

It is important to recognize that the workings of the international monetary system imply real changes in incomes and living standards—changes that cannot be indefinitely postponed. Political leaders are reluctant to sacrifice living standards at home to restore equilibrium in the international balance of payments. As we have seen, these adverse economic changes can feed quickly into political instability that is of direct national security concern. Israel and Mexico in the 1980s provided case studies in the political difficulties caused in part by the workings of the international adjustment mechanism. The trauma of a country adjusting its living standard to "live within its means" internationally raises difficult problems for national security and foreign policy planners. The United States has thus far (1992) not made that painful adjustment; how long it can continue to stave off the inevitable is a key question.

Problems for the 1990s. The economic performance of any nation today depends heavily on world economic developments that are largely beyond its control. In September 1992, the German central bank, the Bundesbank, persisted in its high-interest-rate policy during a speculator's run against its neighbors' currencies (a policy designed to curb the inflationary pressures arising out of German unification), despite the grave problems created thereby for those neighbors and the world economy in general. As a consequence, a number of European countries were forced to leave the EMS temporarily and let their currencies float or sharply devalue them; several observers noted, too, that the American stock market seemed to be responding more to the interest-rate policies of the Bundesbank than those of the U.S. Federal Reserve.

Interdependence is real: we are developing a truly global economy. But we have not yet developed adequate international cooperative mechanisms, or effective supranational institutions, to help intelligently manage interdependence. Nor have we developed sufficient international consensus to guide the resolution of competing national interests.[10] A major threat to U.S. national security lies in this situation. This theme of possible economic or economically induced conflict runs through the economic problems discussed below.

Slow Economic Growth in the Developed World: High Unemployment and Inflation. The long postwar economic expansion was dramatically ended by the worldwide recession of 1974–1975.[11] As the world slowly recovered during the remainder of that decade from the sharp setback, developed nations found it difficult to achieve the rates of economic growth of the prerecession years (Table 14.6). The entry of the postwar "baby boom" children into the developed

Table 14.6 Percentage of Annual Growth in Real GNP

Country	*1961–1970*	*1971–1980*	*1981–1985*	*1986–1990*
Japan	10.6	4.8	3.9	4.8
Germany	4.6	2.7	1.2	3.1
France	5.6	3.6	1.2	2.9
Italy	5.7	3.1	0.9	3.1
Canada	5.2	4.1	2.3	3.2
United Kingdom	2.8	1.8	1.8	3.4
United States	3.8	2.8	2.4	2.8

Sources: Economic Report of the President (Washington, D.C.: U.S. Government Printing Office, 1986 and 1991), p. 378; *IMF Annual Report* (Washington, D.C.: IMF, 1986), p. 6.

countries' labor forces decreased by the mid 1980s; even so, slowed economic expansion, coupled with another global recession at the beginning of the decade, significantly raised unemployment rates. In Europe these averaged 11 percent in 1985, twice the level of six years earlier. Unlike previous economic upswings, the mild economic recovery in the latter 1980s resulted in lowered inflation rates, but the continuing high unemployment in most of Europe, with accompanying social stress, pressured political decision-makers through the latter 1980s and into the early 1990s. The United States fared somewhat better in the 1980s, achieving gains in employment while also keeping inflation under 4 percent from 1983 to 1989. The American economy slowed as the 1990s began, however, with a dip into its recession followed by an agonizingly slow recovery in 1991–1992 (1 percent to 2 percent growth) that left unemployment at 7.5 percent or more by late 1992.

Meeting the challenges of adequate economic growth and employment has been made vastly more difficult for the developed nations by the necessity, simultaneously, to make large-scale adjustments in the structure of their economies, as a consequence of increased international interdependence, accelerating technological change, and increased competition from such NIEs as Korea, Brazil, and Taiwan. Such structural adjustments as shifting from steel and heavy industrial production into services and "high-tech" industries have painful unemployment and other social and political consequences. Inflation, currency volatility, and, in some cases, political instability have increased uncertainty for business decision-makers contemplating long-term investment projects. In the United States, a combination of high consumption and low savings rates with enormous federal budget deficits resulted in a powerful drag on investment rates. Disincentives to investment spending are particularly serious in light of the great need for new investment to provide jobs, develop new sources of energy, reallocate resources, and reduce pollution.[12]

Slow or no growth, inflation, and structural unemployment cause what Daniel Bell calls the "double bind" of the advanced economies: The governments of the developed democracies are expected by their peoples to achieve simultaneously, inconsistent goals; they are deemed responsible both for aiding capital formation and hence economic growth and job creation and for maintaining high levels of current consumption and spending on social programs.[13] Unfortunately, money spent investing in growth and jobs cannot, at the same time, be spent on consumption and government services. In short, it appears that the advanced economies will have difficulty meeting the expectations of their own populations—let alone helping others.

Defense expenditures also compete with the spending for investment and social programs discussed above—as well as for consumption, of course. The economic strains already discussed and the double bind just cited suggest that defense spending will be under continuous pressure, both in the United States and in its allies in the developed world. Yet, despite the collapse of the Soviet Union, American defense budgets will remain substantial, though they will represent a decreasing share of GNP. By 1995, the so-called base force projected by the Bush administration in its 1991–1992 strategy documents would require about 4 percent of GNP; changing priorities and congressional action will likely drive that figure down. This is in sharp contrast to the period FY 1980 to FY 1985, when U.S. defense spending increased at an average annual rate of about 10 percent after inflation, during the largest peacetime build-up in American history—raising the defense budget to 6.2 percent of GNP in FY 1985. This came to an abrupt halt in 1986, however, as mounting budget deficits and apparent mismanagement of the build-up created public pressure to curtail expenditures. From FY 1985 through FY 1990, defense spending declined both in real terms and in percent of GNP—in the latter case from 6.2 percent to 5.4 percent.[14]

In the early 1990s, the developed world as a whole was struggling with lagging growth or recession and, in the case of the United States and Western Europe, with unacceptably high levels of unemployment. Until recently, when one of the three major developed economy units (United States, Western Europe and Japan) was in trouble, one or both of the other two tended to be doing well. By providing trade and investment stimuli, the growing unit or units could help lift the laggard from the trough. Given the current and increasing extent of interdependence, simultaneous recessions (or expansions) may become the distressing pattern of the future.

Chronic Balance-of-Payments Problems. The dislocations caused by balance-of-payments problems in the early and mid 1970s from the first oil price shock had begun to subside when the second oil price shock again disrupted the system in 1979–1980. The current account surplus of the oil exports exceeded $104 billion in 1980, while the LDCs recorded enormous deficits after 1980 (Table 14.7). The LDCs were especially hard hit because of the growing burden of debt service payments due on loans contracted earlier, largely for oil. In the United States, double-digit inflation—and mounting foreign debt—and high interest rates were in large part the legacy of the second shock.

The oil glut that appeared in 1982–1983 eased the situation, and the LDCs, while still in deep trouble from their mounting debt loads, experienced a marked improvement in their balance-of-payments accounts. Despite weathering the second oil shock, however, the United States witnessed an unprecedented decline in its current account balance after 1982. In 1987, the U.S. trade deficit reached a peak of $160 billion, largely attributable to the ballooning merchandise trade deficit (see Table 14.7). U.S. exports stagnated, and imports, especially from other industrial nations, rose rapidly.

The combination, at the start of the 1980s, of worldwide recession and inflation—in considerable part caused by the massive oil-induced wealth transfers—resulted in an enormous increase in international debts (Table 14.8). By the end of 1986, the total external debt of the LDCs reached an estimated $1.035 *trillion,* of which $815 billion was in the form of long-term loans. Three Latin American nations led the list—Brazil ($107.8 billion), Mexico ($102 billion), and Argentina ($53 billion).[15]

In view of these unprecedented magnitudes and high rates of interest, many LDC debtor nations found it impossible to service their debts (i.e., pay back both principal and interest due). Faced with sharply reduced export earnings, they had no recourse—other than default—but to request fresh loans and a rescheduling or stretchout of repayments on existing loans. Despite recurring fears that some major financial institutions would collapse under the debt strain, triggering a chain reaction, ad hoc arrangements, rescheduling, and corrective measures by debtors held the tottering system together through the mid 1980s until reforms could be emplaced.

In 1985, U.S. Secretary of Treasury James Baker proposed a plan by which the LDCs could work out of their debt problems through growth, with the debtors ending subsidies, privatizing inefficient state-owned enterprises, reforming tax systems, and so forth and the private banks, international lending agencies, and governments providing fresh loans aimed at stimulating growth. The Baker plan was widely followed with encouraging but inconclusive results. In 1989, Baker's successor as Secretary of Treasury, Nicholas Brady, again tying debtor reform to fresh lending (and/or conversion of loans into equities or long-term bonds), moved the work-out process forward. Not only did the principal Latin American debtors, for example, produce viable plans to manage their debt, but they also began attracting sizable foreign investments and tens of billions of dollars of "flight capital" that had earlier fled their countries for safer havens. After the pain and sacrifices of more than a decade, by 1992 headlines could read "Bankers Say 'Adios' to Latin Debt Crisis."[16]

The picture was not so bright in the case of the United States' own debt. As noted earlier, by late 1986, the United States had actually become the world's largest debtor nation, owing more than Mexico, Brazil, and Argentina combined. Since 1986, the situation has progressively worsened. The danger in this situation is that the flow of foreign capital could dry up if the American economy is perceived as unduly weakening or if the dollar falls too far. This would push up U.S. interest rates and bring a halt to further economic recovery. A new and deeper recession would then be likely.

If the United States is to reduce its foreign debt, it must export more than it imports. Yet, in the past thirty years the country has had a favorable balance of

Table 14.7 Current Account Balances, 1979–1992 (in Billions of $)

Region	*1979*	*1980*	*1981*	*1982*	*1983*	*1984*	*1985*	*1986*	*1987*	*1988*	*1989*	*1990*	*1991**	*1992 est.*
United States	−1.0	1.9	6.3	−9.1	−40.1	−99.0	−122.3	−145.4	−160.2	−126.2	−106.3	−92.1	−17.6	−92.0
Other industrial countries	−22.4	−63.8	−26.4	−12.9	−3.5	0.4	−5.6	−6.5	−27.5	−58.1	−89.7	−89.0	−70.7	−73.3
Developing countries	6.1	30.1	−48.7	−87.3	−42.7	−12.6	−17.5	−34.1	13.4	−11.3	−19.0	−24.6	−103.8	−64.2
Fuel-exporting countries	56.8	104.0	49.9	−9.6	−13.8	−0.3	1.6	−34.2	−5.5	−20.9	−3.6	10.7	−56.6	−26.9

Source: IMF World Economic Outlook (Washington, D.C.: International Monetary Fund, 1987 and 1991).

* The 1991 figures are seriously distorted by the one-time inclusion of Gulf war contributions to the United States from a number of countries.

Note: Current account balances include official transfers.

Table 14.8 Seventeen Heavily Indebted Developing Countries

Country	Total External Debt* (in Billions of U.S. $)		Debt as a Percent of Exports of Goods and Services, 1990	Debt as a Percent of GNP, 1990
	1985	*1990*		
Argentina	50.8	61.1	405.6	61.7
Bolivia	4.0	4.3	428.7	100.9
Brazil	107.3	116.2	326.8	25.1
Chile	21.0	19.1	181.3	73.5
Colombia	11.3	17.2	183.4	44.5
Costa Rica	4.2	3.8	184.2	69.9
Côte d'Ivoire	8.0	18.0	487.4	204.8
Ecuador	8.5	12.1	371.8	120.6
Jamaica	3.4	4.6	202.6	132.0
Mexico	99.0	96.8	222.0	42.1
Morocco	14.0	23.5	282.5	97.1
Nigeria	19.3	36.1	242.7	110.9
Peru	13.4	21.1	488.3	58.7
Philippines	24.8	30.5	229.2	69.3
Uruguay	3.6	3.7	155.9	46.9
Venezuela	33.6	33.3	158.7	71.0
Yugoslavia	19.6	20.7	67.1	23.7
Total	*445.9*	*522.1*		

Sources: World Bank, *World Debt Tables, 1985–1986* (Washington, D.C., 1986). World Bank, *World Development Report 1992* (Washington, D.C., 1992).
*Estimated total external liabilities, including the use of IMF credit.

trade in only one year, 1969. Reversing this situation will require a major increase in exports, which in turn will necessitate greater productivity at home and better marketing abroad. There are already encouraging signs that these changes are occurring. Merchandise exports grew 64 percent from 1987 to 1991, with nearly two-thirds of this increase coming in the highly competitive capital goods section; from 1985 to 1991, the U.S. share of world exports went from 19 percent to 27 percent.[17] Yet, facing trade deficits of about $90 billion a year in the early 1990s, the United States will have to do even better.

The Developing Nations and the Challenge of Growth. Although the industrial democracies, working within a climate of security and relatively open world trade and in the context of the helpful international economic institutions that were spawned in the aftermath of World War II, have been largely successful in fostering their own and worldwide economic growth, the LDCs continue to be plagued by low growth. The gap between the richest and poorest nations of the world continued to widen. In 1984, for example, it was estimated that the LDCs, while containing just over half the world's population, contributed less than 17 percent of its combined GNP. The noncommunist developed countries in that same year produced almost 60 percent of the total GNP but had only 17 percent of the global population. In per capita terms, the GNP share in the developed world was over ten times the figure among the LDCs. Per capita growth rates in the LDCs through the 1980s were unimpressive, and in many cases any improvement achieved was negated by population increases.[18]

There are a number of notable exceptions to the foregoing generalization, cases in which LDCs have grown successfully, even spectacularly, to the point at which they are ready to leave the LDC ranks—the NIEs, for example. But most underdeveloped or less developed nations lag, cursed by poor policies, poor infrastructure, inept administration, and severe income inequality. Heavy emphasis on agricultural or other primary production as a percentage of GNP and, frequently, a dual economy consisting of a market-oriented industrialized sector alongside a subsistence sector of poor farmers using the crudest technology also often mark these countries.[19] LDCs share a number of economic obstacles that prevent or slow the achievement of higher living standards. Many have very small endowments of the factors of production needed for growth. Often natural resources are scarce or of poor quality, the labor force is poorly nourished, educated, and motivated, and savings are inadequate to create the capital needed for growth.[20]

In addition, the economies of many LDCs are inefficiently managed and organized. Many of them sought, unsuccessfully, to develop along communist or command economy lines. Although they have subsequently adopted, at least partially, a market economy approach, they are having great difficulty—particularly in former Soviet bloc states, in making the transition to markets.

We have already seen that, potentially, international trade can raise incomes in the LDCs by allowing them to specialize in the production of goods in which they have comparative advantage. Likewise, inflows of capital increase the resources available for use in production. While it is true that economic development is a complex social process that cannot be guaranteed by free trade and movement of capital, it is also clear that there is little hope of success in substantially raising living standards around the world in the absence of trade and capital inflows to LDCs. There is, of course, disagreement about how the benefits of trade and capital mobility have been and are distributed. Generally speaking, the LDCs are dissatisfied with the results achieved and are pressing for changes in the terms upon which the exchange of goods and flow of capital will take place in the coming years.

Understandably, the developed countries have been reluctant to meet the LDCs' demands for a "New International Economic Order" that would shift the balance of benefits in the world economy toward the developing states. Yet, the agenda of international politics for the rest of this century is bound to include tensions between the rich and poor nations of the world. Rising expectations of improved living standards around the world and the failure of strong economic growth to relieve abject poverty in many LDCs have increased the potential for confrontation between the developed and the developing world.

Economic Leverage and Economic Security. West German chancellor Helmut Schmidt, in the speech cited in Chapter 1, spoke of the "new economic dimension of national security"—including therein the "necessity to safeguard free trade access to energy supplies and to raw materials, and the need for a monetary system which will help us reach these targets." Some of the problems of attaining the international cooperation needed to achieve these aspects of economic security have been discussed in the preceding sections of this chapter. Although intrinsically difficult, these problems in large part deal with distributing the benefits in a positive sum fashion by which all nations stand to share in whatever economic gains may be achieved.

Economic security has an obverse face; namely, the use of economic power by one nation explicitly to affect the actions and/or behavior of adversary nations. Here we depart from economics in its usual form as the production and distribution of goods and enter the realm of economics as a political and security instrument. This facet of economic security is commonly referred to as "economic leverage" or "economic warfare." In such a relationship, one country seeks to weaken or strengthen another's capabilities—for instance, through denying it certain kinds of trade. Alternatively, a nation may seek not merely to affect another's strength but also to manipulate its behavior, for example, by inducing it to change a particular political course by providing or withholding economic benefits. A clear example of this kind of economic leverage was furnished in 1992 when the Bush administration held up a $10.00 billion loan guarantee that Israel wanted until that country agreed to stop expounding Jewish settlements in the occupied territories. Another version of this form of economics as a political instrument is one in which country *A* explicitly develops or exploits existing economic interdependencies with country *B* so as to bind it in cooperative patterns that will help avert or diminish confrontations in other, noneconomic matters. While providing a potentially useful, long-range approach, this tactic proved unsuccessful during the 1970s when Henry Kissinger was its principal exponent and tried to apply it to inhibit Soviet misbehavior.

The instruments of economic leverage most familiar to students of contemporary world politics include foreign aid, embargoes, boycotts, quotas, tariffs, export controls, subsidies, and preclusive buying.[21] Their use against adversaries has been common in war and in times of severe international tension. During World War II, the United States and its allies used most of the instruments just cited in an orchestrated attack on the viability of the German and Japanese economies. During the Korean War, the United States imposed an embargo on all economic relationships with North Korea and the People's Republic of China. A similar course was followed later in the cases of Cuba and North Vietnam.

Although all the leverage instruments cited in the previous paragraph are theoretically available to policymakers in the 1990s, there is a likelihood that many of them will not be used. (Embargoes, trade controls, and foreign aid are exceptions.) Interdependence makes it possible, even probable that, if you try to hurt an adversary by economic means, you will end up hurting yourself. In 1990, for example, the United States retaliated with high tariffs against the Japanese government for dumping flat screen displays for notebook computers. It thereby protected a tiny American flat screen industry but hurt a much larger U.S. notebook computer industry that depended on Japanese producers for the bulk of its flat screen displays. In succeeding paragraphs the focus will be on embargoes and trade controls.

The United Nations unsuccessfully declared an embargo on all economic relationships with Rhodesia after the white-controlled government in that nation declared its "Unilateral Declaration of Independence" from the United Kingdom in 1968. During the 1980s, attempts were also made to use economic coercion against the governments of South Africa and Poland. The former's policy of apartheid inspired general condemnation, various U.N. resolutions, including an arms embargo in 1977, and widespread pressure on companies that do business there. Despite its status as a political pariah, in 1987 South Africa still had 140 trade partners worldwide and did business with forty-six of the fifty-two members of the Organization of African Unity, which was most strident in its criticism.[22]

The U.S. government imposed economic sanctions on Poland in 1981 and 1982 as punishment for that country's declaration of martial law and crackdown on the Solidarity trade union. These sanctions were not as severe as they could have been, and many U.S. allies did not follow America's lead. Because of Poland's substantial foreign debt, severe economic sanctions could have forced it into default, with traumatic effects on the international banking system. In early 1987, citing Poland's "progress" in reducing repression, the Reagan administration lifted the sanctions entirely and restored Most Favored Nation (MFN) tariff treatment. The Polish government might have been motivated to ease repression by a desire for renewed official U.S. credits and credit guarantees, but it is not at all certain that the sanctions were a prime factor in any changes that were instituted in that country.

Shortly after the Soviet invasion of Afghanistan in December 1979, President Jimmy Carter announced a series of economic countermeasures, which included suspension of further grain deliveries (of about 17 million tons, worth $3 billion), halt of all high-technology transfers, sharp constraints upon Soviet fishing in U.S. waters, and examination of all existing export licenses in order to screen out anything of possible military value. These measures, plus the symbolic gesture of U.S. withdrawal from the Olympics scheduled to be held in Moscow in the summer of 1980, were intended to demonstrate to the Soviet Union that it could not enjoy business as usual while it engaged in blatant aggression.[23]

In the wake of the Soviet takeover of Afghanistan, Carter appealed to America's allies and other nations not to undercut these efforts at economic leverage by replacing American exports with their own; rather, he asked that they join the United States in clamping down on economic relations. Yet, the sanctions imposed against the Soviet Union were not especially effective; certainly the measures did not prompt the Soviets to withdraw from Afghanistan. Allied unwillingness to support the trade sanctions and adjustments in Soviet trade patterns served to blunt the effectiveness of American economic pressure[24]; President Reagan's lifting of the grain embargo against the Soviets early in his administration epitomized the problem of consistency and constancy in the use of this instrument in peacetime.

In the early 1980s, the United States and its European allies clashed sharply over an issue of energy trade. The Soviet Union had proposed the construction of a pipeline to take natural gas from its reserves in northern Siberia to Europe, where it would be sold by long-term contract. The project appealed to many West European countries as a means of reducing their reliance on imported oil and of bolstering their economies by way of the large construction contracts that were anticipated. The United States opposed the project, arguing among other things that it would lead to a dangerous European dependence on the Soviets for energy supplies. By late 1982 the dispute had become severe, with great European resentment over U.S. efforts to block the pipeline through forbidding the participation of European subsidiaries of American companies and the use of U.S. technology or credits. In the end, a combination of pressure from the Europeans and from its own domestic industries forced the United States to back down.

These multiple uses of economic leverage have had limited success. In no case since World War II do they seem to have been decisive in influencing either capabilities or behavior. In part, their mixed record is a result of the difficulties of instituting and maintaining comprehensive economic controls in an era of complex international economic relationships. In part, too, their mixed record reflects the varying degrees of intensity of effort by the countries attempting to use such leverage.

In considerable part, the apparent weakness of economic instruments in decisively influencing political and security affairs has also stemmed from efforts to do too much with too little leverage. Only if a target country has major vulnerabilities and limited options can a persistent, determined, and coordinated use of economic instruments cause it to change direction. Indeed, if economic leverage is inadequate for its projected task or is used crudely, it may backfire, as was the case in 1974 when the Congress insisted, via the Jackson–Vanik Amendment, that the Soviet Union permit free emigration of Jews as a condition of its being granted MFN trade treatment. Prior to that bit of "open diplomacy," the Nixon administration had quietly induced the Soviet leaders to increase Jewish emigration from the Soviet Union from a level of about three thousand a month to thirty thousand a month. After the congressional broad-axe action, the Soviet Union renounced the negotiations leading up to the MFN treaty and reduced Jewish emigration to a trickle.[25]

If peacetime economic leverage through strategic trade controls or embargoes has had so limited effect during the cold war, should not such efforts be abandoned now that the cold war is over, when there is less likelihood of supplier agreements and more confusion about process as economic interdependence deepens? Unfortunately, there are regional threats to be dealt with, as Saddam Hussein has reminded us, and increased dangers of proliferation of weapons of mass destruction to be met. Unwieldy and porous as they may be, strategic trade controls will continue to exist.

Certainly, if the United States is to conduct a peacetime policy of economic pressure or selective technology denial against any adversary or miscreant, it will have to develop new information and control systems as well as new policies. In particular, policy coordination among its friends and allies will have to be strengthened. Technically, the cold war mechanism known as COCOM (Coordinating Committee on Multilateral Export Controls), through which the industrial democracies coordinated their trade controls against the Soviet bloc, could be adapted to this purpose. As of the summer of 1992, the United States was proposing that COCOM establish a special Cooperation Council that could (1) facilitate access by states of the former Soviet Union and its empire to technology previously denied to them, (2) assist those states in creating their own control mechanisms that could be harmonized with COCOM, and (3) provide a forum for joint discussion of common strategic threats.

Reflections on the United States in the World Economy. During the nearly three decades of unprecedented world economic growth after World War II, the United States benefited greatly by its leadership of and increasing involvement in the international economy. Although the American economy has gradually lost much of its earlier preeminence, it is still so far-reaching that the global economic system is significantly affected by the relative health of the U.S. economy and by the actions of U.S. decision-makers. In particular, how the United States deals with its current budgetary and trade deficit difficulties will likely have a decisive effect on the viability of the international economic system.

The chronic trade imbalances and structural problems cited earlier seem certain to put continuing strain on the international monetary system as a whole, as well as on many individual states—including the United States. Similarly, the LDCs' demands for a New International Economic Order will undoubtedly persist. Of greatest importance to world economic growth and stability, however, will be whether the developed Western nations can resolve disagreements among themselves and correct imbalances and structural problems without resorting to protectionist policies. In this context, successfully completing the Uruguay Round of negotiations under the aegis of the General Agreement on Tariffs and Trade (GATT), designed to further trade liberalization on a global basis, is particularly important. Unfortunately, despite six years of effort, by late 1992 the outcome was still in doubt. If the Round fails, the trend toward organizing trade on a regional basis will likely accelerate; so, too, will protectionism.

If a more open world economy is to develop, the United States, because of its economic strength and traditional leadership, will have to continue to play a leading role. By encouraging greater savings and investment, productivity, and the competitiveness of U.S. exports, while controlling its government expenditures, America can strengthen its own economy and its peoples' welfare, as well as the international system. In the process, though, it needs to give continuing attention to the viability of the nation's defense industrial base and its defense technology base, as well as to providing the defense budget required to cope with a still dangerous world. The father of modern economics, Adam Smith, put the point succinctly: "Defense is more important than opulence."

Discussion Questions

1. How can economic performance in itself lead to national security problems?
2. Why does U.S. national security now involve more than safety from military attack?
3. Why does specialization raise real income?
4. Why should U.S. national security policymakers be concerned about developments that hinder or restrict international trade?
5. How do capital movements expand world output?
6. What circumstances can cause foreign aid and loans to assume great importance in the maintenance of U.S. national security? Why?
7. How can the movement of short-term funds create problems for domestic economic policymakers?
8. Why does the clear need for internationally coordinated policies among at least the industrial democracies not lead to the effective concerting of policies? What are your predictions for the future in this respect?
9. Why is the stability of the dollar of direct concern to U.S. national security?
10. Describe how a country's trade balance can affect the value of its currency and how an imbalance can create political instability.
11. What is the "double bind" of the advanced economies? How does it influence defense spending?
12. Why have efforts at economic coercion not been overly successful? Explain the difficulty in coordinating the use of this technique.

Recommended Reading

de Saint Phalle, Thibault, ed. *The International Financial Crisis: An Opportunity for Constructive Action*. Washington, D.C.: Center for Strategic and International Studies, 1983.

Drucker, Peter F. "The Changing World Economy." *Foreign Affairs* 64 (Spring 1986): 768–91.

Economic Report of the President. Transmitted to Congress, January 1992. Washington, D.C.: U.S. Government Printing Office, 1992.

Gilpin, Robert. *U.S. Power and the Multinational Corporation*. New York: Basic Books, 1975.

Hitch, Charles, and McKean, Ronald. *The Economics of Defense in the Nuclear Age*. Cambridge, Mass.: Harvard University Press, 1960.

Kapstein, Ethan Barnaby. *The Political Economy of National Security*. Columbia, S.C.: University of South Carolina Press, 1992.

Kennedy, Paul. *The Rise and Fall of the Great Powers*. New York: Random House, 1987.

Knorr, Klaus, and Trager, Frank N., eds. *Economic Issues and National Security*. Lawrence, Kans.: Regent Press of Kansas, 1977.

Lincoln, G.A., and associates. *Economics of National Security*. Englewood Cliffs, N.J.: Prentice-Hall, 1954.

O'Leary, James P. "Economic Warfare and Strategic Economics." *Comparative Strategy* 5, no. 2 (1985): 179–206

Peterson, Peter G. *Economic Nationalism and International Interdependence: The Global Costs of National Choices*. Washington, D.C.: Per Jacobsson Foundation, 1984.

Ra'anan, Uri, and Perry, Charles M., eds. *Strategic Minerals and International Security*. Oxford: Pergamon Press, 1985.

Schlesinger, James R. *The Political Economy of National Security*. New York: Praeger, 1982.

Wu, Yuan-li. "U.S. Foreign Economic Policy: Politico-Economic Linkages." In *The United States in the 1980s,* ed. by Peter Duignan and Alvin Rabushka. Stanford, Calif.: Hoover Institution Press, 1980.

Yochelson, John N., ed. *The United States and the World Economy: Policy Alternatives for New Realities*. Boulder, Colo.: Westview Press, 1985.

15

Research and Development

Within the context of national security issues, research and development (R&D) has two major challenges. First, it has the challenge of ensuring that a potential opponent cannot (or does not) possess weapons or equipment of such markedly advanced design and capability that we have no defense against its military strength. Second, within currently available knowledge, R&D should ensure that our side has the best weapon or system—one that will minimize the time and cost of performing any required security task. While related, these goals are not necessarily complementary, which introduces legitimate disputes about how best to balance the various trade-offs between quantity and quality or between sophistication and unit cost. "Superior arms provide real advantages, but at some point greater quantity in deployed lower-quality weapons confers the capability to overwhelm the highest quality defense."[1]

This chapter addresses some of the implications that research and development have for defense strategies and forces and indicates the interrelationship of technology problems to other national security topics, such as the decision-making process.

Meaning of R&D. In the fields of science and technology, definitions are neither uniform nor consistent; nor are they universally accepted. However, some common acceptance of basic terminology is needed for our understanding and discussion.

Science in the most general way is defined as "study dealing with a body of facts or truth systematically arranged," pursued without regard for its application.[2] *Technology,* by contrast, deals with the applied sciences and engineering. Thus, technology refers to potential applications of knowledge.

In government programs, the distinction between knowledge and application of knowledge is stated in different terms. *Pure research* is investigation of physical phenomena which may add to our store of knowledge. Any such resulting knowledge may be useful for various purposes, but the rationale for the program is knowledge per se. *Applied research* is an attempt to advance the state of science or technology in a particular field—perhaps, but not necessarily, directed toward certain uses. This often involves the testing of design models or verification of basic theory by constructing laboratory hardware.[3]

Once research has indicated that some scientific principle or new (or improved) design technique is feasible, *development* is undertaken to convert the scientific innovation into an operational element of security policy. If the new development is an entirely new application or requires a completely new system to make it operational, the development stage is usually labeled *weapons systems development*. If the program is smaller or involves only a *part* of a system, it is called *component development*. Because of the complexity of modern weapons systems, this distinction can be somewhat arbitrary.[4] The debate over the precise meaning of the 1972 ABM Treaty stems in part from its use of such a distinction with regard to the development of defensive systems.

In a generalized sense, it is fair to say that *research and development* are governmental applications of the general terms *science* and *technology*. Research is concerned with increasing knowledge, and development is concerned with finding ways to apply this knowledge. A final definitional distinction is that between *development* and *production*. Development is concerned with producing a small number of things that contain the proper scientific and engineering qualities to meet a defined need. These ''prototypes'' are tested and evaluated to determine how well the product will withstand actual operating conditions. If a decision is made to utilize the product, *production* is the process of actually building the entire quantity to furnish the armed forces with a complete issue of the product.

Technology is a vital component of a nation's security posture. ''Any power that lags significantly in military technology, no matter how large its military budget or how efficiently it allocates resources, is likely to be at the mercy of a more progressive enemy.''[5] Given the significance of technology, sheer weight of production will likely not compensate for marked technological unpreparedness. *Within limits,* ''in modern war the technological qualities of weapons are clearly more important than the number of battalions and their numerical combat strength.''*[6] Thus, technological preparedness is generally a necessary, if not sufficient, condition for having other national security issues to address. Note the qualifications on these statements. While it is unavoidably true that the abstract claim of necessity for ''technological sufficiency'' is valid, security decisions are

*Note that the overriding importance of technology, at least in *all* aspects, is debated later in this chapter. What these questions do imply is the necessity to protect against *marked* technological inferiority.

not made in the abstract. They are instead made at specific points in time about specific projects, capabilities, and weapons systems.

Thus, in the mid 1980s, there was an extensive debate about how to maintain the viability of the oldest leg of the U.S. strategic triad, the bomber force. Aware that the aging B-52 were rapidly losing their ability to penetrate the increasingly potent Soviet air defense network, planners considered two very different options, the B-1 bomber and the long-range cruise missile. Advocates of the B-1 bomber cited as arguments for its procurement its base for further technological improvements, its ability to maintain survivability of the manned bomber for another decade, and the complicating factor it causes for the defense.

Cruise missile advocates, on the other hand, argued that cruise missiles provide the same capabilities as the B-1 with much less investment. Penetration and terminal accuracy can be achieved with no new base hardware system procurement. The desired complications for the opponent's defense can be achieved both by saturation (made possible by lower unit cost) and by the cruise missile's nonballistic trajectory (which confuses antimissile radars).

From a technological standpoint, assuming both types of weapon provide the needed capability, the much higher additional cost of the B-1 is justified only by the general advancement in the technological base it creates, versus the exploitation of refinements of current technology via the cruise missile. The Carter administration canceled the B-1 bomber program because of its high cost and doubts regarding its ability to penetrate Soviet airspace in the 1990s. The Reagan administration restarted the program in 1982, seeing the B-1 as a means of maintaining manned bomber capability until the B-2 Stealth bomber (specially designed and constructed to evade radar detection) became available in the 1990s. But, as the B-1s entered the force in the late 1980s, it became evident that their advanced electronic countermeasure systems often interacted in unexpected ways, negating their effectiveness. This problem is enormously expensive to correct, and with the end of the cold war probably it will not be corrected. This situation has forced a sharp curtailment of B-1 production. Clearly, the recent history of this aspect of American strategic forces demonstrates the difficulty of the choices that are almost constantly facing decision-makers in today's complex technological environment.

In considering issues of military R&D in the 1990s, one cannot lose sight of the point that research advances, development programs, and production runs all use up scarce resources. Since defense resources are declining, at least early in the decade, one must choose which of many competing programs—at various stages—are worthy of the limited amount of resources available. Thus, to optimize national return for expenditures in R&D, nations must carefully develop a *strategy,* or overall coherence, for their technology programs.

Sources and Types of American R&D. Each of the categories of research, development, and production to be conducted in pursuit of national security must be funded and staffed. Sources of support for these activities are scattered, further adding to the problem of coordinating research efforts and ensuring that sufficient amounts of effort and resources are allocated to the necessary tasks.

The federal government is the chief source of military-oriented R&D support, requesting $30 billion for R&D in the FY 1993 defense budget.[7] The private sector, for a variety of reasons, also conducts scientific and technological research. While these private sector programs are not necessarily aimed specifically at producing strategic technological advances, the "fact is that many lines of basic research can be regarded as of great strategic importance. . . . No one can predict the ultimate use of any research in any of the pure sciences."[8]

There are important limitations, however, on support for private sector research. Given the uncertainty of even the existence of positive results—let alone their commercial application—particularly in basic research fields, it is obvious that the "risk" of privately financing research programs sometimes exceeds that which the business firm finds prudent.* This leaves the federal budget as the "last resort" source of basic research funds. In addition to the factor of investment risk for industry, some research encounters problems of application. Thus, discoveries and developments that the Defense Department might find highly useful, such as refinements in technology applicable to space weapons, may simply hold little interest for the commercial industrial sector.

This situation causes the defense, space, and nuclear areas of research and development to be very largely dependent on governmental funding. Moreover, since defense, space, and nuclear R&D are characterized by high costs and high risks, during the cold war only the United States and Soviet Union were able to allocate sufficient resources to pursue such programs across a broad spectrum of feasibility. This did not mean that there were no significant programs in nuclear or space technology in other nations; however, the basic research in these fields conducted outside the United States and the Soviet Union was relatively small.

With the collapse of the Soviet Union, only the United States allocates large resources to defense, space, and nuclear R&D, but even the U.S. effort has declined markedly. For example, between 1985 and 1992, the Department of Defense R&D expenditures declined by about 10 percent in real terms.[9] Beyond specific programs in these very-high-risk fields, private sector research can have considerable impact. Research across a broad spectrum has economic potential in the industrial sector, and firms will not hesitate to push into areas of potential profit advantage. The important qualification is that in most cases they will hesitate to fund programs that have *no foreseeable or only very long-run* profit return. Even with a foreseeable profit return, however, the unit cost of most research is so high that only the largest corporations can fund it. Thus, only the highly industrialized nations can undertake substantial research and technological exploration.

Because of the differing reasons various agencies and organizations have for supporting research, the problems of maintaining a coherent framework of

*Management economics theory tells the corporation that it ought to see positive returns on research capital within ten years, which leaves industry with a compound trade-off in terms of both the nature and the subject matter of research.

progress are multiplied. For instance, basic research is "cheap" in relative terms.* As noted above, however, the applications are often so difficult to discover that there is no available return within the time frame relevant to corporate balance sheets. As a result, corporate managers, whose progress and future are measured by those balance sheets, are reluctant to allocate scarce resources to speculative, pure research efforts. Typically, only three to five percent of industrial research is basic in nature.[10] Consequently, when, in the late 1960s, the federal government downgraded its priority for basic research funds, the result was a general "reduction in basic research and high advanced . . . projects."[11] Federal support for basic research again grew significantly in the 1980s, but not in areas that promote economic growth. Throughout the 1980s, defense took an increasingly larger percentage of the federal R&D budget and the research it funded became much less applicable to civilian fields. With the end of the cold war, the emphasis shifted. In the 1990s, even basic defense R&D funds were being directed toward dual-use technologies, that is, technology that can enhance both national security and industrial competitiveness.

In applied research, by contrast, the private and public sectors both contribute heavily. In fact, in 1992 industry provided slightly more than 50 percent of this kind of total national investment. Here the adage that one will likely not fully anticipate the results of one's own research holds true: many of the advances in military technology were unanticipated effects of other research programs. The United States spent some $40 billion on applied research in 1992.[12] Even at these comparatively high expenditure levels, there are two severe resource limitations: not all potentially fruitful variations of a principle can be explored simultaneously, and any discovery is in danger of being outdated before it can be developed, due to the increasing speed of technological change. Therefore, there are always troublesome trade-off decisions on whether to delay production of a new design awaiting more refinement or to push into procurement with what may turn out to be an inferior model.

Adapting scientific designs into optimal methods of meeting strategic needs is a further challenge. This is the function of the next step in the normal development process—test and evaluation. Test and evaluation (T&E) is the process by which experimental and prototype models of equipment are examined to see how well they actually fulfill the performance needs for which they have been designed and to provide guidance for further development.

Devising and producing new defense weapons systems is a complex process. Ideally it is a rational decision process, initiated by defense planners, taking the following course. A need or required task performance (called a qualitative material requirement, or QMR) is established by force planners. This request is then sent to the Office of the Undersecretary of Defense for Acquisition, which surveys all ongoing related research projects to see whether some application of existing basic research efforts could perform the required task. If none is

*In basic research, the hardware costs are low since no working models on actual scale are required. Laboratory facilities needed are of the general rather than specialized variety, and are more likely to be already available.

available, and the need has a sufficient priority, a research project will be initiated to investigate the potentially feasible approaches for developing the required capability. If a requirement is specific to one of the services, that service will oversee the project. Otherwise the project will be managed directly by the Department of Defense (DOD).

Once the requisite scientific principles are established, the project moves from research into development. A special task group (known as a *project team*) is organized to design and build (usually in conjunction with a contracting corporation) working models of actual equipment which can perform the required task. These groups are normally at a branch-of-service level (for example, the artillery branch of the army), and funds are allocated in the DOD budget. Thus, the project-manager is responsible both to the particular service and to DOD for the progress and cost of the project.

The final version of the equipment is submitted for test and evaluation. T&E functions are supervised by the DOD director of operational testing and evaluation, who is independent of the undersecretary for acquisition and reports directly to the secretary of defense. Finally, if the equipment performs to specified standards under rigorous test conditions, and the task is still needed by the force planners, a decision to procure in quantity will be made. In the case of major systems, a new project manager will establish a task force to supervise the building of the weapons system by the corporation submitting the best bid.

Overall, this organization and development cycle is designed to translate requirements into equipment efficiently. The difficulties are introduced by the variances of the real world from the idealized model. Some of these variations will be discussed later in this chapter.

R&D in the National Security Context. During the cold war, technology underlay much of the struggle for national security. As Leonid Brezhnev, the leader of the Soviet Union during the height of the cold war, pointed out in the late 1970s. "The center of gravity in the competition between the two [U.S. and U.S.S.R.] systems is now to be found precisely in [the field of science and technology]."[13]

With the collapse of the Soviet Union, the United States clearly has a substantial lead in military technology over the rest of the world. This technological supremacy was demonstrated in the Gulf war, when the United States relied primarily on its technological advantage to lead the rout of the fourth largest army in the world in a few days. The challenge for the United States for the remainder of the decade is how to maintain that technological edge in an era of shrinking defense budgets and worldwide proliferation of military technologies. To help accomplish this task the Pentagon developed a list of critical technologies.

Modes of war-fighting and war prevention have become inextricably linked to the sophistication and scientific currency of weapons systems. Moreover, we live in an age when a system of international stability could crumble away virtually overnight because of a "breakthrough" in weapons technology. It is no longer sufficient to be able to outproduce a potential opponent in the past decade's weapons. Arms competition has become as much qualitative—or more so—as quantitative.

The level of R&D, to include the establishment and maintenance of a strong technology base and leadership in scientific investigation, is a principal determinant of the future technological capability of a state. This capability, in turn, becomes an important indicator of the future power of the state. If there is an inadequate base for future advancement and continuing progress in technological fields, the military component of national power will erode as technology passes it by. Alternatively, the state will become dependent on importing sophisticated defense systems and thus less free in its policy options.

Once the technological capability to maintain adequately modern weapons has escaped, problems of national security multiply. Not only is a nation confronted by the threat of defeat in an actual war, but it loses some freedom of maneuver in international politics. Dependency on foreign technology introduces new pressure elements in a state's policy calculus, and lack of a credible military force may negate the utmost efforts of skilled negotiators. Nations today view the technological potential and capabilities of opponents as major factors in capability assessments.[14]

Even without reference to either specific research areas or specific applications, the existence of a generic societal orientation toward technology has some potential advantage. In such cases, there is always a chance for advance from the marriage of available systems, as, for example, the TV-guided "smart bombs." A technologically oriented society will more quickly discover such associations. The broader the general technological base of the society as a whole, the greater the occurrence of "applications associations," some of which may have military utility. (See Table 15.1 for a list of technologies critical to defense.)

Technology can become a vital component of national security in two distinct ways. First, a successful technological breakthrough could have a major impact on security. A breakthrough could at the very least increase the burden on potential opponents to augment expenditures in other areas to compensate for or to offset the breakthrough. For example, development of space-based antiballistic missile technology could prevent renegade nations or terrorists from threatening this nation or its allies with nuclear-tipped ballistic missiles.

Less obviously, technology can support national security even if it does not provide sudden major advances. It can (and does) provide refinements and improved production applications of existing technology, which in turn provide improvements in force effectiveness. One example of this phenomenon is the use of the semiconductor chip (one type of which is familiar as the core of pocket calculators) in military radios. Not only has performance been enhanced, but stability under some adverse operating conditions has also been improved.

A second major component of technology's contribution stems from the uncertainty inherent in newness and change. A sizable R&D program, even if it is unsuccessful in gaining breakthroughs in most of its areas of effort, contributes the possibility of associated successes or surprise advances. This introduces a degree of uncertainty into a potential adversary's calculations, intensifying its

Table 15.1 Technologies Critical to Defense

Technology	Description
Semiconductor materials and microelectric circuits	Production and development of ultrasmall integrated electronic devices, high-speed computers, sensitive receivers, automatic control, etc.
Software engineering	Generation, maintenance, and enhancement of affordable and reliable software in a timely fashion
High-performance computing systems	High-performance computing systems having 10^3-fold improvements in computation capability and 10^2-fold improvements in communication capability by 1996
Machine intelligence	Incorporation of aspects of human "intelligence" into computational devices which enable intelligent function of mechanical devices
Simulation and modeling	Visualization of complex processes and the testing of concepts and designs without building physical replicas
Photonics	Includes ultra-low-loss fibers and optical components such as switches, couplers, and multiplexers for communications, navigation, etc.
Sensitive radar	Radar sensors capable of detecting low-observable targets, or capable of noncooperative target classification, recognition, and/or identification
Passive sensors	Sensors not needing to emit signals to detect targets, monitor the environment, or determine the status of condition or equipment
Signal and image processing	Combination of computer architecture, algorithms, and microelectronic signal-processing devices for near-real-time automation of detection, classification, and tracking of targets
Signature control	Ability to control the target signature (radar, acoustical, optical, or other) and thereby enhance the survivability of vehicles and weapon systems
Weapon system environment	Detailed understanding of natural environment (both data and models) and its influence on weapons system design and performance
Data fusion	Machine integration and/or interpretation of data and its presentation in convenient form to the human operator
Computational fluid dynamics	Modeling of complex fluid flow to make dependable predictions by computing, thus saving time and money previously required for expensive facilities and experiments
Air-breathing propulsion	Lightweight, fuel-efficient engines using atmospheric oxygen to support combustion
Pulsed power	Generation of repetitive, short-duration, high-peal power pulses with relatively lightweight, low-volume devices for sensors
Hypervelocity projectiles	Ability to propel projectiles to greater-than-conventional velocities (over 2.0 km/sec), as well as understanding behavior of projectiles and targets at such velocities
High-energy-density materials	Compositions of high-energy ingredients such as explosives, propellants, or pyrotechnics
Composite materials	Two or more constituent materials combined together in a manner to produce a substance possessing selected properties superior to those of individual components
Superconductivity	Makes use of zero-resistance property and other unique properties of superconductors for creation of high-performance sensors, electronic devices and subsystems, and supermagnet-based items
Biotechnology	Systematic application of biology for an end use in military engineering or medicine
Flexible manufacturing	Integration of production-process elements aimed at efficient, low-cost operations for small-, as well as high-, volume part-number variations, with rapidly changing requirements for end-product attributes

Source: The U.S. Department of Defense Critical Technologies Plan of 1991 (May 1, 1991).

sense of risk over particular policy alternatives. A further fear generated by the "unknowable" arising out of possible technological breakthroughs is that a breakthrough would make obsolete much of the nation's standing military force. Even if such a breakthrough did not result immediately in military defeat, the cost of rebuilding a security force from the ground up in a very short time would be prohibitive. (Of course, there can be an obverse side to this argument stating that uncertainty breeds caution; in some instances it may impel one's opponent to make extraordinary and destabilizing efforts to reestablish certainty or at least to reduce risks in the new situation.)

Critics of research on the various defensive systems included in the global protection against limited strikes (GPALS), the successor to the strategic defense initiative (SDI), often cite the immense technical barriers to be overcome as a reason for ending or severely restricting such work. But the uncertainty of technological progress, mentioned above, virtually requires that the United States maintains active research programs in these areas. This is necessary in order to discover what possibilities exist and to guard against unexpected breakthroughs that could seriously weaken U.S. security.

The implications of a true breakthrough pose a dilemma. Given the lengthy lead time from concept to application and the high rate of technological change in the world, planners of the first nation to discover a concept will be reluctant to concede the initiative to the second discoverer, yet they *could* err by "locking themselves in" to the development, procurement, and deployment of a *first-generation* system. (A first-generation system is the earliest operational prototype.) An opponent, in response, could concentrate instead on the development of more advanced *second-generation* applications and, by skillfully collapsing technological stages into each other, could balance the capability with a more advanced system in almost the same time frame. Historically, this case is illustrated by the "missile gap" of 1958–1962. The Soviet Union, by launching sputnik, demonstrated the technological capability to build an intercontinental-range ballistic missile. Immediately thereafter, Soviet spokesmen began implying that the Soviets were deploying first-generation intercontinental ballistic missiles (ICBMs)[15]; in fact, they were not. The United States, uncertain about the truth of Soviet statements, rushed missile programs to completion and deployed first-generation ICBMs to counter the supposed threat.* Both elements, the problem of uncertainty and the fear of technological breakthrough, contributed to the U.S. reactions. In retrospect, the result of this situation was counterproductive for both sides. The Soviet Union suddenly found itself on the inferior side of the strategic balance, faced with a larger U.S. missile force than anticipated. The United States, as a result of its rush to redress, found itself with a costly and obsolete first-generation missile force that had to be phased out and replaced.

The debate in the United States in the 1990s over early deployment of defensive systems contains elements of this same dynamic. By emphasizing

---

*The United States, however, concurrently continued work on more advanced technology. This led to an earlier development of second- and third-generation systems, which still constitute most of our current strategic forces.

systems that can be put in place in the mid 1990s, the United States would be committing itself to a first-generation defense of limited effectiveness. A natural result of this approach is a shift in attention and funding away from more advanced technologies.

International Trends in R&D. The multiplicity of potential areas for research and development leads to a further dilemma in the allocation of resources. Because of its $4 trillion federal debt, in the early 1990s the United States could not afford to invest in virtually every promising area as it once did. It had to make choices and be as concerned about its economic as its military strength because national security is a combination of strength in both of these areas.

During the cold war the Soviet Union did not match the annual effort of the United States in the R&D area. However, the Soviet Union focused some 80 percent of its R&D in the defense area, where it appears to have outpaced the United States in spending from 1970 through 1985. It was in large part this overemphasis on defense and neglect of economic investment that eventually contributed to the collapse of the Soviet empire and the Soviet Union itself.

On the other hand, the remainder of the industrialized Western nations, due in part to their ability to depend for elements of their defense on the United States, have tended to concentrate their research efforts in the commercial sector. Although France, for example, engages in some nuclear and space research, this constitutes less than half its research funding. Japan pursues a "national policy which regards R&D primarily as an instrument of economic growth."[16] Thus, to the extent the United States continues to focus its R&D efforts primarily in the defense sector, it may endanger its ability to remain competitive with its allies in the international marketplace.*

Examination of trends in U.S. research outlays in light of this problem emphasizes the growing magnitude of the difficulty. It is generally recognized that technological innovation is essential if one wishes to compete successfully in the increasingly competitive world economy. Although private R&D funding in the United States in nondefense areas grew significantly in the 1980s, the federal government did not fully join in the effort. Overall government R&D has increased significantly, but additional resources have largely gone to the defense sector. The percentage of federal R&D expenditures devoted to defense rose from 47 to 68 between 1980 and 1990, resulting in actual decreases in other areas of research. Even in the early 1990s, with the cold war over, the percentage of defense-related R&D was still fifty-seven percent.[17] Energy and environmental R&D in particular suffered severe cuts in the amount of funds allocated by the federal government. The government's assistance to the private sector has largely been in the form of tax incentives, but there are many who argue that it must take a more active role if economic growth is to be spurred. Budgetary constraints

*Evidence of the impact of this problem can be obtained from comparatively charting commercial sector R&D as a percent of GNP against balance-of-trade figures, although the two may not be causally linked.

operate against this approach, however, and were slowing funds going to both tax incentives and defense R&D by the early 1990s.

During the 1990s, the R&D portion of the defense budget will likely decline along with the rest of the defense budgets. By 1997, the R&D budget is projected to be 25 percent below its 1990 level in real terms. Since almost 70 percent of all federal support for R&D at the beginning of the 1990s was for defense-related purposes, this will mean a drop in total federal support for R&D unless the federal government changes its current policy. Some have proposed that all federally supported R&D, including defense, be centrally funded. Others have suggested allowing defense facilities, like the Pentagon's seventy-five R&D labs, to work on problems of economic competitiveness. Still others have suggested that the United States develop an industrial policy that would both enhance our international economic position and protect our declining defense industrial base.

As noted earlier, nations have their own distinctive technology policies—explicit or implicit—and it is not unusual that these sometimes clash with their foreign policy interests. The problem of subordinating coordinating technology strategy with foreign policy was demonstrated in the FSX controversy between the United States and Japan. The U.S. Defense and State Departments wanted the General Dynamics Corporation to provide some of the technology from the F-16 to the Japanese to use in developing their new fighter, the FSX. In return, the Japanese would allow General Dynamics to produce about 40 percent of the new fighters. Defense and State felt that this technology transfer and coproduction would enhance the Japanese–U.S. security treaty. In essence, on the other hand, the Department of Commerce and the U.S. Trade Representative (USTR) argued that the FSX arrangement would allow the Japanese access to critical aerospace technology with which they could create a domestic aerospace industry to compete with our own. Eventually, a compromise among Defense/State and Commerce/USTR was worked out that limited the amount of technology that was transferred. While this case suggested that, in the post–cold war era, trade and technology will be treated as being as important as national security, it also suggested the difficulty of coordinating these key aspects of overall policy.

Strategy and Technology. We have already seen how technology is an indicator of future national capability and how it is necessary to differentiate between *knowledge* and possible *applications* of knowledge in defense areas. We have summarized the view of some observers that current trends in R&D may harbor significant policy problems for the United States. Next, we will address the link between technology and security strategy. The linkage is not restricted to the area of equipment modernization. To concentrate on applications may be to ignore investigation of new principles which will make current weapons systems obsolete, although such advance is not frequent. "Technology flows on without regard for human intentions, and each technological breakthrough offers the possibility for decisive advantages to the side that first exploits it."[18] The nature of this dynamism is such that it cannot be controlled unilaterally. For example, even if the United States chooses not to pursue development of space-based strategic defensive systems to defend itself against an accidental launch of an ICBM, the scientific principles that made such weapons possible are not going to evaporate—and, in due course, some other nation or coalition could pursue the possibilities.

Elements of technology are interdependent. This statement has two meanings. First, an advance in field *A* may make no sense unless there is also an advance in field *B;* it is useless, for example, to develop a new thermonuclear warhead if one does not develop an appropriate delivery system to launch and guide it. Second, advances in one field frequently suggest associated moves or applications in others; therefore, a decision not to pursue certain areas of research is no guarantee that the technology of the field will remain static, that others will make the same or parallel decisions.

Several contemporary "weapons technology" issues illustrate these points. One of the most significant is in laser technology. The U.S. approach to laser application has been primarily one of using it as an adaptation of current systems. As an example, we use lasers to provide terminal guidance for precision-guided munitions (PGMs), which creates the effect of significantly enhancing the utility of the basic munition by virtue of increased accuracy but which does not constitute a "new concept" for the battlefield.

These laser-guided weapons, fired from aircraft like the F-117A and the F-16, proved highly effective in the Gulf war. Within a matter of days they rendered useless the very sophisticated Iraqi air defense and command and control systems. It is estimated that of the 2100 laser-guided bombs dropped by the F-117As, 1700 fell within 10 feet of the intended target. Soviet scientists, on the other hand, did not develop laser-designator or laser-optical systems, but rather tried to create a whole new weapons concept, that is, charged-particle beams. Before the collapse of the Soviet empire, the Soviet Union had not yet incorporated charged-particle beams into their inventory. Thus, had war between the superpowers broken out in the late 1980s or early 1990s, the Soviets could have been at a decided technological disadvantage vis-à-vis the United States, because the U.S. applications were within the state of the art, while Soviet applications were open-ended. But, had the cold war lasted until the twenty-first century, the Soviet strategy might have given them a technological advantage over the United States.

From the American standpoint, several attempts at creating a national strategy for technology have been tried, with less than total success. Without central management of the entire economy, and lacking the ability to use classified security items in the civilian sector without compromising their security, the United States is less able to rationalize its overall R&D effort than some other countries. Several U.S. governmental offices have attempted or are attempting to organize and coordinate R&D, with varying degrees of success. At the White House level, R&D staffs have been created, dissolved, and created again. The latest version, the Office of Science and Technology Policy (OSTP), was established in the executive office of the president in 1976 to "serve . . . as a source of scientific, engineering, and technological analysis . . . involved in areas of national concern . . . [and] evaluate the scale, quality, and effectiveness of the Federal effort in science and technology.''[19]

Until the end of the cold war, OSTP had very little impact. However, in the early 1990s it began moving tentatively toward creating a national technology policy. For example, in 1990, it issued a statement on U.S. technology policy that said the federal government had responsibility for participating with the private sector in precompetitive research on generic enabling technologies that have the potential to contribute to a broad range of government and commercial applications. As a result of this policy, the DOD alone spent over $300 million in the early 1990s participating in consortia and other partnership arrangements in developing precompetitive, dual-use technologies.[20]

At the defense level, the undersecretary of defense for acquisition (as well as his predecessor, the undersecretary for research and engineering) has an advocacy function to analyze and defend research proposed by the DOD. Unfortunately, the advocacy function on behalf of the DOD tends to discredit the office's analysis function in the eyes of Congress. In 1972, Congress created its own Office of Technology Assessment (OTA) to provide it with an independent source of analysis and advice on R&D questions. The OTA began its operations in 1974, but has had only limited success in performing those functions.

Although total R&D expenditures climbed steadily in the 1980s, many sectors of American industry were either slow to appreciate the need for higher levels of funding or simply unable to supply the required capital. The situation was exacerbated by the problem of lead time in technology. One area of consistent U.S. concern has been to lower the ''lag time'' from discovery of a concept to production of an item incorporating the concept. Despite continuing work on this problem, the current average time from concept to design to prototypes is about five to seven years. Thus, even if the U.S. government successfully reorganized and rationalized the overall national R&D effort, the effects would not be felt for some time. Significant lag times play a major role in the development of military technologies, which frequently take even longer to evolve. Many of the weapon systems that were employed by U.S. military forces in the Gulf war were conceived and developed during the Carter administration, or even earlier. Similarly, many of the research programs initiated by the Reagan defense build-up of the 1980s will not reach the procurement stage until the mid to late 1990s.

Finally, no amount of internal review or rationalization of existing efforts can accomplish the external function of establishing critical national priorities in resource allocation. The most efficient program organizer cannot manage a program without the appropriation of R&D money. (For example, the DOD did not include funding for precompetitive research in its amended 1992–1993 budget.) Good internal organization can increase the efficiency of the budget within limits, but it cannot create an appropriate budget. In addition, the research budgets of private corporations tend to reflect economic cycles. In times of narrowing profit margins, research is primarily directed to finding new or more efficient applications rather than to basic research for new knowledge. The recovery of the U.S. economy from the disruption of the 1970s and from the economic recession that occurred during 1981–1982 encouraged a large increase in private R&D. Between 1980 and 1990, industrial R&D expenditures increased by four percent a year in real terms. But when the economy faltered again in the early 1990s, this progress came to an abrupt halt, and in 1992 industrial investment in R&D actually declined as a percentage of revenues.

Decision-making in R&D. As indicated previously, decisions about defense R&D would ideally be made on the basis of an optimal way to implement previously determined strategic requirements. However, as implied above, there is a tendency for the reverse to be true, given the speed and complexity of technological advance. Thus, one debate in this area is the extent to which R&D should determine strategy, and vice versa.*

Two major points are often advanced about the technology "tail" wagging the strategy "dog." First, as new technologies become available, there is pressure in defense circles to procure and deploy them, which can result in revising strategies in two ways. The structure of forces may be adapted to fit the new weapons, driving the nation toward new strategies even though a coherent strategy for employing the weapon may not have been developed. Also, because the newer weapons are almost invariably more expensive (and more sophisticated), a nation can buy fewer of them, requiring a modification of strategy to match the resulting new force levels.

The second point is more complex. Basically, it argues that *deploying* new and advanced weapons systems may be self-defeating. This does not contradict the argument made earlier that a state must maintain its technological capabilities at the leading edge of scientific knowledge. Once a state discovers a new weapons system, there are internal pressures to procure and deploy quantities of the weapon.† "The search for *quality*—for the 'technological threshold'—dominated U.S. force posture during the Cold War and the acquisition system provided many incentives for taking this route."[21] But this practice generated a desperate attempt to counter the weapon by the Soviet Union, with the net result that both sides expended large sums without a net increase in security for either.

At this stage the reader might ask: if deployment of new weapons can be useless, as just suggested, but falling behind in military technology can be fatal; and, further, if technology cannot be unilaterally controlled, then what options are available? One possible response is that the United States should awaken to

---

*In this sense, Maxwell Taylor's *The Uncertain Trumpet* was a critique of defense policy. Taylor argued that we had structured our whole defense program around nuclear retaliation because nuclear bombs were there and were cheap, rather than analyze possible situations in which we might actually be called on to employ military capabilities.

†Sources of this pressure are varied. The industry that has developed the system will press for the large contract for mass production. Both congressional and defense sources will argue that to equip the field army with any but the very latest weapons is to degrade their fighting capability.

the fact that it is really fighting a "war of technology." It may not wish to procure and deploy each new development, but it must continue to engage vigorously in R&D to ensure that it is *able* quickly to build and deploy superior weapons if the need arises. Framed succinctly:

> Technological warfare is the direct and purposeful application of the national technological base . . . to attain strategic and tactical objectives. . . . The aims of this kind of warfare, as of all forms of warfare, are to enforce the national will on enemy powers. . . . The winner of the Technological War can, if he chooses, preserve peace and order, act as a stabilizer of international affairs, and prevent shooting wars. The loser has no choice but to accept the conditions of the victor or to engage in a shooting war which he has already lost.[22]

While those who cite technological war as inescapably decisive overstate their case, viewing technology as a crucial element of power—whether or not procurements follow from a particular technological advance—is sensible. The approach suggests a scenario in which states conduct "research and development races" rather than "arms races."

With the end of the cold war, the pressure on the DOD to develop and procure every new weapons system should decline dramatically. Because it no longer confronts another military superpower, and because the weapons that it developed to confront the Soviet Union are so superior to those of any other potential adversary, the United States should be able to change its approach to weapons procurement. It could safely divert funds from procurement to enhancing its technological base. If it decides to produce a result of technology, the DOD can produce only a few prototypes, as it did with the SSN-2 or Seawolf submarine, or go into limited production as it did with the B-2 bomber (twenty aircraft). Only if the new technology represents such a potential breakthrough that it is a "silver bullet" will the DOD go into full production.

Domestic R&D Issues. Issues of strategy and technology are in one sense conceptual; but research programs do not discover, technology programs do not develop, and procurement programs do not build without budgetary allocation of resources to support them. Many agencies compete for attention in defense budgets, including the armed services, who vie with one another. Within the executive branch, policy planners from the DOD, the State Department, and the NSC all develop threat estimates. "The principal determinant of the size and shape of the United States military budget and force structure ought to be the military requirements, nuclear and non-nuclear, of U.S. foreign policy."[23] Defense planners must compete, however, for the resources to provide these forces, and nondefense agencies do not necessarily share either the view of the threat or the immediacy of the need for resources to counter the threat. Thus, as indicated more fully in Chapter 9, setting national spending priorities within the executive branch of the federal government is a highly competitive process.

The Congress has its own interests bearing on the defense budget and its R&D priorities. "It is particularly difficult for the Congress to achieve either discipline or objectivity on military policy issues because both are so clouded by self-interest."[24] These instances of self-interest may relate to the economic impact of particular defense programs in particular congressional districts, or they may be reflections of military strategy or foreign policy viewpoints held by particular groups of representatives or senators. It is not at all uncommon to find the Congress insisting that "the nation needs" a particular weapons system that the president, the secretary of defense, and the head of the armed services that would use the system all insist they do not need or want.

Various interest "publics," both organized and unorganized, may lobby for particular programs or overall levels of defense preparedness. Though these groups frequently work through congressional members, they also testify and print publications touting their particular viewpoints. Driven, understandably, by the profit motive, defense industries naturally attempt to influence military budgets and force structures. In many cases, defense production may represent a major portion of the entire output of a firm. For example, General Dynamics, which in 1990 was the seventieth largest U.S. company in terms of sales, did about 90 percent of its business ($6.3 billion) with the Defense Department. In the early 1990s, when the Pentagon canceled the second and third SSN-2 (or Seawolf) submarine contracts, the future of General Electric's Electric Boat subsidiary in Groton, Connecticut, was in jeopardy. In order to save Electric Boat and its 20,000 employees, the Congress, under heavy pressure from the Connecticut delegation, refused to accept the Pentagon's cancellation of the Seawolf contracts.

The composite of these pressures and competing interest groups has frequently been referred to as the "military–industrial complex" (MIC). Such a "complex" is identifiable, though it shifts in character and composition from year to year and budget area to budget area. Although it is hardly a sinister conspiracy to usurp the functions of the American government, as some critics charge, its sheer size does make it an influential force in domestic politics. By the early 1990s, employment in defense goods still represented about fifty out of every one thousand workers. As one authority noted, these are often not typical workers; "a mere count of the numbers does not convey that those involved in the defense effort are, on the average, superior from an economic viewpoint. Two out of five physicists outside of teaching, and three out of five aeronautical engineers were employed on defense goods."[25]

A related factor in the impact of the MIC is the relative concentration and weight of defense production in various high-technology industries. If defense procurement of underwear is curtailed next year, the looms of the industry certainly will not stop. Even if production is off, there are other types of clothing which could absorb unemployed mill workers, and lateral transfers are possible. The airframe industry, by contrast, is far more dependent on defense. Not only does defense contracting amount to more than 40 percent of total revenue, but the aeronautical skills of the engineering forces employed are not so easily translatable or readily absorbable in civilian sectors of the economy. Thus, considerations such as the maintenance of skilled employment and an industrial base from which to expand should enter into the decision-making process of defense procurement.

As the United States downsizes its military industrial complex in the 1990s it faces dual challenges. First, the DOD must preserve its capacity to reconstitute or rebuild its force structure if international events warrant. This means having critical technologies and manufacturing capacities available in an era when there will not be very much defense business. Second, the nation must help scientists and engineers employed in defense laboratories and defense industry find productive employment in the commercial sector. If it fails in either of these challenges the results could be disastrous for national security. Without a reconstitution capacity, the DOD may not be able to handle a deterioration in the international system. Similarly, if DOD workers cannot make the transition to the commercial sector, Congress may force the DOD to build unneeded weapons just to keep the workers employed.

Impact of R&D on Weapons Acquisition. As implied earlier, an argument sometimes lodged against developing new weapons is that such weapons, particularly "glamorous" ones, tend to determine the force structure and mission of the armed forces, rather than the other way around. If we develop and procure a new and very expensive aircraft, the air force may feel obligated to devise a role and mission for it. For example, the B-2 stealth bomber was developed in the late 1970s to penetrate supersophisticated Soviet air defenses with nuclear weapons. By the time the B-2 was ready to move into full production, however, the Soviet Union had dissolved, the cold war had ended, and the United States had cut its nuclear arsenal by two-thirds. The air force then justified buying 20 B-2s for nearly $50 billion by assigning them a power projection mission with conventional weapons against Third World nations.

One aspect of this argument is the continued debate over whether one ought to concentrate more on quantity (of relatively simple weapons systems) or quality (highly sophisticated weapons systems) in equipping the armed forces. Given cost constraints, increasing the sophistication and quality of a given type of weapons system almost invariably entails decreasing the quantity of forces. In this trade-off, the argument for quality has generally been persuasive in the United States because the majority of senior officers have argued that neither the threat technology nor the importance of saving American lives permits any compromise with quality. This approach has been successful in the Pentagon and on Capitol Hill, and in the minds of many was vindicated in the Gulf war, where sophistication worked heavily in our favor. This perspective logically implies that the most advanced system available must be provided.

The counter position is that there is little direct correlation between combat effectiveness and sophistication. First, as a weapons system is made more complex, the maintenance requirements will increase, both qualitatively (it requires a more skilled technician to repair a missile computer than to change the tread on a tank) and quantitatively (there are more things to break down). Moreover, the miniaturization of the internal parts of some modern weapons systems may make them too fragile for extended field use. In short, there is a probability that the ''sophisticated'' system will perform at less than design level when it is actually employed.[26] Proponents of this view hold that the high-technology successes in the Gulf war did not invalidate their position. Rather, it was the skill of our people, the ineptitude of our enemy, and our numerical superiority that made the quick, relatively bloodless victory possible.

While not decisively influencing this quality–quantity argument, defense contracting and budgetary procedures contribute to related problems in weapons system acquisition. Since quantity is a discretely measurable item, contracts unequivocally specify amounts. Quality is not so easily definable, particularly before the system is actually built. Therefore, contracts allow more leeway in qualitative considerations. A defense contractor who is actually building the prototype thus has much more of a ''blank check'' in getting the government to subsidize inevitable changes in the system if he argues that such changes constitute a qualitative improvement. ''Any service which considers developing a cheaper [and simpler] tank, ship, or airplane must face the possibility that it is proposing a decrement to its budget and consequently to its overall manpower, influence, and the like.''[27] Thus, to change at all is budgetarily dangerous, and to request change in the direction of less cost is particularly deadly. A much easier strategy is to keep a system that has already been approved and simply modify it to new specifications and roles.* While this strategy has bureaucratic advantages, it tends to generate only marginally useful sophistication at the price of cost overruns.[28]

Results of such ad hoc growth of weapons systems can be damaging in several ways. Not only do maintenance problems increase geometrically, but commanders are very reluctant to train on fragile systems, which results in the soldier-user being unfamiliar with and not confident in the weapon. Also, the size of the maintenance force increases, either drawing personnel strength from the combat units or requiring increases in the overall size of the armed forces.

Further, since there are increasingly limited resources available for the total DOD budget, procurement of more sophisticated (and expensive) weapons can adversely affect combat versatility. As an exaggerated example, consider a total equipment budget of $20 billion for a given fiscal year. If previous budget decisions had already obligated funds for the procurement of a $20 billion super aircraft carrier and associated aircraft, then there could be no other equipment purchased during that entire fiscal year. All other combat equipment requirements would have to come from stocks on hand at the beginning of the year.

The ultimate danger of this ''quality above all'' approach, however, lies in its potential strategic implication. During the cold war, the budgetary process pushed toward procuring and deploying increasingly specialized, and costly,

*The AWACS (Airborne Warning and Control System) was originally designed to provide alternative command and control in strategic exchanges but now is deployed for control of the air war in a theater engagement. Similarly, the Patriot Missile System, which was deployed as an air defense weapon against high-altitude aircraft, was modified to serve as a potential defense against intermediate-range missiles, which it did in the Gulf war.

weapons, and the combat capabilities of the armed forces became slaves to the sophisticated weapons they possessed. This situation inevitably led planners to adopt strategies built around these weapons. Ultimately, therefore, this approach led to weapons systems dictating strategy, the exact reverse of a rational strategic decision-making process. It remains to be seen whether the United States can rationalize its decision-making process now that the cold war is over.

Summary. This chapter has introduced some of the issues of research and development which affect national security in the present era. Competence in advanced science and technology is a component of both present and future military capability. Modern technology is so expensive that nations must carefully marshal and organize their efforts to maximize returns. Weapons systems, as direct military applications of technology, keep getting more complex and more expensive, without necessarily getting any more reliable or useful. However, no state that aspires to military leadership can afford to forgo the expense of pursuing weapons development, for fear that a true breakthrough by potential opponents will leave its military forces vulnerable.

Discussion Questions

1. Why is dependence on imported technology a detriment to national security? Do you see any advantages to such a policy?

2. How has the Japanese and Western European policy of "satelliting" on U.S. technological advances in sophisticated weaponry caused a strain in allied relations? What policy changes would you recommend?

3. List some of the reasons you think U.S. efforts at creating a national strategy for technology have not been totally successful. Should the effort be abandoned? Why or why not?

4. How does interservice rivalry affect the competition for pieces of the R&D budget? Does it affect weapons development?

5. Should defense contracts go to the lowest bidder promising the finest piece of equipment? Explain your answer.

6. How can weapons system procurement drive the strategic decision-making process?

7. Why is it increasingly important that nations develop some overall coherence in their technology programs?

8. Should U.S. policy be to develop quantity (relatively simple weapons systems) or quality (highly sophisticated weapons systems) in equipping its armed forces? Defend your answer.

9. Why has the federal government essentially taken over the responsibility for funding basic research? How can private industry be enticed into spending more money on basic research?

10. Does the end of the cold war strengthen or weaken the case for a national technology policy?

11. How can the Planning, Programming, Budgeting System described in Chapter 9 alleviate some of the R&D problems described in this chapter?

Recommended Reading

Adams, Gordon. *The Iron Triangle: The Politics of Defense Contracting*. New York: Council on Economic Priorities, 1982.

Adelman, Kenneth, and Augustine, Norman. *The Defense Revolution*. San Francisco: Institute for Contemporary Studies, 1990.

Blackwell, James A. *The Defense Industrial Base for a New Strategic Era*. Washington, D.C.: The Center for Strategic and International Studies, 1992.

Brauch, Hans, et al. *Controlling the Development and Spread of Military Technology*. Amsterdam: Vu University Press, 1992.

DeGrasse, Robert. *Military Expansion, Economic Decline: The Impact of Military Spending on U.S. Economic Performance*. Armonk, N.Y.: Sharpe, 1983.

Eagelburger, Lawrence S. *High Technology and American Foreign Policy*. Washington, D.C.: American Enterprise Institute, 1985.

Fallows, James. *National Defense*. New York: Random House, 1981.

Gillman, Katherine. *After the Cold War – Living with Lower Defense Spending*. Washington, D.C.: Office of Technology Assessment, 1992.

Goodwin, Jacob. *Brotherhood of Arms: General Dynamics and the Business of Defending America*. New York: Random House, 1985.

Mayer, Kenneth. *The Political Economy of Defense Contracting*. New Haven, Conn.: Yale University Press, 1991.

McNaugher, Thomas. *New Weapons, Old Politics: America's Military Procurement Muddle*. Washington, D.C.: Brookings Institution, 1989.

Nincic, Mirosav. *The Arms Race: The Political Economy of Military Growth*. New York: Praeger, 1982.

Reischauer, Robert. *The Economic Effects of Reduced Defense Spending*. Washington, D.C.: Congressional Budget Office, 1992.

Seitz, Frederick, and Nichols, Rodney W. *Research and Development and the Prospects for International Security*. New York: Crane, Russak, 1973.

Taylor, Maxwell D. *The Uncertain Trumpet*. New York: Harper, 1959.

Tirman, John. *The Militarization of High Technology*. Cambridge, Mass.: Ballinger, 1984.

Ullman, John E. *The Prospects of American Industrial Recovery*. Westport, Conn.: Quorum Books, 1985.

IV

International and Regional Security Issues

16

The Former Soviet Union

In the preceding chapters we have addressed a range of security issues involving U.S. relations with the Soviet Union and its successor states. Here we examine the complex factors that make the former Soviet Union so important to American national security. Despite the political disintegration of the Soviet Union, for the foreseeable future Russia will continue to possess the ability to destroy a significant portion of the globe with nuclear weapons. Thus, even though the character and aims of the former Soviet Union have been utterly transformed, the future of the region remains extremely important to U.S. defense planning.

The major issues of war and peace in the 1990s will in large part hinge on the fate of the former Soviet Union's transformation to market-oriented, democratic powers. If this transition proceeds relatively smoothly, this will profoundly enhance the prospects for international order and open the way for dramatic shifts in U.S. defense policy. If the transition collapses, and the region descends into chaos or lapses into dictatorship, this too will have obviously important implications for international security and for American security planning.

Our purpose in this chapter is to examine the history of the relationship between Soviet foreign and military policy and capabilities and their impact on U.S. national security interests; we shall briefly review Soviet foreign policy from 1945 to the present and then examine the ongoing transformation of the former Soviet Union, with a particular focus on emerging trends in foreign and defense policy.

From Cold War to Détente

American–Soviet relations in the period 1945 to 1969 are generally described by the term *cold war*. This phenomenon may be defined as an era of tension,

FIG. 16.1 Soviet Union

characterized by intense superpower competition, frequent confrontations, and the virtual absence of cooperative activities.

While hundreds of books have been written on the origins of the cold war, two aspects are worthy of mention here.[1] First, and frequently listed as the chief among all causes, was a set of beliefs, arising out of Soviet ideology, that drastically skewed relations between the Soviet Union and the capitalist world. Among these beliefs were

1. Ownership of the means of production dictates socioeconomic conditions within a particular country. Domestically, private ownership breeds class struggle. Internationally, class struggle dictates that conflict will dominate relations between capitalist and socialist states.
2. The United States is implacably hostile to the cause of socialism. Consequently, the World War II alliance between the United States and the Soviet Union was only tactical and temporary in nature.
3. History follows a predictable linear course wherein capitalism, through violent revolutions, will eventually give way to socialism. Major wars among capitalist states, such as World War II, are precursors of these revolutions.
4. Relations between socialist and capitalist states are governed by the "correlation of forces," a sophisticated and somewhat ambiguous notion of the balance of power, which includes social, political, and other "subjective" factors, in addition to the economic and military power of the states concerned. To assist "the inevitable march of history," Soviet leaders must exploit the correlation of forces, except where such exploitation would endanger vital interests of the Soviet state.

The net effect of these beliefs was to produce a climate of hostility and confrontation; for, as one of America's foremost Sovietologists, George Kennan, has observed, "It is an undeniable privilege of every man to prove himself right in the thesis that the world is his enemy; for if he reiterates it frequently enough and makes it the background of his conduct he is bound eventually to be right."[2]

A second key origin of the cold war can be subsumed under the heading of "collision of interests." As stated in Chapter 1, each state, independently or in concert with others, pursues its own national interest within an international system where "self-help" is a nation's principal recourse. The near anarchical nature of the international system places a premium on the pursuit of power within the system. Given this fact and the very different values embodied in free societies and authoritarian ones, conflict of some type is the inevitable consequence. Thus, conflict of various kinds between the United States and the Soviet Union, accentuated by the largely bipolar nature of international security affairs and the awesome power of the superpower nuclear arsenals, was continuous from 1945 to 1985, when the Soviet Union embarked on a reform path that led to its political collapse in 1991.

The first major collision of interests took place over the fate of postwar Germany and Eastern Europe. Stalin wanted to establish a socialist "sphere of influence" in Eastern Europe and ultimately place Germany under Soviet domination. This policy was designed not only to increase the number of nations in the socialist camp (and thereby validate ideological predictions) but also to provide a friendly "buffer zone" for the territory of the Soviet Union.

The United States was willing to see the establishment of governments friendly to the Soviet Union in Eastern Europe but objected to (and was repulsed by) the forcible imposition of communist regimes throughout Eastern Europe. The survival of a free Germany became a key concern for American leaders, who believed that the addition of any significant portion of Western Europe to the newly expanded Soviet bloc would eventually tip the world balance of power, despite the U.S. nuclear monopoly at the time.

While the United States gradually assumed the commitment to keep Western Europe from the fate of Eastern Europe, its policy was initially, in Walter Lippmann's terminology, "insolvent."[3] After World War II, the American drive to disarm its units and "bring the boys home" shrank overall forces by 1947 to approximately 10 percent of their 1945 strength (from 12 million to 1.3 million).[4] Furthermore, most U.S. units after the surgery were organized for occupation duty, and nearly all American service members were assigned to ill-equipped, under-strength units. At the same time, the Soviet Union maintained about 4.5 million soldiers under arms, nearly all in combat units, the vast bulk of which were deployed in Europe.* The end result of this "position of weakness" was to leave doubt in Stalin's mind about the strength of the U.S. commitment to Europe. Consequently, the United States and its allies were tested by the Soviet Union on numerous occasions: in 1946, over the prolonged Soviet occupation of Iran; in 1946–1947, over threats to Greece and Turkey; in 1948, by the Soviet coup that installed a Communist government in Czechoslovakia; and in 1948–1949, by the blockade of West Berlin by Soviet forces for over a year.

As indicated more fully in Chapter 4, the American response to these crises was incremental, reflecting the slow learning of new great powers. In 1947, the United States announced the Truman Doctrine, proclaiming America's intention "to support free people who are resisting attempted subjugation by armed minorities or by outside pressures." Shortly thereafter, George Kennan, then in the State Department, published a famous article using the pseudonym of "Mr. X," which argued that the United States should aim toward containment of the Soviet Union.[5] In response to the Czech coup and the Berlin blockade, both in 1948, eleven Western European nations and the United States in 1949 signed the North Atlantic Treaty, a collective self-defense pact; this became the basis for the NATO military alliance. (Later, after the rearming of West Germany, the Soviet Union and its Eastern European satellites signed a treaty "On Friendship, Cooperation, and Mutual Aid" in May 1955, creating the Warsaw Treaty Organization.)

Even as the United States was adapting to its new activist role, the international environment produced dramatic changes. First, the Soviet Union exploded its initial nuclear bomb in 1949, undercutting the heavy U.S. reliance on nuclear

---

*The precise extent of Soviet postwar demobilization is still unresolved; that it did not proceed to anything like the American case is, however, clear. See Thomas Wolfe, *Soviet Power and Europe, 1945–1970* (Baltimore: Johns Hopkins University Press, 1970), p. 10, n. 6.

weapons to check Soviet aggression. Also in 1949, the Chinese Communists ejected the Chinese Nationalists, with whom the United States was allied, from mainland China. Finally, after a speech by Secretary of State Dean Acheson, in which South Korea was left outside the U.S. security perimeter, Stalin gave his support to the North Korean Communist invasion of South Korea in 1950.* When U.N. forces—led by the United States—made a successful counterattack and entered North Korea, Communist Chinese forces entered the war. This string of stimuli brought a series of strong U.S. responses. Work began on a thermonuclear bomb, containment was transformed into a global doctrine, and, during the Korean War, NATO forces were strengthened and the groundwork laid for the eventual rearmament of West Germany.

Stalin died just before the end of the Korean War in July 1953. The policies of his successors (for a time, Malenkov, then Khrushchev) showed elements of both change and continuity from Stalin's world view. The changes in Soviet strategy were significant. First, realizing the awesome effects of nuclear weapons, Malenkov, and later Khrushchev, shelved the rhetoric, perhaps even the idea, of the inevitability of war between capitalist and socialist states. "Peaceful coexistence" between the United States and the Soviet Union became a goal, though perhaps not the dominant one, of post-Stalinist foreign policy.

Second, after 1957, Khrushchev insisted on developing a nuclear-oriented force structure at the expense of (temporarily, it proved) the ground forces and the surface navy. Third, in an effort to "embarrass and outflank Western diplomacy," Khrushchev began a major effort to increase Soviet influence with the nonaligned nations of the Third World, many of which were former Western colonies.[6] The doctrine that it was the sacred duty of the Soviet Union to promote and support "wars of national liberation" was enunciated by Khrushchev in January 1961 at the Moscow Conference of Communist Parties:

> What is the attitude of Marxists toward such uprisings? A most positive one. These uprisings must not be identified with wars among states. . . . These are uprisings against rotten reactionary regimes, against the colonizers. The Communists fully support such just wars and march in the front rank with the people waging liberation struggles.†

The most important element of continuity in Soviet policy was the Soviet preoccupation with the settlement of the German question and with Western recognition of the status quo in Eastern Europe. Khrushchev twice tried unsuccessfully to push the West into a settlement, using Berlin as the fulcrum for his efforts. It apparently became clear to Khrushchev that to force a favorable solution to the German and East European problems, indeed to pursue its worldwide aims, the Soviet Union would have to attain strategic parity with the

---

*Soviet sources indicated later that Stalin gave his "blessing" to the North Koreans without giving the matter very much serious thought. Nikita Khrushchev, *Khrushchev Remembers,* trans. Strobe Talbott (London: Andre Deutsch, 1971). pp. 366–73.

†President Kennedy thought that Khrushchev's announcement was so significant that he directed that "all the members of his new administration read the speech and consider what it portended." Roger Hisman, *To Move a Nation* (Garden City, N.Y.: Doubleday, 1967), p. 414.

United States or at least something close to it. To deal with the American president (and to outflank Chairman Mao), the Soviets would have to have the power to threaten the United States directly to the same degree that the United States could threaten the Soviet Union.

In one sense, Khrushchev's problem boiled down to numbers. In 1962 the United States had 720 modern, intercontinental delivery systems. In the most generous estimate, the Soviets then had only 260 delivery systems, most of which were of dubious reliability.[7] In seeking to redress this imbalance, Khrushchev had two options. He could quickly build large numbers of primitive, liquid-fueled intercontinental ballistic missiles (ICBMs) or, as a temporary measure, pending further design advances, he could put some of his plentiful medium-range ballistic missiles (MRBMs) within striking range of the United States. The first option would provide an expensive, and not very effective or timely, solution. The second option, though higher in risk, would be quicker and less expensive.

Khrushchev chose the second option, which led directly to the 1962 "Cuban Missile Crisis," the most dramatic Soviet defeat in the postwar era.[8] Khrushchev's covert missile build-up was discovered before it was operationally ready, and the Soviets, faced with U.S. nuclear as well as local conventional superiority, were forced to back down. While this incident was an essential precursor to the subsequent dampening of tensions between the superpowers, it also taught the Soviets a hard lesson: the shadow of military power was no substitute for its substance. The Soviet Union concluded that to advance its interests and values against an increasingly strong United States, it would have to improve its military forces significantly.

Soviet determination to correct the problems encountered in the Cuban Missile Crisis was reflected in a statement made by Soviet Deputy Foreign Minister V. V. Kuznetsov to an American official shortly after the crisis: "Never will we be caught like this again."[9] Khrushchev was replaced in 1964 by the Communist Party Central Committee, whose members had been alienated by his adventurist foreign policy and his reforms and domestic blunders. His successors, Brezhnev and Kosygin, adopted a more moderate tone and businesslike approach to foreign and domestic problems.

In retrospect, three factors contributed to the subsequent Soviet successes in the foreign policy realm. First, especially during the decade from 1965 to 1975, the Soviet economy prospered, leaving the Brezhnev regime free to purchase both more "guns" and more "butter."* Thus, the military power position of the Soviet Union and the domestic standard of living could be simultaneously

*All estimates of the growth of the Soviet economy are subject to wide margins of error. According to some analysts from 1961 to 1970, the Soviet GNP grew at a respectable 5 percent per annum. In the 1970s, it declined to 4 percent and then to 3 percent; in the early 1980s, it was 2 percent or less and by the mid 1980s it actually began to decline. Robert Byrnes, ed., *After Brezhnev: Sources of Soviet Conduct in the 1980s* (Bloomington: Indiana University Press, 1983). See also Central Intelligence Agency paper, *Gorbachev's Modernization Program: A Status Report,* March 19, 1987, presented to the joint Economic Committee of the U.S. Congress.

improved. Second, the United States became increasingly bogged down in Vietnam, with the result that spending on nuclear forces and on improved conventional capabilities for a war in Europe suffered drastically. At the same time, U.S. policymakers and the public alike turned against the notion of military power. Many in the United States (and in the Third World) began to speak of "American imperialism" in the same tone that they once used to discuss the "red menace." A third factor in the Soviet foreign policy successes sprang from the two noted above: many in the West, including in the United States, began to view the Soviet Union as less fearsome. Herbert Dinerstein wrote in 1970:

> The changes in the internal organization of Soviet political life [since Stalin] have tended to make for fewer rather than more initiatives in foreign policy. . . . Soviet foreign policy has been more active . . . when the Soviet leaders have been worried about weaknesses in the system of socialist states and within the Soviet Union itself. . . . It no longer seems satisfactory to assume that the Soviet Union will take more risks to improve its political position as its military position vis-à-vis the U.S. improves.[10]

In brief, by the later 1960s, it appeared to many as if the West had exaggerated the Soviet threat to its interests; perhaps we could deal with the Soviets, if we would but try to improve relations.

For their own purposes, the Soviets also wished to lessen tensions. The United States, under President Nixon, was making worrisome overtures to the People's Republic of China (since the latter 1950s or early 1960s a de facto enemy of the Soviet Union). The Soviets also saw an opportunity to gain from increased trade with the West, especially where high-technology items, such as computers, and grain were concerned. Soviet leaders must also have been pleased by the West's recognition of the status of East Germany and Eastern Europe, thanks in part to West Germany's conciliatory Ostpolitik. Increasingly, too, both sides saw the opportunity, indeed, the necessity, to limit strategic arms. Thus, the era of détente (or "hot peace," as one analyst later termed it) was born.[11]

Unfortunately, American optimism of the late 1960s and early 1970s proved to be unfounded. Indeed, détente was flawed from the beginning. Each side saw the benefits of détente but not the costs that it would entail. For the United States, détente was widely viewed as a replacement for containment: through the development of a network of policy linkages, the West would somehow enforce discipline on a mellowing Soviet Union. For the United States, as Kissinger said, "Détente [could not] be pursued selectively in one area or toward one group of countries only. For us, détente is indivisible."[12]

For their part, the Soviets believed détente was merely a consequence of the new correlation of forces and of American recognition that the Soviet Union was now the "other" superpower. Brezhnev himself outlined the Soviet definition of détente at the Twenty-fifth Party Congress.

> Détente . . . means above all that disputes and conflicts between countries must not be settled by means of war. . . . Détente does not in the slightest abolish . . . the laws of class struggle. No one should expect that in conditions of détente the communists will become reconciled to capitalist exploitation. . . . We make no secret of the fact that we

> see détente as a path leading to the creation of more favorable conditions for peaceful communist construction.[13]

In effect, the Soviets were telling the United States that détente *was* divisible. One analyst summed up the true essence of the détente which followed in this manner: "Détente [became] the art of trade-offs between competitors, not an arrangement whereby new friends solemnly swore to end the contest."[14]

Return to Cold War

The high point of détente occurred in 1972 when the United States and the Soviet Union signed the Strategic Arms Limitation Treaty (SALT I). By 1973, however, it became obvious that the contest had not ended. In October of that year the Soviets threatened U. S. interests with unilateral intervention in the Arab–Israeli War. Unlike the days of Khrushchev, the Soviet threat was not empty—six airborne divisions stood ready, and the Soviet Mediterranean fleet numbered a near record eighty-five vessels.[15] In response, the United States found it necessary to alert its armed forces throughout the world.

From an American perspective, the Arab–Israeli War damaged, but did not sink, the ship of détente; subsequent Soviet operations in the Third World did. After 1973, with varying degrees of Soviet help, procommunist parties oriented toward Moscow seized power or de facto control in Vietnam, Laos, Angola, Ethiopia, Afghanistan, South Yemen, Cambodia, and Nicaragua. Unlike previous Soviet forays into the Third World, these activities seemed particularly ominous for two reasons. First, the Soviets were no longer content to work through nationalist movements, but rather they began to rely on proclaimed communist or socialist elements. Second, Soviet military moves became increasingly bold. Beginning in 1975, Cuban troops and Soviet arms advisers and technicians became major, direct tools in Africa.[16] In Afghanistan, a Soviet army of about 115,000 troops was sent to preserve the remnants of Marxist power and extend Soviet influence in that country.

The December 1979 Soviet invasion of Afghanistan represented a new dimension in Soviet policy. The invasion marked the first time since the end of World War II that Soviet ground forces had engaged in combat outside the Warsaw Pact area. No longer limiting its intervention to arms, advisers, and proxies, the Soviet Union had now become directly involved in a Third World area. Of key importance, the Soviet invasion brought into question the value and future of a superpower détente that was one-sided in practice.

In reacting to the Soviet invasion, Western governments were alarmed by the opportunities it seemed to create for Soviet policy. First, the Soviet Union had a better position than ever to exploit ethnic rivalries in the area. Turbulent Pakistan seemed an especially vulnerable target. Second, the possession of airfields around Afghanistan's Kandahar region put unrefueled Soviet fighters in range of the critical Strait of Hormuz in the Persian Gulf and limited the usefulness of U.S. carriers in the event of an Indian Ocean conflict or confrontation. Finally, a Soviet presence in Afghanistan could become a basis for the neutralization of the entire region, subjecting governments to the Soviet mixture of ''fear and seduction.''[17]

Soviet operations in Afghanistan also had more general and ominous implications. Earlier operations in Angola and Ethiopia had given Soviet leaders confidence in their logistical capabilities and generalship. Afghanistan was a further opportunity to test equipment (including chemical and perhaps biological weapons) and to prove the mettle of Soviet forces. Success in Afghanistan seemed at the time to increase the Politburo's confidence in the Soviet military establishment, making it more prone to use force in the future.[18]

In the context of their intervention in Afghanistan, the Soviets extended the ''protective custody'' of the Brezhnev Doctrine (which guaranteed the perpetual ''socialist'' character of Soviet satellites) to all of the proclaimed Marxist states in the Third World, such as South Yemen, Angola, Nicaragua, and Ethiopia. The Soviet Union had, in effect, created a rationale for using force in areas of the Third World wherever the correlation of forces would permit them to do so.[19]

The Evolving Soviet Threat. The Soviet Union's effort to build its military establishment, capable of conducting warfare in every conceivable manner, was impressive.

Many explanations have been put forward to account for the continuing Soviet military build-up in this period. For many experts it became difficult to believe that purely defensive aims explained the extraordinary size and continuity of the Soviet effort. In any case, the Soviet Union's military effort was widely perceived as posing a multifaceted military threat to U.S. security interests: in the strategic balance, on the Central Front of Europe, in East Asia, and in the Third World.

The Strategic Threat. Every nation's first goal in its security policy is to protect its homeland. Before the Soviet Union's demise removed the threat, the only physical danger to U.S. territory came from the Soviet strategic arsenal—and vice versa. By the early 1980s, the enormous momentum of the Soviet build-up yielded some clear elements of Soviet superiority. Strategic stability, which was sustained for decades by U.S. preeminence and restraint, naturally became a more acute worry in U.S. military planning and arms control policy.

American analysts were worried by a number of aspects of the build-up. First, Soviet military doctrine stressed the maintenance of damage-limiting, war-fighting capabilities.[20] The implications of this are discussed in Chapter 11. Second, U.S. defense strategy depended on the mutually reinforcing capabilities of our triad, but Soviet advances in missile accuracy, when added to Soviet superiority in total megatonnage, placed the future survival of the U.S. land-based ICBMs in jeopardy. These weapons were thought to be essential to U.S. defenses because they alone could assuredly knock out Soviet missiles in their silos. Some American analysts came to believe that the Soviets could use this U.S. vulnerability to establish ''escalation dominance'' in a war, or that it could be parlayed into a credible nuclear threat in crisis bargaining, in the same way that the Soviets attempted to use the fictitious "missile gap" in 1958 and 1961. A far more capable U.S. missile, the MX (discussed in Chapter 11), was deployed in the 1980s, but in small numbers that could not eliminate the problem of ICBM vulnerability.[21]

Frustration over this continuing vulnerability was one major source of U.S. interest in the Strategic Defense Initiative (SDI) (see Chapter 23). The Reagan administration gave this defensive effort high priority, but it was not alone. Soviet investment in defensive systems—such as air, space, and civil defense—was at a high level for many years. To the Soviet leadership, however, the prospect of a race to master these newest, complex technologies seemed very unpleasant, particularly as they were acutely aware of the research strengths of the West and of the Soviet economy's severe weaknesses in technological innovation.

The Threat to NATO. The independence and prosperity of Western Europe have long been held to be a key to U.S. security. In Europe, until their satellite nations in East Europe departed from their orbit in the great anticommunist revolution of 1989, the Soviets followed an intricate policy of "fear and seduction." On the one hand, the Soviets fostered good economic relations with Western Europe and encouraged European initiatives for continental peace and security.[22] Their object was to move the increasingly independent Europeans away from the grip of American influence. On the other hand, the "fear" side of the equation, the Soviets strengthened their forces in Eastern Europe, modernizing the Warsaw Pact armies, and used coercive naval diplomacy against the Scandinavian countries.

According to NATO's own assessment, by the mid 1980s the alliance's 2.6 million soldiers in 88 active divisions faced 115 divisions, or 4 million Warsaw Pact troops. The Soviet Union and its allies fielded nearly 27,000 main battle tanks versus NATO's 13,500, and 2,250 fighter-bomber aircraft to the Atlantic alliance's 1,960. The ratio of fighter-interceptor aircraft was even better for the pact—over 5:1. NATO was also at a severe disadvantage in armored personnel carriers, antitank guided weapons, and attack helicopters.[23]

This imbalance raised the risk of two scenarios inimical to U.S. interests. First was the danger that the Soviets would parlay military superiority into a decisive military victory, particularly if a war were to remain below the nuclear threshold. This danger was heightened by the development of two powerful Soviet weapons systems, the SS-20 missile and the Backfire bomber, able to strike anywhere in Europe from deep within the Soviet Union; neither was limited under SALT I or SALT II. To offset these weapons, the allies decided in 1979 to deploy new, long-range Pershing II and cruise missiles, while trying to reduce the Soviet threat through negotiations (see Chapter 23).[24] Even the elimination of worldwide SS-20 deployments in the INF (intermediate-range nuclear forces) Treaty, cemented at the May 1988 Moscow summit meeting, did not ease the worries of

U.S. allies, many of whom felt that the parallel elimination of American nuclear missiles only emphasized the imbalance in conventional forces.

Chemical warfare also emerged as a major area of concern for NATO. Force parity—or worse—in both the strategic and tactical nuclear realms might enable the Soviets to exploit their one-sided chemical advantage. One analyst described the implications of the NATO–Warsaw Pact chemical weapons imbalance in this manner:

> As a result of two decades of neglect and an over-reliance upon nuclear weapons, NATO has no credible means of deterring the Soviet Union from using chemical weapons. Even if NATO chose to retaliate in kind, by employing the small stockpile of chemical weapons which has been forward-deployed in Europe, it would also cause havoc in its currently unprotected and unprepared civilian population centers.[25]

Many analysts feared a second scenario, namely, that the developments listed above could have encouraged the "Finlandization" of a Western Europe that was unsure of American support and unable by itself to balance Soviet military power. Finlandization was the label given to the process whereby the countries of Western Europe, for whatever reason, would move away from the alliance with the United States and be transformed into isolated, neutralized states—like Finland—fearful of Soviet military power and hence unable to resist Soviet pressure, especially in the foreign policy realm. The degree to which this described the actual Finnish policy situation is arguable, but the metaphor is useful.[26]

Finlandization could be hastened not only by a perceived weakening in the American commitment, but it could also be spawned by an upswing in Euro-Soviet economic ties or by a European perception that the strategic balance had swung decisively against the United States. This was surely the Soviet expectation in the early 1980s; and the upsurge in European peace movements in that period, which were inevitably directed only against Western defense efforts, was doubtless encouraging to Moscow. Yet NATO's successful INF deployments, despite some public unhappiness, demonstrated that détentist sentiment was not strong enough in Western Europe to prevent concerted alliance action.

The Soviet Threat in East Asia. The Soviet Union was, of course, a major Asian power, and among its successor states, Russia and Kazakhstan will continue to play important roles in Asian affairs. On the eastern marches of the former Soviet Union are a number of states in whose security the United States has a significant stake—Japan, the People's Republic of China, and the Republic of Korea, for example. The Soviet Far Eastern fleet, based in Vladivostok but with ancillary facilities elsewhere in the Soviet maritime provinces and in Cam Ranh Bay in Vietnam, was therefore feared as force with the capability to project power throughout the East Asian region. Detailed discussion of the threats to American interests which arose out of these circumstances appears in Chapter 17.

The Soviet Threat in the Third World. Starting in the mid 1960s, one of the most notable Soviet military developments came in the field of power projection forces—the ability to exert military leverage beyond immediately contiguous areas, that is, in much of the Third World. This problem was intensified by the fact that many key Third World areas are much closer to the Soviet Union than to the United States, and some, such as the Middle East, became subject to direct pressure from nearby Soviet ground forces. The domestic organization of the Soviet Union gave its military leaders the logistical advantage of easy access to its considerable civil aviation and merchant marine fleets. Finally, many areas, such as Sub-Saharan Africa, were easily influenced by relatively small amounts of Soviet military power or proxy forces.

In the Third World, as in Europe, the United States and the Soviet Union engaged in a prolonged competition to advance their interests. The Soviets were eager to expand their influence in the Third World to further their ideological aspirations, to secure access to raw materials (and deny them to the United States in conflict situations), to develop a base and support structure for their navy, and to expel the United States from its "positions of strength," especially on the Soviet periphery.* Soviet willingness to use arms aid and proxy forces, especially Cubans, in stimulating or capitalizing upon hostilities in the Third World was thought by most analysts to pose a significant threat.

Even if arms aid or proxies were not brought to bear, Soviet pressures, it was feared, would encourage weaker states to accommodate the Soviet Union or to remain neutral on political, economic, or military issues on which their support for the West could be important.

For the United States, Soviet operations in the Third World represented challenges to its alliances, raw materials lifelines, and markets, as well as to American principles. The 1980s, however, also revealed certain weaknesses in Soviet policy in the Third World. Although Soviet clients that established Leninist forms of social control seemed less likely than nationalist regimes to break their ties with Moscow, many of them proved unable to consolidate their power at home. The existence of armed popular resistance movements was a continuous challenge to those pro-Soviet governments and created an opening for Western counterpressures on Soviet Third World policies. In Afghanistan, above all, a succession of Soviet offensives escalated the fighting but did not break the back of the Mujahedeen, who enjoyed increasing levels of external aid; meanwhile, the Afghan communist ruling group had virtually disintegrated by the late 1980s. In Nicaragua and Angola, there was a sharp but ineffectual increase in the mid and late 1980s in the supply of Soviet counterinsurgency systems, such as

*The question of Soviet objectives in the Third World is still a matter of dispute among scholars. For different perspectives, see Bruce Porter, *The USSR in Third World Conflicts: Soviet Arms and Diplomacy in Local Wars, 1945–1980* (New York: Cambridge University Press, 1984); Jerry Hough, *The Struggle for the Third World: Soviet Debates and American Options* (Washington, D.C.: Brookings Institution, 1986); and "The Empire's New Clothes: The Soviet Union and the Third World after Afghanistan," *The National Interest,* Special Supplement (Summer 1988).

helicopters, and of air defense missiles designed to help Soviet clients cut off support to insurgent forces from outside.

To counter Soviet military adventures and proxy wars in the Third World, the American government began to support anti-Soviet insurgencies in a policy that became known as the "Reagan Doctrine." This policy forced the Soviet Union to focus considerable resources on sustaining clients as they waged difficult counterinsurgency campaigns. The bill in just one instance—Angola—was estimated at $1 billion in 1986.[27] As a tool to impose defeat or higher costs on Soviet policy, the Reagan Doctrine should be seen as a significant innovation after a decade in which the United States seemed unable to cope effectively with Soviet Third World intervention.

In summary, from Stalin's era to Brezhnev's, the Soviet Union proceeded from a regional power to a power with global pretensions to a global power with the ambition to at least equal the United States in virtually every category of military strength. In expanding its role, the Soviet Union increasingly tended to rely heavily on its only strong asset—its formidable military establishment. On the other hand, the authoritarian nature of the Soviet regime, favorable (i.e., unstable) external conditions, and Soviet support for such conditions did not necessarily guarantee permanent gains; and, as we shall see, these conditions did not save the Soviet leadership from some debilitating weaknesses.

Détente II and the End of the Cold War

Brezhnev's death on November 10, 1982, ushered in a new era in Soviet politics. After a brief interregnum, in which first former KGB chief Yuri Andropov and then Party Secretary Konstantin Chernenko were elevated to the position of General Secretary only to fall ill and die, Mikhail Gorbachev was selected by the Politburo to become the Communist Party's leader on March 11, 1985. At that time, the declining economic performance of the Soviet economy was something that Soviet leaders could no longer afford to ignore publicly. Gorbachev began seeking solutions to the economic ailments, introducing a discipline campaign and an antialcohol campaign, in an effort to boost productivity. Neither of these steps addressed the underlying problems of the hidebound, bureaucratized, centrally planned economy. Gorbachev began casting about for ever more radical ways to restructure the economy and the society. Thus was born his policy of perestroika (restructuring). Although we shall not attempt to trace all of the factors and events that led to the collapse and break-up of the Soviet Union at the end of 1991, the aspects of the transformation relevant to Soviet foreign and defense policy deserve consideration.

After the Chernobyl nuclear accident on April 26, 1986, the Gorbachev government failed to acknowledge for 18 days that there had been a disaster. This policy of obsessive secrecy was totally discredited by the accident, and the gradual opening of the government-controlled press that had preceded Chernobyl was expanded into full-blown glasnost (openness), a policy that had profound effects on the ability of the totalitarian government of the Soviet Union to survive.

As ever more controversial topics became the focus of attention in the official press, criticism of Soviet foreign and military policy—once a taboo—became a more frequent feature of articles in the Soviet media. The war in Afghanistan, which at first was presented to Soviet citizens as a glorious effort to help a fraternal socialist revolution in an underdeveloped neighboring country, was for the first time presented in a new and disturbing light. Soviet television began to show footage of the fighting, and reports of casualties and deaths, hitherto kept secret by censorship, began to be openly discussed. The rising chorus of criticism against the Afghan adventure rapidly extended into other areas. The heavy share of the economy devoted to the military also came in for criticism. The burden of supporting faraway countries like Cuba, Angola, Ethiopia, and other Third World countries at a time of mounting economic difficulties became the subject of public discussion, and the government was forced into a defensive stance. Declaring victory, on May 15, 1988, Gorbachev announced a pullout from Afghanistan, and the last Soviet soldiers were withdrawn on February 15, 1989.

Weaknesses in the economy played a major role in bringing down Soviet rule. In the course of the 1980s, for instance, the Soviet Union encountered a dramatic drop in the price of its energy exports, an increase in the cost of extracting energy, a shortfall in the labor pool, a continuing slump in industrial productivity, and a wide-ranging "generational" leadership succession. Social ills, including alcoholism, corruption, and loss of civic morale, compounded these problems. Food problems, always hard to manage under the Soviet centralized planning system, continued to plague the country. Cheap energy, a rapidly growing workforce, and the exploitation of resources in the developed, European part of the Soviet Union had enabled the country to improve its economic standing and, at the same time, increase its defense outlays during the 1960s and 1970s. But in the 1980s the deterioration of these conditions forced the Soviet leadership to make increasingly painful choices.

Growth in the Soviet workforce declined from 1.5 million per annum in 1980 to 0.5 million in 1985. The Soviet Union was no longer able to solve production problems by "throwing people at them." This exacerbated already poor industrial productivity and increased the importance of either augmenting investments in capital stocks or procuring high-technology capital goods from the West. The labor supply problem was aggravated by the fact that most of the population growth was occurring in Moslem areas, far from the industrial heartland and in places where productivity was, in any case, traditionally low.

The mounting economic crisis was compounded by acute political problems in the Soviet empire in Eastern Europe. Gorbachev encouraged the communist leadership there to embark upon a policy of liberalizing reforms similar to those he was pursuing at home. This triggered a series of changes that proved disastrous for the survival of communism in this key region of the empire. Gorbachev had hoped that, as at home, a policy of reform communism would prove politically attractive in Eastern Europe. But the liberalization that he encouraged only served to destabilize regimes that had been installed by Soviet force of arms and that continued to rest on the support of secret policemen, communist penetration of all institutions of the societies, and ultimately, the presence of Soviet troops. The emergence of the independent worker's movement, Solidarity, in Poland in July 1980 was the precursor of the collapse. Although General Woijech Jaruzelski imposed martial law in December 1981, socialism was exposed as a doctrine lacking any roots in Poland, and it was only a matter of time before its empty superstructure collapsed. Under Mikhail Gorbachev's tutelage, a similar process was set in motion throughout Eastern Europe, leading to the collapse of communist parties in every country in the region, and to the destruction of the Berlin Wall on November 11, 1989, and the reunification of Germany.

For Mikhail Gorbachev, the swift pace of change posed an impossible test of his leadership. Previous attempts at reform in Eastern Europe that got out of control had led to Soviet military intervention as in Hungary in 1956 and Czechoslovakia in 1968 during the Prague Spring. Confronted with a snowballing political crisis in Eastern Europe, Gorbachev opted against the use of military force to try to control the pace of change. Intervention was not an attractive option for a number of reasons. For one thing, previous Soviet interventions had been limited to one country at a time. This was a crisis that involved all of the members of the Warsaw Pact. A military attempt to turn back the clock might well have led to a wider war in Europe. Even a successful intervention, however, would certainly have led to the end of Gorbachev's tenure in office. There was no pretext for military intervention, and any military action would have aimed at attempting to contain political forces that Gorbachev himself had encouraged and set in motion. The outcome was a forced policy of restraint that earned Gorbachev the Nobel Peace Prize in 1990.

By 1991, Gorbachev himself succumbed to the same political forces that had toppled communist regimes in Eastern Europe. His piecemeal economic reform efforts only served to destabilize the Soviet Union's badly ailing economy, and the GNP began to plummet. His political thaw led to a rising chorus of criticism that spared not even the most sacred tenets of Marxist-Leninist ideology. The multinational, multiethnic complexion of the country contributed to the political crisis, as nationalism and separatism engulfed one region after another. The communist party apparatus tried to fight back, and beginning in the fall of 1990, Gorbachev was prevailed upon to switch course and slow the pace of change. But the conservatives remained fearful that his leadership would lead to the complete collapse of central Soviet authority.

On August 19, 1991, one day before a new treaty among the Soviet republics was to be signed, senior officials in the military, the communist party, and the KGB attempted to stage a coup d'état against Gorbachev. Hastily planned, and executed like a comic opera, the attempt failed within days. The coup plotters' only achievement was the very objective that they had set out to avoid: the complete destruction of communist rule and the disintegration of the Soviet state. By December, Gorbachev, discredited by his failed economic policies as well as his association with the very men who plotted against him, was himself pushed aside by Boris Yeltsin. One republic after another declared independence from the Soviet state, and a new post-Soviet, post–cold war era was born.

The New World

One of Boris Yeltsin's initial steps as President of the Russian republic—and the first elected Russian leader in a millenium—was to establish the Commonwealth of Independent States (CIS) among all of the former republics, excluding the three Baltic states and Georgia. Even at this early juncture, the future of this arrangement appears very dim. None of the republics has been willing to delegate power and authority to a central body; instead, twelve new countries have emerged, with Russia the most powerful among them. Although the future of relations among these new countries remains cloudy, some trends are already discernible.

In the area of conventional weapons there have been extraordinary changes. Enforcement of the Conventional Forces in Europe (CFE) agreement, as indicated in Table 16.1, will cut the conventional holdings of the former Warsaw Pact and Soviet republics across the board. There is no longer a central command of the Red Army; the old Soviet army has simply fractured and broken up along republic lines. Although the bulk of the forces belong to the Russian republic, the break-up has been far from smooth. Acute tension arose, for example, over who should inherit the sizable Black Sea fleet, a problem that nearly led to a breakdown in relations between Ukraine and Russia. Although thus far, diplomacy and compromise have won out, future disputes between republics over the control of the old arsenal may not be solved peacefully. These problems and territorial disputes lead many analysts to worry about a bloody "Yugoslav

Table 16.1 Conventional Force Inventories in the Former Soviet Union

	November 1990 Inventories					*Maximums under Conventional Forces in Europe (CFE) Agreement*				
	Tanks	*ACVs*	*Artillery*	*CAC*	*Helos*	*Tanks*	*ACVs*	*Artillery*	*CAC*	*Helos*
Armenia	258	641	357	0	7	220	220	285	100	50
Azerbaijan	391	1,285	463	124	24	220	220	285	100	50
Belorussia	2,263	2,776	1,384	650	82	1,800	2,600	1,615	260	80
Estonia	184	201	29	153	10	0	0	0	0	0
Georgia	850	1,054	363	245	48	220	220	285	100	50
Latvia	138	100	81	183	23	0	0	0	0	0
Lithuania	184	1,591	253	46	0	0	0	0	0	0
Moldova	155	402	248	0	0	210	210	250	50	50
Ukraine	6,204	6,394	3,052	1,431	285	4,080	5,050	4,040	1,090	330
Russia	5,017	6,279	3,480	2,750	570	6,400	11,480	6,415	3,450	890
GoFs*	5,017	9,167	4,228	1,029	432	0	0	0	50	0

*Denotes government forces of the former Soviet Union, technically not in existence after the dissolution of the Union of Soviet Socialist Republics. ACV = Armored Combat Vehicles; CAC = Combat Aircraft; Helos = Helicopters.

Reprinted with permission of Renan R. Lurie.

outcome'' (in reference to the civil war in Yugoslavia) to the dissolution of the old empire.

At the same time that the military has broken up, the defense industry is faced with plummeting budgets and a sharp drop in arms sales. In virtually every category of weapons, deep cuts are planned by the Russian government now so anxious to rid itself of the heavy burden of defense expenditures. According to U.S. intelligence reports, by 1992 Russian defense spending had fallen to its lowest levels in twenty years, with even deeper cuts envisioned.[28] Arms exports tumbled by more than 50 percent from 1990 to 1991, an indicator of the even steeper decline to follow. However, this has raised concerns that Russia will be tempted by third parties to sell more advanced weapons at lower prices.[29]

In response to international and American concern and pressure, the republics agreed in early 1992 to keep the nuclear command and control system of the vast Soviet arsenal under central control. In practice this means that the Russian republic has effective command of the nuclear button. The actual shift of nuclear weapons from their present sites in Ukraine, Belarus, and Kazakhstan onto Russian soil has not yet been accomplished as this book goes to press, and this process could be interrupted by a souring of relations between republics. The 1991 START treaty was finally ratified in July 1992, yet cuts agreed to since its inception brought the levels of nuclear weapons to about half of what START would have allowed (see Chapters 11 and 23). The Bush–Yeltsin agreement of June 1992 provided for the elimination of all land-based missiles with multiple warheads (ICBMs) and set a limit of 3,000 to 3,500 warheads for each side. These deep reductions are scheduled to be reached by the year 2003, or by 2000 if the United States is able to further help in the decommissioning costs (thus far, the United States has allocated $400 million dollars to help Russia live up to its treaty obligations). As was the case with the START treaty, the actual process of destroying the agreed nuclear weapons may be hindered by Russia's economic and technical failings. Although it is possible that the effort might stall, the strong antinuclear sentiments that exist in the Soviet Union—in large part because of the Chernobyl accident—create strong pressures on politicians to opt for denuclearization.

Russia's radical proposals to cut back in nuclear weaponry (in January 1992, Yeltsin had called for a 2,000 to 2,500 limit on strategic nuclear weapons) stem from an appreciation of the cost of maintaining Russia's nuclear arsenal, the desire to gain Western good will and financial assistance, and most importantly, a deideologized perception of the world. Gone are the old ideologically driven imperial ambitions of the Soviet empire. In their place is the desire to become "an ordinary power" that will join the European family of nations.

Challenges for the 1990s. The changes in the political and military environment outlined above cannot be ignored, yet without economic stability, many Western analysts feel that a partial reversion to authoritarianism in the former Soviet republics may be possible. Economic partnerships have been negotiated between the republics and Western companies and governments alike, but until their economies are perceived as stable and committed to reform, full-fledged Western aid and investment will be unlikely. It is still too early to forecast whether Russia and the other republics will succeed in the effort fundamentally to remake themselves into democratic, economically viable nations. However, peering into the future, we can see the outlines of several alternative outcomes. The crucial problems that will determine which outcome is most likely will remain the economy, the multinational character of the societies, and the role of the military in political life.

If radical reform fails to rescue the Soviet Union's broken planned economy, we may witness the most dangerous scenario that could emerge from the chaos.

Thus far, extremist Russian nationalists have remained on the fringes of political life; it is the democrats who have captured the center. But if the economy spirals downward, it is not inconceivable that a Russian version of fascism will gain strength. The program of such a movement would be encapsulated in one simple word, "order." But attempts to impose "order" could result in a new age of terror in a country that has already seen so much political terror in this century. Traditional scapegoats of Russian life, the sizable Jewish minority in the republics, for example, might be blamed for the deepening trouble, and a wave of officially sponsored antisemitism could be set in motion. Tensions between republics would certainly accompany further economic decline, and the potential for violent confrontation between them would grow. Ethnic disputes within the republics—in particular, the treatment of Russians outside Russia*—could lead to a broader conflict among the Soviet successor states. If the remnants of the Soviet military establishment saw a salvation for military institutions in this type of outcome, the stage could be set for a powerful ruling coalition that would bear a strong resemblance to the political constellation that brought nazism to power in Germany in 1933.

If economic reform does succeed, at least to a limited degree, the West might be confronted with a different set of problems, albeit problems that are far less worrisome than the nightmare scenario of Russian fascism. Russia and several other republics are fundamentally wealthy countries. Russia, in particular, is blessed with extraordinary natural resources that include rich agricultural land, massive oil and gas supplies, ample stocks of gold, diamonds, and timber, and many other sources of national wealth. Much of its workforce is highly educated. The Soviet scientific elite is second to none in many key areas of science and mathematics. The economic system of communism squandered these resources and left the country in poverty. But this is not a permanent condition. A successful reform might, over the course of a decade or two, transform the impoverished country in ways that are at present difficult to envision. A revitalized Russia would, of course, be a welcome trading partner with the United States, Japan, and Europe. But a revitalized Russia—150 million strong and holding a potent, although smaller arsenal—might also pose a military challenge in the not-so-distant future. Given Russia's vast land mass, its longstanding martial tradition, and its own sense of greatness, the West cannot have complete confidence that a revitalized Russia will emerge as a force for stability in the world.

The West is now being offered a breathing space in which it can pare down military forces and reinvest resources in revitalizing domestic economies. But if the Western societies fail to remain prepared for military threats that cannot at present be foreseen, then they run the risk of inviting challenges and of squandering all that has been achieved through patience and vigilance in the long cold war.

---

*There are at present 25 million ethnic Russians outside the borders of Russia, representing 20 percent of the population of Ukraine and 40 percent of Kazakhstan's populace. The protection of these Russian minorities is emerging as a central issue in Moscow's foreign policy.

Uncertainty about the future of the former Soviet Union will not disappear any time soon. It is this uncertainty, coupled with the heavy weight of the troubled Russian and Soviet past upon our own perceptions of the region, that should shape Western security policy in the years to come.

Discussion Questions

1. Compare Soviet foreign policy under Stalin, Khrushchev, Brezhnev, Andropov, and Gorbachev. What elements of continuity and change were demonstrated?
2. Did Marxist-Leninist ideology lead or follow Soviet foreign policy?
3. Was Soviet foreign policy inherently expansionist or inherently defensive?
4. Soviet nuclear doctrine stressed a war-fighting policy. How was this different from U.S. policy?
5. Many defense analysts thought that the Soviet Union was attempting to reach "military superiority." To what extent was this correct?
6. What aspects of national security policy now call for enhanced cooperation between the United States and the Soviet Union?
7. In what way has the foreign policy of Russia and the other former Soviet republics changed as a result of perestroika, glasnost, and the end of the cold war?

Recommended Reading

Aspaturian, Vernon. *Process and Power in Soviet Foreign Policy*. Boston: Little, Brown, 1971.

Bialer, Seweryn. *The Soviet Paradox: External Expansion, Internal Decline*. New York: Knopf, 1986.

Brzezinski, Zbigniew. *Game Plan: How to Conduct the U.S.-Soviet Contest*. New York: Atlantic Monthly Press, 1986.

Byrnes, Robert F. ed. *After Brezhnev: Sources of Soviet Conduct in the 1980s*. Bloomington: Indiana University Press, 1983.

"The Empire's New Clothes: The Soviet Union and the Third World after Afghanistan." *The National Interest,* Special Supplement (Summer 1988).

Fleron Jr., J. Frederic, ed. et. al. *Soviet Foreign Policy: Classic and Contemporary Issues*. New York: Aldine De Druyter, 1991.

Gelman, Harry. *The Brezhnev Politburo and the Decline of Détente*. Ithaca, N.Y.: Cornell University Press, 1984.

Goldman, Marshall I. *U.S.S.R. in Crisis: The Failure of an Economic System*. New York: Norton, 1983.

Goldman, Marshall I. *What Went Wrong With Perestroika*. New York: Norton, 1991.

Khrushchev, Nikita. *Khrushchev Remembers*. Translated by Strobe Talbott. London: André Deutsch, 1971.

Mandelbaum, Michael, and Talbott, Strobe. *Reagan and Gorbachev*. New York: Vintage Books, 1987.

Medvedev, Zhores. *Gorbachev*. New York: Norton, 1986.

Pipes, Richard. *Survival is Not Enough*. New York: Simon & Schuster, 1984.

Sivachev, N., and Yakovlev, N. *Russia and the United States*. Chicago: University of Chicago Press, 1979.

Sestanovich, Stephen. "The Hour of the Demagogue." *The National Interest,* no. 25 (Fall 1991).

Ulam, Adam. *The Communists: The Intellectual and Political History of Communism.* New York: Scribner's, 1992.

Ulam, Adam. *Expansion and Coexistence: Soviet Foreign Policy, 1917–1973* New York: Praeger, 1974.

Wolfe, Thomas. *Soviet Power and Europe, 1945–1970* Baltimore: Johns Hopkins University Press, 1970.

17

East Asia

Although developments in East Asia in the recent past have not been quite so spectacular nor been compressed into such a short period as in Europe, those changes have nevertheless profoundly altered the region's political, economic, and security landscape. A sample of the more dramatic developments would include: the Vietnamese invasion of Kampuchea and the short-lived, unsuccessful counterinvasion of Vietnam by China; replacement of the excesses of China's Cultural Revolution with political stability and a decade-long program of market-oriented economic reforms; Japan's steady, superior economic performance that enabled it to become the dominant economic player in the region; spectacular economic growth of the "four tigers" (Republic of Korea, Taiwan, Hong Kong, and Singapore) and subsequently of Thailand and Malaysia; the strong trend toward political liberalization and democracy in the region—frustrated in Myanmar and China by bloody crackdowns but with genuine progress in the Philippines, Thailand, the Republic of Korea, and Taiwan; launching of the Asia Pacific Economic Cooperation (APEC) process as a vehicle for trade liberalization and economic integration; reconciliation between the People's Republic of China (P.R.C.) and the Soviet Union; disintegration of the Soviet Union; easing of tensions on the Korean peninsula; fragile, tentative settlement of the Kampuchean civil war; loss of military bases and consequent withdrawal/eviction of American forces from the Philippines; and erosion of U.S.–Japanese relations—largely as a consequence of rising economic tensions between the two economic superpowers. Taken together, these and a number of other important changes have transformed the context in which America's interests and policies in the region must be pursued.

By the end of 1991, Stephen Bosworth could correctly observe that "For more than four decades U.S. engagement in Asia was based on two pillars: a cold war commitment to Asian security and America's extraordinary economic power. Both of these foreign policy premises are now gone; the cold war ended suddenly and dramatically; American economic hegemony has waned more slowly but with no less drama.''[1] We could add that the U.S. engagement also depended upon a third, related pillar, namely, the willingness of its public to expend resources and undertake risks in the region on behalf of what had been accepted as vital American interests. In light of the disappearance or marked erosion of the first two pillars, a key question for the future is the extent to which this third pillar will still stand. Perhaps the best way to tackle this question is to examine American interests in light of the changed regional and global context.

American Interests in Asia. A principal American interest in East Asia, as in Europe, is that no single nation or coalition of nations should control the resources and people of the region. After the Sino–Soviet split and up until the Soviet collapse at the start of the 1990s, this denial objective in practice was containment of Soviet power. From the 1960s until well into the 1980s, China shared this goal of containing the Soviets; accordingly, American policy toward China in that period gradually shifted from one of earlier hostility to one of strengthening the People's Republic of China as a counterweight to the Soviet Union. (Just as China's policy toward the United States shifted to cooperation against the Soviet bear.)

With the Soviet Union's demise, this American central national security objective can be restated as follows: ''to prevent the reemergence of a new rival, either on the territory of the former Soviet Union or elsewhere, that poses a threat on the order of that posed formerly by the Soviet Union. . . .''[2]

A second American objective is regional stability: maintaining ''our status as a military power of the first magnitude in the area . . . acting as a balancing force and prevent[ing] emergence of a vacuum or a regional hegemon.''[3] Providing a stabilizing influence in East Asia does not necessitate our becoming the policeman of the region; rather, it implies the active sharing of responsibilities and burdens in the region. Secretary of State James Baker has noted that, with removal of U.S.–Soviet competition, in Asia

> the enduring diversity of regional interests and security concerns stand out with even greater clarity. What was a secondary aspect of our Cold War-era security presence is becoming the primary rationale for our defense engagement in the region: to provide geopolitical balance, to be an honest broker, to reassure against uncertainty.[4]

A third significant U.S. regional interest is to promote a stronger and more balanced long-term economic relationship with East Asian countries, both by increasing U.S. access to the markets of the region and by opening investment opportunities there. The free-market economies of East Asia (Japan, the Republic of Korea, Taiwan, Hong Kong, Singapore, Malaysia, and Thailand) constitute the most dynamic economic region in the world. The United States' largest trading partner is East Asia, which is about one third larger than all of Western Europe.

In assessing the likelihood of public support for continuing assertive American pursuit of these regional interests, it is useful to review the roots and history of our past policies there.

History of U.S. Policy toward East Asia. Despite longstanding missionary activities and trade with the area and the pull toward Asia that the Philippine colony represented, America's relations with Asia were tenuous prior to World War II.[5] The western Pacific was not generally perceived as vitally linked to U.S. political, economic, or security interests. It was not until World War II, in fact, that America's national interests became inextricably tied to Asia. The defeat of the Japanese in that conflict, the fragmentation of China in civil war, and the demise of the European nations' Asian colonies left the United States as the major power in the region. American occupation troops remained in and governed Japan. From Korea to Southeast Asia, areas that had been under Japanese control fell under American authority or influence. Associated with this increased military presence was rapidly expanding political and economic involvement.

In the initial postwar period, America was engaged in supporting the transition of European and Japanese colonies to self-government in both Southeast Asia and Northeast Asia (with the exception that it supported France in its attempt to reestablish its rule in Indochina). In China, the United States had early hopes of assisting the Chinese in rebuilding their shattered nation, but these were mostly extinguished when General George C. Marshall's mission (1946), aimed at promoting a settlement between the Communists and the Nationalists, collapsed.

Mao Tse-Tung's success in China against the anticommunist forces of Chiang Kai-shek encouraged others, and revolutionary momentum in the region increased: in the late 1940s Ho Chi Minh launched his Viet Minh forces against the French colonists in Indochina; the Hukbalahap rebellion simmered in the Philippines; and communist-inspired insurgencies occurred in Indonesia, Thailand, Malaya, and Burma. The attack by communist North Korea—the Democratic People's Republic of Korea (D.P.R.K.)—on South Korea in 1950, causing the United States to intervene under the auspices of United Nations was the culmination of this series of political events, behind which most American leaders saw the hand of Moscow—or the joined hands of Moscow and Beijing.

As a result of the regional pressures of communists and its own perspective on communism as an inherently expansionist force, America gradually extended its containment policy, which had originated in Europe, into Asia. President Truman's actions to defend South Korea in 1950 and his associated order to move units of the Seventh Fleet in defense of Taiwan were significant not only in Asia but elsewhere, for this was the first time the United States had had to implement containment by actively committing its own military forces to resist communist aggression and to shore up independent nations.[6]

In this period, it was assumed in the West—particularly in the United States—that the two communist giants, the Soviet Union and the People's

FIG. 17.1 East Asia

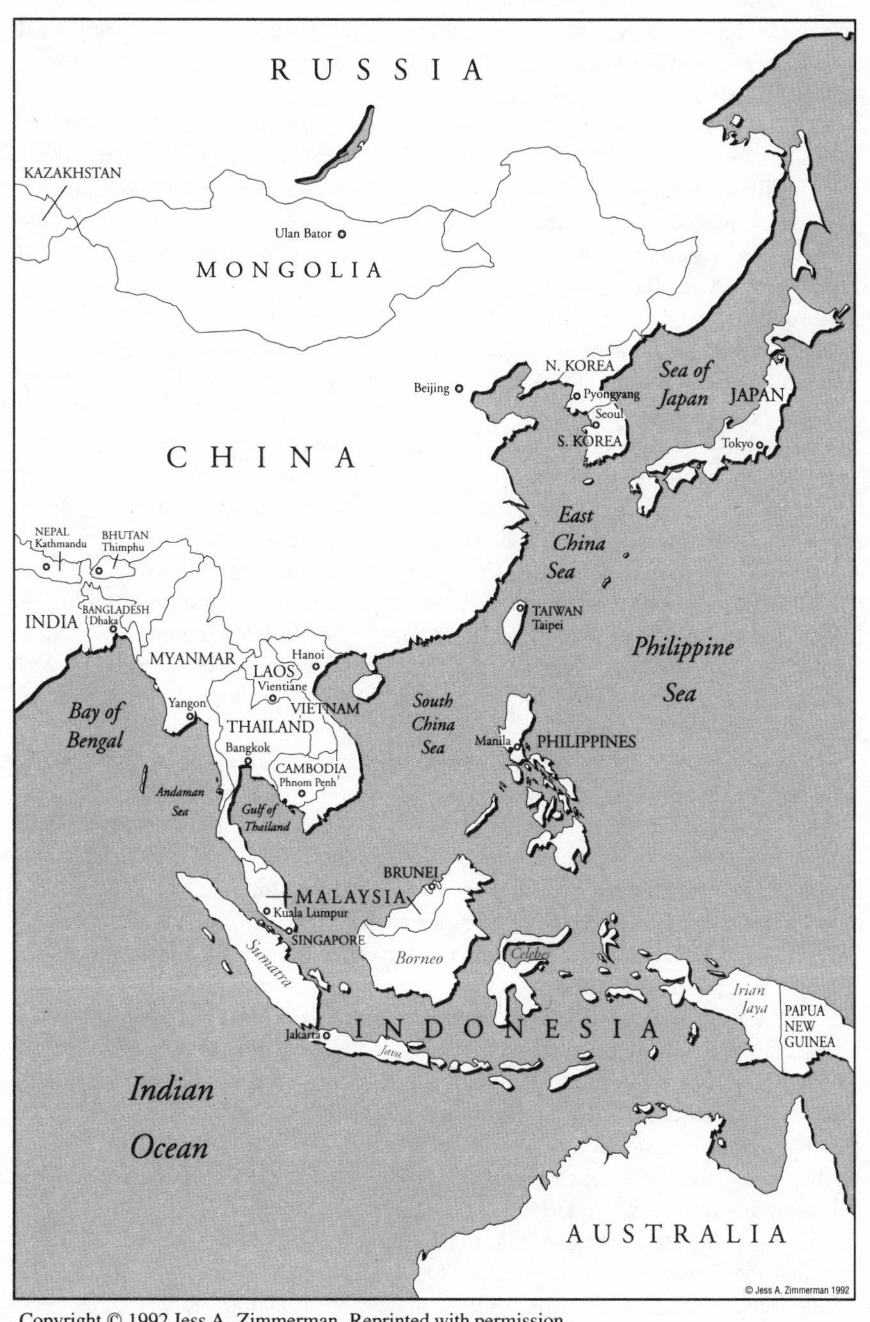

Republic of China, constituted a unified, "monolithic" entity, generally referred to as the Sino-Soviet bloc. American containment policy in Asia was particularly and directly focused on checking the active "Sino" element of the bloc—the People's Republic of China. In the mid 1950s, the United States increased its aid to Chiang Kai-shek on Taiwan and publicly announced assumption of responsibility for helping defend that island.

U.S. logistical support of the French in the early 1950s in their effort to continue to rule in Viet Nam and, after French withdrawal from Vietnam, direct U.S. military assistance to South Vietnam (1955 onward) were also prompted by American preoccupation with containing communism in the region. It was the underlying assumption in Washington that if local communist states emerged throughout Asia, they would be linked ideologically, militarily, and politically with the Soviet Union and Communist China. But, in responding to this perceived threat, as well as to its growing political and economic ties with the region, America found that its interests were being bound ever closer to stability in East Asia—largely bound, that is, to the political status quo.

In addition to supporting countries battling communism, the United States actively encouraged Asian nations to form regional security pacts including the United States. One of the first of these agreements was the 1951 tripartite security treaty with Australia and New Zealand (ANZUS) to provide for mutual aid in the event of aggression and to settle disputes by peaceful means.[7] The second major regional security organization was the Southeast Asia Treaty Organization (SEATO), established in 1954 by the United States, the United Kingdom, Australia, New Zealand, France, Pakistan, the Philippines, and Thailand. SEATO was created as a direct response to the perceived threat of communist expansion in Southeast Asia.

Having consolidated its own revolution, the People's Republic of China began playing an increasingly important role in Asia in the 1950s. China became closely linked with Hanoi and openly supported communist insurgents elsewhere in the region. One of its primary aims was to rid the area of the United States, the only country capable of projecting large-scale military force into the region. For its part, America was prepared to remain in East Asia and to become involved directly in support of other regional states in order to limit the expansion of the People's Republic of China.

In the early 1960s, the United States continued to be deeply concerned about a perceived Sino-Soviet partnership in Asia—and was slow to recognize that in reality a split between the two countries was occurring. Sino-Soviet rivalry was initially expressed publicly as diverging interpretations of communist doctrine, particularly the Soviet policy of "peaceful coexistence." In addition to doctrinal differences, the two became entangled with virulent conflicts between their national interests—particularly over their disputed borderlands.

Chinese talk of world revolution and emphasis on violence in their diatribes against the Soviet Union only served to strengthen apprehension in the United States about P.R.C. intentions. In fact, in a series of actions between 1955 and 1964, including border skirmishes and its first explosion of an atomic device, the

People's Republic of China continually reminded American policymakers of its aggressive potential. With hindsight it is possible to see that the Chinese acted with more restraint than their rhetoric at the time suggested.[8]

Vietnam became central to U.S. containment policy in Asia. When the French departed Vietnam in the mid 1950s, the successor anticommunist regime in the south, the Republic of Viet Nam (R.V.N.), headed by Ngo Dinh Diem, became the beneficiary of that concern. The Republic of Viet Nam (capital in Saigon) was under continual assault, first by guerilla forces (the Viet Cong—VC) under the direction of Ho Chi Minh's communist government in the north, the Democratic Republic of Vietnam (D.R.V.) (capital in Hanoi), and later by regular D.R.V. forces infiltrated in units up to regimental size from the north.

The United States was faced with the choice of seeing South Vietnam taken over by the communists or of providing military assistance to stave off that outcome. Once committed to arms aid to the South, America escalated its military involvement there from a limited advisory role in 1955–1962 to major forces and massive combined arms combat operations in 1965–1970. Altogether, the American effort was intended to provide the Saigon government the time and opportunity to fend off defeat, establish its authority, and stabilize the countryside politically and economically (see Chapter 13). It was an ambitious undertaking.

In 1969, ostensibly because the South Vietnamese government forces, freshly trained and supplied, could deal with VC insurgents and incursions by North Vietnamese regulars, the United States announced a policy to "Vietnamize" the war.[9] It is instructive, however, to examine other elements of U.S. domestic and foreign policies which inspired this policy, for it clearly was not an isolated decision.

By 1968, domestic pressure against U.S. military involvement in Vietnam had become massive. The nation was being ravaged by antiwar riots and demonstrations. Many of America's young, caught also in the throes of the "Youth Revolution," rejected the war, the government that pursued it, and the public and private institutions that supported it. Americans were deeply divided over the ends sought and the means employed in the Vietnam War. In 1968, President Johnson declined to run for reelection because the American public was so dissatisfied with his inability to end the war and deliver on his promises for a "Great Society" at home. Richard Nixon was elected in 1968 in considerable part because he had a "secret plan" to end the war.

By the latter 1960s, other forces were also causing Americans to rethink their nation's role in Asia. The reality of the Sino-Soviet dispute had sunk in, and Washington was faced with the problems and prospects of multipolar, rather than bipolar, politics in East Asia. Another major element in this revised Asian equation was the development of Japan into a major economic power. Previously a passive factor in the area, Japan was becoming a major political and economic force in Asia and was therefore increasingly important to U.S. policy.

President Nixon's 1969 reassessment and revision downward of U.S. responsibilities in Asia, the so-called Nixon Doctrine, his "Vietnamization" of the war in Southeast Asia, and ultimately his 1972 rapprochement with the People's

Republic of China were all driven by political reality, both domestic and foreign. The increasingly bitter Sino-Soviet quarrel and the traumatic experience of the Vietnam War provided the catalysts to bring about a redefinition of U.S. policies in Asia. This redefinition was based on recognition of the need for the United States to reduce its commitments in Asia and to find ways to share the balance of power tasks it had been largely carrying alone.

Throughout the 1970s, America's approach to foreign policy in Asia continued to be based fundamentally on the ideas of the Nixon Doctrine, which called for self-help by others, primarily regional responsibility for regional security and stability, and only residual responsibility by the United States, which was no longer willing to act directly as an international police force in the region. American security assistance would be based henceforth on the willingness and ability of a nation to help itself and on the degree to which others in the region perceived a threat and were willing to assist the nation in question.[10]

Both to facilitate this redirection of policy (and to use Sino-Soviet rivalry as a check on Soviet worldwide ambitions), President Nixon set out to mend relations with America's longtime antagonist in the region, the People's Republic of China. The multipolar relationship that subsequently developed in Asia resulted from this conscious decision to redesign the U.S. policy architecture in Asia.

President Nixon's surprise announcement of Secretary of State Kissinger's visit to the People's Republic of China in 1971 was the first of a number of political and economic shocks to the region that signaled the new direction. While it is probably true that this "Nixon shock" and a subsequent visit to the People's Republic of China in February 1972 by the president were "not at the expense of [Asian leaders'] nations . . . [and] will be in accordance with their long range interests,"[11] it is clear that this new policy thrust, made without consulting America's Asian allies, impelled those same allies to move toward lesser dependence on the United States.

The 1973–1974 oil crisis resulting from the 1973 Arab–Israeli War also served to reemphasize to Asians the necessity of their taking a more independent stance. The rapid collapse of South Vietnam in 1975, after the withdrawal of U.S. ground and air forces and the sharp reduction of military assistance to South Vietnam, further convinced American allies in the region of the necessity to discount the power and promises of the United States. Even though their security treaties with the United States continued, most began seeking greater flexibility in their foreign policies. Finally, President Carter's 1977 decision to withdraw American ground forces from Korea (a decision later placed in abeyance) created particularly strong concern in the area about the constancy of American purposes and power in East Asia.

To these earlier developments in the region must be added the more recent major changes cited in the opening paragraphs of this chapter and, in particular, changes in Soviet policy, starting in 1986. Gorbachev's "new thinking" in East Asia matters, beginning about this time, had called for the Soviet Union to emphasize mutual security, balanced force reductions, and economic cooperation.[12]

Frustrated in his attempts to secure large-scale external economic assistance from the West for the Soviet Far East as a quid pro quo for tension reduction in the area, Gorbachev focused on normalizing relations with China (in the process drawing down military forces along the Chinese and Mongolian borders), began moves toward recognizing South Korea, and withdrew Soviet naval and air units from the major Vietnamese base at Cam Ranh Bay that the Americans had earlier built. Gorbachev was, however, unwilling or politically unable to return the four Ryukuyan islands taken from Japan after World War II (Japan's "Northern Territories"), in part because such a concession might lead to dismemberment of European Soviet territories. Consequently, the Soviet leader was unsuccessful in his wooing of Japanese political leaders and business interests.

In view of the Soviet Union's continued military strength in its Far Eastern territory in the Gorbachev era and in light of the Soviet–Japanese standoff over the Northern Territories, the United States continued to stress its alliances and maintained its forces in the region through the 1980s. The Sino–Soviet rapprochement, formalized in 1989 during Gorbachev's visit to Beijing, reinforced American wariness, as did mounting evidence that the Soviet Union's ally, North Korea, was seeking to build nuclear weapons.

By the start of the 1990s, budgetary pressures and a clear lessening of the Soviet threat had resulted in a roughly 11 percent cut in American forces in the region—to about 135,000. With the 1991 failure of base negotiations with the Philippines, a further slight reduction and redeployment of forces was undertaken in 1992 (to Singapore, Guam, and the United States). The resulting American military posture will undoubtedly be further reduced in the course of the 1990s, but the stakes are such that cuts are likely to be modest.[13]

The Current East Asian Scene. Despite the currents of change in East Asia over the past decade, alluded to at the opening of this chapter, there were nevertheless several elements of geopolitical continuity that provided a degree of stability. First, was the continuing threat of Soviet expansion, which evoked common fears among the region's noncommunist states, particularly in Northeast Asia; second was China's inward focus and military weakness; third was Japan's military weakness, threatening none of its neighbors; fourth was the reassuring military presence of the United States; fifth was the skein of American military alliances that discouraged adventurism by the Soviet Union, China, or lesser communist states; and sixth was the fact that North Korea was stalemated in its aggressive designs by an increasingly strong South Korea and by on-the-ground support by the United States for the South.

Economically, East Asia has become a powerhouse. Although the region, totaling about 1.7 billion people, is much poorer than its western European or American counterparts, its economies have been extraordinarily dynamic and by century's end will begin to approach in aggregate size those of Europe and America. It is the fastest-growing region of the world; indeed, in the 1980s, it was the locomotive that pulled along the rest of the world. Its growth rate averaged between 7 percent and 8 percent over the decade, more than two-and-a-

Table 17.1 Principal Regional Forces in East Asia, 1991.

Country/Service	*Regular Forces*	*Reserves*	*Main Armament*
China, People's Republic (pop. 1,132,072,600)			
Army	2,300,000	1,200,000+	9,250 tks. 2,800 AFV 14,500 arty.
Navy	260,000	115,000	94 subs.
Marines	6,000		56 maj. cbts. 869 other cbts. 880 cbt. acft.
Coastal Defense	27,000		
Air Force	470,000	200,000	4,970 cbt. acft.
Paramilitary	12,000,000		
Japan (pop. 124,096,000)			
Army	156,100	46,000	1,000 tks. 454 AFV 879 arty.
Navy	44,000		17 subs. 66 maj. cbts. 13 ptl. cft. 99 cbt. acft.
Air Self-Defense	46,300		422 cbt. acft.
Paramilitary	12,000		
Korea, Democratic People's Republic (pop. 23,275,600)			
Army	1,111,000	500,000	3,500 tks. 4,200 AFV 5,800 arty.
Navy	41,000	40,000	22 subs. 3 frigates 366 ptl. cft.
Air Force	70,000		732 cbt. acft.
Paramilitary	4,000,000		
Korea, Republic (pop. 44,338,200)			
Army	650,000	500,000	1,550 tks. 730 AFV 4,000 arty.
Navy	60,000	25,400	4 subs. 35 maj. cbts. 83 ptl. cft. 24 cbt. acft.
Air Force	40,000		457 cbt. acft.
Paramilitary	3,500,000		

Table 17.1 Principal Regional Forces in East Asia, 1991. *(continued)*

Country/Service	*Regular Forces*	*Reserves*	*Main Armament*
Taiwan			
(pop. 21,009,000)			
Army	270,000	1,500,000	584 tks.
			1,200 AFV
			1,340 arty.
Navy	30,000	32,500	4 subs.
			33 maj. cbts.
			93 ptl. cft.
			32 cbt. acft.
Marines	30,000	35,000	
Air Force	70,000	90,000	487 cbt. acft.
Paramilitary	25,000		
Vietnam			
(pop. 70,217,000)			
Army (self-defense force)	900,000	3,000,000	1,800 tks.
			1,400 AFV
			2,214 arty.
Navy	31,000		7 frigates
			64 ptl. cft.
Air Force	10,000		185 cbt. acft.
Air Defense Force	100,000		
Paramilitary	3,600,000		
Russia, Far Eastern Military District			
Army			4,400 tks.
			4,950 arty.
Navy*			86 subs.
			54 maj. cbts.
			55 ptl. cft.
			220 cbt. acft.
			99 cbt. hel.
Air Force			930 cbt. acft.
			400 cbt. hel.

Source: International Institute for Strategic Studies, *The Military Balance, 1991–1992* (London: IISS, 1991), pp. 149–153, 165–170, 180–184.

*These figures are for the Pacific Fleet which extends beyond the Far Eastern Military District.

AA = antiaircraft; acft. = aircraft; AFV = armored fighting vehicle; amph. = amphibious; APC = armored personnel carrier; armd. = armored; arty. = artillery; ASW = antisubmarine warfare; ATGW = antitank guided weapons; atk. = attack; bns. = battalions; btrys. = batteries; cbt. = combat; cft. = craft; crvettes = corvettes; destrys. = destroyers; div. = division; frigts. = frigates; hel. = helicopter; hvcrft. = hovercraft; lndg. = landing; mine swprs. = mine sweepers; msl. = missile; prcht. = parachute; ptl. = patrol; regts. = regiments; SAM = surface-to-air missile; sqdn. = squadron; tac. = tactical; tk. = tank; tng. = training; tspt. = transport.

half times that of Europe and America. American trade with the region more than doubled during the 1980s, going from about $140 billion worth at the decade's start to over $300 billion worth at its end.[14]

A reasonably complete analysis of current regional developments would require an in-depth look at a dozen or more countries. In the paragraphs that follow, however, we will only examine five of the key states and then look briefly at Southeast Asia as a whole—rather than at each of the countries in that region.

Japan. Of the major regional actors, Japan has a special relationship with the United States. The roots of this vital and productive relationship extend back to the enlightened postwar U.S. policies of the late 1940s. Despite various strains—in part due to cultural differences, to the asymmetrical nature of the relationship, and to the inevitable economic tensions—both countries' leaders have, for more than four decades, viewed the maintenance of good relations as vital. The Japanese have become aware that their extraordinary economic success in part rests on their relatively open access to the American market and on American military forces as their ultimate protectors. Americans have come to realize that Japan not only plays a key role in regional security and is the major economic force in East Asia but also is vital to the health of the entire international economic system.

For Japan the alliance plays an important role beyond providing a security umbrella and a linkage to the industrial democracies, namely, it also makes a sizable and highly effective Japanese defense effort acceptable to neighbors who remember too well Japan's pre-1945 aggression. From the United States' viewpoint, the alliance and associated deployments of American military forces in and around Japan buttress our nation's basic strategic interests and are a key to the overall power equilibrium in the Pacific.

U.S.–Japanese defense relationships at the start of the 1990s were strong. A high level of trust and mutual respect marked military-to-military relations. Joint exercises, intelligence sharing, and close coordination in operational planning and logistics were the rule. Japan's assumption of responsibility for sea-lane protection out to a 1,000-mile radius from the home islands provided a logical complement to the U.S. Navy's missions of ensuring freedom of the seas and maritime deterrence in the Western Pacific.

But one continuing element of disagreement has plagued the military relationship, namely, the feeling of many Americans that Japan has had a "free ride" in defense, which it has translated into economic advantage. This feeling has led to repeated public and congressional demands that Japan should be spending more on its defense and contributing more financially to the support of American forces underwriting security in the region.

While Japan has undoubtedly gained a competitive advantage through its lesser military spending, it should be noted that the 1 percent of GNP traditionally allotted to defense has enabled it to generate substantial military forces, appropriate to the purely defensive roles that Japan's constitution is interpreted to allow; moreover, any larger forces would deeply worry its neighbors who are fearful of

Japanese rearmament. Also, in 1992 Japan's parliament authorized the development of peacekeeping forces for dispatch abroad; while these forces will initially amount to only a few thousand men, they will likely grow in size and expense and their very existence should help rebut the free-ride charge.

Partially answering the inadequate burden-sharing argument, Japan has been contributing a large and increasing share of the cost of American forces stationed there. In 1992, this "host nation support" amounted to $4 billion and by 1995 is projected to account for 70 percent of the local costs of those forces.[15] Japan has also been increasingly active in a different kind of burden sharing that contributes to international security, namely, the provision of economic assistance to nations that might suffer upheavals if their development efforts fail. By the early 1990s, Japan had become the world's largest donor of economic aid, about half of which was directed to developing countries in the Asia Pacific region.[16]

In contrast to the general warmth in defense matters, economic relations have proven to be a major source of friction between the United States and Japan. To a degree this arises out of the sheer magnitudes involved: the United States is Japan's largest trading partner and Japan is the United States' second largest partner. Japan is the second largest investor in America. Thousands of joint ventures, royalty agreements, and partnerships mark corporate relationships.

But, despite the intensity and scope of economic ties—or perhaps in part because of them—friction has increasingly been the rule in the 1980s and early 1990s. As indicated in Table 17.2, Japan annually sells tens of billions of dollars worth of goods more to than it buys from the United States. This chronic trade imbalance of $40 to $50 billion or so has led to ceaseless American pressures on Japan to "voluntarily" limit exports and remove barriers to imports. Since many of these difficulties stem from the very different ways Japan organizes its economic life from those of the other industrial democracies, "leveling the playing field" for trade and investment has been and will be an extraordinarily demanding task.

By 1992 (when Japan was running an unusually large trade surplus) it had become clear that neither U.S.–Japanese bilateral relations nor the international economic system could long sustain such imbalances. Japan's trade surpluses

Table 17.2 U.S.–Japanese Trade (Billions of U.S. $)

Year	*U.S. Imports from Japan*	*U.S. Exports to Japan*
1983	43.6	21.9
1984	60.4	23.6
1985	72.4	22.6
1986	85.5	26.9
1987	88.1	28.2
1988	93.1	37.6
1989	97.1	44.6
1990	93.1	48.6
1991	95.0	48.1

Source: International Monetary Fund, *Direction of Trade Statistics, Yearbook 1992* (Washington, D.C.: IMF, 1992).

Table 17.3 Japan's Merchandise Trade by Area (U.S. $ million, custom clearance basis)

	with European Community			*with Southeast Asia*		
Year	*Exports*	*Imports*	*Balance*	*Exports*	*Imports*	*Balance*
1980	16,650	7,842	8,808	30,910	31,751	−841
1985	20,016	8,893	11,123	33,248	30,264	2,984
1988	46,873	24,071	22,802	67,109	47,802	19,307
1989	47,908	28,146	19,761	73,516	52,906	20,611

Source: Japan Tariff Association, *The Summary Report: Trade of Japan,* 1990.

with the European Community nations, averaging $20 billion, and with its East Asian neighbors, averaging about $20 billion (see Table 17.3), are perhaps not so immediately threatening to Japan's political relations; but they, too, need correcting. If Japan is to conduct the "global partnership" with the United States to which both sides claim to aspire and if Japan is to play the larger political role that it and others believe its economic strength warrants, then its fundamental trade disequilibria must be addressed.

Korea. Korea is a key building block in a stable, secure East Asia. The interests of four great powers—Russia, China, Japan and the United States—converge there. Korea has traditionally been a bridge (and an invasion route) between Japan and mainland Asia. When President Carter announced in 1977 his intention to withdraw American troops from Korea, deep concern was expressed by Japan's leaders as well as by Korea's. When the United States announced a suspension of such withdrawals in 1979, relief in Tokyo was palpable, for Japan's national interests require a stable, peaceful Korean peninsula. Indeed, until a mutually acceptable unification of Korea occurs, the whole international community's interests are best served by a balancing American military presence there.

North Korea is the world's most mobilized nation, with over a million troops (from a population of only about 23 million), two-thirds of whom are forward-deployed, less than 60 miles from the border. The Democratic People's Republic of Korea (D.P.R.K.) spends at least 20 percent, perhaps 25 percent, of its GNP on its military forces, in contrast to the usual 2 to 5 percent that most nations spend—South Korea's being near the latter figure. The economic strains in the North from this effort are massive and have, together with the inefficiencies of a centralized command economic system, resulted in a stagnant economy barely able to meet the basic needs of its people. In 1991 when the Soviet Union withdrew its subsidies and began demanding market prices and hard currency payment for the oil it had been providing, North Korea suffered a further serious blow.

By the start of the 1990s, the severe economic strains in the North, as well as the collapse of the Soviet Union and communist governments in Eastern Europe and a number of serious diplomatic setbacks, had caused Pyongyang to adopt less autarchic or overtly hostile policies toward the rest of the world, including its South Korean neighbor. By 1992, a serious North–South dialogue about unification was in process, and Pyongyang had launched a major effort to reach out for better relations with Japan, the United States, and other Western powers. Widespread suspicion that the North Korean regime had not abandoned its longstanding goal of communizing the peninsula—by force if necessary—and that it was developing nuclear weapons, however, prompted the international community to remain cautious and skeptical.

Meanwhile, in the South, in the Republic of Korea (R.O.K.), beginning in the 1960s, an "economic miracle" occurred that was especially impressive in contrast to the floundering in the North. In the three decades from 1961 to 1991, per capita GNP in the Republic of Korea grew about tenfold in real terms. In the latter part of the period, political progress was equally impressive. After an extended period of martial law following President Park Chung Hee's assassination in 1979, the political ice began to melt in the latter 1980s, culminating in the first free elections for president at the end of 1987 and for a new national assembly in the spring of 1988.

Political liberalization continued with free local elections in 1991 and a similar round of national assembly elections in early 1992. President Roh Tae Woo, the first fairly elected president of the Republic (in 1987), is the first chief executive to end his term of office honorably, in February of 1993—after a second free presidential election in December 1992. While slowdowns or limited reversals in the process of democratization may occur in the course of the 1990s, the political maturation of the country and the thrust toward broader and freer popular participation appears irreversible.

Since a thriving Republic of Korea is important to the security and well-being of Northeast Asia, the United States has strongly supported the country's political and economic liberalization and its efforts directed toward peaceful unification of the peninsula. During the later 1980s, the R.O.K.'s *nordpolitik,* backed by its increasing economic strength, succeeded in gaining the support, as well, of North Korea's East European and Soviet friends and allies for these same liberalization and unification policies; even the People's Republic of China, in August 1992, accorded diplomatic recognition to the South. Deserted by friends and suffering from a badly limping economy, by the early 1990s the North chose diplomacy rather than obduracy. At the end of 1991, the two Koreas signed a pair of most promising treaties, the "Agreement on Reconciliation, Non-Aggression and Exchanges and Cooperation between South and North Korea," and the "Joint Declaration on Denuclearization of the Korean Peninsula." Whether and when the North's new flexibility will result in early progress toward peaceful unification remains to be seen.

Joining together a democratic, capitalistic South Korea and a Marxist North Korea, dictatorially led by the country's founder, or—in the world's only communist monarchy—by his successor son, in a unified Korea will be incredibly difficult. Despite ethnic homogeneity and strong family ties across the 38th Parallel, the gulf of distrust between the two states is so broad and the dissimilarity of their political, economic, and societal systems so great that full unification is likely to take many years, conceivably decades.

China. The People's Republic of China has had an extraordinarily turbulent life since its birth in 1949, and the turbulence may well continue during the 1990s, when the gerontocracy leading the nation will inevitably be replaced. Under its founding leader, Mao Tse-Tung, China's new communist government imposed a rigid, centralized political, economic, and social system on roughly a billion people who had suffered under feudalism, foreign invasions, civil wars, and weak government for many decades. Mixing Marxism-Leninism with home-grown Maoism, China's leaders developed a unique form of communism. Internationally, they strongly identified China with colonial peoples and Third World states. Initially in concert with, but after the latter 1950s in rivalry with, the Soviet Union, China supported revolutionaries throughout the world. It also aggressively asserted its control over disputed lands, such as Tibet and Sino–Soviet border territories.

In China's eyes, the United States was enemy number one for more than two decades. American assistance to Chiang Kai-shek's nationalist government during the Chinese civil war, followed by combat between Chinese communist "volunteers" and American forces in the Korean War and Chinese logistical and other support for North Vietnam during U.S. involvement in the Indochina conflict, generated mutual hostility and distrust. By the 1960s, however, China increasingly found itself at odds with its Soviet neighbor, with relations reaching a nadir in 1969 when large-scale border clashes occurred along the Ussuri River in Northeastern Manchuria. Even before that time, China had become alarmed at what it perceived as Soviet hegemonic ambitions and tried to enlist the West to check the threat. For its part, the United States was also prepared, by the end of the 1960s, to seek better relations with China in order to check Soviet pressures. The resulting strategic triangle—the Soviet Union, the People's Republic of China, and the United States—provided a tenuous but useful stabilizing element in East Asian relations through the 1970s and 1980s. During that period, China veered from seeking close cooperation with the Americans to an "equidistant" stance between the superpowers, shifting to the latter position as it reappraised the relative strengths and dangers represented by the other two powers.

From the American point of view, from normalization in 1978 to the end of the 1980s, the relationship with China helped provide a check on Soviet adventurism. In the wake of the Soviet invasion of Afghanistan in December 1979, the United States moved to strengthen cooperation with Beijing, to include the sale of "dual-technology" items (dual in that they had both civil and military applications) and limited combat support items for the Chinese military.

Strengthening U.S.–Chinese relations was made easier on both sides by the ending of the Cultural Revolution and its excesses in 1978 and by the rise of Deng Xiaoping with his pragmatic colleagues who took the view that "it doesn't matter what color the chicken is but whether it lays eggs." During the decade of the Deng-led economic reforms (1979–1989) China moved sharply away from the rigid command economy of the previous three decades, instituting land and market reforms and freeing up Chinese capitalist impulses—with the result that per capita income doubled in the decade. Private ventures, to include foreign

"Better dump your excess baggage if you want to make it!"

Reprinted with permission of Renan R. Lurie.

investors and especially in selected ''special economic zones'' in coastal areas, were encouraged. These, together with agricultural and price reforms, resulted by the end of the 1980s in a mixed economy that was roughly 50 percent market-directed and 50 percent government- and party-directed.[17]

Although Deng and the other aging architects of these far-reaching economic reforms made it clear that political life would remain a monopoly of the party, there were limited political reform efforts in the decade, as well. These included multicandidate elections at local levels, opportunities for genuine debate in the National People's Congress, which had long been purely a rubber stamp, and devolution of some economic and political authority to cities, special economic zones and provinces.[18]

The opening to the outside world that China's leaders recognized was essential to attract trade, investment, and technology, together with the market-economy reforms and the limited political reforms, produced popular pressures for still more reform, particularly for political liberalization. These pressures, intensified by a surge of inflation in 1988–1989, produced massive demonstrations in Beijing's Tiananmen Square in May and the first few days of June 1989—which, in turn, led to their bloody suppression on June 4 and the subsequent clampdown on political life and a hiatus in economic reform.

During the 1980s, China's economic progress made possible a leap in its economic interactions with the United States, Japan, and Europe. As shown in Table 17.4, China's trade with the United States more than quadrupled from 1983

Table 17.4 U.S.–P.R.C. Trade (millions of U.S. $)

Year	*U.S. exports*	*U.S. imports*	*Total $*
1983	2,173	2,477	4,650
1984	3,004	3,381	6,385
1985	3,856	4,224	8,080
1986	3,106	5,241	8,347
1987	3,497	6,910	10,407
1988	5,017	9,261	14,278
1989	5,807	12,901	18,708
1990	4,807	16,296	21,103
1991	6,287	20,305	26,592

Source: International Monetary Fund, *Direction of Trade Statistics, Yearbook 1992* (Washington, D.C.: IMF, 1992).

to 1990. In the process, an imbalance in trade developed in the latter part of the period to the point that American pressures mounted against China's restrictions on imports and against its export practices. Charges of prison labor in export industries, violation of property rights, and deceptive third-party routing of exports, joined with continued American unhappiness about human rights practices in China, especially after the Tiananmen Square incident, led to a deterioration in the bilateral relationship that had flourished during most of the 1980s.

President Bush successfully extended Most Favored Nation (MFN) treatment to China into 1992, despite strong congressional opposition after the Tiananmen Square incident, but further cooling in bilateral relations of what had been a warming trend all through the 1980s seems likely in the future. If China's increases in military spending and purchases of Soviet/Russian high-tech military equipment that marked the start of the 1990s continue, and if China continues its missile exports to unstable areas, the prospect is for even chillier relationships. This will especially be the case if the People's Republic of China acts aggressively to enforce its claims to the contested Spratly Islands in the South China Sea—claims that it reasserted in February 1992 with the statement that it was ready to use force to back the claims, if necessary.

If the projected 1997 reversion of Hong Kong to Chinese control (and subsequent governing practice) proceeds smoothly, the outcome will both provide an extraordinary economic asset to the People's Republic of China and also reassure the world—and particularly Taiwan—about the prospects for the long-term peaceful unification of the two Chinas across the Taiwan Straits.

Taiwan. The United States has had a strong, positive relationship with the government of Taiwan ever since its leaders fled the Chinese mainland in the last stages of the civil war and established the Republic of China on the island. American protection and economic and military aid helped the tiny republic to sustain itself in the face of Chinese threats and to launch a successful development program that far outstripped the accomplishments of the mainlanders.

Although it insisted there was only one government of China, its own (just as the Chinese communists did), there was no prospect that it could overturn the Beijing government. Nevertheless, it firmly withstood the People's Republic of China's efforts to isolate and undermine it—efforts that increasingly bore fruit until only a handful of countries, mostly tiny ones, recognized Taiwan by the mid 1980s.

The long-expected normalization of U.S.–P.R.C. relations at the end of 1978 had little immediate effect on Taiwan's political and economic status. Although that normalization entailed "ending U.S. recognition of the Republic of China on Taiwan, termination of the U.S.–Taiwan mutual defense treaty [and] withdrawal of the remaining U.S. troops on Taiwan,"[19] even Taiwan's defense position did not seem unduly shaken in the aftermath. This outcome was due in part to the U.S. Congress' promptly following the termination of the formal treaty with the passage of the Taiwan Relations Act (April 1979), which stipulated that the United States was vitally interested in the continued peace and well-being of the people of Taiwan. This act, which some have viewed as the "functional equivalent" of a treaty, also directed the president to report to Congress on any threat to these interests.

During the 1980s, Taiwan's security for the near term seemed reasonably assured for a number of reasons. The People's Republic of China was preoccupied internally and reaching out to the West for capital and technology in a way that made a military effort against Taiwan unlikely, and Taiwan had increased its own defense efforts—including air defense—to the point that a direct attack by China would be very expensive. We should note, however, that despite Taiwan's relative security from direct attack, the threat of a naval blockade by the People's Republic of China remained worrisome. With one of the most dynamic economies in the world, Taiwan is heavily dependent on international trade, and a naval blockade would quickly defeat it—unless friendly powers, such as the United States, broke the blockade.

By the early 1990s, China had begun a military build-up that deeply troubled Taiwan. Beijing substantially increased its defense budget and began an aggressive procurement program abroad, particularly from Russia. In 1992 it reportedly ordered 72 Sukhoi 27 and 24 Mig 31 planes from Russia—that country's latest and most powerful versions. According to Taiwan's Vice Foreign Minister, Beijing was also seeking Ilyushin long-range transport planes and T-72 tanks, again Russia's top-line equipment. If these purchases were completed, they would "affect the military balance across the Taiwan Straits" the Vice Minister reported to Parliament. Beijing has also reportedly obtained advance military technology and the rights to build more of the high-performance weapons in its own factories.[20] In this context, it is noteworthy that in September 1992 President Bush announced that the United States was prepared to sell 150 F-16 aircraft to Taiwan, a move that would sharply bolster Taiwan's capability; an undisclosed number of the aircraft would be built in Taiwan.[21]

At the same time that it was sending disquieting military signals, Beijing was showing a relatively benign political and economic face to Taipei. Taiwanese investors, mainly operating through Hong Kong, were openly permitted to trade and invest in the People's Republic of China, particularly in Southeast China. By 1992, these investments were estimated to be worth $2.5 billion; accompanying these have been thousands of joint venture and licensing agreements that have helped the Southeast grow at 15 percent to 20 percent annually.

Although China has continued to insist adamantly that any country wishing to have diplomatic relations with it must first break off diplomatic relations with Taiwan, it has eased somewhat its objections to Taiwan's membership in international organizations. In 1991, for instance, Taiwan became a member of the intergovernmental Asia Pacific Economic Cooperation organization (APEC) at the same time that the People's Republic of China and Hong Kong were admitted. For its part, Taiwan has been progressively easing its conditions on cross-straits relationships; in mid 1992, its parliament passed a bill removing most of the remaining legal barriers to trade, investment, travel, and cultural relations with the People's Republic of China.

Taiwan's vibrant economy has not only provided a substantial and increasing standard of living for its people but has also built a solid base for a vigorous "economic diplomacy" that has been remarkably successful in offsetting its political isolation. As the world's thirteenth largest trader, with the world's largest foreign exchange reserves (over $80 billion as of 1991), Taiwan has been able through its economic influence to mitigate the loss of diplomatic relations with all its East Asian neighbors and virtually all of the rest of the world. (As of 1992, with the loss of the Republic of Korea's recognition, only twenty-eight smaller countries still maintained diplomatic relations with the Taipei government.) With its economy growing about 9 percent annually over a thirty-year period and with persistently large trade surpluses, Taiwan has become a major investor in the region, including the People's Republic of China.[22]

Along with this economic success story has been step-by-step political liberalization. The earlier "hard authoritarian" party and government structures under the Kuomintang party of Chiang Kai-shek, dominated by refugee mainlanders, evolved in the course of the 1980s into a multiparty "soft authoritarian" pattern. In 1988 the first Taiwanese-born president, Lee Teng-hui, was elected in an open contest, challenged by the new (1986) Democratic Progressive Party.[23] Although the Kuomintang seems likely to remain the dominant party for years, the march toward democracy seems irreversible, barring war with the mainland or a local upheaval over Taiwan independence—both of which are unlikely.

Vietnam. Emerging victorious and unified in the mid 1970s from the struggle with the United States, Vietnam was a badly battered country. It was widely expected that, after political consolidation, its communist leaders would be engaged for the next decade or more in rebuilding their shattered economy. Contrary to these expectations, Hanoi had additional priorities, namely, the extension of Vietnamese control over the other two Indochinese states, Laos and Kampuchea (Cambodia).

Even before the end of the Vietnam War, Hanoi's troops were emplaced in Laos, supporting the communist Pathet Lao. After the American departure from the peninsula, the Vietnamese in effect continued their control of the governmental reins with their Lao clients in apparent authority. In Kampuchea a different approach was necessary. There, the incredible brutality of the communist Khmer Rouge forces had alienated that part of the population that they did not actually kill. (Estimates vary, but it appears that the Khmer Rouge killed, in one way or another, perhaps 1 to 2 million of their fellow citizens, out of a total population of only 6 to 7 million.[24]) It was possible, therefore, for the Vietnamese to invade the country with minimal opposition. In 1978 they marched in virtually as liberators, resuming their historic thrust toward the rich rice lands of the Khmers, which France had interrupted more than a century before when it colonized all of Indochina.

Although Vietnam succeeded in installing a puppet regime in Phnom Penh, headed by a former Khmer Rouge leader, Hun Sen, it was unable to gain control of the entire countryside. Khmer Rouge guerrillas plus two Khmer nationalist factions, one headed by the former head of state, Prince Sihanouk, and one headed by former premier Son Sann, continued to battle the Hun Sen forces and each other. After twelve years of civil war and devastation and the flight of tens of thousands of refugees, the ASEAN and the U.N.'s "Perm Five" (the five permanent members of the U.N. Security Council) produced a cease-fire and a peace agreement signed by the Hun Sen government and the three guerilla factions. Under the agreed plan, the United Nations would play a central role in disarming the four warring factions (the Vietnamese troops having been withdrawn in 1990), in monitoring interim peace arrangements, and in organizing and supervising free elections.

Khmer Rouge noncooperation, however, stalled the entire agreed process, and by late 1992 it was not clear whether the ambitious U.N. undertaking would be able to proceed or whether a complete breakdown would ensue, with the Khmer Rouge as the most potent military force again on the road to dominating the country. In that terrible eventuality, a reintroduction of Vietnamese forces is conceivable though unlikely.

Although relieved by 1990 of the burden of keeping its troops in Cambodia, the Vietnamese economy was hit at about the same time by the withdrawal of Soviet aid and subsidies worth perhaps $2 billion annually. (Moreover, the Soviets demanded repayment of their $17 billion debt!) Its Marxist-style command economy had already been failing and its leaders had been attempting to shift to a "mixed economy," in which private enterprise and markets would play a major role. By 1991 these efforts had resulted in perhaps 40 percent of the GNP being generated by the private sector.

Given its economic reforms, resource richness, talented and inexpensive labor force, and its attempts to open to the world, foreign investment began to flow into the country in the early 1990s (see Table 17.5). The United States and, through its influence, the international lending agencies have held back, though the restraints (in the U.S. case, largely over prisoners-of-war and missing-in-action difficulties stemming from the U.S.–Vietnam War) seem likely to be lifted in the next year or two.

Table 17.5 Top 10 Investors in Vietnam, August 1992 ($ million)

	Projects	*Invested Capital*
Taiwan	57	755.4
Hong Kong	84	460.5
Netherlands	5	258.5
United Kingdom	9	189.8
Australia	17	170.7
CIS	36	168.6
France	24	167.0
Japan	24	159.4
South Korea	13	125.5
Canada	9	95.8

Source: Asian Wall Street Journal, 3 August 1992, p. 1. Data from the State Committee for Cooperation and Investment, Hanoi.

Recognizing that not only Soviet economic aid but also Soviet political and military support are irretrievably gone, Vietnam's leaders have been attempting to broaden its international relationships, particularly with its ASEAN neighbors and with Japan and the United States. Without the Soviet card to offset China's large and sometimes threatening presence on its borders, it has been anxious to acquire full ASEAN membership and to develop new political and economic ties with a suspicious United States—or at least to accommodate the United States on POW–MIA affairs enough to remove the U.S. veto on aid from multilateral agencies.

In light of the downfall of communist regimes in Europe, Hanoi's rulers have resisted any reforms that might moderate the country's rigid Leninist political system. To a marked degree their behavior toward economic and political liberalization seems to be the same as China's—hesitant and pragmatic movement in the former and minimal, yet unmistakable, changes toward the latter. With the Cambodian venture behind them and needing to motivate their people in the task of economic development, the country's leaders may begin to move toward "soft authoritarianism" over the decade, but there was little sign of that by late 1992—despite rumblings of factionalism in ruling circles.

Neither are there signs that Vietnam is likely to threaten any of its neighbors soon. But sheer size, geographic position, military prowess, and economic potential make Vietnam an important regional player to be treated with caution. Depending on its ambitions in Indochina and its willingness to turn its attention to nation-building, it can become a factor for regional stability or instability in the course of the 1990s.

Russia. Chapter 16 deals at length with Russia and American national security considerations concerning it, but some special attention to Russia's place in East Asia is warranted. Moscow has apparently not firmly settled upon its policies in the East Asian region. It is sending contradictory signals; it is apparently torn, on the one hand, between attempting to retain the Soviet Union's earlier great power status in the region through a continuing large-scale military presence and, on the other hand, seeking a low military profile and a highly focused economic role in the region. The former approach seems to be favored primarily by conservatives, nationalists, and military figures, although Foreign Minister Kozyrev may also be in this camp, for he has been resurrecting familiar Soviet proposals for multinational regional security arrangements. The second approach, forgoing military power and seeking integration into the regional economy, is clearly held by the architects of Soviet economic reform, technocrats, and at least some of the democratic leadership; Boris Yeltsin appears to be in this camp, as well, although he is constrained by tactical considerations.

During the cold war years, the Soviet Union built a major military complex in its Far Eastern territories, a complex which now is Russian. It consists of a major fleet with all of the associated shore facilities and naval aviation. The Far Eastern fleet, the largest of the four Soviet fleets, was built to challenge American control of the Pacific Ocean and to provide a significant part of the ballistic missile threat to the American homeland. SLBM submarines, operating out of the relatively secure waters of the Sea of Okhotsk, continue to be a threat under the Russian flag.

Russian non-SLBM submarines and naval surface forces are formidable in terms of quantity and quality but are being drawn down or inactivated with the drastic cuts in the Russian defense budget. Even so, the residual Russian naval forces in Northeast Asia are large when compared with the forces of other East Asian states. As indicated in Table 17.1, Russian air force, marine, and army units are also still relatively numerous.

Given Russian foreign policy, with its emphasis on international cooperation rather than confrontation and its stress on building peaceful relations with prospective donors, there is very little prospect that any of these forces will be used aggressively—even in demonstrations. Indeed, with Russia's severe economic constraints, its forces are doing very little exercising or training—for example, naval units are virtually tied to their docks. In short, while still formidable, these forces present nothing like the danger they did a few years ago.

Russia's military assets in the region are generally viewed by the other East Asian states as nonthreatening. Japan is a partial exception; in view of the continuing dispute over the four southern Kuril Islands that Russia occupies and claims, Japan is understandably nervous about any substantial Russian forces in the region. Although periodic discussions between Japanese and Soviet or Russian leaders about these "Northern Territories" have occurred, the sensitivity of the claims on both sides is so high that there is little prospect for an early resolution of the dispute.

Having concluded that it could no longer contest the predominance of the American navy in the Pacific, at the end of the 1980s the Soviet Union began liquidating its military base at Cam Ranh Bay, as noted earlier in this chapter. Russia has continued the evacuation of Cam Ranh, so that it will no longer have facilities from which to launch air reconnaissance or power projection forces into the South China Sea or the Southwest Pacific.

In the latter 1980s, Gorbachev attempted, in addition to projecting a strong political and military presence in East Asia, to engage the other regional powers in building up the Soviet economy in the region. He was singularly unsuccessful in getting the economic help he sought. President Yeltsin has had only limited success in getting economic help, even though the military component of Russian foreign policy has been downgraded. Despite growing South Korean trade and investment and cross-border trade with China, the unavailability of large-scale Japanese involvement (because of the Kuriles dispute and the inadequacy of local infrastructure), it is likely to be well into the next century before there is significant development of the Russian part of the region.

Apparently apart from strategic calculations, Russia is engaged in large-scale arms transfers in the region that could prove seriously destabilizing. The roots of this policy are clearly economic—both a search for badly needed hard currency and an effort to preclude Russia's military–industrial facilities from shutting down and adding to the ranks of the unemployed. Top-of-the-line aircraft, both MIG 29s and Sukhoi 27s, are being offered at bargain prices, along with the latest T72 tanks, self-propelled artillery, multiple rocket launchers, and antiaircraft missiles. As of 1992, China was the leading buyer, but there is a likelihood that various Southeast Asian nations will join in, fueling incipient arms races in the region. North Korea may also become a purchaser, with profoundly negative consequences for the region, although Pyongyang's lack of foreign currency to pay for the acquisitions will probably preclude such a development.

Southeast Asia. From Burma to the Philippines, all of Southeast Asia except Thailand was in the grip of colonial powers (the United Kingdom, France, the Netherlands, and the United States) until World War II. After the defeat of the Japanese, who had overrun most of the area, and the colonial powers' withdrawal, (except for France, which lingered on in Indochina), the new nations faced the task of repairing war damage, building new institutions, suppressing communist insurgencies, and creating viable economies. After limping starts, they had mostly met these challenges by the 1960s. By the latter 1960s, six of the region's nations (Thailand, Malaysia, Singapore, Indochina, the Philippines, and Brunei) had concluded that their interests—particularly economic ones—could best be served by intensifying cooperation. Accordingly, in 1967 they formed the Association of Southeast Asian Nations (ASEAN). Burma, which had virtually withdrawn from international life, and the three Indochina states, locked in warfare, were the only nations in the region that did not join.

Although slow to institutionalize itself, ASEAN became an increasingly important political instrument, particularly in the latter 1970s. At that time, worried over the American withdrawal from Southeast Asia and the takeover of Vietnam, Laos, and Kampuchea by communist forces, the ASEAN nations launched a series of cooperative political and economic initiatives, at the same time disclaiming any intention of forming a military alliance.

The fears of the ASEAN countries about stability in their region were underscored in 1978 and 1979 by the Vietnamese invasion of Kampuchea and the installation of a puppet regime there by the invaders. Since the Vietnamese armed forces were substantially superior to those of the ASEAN states, taken singly or together, there was little the nations could do to confront the threat directly. Instead, they drew closer together and waged a diplomatic campaign against Vietnam, encouraging the United States to reassert a stronger role in the region.

Although China, as the foe of Vietnam and the ally of Kampuchea, might also have seemed to be a logical protector of the ASEAN states' interests, the People's Republic of China tends to inspire as much concern as it does confidence in the region. Southeast Asian worries about China arise in part from the People's Republic of China's earlier sponsorship and support of local communist insurrections and in part from the 18 million or more ethnic Chinese in the area who are sometimes feared as potential sympathizers and cooperators with their ethnic homeland. In part, too, the sheer demographic weight of their giant neighbor worries the regional states.

China's posturing regarding its claims to the Spratly Islands and other contested sites in the South China Sea has done little to reassure the region. Taiwan, Vietnam, the Philippines, and Malaysia, as well as China, have claims to some or all of the islands. While the islands have little, if anything, above water to contest, the promise—probably highly exaggerated—of petroleum and other resources on and under the sea bed keep this a contentious issue. Adding to its neighbors' concerns, China began the exploration and drilling of nearby contested sites in 1992, threatening to use force if it ran into interference.

Since the South China Sea is a major thoroughfare for shipping through the region, conflict over the islands could be doubly disastrous. Although the United States has a strong interest in keeping sea lanes open, there is little prospect that it will become involved in specific territorial claims. There is some likelihood that the countries concerned will be able to compromise, setting sovereignty issues aside and cooperating on the economic development of the contested areas; but the discovery of significant petroleum deposits in the area would probably override such sensible efforts.

The 1991–1992 withdrawal of U.S. forces from Clarke Air Base and Subic Bay Naval Base in the Philippines raised fresh concerns among most of the regional states about a possible power vacuum. There is widespread concern that Japan or China will fill that vacuum. The United States has, however, declared its intention to maintain security arrangements and treaties in the region, as well as a sizable continuing forward-presence; given past experience, the regional states are understandably nervous about the durability of those intentions.

Although the three Indochina states (Vietnam, Kampuchea, and Laos) have always been considered part of Southeast Asia, they have been left out of the marked economic and nation-building successes of the rest of the region. While most of the countries of the ASEAN have experienced remarkable growth over the past two decades, with growth rates around 8 percent to 10 percent for the latter half of the 1980s, the Indochina states have remained one of the world's poorest regions. Both to integrate them into the regional economy and to minimize possible future political and security problems, especially with Vietnam, the ASEAN states have been reaching out to them. ASEAN gave Vietnam observer status in the organization in 1992. If Vietnam continues to cooperate in resolving the Kampuchean civil war, full membership will likely follow soon. If and when the Kampuchean civil war is finally ended, that country will desperately need ASEAN assistance, including membership.

In view of the region's rapid economic progress and growing interdependence in the 1980s, further consolidation of ASEAN can be anticipated in the 1990s. Indeed, at the ASEAN summit meeting of January 1992, the organization created the ASEAN Free Trade Area (AFTA), which is intended to lower tariffs among the ASEAN countries, over a fifteen-year period, to virtually zero levels. On the political level, there is also increasing activity. The ASEAN Post-Ministerial Summit (ASEAN-PMC), held annually in different member countries, is becoming a forum for senior diplomats to discuss a whole range of political and security subjects, not only for Southeast Asia, but for the entire Pacific rim.

Policy Challenges in the 1990s. Perhaps the most important near-term challenge for the United States in East Asia is to define its role in the region. As the foregoing sections suggest, America's influence has been waning and its policy options narrowing for more than two decades. In considerable part, this has been the consequence of the higher priority in terms of time, attention, and resources given by American political and business leaders to other parts of the world; in part, the result of the strengthening of other regional actors, particularly Japan, who have increasingly replaced the United States as principal trading partners and investors, and—in Japan's case—provider of assistance; in part, because of the United States' inability to get its own house in order. ''Asian leaders find it incomprehensible that the United States does not recognize the inevitable consequences for its national power over its mounting debt, declining savings rate, crumbling infrastructure, growing income disparities, and inadequate educational system. . . . [I]f the United States is to continue to influence favorably the future economic and security structures of a region as dynamic as the Asia-Pacific, much will depend on its own economic strength, renewed social cohesion and the foresight of its political leadership.''[25]

A central part of the task of defining America's future role in East Asia will be to decide what kind of relationship it should have with the two principal regional powers—Japan and China—and how best to pursue such relationships. With Japan, the case for an intimate partnership regionally and globally is clear, but both history and the strongly competitive nature of the economic dimension of the relationship will make such a partnership difficult to attain. With China, the problem of creating a long-term relationship is far different but at least as difficult, for it involves human rights and possible military confrontation, as well as trade. American efforts to isolate China after the Tiananmen Square incident expressed most clearly through repeated congressional attempts to deny it MFN status, seem likely to culminate in isolating the United States instead; although other nations decry the repression and bloodshed exemplified by Tiananmen, they are not prepared to forgo normal relations with the People's Republic of China as a consequence. For both of these key relationships, a broader and more informed debate needs to occur within the United States about what we should seek and how to go about doing so; thereafter or contemporaneously, a broader and deeper dialogue between the United States and each of these Asian giants needs to take place.

Since the United States is, and will remain, a Pacific nation, it will have to pay increasing attention to both its economic and security interests in the region—even as it tends to its interests elsewhere in the world. Yet, measured in regional trade and investment, the United States' economic attention has been slipping at the same time that its military strength in the region has also been decreasing.

Although East Asia has been relatively quiescent in the 1980s, except for Cambodia, Americans cannot afford to continue to take it for granted in the 1990s. There are too many questions about possibly dangerous developments in the region to assume that peace and progress will reign. Economically, the United States will need to invest and trade more and take a vigorous role in promoting regional economic cooperation. The Asia-Pacific Economic Cooperation (APEC) organization, which was launched in 1989, essentially as an Australian initiative, will require special nurturing. As noted in Chapter 12, APEC can become not only an instrument for liberalizing regional trade, but also for providing a defense against narrower economic groupings in the region and exclusive regional arrangements elsewhere. It is in the interests of neither the United States nor its East Asian neighbors for an inward-looking, protectionist Yen bloc to develop in counterpoise to the European Community and the prospective North American Free Trade Area.

In terms of meeting the regional security challenge through the 1990s, the United States has already spelled out a strategic approach and supporting force structure, the so-called East Asia Strategy Initiative (EASI). Despite the fact that there are a number of important unknown or unknowable developments in the next few years that make regional trends there less predictable than in any period since the Korean conflict, the Department of Defense has produced an overall plan to secure American interests. Six principles underpin it:

- Assurance of American engagement in Asia and the Pacific.
- A strong system of bilateral security arrangements.
- Maintenance of modest but capable forward-deployed U.S. forces.
- Sufficient overseas base structure to support those forces.
- Our Asian allies should assume greater responsibility for their own defense.
- Complementary defense cooperation[26]

It is apparent that American security interests will continue to require a robust U.S. military presence in the region for some time. The Korean situation and the quarrel over the Spratly Islands are indicative of the kinds of regional challenges that may fester and burst into conflict. The EASI provides for a military forward-presence in the region at a somewhat reduced (12 percent) level from the

135,000 troops, ashore and afloat, during the latter stages of the cold war. Unexpectedly, the eruption of Mount Pinatubo and the negativism of the Philippine Senate necessitated adding another 8,000 (to the scheduled 15,000) reduction—but part of those forces are being shifted to other places in the region. Although the loss of the bases is lamentable, the reduced threat in the region and the willingness of other states such as Singapore and Australia to be helpful mitigate the loss. Further Phase II and Phase III cuts are planned in the EASI, post 1992, but they, too, are modest.[27] The planned Phase II reduction in Korea has been placed on hold because of uncertainty about North Korea's nuclear weapons ambitions.

The Administration made plain in its 1992 report to Congress, "A Strategic Framework for the Asian Pacific Rim," that the United States' principal military role in the future will be as a regional stabilizing and balancing force. But whether the American Congress and public can be persuaded to support such a role throughout the decade is a crucial question. Inasmuch as the modest stabilizing and balancing role will require fewer American forces in the region than were deemed essential in the past, when the Soviet threat was high, it seems likely that the necessary broad political support in the United States will be forthcoming—that is, if the nation's political leaders recognize America's strong interests in the region and exercise the required leadership.

Of course the extent to which other nations in the region are prepared to cooperate with and support the United States in a balancing, stabilizing role—and for how long—is crucial. As of 1992, there was a clear regional consensus that an American military presence is desirable. Even the North Koreans, as of mid 1992, were saying that in order to provide a stabilizing element on the peninsula some American troops could remain in South Korea until reunification was accomplished. China, Japan, Taiwan, and the ASEAN nations have also indicated the desirability of the Americans' playing a stabilizing role in the region—although some of the ASEAN nations are less enthusiastic than others about such a role. (All the states in the region would welcome a greater U.S. economic presence, both to offset Japan's very great influence and to provide increased access to American markets, technology, and capital.)

Given the loss of American bases in the Philippines and the inevitable drawdown of U.S. forces in the area, the regional states are searching for some measures to strengthen certainty in their uncertain neighborhood. Accordingly, various nations in both Northeast and Southeast Asia, and Australia as well, are examining possible regional or subregional security arrangements that could contribute to stability. It is clear that such arrangements cannot be alliances, such as NATO; for the lack of a common threat, deep cultural differences, and political distrust preclude such a possibility. It is probable, however, that some further cooperative and coordinating mechanisms will evolve in the course of the 1990s. One of the possibilities under discussion is an Asian adaptation of the Conference on Security Cooperation in Europe (CSCE) that helped dampen the cold war in Europe. In this context, particular attention is being given to confidence- and security-building measures (CBMs/CSBMs) or, more narrowly, arms control. The most likely short-term development, however, is a further strengthening and broadening of the ASEAN-PMC. But more formal regional or subregional security arrangements or institutions could well emerge later in the decade.

Discussion Questions

1. What are the principal goals of the People's Republic of China? How would you rank its development goals versus the People's Republic of China's desire to obtain great power status?

2. How do you think the People's Republic of China views the rest of Asia, and how does the rest of Asia look at the People's Republic of China?

3. How would one describe the East Asian system of nations of today? How are power relationships there changing, and how can equilibrium and stability be maintained?

4. Identify the national interests of the United States in Asia. What are the national interests of the People's Republic of China, and what, if any, mutual interests encourage U.S.–P.R.C. cooperation?

5. What type of role should the United States encourage the People's Republic of China to play in Asia? Should the United States encourage the People's Republic of China and Japan to work more closely together on various matters, or would a strong Sino-Japanese relationship upset the present equilibrium in Asia?

6. How would one describe U.S.–Japanese bilateral relations? How important is the relationship between the United States and Japan? How might this relationship change in the future?

7. What type of role will Japan likely pursue in Asia? Does Japan's economic strength warrant it a larger political role in the world? How might Japan go about expanding its political role in Asia and the rest of the world without being perceived as threatening?

8. What impact would a unified Korea have on the rest of Asia? What can the countries of the region, including the United States, do to further the cause of Korean unification?

9. How does the withdrawal of U.S. military bases from the Philippines influence the security situation of the Asia-Pacific region?

10. What are the implications of a settlement to the Cambodian conflict for the rest of Southeast Asia? Do the Indochinese states belong in ASEAN? What impact would their membership have on ASEAN? On the region?

Recommended Readings

Alves, Dora, ed. *Change, Interdependence and Security in the Pacific Basin, The 1990 Pacific Symposium*. Washington, D.C.: National Defense University, 1991.

Barnett, A. Doak. *The Makings of Foreign Policy in China*. Washington, D.C.: Brookings Institution, 1982.

Bean, R. Mark. *Cooperative Security in Northeast Asia: a China-Japan-South Korea Coalition Approach*. Washington, D.C.: National Defense University, 1990.

Bullock, Mary Brown, and Litwak, Robert S., eds. *The United States and the Pacific Basin: Changing Economic and Security Relationships*. Washington, D.C.: Woodrow Wilson Center Press, 1991.

East Asia, the West, and International Security: Prospects for Peace, vols. 1, 2, 3.

Proceedings of the Twenty-eighth IISS Annual Conference, Kyoto, Japan, September 1986. London: International Institute for Strategic Studies, 1987.

Gong, Gerrit W., and Grant, Richard L., eds. *Security and Economics in the Asia-Pacific Region,* Significant Issues Series, vol. XIII, no. 9. Washington, D.C.: Center for Strategic and International Studies, 1991.

Grove, Eric, ed. *Global Security: North American, European, and Japanese Interdependence in the 1990s*. Washington, D.C.: Brassey's, 1991.

Harding, Harry. *A Fragile Partnership: The United States and China Since 1972*. Washington, D.C.: Brookings Institution, 1992.

Lardy, Nicolas R. *China's Entry Into the World Economy*. Lanham, Md.: University Press of America, 1987.

Macciarola, Frank J., and Oxnam, Robert B., eds. *The China Challenge: American Policies in East Asia*. New York: Academy of Political Science, 1991.

Pacific Rim Security Cooperation. Seoul, South Korea: Institute of Foreign Affairs and National Security, 1992.

Polomka, Peter. *The Two Koreas: Catalysts for Conflict in East Asia?* London: International Institute for Strategic Studies, 1986.

Rich, Michael D., and Morris, Mary E. *Security in East Asia*. Santa Monica, Calif.: Rand, 1986.

Security in South-East Asia and the South-West Pacific: Challenges of the 1990s. IPA report no. 29. New York: International Peace Academy, 1989.

18

The Middle East

As in other regions of the world, the end of the cold war has had profound implications for The Middle East.* Nowhere was the changing strategic relationship between the United States and the Soviet Union made clearer than in the reactions of the two superpowers to the Iraqi invasion of Kuwait on August 2, 1990. Determined to take a stand against naked aggression and to protect U.S. access to oil at affordable prices, the Bush Administration was able to receive assurances from a debilitated, distracted Soviet leadership that it would neither veto U.N. resolutions to use force to liberate Kuwait nor commit military forces to block a United Nations-sponsored coalition effort. Thus, the United States was relatively unimpeded in constructing an international coalition abroad and a political consensus at home to use force as needed to defend U.S. and international interests in the Persian Gulf region.

U.S. Interests. Reliable access to energy supplies has been a continuing major national interest of the United States in the region, and as early as the Franklin D. Roosevelt administration, American policy toward the Middle East was largely aimed at protecting that interest. The Roosevelt administration recognized the

*The "Middle East" is an imprecise term, used to denote the general area of predominantly Moslem culture on the southern and eastern shores of the Mediterranean and on both sides of the Persian (or Arabian) Gulf. The term is used in this chapter to include Egypt, Israel, Jordan, Lebanon, Syria, Turkey, Iraq, Saudi Arabia, Kuwait, Bahrain, Qatar, the United Arab Emirates, Iran, Oman, Yemen (the unified state formed by the merger of the Yemen Arab Republic and the People's Democratic Republic of Yemen), and Sudan. We do not include the North African states of Libya, Tunisia, Algeria, and Morocco.

FIG. 18.1 Middle East

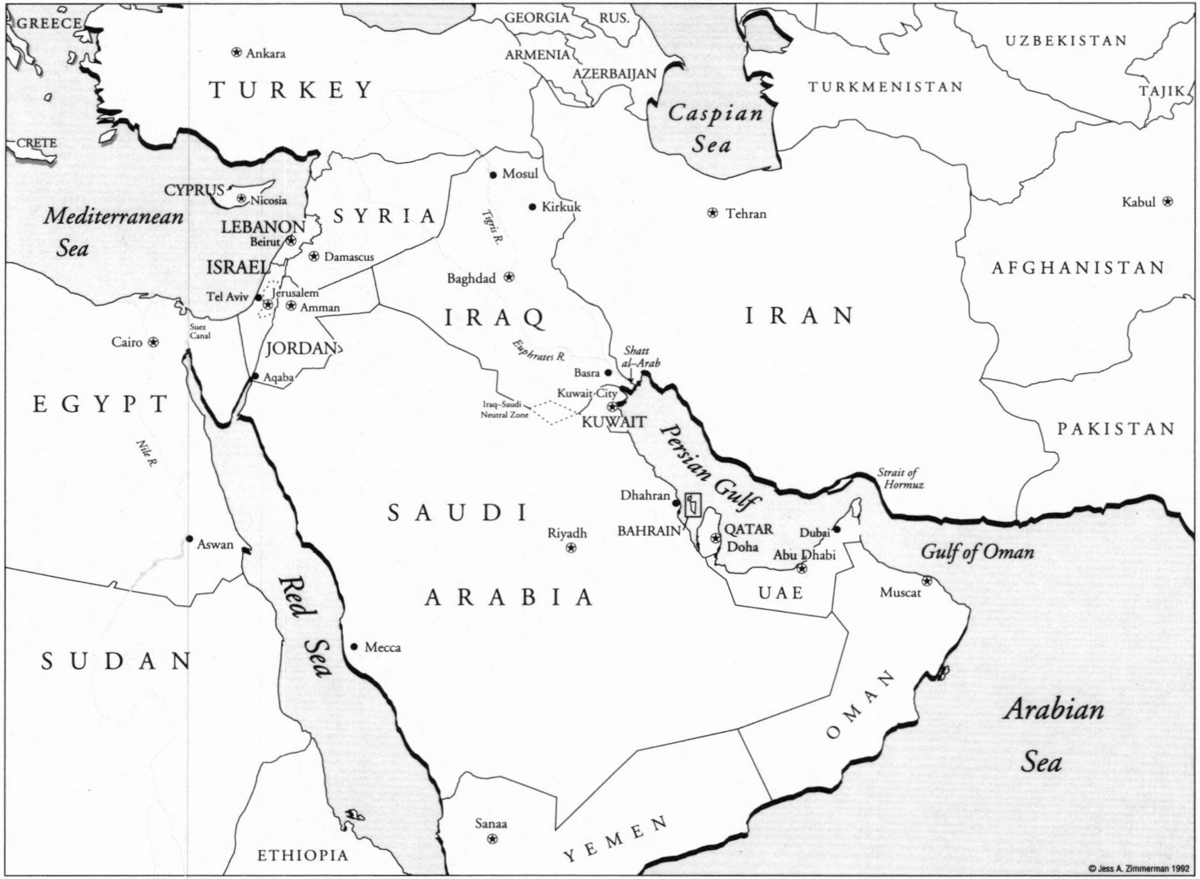

vast potential of oil reserves on the Saudi Arabian peninsula and forged a relationship with the kingdom of Saudi Arabia to help ensure its stability.

Immediately after World War II, the Truman administration made a commitment to the survival of the newly created state of Israel. Ensuring the security of the democratic state of Israel has since been a second major U.S. interest in the region. Pursuit of these two interests from 1948 onward has been difficult because of the view held by most Arab states—abetted by their ability to secure military support from the Soviet Union in the cold war context—that the Jewish state should be destroyed. Over the decades, the United States has had to maintain a precarious balance between pursuit of these two disparate interests. But both have long been regarded as vital national interests and every Congress and administration has had to wrestle with the contradictions involved.

Prior to the 1967 Arab–Israeli War, U.S. interests in the Middle East, while important, were relatively minor as compared with those in Europe and Asia. The positions of Turkey and Iran on the southern border of the Soviet Union gave them a certain strategic value in the context of containment policy, and attempts were made to incorporate them into the network of Western alliances. For essentially moral and domestic political reasons, the United States played an influential role in the creation of Israel in 1947–1948, and after 1948 it remained committed to the new state. At the same time, largely for trade and balance-of-payment reasons, the United States worked to protect and improve the position of American companies developing the oil resources of the Persian Gulf and North Africa. Finally, the United States sought to preserve overflight and transit rights through the Middle East to areas of greater strategic importance.[1]

Since the interests of the United States in the area at that time were limited, its direct involvement in Middle Eastern affairs also tended to be limited. Regional crises that threatened to affect U.S. security interests, such as the Soviet occupation of northwestern Iran (1945–1947), the Suez War of 1956, and the Cyprus Crisis of 1967, occasionally provoked a vigorous response. For the most part, however, the United States sought to escape becoming entangled in local affairs, avoiding, for example, the role of principal arms supplier to Israel or the Arab states. Generally, American policymakers evaluated specific events in the Middle East in terms of how they affected U.S. interests elsewhere and reacted to them—or ignored them—accordingly. Little effort was expended on dealing with the underlying causes of such events or on developing a comprehensive policy for the region as a whole.

Starting in the mid 1960s, however, a series of political and economic changes in both the Middle East and the rest of the world combined to increase the importance of the region to U.S. national security. Among such changes were the enormous increase in oil consumption throughout the world, particularly in the industrialized nations, Israeli occupation of Arab lands in the 1967 war, announcement of British withdrawal from the Persian Gulf area in 1968, and the growth of the role of the Soviet Union in the area.

The cumulative impact of those changes on the relationship between the United States and the states of the Middle East was threefold. First, several U.S.

interests in the region, which previously had been of only marginal concern to government policymakers (although not necessarily marginal to the domestic American political and economic groups most concerned with them), were elevated to the level of vital national interests. The availability of Middle Eastern oil is the best example of such an interest. Second, the growing Soviet presence and declining British power made it important that alternative means be found to protect these newly important interests in the region. Third, the various U.S. interests in the Middle East, which previously had been treated by policymakers as essentially separate, such as Israel and Persian Gulf oil, increasingly became intertwined.

On August 2, 1990, less than two years after the end of its devastating, but inconclusive, eight-year war with Iran, Iraq stunned the world with a lightning armored thrust into the tiny kingdom of Kuwait. Within 48 hours the Iraqi blitzkrieg was over, Kuwait became the "19th province" of Iraq, and the world faced its first crisis of the post–cold war era. The United States quickly took the lead in the United Nations, organized a global coalition to oppose Iraqi aggression, and on January 16th, 1991, launched operation "Desert Storm." The result was the liberation of Kuwait by allied forces numbering over three quarters of a million troops, thousands of aircraft, and nearly two hundred warships—all in a brief, brilliant 44-day campaign.

The Persian Gulf war became the precipitating event for a new era, both for the region and the world as a whole. Coming as it did at the end of the cold war,

Table 18.1 The Middle East: Basic Economic Indicators

Country	*GDP (1990) (billions of dollars)*	*Population (millions)*	*Area (thousands of square miles)*
Algeria	45.43	26.3	919.6
Bahrain	4.01	0.5	0.2
Egypt	39.45	56.0	386.7
Iran	59.49	53.8	636.0
Iraq	40.78	19.9	167.9
Israel	51.22	4.8	8.0
Jordan	3.87	4.3	37.7
Kuwait	25.31	2.1	6.9
Lebanon	3.37	2.7	4.0
Libya	28.96	4.8	679.4
Morocco	25.36	25.4	274.5
Oman	9.16	1.5	82.0
Qatar	7.05	0.4	4.2
Saudi Arabia	87.97	10.6	830.3
Syria	17.41	12.8	71.5
Tunisia	12.42	9.2	63.2
United Arab Emirates	33.67	1.7	32.3
Republic of Yemen	7.98	11.5	217.8

Sources: International Institute for Strategic Studies, *The Military Balance: 1991–92* (London: Brasseys, 1991) and *The Economist World Atlas and Almanac* (London: Economist Books, 1991).

it may come to be judged a turning point in history. For the first time, the United States became massively involved militarily on the ground in the Middle East, thus becoming a significant part of the balance of power in the Persian Gulf. It cannot henceforth extricate itself without affecting that balance.

Significantly, for the first time, too, the United States found itself unopposed in a regional conflict by its archenemy of the cold war, the Soviet Union. Although the Soviet Union attempted to broker a separate, negotiated solution to the Persian Gulf crisis, the attempt failed, and it found itself allied with the United States and the West for the first time since World War II. And soon after the Gulf war the Soviet Union itself dissolved into a loose confederation of independent states, with some even declaring complete independence.

The fundamental restructuring of the world order altered relationships in the Middle East. The more traditional Arab societies of the Gulf region that had attempted to keep themselves shielded from outside influences suddenly found themselves deluged with hundreds of thousands of non-Arabs who had come as defenders of the Saudi kingdom or liberators of the Kuwaiti emirate. The coalition military's forces and the foreign business people who arrived in the wake of the war brought their own concepts of democratization and pluralism to challenge the region's conservative political cultures. Partly as a consequence, the 1990s promise to produce a far different set of outcomes for the political processes, the military balance of power, and the social structures of the Middle East.

The growing linkage between its increasingly important interests in the region has produced a number of thorny problems for the United States as it has continually found itself trying to reconcile interests that appear to be mutually contradictory but that must be pursued simultaneously. Let us turn to an examination of those interests.

Oil Interests. As Table 18.2 shows, the Middle East is the most important source of world oil exports. Although Syria and Turkey are small producers, the overwhelming bulk of the area's production and reserves is found in the Persian Gulf area. Three-fourths of Japan's and two-thirds of Western Europe's oil imports originate in this unstable region. In the early 1990s, only about 12.2 percent of U.S. imports came from the Gulf area; but, of course, if Gulf oil exports were cut off because of regional hostilities, insurgencies, terrorism, or a variety of other reasons, the impact on world energy supplies would be severe, and Japanese and Western Europeans would be competing with Americans for supplies located elsewhere.

Not only is the Gulf region overwhelmingly predominant in the world's supply picture at present, it will continue to play this vital role at least to the end of the century. Well over one-half, perhaps two-thirds of the world's proven reserves are found in the area. Moreover, none of the significant producers—Saudi Arabia, Iraq, Kuwait, Iran, and the United Arab Emirates—is a large consumer. Hence, over 90 percent of the oil produced there is available for export.

The West's energy stake in the Middle East provides a strategic dimension to

Table 18.2 World Oil Production (in Thousands of Barrels Daily)

Region	*Production*				*Percentage of World Production*			
	1990	*1988*	*1985*	*1979*	*1990*	*1988*	*1985*	*1979*
Middle East	16,696	14,482	10,870	21,857	27.7	25.0	19.1	33.1
Former USSR, Eastern Europe, China	14,577	15,467	14,650	14,364	24.1	26.7	25.7	21.8
North America	8,549	9,537	12,185	12,010	14.0	16.5	21.4	18.2
Africa	5,977	4,969	5,285	6,704	9.9	8.6	9.2	10.1
South/Central America	6,975	6,217	6,655	5,558	11.6	10.7	11.7	8.4
Far East and Australia	2,891	2,640	3,280	2,974	4.8	4.6	5.7	4.5
Western Europe	4,100	3,956	3,940	2,380	6.8	6.8	6.9	3.6
Total	*60,385*	*57,832*	*56,865*	*65,847*				

Sources: Oil and Gas in 1979, Shell Oil Co., April, 1980; *Statistical Review of World Energy, 1986,* British Petroleum, 1986; *OPEC Annual Statistical Bulletin, 1990,* Organization of Petroleum Exporting Countries, 1990.

Note: Percentages do not total 100 because of rounding.

regional competition in the post–cold war era. As James Schlesinger has written, "This larger dimension places in proper perspective such matters as fuel shortages and economic performance—for it has the power to determine the political destiny of mankind. . . . The underlying implications are stark."[2]

American oil companies have been actively involved in the Middle East since 1933, when Standard Oil of California obtained its first concession in Saudi Arabia. By 1966 the United States had invested slightly over $3 billion in oil operations throughout the Middle East and North Africa. That investment was extremely profitable. In 1966 alone, U.S. income from direct investments in oil operations in the Middle East amounted to over $1 billion. Such profits, in turn, played a major role in maintaining the favorable balance of payments that the United States enjoyed during most of that period.[3] Yet, despite its deriving substantial benefits from the revenues obtained from the production and sale of Middle Eastern oil, the United States itself made relatively little direct use of the oil. Until the late 1960s, America's energy needs were largely met by domestic oil, gas, and coal production—supplemented to a moderate degree by oil imported from Canada and Latin America. Most of the oil produced by U.S. companies in the Middle East was sold in Western Europe and Japan.

By 1965, however, petroleum consumption was beginning to rise rapidly throughout the world. For example, in the decade between 1964 and 1974, U.S. consumption rose roughly 60 percent—from 10 million barrels per day (mb/d) to 16.2 mb/d. During the same period, Japan's daily consumption rose even more dramatically—from 1.5 mb/d to 5.3 mb/d. Consumption in the industrialized countries of Western Europe also rose steeply.[4] Furthermore, a number of developing countries began to use significant amounts of oil in their efforts to industrialize.

Reprinted with permission of Renan R. Lurie from his book *Lurie's Worlds*, 1970–1980. University Press of Hawaii and King Features Syndicate, Inc.

The rapid increase in world oil consumption after 1965 affected U.S. interests in the Middle East in two ways. First, domestic American oil production could not be expanded rapidly enough to keep pace with growing domestic consumption; indeed, U.S. production peaked in 1970 and began a slow decline thereafter until oil began to flow from Alaska in mid 1977 and temporarily halted the slide. The United States resorted increasingly to imported oil to satisfy its growing appetite. Since oil production by traditional foreign suppliers such as Venezuela and Canada was limited, an ever larger share of America's exploding imports came from the Middle East. By 1990 the share of U.S. oil consumption imported was about 50 percent, including roughly 2 mb/d from the Middle East.

Although the U.S. economy would likely not collapse were it to be deprived of oil imports, it would suffer severe dislocations. As indicated above, key allies such as Japan and the Western European countries are far more dependent than we on Middle Eastern oil; in all likelihood a prolonged interruption in their imports would literally bring about their economic collapse. Since the economic health and political stability of Western Europe and Japan are vital to U.S. national security, it is crucial to us that they have access to adequate supplies of Middle Eastern oil.

Second, the rapid increase in world oil consumption after 1965 fundamentally altered the conditions governing the production and distribution of oil. Before then, the major oil companies had been able to ensure that the supply of oil slightly exceeded demand. By 1970, however, the supply of oil was not increasing fast enough to keep up with escalating demand, and competition among consumers for available oil intensified.

Producing nations gradually realized that the market for oil had become a "seller's market" and took advantage of the new conditions to nationalize the oil business and to raise prices. Between 1968 and 1975, the average price of oil increased from less than $2 per barrel to roughly $11 per barrel.[5] Most of this increase occurred at the end of 1973 and in early 1974 when prices were quadrupled following an embargo by Arab producers against the Americans (and the Netherlands) because of their support for Israel during the 1973 Arab–Israeli War. In the United States and other importing nations, such steep increases led to serious balance-of-payments problems and contributed to inflation. U.S. policymakers belatedly realized that they had a strong interest in ensuring reliable access to Middle Eastern oil at acceptable prices.

The phenomenal rise in the price of oil after 1968 had the effect of transferring unprecedented sums of money to the governments of the Middle Eastern oil-producing countries. But marked decreases in consumption and the glutted oil market of the early 1980s led to sharply reduced prices and revenues. Saudi revenues had fallen from nearly $100 billion in 1980 to only $17 billion in 1986. Moreover, by the late 1980s and early 1990s, wars and arms races had further eroded the oil-rich Arab state coffers. In April 1992, Saudi Arabia experienced unprecedented difficulty in financing major arms purchases; it had to borrow $2.7 billion to make payments on its 1988 al-Yamamah arms deal with Britain.[6]

The turbulent 1970s with their dramatic price jumps and the Iranian revolution, which temporarily cut world supplies by over 4 mb/d, called into question the West's drift into heavy dependency on Middle East oil. Then, in 1980, the Iran–Iraq War broke out, posing a fresh threat to oil supplies, for both sides attacked the other's production and refinery facilities. Despite the consequent loss of about 3 mb/d of exports, oil was initially plentiful, for there were unprecedented stocks on hand throughout the world. Nor did the years of conflict, including a heated "tanker war" in the Persian Gulf beginning in 1984, seriously threaten oil flows from the Gulf. Pipelines now can divert 1 to 2 mb/d of Saudi and Iraqi oil to the Red Sea, but the 8 mb/d or more exported through the Gulf still account for a major proportion of the free world's oil consumption and over 40 percent of the oil in world trade. Hence, effective closure of the twenty-eight-mile-wide Strait of Hormuz at the Gulf's entrance, which might well occur in several contingencies, could bring chaos to the economies of Europe and Japan. The risk during the Persian Gulf crisis of 1990–1991 was not only that the conflict would interrupt the supply of oil, but also that if Saddam Hussein were to gain control over Arabian Gulf oil reserves *and* the choke point of the Strait of Hormuz, he would have been in a position to set a monopoly price on the world's oil.

Strategic Interests. After World War II, the Middle East was an area of strategic competition between the United States and the Soviet Union, as it had earlier been between Britain and Russia or Britain and Germany. Traditionally, the primary U.S. strategic goal in the Middle East was simply to keep the Soviets out. For their part, the Soviet designs upon the Persian Gulf area long predated the predominance of oil in international politics. They were tellingly expressed by Soviet Foreign Minister V. M. Molotov in 1940 at the time of the Ribbentrop–Molotov accords, when the Nazis and the Soviet Union temporarily agreed on their respective shares of the world they planned to dissect. Molotov's statement at the time was that "the area south of Batum and Baku in the general direction of the Persian Gulf is recognized as the center of the aspirations of the Soviet Union."[7] Unsuccessful Russian efforts immediately after World War II to extend their hegemony in that direction by annexing territories in eastern Turkey and western Iran provided one of the opening volleys of the cold war. The rise of Middle East oil as the engine of industrialization merely added an important dimension to that longstanding Russian aspiration for direct access to the warm waters of the Persian Gulf and the Indian Ocean.

American policies in the Middle East were largely responses to the perceived Soviet threat. Between 1945 and 1955, the greatest danger seemed to come from direct Soviet military and political pressure on the countries along its southern border. Consequently, both Turkey and Iran were given large amounts of military and economic aid. Turkey was incorporated into NATO in 1952, and in 1955 both Iran and Turkey joined the Baghdad Pact.*

After the Egypt–Czechoslovakia arms deal of 1955 and the Suez Crisis of 1956, another threat came to the fore: internal subversion fomented by the Soviet Union and its "clients" in the region. The United States responded by continuing to provide aid and by pressing for internal reforms that would reduce the appeal of subversive doctrines. As Soviet influence grew in the area, particularly in Egypt, economic assistance was increasingly used in the competition for position. However, the most dramatic response to the perceived threat of Soviet penetration in the area came in 1957 when the United States promulgated the Eisenhower Doctrine.[8] In it the United States pledged that it would come to the aid, with military force if necessary, of any Middle Eastern country threatened by the forces of "international communism." The doctrine served as the basis for committing U.S. troops to Lebanon in 1958 at the request of President Chamoun.

After the 1967 Arab–Israeli War, a further threat came from the massive quantities of conventional weapons, accompanied by Soviet technicians and military personnel, which the Soviet Union sent to sympathetic regimes such as Egypt, Syria, and Iraq. The United States responded by building up the military power of its own friends in the region: Israel, Iran, and, to a much lesser degree, Saudi Arabia and Jordan.

---

*The original members of the Baghdad Pact were Iraq, Turkey, Iran, Pakistan, and Great Britain. Although instrumental in creating the pact, the United States never became a formal member. Iraq withdrew from the pact after the 1958 revolution.

When Britain announced in 1968 the planned withdrawal of its small but important military forces in the Gulf region, it was apparent to all that instability would be the likely result, with a probable strengthening of Soviet influence. Accordingly, the United States—by this time embroiled in Vietnam—sought to bolster the principal friendly states in the area, namely Saudi Arabia and Iran, with the expectation that they would provide a stabilizing influence. This "two-pillar policy" was shaky from the start, for the Shah of Iran had his own ideas of reestablishing Persian predominance in the region, and the Saudis, despite their economic and cultural influence, lacked the strength to protect themselves, let alone protect others. Moreover, as events a decade later would show, the Iranian pillar, while outwardly sound, was fatally weak at its center and could not bear the policy weight and hopes placed upon it.

The Western desire to contain and minimize Soviet influence in the Middle East was intensified by the Soviet naval build-up in the Indian Ocean and by the increasing Soviet role in the Horn of Africa. From approximately 1970 on, American efforts to limit Soviet influence in the area were increasingly tempered by reluctance to become involved in a military confrontation as a result of conflict in the Middle East. A series of events, starting with the commitment of Soviet pilots and missile troops to Egypt in 1970 after its "war of attrition" with Israel, and including President Nixon's global military alert on October 25, 1973, apparently convinced both American and Soviet policymakers that the danger of such a confrontation was very real.[9]

U.S. Interests in Israel. Since 1948, one of the most enduring features of U.S. policy in the Middle East has been a commitment to the security of Israel. This has been true despite periodic contentions between the two nations, such as that which occurred when Israel invaded Egypt in 1956, or when Israel pressed ahead with settlements on the West Bank of the Jordan River after the Camp David peace accords at the end of the 1970s. Israel has been characterized by its supporters as a reliable ally and a democratic bridgehead in an otherwise anti-American, undemocratic region. Alternatively, some have described it as a regional police officer and potential U.S. surrogate that could be used to keep radical, pro-Soviet states, such as Nasser's Egypt, in line. Sometimes associated with those rationales was the view that, in a Middle East crisis, U.S. support for Israel has been deemed essential to maintaining the credibility of U.S. commitments abroad.[10]

While all these points contained elements of truth, the *intensity* of the American commitment to Israel's security is often more a function of U.S. domestic politics than strategic reasoning. Domestic support for Israel exists in two forms. First, and clearly important, is the broad, general sympathy for Israel which characterizes a large portion of the American population. This basic view tends to be shared by both policymakers and their constituents and is usually independent of any specific developments in the Middle East—although Israel's accelerated settlement of the occupied West Bank area, its 1982 invasion of Lebanon, and its forcible suppression of Palestinian aspirations have eroded that base in the past decade.

The second source of U.S. domestic support for Israel is the highly publicized "Jewish lobby." The Jewish lobby is a coalition of social, cultural, and political groups which seeks to inform American opinion and to influence U.S. policies on subjects of particular interest to the American Jewish community, the most important of which is American support for Israel. Although representing only a tiny portion of the American population, the lobby is highly organized, well financed, and extraordinarily persuasive.[11] (There are other "ethnic" lobbies in Washington as well, such as the Greek lobby that succeeded in cutting off American military aid to Turkey, but these other groups are pale shadows in terms of influence.)

Since 1966, American policies in support of Israel have changed character. Between 1948 and 1966, the United States provided Israel with large amounts of financial and economic aid but relatively little military aid. At the same time, it repeatedly sought to draw Israel and its Arab neighbors into cooperative technical agreements that could serve as a basis for eventual coexistence. In 1966, responding to Israeli fears of increased Soviet arms deliveries to Egypt and Syria, the United States altered its arms supply policy by agreeing to provide Israel with large quantities of modern military equipment. Despite its overwhelming victory in 1967, Israel was incapable of using its military superiority to obtain a secure peace; rather, as the Europeans—who had been its principal suppliers—withdrew their support, Israel's demands on the United States for support increased. During the 1973 Arab–Israeli War, Israel received an emergency package of $2 billion worth of U.S. arms, some of which were taken directly from U.S. operational reserves in Germany.[12]

Although by 1974 the United States was again trying to use its influence to obtain a mutually acceptable settlement to the Arab–Israeli conflict, it also continued to supply large quantities of military aid to Israel.* Secretary of State Kissinger's effort to use American arms aid as a bargaining lever with Israel during negotiation of the Sinai peace accords in this period (1974) illustrated both the importance of the instrument and the strength of the Jewish lobby. During the bargaining, Israel's supporters obtained the signatures of seventy-four U.S. senators instructing the Secretary of State to stand "firmly with Israel in the search for peace in future negotiations," and asserting that "this promise is the basis of the current reassessment of U.S. policy in the Middle East."[13]

After the 1973 war, a primary Israeli security goal was to acquire sufficient military resources to conduct a successful three-week "war of annihilation" against the combined forces of Egypt, Syria, Jordan, Iraq, and Saudi Arabia without having to rely on continuing external (i.e., U.S.) support. By 1977, U.S. military aid had enabled Israel essentially to achieve that goal. This assurance of

---

*Part of the Israeli price for cooperating with Secretary Kissinger's step-by-step diplomacy in 1973–1974 was a U.S. commitment to substantial increases in arms deliveries. Israeli strategists anticipated receiving $2.5 billion worth of U.S. military assistance annually up to approximately 1990. See McLaurin et al., *Foreign Policy Making in the Middle East* (New York: Praeger, 1977), pp. 213–214. From FY 1977 through FY 1986, such military aid did, in fact, average $1.55 billion per year. See DOD Security Assistance Agency, *Foreign Military Sales*, September 30, 1986, pp. 24–25.

supply, combined with Israel's military predominance in the region, seriously reduced the possibility of American pressure toward diplomatic flexibility, as did the subsequent removal of Egypt—via the Camp David accords—as a possible opponent, and indeed it gave Israel the option of redressing any perceived changes in the regional balance of power by launching a "preventive war," without having to worry about short-term U.S. supply pressure or restraint.[14]

The June 1982 Israeli invasion of Lebanon was in part the consequence of this absence of a basis for American pressure on Israel. Israeli forces invaded southern Lebanon and eventually laid siege to West Beirut, forcing the withdrawal of Palestine Liberation Organization (PLO) forces, all without recourse to external military support. U.S. protestations over civilian casualties and use of U.S. weapons restricted by agreement to defensive purposes were not heeded. As a result, both Israel and the United States were drawn into the quagmire of Lebanon's civil war, and both incurred serious human and political costs before they were able to withdraw.

As in previous periods following an Arab–Israeli war, the pace of quantitative and qualitative build-ups in military equipment across the Middle East accelerated after the Lebanon crisis of 1982–1983. By the early 1990s, the region was one of the most heavily armed in the world (Table 18.3).

Factors Affecting Regional Stability. The ability of the United States to pursue its interests in the Middle East has been affected significantly by a number of regional issues already mentioned. However, such highly visible issues have been only part of the problem. Underlying, and to a certain degree causing, such issues is the general political and social instability that characterizes much of the region.

Sources of Instability. Most Middle Eastern states are relatively recent creations, although the peoples living within them may have been there for a very long time. Many of the states were either created or significantly altered in a highly arbitrary fashion by the European powers that dominated the region after World War I.* Furthermore, the political systems set up to govern the new entities often owed more to the values and ideals of the Europeans, than they did to those of the vast bulk of the people governed by them. Thus, monarchies were established in Egypt and Iraq, while Syria became a secular republic. Only in the Arabian Peninsula and, to a much lesser extent, Iran did traditional political institutions maintain their vitality.

The way most Middle Eastern states were formed created inconsistencies that led to major problems once European control was removed. Borders had generally been drawn to satisfy the interest of the European powers and not according to

*For example, Iraq was formed in 1920 when the former Ottoman provinces of Baghdad, Basra, and Mosul were granted to Great Britain as a League of Nations mandate. It did not become an independent state until 1932. Prior to World War I, Iraq was a geographic term with virtually no political significance.

Table 18.3 Principal Regional Forces in the Middle East, 1992

Country/Service	*Regular Forces*	*Reserves*	*Main Armament*
Egypt (pop. 56,018,800)			
Army	290,000	500,000	3,190 tanks 3,360 AFV 1,258 arty.
Navy	20,500	14,000	5 maj. cbts. 4 attk. subs. 39 ptl. cft. 17 armed hel.
Air Force	30,000	20,000	495 cbt. acft. 74 armed hel.
Paramilitary	374,000		
Iran (pop. 53,766,400)			
Army	305,000	350,000	700 tks. 750 AFV 1,000 arty.
Navy	18,000		8 maj. cbts. 29 ptl. cft.
Air Force	35,000		213 cbt. acft.
Revolutionary Guard	170,000		
Paramilitary	1,047,000		
Iraq (pop. 19,854,600)			
Army	350,000		2,300 tks. 2,000 AFV 1,000 arty.
Navy	2,500		16 ptl. cft.
Air Force	30,000		230 cbt. acft.
Israel (pop. 4,822,000)			
Army	104,000	494,000	4,488 tks. 5,900 AFV 1,420 arty.
Navy	9,000	1,000	3 attk. subs. 65 ptl. cft.
Air Force	28,500	9,000	603 cbt. acft. 94 armed hel.
Paramilitary	6,000		
Jordan (pop. 4,275,000)			
Army	90,000	30,000	1,131 tks. 1,160 AFV 242 arty.
Coast Guard	300		1 ptl. cft.
Air Force	11,000		113 cbt. acft. 24 armed hel.
Paramilitary	231,000		

Table 18.3 Principal Regional Forces in the Middle East, 1992 *(continued)*

Country/Service	*Regular Forces*	*Reserves*	*Main Armament*
Saudi Arabia (pop. 10,600,000)			
Army	45,000		700 tks. 2,200 AFV 499 arty.
Navy	9,500		8 frigates 12 ptl. cft.
Air Force	19,000		253 cbt. acft.
National Guard	55,000		
Paramilitary	11,000		
Syria (pop. 12,748,800)			
Army	300,000	392,000	4,350 tks. 3,750 AFV 2,186 arty.
Navy	4,500	8,000	3 subs. 2 frigates 25 ptl. cft.
Air Force	40,000		651 cbt. acft. 100 armed hel.
Paramilitary	9,000		
Yemen (pop. 11,500,000)			
Army	60,000	40,000	1,275 tks. 970 AFV 547 arty.
Navy	3,500		27 ptl. cft.
Air Force	2,000		101 cbt. acft. 20 armed hel.
Paramilitary	40,000		

Source: International Institute for Strategic Studies, *The Military Balance, 1991–1992* (London: IISS, 1991), pp. 98–123. For abbreviations see Table 17.1.

significant local criteria.* As a result, some ethnic or cultural groups that traditionally conceived of themselves as a community were split among two or more artificial political entities. In other cases, cohesive linguistic or religious minorities were incorporated into states dominated by their traditional antagonists. Trading patterns and tribal migration routes were disrupted. As a result, the level of national cohesion and political solidarity in the states of the Middle East

*Two cases of such arbitrarily drawn boundaries were to become particularly troublesome. First, Ottoman Syria (predominantly Sunni Moslem Arabs) was carved up into the states of Palestine, Transjordan, Syria, and Lebanon, with a sizable part also incorporated into Turkey. Second, the substantial Kurdish community was split up among Iran, Turkey, and Iraq. Kurds thus became a dominated minority in all three states.

tended to be low. In all parts of the region, the primary focuses of loyalty were the family, village, and tribe. Beyond that, ties of regionalism, ethnic and cultural solidarity, and religion competed vigorously with the new states for popular allegiance.

The problems created by such conflicting loyalties were accentuated by the growth of intense feelings of nationalism which had spread throughout the region by the end of World War II. Although virtually all the nationalists could agree that the corrupt, European-dominated old order had to be destroyed, their conflicting loyalties made it difficult for them to develop alternative systems to replace it. Some nationalists favored creating a state based on an Islamic revival that eventually would incorporate all Moslems from West Africa to Indonesia. Others thought in terms of a pan-Arab movement that would unite all Arabs—Moslem and Christian—into a single state. Still others sought merely to rejuvenate the existing states on either an Islamic or a secular basis. No nationalist group was willing to relinquish the power it had obtained to other nationalist groups whose ideas differed in any way from its own.[15]

Their colonial origins and such basic disagreement over the legitimate scope, goals, and methods of political activity had two important effects on the new nationalist regimes. First, it became virtually impossible for such regimes to create political institutions capable of transferring power or resolving differences over basic policies. At the same time, the constituency of each significant version of nationalism reached beyond the boundaries of any state it happened to control. For example, the Ba'th party, which ruled Syria in the mid 1960s, had to cope with a large group of Syrian nationalists whose primary loyalty was to President Nasser of Egypt, but they also enjoyed the support of many sympathizers in Iraq, Jordan, and Lebanon. (The generalizations in this entire section apply widely in the Moslem portions of the region, i.e., to the vast bulk of area; Israel had a unique origin and has an entirely different set of internal policy dynamics.)

Such conditions contributed to the insecurity of the new nationalist leaders, placing a premium on conspiratorial methods and violence as a way to obtain political power. Leaders sought to provide themselves with a measure of security by forcefully suppressing their opposition while at the same time presenting the best possible set of nationalist credentials to their people. In practice, that meant taking a stronger stand in favor of rapid economic development and against the foreign influence of the former colonial powers, Israel, and the remaining "traditionalist" regimes in the region. Such steps taken by a Middle Eastern leader to increase domestic legitimacy automatically posed a threat to the internal security of his neighbors, who usually were trying to build support in the same way. As a result, minor incidents and differences often took on much greater importance than was warranted. Border clashes and attempts to subvert rival regimes, either through propaganda or the distribution of arms and subsidies to potential dissidents was common.[16] Though smaller in scale, hostilities between and among Arab states have been much more frequent, for example, than Arab–Israeli wars since World War II.

Such problems were further enhanced by the tensions caused by economic change. After World War II, even the most traditional Middle Eastern governments found it necessary to advocate far-reaching economic development programs, if for no other reason than that of self-defense against nationalist pressure. In several countries such programs involved major land reforms, the development of heavy industry, and the growth of state ownership and bureaucratic controls over the economy. Increased taxes, scarcities, and heavy inflation seemed, inevitably, to accompany the new economic policies. The dissatisfaction created by such situations could easily be converted into political unrest.*

In the oil-producing countries, the problems caused by economic development were somewhat different but no less acute. The vast funds generated by the oil industry enabled them to initiate major economic development programs that destabilized the traditional societies and political norms that characterized most of them. Moreover, the shortage of skilled technicians and laborers in the producing countries forced their governments to bring in many foreigners. By the latter 1970s, Americans, Europeans, Egyptians, and Palestinians played key roles in the economies, bureaucracies, and educational systems of the oil-producing countries of the Arabian Peninsula. Yemenis, Pakistanis, and Indians made up much of the unskilled labor force. The role of foreigners in Iraq was far less pervasive but still important. In Iran, the pressure of large numbers of highly visible Westerners was one of the precipitants of the revival of militant Islam and the destruction of the monarchy.

One of the most profound and persistent of the many regional problems in the Middle East is the Arab–Israeli conflict. The special relationship between the United States and Israel, the universal antipathy of both nationalist and traditionalist Arabs to Zionism, and the high level of militarization which characterizes the conflict all make it worthy of special mention.

The Arab–Israeli conflict has its recent roots in the late nineteenth century, when increasingly large numbers of Jews sought to escape from oppression in Eastern Europe by emigration to Palestine. In 1917, prominent British Zionists, led by Chaim Weizmann, induced the British foreign secretary, Lord Balfour, to issue an open letter pledging the British government to "view with favor the establishment in Palestine of a national home for the Jewish people."[17] (Further intensive lobbying by the World Zionist Organization obtained the inclusion of the Balfour Declaration in the text of the League of Nations Mandate for Palestine, granted to Great Britain in 1920.)

The British government delegated the task of supervising the establishment of the Jewish national home to the World Zionist Organization, which created a number of special agencies to do so. Between 1922 and 1946, largely as a result of their efforts, the Jewish population of Palestine rose from 84,000, comprising 11 percent of the total population, to 583,000 comprising 31 percent of the total. Jewish landholding during the same period increased from 2.6 percent to 7

*For example, between 1951 and 1958, the Iraqi monarchy devoted most of its development funds to extensive flood control projects. Although such projects were of tremendous long-term benefit to Iraq, the failure of the regime to devote more funds to conspicuous short-term projects such as public housing was an important stimulus behind the 1958 revolution.

percent of the total area of Palestine and consisted almost entirely of fertile agricultural land along the coast and in Galilee.[18] Inevitably, in many cases the growth of the Jewish community was achieved at the expense of the Arab population of Palestine—or at least the Arabs intensely believed so.

Arab resentment, combined with a growing awareness of ultimate Jewish political aims, led to a series of bloody riots culminating in the Arab Revolt of 1936. Although the British eventually crushed the revolt, many Jewish settlers were not satisfied with the zeal shown by the British authorities in protecting Jewish interests. By 1938, several clandestine Jewish military groups had been created which conducted terrorist operations against both the Arabs and the British.[19] By 1947, the level of violence had risen to such a degree that Britain decided to give up its mandate and turn the problem over to the United Nations.

On November 28, 1947, with leadership from the United States, the United Nations voted to partition Palestine into two states. The projected Jewish state was to contain 55 percent of the total area of Palestine (the population of the Jewish area was 56 percent Jewish and 44 percent Arab), while the projected Arab state occupied 45 percent of the land (of which the population was 98 percent Arab and 2 percent Jewish). After much debate, Jewish leaders, led by David Ben-Gurion, accepted the U.N. plan and launched a series of military operations designed to consolidate areas placed under Jewish control, while Palestinian leaders rejected the plan and began to attack isolated Jewish settlements.[20] The conflict quickly escalated into a full-scale war, with the armies of five neighboring Arab states intervening haphazardly on the side of the Palestinians while the Israelis obtained sizable quantities of arms and unofficial military assistance from the United States and Europe.[21]* By April 1949, Israel had defeated the combined Arab forces and in the process gained control of a great deal of territory that had not been assigned to it in the original partition plan. Furthermore, over seven hundred thousand Palestinian Arabs had been expelled or fled from their homes and were living as stateless refugees in neighboring Arab countries.

The 1948–1949 Arab–Israeli War was ended by an armistice signed on July 20, 1949. Many Arabs felt that the very existence of Israel was a violation of Arab rights and wanted it destroyed as soon as possible. Others desired to gain revenge for the defeat suffered. Such feelings generated an unremitting hostility toward Israel, leading to continual raids and terrorist attacks on it. In 1964, the Palestine Liberation Organization was created and promptly began conducting the same type of terrorist campaign against Israel that the Israelis had conducted against the British and Arabs before 1948.

On the other hand, some Israelis were not satisfied with the amount of territory occupied by Israeli forces in 1948. These ultranationalist and religious party

*For example, Zionist private arms purchasers were able to provide the Israeli forces with tanks, artillery, and B-17 heavy bombers from the United States as well as Messerschmidt 109K fighters from Czechoslovakia. Furthermore, approximately ten thousand foreign volunteers are estimated to have served in the Haganah in 1948–1949. During that period, all Arab and official Israeli arms requests were blocked by an embargo declared by the United States and Britain.

elements desired to extend Jewish control over all of biblical Israel. Other Israelis felt that it was essential to seize and retain additional Arab land in order to settle the new waves of Jewish immigrants who were expected to arrive in due course and to provide space for future defense of urban centers. Consequently, they were unwilling to make territorial or legal concessions to the Arabs—particularly concerning the Palestinians. Israel responded to Arab threats and harassment with punitive raids against neighboring Arab states in the hope that such displays of superior force eventually would compel Arab leaders to accept the presence of Israel on Israeli terms.[22]

As each side sought, and eventually obtained, outside military assistance to strengthen its position, the level of hostilities rose. Major wars were fought in 1956, 1967, 1973, and again—on a smaller scale—in 1982. Although Israel gained a military victory in each war and greatly augmented its territory in the 1967 conflict, the cost of obtaining such victories rose steadily. Most importantly, the military victories did not ensure Israeli security. For example, though not a participant in the Persian Gulf war of 1990–1991, Israel was attacked by Iraqi Scud missiles. Only through intense U.S. diplomacy was Israel persuaded not to respond militarily in ways that would certainly have widened the war.

Through the late 1970s and into the late 1980s, Israel and its front-line Arab adversaries maintained high military readiness despite severe economic stress.* Serious Islamic-based unrest broke out in Syria early in 1982, and unprecedented fissures in Israeli society resulted from the invasion of Lebanon. Despite the great efforts made, neither party was able to impose its own version of justice and security on the other. However, both sides continued to maintain large military forces and, with the exception of Egypt, following on President Sadat's peace initiative in November 1977, refused to compromise on basic issues such as Palestinian rights, West Bank territorial concessions, and recognition of Israel.

Before 1967, the Arab–Israeli conflict had relatively little effect on U.S. interests in the Middle East; Great Britain and, to a lesser degree, France were the principal Western states involved; the Soviet Union and its satellites were important suppliers to key Arab states. U.S. policy treated the oil-producing countries of the Persian Gulf, the northern tier states (Iran, Iraq, Pakistan, and Turkey), and the nations directly involved in the Arab–Israeli conflict (Israel, Egypt, Syria, and Jordan) as separate areas. Obviously, U.S. support for Israel antagonized the Arab world. During most of that period, however, the oil-producing states felt that the Arab nationalist regimes in Egypt, Syria, and, after 1958, Iraq posed dangerous threats to their own security. Thus, they were willing to cooperate with the United States, despite its support for Israel.

---

*Inflation in Israel at the end of 1980 was approximately 120 percent annually; J.C. Hurewitz, "The Middle East," *Foreign Affairs* 59, no. 3 (1980): 574. Much of the inflation was caused by vast expenditures for defense purposes. See Don Peretz, "The Earthquake: Israel's Ninth Knesset Elections," *Middle East Journal*, no. 31 (Summer 1977), p.8. In January 1978, a major riot broke out in Cairo in which crowds chanted, "Oh hero of the crossing [of the Suez Canal in 1973], give us our breakfast." The riots were caused by the attempts of the Egyptian government to eliminate subsidies that kept the price of food at artificially low levels. President Sadat had to use the army to quell the crowds.

The crushing defeat suffered by the Arabs in 1967 fundamentally changed the political balance in the Arab world. Israeli occupation of Arab lands increased Arab antagonism toward Israel to the point at which it increasingly took precedence over internal Arab or nationalist–traditionalist disputes. In their search for support against Israel, nationalist leaders such as President Nasser modified their regional policies so that they no longer threatened the legitimacy of traditional regimes such as Saudi Arabia. The gradual rapprochement between nationalist and traditionalist regimes was demonstrated in early 1973 with the creation of the informal Cairo–Riyadh axis. The Egyptian–Israeli peace treaty, signed in March 1979 in Washington, D.C., disrupted that axis, with the Saudis joining the other Arabs in opposing Egypt's separate peace with Israel. After a brief period of Arab solidarity under Iraqi leadership, longstanding divisions in the Arab camp resurfaced. Syrian and Libyan support of Iran against Iraq in the Gulf war, contrary to the interests of the Saudis and other gulf Arabs, highlighted this factionalization.[23]

As implied in the preceding paragraph, a sea change in Arab–Israeli affairs occurred in the late 1970s as a result of Egyptian President Sadat's determination to break Egypt out of the disastrous cycle of wars with Israel. His historic peace-making journey to Jerusalem in November 1977, followed by the American-engineered Camp David accords between Israel and Egypt in September 1978, transformed the Middle Eastern political and strategic landscape—the Egypt–Israel Peace treaty of 1979 simply codified this change. In return for restoration of its Sinai territories (captured by Israel in 1967) plus an Israeli promise of autonomy for the predominantly Palestinian West Bank area (also captured in 1967), Egypt shifted from its support of pan-Arab military confrontation to policies of political accommodation and economic cooperation with Israel.

The Egyptian–Israeli peace survived a sustained period of strained relations over Israel's invasion of Lebanon and a dispute over a corner of the Sinai Peninsula (Taba), that was eventually submitted to international arbitration. The other Arab states have proven too weak militarily and too divided politically to challenge Egypt's arrangement with Israel. Meanwhile, regional pressures led Jordan to resume formal ties with Cairo; and other countries, particularly Iraq, renewed wide-ranging trade and political–military contacts with Egypt.

No serious progress was made in the 1980s in resolving the thorny Palestinian problem. Various attempts to focus attention on this central aspect of the Arab–Israeli peace process (e.g., President Reagan's abortive September 1982 peace initiative and his call for an international peace conference in early 1987) ran into a brick wall in the form of the greater-Israel governments of Prime Ministers Begin and Shamir. This left a principal source of regional instability intact, with the possibility that open hostilities could resume at any time. But in 1992, in the aftermath of the Persian Gulf war, U.S. Secretary of State James A. Baker attempted once again to bring the sides together, this time with a new, pragmatic Israeli prime minister, Itzhak Rabin, on one side of the table and more flexible Palestinians and Syrians on the other. With $10 billion in U.S. loans guarantees in the balance, Rabin sought to curtail expansion of Israeli settlements on the West Bank (a particular thorn in Arab sides) and to generate other reconciliation measures toward the Palestinians. The outcome of these efforts remains to be seen.

Iran's Role. Arabs and Iranians have coexisted uneasily within the framework of Islam since the Arab conquest of Iran (formerly Persia) in the seventh century A.D. Whenever subsequent Iranian empires were strong, they dominated Arab-inhabited lands on both sides of the Persian Gulf. On the other hand, when such empires were weak, local Arabs quickly threw off Iranian control. It was during such a period of Iranian weakness in the early nineteenth century that Great Britain established its control over the Arab side of the Gulf. The series of treaties signed by the British with various Persian Gulf rulers had the effect of "freezing" the transitory political situation, which then became a permanent system guaranteed by British power.

Arab–Iranian tension in recent decades stems partly from Arab fears that an increasingly strong Iran will seek to reassert its traditional hegemony over the Gulf. Three factors have combined to intensify such fears. First, between 1968 and 1971, Britain abandoned its role as protector of the Arab states in the Persian Gulf. Although Britain's physical presence in the area after World War II was minuscule, it still served as a deterrent to the ambitions of regional powers such as Iran, Iraq, and Egypt. Second, by 1970 Arab leaders were aware of the Shah's concern over the relatively low level of proven oil reserves in Iran. Although the Shah's stated intention to industrialize Iran before the oil ran out seemed to them all well and good, Arab leaders were not convinced that he would abstain from using force to gain control of Arab oil once Iranian supplies began to fail.

The third, and perhaps most important, factor behind Arab fears of Iranian ambitions was the rapid growth of Iran's capability to achieve them through the use of force. U.S. military assistance had enabled the Shah to expand and strengthen his armed forces considerably after World War II. In American eyes, such forces were designed primarily for internal security and to defend against direct Soviet attacks or, later, to provide one Middle Eastern pillar of regional stability—Saudi forces were to form the other. In the late 1960s, however, the Shah began to purchase large quantities of arms designed to provide Iranian forces with a significant offensive capability. Among such purchases were U.S. destroyers and antisubmarine aircraft, British hovercraft, and several other systems that could only be used in the Persian Gulf or its approaches.* To the

*In 1969, the United States terminated its program of military grants to Iran. All future arms transfers were to be handled on a commercial basis. Ironically, although that action was at least partially intended to limit Iran's acquisition of modern arms, it had the opposite effect. When Iran oil revenues soared after 1973, the Shah was able to embark on a spending spree. See Shahram Chubin and Sepehr Zabih, *The Foreign Relations of Iran* (Berkeley and Los Angeles: University of California Press, 1974), pp. 109–12.

Arabs, it seemed that those forces were oriented directly at them. Neighboring Iraq was particularly sensitive.

From the Iranian point of view, such a military build-up was necessary in order to provide security for vital Persian Gulf oil fields and tanker facilities. The Shah had serious doubts about American effectiveness in the area, the internal stability of the Arab states of the Persian Gulf, and those states' ability to defend themselves or to contain subversion. If necessary, he intended to take action himself. Yet Iranian diplomacy went to great lengths to convince Arab rulers that Iran's military power posed no threat to them. At the same time, however, the Shah did not hesitate to use force to seize three Arab islands in the Persian Gulf in 1971, or to give substantial military support to the Kurdish rebels in Iraq prior to the 1975 Iraq–Iran agreement.[24]

The Arab states responded to the growth of Iranian power in several ways. Some countries, such as Saudi Arabia and Iraq, replied by seeking foreign assistance in building up their own forces, although they never could hope to match Iranian manpower. The Arab reaction to Iranian intervention in Oman's Dhofar Rebellion in 1973 was in many ways characteristic of the unease about Iran. On the one hand, Arab leaders were happy to see Iranian troops suppress a radical movement threatening them all; on the other hand, the presence of Iranian troops on Arab soil was both an embarrassment and a source of dangerous unrest among Arab nationalists.

The Iranian revolution of 1978–1979 upset all the old assumptions, both in Iran and elsewhere in the region. The Shah's accelerated economic development program, carried out largely along Western lines with a heavy infusion of Western technicians and values, had proven profoundly destabilizing. Traditionalists, who felt themselves endangered (the Moslem clergy, landowners, and bazaar merchants, for example), joined in opposition with the disadvantaged (the middle classes and the poor, who suffered from the inflation attending accelerated modernization) and the displaced (primarily the expeasants flocking to the cities in search of jobs in the mismanaged industrial sector).

The precipitating cause of the Shah's downfall was his attempt to crush religious opposition to his rule. At least since the start of the eighteenth century, when Shi'ism was formally adopted as the state religion, Iran's secular rulers had been uneasy partners with its Islamic leaders. In contrast to the Sunni sect of Islam, predominant in Saudi Arabia and most of the rest of the Moslem world, Shi'ism has enough of a hierarchical structure to permit its leaders to impose an alternative authority system. Although Iran's rulers have for centuries shared power with religious leaders, the Shah, who was convinced that the mosque stood against his modernization efforts, squeezed down on the clergy in matters of land reform, religious endowments, schools, and so forth. For a variety of reasons, including the mosque's role as the one secure rallying point and meeting place for all the forces opposed to his rule, the Shah found himself confronted with a genuine popular revolution under the banners of resurgent Islam.

Contributing to the Shah's demise was his increasingly repressive and authoritarian rule in the face of a sizable, politicized middle class. Unfortunately for the regime, partial development successes had helped create the very forces that made authoritarianism no longer tenable. Unwilling to share power with the middle class and alienated from traditionalist support, the Shah became increasingly isolated. By and large his answer to demands that he broaden political participation was repression, further intensifying his problem. Corruption, frustrated popular expectations, the Shah's ill health, and American vacillation about supporting a repressive, corrupt regime added to the brew. The result was massive demonstrations and riots in the streets of Teheran and other major cities, culminating in early 1979 in the Shah's flight and the Ayatollah Khomeini's triumphant return from exile in France to establish a "pure Islamic state."[25]

In large measure, the chaos attending the new regime's birth continued into the 1980s. Especially noteworthy in this regard was the disintegration of the once large, well-armed, and reasonably well-trained Iranian armed forces. Although they had mostly stood aside during the revolutionary upheaval rather than make a widely expected bid for power, the military's senior leaders were executed or retired, or they fled into exile. While many in the lower ranks deserted en masse, revolutionary guards and militia seized the nation's arsenals and distributed their contents. Western technicians, essential to maintaining the advanced weapons systems the Shah had purchased, were pushed out and returned home as quickly as possible. In short, Iran's own defenses became severely weakened; indeed, the Shah's ability to hold the country together by means of the armed forces became doubtful.

At the same time, the new government went out of its way to antagonize and humiliate its traditional ally, the United States. The Ayatollah singled out the United States as "Satan"—the source of religious and cultural pollution, the reason why its lackey, the Shah, could corrupt and repress the nation, and the fount of all evil. Caught up in this ideological crusade and with at least tacit support from the regime, a group of several hundred "students" stormed the U.S. embassy in Teheran in November 1979, taking over fifty American diplomats and marine guards hostage in the process. The United States was able to rally international opinion and law to its side regarding the ancient right of diplomatic immunity, but the Iranians took no notice. Since its economic leverage (essentially, freezing assets and halting trade) was inadequate, and since it was unwilling to use force or agree to Iranian terms for the hostages' release (which included apologies and the return of both the Shah and the billions of dollars the former ruler had purportedly stolen from the Iranian people), the United States was checkmated.

To exploit Iran's weakened, isolated condition and probably as well to preempt Iran's incitement of Iraq's large Shi'ite population, Iraq launched a series of ground and air assaults against Iran in late September 1980. By the end of the month, these assaults had penetrated well into Iran, raising the possibility of an Iranian government collapse and fragmentation of the state. Oil facilities on both sides were destroyed in the first days of fighting, resulting in the temporary loss of over 3 mb/d of oil to the world's markets. But Iraq was unable to prevail over Iran's weakened forces and was forced to withdraw in 1982. Iranian counteroffensive measures against Iraq began immediately and continued on at least an annual basis, producing some of the largest land battles since World War II and resulting in massive casualties, particularly Iranian casualties. (The credibility of U.S. attempts to help terminate the war suffered sharply with the revelation of very small but politically explosive U.S. arms sales to Iran in 1985 and 1986—the Iran–Contra debacle.) Both exhausted, Iran and Iraq mutually agreed in August 1988 to stop the fighting and both sides declared victory!

Other Regional and Extraregional Developments. Turkey occupies a key position in the Middle East, both geographically and functionally. The bridge between Europe and Asia, during the cold war, it was also a barrier between the Soviet Union and the Mediterranean. Simultaneously, it forms the southeastern anchor of NATO and the West's strongest link to what were considered the "northern tier states" of Iran and Pakistan. As noted earlier, the cold war began with the Soviet Union's demands on the Dardenelles Straits and its effort to annex territory in eastern Turkey and Iran.

Yet Turkey has been an uneasy member of the NATO alliance since joining it in 1951, both because of the Turkish exposed flank position and because of the strains within the alliance as a result of continuing Greek–Turkish hostility. The island of Cyprus has been a particular source of contention as the Turks sought to protect the interests of the Turkish minority there against the Greek majority. In 1967 it required strong American pressure to forestall armed Turkish intervention in Cyprus. By 1974 the situation on the island had deteriorated (as had America's influence) to the point that pressure from the United States was no longer sufficient to stave off a Turkish assault. The ensuing warfare on Cyprus ruptured the NATO southeastern flank as Greece withdrew its forces from the alliance, threatening counteraction, and as the United States ceased all economic and military support for Turkey. American intelligence-gathering facilities, which were important in monitoring Soviet communications and missile tests, were also casualties as the Turks reacted to U.S. pressure by halting all American operations within its borders. Partly as a consequence of strained relations with the United States and its other Western allies, Turkey also moved in the 1970s to reduce tension between itself and the Soviet Union. Increasing Soviet trade and economic assistance culminated in 1978 in a twenty-year Soviet–Turkish accord on friendly relations and cooperation.[26]

At the same time that Turkey's ties to the West, particularly to the United States, were deteriorating, so was its political and economic health. By 1980, violence generated by both leftist and rightist factions was claiming about one thousand lives a year; inflation was at a 40 percent annual rate, and inability to pay for needed imports, particularly oil, had brought economic life to the point of near collapse. Violence and political and economic troubles continued to mount, culminating in September 1980 with a military takeover of the government. Miliary coups are familiar phenomena in Turkey, having occurred roughly once a decade as politicians failed to govern effectively.

Civilian rule was restored in 1983, and the military again returned to its traditional guardian role, while political stability and economic growth also returned. Turkey's relations with NATO regained their intimacy and the Turks veered from the 1970s path of accommodation with the Soviet Union. Ingrained Turkish suspicion of Soviet intentions, restimulated by the Soviet occupation of Afghanistan in 1979, led it to allow modernization and expansion of U.S. military bases near its eastern border. During the Persian Gulf war it permitted extensive use of its military facilities by the U.N. coalition. Turkey continues to find common security interests with the United States in the post–cold war era in guarding against any resurgent regional threat from Iraq, in balancing the potential power of Iran and in keeping a lid on the Balkan crisis in southern Europe.

Two other major developments affecting the region in the 1980s occurred on its flanks: in the Horn of Africa and in Afghanistan. In the Horn (comprising Ethiopia, Djibouti, and Somalia), at the close of the 1970s, the Soviet Union had established a position of strength deeply worrisome to both the West and the neighboring states on both sides of the Red Sea. Cuban proxy forces and Soviet arms and advisers helped Ethiopia to defeat a Somali-supported revolt in its eastern Ogaden territories (1978) and to check the longstanding Eritrean independence movement (1979). Accompanying these African adventures of the Soviet Union and its Cuban proxies were pro-Soviet developments in the two Yemens across the Strait of Bab el Mandeb. In both Western and Arab capitals, the concern grew that the Soviet Union was engaged in a giant pincers movement directed at Middle Eastern oil resources.

The other arm of the pincers took initial shape in April 1978 when a communist coup in hitherto neutralist, but Soviet-leaning, Afghanistan occurred. Despite significant Soviet assistance and the proximity of Soviet armies, anticommunist Afghans turned on their new Marxist masters in an escalating insurgency. By the autumn of 1979, it had become clear that the Afghan communist regime could not survive as its army melted away in desertions and its civilian support similarly evaporated. Faced with the choice of seeing a client regime disappear or massively intervening to support it—perhaps seizing the opportunity to position itself more favorably for a subsequent move into the Middle East proper—the Soviet Union chose intervention. In December 1979 it invaded with the first echelons of what quickly became an 80,000-troop intervention force (and which subsequently increased to 115,000 to 120,000 troops).

Afghan resistance, which had been on the point of bringing down the native communists, rallied against the Soviet occupiers. Despite massive firepower and the mobility that helicopters and armored vehicles gave the Soviet forces, by mid 1987 they had made little or no progress in subjugating the Afghans. Various Moslem states sent the rebels arms and money as did the United States through neighboring Pakistan. After nearly eight years and at great cost, the Soviets had undermined their own Afghan instruments, deeply frightened other regimes (within the reach of the Soviet conventional forces), and galvanized the West into a series of counteractions.

In February 1988 Mikhail Gorbachev declared Soviet intentions to withdraw from Afghanistan and by 15 February 1989, after some 15,000 casualties, the withdrawal was complete. Similarly, the Soviets abruptly halted the other arm of its "pincer," forcing the Ethiopian government to negotiate with its Eritrean foes.

Fundamentalism versus Secularism. The rise of Islamic fundamentalism as a dynamic movement for political change in the Middle East was dramatically demonstrated by the growing turmoil in prerevolutionary Iran in the early 1970s. It was clearly triggered by the growing perception that Shah Reza Pahlevi was determined to transform Iran into a modern secular autocracy with leanings to the non-Moslem West. Once the Shah was successfully deposed in 1979 and replaced by a Khomeini-led theocracy, the appeal of fundamentalism quickly spread to the Shi'ite and other Moslem sects, most notably in Egypt, the Sudan, the Mahgreb states of North Africa, and in South and Southeast Asia. In the 1990s it has become a political force in the Moslem republics of the former Soviet Union.

What is Islamic fundamentalism? In simple terms it is a belief in the literal application in everyday life, enforced by government, of the *Sharia*—the code of conduct laid down in the Koran, as interpreted by "holy men" or mullahs. In practice, it is antidemocratic, puritanical, xenophobic, and occasionally violent. But in broader terms it is best understood as a religiously based alternative to nationalism.* As such, it finds fertile ground in the Middle East for the following reasons:

1. The nation-states in the region have artificial boundaries that were drawn in colonial times without regard to ethnic or religious homogeneity or to economic viability.
2. The Moslem states of the region have an authoritative tradition resistant to popular participation in the governance process.
3. There is a common perception in the Arab world and Iran that all political and social change must be consistent with Islamic principles.

The power of the concepts and ultimate goals of Islamic fundamentalism are poorly comprehended in the non-Moslem world. Americans and Europeans are inclined to prefer the region's more familiar secular autocracy over unpredictable theocracy, especially in countries of strategic significance to them. There is also a proclivity in the West to equate fundamentalism with international terrorism,

*The relationship between fundamentalism and nationalism as factors in international security is ably discussed by Vitaly Naumkin (Paper I) and Bassma Kodmani-Darwish (Paper II) in "International Security and the Forces of Nationalism and Fundamentalism," International Institute for Strategic Studies, *Adelphi Papers 266*, Winter 1991/1992, Nuffield Press Ltd., Oxford, Great Britain. A classic text on the various Islamic sects in the context of the overall political culture of the Arab world is Albert Hourani's *A History of the Arab Peoples* (Cambridge, Mass.: Harvard University Press, 1991).

ignoring the reality that the two are largely unrelated. Fundamentalist Iran has demonstrably sponsored terrorism abroad, but so too have other regional powers (e.g., Libya, Iraq, and Syria) whose leaders resist fundamentalism. There is gathering evidence that all four of these states are currently seeking to shed their terrorist image in a new global environment that subordinates political machoism to economic success.

A decline in terrorism, however, will not nullify fundamentalism as a threat to U.S. security interests in the Middle East, because its primary targets are secular regimes in the oil-exporting states of the region. A fundamentalist overthrow of such regimes, whose pragmatism (and fears of just such an event) have led them to cooperate with the oil-consuming democracies, could dangerously politicize the petroleum industry, with potentially devastating impact on the global economy. Moreover, fundamentalist regimes would be more hostile both to democratic experimentation and the state of Israel.

The hard truth is that the vast majority of people in the Middle East are, with considerable justification, disenchanted with their national governments. That majority is swelled by widespread Palestinian diaspora, which has no government of its own. Fundamentalism provides a spiritually orthodox rallying ground for the disaffected majority throughout the Arab world.

It will likely thrive unless and until the secular regimes can satisfy the majority that they can outperform fundamentalism in delivering economic opportunity and social justice to their citizens.[27] That is far from impossible, but will require a sense of urgency and enlightenment that is uncommon among the region's autocrats.

The Soviet Role in the Middle East The Soviet Union played a particularly significant role in the Middle East during the cold war, beginning in 1955, when it agreed to supply military equipment to Egypt via Czechoslovakia. Soviet interests in the region were global as well as regional. The Soviets tried to eliminate U.S. influence throughout the region, without risking a superpower confrontation in the process. They wanted to secure their own southern borders; at the same time, they felt that access to the Suez Canal and to facilities in the Indian Ocean would increase their ability to exert counterpressures.[28]

The Soviet Union had no compelling economic interests in the Middle East comparable to those of the United States, but they saw by the 1970s that that was going to change. Older Soviet oil fields were becoming depleted, and the Soviet government's enormous investments to develop new fields, largely in Siberia, had been slow to pay off. Consequently, in the 1980s the Soviet Union ceased being an exporter to nations outside the Soviet bloc, and is likely to become a net importer in the 1990s.[29]

From World War II on, Soviet policy in the Middle East was faced with a dilemma. The Soviet Union could seek to use its developing position in the Middle East to subvert the states there and hope eventually to bring local communists to power, or it could support noncommunist regimes, thus enabling them to cooperate effectively with the Soviet Union against the United States and its interests. (To their regret, the Soviets found that regimes they helped also tended to use their new strength to crush their domestic communists.)

During the cold war the Soviet Union generally chose to support existing Middle Eastern regimes rather than subvert them. Such support took two forms. First, the Soviets provided friendly governments with the military and political support needed to suppress internal unrest and external threats. The classic example of such support occurred after the June 1967 Arab–Israeli War when the Soviet Union rushed large quantities of arms to Egypt to bolster Nasser's sagging regime.[30] (By October 1967, an estimated 80 percent of Egyptian equipment losses in the June war had been replaced.) Second, at the same time, the Soviets provided technical and financial support for the economic development programs that played such an important role in many Middle Eastern states. Apparently, they believed that such support not only increased the strength of friendly regimes but also generated social changes that would lead to increased Soviet influence in the region.

The Soviet Union did achieve occasional successes in the area by following such policies. It also capitalized on Arab resentment of American support for Israel and succeeded, in part, in allaying Arab fears about its intentions by providing countersupport. Yet, most Middle Eastern countries saw more economic advantages to dealing with the United States, Western Europe, and Japan than in dealing with the Soviet Union. Even Iraq, which maintained a variety of close ties with the Soviet Union, cultivated extensive economic and military relations with the West and restored diplomatic relations with the United States in 1984.

Middle Eastern leaders also found that Soviet political and military support, although sometimes useful, was of limited effectiveness in dealing with the problems they faced. Soviet aid to one country often triggered even greater U.S. (or Saudi) aid to its rivals. Soviet unwillingness to push for power for local communists ensured that, regardless of the value of Soviet aid, political authority remained in the hands of local leaders. Such leaders tended to be concerned primarily with their own or regional problems and responded to Soviet wishes only when such wishes suited their own purposes.[31] When Arab leaders deemed Soviet wishes and pressures to be oppressive, they cooled the relationship, even ejecting Soviet advisors, as happened in the case of Egypt.

Perhaps the most important check on the influence of the Soviet Union in the Middle East was the fear and distrust it automatically inspired in the region. This aversion was compounded partly by the sheer size of the Soviet Union and its proximity, partly by its antireligious values, and partly by its record in dealing with its southern neighbors—particularly with the Iranians and Turks after World War II and with the Afghans in the 1980s. Nevertheless, the Soviet Union consistently constrained U.S. policy in the Middle East during the cold war. Soviet support to nations and groups dissatisfied with the status quo, such as Syria and the PLO, made it impossible for policymakers to ignore the desires of such nations and groups. The Soviet Union also gave local regimes an alternative if U.S. pressure for a given policy became distasteful. From the Persian Gulf to the Arab–Israeli peace process, the Soviets took an active role that was difficult for the West to ignore.[32]

But as we have seen, the influence of the Soviet Union in the region sank during the Persian Gulf crisis. It virtually ended with the Persian Gulf war. The subsequent collapse of the former Soviet Union has also eroded Israel's role as a strategic asset to the United States. That role was defined not only in terms of the long-term commitment by the U.S. to Israel's security, but also in terms of Israel's staunch anti-Soviet orientation in the region.

The Influences of Other States. Western Europe and Japan provide alternative sources of financial, economic, and military support to the Middle East, although their political influence in the region has been limited. The high oil dependence of these nations makes them, in turn, vulnerable to counterpressures from the region. For example, the reported Japanese willingness to pay virtually any price for Middle Eastern oil greatly strengthened the negotiating position of OPEC in 1973.[33]

Along with the United Kingdom, France has played, and will likely continue to play, a significant role; it has, for example, provided advanced military equipment to several Arab states when both the United States and the Soviet Union were unwilling to do so.* However, the importance of the Europeans and Japanese is limited by the fact that none of them has the capability to supply the Middle Eastern states with the range of economic or military support they desire. Sheer size, strength, and importance of interests ensure that the United States will continue to be the principal external power in the Middle East. Others, such as India, China, or a reborn Russia, may have the potential to shape events in the future, but it will be well into the twenty-first century before that potential can be translated into dominant influence.

The Rise and Fall of Iraq The land and peoples of the area now associated with the state of Iraq have a long and glorious history.[34] Ancient civilizations in the Tigris–Euphrates region provided many early advances into modernity including handwriting, brick-making, and the rule of law. But there is also an inglorious side to Iraqi history, characterized by neglect of the people's needs and unspeakable acts of terror and violence. Some of the most feared warriors of old came out of this region. This martial heritage became the source of many military innovations that revolutionized warfare including the discovery of bronze, the first conscripted armies, the forging of iron into weapons and the invention of the chariot.

Britain administered the region under its colonial empire until 1932 when it established Iraq as the first sovereign state in its Arab mandate territory that was

---

*France supplied Israel with the bulk of its arms between 1950 and 1965 when both Britain and the United States were not major suppliers.

established pursuant to the terms of the settlement of World War I. The grant of sovereignty was aimed at appeasing a restless populace, while affording British forces continued access to the region. The British tried to implant a constitutional monarchy, but it lasted—in name only—until 1958, when the regime was overthrown in a military coup. That coup occurred in part because of animosity engendered by British support for the United Nations' partitioning of Palestine after World War II.

Although Saddam Hussein was by the early 1970s a member of the ruling triumvirate of Iraq's governing Ba'ath party, he had played only minor supporting roles in military operations against Israel and other opponents. Yet he understood the use of force and was highly skilled at intrigue—and totally ruthless. Beginning in 1976, he gradually consolidated his rule over the country and began to exploit it for his own purposes. He undertook an ambitious economic reform program, ostensibly to rebuild the country, but turned out to be more interested in funding a military build-up than in advancing the population's welfare. By 1979 he had become Iraq's sole leader, purging the party and the military and killing hundreds of potential opponents in the process.

Saddam used the pretense of an old border dispute with Iran to strike immediately at his most threatening rival for influence in the region. Saddam attacked in the belief that the ancient enemy, just emerging from the chaos surrounding the overthrow of the Shah, was at its weakest point. The resulting war was indecisive, with both sides launching air and ground attacks that resulted in heavy casualties but no decisive advantage for either. Both sides obtained ballistic missiles, which they fired at each others' cities, sometimes employing chemical warheads. Then, in the spring of 1988, Iraq launched a series of lightning offensives against an exhausted Iranian army, bringing the war to a close with a negotiated settlement of the original boundary dispute that was basically back at the starting point.

Despite its stalemated outcome, the Iran–Iraq War tipped the military balance in the Middle East decisively in Iraq's favor. The amassing of tanks, artillery, and aircraft with a large number of men under arms gave Saddam the most potent military force in the region. In spite of his country's war damage and suffering—recovery from which the United States and others believed would absorb his attention for years—Saddam promptly began a military rebuilding campaign aimed at preparing his forces for the next target: the Arabian Peninsula, or more immediately, Kuwait.

The Iraqi enmity with Kuwait had three main elements. First, there was a pretense of a border dispute, which had in fact been settled long ago. Second, Iraq accused Kuwait of stealing oil from the Rumaila oil field that the two countries shared across their common border. Finally, Iraq accused Kuwait of producing too much oil overall, undermining pricing agreements reached in the councils of the Organization of Petroleum Exporting Countries (OPEC). It seems likely, however, that the invasion was not merely to deal with these issues but was aimed at controlling the oil resources of the Arabian peninsula as a part of a grand scheme to unite the Arab world under Saddam's—the modern Saladin's—

leadership. He undoubtedly expected that the rest of the world, led by the superpowers that were focused on their post–cold war disengagement from each other, would look the other way.

The Persian Gulf War The August 1990 invasion of Kuwait precipitated a crisis in the international security system—a crisis not only about the taking of a small country, but also, fundamentally, about whether the world would allow control of a major fraction of world's oil production and perhaps one-half of its oil reserves to fall into the hands of a ruthless aggressor. Kuwait would likely be only a way station to conquest or intimidation of the Arabian Peninsula. With a strong lead from the United States, the bulk of the world responded by condemnations through the United Nations and by a variety of economic sanctions. Yet, for all the urgency of the situation, the crisis settled into an anxious waiting game that lasted for four and a half months, while diplomatic and economic efforts to reverse the aggression were pursued, fruitlessly.

Military mobilizations and deployments proceeded on both sides, as the potential battlefield took shape across the Persian Gulf and the Arabian desert. By the end of December 1990, most of the rest of the world had come to support military action through an unprecedented series of U.N. Security Council resolutions authorizing the use of military force, if necessary, if Iraq did not withdraw from Kuwait, immediately and unconditionally. Last-minute diplomatic efforts failed to resolve the crisis and the world—or more accurately, forces from 18 nations—was plunged into regional war on January 16, 1991.

It was a revolutionary military campaign.[35] It began with an air assault that raged for some forty days, with the allied air forces first clearing the skies of any hostile threats, then systematically destroying strategic military targets in Iraq and Kuwait. Within two weeks, the Iraqi army in Kuwait was cut off from its command and control linkages and most of its logistical lifelines. Only the continuing threat of Iraqi Scud missiles aimed at key Israeli and Saudi cities endangered the effectiveness of the coalition, but by the third week of the air campaign actual launches of Iraqi Scud missiles were reduced to zero.

The complex ground campaign began on February 23. In a remarkable 100-hour assault and flanking maneuver, allied forces encircled and defeated the Iraqi army before Saddam's generals fully realized what had happened to them. It was an utter defeat of a once-formidable army.

Fearful that complete destruction of Iraq's forces would sow chaos and perhaps result in a breakup of Iraq, causing unnecessary casualties and leaving an unstable postwar balance of power in the region, the allies allowed a substantial portion of the Iraqi army to escape. Saddam was able, as a consequence, to reconstitute a sizable force that he used a few months later in defiance of the ceasefire agreements to put down uprisings of Shi'ites opposed to his regime in the south, and of the long-suppressed but rebellious Kurds in the north. In response, and after much Kurdish suffering, the United Nations imposed a protective area in Iraqi Kurdistan and provided humanitarian relief backed up with armed force provided by the United States and the United Kingdom. After

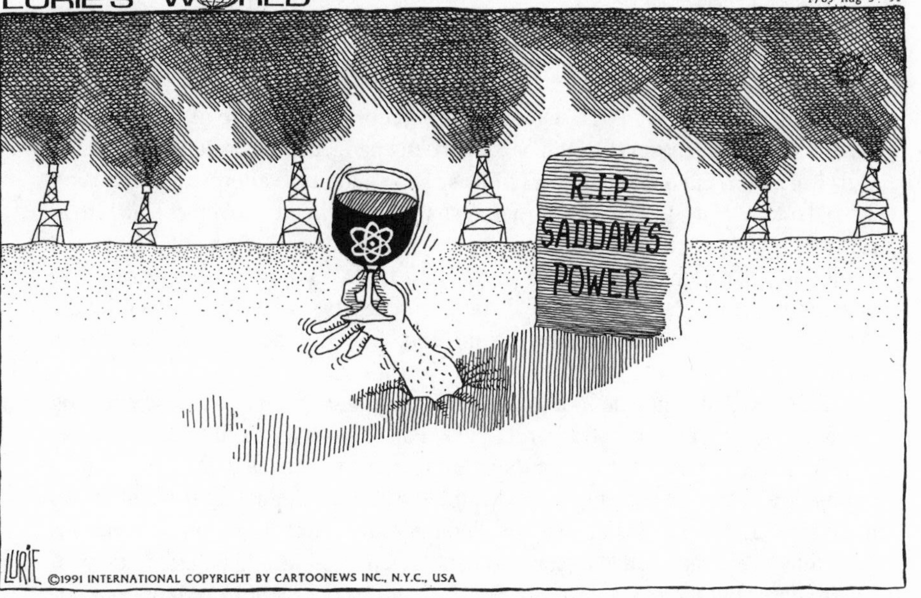

Reprinted with permission of Renan R. Lurie.

protesting vainly until the summer of 1992, while Iraqi forces sporadically killed Iraqi Shi'ites, the international community threatened retaliation and imposed, finally, a "no fly zone" over Iraqi territory south of the 36th parallel—enforced by U.S., French and British warplanes.

Despite continuing sanctions that proved painful to Iraq's people and damaging to its economy, Saddam continued through 1992 to resist full compliance with the ceasefire agreement's call for destruction of all Iraq's missiles and chemical, biological, and nuclear weapons and their manufacturing facilities. If the standoffs continue or escalate there could well be a renewal of the war at some juncture, or at least of the air campaign which the allies used so successfully before.

The Aftermath of the Persian Gulf War. The aftermath of the Persian Gulf war—itself coming in the aftermath of the cold war—presented unprecedented opportunities in the Middle East, including Arab–Israeli peace-making carried forward decisively, united action against potential aggressors, the modernization of most of the regional societies, and a mutually beneficial use of the region's economic potential.[36]

The United Nations emerged from the Gulf war with new credibility in the international security system. It will not automatically triumph in future crises, for it was the combination of the flagrant character of aggression and the skillful and determined leadership of the United States that made the U.N. action feasible. The war may have set a significant precedent in forcing Iraq to yield a measure of its sovereignty, through allowing allied creation of protected zones in Kurdistan and in permitting virtually unrestricted rights of inspections to the U.N. Special Commission to verify the destruction of Iraqi weapons of mass destruction.

The dynamics of the Arab–Israeli confrontation and the role of the Palestine Liberation Organization (PLO) have also been changed as a result of the Persian Gulf war. Born out of twenty years of frustration and in the aftermath of the 1967 Arab–Israeli War, the PLO—as a transnational militant movement aimed at restoring Arab sovereignty over the occupied territories—brought together a number of disparate Palestinian groups. The PLO's mission has been extremely difficult to accomplish in the face of tough suppressive measures adopted by the Israeli occupiers and in light of the inherent fractures among the Palestinian people.

"Palestinians" include not only persons living in the lands seized and occupied by Israel in the 1967 war, but also Palestinians living in Israel-proper as Israeli citizens, governed by the laws of Israel, as well as a large irredentist population dispersed throughout the Middle East, with significant concentrations in Jordan, Lebanon, Syria, and the Persian Gulf. Not only have the various Palestinian populations had to contend with Israeli resistance to their assertions of sovereignty, but they have also suffered from an inconsistent pattern of commitment and support from Arab states to those claims of sovereignty.

Since 1967 the various Palestinian factions have come together irregularly in the Palestinian National Council. Its power to develop a consensus is held by a leadership core centering on Yassir Arafat, the Chairman of the Fateh Central Committee and of the PLO, which is a coalition of factions. As the years of occupation became decades and the PLO proved helpless to relieve their plight or to halt the multiplying Jewish settlements on the West Bank, Palestinian despair generated a number of local paramilitary organizations whose leadership was largely outside the control of Arafat and the PLO. Their "uprising" (or Intifada) reaction to Israeli rule became increasingly violent. By 1988 Jordan's King Hussein, unable any longer to control the 1.5 million Palestinians to whom he had been providing succor, abandoned his calls for a political settlement for an independent West Bank under Jordanian supervision and accepted the 1947 partitioning of the area. In late fall of 1988 the Palestinian National Council, on behalf of the Intifada, declared Palestinian sovereignty over the occupied territories. Increasingly it fell to Palestinians living in the occupied territories to represent their cause.

During the Persian Gulf war the Palestinians were caught in a dilemma. On the one hand, the enemy of Israel, Iraq, was their enemy; the PLO led the cheering as missiles fell on Tel Aviv. Yet Saddam's Scud missiles fired at Israel were landing on land claimed as Palestinian territory and were causing damage and harm not only to Israeli but also to Palestinians and their property in Israel and in the occupied territories. Moreover, the clear pro-Iraqi tilt most Palestinians showed earned them the hostility of the Saudis, Kuwaitis, and other Arabs who had supported them over the years. It also cost them sympathy in the United States and other Western nations. Still, the United States, judging the situation after the war as propitious, began a fresh effort to get Middle East peace talks, centering on the Palestinian question, under way. New Palestinian leaders proved to be instrumental in moving the process forward and in articulating the Palestinian cause in the talks which ensued under the Baker initiative. The PLO was relegated to a supporting role, perhaps permanently.

The United States emerged from the Persian Gulf war as the clearly preeminent power in the region. In the near term, there will probably be few direct threats to U.S. interests emanating from the region. Nonetheless, for the longer term it is important that all regional actors understand that the United States continues to have vital interests in the Middle East and that it will stay engaged. For example, the United States has developed an important security relationship with Saudi Arabia in particular, a relationship that will have special value until the roles of Iran and Iraq are clarified and the Arab states of the region develop more security arrangements. The Saudi relationship will be essential in the event that U.S. military forces need to be returned to the region.

Policy Challenges in the 1990s. The events cited in the preceding pages suggest that the Middle East will be turbulent for years to come. While such developments provide ample grounds for pessimism, some of the more recent ones—in particular the series of Arab–Israeli peace conferences under way as of 1992—also present opportunities. Seizing those opportunities will require a broad understanding of, and sustained involvement in, the region by the United States.

Paradoxically, the very complexity of American interests in the Middle East contributes to one of the greatest assets that the United States has in the region. These varied interests have forced U.S. policymakers to cultivate good working relations with most states in the Middle East. At the same time, virtually every significant political group in the Middle East has found some area—economic, political, scientific, or military—from which it can derive benefits from maintaining good relations with the United States. With the exception of the Ayatollah's Iran, the former South Yemen (P.D.R.Y.), and some factions within the PLO, none of these groups ever rejected the United States in the way various Middle Easterners reject each other and outsiders generally. The resulting U.S. ability to exert influence on both sides of most regional disputes is a powerful diplomatic and security asset.

The conjunction of high stakes in the area, persistent instability, and logistical difficulty makes the Middle East perhaps the single most challenging area for the United States in the remaining years of this century. In meeting those challenges, the United States has formidable assets, both in the region and of value to the region. If those assets are used wisely, not in an attempt to ensure stability—which in the Middle East is as enduring as a summer snowstorm—but to promote peaceful change, there is hope.

Discussion Questions

1. How have U.S. economic interests in the Middle East changed during the past twenty years?

2. How does the special relationship between the United States and Israel affect U.S. relations with its other allies in the Middle East?

3. How did the 1967 Arab–Israeli War change the nature of the Arab–Israeli conflict? How did it affect the U.S. role in that conflict?

4. What policies could the United States adopt in order to prevent any further large increases in the price of oil? What policies could it adopt to prevent production cutbacks or another oil embargo?

5. How did détente with the Soviet Union affect the U.S. position in the Middle East? In particular? How has the disintegration of the Soviet Union changed matters?

6. Compare Israel's post–gulf war position in the Middle East with its prewar position. Would Israel have been better off had it intervened with military forces? Would we?

7. Discuss the advantages and disadvantages for the United States of relying on Israel and Saudi Arabia to further U.S. interests in the Middle East. What advantages or disadvantages would those countries derive from such an arrangement?

8. What are the prospects for Iran in the region? Will it become a regional superpower by the twenty-first century? What are the implications for the United States?

9. What non–Middle Eastern powers, other than the United States, have major interests in the Middle East? How do you expect they will attempt to exert their influence in the region?

10. How important is it for the United States to be closely involved in searching for a settlement to the Arab–Israeli conflict? Should it seek to use its influence to impose a settlement on all parties?

Recommended Reading

Anderson, Roy R., et al. *Politics and Change in the Middle East*. Englewood Cliffs, N.J.: Prentice-Hall, 1982.

Blackwell, James. *Thunder in the Desert: The Strategy and Tactics of the Persian Gulf War*. New York: Bantam Books, 1991.

Congressional Quarterly. *The Middle East,* 7th ed. Washington, DC: Congressional Quarterly, 1990.

Hourani, Albert. *A History of the Arab Peoples*. Cambridge, Mass.: Harvard University Press, 1991.

Hunter, Shireen T. *Iran and the World: Continuity in a Revolutionary Decade*. Bloomington: Indiana University Press, 1990.

Indyk, Martin. "Watershed in the Middle East." *Foreign Affairs: American and the World 1991/92*, 71 (1992), 70–93.

Khadduri, Majid. *Political Trends in the Arab World*. Baltimore: Johns Hopkins University Press, 1970.

Khouri, Fred J. *The Arab Israeli Dilemma,* 2d ed. Syracuse, N.Y.: Syracuse University Press, 1976.

Peterson, J. E. *Defending Arabia*. London: Croom Helm; New York: St. Martin's Press, 1986.

Quandt, William B. *Decade of Decision: American Policy toward the Arab-Israeli Conflict, 1967–1976*. Berkeley and Los Angeles: University of California Press, 1977.

Rustow, Dankwart A. *Oil and Turmoil: America Faces OPEC and the Middle East*. New York: Norton, 1982.

Tillman, Seth. *The United States in the Middle East*. Bloomington: Indiana University Press, 1982.

The United States and the New Middle East: Strategic Perspectives After the Persian Gulf War. Washington, D.C.: Center for Strategic and International Studies, 1992.

Whetten, Lawrence L. *The Canal War: Four-Power Conflict in the Middle East*. Cambridge, Mass.: MIT Press, 1974.

19

Sub-Saharan Africa

As much as any other region in the world, the continent of Africa has been a chessboard on which the United States and the former Soviet Union have strategically maneuvered so as to strengthen their respective positions. At various points in their short histories, certain African nations have assumed critical importance in the foreign policies of the two superpowers. During the cold war, few nations escaped some sort of superpower involvement, in most cases, taking the form of intervention through military or economic assistance; in only a few cases was the presence of external intervention felt. However, since 1989, significant changes in the global balance of power have occurred. In Africa, these changes have been associated with developments in two specific areas: conflict resolution and the "democratization" process. This chapter outlines U.S. interests and policy in the region, examines recent developments against the historical backdrop of the cold war, analyzes the role of intra-African organizations, and concludes with an analysis of how the future of Africa will be affected by a number of destabilizing forces—economic underdevelopment, autocratic rule, and unsettled conflicts.

U.S. Interest in the Region. The strategic interests of the United States in sub-Saharan Africa* are limited in comparison with its interest in other areas. Thus, a question sometimes arises about whether or not misjudgments in U.S. policy for the area are terribly damaging. Sub-Saharan Africa is neither a

**Africa* and, more precisely, *sub-Saharan Africa* are used herein to denote all of Africa except the North African states of Egypt, Libya, Tunisia, Algeria, and Morocco.

crossroads of world power or trade, nor a natural place for confrontation between world powers. It is (for the most part) underdeveloped. In the entire region, not a single nation is a significant military threat to the United States or its non-African allies. Only a few African nations possess even significant regional power. Nonetheless, the United States has important, even critical concerns in Africa on several levels.[1]

Strategic Position. The huge African continent sits astride one of the world's key shipping lanes—the route for Middle Eastern oil to Europe and America. This makes its littoral status of geopolitical interest to Western oil-importing powers and consequently to their potential adversaries. The East African coastline is similarly important for communications with the Indian Ocean, where regional rivalry is growing. African ports and bases, particularly those close to the major sources of Middle East oil, are becoming increasingly important.

International Politics. As nearly a third of the world's sovereign nations are on the continent, Africa has contributed to a transformation of the character and scope of international affairs since the mid 1960s. African nations play a large role in seeking change in the international order through increasingly active participation in conferences of nonaligned nations, the United Nations and its specialized agencies, the North–South dialogues on aid, trade, and investment, and numerous other forums. In many functional areas the United States has an interest in African support—the world environment, the future of the oceans, nuclear nonproliferation, energy, and population growth, for instance.[2]

Economic Interdependence. Sub-Saharan Africa's role in the world economy is small by U.S., European, or East Asian standards. U.S. trade ($4.1 billion in exports and $12.7 billion in imports in 1990) and direct investment ($1.94 billion in 1990 in the sub-Saharan region, including South Africa) constitute but a tiny proportion of our national product. These numbers, however, understate Africa's future economic importance. For one thing, a number of our European allies have a significant stake in African economies. In addition, all the Western industrialized nations have a stake in the availability of African fuels and nonfuel materials. For example, in 1985 Nigeria was one of the six leading suppliers of U.S. petroleum imports.[3]

An even more crucial concern than oil from south of the Sahara is long-term Western access to Africa's enormous mineral deposits. In the noncommunist world, Africa yields over half the production of seven crucial minerals—chromium, cobalt, industrial diamonds, germanium, manganese, platinum, and vanadium—and is a major source of several other commodities.[4] European dependence considerably exceeds that of the United States, with its sizable strategic stockpiles and its own mineral wealth. The location of most of the mineral deposits in the troubled areas of southern Africa is a policy concern of all industrial powers.

FIG. 19.1 Africa

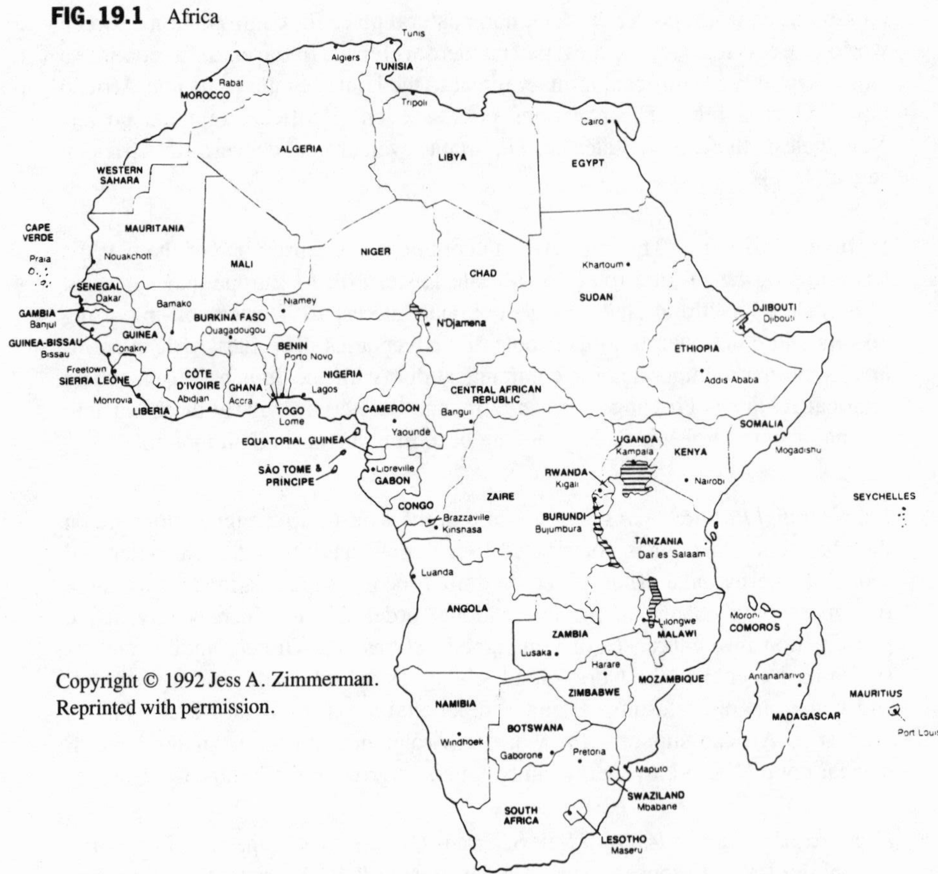

Unstable Arena for Conflict. The very weaknesses that preclude African states from posing a security threat to the United States invite regional strife and outside intervention. The general instability of African regimes stems from a host of problems—poverty, tribalism, secessionist and irredentist movements, and inadequate institutionalization, to name a few. Before the ending of the cold war, these considerations, along with the notion that these were African problems best left to Africans, competed with the fear that Soviet exploitation of such instability would be to the detriment of U.S. interests in Africa and, more broadly, of U.S. credibility worldwide. On the other hand, there are critics of the "credibility doctrine" who believe that the application of such a doctrine to Africa tempts the United States to react in areas of minimal interest or where other nations dictate the timing or interest at stake. Of particular interest in this context was the demonstrated willingness of the Soviet Union (and its Cuban proxies) to intervene militarily in local conflicts such as Angola (1975) and Ethiopia (1979) in relatively large numbers and for prolonged periods.

Values at Stake. U.S. interest in Africa is not only material and strategic. It bears strong threads of cultural, political, and moral values as well. Fundamental American norms of freedom, justice, and peaceful order create sympathy with African anticolonialism, nationalism, and pan-African solidarity. Other American values—democracy, human rights, free enterprise—encounter fewer parallels in the numerous single-party and military regimes of Africa, although this is clearly changing.

The issue of majority rule in southern Africa tends to bring these varying values into focus. The size and sensitivity of the American black population and its emergence as a major internal American political force give the United States special moral and political interests in southern Africa. Strategic and economic interests accentuated the urgency we attached to finding solutions to the struggle in Zimbabwe (Rhodesia). In that case, the United States acted as an anxious, honest broker among the contending parties, a posture that was helpful in obtaining a solution serving as a counter to possible Soviet and Cuban use of force. The United States has also sought to play a constructive role in the controversy over the former German colony of Namibia (also known as South-West Africa), which was made a South African mandate by the League of Nations in 1920. Although the United Nations revoked the mandate in 1966, South Africa has continued to rule over the territory, which encompasses some nine hundred thousand blacks and one hundred thousand whites. In 1977 the United States took the lead as five Western members of the U.N. Security Council (the United States, the United Kingdom, France, West Germany, and Canada) formed a "Contact Group" for the purpose of resolving the Namibian conflict and finding an internationally acceptable solution to the problem. It is also true, however, that moral and domestic political factors helped shape U.S. policy in those crises and in our antiapartheid stance vis-à-vis South Africa.

The Historical Context of U.S. Policy. Prior to 1945, the history of sub-Saharan Africa and its inhabitants was usually addressed as part of the colonial history of the European states. The weakening of colonialism caused by World War II, plus the rapidly changing international power equation, led to most African states achieving independence in the 1960s. The United States for the most part warmly embraced that independence. As France, Belgium, Portugal, and Britain granted sovereignty to some three dozen nations, the United States offered goodwill and modest amounts of aid and investment. American sympathy for self-rule and hopes for African democracy and development were perhaps symbolized best by the creation in 1961 of the Peace Corps. Prior to the genesis of the Peace Corps, however, several administrations had affirmed the American commitment to contain communist aggression worldwide, particularly in the developing world. Thus, U.S. policy for sub-Saharan Africa by the early 1960s had taken the dual nature that it maintained for more than two decades—support for socioeconomic development in sovereign states (preferably democratic ones) linked to the West and opposition to intrusion by communist powers. Since the collapse of communist power in Eastern Europe and the former Soviet Union, this latter policy thrust has taken the more general form of opposition to any intrusions by outsiders.

In order to understand the 1990s environment of U.S. policy toward this region, it is useful to review its general evolution over the past twenty-five years. Many factors favored U.S. and Western interests in Africa. In general, the British and French (but not the Belgians) left in their colonial wake a Western-educated elite and a legacy of Western institutions, including private enterprises, civil services, and governments that (at least at the outset) possessed the formal trappings of democracy. Trade links, almost exclusively Western at the time of independence, were reinforced by special market arrangements such as French association and British commonwealth agreements. Europe and America provided African military organization, training, and equipment.

On the other hand, several factors tended to undermine the Western position. Colonial rule and, in some instances, the bitterness of the independence struggle brought anti-Western leaders to power in several countries.* Also, the new African states were institutionally weak at their center. Their largely arbitrary, inherited boundaries contained diverse peoples whose tribal loyalties generally far outweighed any national identity. Many African national leaders found it appropriate, expedient, or essential to articulate anti-Western themes of neocolonialism and neoimperialism to keep attention focused on the "national struggle." This line, plus the poverty of most sub-Saharan African countries, persuaded responsive audiences that they were continuing victims of capitalist exploitation. Meanwhile, multiparty democracy quickly waned in the face of domestic social heterogeneity, traditional nondemocratic ways, and the weakness of central national institutions.† The military coup became a widespread phenomenon, occasionally bringing to power leaders espousing socialist or Marxist doctrines.[5]

The predominant trend in Africa, however, was neither pro-Western nor anti-Western. As diverse as the new states were domestically, a distinctive Africanist style in international affairs emerged, represented most prominently by the Organization of African Unity (OAU). Created in 1963, the OAU came to include the five countries of North Africa and all independent black-ruled states and adjacent islands as members (thus excluding South Africa and, until recently, Namibia [1990] and Rhodesia/Zimbabwe [1980]). Its core principles have been African unity (both internally and internationally), socioeconomic development, respect for the territorial integrity of all member states, independence from external influence, elimination of all forms of colonialism, and support for the principles of the United Nations. The OAU has achieved its

*These anti-Western stances were often subject to mellowing with time. The postindependence regimes of such countries as Guinea, Algeria, and Mozambique, which were initially suspicious of the West due to a combination of ideology and unpleasant memories of the former colonial power, have since moved toward a greater openness with respect to the capitalist world.

†In 1987, multiparty polities in sub-Saharan Africa numbered nine—Botswana, Gambia, Liberia, Madagascar, Mauritius, Senegal, South Africa, Sudan, and Zimbabwe. In 1992, multiparty polities in Sub-Saharan Africa numbered twenty-seven (see Table 19.1).

establishing acceptance of boundaries inherited from the colonial era and moderating several inter-African disputes.*[6] Nonalignment with the East or the West came to characterize the OAU despite the proclivities of individual members. African nationalism with its opposition to all foreign domination, remains the strongest deterrent on the continent to foreign penetration or influence. Awareness of this has generally resulted in U.S. support for the OAU as an institution of African solidarity.

Until recent years U.S. policy in Africa has fluctuated between attempts to help Africans solve Africa's problems, thereby reducing the potential for outside interference, and efforts to counter directly Soviet adventurism. Lacking leverage or suitable instruments, the United States has faced great difficulty in accomplishing its objectives by the first course. The second approach has encountered frequent difficulties as well. For example, in May 1978 the United States supported the efforts of France and Belgium to counter a cross-border invasion of Zaire's mineral-rich Shaba region by Angola-based Zairian exiles (who, it was feared, might be receiving Cuban backing). Because the attackers were former inhabitants of the area with a long history of antigovernment activity on a nonideological basis, and because there was a demonstrated preoccupation for the safety of Europeans in the region, our efforts were viewed by some Africans as support for a corrupt regime and not a legitimate response in the African context.[7] More recently, the 1986 decision by the Reagan administration to supply covert military aid (including antitank weapons and antiaircraft missiles) to Jonas Savimbi's UNITA guerilla movement was widely denounced by Africans. U.S. support for UNITA, which had been engaged from 1975 to 1991 in a civil war with the formerly Marxist-Leninist government of Angola, was viewed by many African governments and movements of disparate ideological leanings, as well as by some groups in the United States, as an attack on a sovereign, black-ruled state and an instance of U.S. collaboration with South Africa.

The Eisenhower and Kennedy administrations actively sought to cultivate friendly regimes in Africa by promoting independence and encouraging the installation of Western-oriented governments and continued Western economic ties. When this approach ran afoul of postcolonial turmoil in the Congo (now Zaire), the United States intervened with its Western allies and nonaligned nations (under U.N. auspices), in large measure to counter Soviet influence—as described in Chapter 22.

For a time during the Kennedy years it appeared that Africa might become a testing place for U.S. intervention against the threat of communist "wars of national liberation"; instead, Vietnam provided that focus. Starting in about 1965, as American preoccupation with Southeast Asia grew, American attention to Africa entered a period of "benign neglect." That same year saw whites in

*There are, of course, some notable exceptions to OAU success in these areas. The dispute between Chad and Libya over the latter's occupation of northern Chad, the conflict over the Western Sahara, and Tanzania's 1979 military intervention in Uganda to help overthrow Idi Amin provide examples of tough issues not resolved by the OAU.

southern Rhodesia proclaim a unilateral declaration of independence from Britain, with the 5 percent minority of whites in total charge.

During the next decade, U.S. inaction with respect to Portuguese colonies came to be viewed in Africa as support for the NATO ally's colonial policy. The Nixon administration, persuaded that the Portuguese and local whites would continue in power for some time, attempted to straddle the issue of black–white interests. Rather than actively undermining the status quo, as some would have preferred, the United States was resolutely ambiguous. Meanwhile the Vietnam War dragged painfully on, attracting both African opposition and African fears that America's failure there would undercut its capacity to act as a global power. U.S. support for Israel during its 1967 and 1973 wars with Arab states alienated several African states with a strong Islamic heritage.

Thus, by the early 1970s, as the great sweep of independence in Africa approached the borders of Angola, Mozambique, Rhodesia, and Portuguese Guinea, American enthusiasm for such change seemed questionable to many Africans and non-Africans alike. Importantly too, by the late 1960s most anticolonial forces had found that the Soviet Union and the People's Republic of China were prepared to give them significant backing, particularly in military supplies and training. Although the United States (and Europe) far exceeded the communist states in establishing trade links and in providing nonmilitary aid, these positive elements of American policy were partly overshadowed by the Vietnam War, the Portuguese connection, failure to maintain U.N. sanctions on Rhodesia,* and perceived indifference to South African apartheid.

The April 1974 coup in Portugal shattered the status quo in southern Africa and the U.S. policy that assumed its continuance for years to come.[8] Over the next nineteen moths, all five Portuguese African colonies gained independence.† Unprepared for this sudden turn of events, the United States in 1975 nonetheless attempted to influence the outcome in Angola, where three liberation movements contested for power. Despite the administration's efforts, however, American clandestine support for two non-Marxist groups, National Union for the Total Liberation of Angola [UNITA] and the National Front for the Liberation of Angola [FNLA], was ended—for the time being—by the U.S. Congress. Meanwhile, more than fifteen thousand Cuban troops and Soviet advisers poured into Angola, enabling the Soviet-aligned Marxist faction to defeat the two opposing groups and to gain OAU recognition by February 1976.

In the following October, the new regime signed a treaty of friendship and cooperation with the Soviet Union, and in 1977 Cuban troop withdrawals were stopped and the Cuban presence began to become more entrenched. In December of that year, the ruling party formally proclaimed its adherence to Marxism-Leninism. (Meanwhile, the government pragmatically maintained cordial business relations with Gulf Oil, thereby ensuring the badly needed revenues gener-

*From 1972 to 1977, the Byrd Amendment effectively mandated U.S. importation of Rhodesian chrome.

†The five were Guinea-Bissau (September 1974), Mozambique (June 1975), Cape Verde Islands (July 1985), Sao Tomé and Príncipe (July 1975), and Angola (November 1975).

ated by petroleum exports from the country's Cabinda region.) In 1981, UNITA, with considerable help from South Africa, revived as a serious threat to the Luanda regime. In 1985, the U.S. Congress voted to end the nine-year-old ban on U.S. security assistance to Angolan groups, that is, to UNITA.

Angola's civil war and the assumption of power by Marxist regimes in Mozambique (1975) and Ethiopia (1974) signified a new era in Africa. The Soviet Union had demonstrated a major strategic logistics capability. Along with its Cuban ally, it had intervened directly and decisively in Africa. The "liberation struggle" had shifted southward, and soon-to-be-independent Zimbabwe (Rhodesia) was suddenly ringed by black-ruled states willing to tolerate or promote insurgent groups. In the succeeding three years, the guerilla war against Rhodesia intensified to the point at which its white-dominated government had to submit to growing pressure and turn over power to the black majority after British-supervised elections (1980).

Somewhat earlier, Lt. Colonel Mengistu declared his regime in Ethiopia to be Marxist, following his successful coup in 1974. In late 1977 and early 1978 a significant infusion of Cuban troops and Soviet material and advisers enabled his forces to defeat local guerrillas and Somalis and to drive them from Ethiopia's Ogaden region. In the same period, the Ethiopians temporarily checked the longstanding Eritrean rebellion to a degree unknown before Soviet assistance was provided. In September 1984, after years of pressure from Soviet advisers eager to cement Ethiopia's links with the East, the military regime established a single ruling party, the Workers' Party of Ethiopia. However, this move did not stop the regime from accepting Western famine aid a few months later.[9]

Conflict Resolution. At the risk of oversimplifying a complex historical sequence, it can be said that the African component of the cold war symbolically ended on December 22, 1988. It was on that date that officials of South Africa, Cuba, and Angola met in New York to sign the agreements that initiated Namibia's U.N.-monitored transition to independence, as well as the phased departure of all of the 50,000 or so Cuban troops in Angola. These agreements, largely negotiated over a period of several years by U.S. Assistant Secretary of State for African Affairs Chester Crocker (with critical Soviet support in the latter stages), embodied an implicit recognition on the part of Washington and Moscow that neither would gain from further military competition in Africa.

As noted earlier, this has not always been the case concerning superpower involvement in Africa. From 1957, when Ghana gained its independence, until the mid 1980s, both U.S. and Soviet policymakers formulated their regional strategies in an effort to counter both the presence and threat of their respective ideological opponents.[10] Throughout the 1960s and mid 1970s, U.S. presidents and secretaries of state became involved in African issues when the perceived Soviet threat seemed greatest. At times, the inability of the two superpowers to cooperate over key African issues led to the failure of attempted agreements on non-African issues. An example of this was the first breakdown of U.S.–Soviet détente in 1975, when Cuba began its support of the socialist-oriented Popular

Table 19.1 Types of Regimes in Sub-Saharan Africa, 1992

Multiparty Polities	*Transition to Multipartyism*	*One-Party States*	*Undefined*
Benin	Angola	Central African Republic	Liberia
Botswana	Ethiopia	Chad	Sierra Leone
Burkina Faso	Ghana	Djibouti	Somalia
Burundi		Lesotho	Sudan
Cameroon		Madagascar	
Cape Verde		Malawi	
Congo		Swaziland	
Cote-d'Ivoire		Tanzania	
Equatorial Guinea		Uganda	
Gambia			
Guinea			
Guinea-Bissau			
Kenya			
Mali			
Mauritania			
Mozambique			
Niger			
Nigeria			
Rwanda			
Sao Tomé and Príncipe			
Senegal			
Seychelles			
South Africa			
Togo			
Zaire			
Zambia			
Zimbabwe			

Sources: "Africa's Experiments," *West Africa,* May 25–31, 1992, pp. 870–871. African Studies Program, CSIS.

Movement for the Liberation of Angola (MPLA) against vociferous U.S. disapproval. Without question, Cuba's actions adversely affected U.S.–Soviet relations. This was further evident in the SALT II talks, when (according to former U.S. National Security Advisor Zbigniew Brzezinski) Soviet intervention in the Ethiopian–Somali conflict led to the subsequent U.S.–Soviet tension that "buried [SALT II] in the sands of the Ogaden."[11]

In retrospect, the ascent to power of Mikhail Gorbachev in the Soviet Union in 1985 signaled a turning point in the cold war in Africa. As Leonid Fituni observes, Gorbachev's "new thinking" called for the "abandonment of confrontational politics, priority attention to the resolution of regional politics, a deemphasis on ideology as a key factor shaping diplomatic relationships, and a search for compromises on potentially inflammatory issues."[12] In practical terms, this meant a significant change in the approach taken by the Kremlin to Third World affairs. A series of high-level contacts between Moscow and Washington were quickly established. The first tangible results of these contacts were the December 1988 agreements on Angola and Namibia. On May 31, 1991, another historic milestone was reached when the following Joint Statement on U.S.–Soviet Cooperation on Conflict Resolution in Africa was released at the signing of the peace accords that brought Angola's sixteen-year civil war to an end:

> We have just witnessed here in Lisbon the settlement of the Angola conflict, which was achieved through negotiations under Portuguese stewardship.
>
> Last year's achievement of Namibian independence, the establishment of peace in Angola, and the intensification of peace-making activities in other parts of the continent have demonstrated that negotiations are replacing armed struggle as the principal political trend in Africa. The future of Africa largely depends on how quickly wars can be ended and new political structures developed to resolve and prevent conflict.
>
> The United States and Soviet Union express satisfaction with their increasing cooperation, which is aimed at assisting African countries in restoring peace in various regions of their continent. The US and USSR stand ready to work together with the international community and especially African countries and the OAU [Organization of African Unity] to resolve armed conflicts through political means. In this context, the UN has a valuable role to play in peace-making and peace-keeping, as it has demonstrated in Africa. Our two countries are determined to play a constructive role in ending conflicts in Africa, and will cooperate in promoting political resolution of disputes, strengthening democracy and economic development, combating hunger and disease, and enhancing environmental stability.[13]

The changed tone in superpower involvement in Africa was further demonstrated in mid 1991, when both U.S. and Soviet officials were active in on-the-ground consultations relating to the resolution of conflicts in Ethiopia and Somalia. Further cooperation was evident in the support from both Washington and Moscow for the Italian-chaired peace talks aimed at ending the unresolved war in Mozambique, where a former Marxist government and ally of Moscow continues to battle against a rebel army that had at one time sought support from Washington.

The end of the cold war has also signaled the end of the competition between the United States and the Soviet Union to validate their respective systems of government by encouraging African nations to adopt their own or similar ideologies. Some Africanists are tempted to view the failure of the United States and the Soviet Union to instill their respective ideologies in Africa as a vindication of their insistence that neither communism nor capitalism has been particularly relevant to the African continent. As to the future, Leonid Fituni contends that Russia, in its preoccupation with regional issues closer to home, will be primarily concerned with commercial interests.[14] For the other former Soviet republics, it is likely that foreign policy toward Africa will be developed on ad hoc bases (e.g., Muslim republics forging links with Muslim-dominated nations in Africa). The same will probably also hold true for the United States as it faces domestic economic difficulties that limit its ability to extend itself overseas. Corporations based in the United States will undoubtedly continue to invest in countries where returns are greatest, although future investments will increase if many African nations are able to create more reliable and stable environments for foreign investment.

Overall, the end of the cold war has transformed the structural relationships between the superpowers and Africa considerably. Without question, there is now a decreased ability of either the United States or the former Soviet republics to directly influence African affairs. Most of the assistance that might filter to Africa over the next several years is likely to be either conditioned or related to human rights and economic reforms. Other issues on the agenda for major power cooperation in Africa include research and help with the acquired immunodeficiency syndrome (AIDS), the debt crisis, political instability, the environment, and the cooperative role to be played by the major powers within foreign donor agencies.

Several external actors may figure prominently in the changed environment of Africa. Already, Portugal has emerged as a low-key mediator in the Angola–Namibia talks, and both Italy and the Vatican have made attempts to expedite Mozambican peace talks. In the vacuum created by the partial retrenchment of U.S. and Soviet positions, a set of actors primarily pursuing economic objectives has entered the scene. Among the most notable are Japan, Germany, and several Nordic countries. The presence of former colonial powers such as Belgium and Great Britain has also continued, although both seem to be eager to cut those links with Africa which are no longer politically or economically profitable.

France continues to maintain its political, economic, and social linkages with its former colonies. Through the Communaute Financière Africaine (CFA) franc zone, Paris has historically exerted influence, especially among West African states. While France's presence will undoubtedly be felt in the future, its public role may be diminished. Recently, France has been the target of attacks by other nations for its propping up of less-than-democratic leaders. In an attempt to shed itself of this image, President François Mitterrand has applied pressure on its client states to democratize, or lose vital French financial assistance.

French military presence also continues to be felt in Africa. Six nations (Djibouti, Chad, the Central African Republic, Senegal, Gabon, and Côte d'Ivoire) host French troops on a permanent basis. Further, in Paris, a 48,000-strong rapid-deployment force stands ready to intervene in any African nation where French nationals are at risk. The rule which seems to have emerged regarding French military involvement in Africa is that the French will respond only to external threats to the security of their client states in Africa; internal tensions must be eased without French assistance.[15]

Several other actors should be noted. In the past, China has been involved in Africa, most notably in its support for Roger Mugabe's Zimbabwean African National Union (ZANU) during the late-1970s struggle for independence in Zimbabwe. China has also played a role as an arms dealer. Israel has worked arduously to strengthen its ties with South Africa with a fair amount of success. Israeli relations with Ethiopia have also improved, in large part because of the Falasha resettlement program. Although the generally pro-Arab stance of most African states in the Arab–Israeli conflict has made Israel somewhat of a pariah state in Africa, Israel's financial and technical value may make it more attractive as a future friend or ally. Iran may also play a more extensive role in influencing the course of events in Africa. Teheran has already forged strong links with the al-Bashir regime in Khartoum, and it has made public its intent to spread its distinct brand of Islamic fundamentalism throughout Africa. Khartoum is geographically strategic for Iran, primarily because it serves as a point from which Teheran can deliver its message to the vulnerable neighbors of Sudan.

As an individual actor, former U.S. President Carter and his Conflict Resolution Program in the Carter Center at Emory University have been especially active in overseeing democratic elections in Zambia and in various economic development efforts elsewhere in the region. It is reasonable to expect further participation by the Center in the future, perhaps in supervising national conferences and elections.

African Initiatives. For years, many African nations were hesitant to undertake actions on the African continent without first consulting with their non-African mentors or allies. This was especially evident in France's prominent role in influencing events in West Africa. Now, with the conclusion of the cold war, more African states are demonstrating an increased readiness to deal with conflict resolution and questions of economic integration. Such prominent individuals as former President of Nigeria Olusegun Obasanjo have stepped to the forefront. His intercontinental African Leadership Forum has been active in promoting African interests and raising public consciousness. A renewed respect for the OAU and other regional organizations can be also seen. As described in the publication *West Africa* in June 1991:

> There was a time when OAU summits were in danger of becoming mere annual jamborees for African heads of state. That was when the Cold War was at its chilliest and there was a feeling that somehow the continent's destiny would be a part of a bargained resolution of superpower rivalry. . . . Now, the OAU is a necessity.[16]

This renewed sense of purpose can be seen in the higher attendance and the more ambitious agenda adopted at the 1991 OAU summit. All told, there were thirty-four heads of state in attendance, with only three countries not represented by delegations. At that summit, agreements were reached that called for the creation of the African Economic Community (to deal specifically with the African debt crisis) and a new commitment to end all African wars. Perhaps the most significant achievement of the summit was the tacit acceptance of Nigeria's domination of the sixteen-nation Economic Community of West African States' five-member Economic Community of West African States Cease-Fire Monitoring Group (ECOMOG). This force was dispatched to Liberia in August 1990 to impose and monitor a ceasefire in the war-torn capital of Monrovia. While it has had only limited success in achieving its stated purposes, the ECOMOG force is an important example of African cooperation.

African states have also made overtures to other international organizations. Like most Third World nations during the cold war years, African states were active in the U.N. General Assembly. Starting in the mid 1960s, African states consistently introduced resolutions addressing such critical African issues as refugees, deforestation, and drought. African states led the movement to impose sanctions against Rhodesia in the late 1970s, and it was the work of these same African states that ensured that the situation in South Africa and the Western Sahara remained on the annual General Assembly agendas. Together, the African states comprise nearly one-third of all members of the General Assembly—where the crucial fact is that each state is equal (i.e., each state has one vote). In recent years, attempts have been made by African representatives to the United Nations to unify the African bloc and thus make it the most powerful political entity within the General Assembly.

In early 1992, Boutros Boutros-Ghali of Egypt was elected to succeed Javier-Perez de Cuellar as Secretary General of the United Nations. For Africa, this was a clear signal that their role in U.N. activities is significant, and that their role will continue to be critical. However, some Africans have protested that the selection of a North African Secretary General from among the pool of candidates (which included key sub-Saharan African representatives) was a deliberate attempt by the Security Council members holding veto power to ignore qualified sub-Saharan candidates. It is the hope of most Africans that Boutros-Ghali will work to place African issues at the top of his agenda.

Democratization. The winds of change sweeping across the African continent have been characterized by some as evidence of Africa's "second revolution." This second revolution is understood to be the movement away from and popular rejection of the autocratic rule typical of most African states during the first three postcolonial decades. While it is tempting to consider this repudiation of authoritarianism as the first stage of a more dramatic "democratization" movement spreading across the continent, caution should be exercised in formulating any solid conclusions about the fate of democracy in Africa.

A series of clearly discernible factors has thus far helped propel the "democratization" movement. First, the justifications offered historically as defenses of authoritarian rule (e.g., strong central government is necessary to quell ethnic, religious, or regional tensions) are no longer popularly accepted. Second, the end of the cold war has left several of Africa's least legitimate leaders (Ethiopia's Mengistu before he fell, Zaire's Mobutu, and to a lesser extent, Kenya's Moi) without critical superpower support. Third, the increased power of the print and electronic media to make information available to populations has inspired more democratically oriented or mass-oriented organizations to mobilize. Fourth, an increasingly obvious trend among external donors (France, the United States, Great Britain, and the World Bank) to condition economic assistance on certain criteria of "good governance" has forced many African states seeking financial aid to initiate serious policy reform. Although the governance criteria are implicitly based on Western concerns for human rights and fundamental freedoms (e.g., freedoms of speech, press, and assembly), the World Bank's explicit standards which must be met by potential recipients are accountability, predictability, the rule of law in government, and the absence of any factors which could interfere with economic recovery.[17]

Historically, Africa's social differentiation and political organization have

Table 19.2 External Debt in Sub-Saharan Africa (in Millions of Dollars)

Country	*1980*	*1985*	*1989*
Benin	417	812	1,177
Botswana	133	334	513
Burkina Faso	334	538	756
Burundi	166	446	867
Cameroon	2,513	2,940	4,743
Cape Verde	20	97	130
Central African Republic	195	348	716
Chad	218	186	368
Comoros	44	133	176
Congo	1,496	3,033	4,316
Côte d'Ivoire	5,848	9,746	15,412
Djibouti	32	144	180
Equatorial Guinea	76	159	228
Ethiopia	804	1,869	3,013
Gabon	1,513	1,207	3,176
Gambia	137	245	342
Ghana	1,314	1,898	3,028
Guinea	1,117	1,438	2,176
Guinea-Bissau	132	304	458
Kenya	3,530	4,309	5,690
Liberia	686	1,247	1,761
Lesotho	71	173	324
Madagascar	1,257	2,460	3,607
Malawi	821	1,018	1,394
Mali	733	1,468	2,157
Mauritania	845	1,502	2,010
Mauritius	467	629	832
Mozambique	NA	2,863	4,737
Niger	863	1,208	1,578
Nigeria	8,934	19,551	32,832
Rwanda	190	369	652
Sao Tomé and Príncipe	24	62	131
Senegal	1,468	2,559	4,139
Seychelles	84	98	168
Sierra Leone	430	724	1,057
Somalia	660	1,639	2,137
Sudan	5,163	9,127	12,965
Swaziland	206	238	282
Tanzania	2,572	3,867	4,918
Togo	1,045	937	1,185
Uganda	733	1,171	1,808
Zaire	4,860	6,027	8,843
Zambia	3,266	4,639	6,874
Zimbabwe	786	2,465	3,688

Source: World Bank, *World Debt Tables, 1990–91: External Debt of Developing Countries,* vol. 2 (Washington: International Bank for Reconstruction & Development, 1990), pp. 1–429.

NA = not available.

encouraged a narrow base of popular support for decision-making. According to Dr. Adebayo Adedeji, former executive secretary of the Economic Commission for Africa, democracy in Africa must be linked to political and economic empowerment, accountability, economic justice, and an internalization of these values. Adedeji calls his formula for empowerment and accountability the "five Cs"; to have democracy, a nation must have a government guided by popular consent, consensus, commitment, conviction, and compromise.[18] At present, few states meet these conditions. The African Governance Program of the Carter Center (as of early 1992) has increased the number of African countries classified as democratic to nine (Benin, Botswana, Cape Verde, The Gambia, Mauritius, Namibia, Sao Tomé and Príncipe, Senegal, and Zambia). Another thirty-one states are, according to the Carter Center, in some form of transition away from authoritarian rule. Starting with Benin in 1990, many of the francophone countries have either convened or considered the organization of a "national conference" composed of representatives from government, opposition political parties (if legally recognized) or political associations, civic associations, trade unions, and any other elements relevant to the "democratization."

However, the transition away from either a military-dictatorship or authoritarian regime to a more democratically oriented government has not been easy. Years of autocratic rule have, in most cases, created regimes characterized by decay, corruption, and out-of-control bureaucracies. Perhaps the two greatest challenges to democracy and stability have been the questions of how to ensure transitions and national reconciliation following elections, and how to create armies that are accountable and loyal to civilian governments. Nonetheless, some African countries have turned to the cleansing experience of a national conference in the hope of stimulating growth and ensuring stability. The national conference held in Benin in 1990 has served as the model for other nations to follow. Under pressure from Paris, Mathieu Kerekou, the Marxist dictator of Benin, organized an interim government which supervised a peaceful transition in government.

Following Benin's example, Togo, Congo, and Zaire have also organized national conferences. Unfortunately, none of these countries has shared Benin's democratic success. In Togo, the democratic process has been strained. General Gnassingbe Eyadema, former president (stripped of all but ceremonial powers on August 28, 1991), continues to control loyal military forces which threaten the rule of appointed president Joseph Koffigoh. After the national conference, violent demonstrations occurred regularly. Congo's interim Prime Minister André Milongo also struggled against the legacy of former President Denis Sassou-Nguesso's highly authoritarian rule. Zaire's transition to democracy will undoubtedly be the most difficult. Since mid 1991, President Mobutu has appointed three different prime ministers in a desperate attempt to cling to power. Inflation, unemployment, and an enormous foreign debt have crippled the Mobutu regime. Popular protests have been regular and vehement in demanding democracy and governmental accountability. Recently, Niger and Mali have considered (with some trepidation, in light of the troubles of other francophone nations) the national conference idea.

This phenomenon of national conferences is one that is so far unique to the francophone states, although nonfrancophone states have also considered the democratic option. Chief among these is Nigeria, which planned to have a democratically elected president by the summer of 1993. Other nations with tentative near-term plans for democratic elections were Angola (which held them on September 29 and 30, 1992) and Ethiopia (referendum on the status of Eritrea by late 1993).

Only Zambia, which held successful democratic elections in late October 1991 to elect former trade union leader Frederick Chiluba, demonstrated that the transition to democracy can be peaceful and quick. On October 31, 1991, Chiluba and the Movement for Multiparty Democracy (MMD) defeated Kenneth Kaunda and his United National Independence Party (UNIP), which had ruled the country since independence in 1964 (and ruled it as a one-party state from 1972). Throughout the 1970s, Zambia was wracked by economic crises: the price of copper, Zambia's main export, fell drastically; oil prices rose, raising transportation costs for Zambian exporters; deficit spending by the government reached 10 percent of the gross domestic product, setting off an inflationary cycle; and foreign debts to external creditors rose to over $7.5 billion. These setbacks, compounded by ineffective government control of marketing boards, fueled public discontent.[19] An aborted military coup in 1990 forced Kaunda to schedule the 1991 elections which eventually removed him from power.

The Case of South Africa. The apartheid system of government that has existed in South Africa since 1948 is being dismantled after years of struggle, with hope that President F. W. de Klerk will follow through on his 1989 promise to ensure that the presidential vote in 1994 would not exclude nonwhites. The pace of reform pursued by de Klerk left almost no one unsurprised.

A referendum of March 17, 1992, in which 68.7 percent of the more than 2.3 million white voters casting ballots endorsed the negotiations taking place between the South African government, the African National Congress (ANC), and seventeen other organizations, provided a clear sign that the process of change that started before 1990 was finally irreversible. The single question on the ballot was: "Do you support continuation of the reform process which the State President began on February 2, 1990, and which is aimed at a new constitution through negotiations?"

The first milestone was passed on February 2, 1990, when President de Klerk dramatically accelerated the dismantling of apartheid by announcing the "unbanning" of all opposition groups, including the ANC. Nine days later, ANC leader Nelson Mandela walked out of prison, after more than twenty-seven years of incarceration. Thereafter, the government, the ANC, and a broad array of other political and quasipolitical organizations established the Convention for a Democratic South Africa (CODESA), a forum in which the adoption of a democratic, nonracial constitution and the process leading to elections are being negotiated. The March 1992 referendum represented an important second milestone on the path to that objective.

Table 19.3 Principal Regional Forces in Sub-Saharan Africa, 1991

Country/Service	*Regular Forces*	*Reserves*	*Main Armament*
Angola*			
(pop. 10,323,600)			
Army	91,500	50,000	500+ tanks
			125 AFV
			505 arty.
Navy	1,500		17 ptl. acft.
Air Force	3,000		160 cbt. acft.
			40 armed hel.
Paramilitary	7,000		
Chad			
(pop. 5,827,400)			
Army	17,000		63 AFV
Air Force	200		4 cbt. acft.
Paramilitary	5,700		
Ethiopia			
(pop. 50,628,200)			
Army†			300+ tks.
			350 AFV
			400 arty.
Navy†			2 frigates
			16 ptl. cft.
Air Force†			68 cbt. acft.
Kenya			
(pop. 26,024,200)			
Army	19,000		76 tks.
			88 AFV
			56 arty.
Navy	1,100		7 ptl. crft.
Air Force	3,500		26 cbt. acft.
			38 armed hel.
Paramilitary	4,000		
Mozambique			
(pop. 16,386,000)			
Army	45,000		80 tks.
			230 AFV
			200+ arty.
Navy	1,000		24 ptl. crft.
Air Force	7,000		43 cbt. acft.
			6 armed hel.
Paramilitary	5,000		

Table 19.3 Principal Regional Forces in Sub-Saharan Africa, 1991 *(continued)*

Country/Service	*Regular Forces*	*Reserves*	*Main Armament*
Nigeria (pop. 122,519,000)			
Army	80,000‡		257 tks. 290 AFV 459 arty.
Navy	5,000		2 frigates 95 ptl. crft.
Air Force	9,500		95 cbt. acft. 15 armed hel.
Paramilitary	12,000		
South Africa (pop. 37,354,200)			
Army	50,000	635,000§	250 tks. 4,600 AFV 350 arty.
Navy	4,500	2,000	3 subs. 40 ptl. crft.
Air Force	10,000	27,000	259 cbt. acft. 14+ armed hel.
Medical Corps	8,000		
Paramilitary	97,000		
Sudan (pop. 26,083,200)			
Army	65,000		230 tks. 286 AFV 137 arty.
Navy	500		2 ptl. crft.
Air Force	6,000		51 cbt. acft. 2 armed hel.
Paramilitary	3,000		
Tanzania (pop. 27,567,400)			
Army	45,500	10,000	90 tks. 75 AFV 375 arty.
Navy	800		21 ptl. crft.
Air Force	1,000		24 cbt. acft.
Paramilitary	101,500		
Zambia (pop. 7,134,000)			
Army	16,000		60 tks. 88 AFV 153 arty.
Air Force	2,000		81 cbt. acft. 5+ armed hel.
Paramilitary	1,200		

Table 19.3 Principal Regional Forces in Sub-Saharan Africa, 1991 *(continued)*

Country/Service	*Regular Forces*	*Reserves*	*Main Armament*
Zimbabwe (pop. 10,270,000)			
Army	51,600		43 tks. 198 AFV 40 arty.
Air Force	3,000		64 cbt. acft.
Paramilitary	38,000		

Source: International Institute for Strategic Studies, *The Military Balance 1991–1992* (London: IISS, 1991), pp. 124–148. For abbreviations, see Table 17.1.

*These figures represent government forces prior to a June 1991 agreement under which the government and UNITA agreed to merge their armed forces to form a 50,000-strong National Army. UNITA forces included 28,000 regulars and a militia force of 37,000.

†Following the defeat and dissolution of the former government of Ethiopia by forces of the Ethiopian People's Revolutionary Democratic Front (EPRDF) and Eritrean People's Liberation Front (EPLF), no national armed forces have yet been formed. Approximate troop strength of two are assessed at: EPRDF—65,000; EPLF—60,000. Equipment formerly held by the government is now largely in the hands of EPRDF and EPLF. No recognizable organization of either the Navy or Air Force remains.

‡As part of the transition to civilian rule, Nigeria will be cutting its armed forces by approximately 40,000 men.

§Includes 360,000 Citizen Force Reserves, 135,000 Active Citizen Force Reserve, and 140,000 Commando Force.

The decision to hold a referendum was reached by de Klerk and his small inner circle of advisers immediately after the defeat suffered by the governing National Party in a by-election that registered a 11.2 percent swing from the National Party to the Conservative Party—results that were much worse than the government had anticipated. This by-election was one of a series that had shown an unmistakable loss of support for the National Party. Confronted with the Conservative Party claim that he no longer had white support and had to call for a new parliamentary election, de Klerk believed that he had to go back to the white voters to obtain a mandate enabling him to continue negotiating with the ANC from a position of strength.[20]

By mid 1992, the key question for future negotiations was the size of the majority necessary to ratify a new constitution. This was only part of the larger question of how to end the confrontation between the South African government and the African National Congress. de Klerk favored a power-sharing arrangement whereby a majority would control the country but would be forced to deal with coalitions, mainly whites, that would have representation in a future government. The ANC favored outright majority rule but supported a bill of rights to protect minorities. CODESA was the forum to resolve these questions. A primary concern of both parties was the time frame that CODESA had to be allotted to draft an agreeable constitution. The ANC suggested six months while some government officials spoke in terms of ten years. This issue remained unsolved by the end of 1992.

"Finally we're all together!"

Reprinted with permission of Renan R. Lurie.

On the military side, South African Defense Forces (SADF) will soon face the challenge of combining forces with the ANC's Umkhonto we Sizwe (Spear of the Nation) as well as, perhaps, with Mangosuthu Buthelezi's Inkatha and the Azanian People's Liberation Army. Some sort of melding of South African Defense and Umkhonto forces will be necessary to reassure South Africa's two major constituencies that the new national military will not act against the interests of either group. Although Minister of Defense Malan expressed skepticism about such a merger, his statement was viewed as a short-term reaction. Some SADF officers have said privately that either Malan or his successor would negotiate specific integration issues with Umkhonto.

Military amalgamation raises a range of difficult and likely divisive ideological, structural, and personnel issues. Can two competitors, historically and sometimes violently identified with opposing views, and oriented toward markedly different military methodologies, support a government answerable to all South Africans?

The army will be the focus of concern, because the ANC has very few personnel trained in air and naval operations. A black-dominated government would understandably be concerned about an enemy within the gates—e.g., dissident officers at the operational level who might stage mutinies, commit sabotage, or simply slow down the bureaucratic process. And former Umkhonto members would likely find it psychologically difficult to cooperate with and take orders from former dominant SADF personnel.

A central issue of structure is whether the much smaller Umkhonto should be integrated into the existing SADF or whether a totally new force should be formed (as in Namibia, where the postindependence government headed by President Sam Nujoma ordered members of both the SWAPO military wing and the South West Africa Territory Force to disband and then apply to join the country's new defense force as raw recruits).[21]

Although the process of political change and its likely outcome are uncertain, all sides were clear on the fact that minority domination of South Africa would soon come to an end. The mechanisms were in place, but by the end of 1992 the modalities and time frame had yet to be negotiated.

Economic Component of Democratization. One further key question is whether the success of democracy in Africa is linked to economic growth and stability, and whether one can be achieved independently of the other. According to the World Bank, as of 1990, twenty-four of the twenty-six most severely indebted low-income countries (annual income per capita less than $580) are in Africa.[22] In addition, thirty out of fourty-four borrowing countries in Africa have resorted to some sort of rescheduling of debts because they have been unable to service them at the original rates. Only nine nations (Botswana, Burkina Faso, Chad, Djibouti, Lesotho, Mauritius, Rwanda, Seychelles, and Swaziland) are not facing a foreign debt. Clearly, economic poverty and economic hardship have made it difficult for many African leaders to implement innovative plans of reform.

Throughout the 1980s, many African nations adopted stabilization programs which aimed, in various ways, at promoting long-term economic growth. However, western investors have been slow to respond favorably to Africa as an environment for long-term investment. Some African presidents have launched their own liberalizing measures so as to decrease capital flight, "brain drain," and severe foreign debts. One element of the contentious debate that has resulted from these stabilizing measures has been whether economic development is necessary for democratization. In any case, a more stable economic environment would undoubtedly facilitate any attempts at liberating the political system.

The question of how loans should and will be made, whether through an international lending organization or bilaterally, is also important. As the rescheduling of loans made by either of the international lending institutions (the International Monetary Fund or the World Bank) continues, these lending institutions have more seriously considered "conditioning" loans. In so doing, lending institutions would establish certain criteria (e.g., transparency and accountability in government, rule of law, free press, etc.) with which potential donor nations would need to comply to qualify for loans. This issue of conditioning loans has been hotly debated, and this debate will likely continue.

For the first time in Africa's postcolonial history, the continent has the opportunity to operate without the veil of superpower confrontation looming overhead. Political accountability, good governance, economic development, and ethnic conflicts are now emerging as the central issues, whereas autocratic rule, financial mismanagement, and ideological slogans once dominated Africa. Each country must begin to chart its course toward a more constructive future, otherwise the marginalization of the continent will continue unabated. American national security is unlikely to be directly challenged by evolving trends or events on the sub-Saharan scene. Yet a peaceful, developing Africa as an important building block of a less dangerous, more cooperative new world order is very much in the U.S. interest and worth increased attention and effort.

Discussion Questions

1. What has been the legacy of the cold war in Africa? How has it affected countries like Angola, Ethiopia, and Mozambique?
2. Have U.S. strategic interests in the region changed since the ending of the cold war?
3. How can the United States promote democracy or greater political accountability in Africa? Through what mechanisms can this be accomplished?
4. Without the interest of the superpowers, will Africa be further marginalized in the global economy?
5. Will South Africa successfully complete its transition to majority rule? What is the future for foreign investment in South Africa? What impact did American sanctions have on changing the apartheid system in South Africa?
6. How can African states attract foreign investment in an increasingly competitive world economy? What are the prospects for genuine free economic zones in Africa?
7. Should the United States make human rights the cornerstone of its foreign policy toward Africa? Why?
8. Can and will African militaries extricate themselves from politics? Is there a greater chance of military takeovers of fragile democracies?
9. Can the United States cancel African debt as a means to promote a new beginning for the continent? Should it try?
10. What African forces/factors will likely shape the future of the continent, and what impact will they have on U.S.–African relations?

Recommended Reading

Africa South of the Sahara, 1992. London: Europa Publications, 1991.

Albright, David. *Soviet Policy toward Africa Revisited*. Washington, D.C.: CSIS Significant Issues Series, Georgetown University, 1987.

Clough, Michael. "Africa in the 1990s." *CSIS Africa Notes,* no. 107 (January 29, 1990).

Clough, Michael. *Free at Last?: U.S. Policy Toward Africa and the End of the Cold War*. New York: Council on Foreign Relations Press, 1992.

Deng, Francis M., and Zartman, I. William. *Conflict Resolution in Africa*. Washington, D.C.: Brookings Institution, 1991.

Foltz, William J., and Bienen, Henry S., eds. *Arms and the African*. New Haven, Conn.: Yale University Press, 1985.

Futuni, Leonid. "Russia's Third Discovery of Africa." *CSIS Africa Notes,* no. 134 (March 1992).

Kitchen, Helen. *Some Guidelines on Africa for the Next President*. Washington, D.C.: CSIS Significant Issues Series, Center for Strategic and International Studies, 1988.

Kitchen, Helen. "Some Thoughts on the U.S. Policy Process." *CSIS Africa Notes*, no. 119 (December 28, 1990).

Laidi, Zahi. *The Superpowers and Africa*. Chicago: University of Chicago Press, 1990.

Lancaster, Carol. "The New Politics of U.S. Aid to Africa." *CSIS Africa Notes*, no. 120 (January 1991).

Lee, Robin, and Schemmer, Lawrence, eds. *Transition to Democracy*. Cape Town, South Africa: Oxford University Press, 1991.

Libby, Ronald T. *The Politics of Economic Power in Southern Africa*. Princeton, N.J.: Princeton University Press, 1987.

Lowenkopf, Martin. "Some Lessons from the Past and Some Thoughts for the Future on U.S. Policy in Africa." *CSIS Africa Notes*, no. 132 (January 1992).

Marx, Anthony W. *Lessons of Struggle: South African Internal Opposition, 1960–1990*. New York: Oxford University Press, 1992.

McCormick, Shawn H. "Angola: The Road to Peace." *CSIS Africa Notes*, no. 125 (June 6, 1991).

Ottaway, Marina. "South Africa After the Referendum." *CSIS Africa Notes*, no. 135 (April 1992).

Said, Abdul A. *The African Phenomenon*. Boston: Allyn & Bacon, 1968.

The World Bank. *World Development Report, 1991*. New York: Oxford University Press, 1991.

20

Latin America

The bases of U.S.–Latin American relations are changing rapidly. Dominance of the hemisphere by the United States, though never as all-encompassing as sometimes alleged, has diminished significantly in the past twenty-five years. The longstanding stereotype that the "colossus of the North" could freely impose its will on its weak and dependent neighbors to the south is clearly no longer valid, if indeed it ever was. As we approach the beginning of the twenty-first century, the United States is struggling to adapt its perceptions and policies to a vastly changed global reality, of which the Latin American nations are a part.

During the cold war period Latin America had ridden a roller coaster in terms of U.S. attention and interest, a familiar pattern in U.S.–Latin American relations. At times, U.S. policy had been intensely focused on the region as presidents worried about the vulnerability of the region to communist ideologies and Soviet influence. At other times, Americans turned their attention elsewhere and the region became an object of benign neglect. While there are important cold war legacies, from Castro's Cuba to the *Sendero Luminoso* (Shining Path) insurgency in Peru, the remarkable fact about Latin America at the end of the twentieth century is not continuity but the political and economic transformations occurring across the region. In turn, these changes are having a significant impact upon U.S.–Latin American relations at every level.

While it is convenient for North Americans to think of Latin America as a whole, it is in fact a diverse region with many cultures and heritages. Mexico, while culturally "Latin" is geographically part of North America, along with the United States and Canada. The Caribbean Basin, also called the Circum-Caribbean, includes the islands of the Caribbean Sea and nearby Atlantic Ocean as well as the four Central American countries, Panama, Belize, Venezuela, and Colombia. Among the Caribbean islands one finds French, English, Spanish and Creole languages spoken. Panama and Belize are often included among the Central American nations, in addition to Costa Rica, El Salvador, Guatemala, Honduras, and Nicaragua.

There are further divisions within South America itself. The Andean nations consist of Ecuador, Peru, Bolivia, Colombia, and Venezuela. The countries of Argentina, Chile, Uruguay, and Paraguay are considered part of the Southern Cone. Brazil has long been regarded as a unique entity within the region because of its size, Portuguese language and heritage, and independent economic and foreign policy.

Latin America has tremendous economic and political potential. Resource-rich Brazil has the tenth largest economy in the world and has become a major trading nation. After the Middle East, Latin America probably has the world's largest resources of petroleum. Mexico is the United States' third largest trading partner and will provide a market of some one hundred million people by the end of the century. Chile, Argentina, Venezuela, and Colombia are all potentially vibrant newly industrialized countries (NICs).

During the 1980s almost every Latin American country underwent a transition from authoritarian regimes to democratic rule. In Central America, Nicaragua returned to democratic leadership after more than a decade under Sandinista rule. In El Salvador a historic ceasefire and peace process, under U.N. auspices, promises an end to more than a decade of civil war. While many of these new democracies are fragile and a great deal of uncertainty attends these transitions, they hold the promise of a new era of economic growth, political stability, and interamerican cooperation. Increasingly, Latin America can also boast of a politically and socially modernized middle class, helping to make the region an increasingly dynamic actor on the international stage. Such a vibrant environment may at times be a challenge to the United States, but in the long run, given hemispheric cooperation, it could also present a major opportunity for strengthening the United States, economically and strategically.

Yet there are a host of regional problems, some familiar and others new, with which the United States is inevitably involved. Economically, many Latin American nations still stagger under the strains of enormous debt. Tremendous disparities between rich and poor continue to grow wider with time. The heightened concern for environmental issues, such as deforestation and global warming, have increased tensions not only within nations such as Brazil, but among the nations of the region. These economic and environmental issues contribute to political and social instability in the region and exacerbate such problems as massive flows of refugees, illegal immigrants, and narcotics traffic.

U.S. Interests in Latin America. Since the early nineteenth century, the primary interest of the United States in Latin America has been to have a peaceful southern flank. This objective led directly to President James Monroe's official warning against incursion by European powers into the Western Hemisphere.

FIG. 20.1 Central and South America

"The American continents . . . are henceforth not to be considered as subjects for future colonization by any European power."[1] Monroe went on specifically to warn the "allied powers" that "we should consider any attempt on their part to extend their system to any portion of this hemisphere as dangerous to our peace and safety."

President Polk, in reaffirming the Monroe Doctrine in 1845, added a corollary

Table 20.1 Basic Statistics for Latin America

Country	GDP (1990) (billions of dollars)	Population (millions)	Area (thousands of square miles)
Argentina	64.69	33.1	1068.3
Belize	0.37	0.2	8.9
Bolivia	5.13	7.4	424.2
Brazil	330.29	153.1	3286.5
Chile	27.64	13.1	292.3
Colombia	39.39	31.7	440.8
Costa Rica	5.70	3.0	19.6
Cuba	33.84	10.7	42.8
Ecuador	10.79	11.0	104.5
El Salvador	5.11	5.4	8.1
Guatemala	7.56	9.3	42.0
Guyana	0.37	0.8	83.0
Honduras	4.04	5.3	43.3
Mexico	193.84	91.0	761.6
Nicaragua	2.46	3.9	50.0
Panama	4.71	2.4	29.8
Paraguay	5.50	4.4	157.0
Peru	17.22	21.2	496.2
Surinam	1.40	0.4	63.0
Uruguay	9.14	3.1	68.0
Venezuela	47.70	20.1	352.1

Sources: International Institute for Strategic Studies, *The Military Balance: 1991–92* (London: Brasseys, 1991) and *The Economist World Atlas and Almanac* (London: Economist Books, 1991).

forbidding the voluntary transfer of territory by an American state to a European power. Other presidents further spelled out the implications of the doctrine; for instance, Grover Cleveland's secretary of state in 1895 said, "Today the U.S. is practically sovereign on this continent, and its fiat is law upon the subjects to which it confines its interposition." Teddy Roosevelt in 1904 asserted that the doctrine carried "the exercise of an international police power" in the Western Hemisphere—a corollary subsequently used to justify military intervention in the Caribbean basin.

Although many Latin Americans originally welcomed the doctrine (and at the Lima Conference in 1847 in effect endorsed it), disenchantment set in over the decades. It was not until World War II that the American nations as a whole agreed that an assault by a non-American nation upon the territory or independence of any American state "is an act of aggression against all the other American states."[2] This principle was established through the Inter-American Treaty of Reciprocal Assistance (the Rio Pact), signed in 1947, the first postwar American alliance. A year later the Charter of Bogota created the Organization of American States (OAS). The Rio Pact reflected not so much the evolving conflict with the Soviet Union as the experience with the Axis powers during World War II and the desire to codify and strengthen complementary interests. The United States had an interest in preserving order and the status quo in the region against challenges from both within and without. The Latin American nations too were concerned with protecting the status quo, but were equally concerned with institutionalizing their special relationship with the United States, hoping that increased U.S. attention would mean more financial resources for addressing longstanding economic and social problems. Restraining the United States' interventionist impulse was also high on their list of objectives.

Ironically, almost before the ink was dry on the pact which in effect had codified basic principles of the Monroe Doctrine, Latin American governments began to distance themselves from the treaty, viewing it as a license for American imperialism. U.S. intervention in Guatemala in 1954, the failed Bay of Pigs operation in 1961, and the 1965 intervention in the Dominican Republic reinforced Latin American wariness. The general ineffectiveness of the OAS as an organization for resolving regional conflicts is in part a consequence of Latin American suspicions regarding U.S. intentions. But, despite such Latin American misgivings, the United States has continued to view the Monroe Doctrine as an integral part of its defense policy and as a signal that it will not tolerate a military threat from the south.[3]

The longstanding lack of a military threat in and from Latin America has facilitated the deployment of U.S. power in other regions. This was important to the United States, particularly during the cold war period, for resources deployed in defending against a Western Hemisphere–based opponent would not be available for the defense of Europe, Japan, or the Middle East. Thus, the United States strongly resisted Soviet efforts to place offensive nuclear weapons in Cuba in 1962 and viewed with deep suspicion any Latin American governments seeking close ties with the Soviet Union and the Eastern bloc nations. In fact, since 1959 when Fidel Castro fomented his revolution, a paramount concern for U.S. policy has been to avoid a "second Cuba" in Latin America. Keeping the southern flank secure also explains continuing U.S. efforts to prevent historic rivalries among Latin American countries from degenerating into armed conflict. Moreover, war in the region, as the 1982 Falklands/Malvinas War between Argentina and the United Kingdom demonstrated, forces Washington to make choices among allies.

Historically, a second major U.S. interest in Latin America has been the continuing operation and defense of the Panama Canal. To protect the canal, the United States acquired territory and built bases in the 1900–1930 period. The importance of these investments was shown by the great utility of the canal in both World War II and the Korean conflict. However, the potential wartime role of the canal declined in the 1950s as U.S. aircraft carriers became too large for the locks to handle, and in the mid 1960s, as the Soviet Union deployed nuclear delivery vehicles capable of reaching the vulnerable locks. While still useful in deploying warships prior to general war hostilities and in moving cargo inexpensively between the Atlantic and the Pacific, the Panama Canal is no longer as important a security consideration as in past decades. Yet, because the 1978 Panama Canal treaties transfer almost complete control of the waterway to Panama by the year 2000, the canal's nonavailability could represent a major complication for U.S. military planning.

A third area of concern to the United States is stability in the Caribbean basin—a longstanding interest which in recent years acquired new force. During the 1980s, Central America and several Caribbean islands received considerable U.S. attention. While the international political context has changed significantly since 1988 and apparently lessened the need for U.S. attention, turmoil in the area persists. The upheavals in Haiti in 1992, when a military coup overthrew a democratically elected leader, underscores the continuing seriousness of the problems yet to be addressed in the subregion and the refugee and other consequences for the United States of not addressing them. Indeed, instability elsewhere in Latin America leading to refugee flows is likely to be a major U.S. concern throughout the decade.

A fourth major continuing U.S. interest in Latin America has been economic: oil, raw materials, trade, and investments. Despite the difficulties Latin America experienced during the 1980s, it remains one of the more vibrant developing regions of the world. The region provides about 12 to 15 percent of both U.S. exports and imports and is a major supplier of raw materials. During World War II, it was the primary source for the United States of a number of strategic minerals and petroleum. It has continued to provide most of these same materials to the industrialized North over the past five decades.

Latin Americans are ambivalent about their economic ties with the United States; they fear northern economic domination, yet they need capital, technology, and—in some cases—key skills from the United States. For their part, many U.S. companies view Latin America as a region of uncertain political stability but above-average potential for investment and trade. During the 1980s there was not only a sharp rise in the number of assembly plants (maquiladoras) located by U.S. and Japanese companies in Mexico and Central America, but a rise in Japanese and German investment in such countries as Chile, Brazil, and Mexico.

Growing recognition of the mutual benefits to be gained from strengthening economic relationships among the countries in the hemisphere has sparked several new initiatives from both U.S. and Latin American leaders. In 1982 the Reagan administration proposed the Caribbean Basin Initiative (CBI), a long-term program for increasing trade and economic development through investment incentives and reduced trade barriers for regional export. By emphasizing a comprehensive regional policy that relies more on the active participation of the Caribbean basin states, this approach presented some interesting departures from past policy initiatives. Nonetheless, it languished throughout much of the 1980s. However, in 1990 the Bush administration announced an even more comprehensive plan, the Enterprise for the Americas Initiative (EAI), which incorporated much of CBI into a policy that envisioned a more integrated regional economy with stronger trade ties, investment opportunities, and overall economic growth. The EAI has been greeted with marked enthusiasm by countries throughout the region and represents the first step in a new era of economic cooperation between the United States and its neighbors to the south. In February 1991, leaders from Canada, Mexico, and the United States announced their intention to negotiate a North American Free Trade Agreement (NAFTA) as a means not only of increasing trade among the countries, but also of improving employment and income levels. NAFTA was signed on December 17, 1992 and at the time of this writing it is awaiting ratification. (See Chapter 14 for a brief discussion of NAFTA.)

A fifth prime interest of the United States has been to promote democracy and human rights in Latin America. Largely given lip service or pursued only episodically by the United States in earlier years, this interest became a dominant one during the latter 1970s and an important one in the 1980s. By the 1960s, the three traditional pillars of Latin American societies, namely the church, oligarchy, and the military, were no longer monolithic institutions upholding the status quo and enforcing a common ideology. Moreover, new social groups and new educational, demographic, and economic forces were growing up beside, and in some cases eclipsing, the traditional pillars. The resulting deepening and diffusion of power meant that most Latin American nations acquired a broader, more secure base for democracy in the period. By the late 1980s, a tide of democratization had swept the area; but, although some countries, such as Venezuela and Chile, had had longstanding democratic traditions, for most countries, the institutions and practices of democracy were immature and weak. In any case, the long era of military and oligarchic rule has left an imprint, with the consequence that civil–military relations are not yet in balance and human rights abuses are still all too frequent.

Traditional Patterns in Hemispheric Relations. If the notion of a U.S. "special relationship" with Latin America had any significance in the past, it was more applicable to the Caribbean basin area than to the region as a whole. The United States played a central role in detaching Panama from Colombia in 1903. The newly independent Panamanians, apprehensive that Washington's enthusiasm for their independence might fade, accepted President Theodore Roosevelt's terms for constructing a transisthmian canal. Most controversially, Panama ceded control over the waterway "in perpetuity" to the United States, as well as control over a ten-mile-wide strip bisecting the country. From the perspective of U.S. war-making capabilities, the canal dramatically eased the problem of naval deployment between the Atlantic and Pacific theaters. Consequently, as noted earlier, defense of the canal became an overriding U.S. policy objective in the Caribbean area. Other Caribbean initiatives by the United States, including the acquisition of Puerto Rico and the virtual acquisition of Cuba (and hence a naval base at Guantanamo) as a result of the Spanish–American War, solidified U.S. control of the Caribbean and the approaches to it.

President Wilson purchased the Virgin Islands in 1916, justifying their acquisition as necessary for defense of the Panama Canal. The same concern for the canal caused Washington to be increasingly worried that chronic political stability might tempt Europeans to reintroduce military forces into the Caribbean basin. Largely to avoid such a possibility, the United States assumed the role of Caribbean police officer. Between 1900 and 1933, U.S. armed forces intervened in Panama, Cuba, Nicaragua, Mexico, Haiti, and the Dominican Republic. Far from apologizing for these interventions, Washington explicitly stated its right to carry them out by the so-called Roosevelt Corollary to the Monroe Doctrine.

United States economic interests in the Caribbean basin also grew substantially during the first half of the twentieth century. U.S. corporations invested billions of dollars in Cuban sugar, Mexican petroleum, and Central American bananas. Protection of these investments became an important policy objective, and an influential school of thought about U.S.–Latin American relations maintains that economic factors were more important than political or strategic considerations as causes of Washington's Caribbean military adventures.[4]

In any case, all Latin Americans gave high priority to discouraging the United States from intervening militarily south of the Rio Grande. During the 1930s, Washington gradually abandoned the doctrine of unilateral military intervention in Latin America, replacing it with the so-called Good Neighbor policies of President Franklin Roosevelt.[5] In return, the Latins threw their support behind the European and Asian policies of their northern neighbor.

Venezuela's location on South America's northern coast, and its importance as a source of petroleum for New England and the Middle Atlantic states, caused Washington to treat Caracas as essentially part of its Caribbean basin preserve. Neighboring Colombia has also sometimes been so treated. The rest of South America was perceived by Washington policymakers as a special sphere of influence, although one of less strategic importance. Except in Brazil, the South American investments of U.S. corporations were less extensive than in the Caribbean area, and the continent's southern and western nations were far from the Panama Canal.

In South America, as in the Caribbean basin, the United States largely had things its own way between 1900 and 1960. During World War I, South American governments either declared war on the Central Powers or maintained a pro-Allied neutrality. In World War II they declared war on the Axis powers (though generally belatedly), and between 1947 and 1970 they sided with Washington against Moscow in the cold war. Economically, most South American countries remained eager to supply raw materials for the United States. They also encouraged U.S. investment. By 1960, Latin America accounted for $8.1 billion, or 26 percent, of all U.S. foreign investment (in 1990 investment in Latin America, at $72 billion, was still 17 percent of the U.S. total).[6] Also, large numbers of Latin Americans, especially military officers and children of elites, were attending U.S. universities and professional military schools. Until the late 1950s, virtually all of Latin America remained essentially Washington's special preserve.

Brazil, dramatically different from its Spanish-speaking neighbors, long considered itself joined with the United States in a unique partnership. This perception figured significantly in the decision of President Getulio Vargas to send a Brazilian division to Italy during World War II.[7] On the other hand, Washington generally took the Brazilians for granted. Along with the other Latin Americans, they received periodic pats on the head as long as they did not ally with an extrahemispheric power or threaten hemispheric peace.

Latent anti–United States feelings throughout the region, never far below the surface, were expressed more openly and with greater frequency after 1960. The Roosevelt Corollary had been neither forgotten nor forgiven; the area's terms of trade with the United States had shifted so that ever larger quantities of Latin raw materials were needed to purchase U.S. manufactured goods; and Latin resentment increased against the continual repatriation of profits by U.S. investors. In 1961 Fidel Castro nationalized, without compensation, all U.S. investment in Cuba. Subsequently, after Castro repulsed the half-hearted, CIA-sponsored Bay of Pigs invasion by Cuban exiles and declared himself a Marxist-Leninist, many Latin Americans felt freer to express their grievances. With Castro's support, various disaffected elements launched guerrilla warfare that sought to duplicate the Cuban Revolution in selected Caribbean and South American countries (see Chapter 13 for a discussion of "revolutionary warfare"). For the first time in more than half a century, the United States faced an important political, economic, and military challenge in the Western Hemisphere.

After the Bay of Pigs fiasco in 1961, the United States began responding differently and more firmly to Castro and his Soviet allies. The widely publicized Alliance for Progress launched by the Kennedy administration was intended to address Latin American economic grievances but also to help meet U.S. political and security concerns. President Kennedy's success in facing down the Soviet Union in the 1962 Cuban Missile Crisis discredited Soviet military power in the area while rebuilding confidence in U.S. regional leadership. The 1965 Dominican Republic intervention by the Johnson administration also demonstrated U.S. resolve, although it also awakened old fears associated with the Roosevelt Corollary.

Changing Patterns of Hemispheric Interaction. Relative quiescence prevailed in U.S. policy for Latin America in the late 1960s and early 1970s. As the Alliance for Progress faded in importance, Vietnam, China, the Middle East, and the energy crisis consumed the attention of the United States. As compared with Southeast Asia, our southern flank appeared secure. Crises that emerged during that period were relatively easy to dispose of: the Dominican Republic in 1965, Trinidad and Tobago in 1970, and Chile in 1973.

One of the few comprehensive attempts at charting policy for Latin America during this period was the "Rockefeller Report," commissioned by President Nixon in 1969. Recognizing the importance of Latin America for U.S. security, Nelson Rockefeller proposed a major commitment of U.S. attention and resources to the region. President Nixon quickly dismissed the report, however, because he felt that Latin America did not warrant such a special regional approach.

The 1967 death of Che Guevara, Cuba's foremost exponent and exporter of revolution, carried perhaps the most important consequences for the lack of U.S. policy attention to Latin America. Che's death was mistakenly read as indicating the death of revolutionary activity in the region, even though Latin American insurgent movements were festering underground. In fact, while public attention was turned elsewhere, political violence attained new heights in Guatemala in the late 1960s and early 1970s and took a dramatic worsening turn in the form of terrorism in the Southern Cone and Brazil during the same period. Unrest in El Salvador and Nicaragua in the late 1970s was suggestive of the explosions to follow but was almost entirely neglected as a security threat by the United States.

When a coherent U.S. policy toward Latin America reappeared, it took the form of President Carter's human rights thrust and his administration's push for more pluralistic societies in the region. Repressive regimes in Central America and the Southern Cone became the almost exclusive targets of U.S. attention. American diplomacy in this period was largely predicated on the assumption that the United States could use its economic and political influence to modify the behavior of its recalcitrant Latin neighbors. While this policy approach emphasized fundamental moral concepts for which the United States stands, the inherent difficulties in applying it firmly and consistently limited its effectiveness.

The period between 1978 and 1990 was a time of extraordinary political change in Latin America as a whole. In the late 1970s and early 1980s, even as Argentina, Guatemala, Nicaragua, and El Salvador were in the throes of bloody internal conflicts there were elections in the Dominican Republic and a return to democratic government in Peru and Ecuador. By the end of 1990, democratic transitions had taken place in virtually every country in South and Central America. While democracy is only barely rooted in a number of these countries and insurgencies continue in Guatemala, Peru, and Colombia, a new sense of stability and hopefulness has settled over the region.

Changes in the global economy during the 1980s also reverbrated in the region. Oil-price shocks, rising interest rates, a strong U.S. dollar, worldwide recession, and deteriorating terms of trade combined with mismanagement of bloated domestic economies to bring economic growth to a halt and worsen already serious debt burdens. The gravity of the situation came to international attention in 1982 when Mexico announced it could no longer pay its debt service obligations. It quickly became clear that a number of Latin American countries were severely affected by the debt problem, more so than those in any other region of the world. The debt crisis served to emphasize two important points. First, it demonstrated the interdependence of the United States and Latin America. More than a faddish slogan, interdependence meant that the potential value of U.S. trade and investments in Latin America and the ability of Latin American countries to maintain a reasonable level of economic growth and stability were inextricably intertwined. The United States could no longer ignore Latin American economic stagnation and underdevelopment. Second, the solutions to the debt crisis required strong political leadership just at the time when many of these countries were in the midst of delicate political transitions. Political leaders needed widespread backing for tough policies that imposed economic hardship on many parts of the population in order to undertake the required structural adjustment and reform measures. The potential for unrest and increasing instability arising out of economic difficulties was demonstrated by the rioting that broke out during 1989 in Venezuela, a country with a longstanding tradition of democratic institutions and practices. Thus, U.S. policy has increasingly had to take into account both the economic realities of the region and their political implications.

Despite its weakened economic condition, Latin America's relative political stability in the 1980s has increased its flexibility in international affairs. As the world was hit by the 1979–1980 oil crisis, Mexico's and Venezuela's diplomatic leverage increased in proportion to their petroleum reserves. These two countries joined with Panama and Colombia in 1983 to form the Contadora Group, which sought to bring about a regional settlement of the civil war in Nicaragua. Significant in this and a number of other developments is that the Latin American nations were developing a sense of strategic interests that did not always coincide with those of the United States. Brazil began to sell arms to U.S. adversaries such as Libya. Argentina declared war on a major U.S. ally in 1982. In 1981, the Mexican president, José Lopez Portillo, recognized the Salvadoran insurgents as a legitimate political force. Actions such as these underscore the increasingly independent foreign policies of the Latin nations.

Subregional Review

Central America. In contrast to the previous decade, during the 1980s the United States was intensely focused on Central America as an area of strategic interest. The 1970s had been a time in which not only had the United States paid scant attention to developments in Central America, but a time as well in which the tensions within several of these countries had mounted ominously. When the hated, increasingly repressive regime of Somoza was toppled in 1979 by a coalition of armed opposition groups within Nicaraguan society, much of the hemisphere celebrated. But when the Sandinista junta quickly emerged as Somoza's successor, U.S. policy crashed on the shoals of ambivalence. The wisdom of the Carter administration's attempt at accommodating the Sandinistas between 1979 and 1981 will continue to be debated, but it was clearly rejected as an approach by the Reagan administration. By the end of Reagan's first year, all U.S. aid had been cut off and the CIA had been authorized to build and train an opposition group to the Sandinistas, which eventually became known as the contras.

Over the next eight years, U.S. support for the contras became a highly contentious issue, not only between President Reagan and the Congress, but also in Latin America itself. In 1982, the first of the Boland amendments, barring further monies from being spent to undermine the Nicaraguan government, was passed by the U.S. Congress. In 1983, the need for greater public and congressional support for the administration's policy led President Reagan to establish the National Bipartisan Commission on Central America, chaired by former Secretary of State Henry Kissinger, which produced a unanimous, potentially useful but mostly ignored report. In 1984, a group of four Latin nations—Mexico, Panama, Venezuela and Colombia—presented the first in a series of peace initiatives to help resolve conflict within the region. However, Nicaraguan resistance and U.S. opposition doomed this Contadora initiative.

In the summer of 1987 a bold new proposal from Costa Rican president Oscar Arias revived prospects for a regional peace settlement. The increasing flow of Nicaraguan refugees into Costa Rica and growing uncertainty about the future of U.S. policy in the region, in the wake of the unfolding Iran–Contra scandal, motivated President Arias to formulate a fresh approach to the conflicts in the region. The accord, calling for across-the-board ceasefires, democratization, suspension of all external aid to insurgents, refugee repatriation processes, and regional arms reduction, was signed in August 1987 by all five Central American presidents. Significantly, the United States was taken by surprise when the initiative was announced in March 1987 and was kept at arm's length during the negotiations that led to its adoption five months later. In 1988–1989, under U.N. auspices, the peace process began to be implemented and the Nicaraguan civil war came to an end. In February 1990 Violeta Chamorro, candidate of the United Nicaraguan Opposition (UNO), was elected president of Nicaragua in a surprise victory over Sandinista National Liberation Front (FSLN) leader, Daniel Ortega, who had served as president of the country since the overthrow of Somoza. This event served to put an end to an eleven-year confrontation between the United States and this small Central American nation. (Nonetheless, critics in the United States continued to block economic aid to Nicaragua, charging that Chamorro had not done enough to control the state security forces, which remained largely in the hands of the Sandinistas as of mid 1992.)

Buoyed by success in Nicaragua, the Arias Peace Plan also became the basis for an agreement to end a bloody civil war in El Salvador. In January 1992 the democratically elected government of Alfredo Cristiani signed a peace accord with the leaders of the Frente Farabundo Marti Liberacion Nacional (FMLN), the coalition of insurgency groups that had been at war with the government since 1980. The Salvadoran accord has the potential of bringing peace to a small country that experienced more than 75,000 civilian deaths during the 1980s. However, the bitterness of the conflicts within Salvadoran society make the ultimate success of this venture a matter of high uncertainty. Some of the same dynamics and tensions exist in neighboring Guatemala as well. Although there have been attempts by the government of Jorge Serrano to reach an end to the fighting between the Guatemalan military and a thirty-year-old insurgency, progress has been slow and uneven.

In 1988, the Panamanian strongman, Manuel Noriega, previously considered an asset to the United States, began to pose a serious problem because of his involvement in drug trafficking and other illegal operations in the region. After various unsuccessful attempts to remove him from office, including an election which he nullified, the United States mounted a military operation in December 1989 to capture him and bring him to the United States where he could be tried on charges of drug smuggling. In 1992 he was convicted and sentenced to prison.

The U.S. operation, while successful on one level, was harshly criticized both domestically and internationally, once again raising the specter of U.S. interventionist impulses in the region.

The Caribbean. The Caribbean subregion is primarily characterized by small states with large humanitarian and economic problems (thirty-two political entities with a combined population of approximately 31 million). Overall, the region is poorly endowed economically. Unstable tourism revenues, relatively high energy prices, and a drop in the demand and prices for major exports such as sugar and bauxite have put a tremendous strain on regional economies. Severe income disparities and rapid demographic growth have added fuel to a depressed socioeconomic situation, resulting in major population outflows. In a few cases, such as in Haiti and Cuba, refugee flows have attained dramatic proportions and strong political overtones.

The United States' determination to prevent "another Cuba" and to ensure freedom of navigation in the approaches to the Canal and throughout the Gulf of Mexico and the Caribbean Sea (through which about half of U.S. oil imports pass) have led to periodic U.S. military action in the region. The deployment of the 82nd Airborne Division to the Dominican Republic in 1965, of U.S. warships to Trinidad and Tobago in 1970, and of seven thousand troops to Grenada in late October 1983 are examples. The military operation in Grenada, a political stroke that occurred within days of a major U.S. military debacle in Beirut, sent a strong message about American resolve throughout the region. It powerfully emphasized the point that Washington would not tolerate overt Cuban meddling in an American security zone. (Cuban and other Eastern bloc advisers and materiel had generated a miniarsenal on the island that could have become a highly destabilizing proxy in the Caribbean basin as a whole.)

Cuba remains in many ways the subregion's focal point in terms of U.S. national security, primarily because it is governed by a Marxist regime and lies only ninety miles off the coast of Florida. Although it has a population of only 10 million and is about the size of the state of Virginia, Cuba enjoyed considerable global influence during the 1960s, 1970s, and early 1980s. At one time Fidel Castro actively supported numerous leftist movements and regimes throughout the region and elsewhere, disbursing advisers of various sorts and serving as a safe haven and center of coordination for assorted revolutionary movements. The level of such activities declined dramatically, however, as financial support from the Soviet Union dwindled severely during the late 1980s and Cuba's domestic problems became more pronounced.[8]

In addition to continuing economic and security concerns, the problems facing most of the Caribbean island states over the next several decades will center around arresting decay in and strengthening established democratic and parliamentary infrastructures created during a relatively recent colonial experience. In this context, Puerto Rico may present a particularly sensitive problem due to continued civil unrest, sabotage, and terrorism. The most difficult challenge,

"First fill in the documents in triplicate, sign them, and send them to us by certified mail."

Reprinted with permission of Renan R. Lurie.

however, will probably be Haiti, which for decades has been the poorest country in the Western Hemisphere. Here, the ruthless and despotic misrule of the Duvalier era has guaranteed that the road to economic viability and democratic governance will be long and difficult. The December 1990 election of Jean-Bertrand Aristide and his ouster via a military coup the following year demonstrate that political stability is still a distant possibility. The turmoil within the country has drawn in the Organization of American States, which is attempting to adjudicate conflicting interests and establish a process for a peaceful transition to democratic rule. Whether the traditionally weak OAS will be able to exert sufficient pressure on the dominant military forces within the country remains a matter of speculation.

Mexico. The two-thousand-mile border between the United States and Mexico is the longest one between a developing nation and an advanced industrial one. The obvious result of this geostrategic fact is an extensive and delicate network of interaction between the two entities. As noted in a 1980 Rand report:

> Mexico's new importance derives from the massive economic, social and cultural interconnections growing throughout the U.S. borderlands and extending deeper into both countries. . . . The asymmetry of national power and the disparity of socioeconomic conditions between the two bordering nations is among the greatest in the world. . . . Thus, the borderlands could become the melting pot or the boiling caldron of future U.S.–Mexican relations.[9]

Mexico has recently been enjoying a level of political and social stability and economic prosperity seldom experienced elsewhere in Latin America. Economic liberalization and restructuring has brought consistent gross domestic product growth (3.9 percent in 1990) and gradual political reform. The United States has benefitted economically and geopolitically from this progress; among other benefits, our peaceful southern neighbor is our third largest trading partner. Few developments would be more disastrous for U.S. interests than a serious deterioration of Mexico's economy and political stability.

Mexico's traditional view of its security problems has focused on the threat by the United States to its northern borders. In contrast, until recently, it has not considered Central America either as a problem for its security or within the scope of its national ambitions. Today, fears of U.S. expansionism have generally receded into the background, but they do remain in the Mexican psyche.

Contemporary Mexican policy continues to strike a balance between independence from and cooperation with the United States in global and regional affairs. Thus, the United States is both Mexico's primary security guarantor and its most important psychological threat. However, the prospect of Mexico becoming part of the North American Free Trade Agreement (NAFTA) has begun to alter significantly the nature of U.S.–Mexican relations. It represents a fundamental shift in Mexico's posture from studied detachment to explicit connection in terms of its political relations with the United States. Even so, cooperation on the traditional problems which stem from the unique dynamics of the border—especially drug interdiction and immigration policy—will continue to be an essential part of U.S.–Mexican relations.

Colombia and Venezuela. The two nations on the northern rim of South America form an important security bloc in the middle of the Western Hemisphere. Colombia and Venezuela have their own geopolitical vision of the Caribbean region, with spheres of interest encompassing the Panama Canal, the Atlantic approaches to the Caribbean Sea, and the security of the Guyanas. This regional view was a significant factor in their joining in the formation of the Contadora Group, indicating their clear interest in projecting themselves on a regional scale.

That Colombia and Venezuela maintain democratic governments amidst serious foreign debt pressures, insurgency, and a virtually uncontrollable narcotics industry is remarkable. Relatively sound economies and strong civilian institutions permit both to survive, despite continuous threats to their constitutional governments. In the latter 1970s and 1980s, insurgent groups such as the M-19 in Colombia generated serious internal security problems. Compounding this situation is an increasing direct overlap between the insurgents and the cocaine industry. The activities of Colombian narco-guerrillas have heightened border security concerns, resulting in greater Venezuelan vigilance. In the early 1990s, Venezuela became an important processing and distribution point for cocaine headed for the United States and Europe. Nonetheless, Venezuela is the

United States' second largest trading partner in the Western Hemisphere and a reliable source of petroleum, an important fact underscored during the Persian Gulf war of 1991.

The Andean Countries. The Andean states of Bolivia, Ecuador, and Peru have traditionally been relegated to minor status in U.S. strategic thinking. This situation shifted in the late 1970s and 1980s as events in the subregion took on a new character. Drug trafficking in Bolivia, Peru, Colombia, and Venezuela is a multi-billion-dollar export industry. This flow of cocaine and other substances has been directed primarily at the U.S. market but represents a law-and-order threat in the region as well as in the United States. This has been particularly true in Peru, where political violence and guerilla warfare are wrestling with a young democracy. In 1990 Alberto Fujimori was elected president on a platform of returning political and economic stability to the country. However, in 1992, frustrated by inability to enact his reforms, he suspended the constitution and dissolved the legislature and courts. While his actions were overwhelmingly popular with Peruvians, it is not yet clear whether his unconventional approach will lead to stability or will further fuel the insurgency movement by playing into its efforts to destroy the social and political fabric of Peruvian society.

Maoist in orientation, the Peruvian *Sendero Luminoso* (Shining Path) guerrillas have gained significant support from the largely neglected Indian communities of the Ayacucho region. Since 1982, levels of Sendero violence have increased dramatically, resulting in over 24,000 civilian and military casualties and about $20 billion in economic damage.[10] While insurgency is not a major threat in Ecuador, internal political conflicts there have seriously threatened this other young democracy, as exemplified by the 1987 kidnapping of President Fabres Cordero by rebellious air force officers.

Another striking example of the threat of instability is Bolivia. When President Victor Paz Estenssoro came to power in 1985, he faced a staggering 2,000 percent annual inflation rate. While Estenssoro was able to institute a program of harsh austerity measures and structural adjustment that brought inflation under control, the devastated economy was a key factor in the proliferation of the drug trade in this, South America's poorest nation. To address the narcotics threat, a joint U.S.–Bolivian antidrug campaign was started in 1986. While drugs still pose a threat to Bolivia's future, the country has achieved a remarkable degree of political and economic stability despite its handicaps.

The Southern Cone. Chile and Argentina are the most distant partners of the United States in the hemisphere, in both geographic and diplomatic terms. Neither country has ever warmly interacted with the United States—particularly in recent decades. Until the past few years, repressive military governments in both countries helped generate a distant, uneasy relationship with Washington.

A striking example of this unhappy situation occurred in 1982 when the military government in Buenos Aires decided to act on Argentina's claim to the

Malvinas/Falkland Islands. By doing so, it provoked a war with Britain and placed Washington in an awkward diplomatic situation. The strength of the U.S.–U.K. alliance was such that Washington had to support the United Kingdom's successful campaign against Argentina, much to the latter's chagrin. Elected one year after Argentina's defeat, President Raul Alfonsin was faced with the virtual reconstruction of a once-prosperous nation shattered by forty years of irresponsible rule. Alfonsin made significant strides in implementing democracy, including putting former military leaders on trial for gross human rights violations. However, a series of rebellions by military officers during his last two years in office, though unsuccessful, made the democratic transition more uncertain. A chaotic, overheated economy weakened his ability to rule and he resigned prematurely in order to allow the newly elected president, Carlos Menem, to take office in 1989. After a period of difficulties and confusion that included another unsuccessful military rebellion, a degree of stability and growth has returned to the Argentine economy, and the armed forces have begun a process of modernization that seems promising. By 1992, after nearly half a century of economic profligacy and political chaos, the country seemed poised to reemerge as an economic power in the Southern Cone.

After the return of democracy to neighboring Argentina, American attention shifted to Chile and its deplorable human rights record. Since the overthrow of Allende's Marxist government in 1973, Chile had been ruled by the iron fist of General Augusto Pinochet. Events took a surprising turn in 1989, however, when Pinochet was defeated in a national referendum on his rule, leading to democratic elections at year's end. Although Pinochet tried to keep tight control of the transition process, he nonetheless honored the mandate to return to democratic rule. The primary challenge of the new government of Patrice Aylwin was to maintain the sound and growing economy bequeathed by the Pinochet regime. And, while Pinochet did not totally release his grip on the machinery of government, the new Chilean democracy has seemed to be moving toward consolidation. This transition made it possible for other countries, including the United States, to refocus on Chile's considerable economic achievements over the past two decades and to consider new ways to strengthen their investment and trade ties.

Brazil. Brazil is the sole Latin American nation capable of aspiring to a major global role. The sixth largest state in the international system, Brazil is endowed with plentiful resources, including uranium, bauxite, copper, iron, and gold. This former Portuguese colony is second only to the United States as the world's largest agricultural commodities exporter. Also a major exporter of weapons, Brazil sells aircraft, tanks, and missiles to over thirty countries yielding 380 million dollars of annual revenue.

Brazil's development has transformed the balance of power in the southern portion of Latin America, historically an area of intense Brazilian–Argentine rivalry. At the end of the colonial era, Buenos Aires controlled territories currently comprising Bolivia, Paraguay, Uruguay, and part of southern Brazil. During the struggle for independence, these areas—assisted by Brazil—resisted efforts by Buenos Aires to incorporate them into the new Argentine nation. Nevertheless, Buenos Aires historically considered them as special spheres of influence. Since 1950, however, continued internal political strife and accompanying economic stagnation have made Argentina increasingly less able to project power beyond its frontiers. The century-old parity between Argentina and Brazil has given way to clear and growing Brazilian superiority. Perhaps because of that fact, since 1979, Brazilian–Argentine relations have achieved a state of unprecedented cooperation, after decades of rivalry.[11]

Until 1982, Brazil was justly pointed to as a model of rapid growth. But this "miracle" began to fade during the early 1980s as the country struggled under an enormous external debt burden and growing domestic political uncertainties. By 1985 as Brazil joined the ranks of nations moving from authoritarian to democratic rule, inflation had jumped to 200 percent annually and new foreign investment in the country had virtually come to a halt. However, in March 1990, when Fernando Collor de Mello took office as the first directly elected president in twenty-nine years, he instituted a program of economic stabilization and reform designed to rejuvenate Brazil's sagging economic fortunes. By 1992, however, uncertainty again prevailed with the president facing impeachment on corruption charges and the political system in turmoil.

Eager to expand its influence in South America and recognizing that a special relationship with Brazil could prevent the emergence of an inter-American system in opposition to U.S. policy, the United States long gave special attention to Brazil. This led to the famous "unwritten alliance" that characterized relations between the two countries until the 1970s. Over the past two decades, however, Brazil's desire to play a more autonomous role in international affairs has sundered this informal alliance—though relations have generally remained amicable.

Extrahemispheric Relations. Over the past generation the countries of Latin America have begun diversifying their trade, investment, and security relationships globally, in order to reduce their dependence upon the United States. In their search for technology and associated foreign investment they have looked to Europe and Japan, asking in return that European and Japanese markets be opened to Latin American finished goods as well as raw materials. In addition, there has been a significant increase in their trade with other developing countries and less reliance on the more industrialized nations. Regional trade agreements are also altering Latin American economic and political dynamics, stimulating growth and in turn creating new entrepreneurial classes within countries, introducing new opportunities and new tensions within societies, and shifting the balance of power among nations.

The search for technology, foreign investments and financial credits from diversified sources is central to Latin American economic policies. During the 1970s, Latin America's nations sought primarily to reduce the gap between themselves and the industrialized nations while decreasing their dependence on the United States. To do so, many of them borrowed heavily and not always wisely. The changing economic realities of the 1980s forced most of them to take a much more pragmatic, though economically and politically painful, approach to economic stability and growth. In particular, debt repayment, even with generous rescheduling by their creditors, has been difficult; with a $420 billion external debt and the highest debt service ratio among the regions of the world,[12] most struggle to keep afloat.

The Latin American nations are involved in a rich array of relationships with important U.S. allies. Spain, whose political and cultural ties with Latin America go back to the fifteenth century, has been an especially important dialogue partner for the region; it even hosted a Contadora negotiating session in Madrid. During the 1980s, European political parties and their foundations began to work extensively in Latin America, establishing relationships with labor unions, sister political parties, and business organizations in the region. Japan has increasingly become a major economic player in Latin America. It has funneled money to the region through multilateral development banks as well as directly through foreign aid and direct investment. The Japanese have also shown an interest in maintaining or managing the Panama Canal.

Latin American relations with Africa, Asia, and the Middle East have crystallized along several dimensions during the past fifteen to twenty years. Economically, Brazil and several Spanish-speaking countries have begun selling manufactured goods and development technology to Africa and the Middle East. Of particular significance has been China's acquisition of Brazilian computers. Although trade between Latin America and other developing countries will expand in the future, except for the Brazilian dependence on petroleum these economic relationships will remain secondary.

Politically, stronger ties among the developing nations could provide important leverage in Latin American efforts to gain economic concessions from the industrial North. Eager to capitalize on that leverage, Latin American countries participate as members of the South during North–South dialogues in international forums. By the 1990s, despite their high foreign debt and concomitant debt service requirements, the economies of Latin America were among the strongest within the developing world.

Military Issues. Although Latin America is not nearly so militarized a region as, say, Northeast Asia or the Middle East, internal security threats and historic conflicts have left the region with bloated military establishments often armed with sophisticated weapons. The new tasks for many Latin American countries include streamlining and professionalizing their armed forces, reorienting force missions from internal to external security, and establishing new norms that institutionalize the primacy of civilian rule. In several countries continuing insurgencies will hamper these needed military reforms and threaten the consolidation of democratic rule.

Table 20.2 Regional Forces in Latin America, 1992

Country/Service	Regular Forces	Reserves	Main Armament
Argentina (pop. 33,082,400)			
Army	45,000	250,000	500 tks. 630 AFV 777 arty.
Navy	25,000	77,000	4 atk. subs. 1 acft. carrier 6 destroyers 41 cbt. acft 10 armed hel.
Air Force	13,000	50,000	176 cbt. acft. 14 armed hel.
Paramilitary	28,000		
Brazil (pop. 153,071,400)			
Army	196,000	1,115,000	520 tks. 995 AFV 930 arty.
Navy	50,000		5 atk. subs. 1 acft. carrier 6 destroyers 15 cbt. hel.
Air Force	50,700		313 cbt. acft. 8 armed hel.
Paramilitary	243,000		
Chile (pop. 13,124,000)			
Army	54,000	45,000	477 tks. 520 AFV 548 arty.
Navy	25,000		4 atk. subs. 10 maj. surf. ships 6 cbt. acft. 4 armed hel.
Air Force	12,800		107 cbt. acft.
Paramilitary	27,000		
Colombia (pop. 31,742,400)			
Army	115,000	100,000	12 tks. 126 AFV 200 arty.
Navy	12,000	15,000	2 atk. subs. 5 maj. surf. ships
Air Force	7,000	1,900	68 cbt. acft.
Paramilitary	81,500		51 armed hel.
Costa Rica* (pop. 2,973,200)			
Civil Guard	4,300		
Rural Guard	3,200		

Table 20.2 Regional Forces in Latin America, 1992 *(continued)*

Country/Service	*Regular Forces*	*Reserves*	*Main Armament*
Cuba			
(pop. 10,712,200)			
Army	145,000	135,000	1,770 tks.
			670 AFV
			1,600 arty.
Navy	13,500	8,000	3 atk. subs.
			3 maj. surf. ships
Air Force	22,000+	12,000	162 cbt. acft.
Paramilitary	1,569,000		85 armed hel.
El Salvador			
(pop. 5,360,000)			
Army	40,000		12 tks.
			98 AFV
			56 arty.
Navy	1,200		
Air Force	2,400		42 cbt. acft.
			27 armed hel.
Paramilitary	36,000		
Guatemala			
(pop. 9,329,200)			
Army	37,000	4,500	10 tks.
			40 AFV
			153 arty.
Navy	1,200		
Air Force	1,400	200	16 cbt. acft.
			6 armed hel.
Paramilitary	510,100		
Honduras			
(pop. 5,319,800)			
Army	14,400	50,000	12 tks.
			88 AFV
			28 arty.
Navy	1,000		
Air Force	2,100		48 cbt. acft.
Paramilitary	5,000		
Mexico			
(pop. 91,024,000)			
Army	130,000	300,000	50 tks.
			260 AFV
			118 arty.
Navy	37,000		3 destroyers
			9 cbt. acft.
Air Force	8,000		113 cbt. acft.
			25 armed hel.
Paramilitary	14,000		

Table 20.2 Regional Forces in Latin America, 1992 *(continued)*

Country/Service	*Regular Forces*	*Reserves*	*Main Armament*
Nicaragua			
(pop. 3,923,600)			
Army (reorganization in progress)	27,000		157 tks. 139 AFV 96 arty.
Navy	1,500		
Air Force	2,000		16 cbt. acft. 9 armed hel.
Panama†			
(pop. 2,438,400)			
National Police	11,000		Small arms only
National Maritime Service	300		
National Air Service	200		
Peru			
(pop. 21,170,600)			
Army	72,000	188,000	460 tks. 525 AFV 290 arty.
Navy	18,000		10 subs. 12 maj. surf. ships 8 cbt. acft. 14 armed hel.
Air Force	15,000		113 cbt. acft. 10 armed hel.
Paramilitary	70,600		
Venezuela			
(pop. 20,057,400)			
Army	34,000		185 tks. 255 AFV 280 arty.
Navy	11,000		2 atk. subs. 6 maj. surf. ships 6 cbt. acft. 6 armed hel.
Air Force	7,000		106 acft. 26 armed hel.
National Guard	23,000		

Source: International Institute for Strategic Studies, *The Military Balance, 1991–1992* (London: Brasseys), pp. 185–208. For abbreviations see Table 17.1.

*No armed forces. Figures are for Security, Interior, and Police Ministries.

†Panama's defense forces are undergoing large-scale reorganization following Operation Just Cause.

While American global security is based on a peaceful and stable Latin America, the United States has tended to neglect, if not ignore, Latin American national security matters in times of relative peace. In the nineteenth century, when several major Latin American conflicts over territorial disputes occurred, the United States was not in a position to influence events significantly. Once Washington gained undisputed military and economic preeminence in the hemisphere, its power was used to discourage Latin American nations from resorting to force in disputes among themselves. A major exception occurred during the mid 1930s, when Paraguay and Bolivia battled over the Chaco Province and its potentially rich petroleum deposits. Paraguay's victory marked the last successful use of arms to transfer territory from one Latin American country to another.

Articles 6 and 7 of the Rio Pact commit all signatories to respect existing international boundaries. Thus, in 1969, when Salvadoran troops occupied areas of Honduras, allegedly to protect El Salvador's nationals who had settled on the Honduran side of the frontier, the status quo antebellum clause of the Rio Pact provided procedures and principles for settling the conflict.[13] With this one brief exception, the U.S. and Latin American joint commitment to the doctrine of nonforceable transfer of territory has held.

Four current problems in Latin America involve military considerations. First, although less pressing than during the 1960s, challenges to internal order persist, including guerrilla warfare. The Castro revolution of 1959 demonstrated that small, efficiently organized and politically directed forces could employ irregular warfare to defeat established armed forces and create the opportunity for total societal reorganization. Washington and most Latin American governments assign high priority to preventing another guerrilla movement from repeating the Cuban experience.

Despite earlier success against insurgents, Latin American leaders have not discounted the possibility that irregular warfare might again seriously threaten their countries. They are paying increased attention to some of the root causes of such warfare and to solutions which emphasize negotiation and increased opportunities for political participation. Long-term patterns of racial discrimination as well as deep poverty also seem to feed rebellion and guerilla resistance. By the early 1990s, the countries with the most virulent insurgencies were Peru, Colombia, and Guatemala, each of which also had significant exploited indigenous populations.

Border disputes and conflicting territorial ambitions form a second set of military issues of importance in Latin America. Tensions between Peru and Chile have persisted since the latter's territorial conquests in the War of the Pacific (1879–1884). Bolivia, forced to surrender its outlet to the sea in the same conflict, has continually pressed Chile and Peru for a Pacific port.[14] In northern South America, Colombia and Venezuela remain at odds over the location of their boundary in the potentially oil-rich Gulf of Venezuela. Even so, the number of bilateral disputes among nations of the hemisphere is at an all-time, historic low.

The third basic military issue concerns globally oriented missions for which

Latin militaries might prepare themselves. Because of Brazilian participation in World War II, the idea of integrating some Brazilian troops in NATO European defenses was occasionally raised during the cold war. But Western strategists considered that South American armies and air forces would only have been available to defend their national territories during any global confrontation, so the idea was never seriously pursued. Between 1945 and 1960 no credible military threat to Latin America existed, so the equipment and training of the region's armed forces were not matters of great concern in Washington (or in Western Europe). In the 1960s, when guerrilla warfare became a problem, the United States supplied counterinsurgency technology and training; but, other than that, Latin Americans generally received only training and obsolescent equipment from the United States, useful only in defending their homelands against similarly armed neighbors—or, perhaps, in U.N. peacekeeping.[15]

Defending Latin America states against interstate war, even given the remoteness of such an eventuality, gave rise to institutions and arrangements known collectively as the Inter-American Defense System. The system's authority, the Inter-American Defense Board, has always been headed by a U.S. general officer. Lack of U.S. interest and Latin American concern about Yankee intervention have kept the Inter-American Defense Board weak. It persists, however, as a mechanism through which Rio Pact members could cooperate militarily if they were so inclined. The Falklands/Malvinas War and the Grenada incident demonstrated all too clearly the weakness of the Inter-American Defense Board, which was irrelevant in both crises.

The School of the Americas, now in Georgia and formerly in Panama, is an important U.S. training center that has, since the early 1960s, graduated thousands of Latin Americans from its rigorous courses in counterinsurgency, infantry tactics, and many other fields. At sea, the annual UNITAS exercise in the South Atlantic has facilitated naval cooperation between the United States and Latin America. Thousands of Latin American officers have also attended U.S. military service schools, and U.S. military training missions have operated in many Latin American countries during much of this century. The payoff for Washington was that these efforts would help deliver Latin American support for the United States during the cold war, as well as in the case of aggression against a Western Hemisphere nation.

Latin America armies appear to believe that their most important extracontinental mission is to make it unattractive for the United States to interfere militarily in the South. In this context, Latin Americans cast a nervous glance at U.S. dependence on their energy and raw materials, even as they welcome the increased export earnings.

In examining possible extrahemispheric roles for the Latin American military, Cuba's African involvement stands out as unexpected and dramatic.[16] Brazil contemplated involvement in Portugal's African territories during the early 1970s but abandoned the idea as beyond its logistical, military, and economic capabilities. Yet Cuba, far smaller, more vulnerable and less industrialized than Brazil, for years managed to maintain a significant military presence in Angola and

Ethiopia; of course, it could do so only because of extensive Soviet funding, supplies, and support personnel. The Angolan and Ethiopian interventions occurred because of a unique confluence of Castro's self-image as a twentieth-century revolutionary and of Soviet interest in an African presence. It was adventurism that seems highly unlikely to be replicated by Cubans or any other Latin Americans.

Acquisition of weapons and training, the fourth military issue, is greatly affected by Latin expectations of guerrilla activity, relations with neighboring states, and anticipated extrahemispheric missions. Until World War II, Europe dominated the South American arms trade. Between 1945 and 1970, U.S. training and equipment predominated. Initially Washington supplied surplus conventional arms from World War II and Korea, but during the 1960s the emphasis shifted to counterinsurgency-related items.[17] In the early 1970s, as most Latin American militaries began replacing their antiquated conventional equipment, Washington reduced foreign military grants and sales to the region. In addition, Congress prohibited the sale of advanced conventional weapons to Latin American forces irrespective of those nations' perceived needs. In contrast, the French, British, Germans, Italians, and Soviets actively merchandised their most advanced aircraft, tanks, and destroyers. The acquisition of Soviet-made tanks and aircraft by Peru in the 1960s broke the "Western" monopoly on military sales to South America. During the past two decades, most Latin American countries have received progressively less U.S. military training and equipment.

Dependence on Northern arms suppliers implies that sophisticated weapons can be employed by Latin Americans for any length of time only with the support of these suppliers. Recognizing this, in the early 1970s Brazil and Argentina, the region's most industrially advanced states, accelerated already substantial efforts to develop a domestic arms industry.[18] At one time, Argentina's greater technological sophistication gave it an advantage in such undertakings, and historically it could rely on superior equipment and training to offset Brazil's larger numbers. By 1970, however, the qualitative differences between the two militaries had narrowed dramatically. Rapidly growing Brazilian industries have since outperformed their Argentine counterparts in defense-related production to the point that Brazil now produces most of its own equipment and has become a major arms exporter. Several other Latin nations are also arms producers and exporters, on a smaller scale.

Argentine military leaders long argued that only by acquiring nuclear weapons could their country maintain a military force capable of discouraging Brazilian adventurism. Argentine interest in nuclear energy had begun in 1950, when President Juan Peron created the National Atomic Energy Commission.[19] In 1958, it operated South America's first research reactor, and ten years later built the region's first and only nuclear reprocessing plant. In 1968, Argentina began construction of the Atucha I nuclear power facility, which it put into operation in 1974. The military potential of Atucha I, and the prospect of falling even further behind Argentina in this area, caused alarm throughout Brazil. Thus, in 1975

Brazil signed an agreement with West Germany which would satisfy Brazilian projected demand for atomic energy through 1990 and provide the technological base for manufacturing nuclear weapons. However, in late 1985 an agreement between Brazil and Argentina to discuss mutual inspection of nuclear facilities slowed considerably the race to develop nuclear technology. In 1987 the two countries issued a joint declaration that they would use nuclear energy for peaceful purposes only.[20] While there is still some mistrust and worry that either one or both of these countries is proceeding clandestinely with the development of a nuclear capability, the lessening of tensions between these two nations and their distressed economies make the problem of nuclear proliferation seem remote.

Future Challenges in Latin America to U.S. National Security. It is clear that as the twenty-first century approaches, the United States can neither ignore nor take for granted its Southern neighbors. The various currents running in Latin America require the United States to define clearly its position on hemispheric matters and to work vigorously in concert with others to shape them. The key national security challenges that lie ahead are diverse and complex, requiring American policies that are multidimensional and oriented toward the long term. They involve issues that range from drug trafficking and insurgency to democratic consolidation and economic development. The current ebbing of large-scale global threats provides an opportunity in the Western Hemisphere to build the kind of solid relationships among the countries in this region that will preclude the need for approaches that have characterized U.S. policy toward Latin America in the past. Issues such as continuing access to the Panama Canal after 1999, ongoing insurgent movements that feed on the poverty and despair of the region, drug trafficking, fragile democracies facing daunting economic challenges, economically driven immigration, and clashing environmental and economic interests present pieces of a puzzle that will be a significant challenge for U.S. policymakers through the 1990s.

The biggest question marks for the United States will likely be Cuba and Panama. While Castro has been able to retain unchallenged control of the political, economic, and military structures of Cuban society for nearly 35 years, the time of transition to a post-Castro Cuba is on the horizon. How soon such a transition will come, and whether it will bring changes that are large or small, violent or peaceful, dramatic or pedestrian, remains a matter of speculation. Clearly the United States should be ready to adjust its Cuban policy to respond appropriately to this inevitable process. A second challenge to U.S. policy in the region that will likely be a major source of difficulty is Panama. The results of the canal treaties of the late 1970s will come into play during the 1990s, with uncertain strategic results for the United States. Although the removal of Noriega in late 1990 eased some of the volatility, the unsatisfactory political and economic situation in the aftermath of the U.S. military operation indicates that further trouble lies ahead in that sensitive country.

The Caribbean basin as a whole suffers from internal political strains and severe economic problems. Without outside help through a major, long-range aid, trade, and investment effort, these states are not likely to succeed in meeting their citizens' basic needs. Political upheavals, widespread suffering, and refugee flows are likely consequences with which other Latin American countries and the United States must cope—unless, that is, the aid and other measures in the CBI are successfully pursued. Mexico, bordering the Caribbean region and in the midst, in the early 1990s, of fundamental political and economic reforms, is a promising exception to these forecasts. Indeed, by the latter part of the decade, Mexico may be able to play a more vigorous and helpful stabilizing role in the Caribbean basin subregion.

With the exception of the military operation in Panama in December 1989, there has been a clear trend in recent years away from confrontation and toward negotiated settlements of longstanding conflicts—a trend which seems likely to continue. With the change of government in Nicaragua and the dramatic transformations in Eastern Europe and the former Soviet Union, U.S. attention has been able to shift away from the Central American and Caribbean areas that were so turbulent in the 1980s. The principal challenge ahead will be to work with the various regional powers to bring political and economic viability to the entire region.

In this challenge just cited and in other respects, the 1990s represent a new era for the United States in its relationships with its neighbors to the south. Hemispheric defense in the 1940s or 1950s sense is neither needed nor possible in the future. But cooperation in defense matters, including intelligence and arms supply, between principal South American states and the United States continues to be desirable. A stable southern flank, comprising both South America and the Caribbean basin and without the presence of hostile extrahemispheric states or their proxies, still remains a fundamental condition of U.S. security—one which will require continuing, even increased, effort and understanding on the part of both the U.S. public and policymakers.

Discussion Questions

1. Historically, what terms have been used to describe the relation(s) between the United States and Latin America? How relevant are they today?

2. At least until World War II, U.S. influence in Latin America was greatest in the Caribbean basin area. Why? How did this relate to security questions of that time? And now?

3. Brazil's economic and geographic preponderance in South America directly affects Latin American development plans, both overall and those of individual countries. Examine the La Plata River basin and the Amazon basin development from Brazilian and other Latin American perspectives.

4. What general problems in Latin America involve military considerations? How do these problems affect existing security arrangements with the United States?

5. What are the severe internal problems that constrain emergent Brazil's influence beyond its borders? What effects do they have?

6. What are the obstacles which the new democracies in Latin America confront as

they move toward consolidation? Discuss the role of the United States in supporting these transition and consolidation processes.

7. How has the end of the cold war affected U.S. relations with the countries of Latin America? What are the prospects for and what will be the salient features of U.S.–Latin American relations in the future?

8. Is the definition of "security" changing? What traditional security concerns remain for the United States in Latin America? What security concerns have diminished during the past decade? What new concerns have emerged?

9. What kind of relationship with Mexico will be most productive for U.S. interests in the short and long runs?

10. Is a political-security equivalent to the North American Free Trade Agreement possible or even desirable? Can the Rio Pact and the Organization of American States be made to serve the mutual interests of both the United States and the countries of Latin American? What would it take to realize an effective regional security arrangement?

Recommended Reading

Atkins, G. Pope, ed. *South America into the 1990s: Evolving International Relationships in a New Era*. Boulder, Colo.: Westview Press, 1990.

Best, Edward. *U.S. Policy and Regional Security in Central America*. New York: St. Martin's Press, 1987.

Best, Edward. *The Hovering Giant: U.S. Responses to Revolutionary Change in Latin America,* rev. ed. Pittsburgh: University of Pittsburgh Press, 1985.

Blachman, Morris J., LeoGrande, William M., and Sharpe, Kenneth, eds. *Confronting Revolution: Security Through Diplomacy in Central America*. New York: Pantheon, 1986.

Child, Jack. *Geopolitics and Conflicts in South America: Quarrels among Neighbors*. New York: Praeger, 1985.

Fauriol, Georges A., ed. *Security in the Americas*. Washington, D.C.: National Defense University Press, 1989.

Freedman, Lawrence, and Gamba-Stonehouse, Virginia. *Signals of War: The Falklands Conflict of 1982*. Princeton, N.J.: Princeton University Press, 1991.

Goodman, Louis W., Mendelson, Johanna S. R., and Rial, Juan, eds. *The Military and Democracy: The Future of Civil-Military Relations in Latin America*. Lexington, Mass.: Lexington Books, 1990.

Green, James R., and Scowcroft, Brent. *Western Interests and U.S. Policy Options in the Caribbean Basin*. Boston: Oelgeschlager, Gunn, & Hain, 1984.

Hayes, Margaret Daly. *Latin America and the U.S. National Interest: A Basis for U.S. Foreign Policy*. Boulder, Colo.: Westview Press, 1984.

Leiken, Robert S., ed. *Central America: Anatomy of Conflict*. New York: Pergamon Press, 1984.

Lowenthal, Abraham F. *The Dominican Intervention*. Cambridge, Mass.: Harvard University Press, 1972.

Lowenthal, Abraham F. *Partners in Conflict: The United States and Latin America in the 1990s,* rev. ed. Baltimore: Johns Hopkins University Press, 1990.

Mazarr, Michael. *Semper Fidel: America & Cuba, 1776–1988*. Baltimore: Nautical and Aviation Publishing, 1988.

O'Donnell, Guillermo, Schmitter, Philippe, and Whitehead, Lawrence, eds. *Transitions*

From Authoritarian Rule: Prospects for Democracy. Baltimore: Johns Hopkins University Press, 1986.

Rangel, Carlos. *The Latin Americas: Their Love–Hate Relationship with the United States*, rev. ed. New Brunswick, N.J.: Transaction Books, 1987.

Rockefeller, Nelson A. *The Rockefeller Report on the Americas*. New York: Quadrangle Books, 1969.

Remmer, Karen L. *Military Rule in Latin America*. Boston: Unwin Hyman, 1989.

Weintraub, Sidney. *A Marriage of Convenience: Relations Between Mexico and the United States*. New York: Oxford University Press for the Twentieth Century Fund, 1990.

Whitaker, Arthur P. *The Western Hemisphere Idea: Its Rise and Decline*. Ithaca, N.Y.: Cornell University Press, 1984.

Wiarda, Howard J. *The Democratic Revolution in Latin America: History, Politics and U.S. Policy*. New York: Holmes and Meier, 1990.

21

Europe

The history of U.S. security policy toward Europe is tied inextricably to the East–West confrontation arising from the ashes of World War II and to the consequent development of the policy of containment and the North Atlantic Treaty Organization (NATO). It was inevitable, therefore, that the dramatic changes that swept the European continent in 1989, unleashed by Soviet Secretary General Mikhail Gorbachev's perestroika, would cause a fundamental realignment of U.S. policy in that part of the world. The United States still has strong interests in Europe, however, and its future policies there will undoubtedly retain clear elements of continuity with the past.

U.S. Interests in the Region. In light of the dramatic transformations on the European continent since 1989, a logical question is: What are U.S. security interests on the European continent? Five major interests can be identified. First, the United States is tied to the security of fourteen European states (plus Canada) through its membership in the North Atlantic Treaty Organization, which calls for it to come to the defense of its NATO allies. Second, because of the large volume of trade carried out across the Atlantic, the stability of this region and security of transatlantic lines of communications remain key U.S. interests to be safeguarded. In 1991, 24 percent of all U.S. exports went to the European Economic Community (EC), while 18 percent of total U.S. imports were from the EC.[1] Third, the United States has an interest in remaining engaged in the region to counterbalance the major successor states to the former Soviet Union, which, despite undertaking arms reductions, retain a large conventional and nuclear arsenal still capable of threatening the United States—if intentions should change.

Fourth, Europe's geographical proximity to other regions in which U.S. vital interests lie—particularly the Middle East—makes it of strategic value for the United States. The ability to maintain prepositioned forces on the European continent and to rely on the logistical support of its NATO allies allows the United States greater strategic reach by enabling it to deploy its forces more quickly to neighboring regions when needed. The importance of this was evident during the U.S.–led military campaign against Saddam Hussein in 1991, when, aided by its NATO allies, the United States moved the Seventh Army Corps from Germany to the Persian Gulf to augment its forces there.[2] Finally, remaining engaged in European security can further other U.S. political objectives. Retaining a U.S. security presence on the continent will allow the United States to exercise political leverage on other aspects of U.S.–European relations:

> Just as domestic economic revival is a necessary foundation for foreign and defense policy, so an active U.S. engagement in the world provides critical influence in the economic field. The United States obviously will not form up armored battalions and march on Brussels to demand an open market or an agreement on the Uruguay Round and its successor round. . . . By continuing to play a leading role in NATO, however, and by demonstrating the seriousness of our purpose in Europe, we can build goodwill—and obtain influence—that will flow into economic issues.[3]

Thus, despite the change in East–West relations, European security will continue to be vitally important to the United States, even if the instruments of U.S. security policy toward Europe, such as the level of military forces maintained on the continent, change. In order to explore post–cold war U.S. security policy in this region, however, we should first review the principal changes that have occurred since the end of World War II.

Historical Context. By the latter 1940s, the structure of the international system, at least with regard to Europe, was strongly bipolar; only the United States and the Soviet Union had sufficient capabilities to play significant political–military roles. Their attempts to organize Europe so that it would satisfy their perceived vital interests clashed strongly, even before World War II ended. Furthermore, ideological differences between the two nations, muted during the war in the pursuit of coalition strength, regained their earlier importance by the war's end. Faced with growing Soviet intransigence and bellicosity in Central and Eastern Europe, and with Soviet threats directed against Western and Southern Europe as well, the United States felt compelled to respond. It had attempted in two wars to maintain equilibrium in Europe; it could not afford to withdraw when this equilibrium was again threatened. America's first response was against growing communist insurgency and pressure in Greece and Turkey. The consequent Truman Doctrine (1947) stated that the United States could survive only in a world where aggression and totalitarianism were neither allowed to expand against the institutions of free nations nor to undermine international peace. Within a year, the United States acted to bolster its words, sending military assistance and military advisers to Greece and Turkey.

FIG. 21.1 Europe

As explained in Chapter 4, the Truman Doctrine, a classic response to a disequilibrium of power in a tight bipolar world, was the opening move in what came to be known as the policy of "containment," by which the United States sought to confine the power of the Soviet Union to its existing boundaries. In pursuit of this policy, the American military presence in the Mediterranean area and in Europe was designed to deter and to defend against Soviet expansionism, allowing the Southern and Western Europeans to recover from the physical and economic devastation of the war. Recognizing that the Western European nations were essential actors in building and maintaining an equilibrium of power and that economic and social recovery were vital to European security, the United States formulated the Marshall Plan, a massive economic aid program intended to restore Europe to economic vitality.

As hostility between the Western powers and the Soviet bloc increased, it became clear to the West that a security arrangement going beyond economic cooperation and assurances of common interests was necessary. The Soviet-supported coup in Czechoslovakia (1948) and the Berlin Blockade (1948–1949) convinced Americans and Europeans alike of the need for a defensive military alliance. Accordingly, in 1949, the common interests and goals of the United States and Western European nations (with the exception of West Germany, which joined in 1955) were formalized in the North Atlantic Treaty Organization. NATO was designed as a collective defense organization, providing that an attack on one would be considered an attack on all. The new alliance's strategic policy stressed deterrence of Soviet aggression by alliance forces on the ground, supported by U.S. strategic nuclear weapons. NATO also provided for a joint command structure with joint planning and forces-in-being. NATO represented America's first peacetime military alliance; as such, it was rooted primarily in the concept of deterrence, as explained in Chapter 11.

The build-up of conventional forces in Europe was slow. Initial unwillingness on both sides of the Atlantic to return to large, expensive military forces and belief that America's dominant nuclear power was sufficient for deterrence meant that NATO conventional forces were at first starved. The North Korean invasion of South Korea in 1950, believed to have been instigated by the Soviet Union, however, convinced the alliance of the need to develop a substantial conventional force capable of repelling a potential Soviet invasion—which many believed the Korean invasion portended. NATO strategy began to emphasize defense as well as deterrence.

NATO has been a successful, if not always harmonious, alliance. At different times in its history, geopolitical developments have tested intraalliance relations; at each such juncture, the alliance has been able to adapt and survive. An early cause of intraalliance debate centered on the credibility of the U.S. commitment to European security in the face of Soviet attainment of nuclear parity with the United States. As the Soviet Union developed strategic weapons that threatened to destroy the United States if a nuclear war occurred, the American commitment to Europe became—theoretically at least—more expensive and the credibility of the American deterrent more doubtful. A speech by Henry Kissinger at a Center for Strategic and International Studies conference on NATO encapsulated the strategic dilemma confronted by the United States:

> Our European allies should not keep asking us to multiply strategic assurances that we cannot possibly mean or if we do mean, we should not want to execute because if we execute, we risk the destruction of civilization. Our strategic dilemma is not solved by verbal reassurances; it requires redesigning our forces and doctrine.[4]

To solve this strategic dilemma, the United States and its European allies repeatedly searched for a credible nuclear policy for the alliance; but this was a source of more intraalliance problems. An attempt at building a European multilateral nuclear force (MLF) failed in the mid 1960s, leading to a NATO nuclear deterrent comprised primarily of U.S. theater nuclear forces (TNF) as well as the U.S. strategic deterrent. TNF achieved an essential goal for the European allies in that it linked, or "coupled," the conventional defenses along the East–West frontier with American strategic forces.

But the modernization of such theater nuclear systems, made necessary by the introduction of Soviet intermediate-range nuclear missiles aimed at Western Europe, caused yet more friction within the alliance. As a result, NATO adopted in 1979 a "double-track" policy, by which it would undertake modernization of TNF simultaneously with bilateral negotiations between the United States and the Soviet Union on reducing this category of weapons. The resulting talks on intermediate-range nuclear forces (INF) began in 1981 and concluded in 1987 with the signing of the INF Treaty by President Ronald Reagan and Secretary General Gorbachev.

NATO's strategy of "flexible response" also generated alliance problems (see Chapter 4 for a discussion of this strategy). Flexible response included the option of meeting a Soviet conventional attack, at least initially, by fighting a large-scale conventional defense in Europe—a prospect that raised great concern in the countries whose territories stood to be devastated by such a war.[5] In addition, flexible response raised again the nuclear dilemma of the alliance: increasing the capability for conventional defense, which the United States emphasized as needed for the strategy, could imply less than full readiness to escalate to the use of nuclear weapons, thus causing declining trust in nuclear deterrence.

During much of this period, as NATO coped with the changes in doctrine necessitated by technology and an ever-shifting geopolitical environment, a debate on the sharing of the burden of common defense also engaged the allies. It was a problem seemingly unavoidable for an alliance composed of a superpower, some medium powers, and smaller powers with sometimes divergent goals.[6] The smaller NATO nations generally let their larger neighbors take the lead and pay the costs. The French developed and deployed their own strategic weapons, the *force de frappe,* and withdrew their forces from the military command of NATO in 1966, thus diminishing the capabilities of a concerted flexible defense in Europe. The Greeks and Turks engaged in a longstanding dispute over Cyprus and at times decreased their cooperation with NATO. Increasingly, the initiatives and the financial and other burdens largely shifted to the Germans and the United States, with the British also bearing a considerable share.

European security planners in the late 1980s appeared prepared to continue on the path of intraalliance negotiation and fine-tuning of NATO's conventional and nuclear strategies when the European security landscape began to be significantly affected by Soviet "new thinking." The first demonstration of change in Soviet intentions occurred in the field of conventional arms control—an area that had languished in East–West relations even as the United States and the Soviet Union concluded a number of nuclear arms control treaties.

Negotiations to limit conventional military arsenals in Europe had occupied NATO and the Warsaw Pact countries for thirteen years with little result until 1986, when Gorbachev, in response to a NATO proposal, called for phased reductions of ground and air forces in a region stretching from the Atlantic to the Urals (ATTU). Also contained in the Soviet proposal was the notion that the Soviet Union would accept on-site inspections to verify reductions. Confidence in Soviet peaceful intentions was further enhanced in 1988 by the announcement that the Soviet Union would undertake unilateral reductions of its forces in the ATTU region. With the opening of the Conventional Forces in Europe (CFE) negotiations in March 1989, NATO and the Warsaw Pact finally began marching toward a goal that had proven elusive for sixteen years.

As the cold war began to draw to a close in 1989, the conventional arms control process that had been revitalized in 1986 exemplified how much Gorbachev's actions had transformed the European security environment in a few short years. The CFE talks, which opened formally in March 1989, reached impressive results with the signing of the Treaty in November of the next year: over 125,000 battle tanks, armored combat vehicles, artillery, combat aircraft, and attack helicopters would be destroyed—greatly downgrading the threat of large-scale, surprise conventional attack by limiting the weapons systems most conducive to it. (See Table 21.1.)

But by the conclusion of the negotiations, the Warsaw Pact had broken up and Germany was approaching unification, making the ceilings attained by the CFE negotiations appear too high. Negotiators and the policy community coped with these new challenges by first devising a "sufficiency rule" that would allow the Soviet Union to retain only one-third of the systems in the ATTU region and by setting a cap on the armed forces of a united Germany. Yet another challenge to the new conventional arms control regime emerged with the subsequent dissolution of the Soviet Union, which placed the command and control of the Soviet arsenal in question. Further negotiations among seven former Soviet Republics—Russia, Byelorussia, Ukraine, Moldova, Georgia, Armenia, and Azerbaijan—were necessary to establish command and control of the former Union's military assets—and how the conventional reductions would apply—before the CFE Treaty could be ratified and come into force.

Just as the arms control process was forced to adapt to the changing security environment, so was the Western security framework that had evolved over forty-six years of East-West confrontation and cold war. In view of the sharply declining threat from the Soviet Union caused by conventional arms control negotiations and arrangements, unilateral Soviet military withdrawals, the dissolution of the Warsaw Pact, and the unification of the two Germanies, the policy of forward-defense that had characterized Western defense policy in Europe appeared no longer relevant to the situation. The Soviet military withdrawals extended the warning time available to the West to organize a defense, should a threat from the Soviet Union reemerge. In addition, it was incongruous to maintain forces positioned along the old East–West border that now ran through an allied country. And, moving the border eastward also appeared to be an

Table 21.1 Conventional Weapons in Europe Before and After CFE.

	Tanks	*ACVs*	*Arty*	*Aircraft*	*Helos*	*TOTAL*
NATO:						
Belgium	359	1,381	376	191	0	2,307
	334	*1,099*	*320*	*232*	*46*	*2,031*
Denmark	419	316	553	106	3	1,397
	353	*316*	*553*	*106*	*12*	*1,340*
France	1,343	4,177	1,360	699	418	7,997
	1,306	*3,820*	*1,292*	*800*	*352*	*7,570*
Germany	4,726	3,103	2,462	626	206	11,123
	4,166	*3,446*	*2,705*	*900*	*306*	*11,523*
Greece	1,879	1,641	1,908	469	0	5,897
	1,735	*2,534*	*1,878*	*650*	*18*	*6,815*
Iceland	0	0	0	0	0	0
	0	*0*	*0*	*0*	*0*	*0*
Italy	1,246	3,958	2,144	577	168	8,093
	1,348	*3,339*	*1,955*	*650*	*142*	*7,434*
Luxembourg	0	0	0	0	0	0
	0	*0*	*0*	*0*	*0*	*0*
Netherlands	913	1,467	837	196	91	3,504
	743	*1,080*	*607*	*230*	*69*	*2,729*
Norway	205	146	531	90	0	972
	170	*225*	*527*	*100*	*0*	*1,022*
Portugal	146	244	343	96	0	829
	300	*430*	*450*	*160*	*26*	*1,366*
Spain	854	1,256	1,373	242	28	3,753
	794	*1,588*	*1,310*	*310*	*71*	*4,073*
Turkey	2,823	1,502	3,442	449	0	8,216
	2,795	*3,120*	*3,523*	*750*	*43*	*10,231*
U.K.	1,198	3,193	636	842	368	6,237
	1,015	*3,176*	*636*	*900*	*384*	*6,111*
Canada	77	277	38	45	12	449
	77	*277*	*38*	*90*	*13*	*495*
U.S.A.	5,904	5,747	2,601	704	279	15,235
	4,006	*5,372*	*2,492*	*784*	*518*	*13,172*
TOTALS	22,092	28,408	18,604	5,332	1,573	76,009
	19,142	*29,822*	*18,286*	*6,662*	*2,000*	*75,912*
Former Warsaw Pact (not including former Soviet Union):						
Bulgaria	2,145	2,204	2,116	243	44	6,752
	1,475	*2,000*	*1,750*	*235*	*67*	*5,527*
Czechoslovakia	1,797	2,538	1,566	348	56	6,305
	1,435	*2,050*	*1,150*	*345*	*75*	*5,055*
Hungary	1,345	1,720	1,047	110	39	4,261
	835	*1,700*	*840*	*180*	*108*	*3,663*
Poland	2,850	2,377	2,300	551	29	8,107
	1,730	*2,150*	*1,610*	*460*	*130*	*6,080*
Rumania	2,851	3,102	3,789	505	13	10,260
	1,375	*2,100*	*1,475*	*430*	*120*	*5,500*
TOTALS	10,988	11,941	10,818	1,757	181	35,685
	6,850	*10,000*	*6,825*	*1,650*	*500*	*25,825*

Note: Numbers in italic indicate post CFE levels. See Table 16.1 for data regarding ex Soviet republics.

Source: The Arms Control Association. *Arms Control Today*. June 1992, p. 32.

ineffective solution, for it would have implied that the non-Soviet former Warsaw Pact states were still the enemy when they were trying to democratize their political systems. Therefore, NATO needed to undertake a basic reassessment of its military and political strategy.

NATO responded to the challenge created by the new environment by extending diplomatic liaison with the states of Central and Eastern Europe and announcing a fundamental political and military review at the London Summit of July 1990. The outcome of the NATO review was twofold. First, a new relationship with the states of the now defunct Warsaw Pact was established at the Copenhagen meeting of the North Atlantic Council (NAC) in June 1991 and refined at the Rome Summit of November 1991. Second, a new strategic concept for the Alliance was also unveiled in Rome.

The essence of NATO's political approach to the former Warsaw Pact states is encapsulated in the NATO Copenhagen communique:

> Our own security is inseparably linked to that of all other states in Europe. The consolidation and preservation throughout the continent of democratic societies and their freedom from any form of coercion or intimidation are therefore of direct and material concern to us.[7]

Although establishing NATO's concern for the security of the states of Central and Eastern Europe, the Copenhagen communique stopped short of a security guarantee to these states. The Rome NATO Summit created the North Atlantic Cooperation Council (NACC), a thirty-seven-member forum which meets annually at the level of foreign minister, to promote dialogue between the traditional NAC and the newly independent nations of the former Soviet bloc. The new relationship stops with dialogue and consultation; the reasons for this lay in the complex dynamics of the new European security landscape. In 1991, before the dissolution of the Soviet Union, extending NATO membership to the Central and East European countries would have created insecurity for the Soviet Union at a time when the West was encouraging continued reform in that country. In addition, expanding NATO membership would have required a redefinition of the Alliance and its purposes; for example, whom would it defend against and what would its response be to conflicts between ethnic factions within the national borders of some of its members?

NATO's new strategic concept, as defined at the Rome Summit, was based on the premise of an altered security landscape in which the threat of a massive attack had been replaced by risks to allied security arising from instability due to ethnic rivalries and territorial disputes. It established a new force structure for NATO that would "move away. . . . from the concept of forward defence towards a reduced forward presence, and . . . modify the principle of flexible response to reflect a reduced reliance on nuclear weapons."[8] The structure of NATO forces would also change to reflect the new environment. Thus, the new strategic concept called for smaller forces, with reduced readiness but augmentation capabilities, and with greater flexibility and mobility to be able to respond to crises or threats originating against any ally.

The continuing process of change in Europe and globally as a result of the disintegration of the Soviet Union and related developments, will require continuing adaptation of U.S. policy objectives and instruments. An analysis of future U.S. national security interests and policies in Europe should begin with an examination of two parallel and defining processes on the continent: disintegration in the East and integration in the West.

The New Context of European Security: Disintegration in the East. The dissolution of the Soviet Union in December 1991 changed the European security landscape profoundly and overthrew the assumptions that governed the transatlantic security framework throughout the post–World War II period. The end of the Soviet Union, the drastically improved climate between the United States and the successor government in Russia, and the conventional arms control and accompanying verification regime negotiated in 1991 together removed the threat of a massive attack on the territories of the Western allies by a single, well-defined enemy. With the end of the cold war, however, new challenges to European security emerged, namely, longstanding ethnic tensions and nationalist claims that had been suppressed by the cold war. Dismantling of the Soviet threat produced a lower level of threat, but, at the same time, a more unstable environment.

In the aftermath of the revolutions of 1989, the literature on European security that attempted to sort out the implications of the dramatic changes for European security listed four potential sources of instability.[9] First was the preoccupation with a residual threat from the Soviet Union or a successor state, whose military capabilities remained substantial. The second involved the future of the united German state. Various scenarios were articulated about the possibility that Germany would reassert itself on the European continent, either as a result of insecurity stemming from regional instability or as conscious attempt to exploit the "power vacuum" left by the end of superpower rivalry. Other analysts described a different type of threat emanating from Germany, which would result from Germany developing a new Ostpolitik with the Soviet Union that would render NATO ineffective.[10] The third threat to the European security environment was described as the potential for conflict arising from the ethnic and nationalist tensions in Eastern Europe, which stood to be heightened by the economic strain of transforming centrally planned economies to market societies. The fourth area of concern was the potential for mass migration from areas east and southeast of Western Europe as a result of regional political and economic instability.

By 1992, scenarios for instability involving Germany or a remilitarized Soviet successor state appeared somewhat less threatening. Realization of the single European market—the "EC 92" process—and the negotiation of the Maastricht Treaty of European economic, monetary, and political union further integrated the German state into a European house. In addition, the enormity of the commitment that the Federal Republic of Germany had undertaken in absorbing the German Democratic Republic had begun to be felt in the unified German state in the form of worrisome inflation and a widening fiscal deficit—a result of increased public borrowing to finance the reconstruction of the eastern Ländern (the political subdivisions of the territory). In sum, in the near term, Germany appeared both well on the way to integrating within a wider European framework and less willing to pursue an active foreign policy toward the East that might diverge from that of the other Western countries.

The prospect of an aggressive Soviet successor state also appeared less pressing by 1992. The Soviet Union formally dissolved in December 1991, first leaving the Soviet military machine under the control of the newly established Commonwealth of Independent States (CIS) and eventually (in June 1992) leading to a division of the conventional military assets of the former Soviet Union that came under the CFE Treaty among seven former Soviet republics. Still, the large residual "Soviet" conventional and nuclear arsenal posed a danger to U.S. security interests. Of particular concern was the potential for the proliferation of nuclear and conventional weapons technology arising from the extensive arsenals and know-how of the former Soviet states. They also harbored the danger of regional instability due to political, economic, and ethnic tensions that threatened to derail the process of transforming a centralized system into independent states.

Indeed, instability arising from ethnic and nationalist tensions was no longer just a prospect by 1992: It had become a reality as a result of conflict in Yugoslavia, and on territory that once made up the Soviet Union, such as Nagorno-Karabakh, South Ossetia, and Moldova. Migration, although not yet having materialized as a major threat to the West European states, also became a more pressing source of concern in Europe by 1992, as the conflict between Serbs, Croats, and Muslims in Bosnia-Herzegovina intensified. Refugees from the war in Bosnia-Herzegovina and Croatia were estimated at 2.2 million in July 1992.[11] Thus, by the middle of 1992, as the U.N.-sponsored peace negotiations and U.N. peacekeeping efforts flagged in the Balkans, the major cause of insecurity in the European region appeared to be the political disintegration occurring in Eastern Europe.

The essence of the European security problem appears to be that the majority of the conflicts will occur within national borders and, thus, strain the ability of other nations to intervene. Although U.N. actions to protect the Kurds in Iraq set a precedent for international intervention against a government's abuse of its citizens, and although the principles established by the Helsinki Final Act and the Conference on Security and Cooperation in Europe (CSCE) justify intervention, such interference holds dangers of its own.[12] Intervention in intrastate conflicts could lead to greater instability if it draws in outside participants with competing objectives. Not to intervene, however, creates or contributes to other problems.

First, the conflict could spill over national borders; this is a particularly potent threat in Eastern Europe and the Balkans, where ethnic ties cross national boundaries. In the Balkans in 1992, for example, there was the potential for Albania, Bulgaria, and Greece to become involved in disputes with Serbia if the conflict in the former Yugoslavia spread to Kosovo or Macedonia. Second, the stability of neighboring nations can be affected even without entering the conflict. Refugees from conflict-torn areas in Eastern Europe could strain the capacity of West European nations to absorb them and potentially destabilize other East European countries already coping with the economic difficulties created by a transition to market economies. Third, the humanitarian factor needs to be considered. As Stephen Flanagan highlights, "how can we speak of having achieved a new European order when the images of the slaughter at Vukovar, Dubrovnik, and elsewhere in Yugoslavia are on the front pages of newspapers and on the conscience of the Continent?"[13] It would be sadly ironic if, having created the conditions for the dissolution of the Soviet hold over Eastern Europe, the United States and its allies would choose to witness, uninvolved, the destruction of lives and civilization arising out of the end of the cold war.

Given the new geopolitical environment, the international community—and U.S. security policy—must come to terms with a number of issues generated by the Yugoslav experience: How should America respond to conflicts involving ethnically based claims of sovereignty? When does this type of conflict cease to be purely an intrastate matter and become an interstate concern? What are the costs of nonintervention in conflicts that may spill over into international ones? The 1991–1993 crisis in the Balkans indicates that relying on exhortation has political and strategic costs. Limiting intervention to the provision of peacekeeping forces, once a ceasefire has been achieved, in some cases merely amounts to endorsement of the territorial gains of the aggressor.[14] In effect, by not intervening to stop aggression in the first place, the international community is sending a signal to other potential aggressors that violation of the sovereign claims or rights of others will be condoned.

What kind of intervention could make sense? Peacekeeping efforts by the United Nations and negotiations among opposing parties proved ineffective in the case of Yugoslavia. But joint or international action beyond peacekeeping appears unlikely to occur in other cases similar to Yugoslavia, where the vital interests of other states are not immediately evident and do not coincide.[15] The lessons of the Balkans of the early 1990s for European security are twofold: the essentiality of conflict avoidance and the importance of conflict containment. In this twin context, the evolution of the European Community (EC) and of European and transatlantic political and security institutions will play an important role.

Integration in the West. As the end of the cold war encouraged centrifugal forces in Eastern Europe, Western Europe advanced toward greater economic and political integration. Progress in the "EC 92" process has been the elimination of all barriers to the free flow of goods, services, capital, and labor among the twelve EC members introduced by the Single European Act of 1986 and agreement on the modalities for monetary union and greater political integration through negotiation of the Maastricht Treaty in December 1991. The process of

European integration has shaped and will continue to shape the European political and security landscape in two significant ways: by acting as a magnet for the East European economies and by aligning the foreign as well as domestic policies of the member states. Analysis of the development and future prospects of the EC, therefore, must be an integral part of the continuing process of U.S. foreign and security policy formulation.

The European Community had its origins in the European Coal and Steel Community (ECSC), developed in 1951 as part of a plan by Jean Monnet to revitalize the steel industry in post–World War II France by ensuring access to German coal and coke—and, at the same time, to end centuries of Franco-German competition by organizing joint control of key mineral resources. The ECSC, which included Italy, Belgium, Luxembourg, and the Netherlands, as well as France and Germany, created an impetus for a common internal market among its members, leading to the European Economic Community (EC) that was instituted for this purpose by the Treaty of Rome (1957). The development of the European Community from an organization of six members to a common market of twelve countries has occurred incrementally and falteringly; but by 1992, the Community appeared positioned to become a significant actor on the European geopolitical landscape. Two factors largely account for this development: the prospect of Community enlargement and of the development of a common Community foreign and security policy.

The success of the EC has proven to be a strong a magnet for the rest of Europe—the East European countries and the countries which in cold war terminology were neutral or nonaligned. Austria, Finland, and Sweden have applied for membership to the EC, and are likely to gain acceptance by 1996, potentially joined by Norway and Switzerland. Poland, Hungary, and the Czech and Slovak Republics have concluded special agreements with the EC and are likely to seek full membership by the end of the decade. For some, the challenge created by the end of the cold war is one of choosing such enlargement or "widening" versus "deepening" (i.e., strengthening the Community's authority over current member governments). Another perspective holds that, in order to prepare for widening, the EC should first deepen by shoring up its decision-making authority. Development of a common foreign and security policy is one aspect of this process of "deepening."

Thus, the Maastricht Treaty calls for a common foreign and security policy which "shall include all questions related to the security of the European Union, including the eventual framing of a common defence policy, which might in time lead to common defence." The Treaty also designates the Western European Union (WEU)—a group of nine EC countries that are also members of NATO—as the organization that would "elaborate and implement the decisions and actions of the Union which have defence implications" and establishes it as the link between NATO and the EC.[16]

There are other practical reasons pushing the EC members toward common foreign and security policies, the most immediate of which in 1992 was the challenge presented by real and prospective immigration from regions east and

"Now that I've united myself, I'll help you do the same."

Reprinted with permission of Renan R. Lurie.

south of the Community. With internal borders down, migration into one country of the EC had by 1992 become a problem for all, highlighting the need to coordinate policies vis-à-vis the countries of emigration.

Far from establishing the future scope of the EC in foreign and security matters, the provisions of the Maastricht Treaty present new challenges for the Community. To a large extent, EC authority on defense matters will depend on the evolution of its ties to the WEU and on the development of the 1991 Franco-German initiative to form a joint army corps. In this context, it is important to note the wide variety of opinions among European countries about how to organize for defense. There are those within Europe who would like to retain a strong transatlantic link in European security matters and who argue for a stronger WEU, but one still part of a transatlantic framework. There are also those who envisage the gradual disassociation of European defense from the transatlantic framework. This is a view held largely by proponents of the "Eurocorps"—an all-European defense force based on the Franco-German proposal for a joint army corps. The prospect of entry into the EC of such nations as Sweden, Austria, Finland, and Switzerland and of the former Warsaw Pact countries also raises questions about the development of a common EC foreign and security policy. Finally, the evolution of other European and transatlantic security institutions—NATO, the NACC, and the CSCE—as well as the WEU will likely determine how much authority the EC will be able to assume in the field of foreign and security policy. It may, therefore, be useful to examine the prospects of such institutions in order to assess the relative security responsibility of the EC and the United States in the future.

Institution Building as Response to Political Changes. The transatlantic security debate in 1992 focused to a large extent on the development of alternative institutions for the management of Europe's security. Despite a heated debate between the United States and Europe, and especially between the United States and France, on the merits of NATO versus the WEU, the relevant question was more likely the extent to which different organizations, including NATO, NACC, the WEU, and CSCE, would interact in forestalling or managing crises in post–cold war Europe.

At the beginning of 1992, the WEU appeared positioned to become the security arm of the European Community. The Maastricht Treaty negotiated by the twelve members of the EC referred to it as the link between NATO and the European Community, and NATO itself had endorsed the EC–WEU initiative in its Oslo Communique of 1992. One question regarding the future role of the WEU is its ability to transform itself from an alliance of nine members—currently Belgium, Great Britain, France, Germany, Italy, Luxembourg, the Netherlands, Portugal, and Spain—to the representative, in matters of defense, of the twelve members of the Community, including neutral Ireland. A further complicating factor is the prospective enlargement of the EC, which would bring under its wing former neutral or nonaligned nations, such as Austria, Sweden, and Switzerland. Finally, the inability of the European Community in 1992 to secure support for joint action by the WEU to protect peacekeeping operations in the Balkans revealed continuing rifts among the twelve members of the EC in foreign policy objectives and security interests.[17] Clearly, the ability of the WEU to become the security organization envisioned by the Maastricht Treaty will centrally depend on whether the EC member states can agree on joint security interests and objectives. In this context, the rejection by the Danish electorate in June 1992 of the Maastricht Treaty offered a setback to greater EC coordination in foreign policy matters.

European and transatlantic dialogue regarding the EC's future security tasks was also tested in 1991–1992 by reactions to the already mentioned Franco-German initiative for building upon the existing Franco-German brigade to establish a army corps of up to 50,000 men. The Franco-German corps was conceived as the basis for a larger defense force that would include personnel from other WEU members. This so-called Eurocorps did not, however, have full backing from all members of the European Community. Great Britain and Italy, for example, tabled a different proposal for the development of a European security identity which emphasized NATO's role in European defense. In addition, the Eurocorps plan has certain weaknesses that, unless remedied, could undermine its development into a European defense force. First, the Franco-German initiative does not include French nuclear weapons and thus does not address the issue of a European nuclear deterrent. It is questionable whether a European defense identity can be built without addressing the issue of who has authority over the use of a nuclear deterrent. Second, its proponents have not articulated a clear mission for the Eurocorps which augments or differs from NATO's: Its role in contingencies outside NATO's traditional area of action is limited by Germany's constitutional constraint on deployment of forces abroad.

The early debate about the preeminence of the CSCE in European security appeared to fade in 1992 as the organization demonstrated its limitations in dealing with the violent disintegration of Yugoslavia. Specifically, the CSCE's decision-making structures and procedures, which require unanimity, prevented it from acting decisively and in timely fashion in responding to the crisis in Yugoslavia. The CSCE Council of Ministers, for example, which can meet at least annually to discuss any issues relevant to security in Europe, was limited from acting during the crisis in Yugoslavia by the fact that it was chaired by Germany—a state which is viewed with suspicion by Yugoslavia.[18] The CSCE officially sponsored the observer teams in Yugoslavia, but it delegated most of the mediation efforts among the parties in Yugoslavia to the EC and peacekeeping duties to the United Nations. The CSCE is caught in a dilemma: Its inclusive membership which imbues it with the legitimacy to intervene in crises also limits its capacity for action.

Plainly, Europe lacks an institution with both the will and the capacity to intervene in European security crises arising outside the NATO framework. Despite NATO's strategy evolution, it has at best a limited role in crises that do not involve a threat to the common defense of the Alliance. In establishing the NACC, NATO has created yet another link between the West and the states of Central and Eastern Europe and the former Soviet Republics; but it is one based on dialogue, it is not a security guarantee. The Alliance's link with the CSCE, established in June 1992, goes further; the NATO Oslo Communique specifies: "we are prepared to support, on a case-by-case basis in accordance with our own procedures, peacekeeping activities under the responsibility of the CSCE, including by making available Alliance resources and expertise."[19] However, based on the U.S. and European response to the conflict in the former Yugoslavia, by mid 1992 it was doubtful that the allies would respond by authorizing joint intervention beyond peacekeeping.

Although the CSCE's link with NATO can partially fill the void in European security, further evolution of such institutional arrangements will be required by the emerging European security environment. The post–cold war European security landscape requires institutional fluidity. Different organizations will have different roles to play at different times. More often than not the new European security framework will require temporary, as well as permanent, linkages among various organizations. The CSCE, for example, may function as a legitimizing institution for the actions of another entity that is more empowered to act, such as the EC or NATO. This is a framework for European security that was envisioned by the United States as early as 1989; in a speech given by Secretary of State James Baker in Berlin it was emphasized that no one institution would be able to further the stated goal of a "Europe whole and free," but that the EC, the CSCE, and NATO all would have their individual roles to play in the new Europe.

Post–Cold War U.S. Security Policy toward Europe. In response to the altered European (and other) geopolitical environment, the U.S. Defense Department has articulated a concept of "forward-presence." It is based on the premise that retaining a U.S. force presence abroad—albeit reduced—will bolster the credibility of the intent of the United States to respond to crises, thereby decreasing the likelihood that such crises will occur in the first place.[20] Forward-presence also recognizes nonmilitary means:

> [T]he new role of forward presence forces, properly understood, is not to defend U.S. interests directly but to provide leverage for diplomatic and economic instruments of policy. They do this by creating, for adversaries and allies alike, the perception that the United States is strongly committed to the preservation of its interests in each region of the globe.
>
> Forward presence recognizes the strategic implications of global integration and interdependence—the relevant choice for great powers now and in the future is either to influence global events or to be influenced by them. Forward presence also recognizes the increased importance of nonmilitary instruments of power relative to the military. Because foreign states have less need for U.S. defensive protection, exports of U.S. security no longer command such an attractive price. On the other hand, because the United States does have strategic interests abroad, many vital, and in its own self-interest, it needs to visually reassure both allies and competitors that it will stand by its interests. Whispered innuendos that the United States is "going home" can fuel false perceptions. Thus, in the language of deterrence theory, these forward presence forces communicate locally and regionally the credibility of U.S. national commitments in the context of a very interdependent world.[21]

The altered European political and security landscape has profound implications for U.S. conventional and nuclear force posture. U.S. conventional forces in Europe are being reduced through conventional arms control from 300,000 to a ceiling of 150,000, but it is likely that U.S. budgetary imperatives will push that number lower. As Don M. Snider has demonstrated, it is possible for the United States to reduce its forces in Europe to well below the 150,000 mark and retain the capability to carry out a forward-presence role.[22]

The changing context of European security also affects U.S. nuclear strategy and policy. The U.S. policy of extended deterrence stemmed from Soviet conventional superiority in Europe. But, partly due to the unilateral withdrawals initiated by Gorbachev in the late 1980s, partly due to the negotiation of the CFE Treaty, and partly as a result of the dissolution of the Warsaw Pact, the likelihood of a conventional war involving the United States or its allies in Europe has been reduced significantly. In the new military landscape, U.S. and allied conventional military power no longer needs a nuclear deterrent to bolster its credibility. Thus, some analysts have argued, as long as the United States and its allies maintain a strong conventional defense, it is possible to reduce or do away with the concept of extended deterrence.

This notion, in turn, has repercussions both for the structure of the U.S. nuclear strategic arsenal and for strategic doctrine. Rivlin, Jones, and Meyer assert that in the absence of a need for extended deterrence, the U.S. strategic arsenal would no longer be required to have a credible capability to attack the forces of the other side; instead, mutual security and stability would be enhanced by the survivability of the forces of each side.[23] Systems such as heavy missiles (e.g., the MX and the SS-18) carrying multiple independently targeted reentry vehicles (MIRVs) lose much of their rationale in these circumstances.

The changes in the European security framework, as well as the dramatic improvement in relations between the United States and Russia, have enabled the unilateral cuts in strategic nuclear systems announced by President Bush and Russian President Boris Yeltsin on June 16, 1992. This accord between the U.S. and Russian leaders lowers the numbers of warheads on strategic systems that were earlier agreed as a result of the 1991 START Treaty to a range of 3,000 to 3,500 by the year 2003 and eliminates all multiple-warhead intercontinental missiles.

The political and security climate in Eastern Europe, the development of a European security identity, and the evolution of transatlantic and European security institutions will all affect the future security framework on the continent. But one key question concerning European security in the future lies outside this framework, namely, what role the United States will choose to play in European security management. Resolving this question will affect, in turn, the development of European security institutions and a European security identity. As the United States explores its future role, a crucial consideration will be the extent to which its interests are at stake in the European security environment—an issue that has been illuminated by U.S. policy toward the conflict in the Balkans, a low-posture policy that encouraged European leadership and the involvement of international organizations. Unless it perceives its interests to be more centrally threatened than in the Yugoslav case, the United States is likely to resort in the future to diplomacy and economic measures and to defer to others on the use of the military instrument.

Increasingly, too, U.S. involvement in European security will be affected by American domestic priorities. The future transatlantic relationship is not going to be defined by the need to defend against common threats, but by responsibility sharing for the management of European security—and the amount of responsibility each side will be willing to accept will be determined to a large extent by the competing domestic priorities that each country confronts. U.S. foreign policy in general, and its policy toward Europe more specifically, will be affected by such domestic constraints as the U.S. debt, the trade and budget deficits, and the perceived loss of economic competitiveness in relation to Western Europe and Japan. These factors have already created domestic pressures that, combined with the need and opportunity to reduce the defense budget, will affect the tools of security policy the United States will be prepared to use in Europe over the next decade.

In short, considering likely developments in European security and the domestic constraints affecting the United States in the first half of the 1990s, U.S. national security policy toward Europe will focus on encouraging European management of crises such as the conflict in the Balkans. As noted above, however, the United States will undoubtedly remain militarily engaged in European security, albeit at a far lower level of forces than has been the case during forty-odd years of cold war. Moreover, the United States will also be using its various nonmilitary means to contribute—whether unilaterally or through international or European mechanisms—to European security. While

NATO will clearly be the key element in the overall transatlantic security relationship through the early 1990s, over the longer run it seems likely that it will mutate into quite a different institution or be displaced from its position of primacy—probably by a mix of other arrangements and processes.

Discussion Questions

1. What basic changes in American foreign policy occurred in 1947? What was the rationale for adopting the policy of containment?
2. Why did the United States lead in the formation of NATO? What are U.S. security commitments under NATO?
3. What factors have enhanced or limited the credibility of NATO?
4. What are the implications of the end of the cold war for U.S. security policy in Europe? How has the dissolution of the Soviet threat affected NATO?
5. How will the new European security challenges affect the overall transatlantic relationship, if at all?
6. Can a system of collective security be created to address the new security challenges on the European continent? If so, how?
7. What role can alternative security institutions—NATO, the CSCE, the WEU—play in the emerging European security landscape? What role can traditional nonsecurity organizations such as the EC play?
8. What should be the role of the United States in preventing and responding to ethnic or nationality-based conflicts on the European continent? What are the problems involved in intervening or not intervening in such conflicts?
9. How will the creation of a European security identity affect U.S. national security objectives and means to carry out those objectives on the European continent?

Recommended Reading

Binnedijk, Hans. "The Emerging European Security Order." *The Washington Quarterly*, Fall 1991.

Brandon, Henry, ed. *The Future of U.S.-European Relations: In Search of a New World Order*. Washington, D.C.: Brookings Institution, 1992.

DePorte, A. W. *NATO Between the Superpowers: The Enduring Balance*. New Haven, Conn.: Yale University Press, 1986.

Facing the Future: American Strategy in the 1990s. Aspen, Colo.: Aspen Institute, 1991.

Grosser, Alfred. *The Western Alliance: European-American Relations Since 1945*. New York: Vintage Books, 1982.

Hunter, Robert E., ed. *NATO—The Next Generation*. Boulder, Colo.: Westview Press, 1984.

Joffe, Josef. "Collective Security and the Future of Europe: Failed Dreams and Dead Ends." *Survival*, Spring 1992.

Olson, Mancur, Jr. *The Logic of Collective Action: Public Goods and the Theory of Groups*. Cambridge, Mass.: Harvard University Press, 1965.

Schwartz, David N. *NATO's Nuclear Dilemmas*. Washington, D.C.: Brookings Institution, 1983.

Sloan, Stanley R., ed. *NATO in the 1990s*. Washington, D.C.: Pergamon-Brassey's, 1989.

V

Approaches to National Security for the 1990s

22

International Forces and Peacekeeping

Preceding chapters have set forth some of the international political and economic realities that challenge the national security interests of the United States. One approach available to meet those challenges is support for international forces. The United Nations Charter provides for multilateral action to preserve or restore peace and sanctions the existence of regional arrangements that deal with the maintenance of regional peace and security; indeed, it indicates that the Security Council may use regional arrangements, as appropriate, for such purposes, under its authority.

Although only modestly effective in the post–World War II era as a whole, the multilateral or international approach has proven to be of critical value in some situations. The challenge for American national security policymakers is to identify paths of multilateral action that directly enhance the security interests of the United States and are perceived by others as legitimately contributing to a stable and just international order.

In the post–cold war era, the international community has essentially three tools at its disposal, *peacekeeping, peace-making,* and *peace enforcement* to control violence between and within states and to resolve the tensions that cause the violence. *Peacekeeping* functions by interposing external military forces or observers between the contending parties or by providing internationally respected teams to monitor events, such as the fairness of crucial elections. Brian Urquhart, who for more than forty years bore much of the responsibility in the United Nations for peacekeeping efforts, says,

> Peacekeeping may be briefly defined as the use by the United Nations of military personnel and formations not in a fighting or enforcement role but interposed as a

mechanism to bring an end to hostilities and as a buffer between hostile forces. In effect, it serves as an internationally constituted pretext for the parties to a conflict to stop fighting and as a mechanism to maintain a ceasefire.[1]

International peacekeeping action can be conceived and led (1) by a superpower, as was the case with the ill-fated U.S.–French-Italian multinational force in Lebanon in 1982; (2) by a regional grouping such as the Economic Community of West African States Cease-Fire Monitoring Group (ECOMOG) in the Liberian civil war, 1990–1991; or (3) by the U.N. Security Council or General Assembly, as has been the case in a large number of instances, starting with the creation of the United Nations Truce Supervision Organization, UNTSO, in 1948, as further described later in this chapter.

Peace-making is the conflict resolution mechanism. It functions through diplomacy and "good offices" and by providing neutral arbiters, mediators acceptable to all the disputants, to assist them in reaching an enduring settlement of their differences. Though the expense of inserting peacekeeping forces can be justified only in the more volatile contingencies, peace-making by the United Nations, regional groupings, and the major world powers is a relatively inexpensive matter and goes on all the time. There is certainly a potential peace-making dimension to every peacekeeping operation, however intractable the underlying tensions may appear to be.

Peace enforcement is the employment of military forces or economic strength to maintain or restore international peace and security. U.N. members, for example, may be called on to interrupt or blockade economic relations, communications, or diplomatic relations; if such measures are not applicable or do not suffice, military force may be applied. The first major utilization of the enforcement power of the United Nations occurred in Korea from 1950 to 1953. Other instances have included the Congo (1960–1964), which is an ambiguous case, for it began as peacekeeping but became peace enforcement; Southern Rhodesia (1966–1971), where the force applied was mandatory economic sanctions in the first instance and then severance of all relations when economic sanctions proved insufficient; and the Persian Gulf war, 1991.[2] These cases, except for Southern Rhodesia, are discussed further in succeeding pages.

With the end of the cold war, the disintegration of the Soviet Union, and the systematic retrenchment of U.S. military capabilities, the era of superpower-led interventions may be nearing its end. Even if the United States retains a substantial and sophisticated force projection potential, the range of "vital" American interests abroad that it must secure has narrowed with the decline of expansionist communism. Moreover, the Gulf war experience made clear the political, military, and cost-sharing advantages of a multilateral approach to conflict suppression under a clear-cut U.N. umbrella. A critical new factor in recent years has been the ability of the five permanent members of the Security Council (the United States, France, the Russian Federation, the People's Republic of China, and the United Kingdom) to work in harmony against threats to peace.[3]

Unity in the Security Council was dramatically affirmed on January 31, 1992, when the Council held in New York the first summit meeting in its forty-six-year history. Characteristic of the collegial atmosphere at that gathering was the remarkable statement of Russian Federation President Boris Yeltsin that "Russia considers the United States and the West not as mere partners but rather as allies" in the search for peace.[4] But of greater relevance to the theme of this chapter was a request by the heads of government, including President Bush, that new U.N. Secretary-General Boutros Boutros-Ghali of Egypt produce by June 11, 1992, a set of recommendations to strengthen the Security Council for the better discharge of its international peacekeeping and peace-making responsibilities.[5]

This chapter will focus on the United Nations's capacities and limitations in fulfilling its peacekeeping and peace enforcement roles. It will also briefly examine the potential of existing and emerging regional security groupings in addressing localized contingencies, as contemplated under Article 52 of the U.N. Charter, but without invoking U.N. intervention.

The U.N. Mandate and Performance since 1945. As global society seeks to construct a stable new world order in an atmosphere of chaotic transition in the former Soviet Union and Yugoslavia, high interstate tension—with nuclear overtones—in various regions, and economic distress in much of the developing world, it is understandably looking to the United Nations to make that new order a peaceful one. It is the only organization to which virtually all nations belong, and the maintenance of world peace is its most crucial task. Does it have the tools to do the job and how effectively has it used them so far?

The U.N. Charter was drafted in 1945 by the winners of World War II bent on preventing World War III. It made provision both to reduce the political, economic, and social causes of conflict and to nip incipient violence in the bud. Chapter V of the Charter established a Security Council to maintain international peace and security with five permanent members, plus six (later expanded to ten) other members to be elected biennially by the General Assembly. Chapter VI outlined the modalities for the peaceful settlement of disputes by negotiations among the parties, by International Court of Justice adjudication, or by Security Council mediation. Chapter VII empowered the Security Council to enforce the peace, if necessary by the use of "air, sea, or land forces by Members of the United Nations," and established a Military Staff Committee of permanent member personnel to advise the Council in such operations. Chapter VII could be invoked only by a majority vote in the Security Council including all permanent members, but it clearly assumed that the old allies would continue to act in concert.[6]

By 1947, however, Chapter VII had essentially become a dead letter, a casualty of the emerging cold war, which effectively prevented U.S.–Soviet agreement in the Security Council. By then the two superpowers were taking opposite sides in virtually every regional dispute. Their cold war horizons had become global, along with their ideological competition for all geostrategically interesting turf. The 1950 peace enforcement action, under Chapter VII, on the Korean peninsula was the exception only because the Soviets were then boycotting the Security Council. After the Soviet Union returned to the Security Council, continued U.N. action to reverse North Korea's aggression was possible only by the Western powers', led by the United States, using their dominant influence in the General Assembly to pass the "Uniting for Peace Resolution," thus shifting responsibility to the Assembly.[7]

It was the eclipse of Chapter VII, and the creativity that the eclipse inspired in successive U.N. secretaries-general and their often more enterprising deputies, that led to the U.N. peacekeeping, peace-making, and peace enforcement processes as we know them today.

What is now called peacekeeping (a term and concept not mentioned in the U.N. Charter) started in 1948 with the monitoring by unarmed U.N. military observers of the truce following the 1948 Arab–Israeli War. That United Nations Truce Supervision Organization (UNTSO) became the forerunner of numerous other observer missions—for example, in Kashmir and Lebanon, places where peacemaking efforts have failed for decades and a minimal, inexpensive "blue beret" U.N. presence could help avert further bloodshed.

The first use of troops in peacekeeping was occasioned by the Israeli–Anglo–French invasion of Suez in 1956. Mandated by the General Assembly to bypass likely Anglo–French vetoes in the Security Council, the first U.N. Emergency Force (now referred to as UNEF I) was a masterpiece of hasty improvisation by then Secretary-General Dag Hammarskjold. It was akin to assembling a sheriff's posse, with troops from Canada, Colombia, Denmark, Finland, India, and Sweden; Swiss civilian and Italian military airlift; and U.S. logistical help.[8]

Essentially, UNEF I set the pattern for future U.N. military peacekeeping operations under cold war conditions. It employed forces largely from nations that were not strongly aligned with either superpower, forces that were under instructions to use their weapons only for self-defense; it was funded by the major Western powers, notably the United States; it pioneered the concept of the peaceful interposition of U.N. forces in buffer zones between the contenders; and it even introduced the blue helmets now worn by all U.N. force contingents.

Above all, UNEF I was successful in deterring Israeli–Egyptian violence for just over a decade. Its effectiveness quickly led to other peacekeeping initiatives in the Congo (1960) and Cyprus (1964), where the problems were more complex and clear-cut success proved elusive.

A big lesson eventually learned from all these early adventures in U.N. peacekeeping was that Blue Berets (military observers) and Blue Helmets can discourage violence but cannot, by themselves, build the foundations of enduring peace. They buy time but solve nothing. Unless accompanied by a sincere commitment of political will among the contending parties for real peace, abetted by U.N. and major power diplomacy (peace-making), the business of peacekeeping can become difficult to terminate. Blue Berets have been in Kashmir since 1949 and Blue Helmets in Cyprus since 1964. This is not failure—it is inhibiting bloodshed—but it is a long step short of a final solution.

That lesson was tragically underlined by UNEF I itself. In May 1967, Egyptian President Nasser ordered the withdrawal of the U.N. force from Sinai and the Gaza. A few weeks later, Israel overran both in the Six Day War.

By the early 1970s, with the demand for U.N. peacekeeping (especially in the Middle East) still strong, the U.N. Secretariat had developed a set of basic preconditions that have been largely applied to all subsequent missions. These were best articulated by former U.N. Under Secretary-General for Special Political Affairs Sir Brian Urquhart, as follows[9]:

- The consent of the parties involved in the conflict to the establishment of the operation, to its mandate, to its composition, and to its appointed commanding officer;
- The continuing and strong support of the operation by the mandating authority, the Security Council;
- A clear and practicable mandate;
- No use of force except in the last resort of self-defense—self-defense, however, includes resistance to attempts by forceful means to prevent the peacekeepers from discharging their duties;
- The willingness of troop-contributing countries to provide adequate numbers of capable military personnel and to accept the degree of risk which the mandate and the situation demand;
- The willingness of the member states, and especially the permanent members of the Security Council, to make available the necessary financial and logistical support.

These self-imposed constraints reflect prudence on the part of a voluntary association of sovereign nations whose most powerful members have been less than totally committed to a multilateral approach to international peace and security. Indeed, both the United States and the Soviet Union over the years routinely vetoed proposed U.N. peacekeeping operations that they perceived as unhelpful to their respective strategic designs; and both have engaged their alliance systems in ill-fated attempts at partisan peacekeeping, as epitomized by the 1982 insertion of a multinational force, including U.S. marines, in Lebanon. In the breakdown of East–West détente between the 1979 Soviet invasion of Afghanistan and the accession to power of Mikhail Gorbachev in 1985, no new U.N. peacekeeping operations could get through the Security Council. In that period, both superpowers fell behind in the payment of U.N. dues and assessments, often in selective boycott of programs of which they disapproved. These arrearages dangerously truncated some ongoing peacekeeping operations and worked hardship on the troop-contributing nations.

Since 1986, there has been growing unanimity among the Security Council's permanent members, facilitating successful U.N. peace-making and/or peacekeeping operations in such former cold war arenas as Afghanistan, Namibia, Angola, and Nicaragua.

Looking back on U.N. peacekeeping in the cold war era, the world can find some reassurance in the resourcefulness of its multilateral instrument for peace. Successive U.N. secretaries-general have found creative ways to work around the East–West confrontation and to plan, fund, man, and conduct a wide array of tailor-made operations that successfully reduced violence in some highly charged situations. With little help—and often hindrance—from the great powers, they demonstrated the effectiveness of a neutral multilateral presence in suppressing conflict while negotiations proceeded. They illuminated what works and what does not in the peacekeeping art. They built respect for multilateralism among would-be aggressors and their targets alike, and ultimately among the great powers.

In sum, the U.N. peacekeepers earned their 1988 Nobel Peace Prize. They preserved through a dangerous generation of bipolarity the 1945 dream of the United Nations as the major contributor to global peace. But in that process more than 700 U.N. peacekeepers gave their lives.[10]

All told, the United Nations has conducted twenty-six peacekeeping operations since 1948. Though not all have been problem-free, and a few have become seemingly interminable (see Table 22.1), it is fair to say that the twenty-six have paved the way for the peace-makers by containing bloodshed that would have made matters worse. Meanwhile, the U.N. Secretariat has acquired a wealth of experience in peacekeeping that should prove an enormous resource in the years ahead.

However, at the turn of the year in 1993, two major U.N. operations—UNTAC (in Cambodia) and UNPROFOR (in the former Yugoslavia)—were clearly floundering, perhaps foundering. A major problem in both regions appeared to be that negotiations among ethnic groups did not seem to provide a proper context in which peacekeeping could proceed.

Turning to peace enforcement actions, the record has been scanty. As already indicated, the machinery for enforcement measures, set forth in Chapter VII, fell prey to the cold war. But military enforcement activities have occurred under the Charter's mandate in Korea, the Congo, and the Persian Gulf.

Despite high costs in blood and money, the enforcement action in Korea recovered the territory in the South that the North had overrun and produced an Armistice Agreement in 1953 that has held. In turn, that uneasy peace has led to the U.S.–South Korean alliance that has since permitted a fledgling democracy and spectacular economic growth in the South. While the U.N. effort did not accomplish its full aims of bringing about a "unified, democratic, and independent Korea," it was a qualified success. A definitive peace treaty between the two Koreas is now a credible prospect in the next few years, especially if another U.N. body, the International Atomic Energy Agency, is able to certify that the suspected North Korean nuclear weapons research program was a misapprehension or has been terminated.

The Congo crisis, which erupted immediately after the former Belgian Congo achieved independence in 1960, led to a quasi-enforcement action. Mutiny in the Congolese army, which threw out its Belgian officers, widespread attacks on European civilians, and general chaos in the countryside led Belgium to reintroduce troops of its own. Fighting between these troops and Congolese army units, the breakdown of essential services and secession of the richest province of Katanga led the Congo's leaders to appeal for U.N. troops—a request to which

Table 22.1 United Nations Peacekeeping Operations: 1948–1992

Acronym	*Type*	*Location*	*Initiated*	*Terminated*
UNMOGIP	Observation	Kashmir	1948	—
UNTSO	Observation	Sinai	1949	—
UNEF I	Interpositional	Sinai	1956	1967
UNOGIL	Observation	Lebanon	1958	1958
ONUC	Interpositional	Congo	1960	1964
UNSF	Interpositional	West Iran	1962	1963
UNIYOM	Observation	Yemen	1963	1964
UNFICYP	Interpositional	Cyprus	1964	—
DOMREP	Observation	Dominican Republic	1965	1966
UNIPOM	Observation	India/Pakistan	1965	1966
UNEF II	Interpositional	Sinai	1973	1979
UNDOF	Observation	Syria/Israel	1974	—
UNIFIL	Interpositional	Lebanon	1978	—
UNIIMOG	Observation	Iran/Iraq	1987	—
UNCOMAP	Observation	Afghanistan/Pakistan	1988	1990
ONUCA	Observation	Central America	1989	—
ONUVEN	Election	Nicaragua	1989	1990
UNTAG	Interpositional	Namibia	1989	1990
UNAVEM I	Observation	Angola	1989	1991
MINURSO	Observation	Somalia	1991	—
ONUSAL	Observation	El Salvador	1991	—
UNAMIC	Observation	Cambodia	1991	1992
UNAVEM II	Observation	Angola	1991	—
UNIKOM	Observation	Iraq/Kuwait	1991	—
UNTAC	Interpositional/Election	Cambodia	1992	—
UNPROFOR	Interpositional	Yugoslavia	1992	—

the Security Council promptly responded positively. Ultimately, 20,000 soldiers (plus 10,000 civilians) were provided from a dozen, mostly nonaligned, nations.

Although initiated as a peacekeeping operation, it was clear from the outset that the endeavor would not be akin to UNEF I, that is, one in which a truce was already in place and a purely defensive U.N. force could be interposed between the antagonists. Nevertheless, the United Nations Operation in the Congo (ONUC) began in the proven peacekeeping way—nonviolent, perfectly defensive. As anarchy spread, and particularly as the secessionist problem worsened and the possibilities of great power intervention grew, the operation changed character. ONUC acquired an air force of Swedish and Ethiopian fighter planes and Indian bombers and it began clearly offensive operations that can only be labeled as peace enforcement. After four years of major effort and in the face of immeasurable political and economic as well as military difficulties, ONUC withdrew. It had essentially accomplished its mission of restoring a semblance of law and order, forestalling civil war, preventing the disintegration of the Congo, and precluding the intervention of outside powers.

The U.N.-mandated multinational force in the 1991 Persian Gulf war accomplished all of its objectives and may seem to have established a prototype for future superpower-led U.N. actions. By its composition, it finessed the traditional and strong reluctance of the United States to put its forces under non-U.S. operational control in a combat situation. But if the United States should again feel compelled to intervene in an overseas conflict, the Korean model might confer more political and risk-sharing advantage. In Korea, the U.S. commander was also the U.N. commander, and still was in 1992, although basic changes in this command structure were under active consideration. He benefitted from U.N. and member nation support without surrendering tactical authority. The key factor is what the Security Council is willing to accept at a given time and in a particular set of circumstances.

U.N. Peacekeeping Issues in the New Environment. Likely elements of the global security environment into the twenty-first century have been explored in earlier chapters. The overall impression is one of widespread instability and conflict potential brought to the fore by the abrupt termination of cold war restraints on regional power behavior. This new anarchic atmosphere was epitomized by the Iraqi invasion of Kuwait, the conflict between Armenia and Azerbaijan and the Serbian assaults on Croatia and Bosnia-Herzegovina. The world is vastly overstocked with lethal weaponry, including nuclear warheads and delivery systems. The scientific brain drain from the former Soviet defense industrial base is a major related concern. Longstanding ethnic, religious, and territorial tensions are apparently on the rise. The gap between the rich and poor nations has widened in many regions. The United States, though clearly the sole remaining global power in security terms, is fast losing its ability and will to address all these problems unilaterally.

Given the foregoing conditions, there is a clear and urgent need for an effective global security system based on multilateralism. The building blocks for this new world order should ideally function at the regional level. The OAS, the OAU, ASEAN, and perhaps a new all-European security arrangement based on a Franco-German agreement and related to the CSCE, provide useful starting points in their respective regions. The Middle East and South and East Asia, however, have been so divided by conflicting interests since World War II that regionwide security cooperation has been out of the question. That is why these regions have been the major loci for U.N. peacekeeping since 1949, and that will likely continue to be the case. Depending on the evolution of events in the former Soviet Union and in Eastern Europe, that part of the globe may also become a major claimant on peacekeeping (or peace enforcement) efforts—as the situation in Yugoslavia in late 1992 would indicate.

There is considerable new hope today, in some circles, for a regional security system in East Asia. With the end of the cold war there is a growing community of interest there, which a Korean peace treaty would further advance. Cooperation in Southeast Asia through ASEAN is already well developed, and there is a mutual economic complementarity between the United States, Japan, and South Korea on the one side, and China, Russia, and North Korea on the other. Also, promising initiatives are under way to strengthen Pacific economic cooperation, encompassing Australasia and Oceania. In such a prospering and interdependent

Waving a finger at Serbia

Reprinted with permission of Renan R. Lurie.

region, the emergence of a regional security grouping by the turn of the century is a plausible prospect. If this happens, the grouping will not be an alliance in the cold war sense, that is, a collective security pact against a common external threat, but rather a looser consultative mechanism to control potentially violent contingencies within East Asia itself, whether by peace-making or peacekeeping.

All regional groupings, however, have inherent limitations in local conflict resolution. Regions are not monoliths; they are mosaics of divergent political, economic, and social systems. Internal divisions in the OAS, OAU, and even in the ethnically homogeneous Arab League, have often hamstrung their peace-making and peacekeeping efforts, as in Namibia in 1989 or Haiti in 1991. Yet, as the former superpowers turn inward, security management vacuums will emerge in many parts of the world that will make regional multilateral efforts increasingly important, both in anticipating and averting crises at an early stage and in developing a tradition of collective regional response to intraregional contingencies. As Javier Perez de Cuellar, former U.N. Secretary-General, noted in a September, 1991 report:

> I must stress here that, for itself, the United Nations is not designed to monopolize the peace process. The role of regional arrangements or agencies in pacific settlement of disputes is explicitly recognized in Articles 33(1) and 52(2) of the Charter. As long as a credible peace process is in motion as envisaged in these two Articles, there can be no cause for complaint that the United Nations is being bypassed. However, when such a process is not initiated or appears to be interminably suspended or to have clearly failed, then there would be little reason why recourse to the United Nations should still be

avoided. Recognizing the central part of the United Nations in the international system should be more than theoretical.[11]

Perez went on in the same report to stress the importance of consistency between the purposes and principles of the regional organizations and those of the United Nations. Only if there is a "mutual rapport" between the two levels, he warned, can the "machinery of peace" function coherently.

Over the long haul, however, the United Nations must serve as the prime mover of that machinery. That is the purpose for which it was founded, and there are no other plausible contenders for the job with a comparable legitimacy and apparatus for conflict resolution, including a universal judicial system. (It is noteworthy that in June 1992 when the Japanese Diet, after long and bitter debate, approved the dispatch abroad of Japanese peacekeeping forces, it specified that their employment could only be under a U.N. flag.)

The crucial question today is whether the U.N. apparatus—and the law, doctrine and resources supporting it—are equal to the challenges likely to lie ahead. The central issues fall under four headings: (1) mandate and missions, (2) military force construction, (3) organization, and (4) funding.

Mandate and Missions. The United Nations is not, of course, itself a superpower; it is a voluntary association of nations. Its every action in the security dimension must meet—and be seen to meet—the constraints of the U.N. Charter and the Security Council resolutions that empower those actions.

The U.N. Charter is now nearly a half-century old. On security matters, it has been amended only once—to enlarge the Security Council from 11 to 15 members in 1965. Though the cold war's end has largely—but perhaps only temporarily—restored the effectiveness of the Security Council, there remains an important constraint in Article 2, Paragraph 7:

> Nothing contained in the present Charter shall authorize the United Nations to intervene in matters which are essentially within the domestic jurisdiction of any state or shall require the Members to submit such matters to settlement under the present Charter; but this principle shall not prejudice the application of enforcement measures under Chapter VII.

Article 2 would appear to prevent U.N. intervention in an intrastate contingency without an invitation from the host government. But what if violence or prospective violence in or originating from that state endangers security elsewhere? A partial answer is found in Article 1, which affirms the purposes of the United Nations to include "to maintain international peace and security," and Article 24, which confers "on the Security Council primary responsibility for the maintenance of international peace and security"—pursuant to Chapter VII. As Major General Indar Rikhe, former head of a number of U.N. peacekeeping operations and military advisor to Secretaries-General Dag Hammarskjold and U Thant, has observed, the U.N. Charter distinguishes between purely domestic conflicts, in which U.N. intervention is prohibited, and domestic conflicts that threaten the maintenance of international peace and security, in which U.N.

intervention is not prohibited. He further noted that the United Nations has often authorized action in regions where a civil war threatened to spread, such as the Congo, Cyprus, and Yemen.[12]

This issue has recently been revisited in the Security Council. On April 5, 1991, the Council's Resolution 688 (from which China abstained) determined that Iraqi persecution of the Kurds "posed a danger to international peace and security" and thus superseded the constraints of Article 2, Paragraph 7. But at the January 31, 1992, summit, People's Republic of China Premier Li Peng declared China's opposition to "using human rights issues as an excuse for interference in our affairs." The question thus boils down, in effect, to a clash between the rights of states and the rights of people. No issue can be more fundamental to the future peacekeeping outreach of the United Nations. And since states, not people, are U.N. members, a neat formula protecting both may remain forever elusive.

Another mandate issue relates to the use of force by U.N. peacekeepers. The current doctrine is to deploy ample force, but to use it only for self-defense. But what if the stable confrontation that made possible a U.N. peacekeeping insertion should deteriorate into wholesale genocide? Must the U.N. force simply hunker down, or should it use its fire power to discourage further offensive action by either party? Should peacekeepers be ready to become enforcers?

A third mandate issue is the conviction of many observers that the spectrum of U.N. peacekeeping missions should be broadened to address such threats to world tranquility as organized terrorism, drug trafficking, environmental disasters, and epidemics. This is in keeping with recent trends in which election monitoring, for example, has become an accepted U.N. role. Such a broader mandate would appear consistent with the spirit of Chapter VI of the Charter and is unlikely to be resisted by the major powers. It would relieve them of burdens that they might otherwise be called upon to assume unilaterally. An important implication is that future peacekeeping missions are likely to engage more civilian (especially police) personnel from the member states and involve greater interaction between the Security Council and the U.N. specialized agencies.

Military Force Construction. A cardinal U.N. principle has been that Chapter VII "peace enforcement" is a job for the mobile, sophisticated, and nuclear-capable forces of the five permanent members of the Security Council, while interpositional peacekeeping is better conducted by contingents from smaller countries (preferably perceived as "neutral") under a U.N.-appointed commander from one of them. Most peacekeeping missions have been largely funded by the major powers and have drawn on their logistical support capabilities—and one or two missions have enjoyed the benefit of U.S. satellite intelligence, but the distinction between enforcement and peacekeeping has been essentially maintained.

In the new environment, however, the rationale for this distinction has been eroding. There is a continuing retrenchment in the military forces of many of the traditional contributors to peacekeeping contingents, and there is a declining justification for excluding Russian, U.S., or other major power forces from the peacekeeping process. The great powers are more interested today in conflict suppression than in force projection into areas of diminished geostrategic significance to them.

Perhaps more to the point in this context is the fact that the United Nations launched two of the largest peacekeeping operations in its history on March 15, 1992. The early plans of Secretary-General Boutros-Ghali called for the insertion of 14,000 Blue Helmets and civilian police into Yugoslavia and perhaps 19,500 into Cambodia. In addition, in the year from Spring 1991 to Spring 1992, 490 U.N. personnel were sent to the Iraq–Kuwait area, 400 to Western Sahara, 500 to Angola, 500 to El Salvador, and 50 to Somalia—making a total of some 36,000 in the field altogether, with an estimated 1992 budget of 2.7 billion U.S. dollars, up from 421 million U.S. dollars in 1991.[13] It will be difficult if not impossible to assemble that many people with adequate expertise, fire power, and mobility without some major power participation. And both operations may need the state-of-the-art intelligence and logistical support that only the United States can provide.

There have been occasional proposals—the most recent in June 1992 by Boutros-Ghali—for a permanent U.N. peacekeeping or policing force under the secretary-general's control.[14] Such a force, recruited from qualified volunteers worldwide, would benefit from unified training, cumulative experience in working together, and rapid deployability. It would perhaps provide the larger member states with a less costly alternative to the maintenance of national forces for the same missions. It is an approach whose day may come, but probably not soon. It would require further attitudinal changes in the major capitals, plus an upgrading in U.N. organization and funding, that would take time.

In the meantime, one logical approach is to enhance coordination between the Secretariat and the troop-contributing nations to develop and train modular national military and police units. Such units should be in a state of sufficient readiness to permit them to be rapidly assembled into peacekeeping forces, tailor-made for each mission, and complete with appropriate intelligence and logistical support. This is eminently feasible, but will require a greater member state commitment to U.N.-directed peacekeeping than is currently in evidence, especially among the Security Council's permanent members.

Organization. There is an overwhelming consensus—not least within the U.N. Secretariat itself—that the organization is ill-equipped today to play the broader peacekeeping role implicit for it in the new global environment.

To start with, there are questions about the appropriateness of the current set of Security Council permanent members. It is at least arguable that Britain and France should be replaced by the unifying European Community (EC) and that Japan—as a major economic power center—should be added. There is also a case for including a leading power (e.g., India) from what has been called the "Third World." The composition of the Security Council could become a contentious issue in the years ahead if the Council's role in global security management expands. The issue was, in fact, raised explicitly by Japanese Prime Minister Kiichi Miyagawa at the January 1992 summit.

Of more immediate concern is the need to strengthen the Secretariat staff sections that must plan and help execute the peacekeeping missions mandated by the Security Council, primarily in the office of the Under Secretary-General for Political Affairs. A five-year U.N. plan for 1992–1997 calls for additional managerial personnel, economies of scale in procurement for peacekeeping, better use of member-country civilian experts, greater efficiency in mission start-up, and enhanced U.N. capabilities to anticipate and analyze emerging threats to peace around the world. All this, of course, will cost money.

Funding. U.N. peacekeeping operations are funded outside the regular U.N. budget under a formula of obligatory assessments that imposes 57.69 percent of the burden on the permanent members. The United States alone is supposed to pay 30.76 percent. Though the organizational innovations mentioned above would fall under the regular budget (U.S. share, 25 percent), by early 1992 the peacekeeping budget suffered from a cumulative arrearage of $380 million in member payments, of which roughly a third was owed by the United States. This did not bode well for the Yugoslav operation—expected to cost over $600 million in the first year—or the biggest ever U.N. peacekeeping operation, Cambodia, which was projected to cost $2 billion over 18 months.[15] And these figures do not include close to a billion dollars of voluntary contributions needed from the member states to rehabilitate Cambodia.

For these important operations, the added bill for Washington alone could well be $5 to $700 million in the 1992–1993 fiscal year. It is problematical whether the administration and Congress, preoccupied with domestic issues in a recession, would come up with such a sum, let alone the cumulative arrearage.

Over the longer haul, it is obvious that the global community should seek a common design for the U.N. security role in the twenty-first century. If it opts for multilateralism, it must be ready to furnish the United Nations with the resources it needs. To do so should not increase the net security costs of the member states, for a stronger United Nations would permit reductions in the national military establishments of the countries whose security concerns include the preservation of peace.

Implications for U.S. Policy. The Clinton administration inaugurated on January 20, 1993, faces a reexamination of U.S. global security strategy. Its range of strategic choices is essentially limited to (1) reliance on multilateralism through the U.N. instrument, (2) primary emphasis on regional collective security arrangements, and (3) a unilateral approach allowing for selective U.S. intervention in external contingencies that threaten vital U.S. interests.

Of course these options are not mutually incompatible. Indeed, the new administration is virtually certain to adopt elements of all three. In the looming global disorder, a redundance of possible responses to threat may prove crucial.

The U.S. Joint Chiefs of Staff (JCS) anticipated this postelection reevaluation through the publication in February 1992 of a twenty-six-page *National Military Strategy* for the 1990s. The JCS proposal called for a self-contained U.S. base force capable of fulfilling four key requirements already agreed upon within the Bush administration—that is, Strategic Deterrence and Defense, Forward Presence, Crisis Response, and Force Reconstitution. The JCS acknowledged the potential value of "ad hoc coalitions" and "U.N. auspices" in areas not covered by existing U.S. alliances, but stressed that "we must also retain the capability to act independently, as our interests dictate." There was no suggestion—nor is there any near-term likelihood—that U.S. forces might operate under U.N. command in any contingency. The ultimate fate of this JCS approach and of the force structure prescribed in it was, of course, dependent in large part on 1992 postelection political and fiscal realities. For the purposes of this analysis, however, the main inference to be drawn from it is that the Pentagon, at least, did not foresee a dominant U.N. role in global security management before the end of this century.

But, assuming that the United States will aspire to global leadership in the next generation, it should now begin to work at creating the elements of a new world order in which threats to the peace anywhere will be countered by prompt and effective multilateral action. And in such an environment, only a central organization of universal membership—with a built-in judicial system—would appear to possess the collective authority for such action.

It thus follows that however the United States decides to defend its national interests in the medium term, one of its long-term objectives should be to upgrade the United Nations as the global security guarantor. This is not a "them-or-us" proposition. The United States took the lead in establishing the United Nations for precisely that purpose. It retains a Security Council veto and unparalleled influence over how the United Nations does its business. If the United Nations fails to discharge its chartered role, nothing much will have been lost in the attempt. But if it succeeds, it can provide the global community with an effective and affordable security system that complements and in some cases can largely replace the military establishments of its member nations.

Discussion Questions

1. What is meant by "peacekeeping"? How does international peacekeeping differ from independent state actions in keeping the peace?
2. What factors influence the effectiveness of an international peacekeeping effort? By what criteria is the effectiveness of an international peacekeeping operation evaluated?
3. What are the relative merits of the multilateral (U.N.-sponsored) and multinational (superpower-sponsored) approaches to international peacekeeping?
4. How, if at all, should the list of Security Council permanent members be changed? Why?
5. Does peace enforcement have a future?

6. What are the inherent limitations of U.N. peacekeeping missions? Should their rules of engagement be liberalized?

7. Can and should there be a time limitation on U.N. peacekeeping missions? Is there a case for shifting their costs at some point to the appropriate regional grouping or the contending parties?

8. Should the scope of U.N. peacekeeping missions be broadened to address international crime, natural disasters, the gross violation of human rights, or nuclear weapons development by states not parties to the Non-Proliferation Treaty?

9. How should the Article 2, Paragraph 7, dilemma be resolved? When, if ever, should the rights of people take precedence over the rights of U.N. member states?

10. By what criteria should the future funding of U.N. security activities be allocated among the member states?

11. Is the historic distinction between interpositional peacekeeping and Chapter VII enforcement valid in the emerging global environment?

12. At what point, if ever, should America's cold war alliance systems give way to a U.N. system of global security management?

13. Would U.S. national security be enhanced or reduced by a gradual shift to multilateralism?

Recommended Reading

Blodgett, John Q. "The Future of U.N. Peacekeeping." *The Washington Quarterly* (Winter 1991), pp. 207–220.

Gardner, Richard N. "The Case for Practical Internationalism." *Foreign Affairs* 66 (Spring 1988).

General Assembly. *Proposed Medium-Term Plan for the Period 1992–1997. Major Programme 1. Maintenance of Peace and Security, Disarmament and Decolonialization*. UN Document A/45/6 (Prog. 2), April 10, 1990.

Hagglund, Gustav. "Peace-Keeping in a Modern War Zone." *Survival* 32 (May–June 1990): 223–40.

Krepon, Michael, and Tracey, Jeffrey P. " 'Open Skies' and UN Peace-Keeping." *Survival* 32 (May–June 1990): 251–63.

Liu, F. T. *United Nations Peacekeeping: Management and Operations*. Occasional Paper no. 4 (New York: International Peace Academy, 1990).

Perez de Cuellar, Javier. "Peace-Keeping in the 1990s." Address delivered to a conference organized by Parliamentarians for Global Action, United Nations Headquarters, New York, November 2, 1990.

Rikhye, Indar Jit. *The Future of Peace-Keeping*. Occasional Paper no. 2 (New York: International Peace Academy, 1989).

Rikhye, Indar Jit. *Strengthening UN Peacekeeping: New Challenges and Proposals* (Washington, D.C.: United States Institute for Peace, 1992).

Urquhart, Brian. *A Life in Peace and War*. (New York: Harper & Row, 1987).

Urquhart, Brian. "The Future of Peacekeeping." *Negotiation Journal* 5 (January 1989), pp. 25–31.

Urquhart, Brian. "Beyond the Sheriff's Posse." *Survival* 32 (May–June 1990): 196–205.

Urquhart, Brian. "New Dimensions in International Security." *Adelphi Papers* 265 (Winter 1991/92).

23

Conflict and Arms Control

The end of the cold war has led many to hope that the problem of international conflict and war will disappear from the list of international policy concerns. As argued throughout this volume, this hope will not be realized. Even with the advent of a new set of international relations in the 1990s, war remains as a problem of international politics, although the threat of the most cataclysmic war in history—that of full strategic nuclear war between the superpowers—has dramatically receded. In theory, international conflict should become easier to manage in the 1990s, with the shift from confrontation to cooperation between the former superpower adversaries, the restoration of the United Nations as an instrument of collective security, and the preponderance of nonexpansionist U.S. military power. But in another sense, it may grow more difficult, with a worsening of regional conflicts, increasing disarray in the former communist world, and the ever-present nuclear specter.

If the problem of war is endemic to history, so too is the desire and capacity for peace. War as a customary means of resolving political disputes has been greatly devalued among the developed societies in the late twentieth century, not just because of its sheer destructiveness but also because of the growth of shared values and a widespread commitment to "life, liberty, and the pursuit of happiness." In the United States, antipathy to the use of force is strong, except as a last resort and for a just cause with just means. Thus, the challenge confronting public policymakers in the United States is the management of international competition and conflict in ways that make war unlikely—especially war involving the United States. Phrased differently, the challenge is to bring to bear the influence and power of the United States to shape the incentives and disincentives to conflict in ways conducive to its amelioration or resolution without resorting to the use of force.

Arms control emerged in the era after World War II as a major U.S. policy tool in this regard. The arms control process itself, that is, the negotiation of the limits of various kinds on military capabilities, became a significant way to conduct political dialogue between deeply divided adversaries. The product of arms control, in the form of formal agreements, made more manageable the armaments competition between the adversaries and contributed to some easing of the economic costs associated with maintaining defenses. In the 1990s, the key question is whether arms control can continue to play a key role in U.S. security policy.

This chapter begins with a review of the problem of conflict in the international system and alternate theories about the sources of conflict. It turns then to the management of conflict, in times of both war and relative peace. This includes a discussion of the history of arms control and an exploration of its potential role in the decades ahead.

Sources of Conflict. From the beginning of recorded time, people have been involved in conflict with one another. Although the human race has progressed in many ways since cave dwellers used clubs against each other, contemporary history and recent events make it painfully clear that people have not yet found a solution to the problem of conflict in society. Yet the highly advanced state of technology of destruction available today makes the control of conflict a necessity.

Three basic schools of thought have developed in the various attempts to discover the causes of conflict and war, namely, those that find the causes in (1) human nature, (2) the characteristics of various types of nation-states, and (3) the structure of the international system. In a major theoretical analysis of the causes of war, *Man, The State, and War,* Kenneth Waltz refers to these three views of the cause of war as different ''images'' of international relations.[1] If conflict is to be controlled, these images must be manipulated: human nature must be altered through social policy, or the characteristics of the nation-state must change to emphasize cooperation over violence in resolving differences, or the international system must provide the means and incentive for cooperative interactions and for constraining violence. As discussed in earlier chapters, significant changes in the post–World War II environment have indeed occurred and continue to transform the arena in which conflict occurs; thus far, however, it is plain that the changes have been insufficient to provide adequate conflict control.

Human Nature. Consider first the active troublemaker, Homo sapiens. The human-nature-is-to-blame school of thought emphasizes the existence of various characteristics of human nature which cause conflict. Malthus observed that while human institutions in society could be the cause ''of much mischief to mankind; . . . yet they are mere feathers that float on the surface, in comparison with those deeper seated causes of impurity that corrupt . . . the whole stream of human life.'' Spinoza considered the passions inherent in humans as the force that draws them into conflict. While Spinoza asserted that reason could moderate passions on occasion, he concluded that passion would generally rule in the internal conflict between the two. Freud believed that conflicts between people are resolved by resorting to violence, ''the same [as in] the animal kingdom, from which man cannot claim exclusion.'' Konrad Lorenz, the noted expert on animal behavior, also asserts that humans have an inherent aggressive instinct, like all animals. Lorenz's theories on aggressiveness in human nature and its moderation or exacerbation by the social environment are, however, essentially based on animal data, rather than on empirical human evidence. Extrapolation from the behavior of tropical fish and geese to that of humans is fraught with risk.[2]

Common to many of the writers of this school of thought is the concept that society's institutions are sometimes capable of holding the aggressive tendencies of human nature in check and at least temporarily overcoming its intrinsic evil. A contrary view is taken by another branch for this school: It emphasizes the role that society and its institutions play in perverting human nature, which they consider good or essentially neutral prior to exposure to the bias of the social environment. Rousseau is perhaps the most noted exponent of this view of human beings as inherently noble creatures whom society corrupts. Mark May provides a more recent statement of this perspective on learned behavior, emphasizing the perverse role of the social environment.[3] By far the most influential exponent of this view of society's crucial role has been Karl Marx; for him the nature of social organization, whether capitalist or socialist, is decisive in determining whether people pursue war or peace.

The human nature school's prescription for lessening the incidence of conflict calls for the development and education of humanity in a direction that emphasizes cooperation as a means of resolving problems. A variant of this approach focuses on the development of a social environment that elicits cooperative behavior and attenuates the aggressive tendencies of human nature.

The Nature of the Nation-State. A second school holds that the values dominant in a certain type of nation-state affect its structure and behavior, producing bellicose actions in international relations. Lenin's view of the imperialistic activities of capitalist states is an example.[4] Lenin believed that the capitalistic states' struggle for markets, resources, and profits inevitably leads them to dominate and exploit the underdeveloped areas of the world. As the potential colonial territory of the world diminished, Lenin foresaw an increased level of competition that would ultimately result in violent conflict among the capitalist nation-states and the end of the capitalist system.

Various other arguments concerning the nature of states have been contributed by more liberal thinkers. Thomas Paine, for example, described war as the work of the unrepresentative governments of nation-states; since the interest of the people lies in peace, governments that make war do not express the true interests of the people through government policy. A democratic form of government is most conducive to peace, he asserted, since the people have more control over policy. Woodrow Wilson expanded this line of thought to advocate an era in which the same moral standards would apply to the actions of nation-states as apply to peoples' individual actions. To achieve this situation, nation-states must become democratic, for democracies are by definition peaceful. While Wilson admitted that the condition of peace would still be based on force when the democratic international community was realized, that force would not be the force employed by individual nation-states but one based on the consent of the governed and the organized public opinion of the world community—referred to by Wilson as "the organized major force of mankind."[5]

Ideologically motivated states are not, of course, necessarily peaceful. An ideology is both a set "of beliefs that give meaning to life" and "an explicit or implicit program of action."[6] The program-of-action component can constitute a threat to nations of differing ideologies whose own programs of action may seek interests that will bring the ideologies into conflict. Nazism, as exemplified in the German Third Reich, was a threat to every other ideology. Even Christian ideology has generated war. Charlemagne and the Crusaders resolved threats to the soul by spreading their Christian faith by fire and sword. The conviction that one's own side is infallibly and unquestionably righteous can overpower the survival instinct itself and remove all reason and restraint from conflict. During the Crusades, the slogan "God wills it!" was used to rationalize and legitimize a vast array of destructive acts completely antithetical to Christianity.

Whatever the ideology or motivation of particular states, the nation-state is the actor that represents and executes both the creative and destructive tendencies of its members. It provides a definition and an embodiment of the legal, cultural, and behavioral values of its members. The sentiment of identification with a nation-state is nationalism, perhaps the single most important form of ideology in the twentieth century. A democratic nation-state is able to strengthen its citizens' identification with it by defining them as sovereign and the state merely as an agent, thus spreading power and responsibility. Indeed, the emergence of the nation-state and of the nationalism it evokes has tended to broaden involvement in war to include total populations.

The political mobilization of the masses in Asia and Africa accompanying the human revolution cited in Chapter 1 has significantly increased the number of nation-state actors in the international environment. The fifty nation-states that constituted the founding members of the United Nations in 1945 represented most of the non-Axis sovereign states of the world at that time. Forty-five years later, the number of sovereignties had more than tripled, with about one hundred fifty-nine belonging to the United Nations. By 1992, the number had grown to one hundred seventy-nine. The growth in the number of states has exacerbated the problem of conflict control, for even the smaller, newly formed states (which may have limited ambitions and claims) make decisions and take independent actions that significantly affect other nation-states possessing extended interests of their own.

The Structure of the International System. Theoreticians who believe that the causes of conflict lie in the nature of the international system assert that war is inevitable owing to the lack of authority above the nation-state, which can dampen inevitable conflicts and adjust varying interests to permit resolution of differences short of violence. Even if a nation-state attempts to be just, others will not accept its bona fides, for its perception of the situation is bound to be affected by self-interest. In this view, international anarchy is thus the major cause of war. It is difficult to rebut the central concept behind this formulation for the problem; yet the existing international system is hardly structureless. Collective security and international peacekeeping arrangements, alliances, international law, and various forms of transnational institutions all act expressly to contain, manage, or diffuse tension and conflict.

Perhaps the most useful way to approach these three explanations of the sources of conflict is to note that they are in essence three different levels of analysis. While one or another may have greater explanatory power in a given instance, all are likely to bear on the case. A comprehensive understanding of conflict is not likely to be gained by limiting one's attention to any single analytical level.

Arms Control. As the destructiveness and costs of war have increased, policymakers have sought additional means to control or eliminate it. These have included the formal negotiated measures between East and West during the cold war, as well as a host of other formal and informal measures, diplomatic initiatives, and international efforts to produce norms of acceptable behavior for states. *Arms control* narrowly defined is just a small slice of these measures, but arms control viewed more broadly should be seen as the full range of policy approaches to the problem of conflict management and avoidance. This section reviews the history of arms control in this broader sense and evaluates its current and future role. Before reviewing history, it may be useful to distinguish between arms control and its related concept, disarmament. Although both assume that nations' security can be furthered by cooperative measures, they represent quite different approaches to conflict control. Disarmament is predicated on the idea that arms cause war and that reducing or eliminating them will contribute to peace. Arms control focuses on a whole range of stabilizing measures (perhaps including arms reductions) that reduce the likelihood or severity of conflict—with the result that in some circumstances an increase of arms or of particular types of arms that would contribute to stability would be welcome from an arms control perspective.

Pre–World War I. Arms control has a long history in human affairs. Limitations on the use of certain types of weapons were included in the Manu law of war in India in approximately 500 B.C. and in the codes of the Saracens over a millennium later. The Rush–Bagot agreement of 1817 between the United States and Great Britain limited the deployment of naval vessels on the Great Lakes and

Lake Champlain, and it remains one of the best examples of a negotiated, successful arms control measure. International conferences were convened at the Hague in 1899 and 1907 to codify the rules of war and establish institutions and procedures for the settlement of international disputes, including the Permanent Court of Arbitration at the Hague, a predecessor to the present International Court of Justice.

The Interwar Years. As the first major international war fought among industrializing states, World War I evoked widespread concern about the future of military technology. The view that military preparations contributed to the outbreak of war and that weapons producers stoked the flames of war while also enriching themselves created intense political pressure after the war for negotiated measures to control and eliminate weapons.

A variety of approaches were explored. Arms limitations were included in the Treaty of Versailles, forbidding Germany from possessing certain types or quantities of weapons. In 1921 the United States convened an international conference to discuss arms limitations, resulting in the Washington Naval Treaty of 1922, which established fixed ratios and tonnage limits for the capital ships of the leading naval powers. In 1925, a protocol was signed in Geneva prohibiting the use in war of poison gas and bacteriological weapons. In 1928, the Kellogg–Briand Pact signatories renounced war as an instrument of national policy. In 1932, after seven years of preparation, a general disarmament conference was convened under the auspices of the League of Nations. Except for the 1925 Geneva Protocol, which remains in force today, each of these arms control measures collapsed in the 1930s in the face of a changing international security environment.

One legacy of this era has been a sharp division of opinions about the virtues of disarmament. The most idealistic have sought to eliminate weapons, either by category or wholesale, seeing them as the source of conflict. In the interwar years, their views supported the abolition of many types of weapons, especially chemical and biological, but have continued in the second half of the twentieth century in the form of efforts to selectively ban certain types of weapons or simply to freeze weapons deployments. In opposition to these views, others have argued that weapons should be seen as symptoms rather than causes of war, and that disarmament may contribute not to security but to insecurity by depriving states of the means to defend themselves and by nourishing the ambitions of aggressors, as the peace movements in Europe and the United States encouraged both Hitler and Tojo. Implicit is the idea that there is or can be a distribution of lands, resources, and other values among nations such that no nation is, or would be, sufficiently dissatisfied to attempt to alter the status quo by force. Advocates of disarmament generally have failed to account adequately for the problems of malevolent intent, aggressive national policies, and an unstable international system outlined at the beginning of this chapter.

Of course, although disarmament is not a panacea to the problem of conflict, there may be instances in which some selective disarmament of outdated, redundant, or otherwise unnecessary systems can bring some elements of security. The United States, for example, unilaterally disarmed itself in the biological area in the 1960s, without perceived risk to its security. Similarly, in 1991 it announced the unilateral withdrawal of all American land- and sea-based tactical nuclear weapons worldwide.

Post–World War II. Arms control and disarmament negotiations resumed after the second world war. Some of the old agenda remained. In the peace treaties after the war, unilateral measures were imposed by the victors upon the vanquished. The Federal Republic of Germany foreswore the right to possess atomic, biological, and chemical weapons, and Italy and Austria had to foreswear the right to V-2 type missiles. Similarly, Japan's constitution, reflecting the views of its American occupiers, forbade the nation's maintaining armed forces and from using "the threat or use of force as means of settling international disputes."[7] The old disarmament agenda also returned, in the guise of multinational negotiations under the aegis of the U.N.-affiliated Eighteen Nation Disarmament Conference.

But with the advent of nuclear weapons and the emergence of significant East–West competition in strategic armaments in the postwar era, arms control took on an entirely new look. In the 1950s, a new generation of analysts began to look at the problems of military strategy and international conflict in a nuclear age. A new and more precise definition of arms control came into use. Arms control was defined as having three purposes.[8]

The first purpose of arms control is to reduce the likelihood of war. Military preparations alone were seen as unable to achieve this goal in and of themselves, although some steps to reduce the vulnerability of forces to successful surprise attack were most useful. Arms control was seen as offering an alternative means to safeguard the nuclear deterrent by limiting surprise attack, diminishing the risks of miscalculation and instability in time of political or military crisis, and eliminating the risks caused by misunderstanding or miscommunication. Implicit in this arms control concept is the notion that, in a nuclear era, stability requires steps to ensure the security of the opponent as well as one's own side in circumstances short of war.

The second purpose is to contain the damage or severity of war if it occurs. This pointed in the direction of force reductions as well as of defenses and other countermeasures, but not if such steps might increase the vulnerability of retaliatory forces or the possibility of war or otherwise contribute to international insecurity.

The third purpose of arms control is to reduce the economic burden of preparations for war. Arms control, it was hoped, would enable policymakers to secure the national interest without expending huge portions of the nation's wealth simply to compete in the fielding of ever better weapons in ever larger numbers.

Arms control rests on the fundamental assumption that the probability of war is in part a function of the kinds and sizes of opposing military forces. For example, during a crisis, with all other things being equal, the probability of war is greater if one side has much larger or qualitatively superior forces, while the probability of war is lower if opposing forces are approximately equivalent in size and quality. Quantitative and qualitative disparities create destabilizing situations, since the stronger side will be tempted to exploit its advantages politically or perhaps even attack, while the weaker side, in expectation of attack and in order to minimize losses, may be tempted to launch preemptive attacks. Even if the stronger side is inclined toward restraint, perception that its weaker opponent might seek to preempt it becomes a persuasive argument for taking the military initiative. Thus, reciprocal expectations of attack under military imbalance start a vicious cycle of expectations, in part by reducing the vulnerability of strategic forces to preemptive attack, so that each nation has little to gain from attacking first but retains confidence in its deterrent and retaliatory capabilities.

Arms control also seeks to reduce the probability of accidents or miscalculations that may precipitate conflict, either through unilateral means or by specific forms of cooperation between adversaries. Unilateral measures include designing safety devices and procedures in weapons systems to guard against accidental or unauthorized use and against theft by terrorists. The U.S.–Soviet development of a direct, head-of-government-to-head-of-government hotline in the 1960s and of nuclear risk reduction centers in the 1980s provides recent examples.

Because the purposes of arms control are complex and difficult to balance, and because they required paying attention to the security, perceptions, capabilities, and actions of the Soviet Union, the U.S. strategic policy community turned to the study of games and the theory generated there about choices made by rational actors with limited amounts of information, facing opponents capable of independent and destructive behavior. Game theory came to play a key role in the study of East–West strategic relations and arms control theory in the 1950s and 1960s.[9]

The 1960s. In 1961, the United States established the Arms Control and Disarmament Agency as an independent entity charged with advising the president on arms control matters and, more generally, with building expertise on problems associated with negotiated measures dealing with international conflict. Under the Kennedy administration, two major arms control agreements were negotiated. The first was the so-called Hot Line Agreement of June 1963, which was a memorandum of understanding between the United States and the Soviet Union regarding the establishment of a direct communications link. The other was the Limited Test Ban of August 1963, which bans nuclear weapons tests in the atmosphere, in outer space, and under water. Both remain in force, with the latter having over 100 signatories.

Growing fears of the spread of nuclear weapons to states other than the established nuclear powers led to the negotiation of two additional agreements. The first was the Latin American Nuclear Free Zone Treaty, otherwise known as the Treaty of Tlatelolco, of February 1967. The other was the Non-Proliferation Treaty (NPT), which commits the states that had not exploded a nuclear device by January 1, 1967, not to build or use nuclear weapons and commits the nuclear weapon states to the eventual elimination of their own weapons. To facilitate verification of compliance with treaty commitments, the International Atomic Energy Agency was created to monitor nonproscribed activities. Both treaties remain in force, although the latter will be the subject of a review conference in 1995 to consider its termination or extension.

Détente I. With the advent of improved relations between East and West at the end of the 1960s and the early 1970s, arms control took on new purposes and guises. Also important to the evolution of arms control policy was the fact that the Soviet Union at this time had gained a strategic nuclear capability that credibly could threaten the annihilation of the United States. This compelled U.S. policymakers to cope with the risks of living with mutual assured destruction (MAD).

The Nixon administration negotiated a series of arms control agreements. In September 1971 the Accidents Measures Agreement was produced, identifying specific steps to reduce the risk of the outbreak of nuclear war between the two superpowers, as was a "hot line" modernization agreement. The Biological Weapons Convention, completed in April 1972, is a prohibition on the development, production, and guidelines stockpiling of bacteriological (biological) and toxin weapons and on their destruction. The following month saw the completion of the Incidents at Sea Agreement on the prevention of incidents on and over the high seas.

But the culmination of this effort was the talks on strategic arms limitations culminating in the 1972 Interim Agreement on strategic offensive arms (SALT I, for Strategic Arms Limitation Treaty) and the Anti-Ballistic Missile (ABM) Treaty of May 1972. The latter imposed strict limits on current and future strategic defensive capabilities and essentially codified the MAD strategic nuclear relationship. The former imposed certain caps on the future development of offensive strategic nuclear systems and sought to channel weapons modernization in ways deemed stabilizing to both parties. These were followed in June 1973 with an agreement on the prevention of nuclear war and in July 1974 with both a protocol to the ABM treaty and further testing limitations in the form of the Threshold Test Ban Treaty, committing the superpowers to limit the size of weapons being tested underground.

Because of the crucial nature of Soviet compliance with these two agreements for U.S. security, the means of effectively monitoring and verifying compliance became a subject of broad and intense interest. Senate consent to ratification was matched by a commitment to spend the necessary funds to substantially improve the national technical means (NTM) for verifying compliance—meaning, especially, observation satellites for counting the numbers of missiles in silos and the number of strategic nuclear submarines under construction and use.

The bilateral U.S.–Soviet arms control agenda of this era was paralleled by a broader East–West arms control agenda focusing on the management of conflict in Europe. Negotiations began in 1972 aimed at Mutual and Balanced Force

Reductions, which immediately stumbled into the very difficult problem of identifying what and how to count, and ran unproductively for well over a decade before being overtaken by events. Negotiations were also conducted during this period to recognize the post–World War II order in Europe, to secure the commitment of the Eastern bloc to Western human rights standards, and to build confidence in the region, which resulted in the Helsinki Communique of 1975 and the creation of the Conference on Security and Cooperation in Europe (CSCE). During this era, the concept of arms control expanded to include appreciation of its role in reassuring the public in both the United States and among allied nations overseas about the safe management of East–West conflict.

These areas of East–West agreement facilitated progress on a much broader international arms control agenda as well. Earlier, agreement had been reached on preventing the militarization of Antarctica (the Antarctic Treaty of December 1959). The Outer Space Treaty of January 1967 provides principles governing the activities of states in the exploration and use of outer space. The Seabed Arms Control Treaty of February 1971 prohibits the emplacement of nuclear weapons and other weapons of mass destruction on the seabed. In May 1977, agreement was reached on the Environmental Modification Convention, prohibiting the military or any other hostile use of environmental modification techniques. Later that year, in November, agreement was reached between the United States and the International Atomic Energy Agency (IAEA) on the application of nuclear safeguards in the United States. In March 1980, the international Nuclear Material Convention was completed, providing for the physical protection of nuclear material.

Return to Cold War. But the return to more frigid relations between East and West, arising out of a continuing massive Soviet arms build-up as well as the extensive use of Soviet military power outside of its territory in the latter 1970s, led to a sharp debate within the United States about the continuing utility of arms control.

Arms control negotiations survived the first signs of the end of détente during Jimmy Carter's presidency. After some early missteps in which the Carter administration sought a departure from past negotiating practice in the form of a dramatic new arms control initiative calling for deep arms reductions, SALT II was completed in June 1979 after seven years of work. It sought to provide equal limits on nuclear delivery systems for both sides, to begin the process of reductions, and to impose restraints on developments threatening to stability (especially on the deployment of multiple independently targeted reentry vehicles—MIRVs—atop ballistic missiles). SALT II was submitted to the Senate for consent to ratification but was withdrawn six months later in January 1980 in response to the Soviet invasion of Afghanistan. It did not enter into force as a binding legal document, although the United States did make a political commitment not to abrogate the terms of the treaty. This commitment in fact outlasted the terms of the treaty had it been implemented formally—SALT II would have expired in 1985, but the Reagan administration agreed to continue to refrain from undercutting its provisions, assuming Soviet reciprocity, while negotiating further reductions.

During this same period NATO also began to confront the serious strategic issues on its agenda. Bilateral U.S.–Soviet negotiations of the détente era prompted among some West Europeans a fear that arms control agreements would weaken the credibility of the U.S. nuclear guarantee to Europe. There was also concern about the Soviet deployment of large numbers of sophisticated intermediate-range SS-20 nuclear missiles targeted on Western Europe. In November 1979, NATO responded with a plan to upgrade its own intermediate-range nuclear forces (INF) by deploying a new generation of ground-launched cruise missiles and highly accurate Pershing II ballistic missiles. A second track toward resolving NATO's strategic problem was begun in the form of U.S.–Soviet negotiations to reduce INF forces on both sides to the lowest possible levels.

The election of Ronald Reagan to the presidency in November 1980 presaged an entirely new approach to arms control. With a return to a more confrontational U.S.–Soviet relationship, arms control came under heavy fire in Washington. Hardliners within the administration criticized arms control as irresponsibly weakening the U.S. military and as giving the Soviets a propaganda forum in which to weaken the will of the West to sustain strategic competition. They also asserted that Westerners had deluded themselves in believing that the Soviet elite shared Western concepts of stability, citing as proof the major ongoing construction and deployment of offensive weapon systems.

The new administration conducted an extensive review of arms control policy, with the result that a new set of goals was articulated. In the strategic nuclear area, emphasis shifted from caps to deep reductions, and it called for negotiation of a Strategic Arms Reductions Treaty (START) providing for cuts of roughly 50 percent. In the European theater, the United States stood firm on its commitment to the zero option—meaning the complete elimination of all INF systems rather than just partial cuts in their numbers—and at one point the Soviets walked out of the negotiations (U.S. INF deployments were carried out in 1984). The new administration also revised thinking on verification approaches, emphasizing the importance of on-site inspections as a supplement to National Technical Means (NTM). It also conducted a highly politicized campaign to publicize allegations of noncompliance by the Soviet Union with existing agreements, resulting in an annual report to Congress chronicling doubts about Soviet compliance in the nuclear and chemical areas.

Given the widespread public interest in arms control issues in the United States and Europe, many observers saw in these policies a thinly veiled attempt to abandon arms control as an instrument of policy. These perceptions combined with the INF deployments in Europe to bring tens of thousands of protestors to various European, as well as American, streets; NATO's maintenance of its solidarity on the INF issue in the face of such popular opposition was a powerful signal of the commitment of its leadership to countering Soviet military moves. In the United States, these perceptions stimulated widespread interest in the nuclear freeze movement, which called for a simple stop to the building and deployment of nuclear weapons. The freeze was dismissed by many as yet another disarmament fantasy, and it was eviscerated politically when it became clear that a credibly mutual and verifiable freeze was not possible. Ronald Reagan succeeded in shifting the terms of the public debate with his famous "star wars" speech of 1983, calling for the deployment of strategic defenses to make nuclear weapons "impotent and obsolete."

Détente II. East–West arms control negotiations began again with an agreement in January 1985 between the United States and the Soviet Union to resume INF negotiations and to initiate negotiations on both START and defense in space. With Mikhail Gorbachev's ascendancy in Moscow and his articulation of "new thinking" about Soviet interests, the possibilities for arms control were transformed. In a major speech in January 1986, Gorbachev set out a new approach to arms control, calling for the abolition of nuclear weapons by the year 2000, and over the ensuing months his government ceded ground on many traditional Soviet positions.

The first result was the agreement in September 1986 on a final document of the Stockholm Conference on Confidence and Security-Building Measures and Disarmament in Europe. Aimed at reducing the risk of armed conflict in Europe, it provided a number of measures designed to increase openness and predictability about military activities there. In this treaty, for the first time, the principle of on-site inspections by foreign teams was put into practice. This was followed in 1989 with the Vienna agreement on the exchange of information, observers, and inspections. In November 1990 a treaty on Conventional Forces in Europe (CFE) was completed, providing for deep reductions and significant restructuring of all East–West military forces between the Atlantic and the Urals.

A bilateral U.S.–Soviet agreement establishing jointly staffed nuclear risk reduction centers was finalized in September 1987. It was followed three months later by the INF treaty, which embodied the zero option. In 1991, START negotiations concluded with a formal agreement between the governments of the United States and the Soviet Union that called for substantial reductions in deployed nuclear forces. A number of other arms control measures were concluded at this time, such as a joint commitment to reduce chemical weapons stockpiles to 5,000 tons. There were also discussions about joint measures to limit the proliferation of unconventional weapons and their delivery systems. Even an agreement on Open Skies, first proposed by President Dwight D. Eisenhower in the 1950s, whereby participating states would have the right to the full use of aerial inspections over each other's territories, was finally ratified in 1992.

This was in essence the golden age of arms control for the United States—a reforming Soviet government sought agreement with the West, largely on Western terms, in order to secure the benefits of a less demanding international environment and some assistance in managing its domestic transition. Some arms control ideas were not pursued, such as control of naval platforms, or were pursued unsuccessfully, such as control of strategic defenses. There was also a marked evolution in thinking about monitoring compliance, with some backing away from the highly intrusive notions proposed in the early Reagan years in favor of more limited mechanisms backed by a rigorous U.S. intelligence process. The Senate's highly visible and demanding review of the INF treaty during its ratification debate suggested the political importance of arms control as well as the anticipation of exercising the Senate's full role as a coequal power in the treaty-making process.

The Post–Cold War Era. But the golden era did not last long, as the entire political framework in which arms control had been developed and pursued in the post–World War II era disappeared with the collapse of the Soviet Union in the second half of 1991. Does arms control remain relevant in this new era?

With regard to East–West relations, arms control may have a continuing importance in three areas. *The first is in the implementation of existing agreements.* At this writing, there are significant doubts about whether the major agreements of recent years—INF, START, and CFE—will be successfully implemented by the successor states of the Soviet Union. The West, and particularly the United States, has tried to ensure that these states assume the responsibilities accepted by the old Union government. It has also sought to use the arms control process as a way to create incentives for the new states to

Reprinted with permission of Renan R. Lurie.

centralize the command and control of the strategic nuclear weapons of the former Soviet military. It may well prove that the arrangements and the allocation of weapons systems among them are simply too difficult for the new geostrategic realities in Europe. On the other hand, it is clear that many of the leaders and publics of the successor states see participation in binding arms control agreements as a key sign of their acceptance and legitimacy as new states in the international system.

Problems associated with the destruction of weapons have emerged as key unanticipated challenges to the implementation of existing arms control agreements. Especially in the area of nuclear and chemical weapons, it appears that Russia has neither the fiscal means nor the technical ability—nor, perhaps, the political will—to undertake the rapid destruction of weapons in environmentally safe ways. This situation sows doubts about the determination of remnants of the old system to continue pursuing the arms control agenda.

A second major arms control topic remaining for the East–West agenda is the pursuit of follow-on agreements. Following the June 1992 Bush–Yeltsin agreement (see Chapter 16), the widespread sense in Washington and the media was that the most ambitious East–West arms control agenda possible was concluded and that the future would not hold significant new agreements. With the rapid drift of international events and ever-changing thinking about the place of nuclear weapons in the post–cold war environment, this sentiment should not go unchallenged. Some interest remains in deeper cuts in the American and Russian nuclear arsenals and, at some future time, in an arms control agreement that also addresses the arsenals of the other advanced nuclear states: Britain, France, and the People's Republic of China (P.R.C.). Further unilateral arms control measures by either Russia or the United States appear unlikely at this writing, given the apparent preference of both states for codifying restraints in formal measures so that they will have the benefits of verification and compliance mechanisms. Some arms control steps, however, such as those related to the redeployment or elimination of short-range nuclear forces, are likely to remain informal in character.

The third 1990s remnant of the old East–West arms control agenda is European security. CSCE remains firmly in place and in Spring 1992 gained a new forum for negotiating arms control measures. Interest also remains strong among some Europeans in a follow-on CFE treaty (called CFE-1A), which would add manpower limitations to the armaments limits of the original agreement. There is a sharp debate within the transatlantic community about whether these various negotiations should be used to deal with problems of possible future force reconstitution and peacekeeping or whether there should be some pause in the effort for negotiated measures and a shifting of emphasis instead toward working with existing transparency and confidence-building measures. The United States appears undecided on this point, although it has rejected any effort to use the CSCE arms control process as a way to negotiate constraints on forces in the continental United States.

But the East–West arms control agenda is only one element of the agenda of the 1990s. A second focus of arms control energy will be the multilateral agenda. Global arms control mechanisms are likely to grow in importance with the breakdown of the bipolar world order and with the industrialization of the developing world and the proliferation of military technology and capability, especially of unconventional weapons.

Efforts to strengthen the existing regimes controlling unconventional weapons will be the top priority. The nuclear Non-Proliferation Treaty (NPT) is facing new trials in the early 1990s with the pull of events in the Middle East, South and Northeast Asia, and the former Soviet Union. Following discovery of Iraq's sizable but secret nuclear weapons program under the nose of International Atomic Energy Agency inspectors, measures associated with strengthened verification and compliance with the NPT are likely to enjoy growing support. In 1995, states parties to the NPT will convene to consider the extension of the treaty either for another twenty-five years or for a shorter period. States opposed to the special rights of the states who had nuclear weapons before 1967 may gather enough political support among the disaffected states of the developing world to throw the extension of the treaty in doubt. The outcome of that debate will be one key determinant of the future spread of nuclear weapons.

The Biological Weapons Convention of 1972 will also face growing scrutiny in the 1990s. Twenty years after it was written, there are increasing doubts about the seriousness with which many states take their commitment to the convention, with reports of between ten and fifteen countries possessing offensive biological warfare capabilities, where they might be seen as "the poor man's atom bomb." The treaty lacks meaningful verification and compliance provisions. The means to strengthen the convention and to boost confidence in its effectiveness have been the subject of periodic review conferences.

In the chemical area, negotiations appear to be leading to the early conclusion of a comprehensive disarmament treaty, the Chemical Weapons Convention. The basic undertaking to destroy existing arsenals and not to build or transfer chemical weapons to others would represent a significant advance on the Geneva Protocol of 1925, which remains in force as an undertaking not to use these weapons. Unlike the Biological Weapons Convention (BWC), it would provide for some verification and compliance mechanisms. Unlike the NPT, it would require disarmament by states of both the developing and the developed worlds. Such selective disarmament by the United States appears consistent not with the ideology of the 1920s but with a prudent reading of national security interests in the 1990s. That is, the United States would be trading away an unused military instrument (last used by the United States when Woodrow Wilson sat in the White House) in exchange for a dampening of the pressures toward chemical weapons proliferation.

A strengthening of these regimes to control unconventional weapons will require concerted and continuing efforts on the part of the United States and its allies. They must make astute use of periodic review conferences to gain consensus about problems and responses. Particular attention must be given to the inspection issue, and whether or how existing verification regimes can be improved to deal with new threats. U.S. thinking about the verification of bilateral U.S.–Soviet treaties has tended to dominate its positions in multilateral forums, but this should change as the cold war recedes, leading possibly to a new openness to more intrusive inspections.

But effective multilateral arms control will require more than just some tightening of the existing legal framework. Complementary policies must be pursued as well. Policymakers should increase the diplomatic attention given to proliferation issues. They must also attend to the military capabilities that will shape the expectations of potential cheaters; this points to the continuing need for investment in technological superiority and defenses against specific types of weapons as well as the preservation of alliances and the political bases for collective security.

The 1990s will likely witness the emergence of a new set of multilateral arms control issues. The 1991 decision of the United Nations to constitute an annual registry of conventional weapons that are traded internationally suggests a growing global interest in arms control transparency measures and in the use of negotiated measures to cope in new ways with the problems of competitive relations.[10] In a way, the registry idea represents a bit of old thinking about arms control—that it is weapons themselves that create security problems. But in a way it also represents a new appreciation of the fact that the uneven flow of arms can and has produced not just competition but war, either by nourishing the ambitions of aggressors or deepening fear among the vulnerable. The effort of the United Nations to police Iraq's compliance with the April 1991 ceasefire agreement—through a U.N. Special Commission (UNSCOM)—points also to the possibility of a growing U.N. role in monitoring and verifying treaty compliance. The UNSCOM's use of information provided by various national intelligence agencies has stirred interest in supporting new U.N. roles in this area.

Is the multilateral agenda of the 1990s likely to enjoy a golden age in the same way as the bilateral U.S.–Soviet agenda of a few years earlier? Probably not. There is a real possibility that arms control negotiations, often paralyzed by East–West division, may now suffer the consequences of North–South division. For some leading states of the developing world, the debate about these various agreements has become a vehicle for contesting the distribution of power and influence in the post–cold war era. They abhor any agreement that preserves the long-term military or economic dominance of the developed world and may prefer to scuttle negotiated measures—or to sign them with the expectation of cheating—rather than be seen acquiescing to the political agenda of the North.

A new set of arms control measures beyond the East–West and familiar multilateral ones is emerging in the early 1990s as a serious possibility—regional measures. The end of bipolarity and superpower preeminence, combined with the proliferation of advanced conventional and unconventional weapons in regions of chronic conflict, has stimulated interest in regional arms control. This is most advanced in Latin America, where Argentina, Chile, and Brazil, building on the Tlatelolco Treaty, agreed in September 1991 to create and police among themselves a zone free of nuclear, chemical, and biological weapons. In East Asia, elements of an informal arms control regime between the two Koreas that overlap with North Korea's entry into the multilateral NPT are beginning to emerge, as described in Chapter 17. In South Asia, the nuclearization of both India and Pakistan has prompted fears of an arms race and war, nudging them to begin a dialogue about informal and formal measures to limit the risks. And in the Middle East—where some limited arms control measures have long been implemented, such as the demilitarization of the Sinai—there is renewed but still very limited interest stimulated by calls of recent years by Presidents Bush, Gorbachev, and Mubarek for regional control measures.

In each of these regions there is active exploration of the models of arms control from the East–West experience. There are many reasons to believe that the achievement of formal negotiated measures will be difficult, especially in the Middle East. Many of the factors critical to arms control in the East–West context—especially the presence of bipolarity and of mutual assured destruction—are not characteristic of those conflicts. On the other hand, the increasing risks associated with war in these regions may create new perceptions of the stakes and risks, as it did in Washington and Moscow, to redefine national interests in ways conducive to arms control.[11] There are important questions about the timing and scale of such undertakings, and whether confidence-building measures really have anything to contribute to historical enmities. But if the East–West experience is any indication, arms control may have as much to contribute in the 1990s as a process of dialogue and signalling about political intent as for its culmination in formal measures in the decade(s) ahead.[12]

The success or failure of efforts to achieve meaningful arms control in regions in conflict will have tangible consequences for the security of the United States. In both Asia and the Middle East, the United States has a direct role as the guarantor of the security of one or more states, and the drift toward war in either region would likely involve U.S. forces. Moreover, a general deterioration of the international security environment would make it much more difficult for the United States to reap the peace dividend at the end of the cold war and would force upon it politically divisive choices about the kind of role it should play in maintaining peace in an anarchic world. There is not a great deal that the United States can do directly to compel the adoption of regional arms control measures, but given its power, influence, and ability to cushion some of the risks for some of the states involved in the negotiations, it can play a key role as a facilitator.

Conclusion. Contrary to the hopes generated by the end of the cold war, the problem of conflict and of war among nations has not disappeared at the end of the twentieth century. Among the developed societies, war has ceased to be viewed as a legitimate instrument of policy, except as a last resort or under collective security provisions. But these societies cannot isolate themselves from the problem of war in regions near and far. In an era of growing interdependence, war can have economic and political repercussions well beyond its locus. Moreover, with the increasing sophistication and reach of military capabilities among states of the developing world, the interests of the states of the developed world can be directly engaged by threat of attack, even when they prefer to remain apart from the conflict.

Given the continued existence of war in the international system, and the potential that the interests and armed forces of the United States may become engaged in such wars, arms control will remain a key American security policy instrument. But not as before. In the narrowest sense, arms control as a body of legal treaties relating to the disposition of the military forces most threatening to the United States is likely to be of less salience in the 1990s with the passing of the Soviet Union. But in a broader sense, arms control as a set of formal and informal understandings and regimes concerning the disposition of military capabilities—either local or global—will continue to have value as a way to counter threats to U.S. security and to reduce the likelihood that U.S. forces will be called upon in last resort.

Thus, we see both an expansion and dilution of the arms control agenda from the perspective of U.S. policymakers in the 1990s. It will likely include many more elements than in the cold war era, although they are of less direct short-term importance for the United States. But they will prove to be critical tools in building a new order of international affairs that is more cooperative than anarchic and that channels the energies of the developing world away from military means of solving conflict and toward the building of stable, prosperous nations and regions.

Discussion Questions

1. Why do nations go to war? Are there major reasons and minor ones? To which of the alternative explanations in the text do you subscribe? Do you have others to suggest? Do the traditional theories of war take into account adequately the problem of weapons—either the sheer destructiveness of nuclear weapons or the uneven flow of conventional weapons?
2. Have the ideological and technological revolutions increased or decreased the prospects for conflict? Are there different answers for the two halves of the twentieth century?
3. Define *conflict control* and explain the importance of shared interests for this concept.
4. What is the difference between arms control and disarmament as approaches to conflict control?
5. What principal bureaucratic actors in the U.S. government are involved in the arms control process? What perspectives are they likely to bring to bear in the intragovernmental bargaining process?
6. What accounts for the short-lived success of some arms control measures and the relative durability of others? Identify salient political, military, and technological factors.
7. Surveying arms control efforts of the last one hundred years, has it on balance made a positive or a negative contribution to international security and to U.S. national security?
8. How has thinking about the verification of arms control agreements changed in recent decades?
9. What lessons of the East–West nuclear relationship are important for understanding the future of regional conflict?

10. What lessons of the East–West arms control experience are applicable to regions of conflict in the developing world?

11. What security and political risks should the United States be willing to run in the post–cold war era to advance a broader international arms control agenda?

Recommended Reading

Arms Control and Disarmament Agency. *Arms Control and Disarmament Agreements: Texts and Histories of the Negotiations*. Washington, D.C.: U.S. Government Printing Office, 1990.

"Arms Control: Thirty Years On." *Daedalus,* special issue (Winter 1991).

Berkowitz, B. D. *Calculated Risks: A Century of Arms Control, Why It Has Failed, and How It Can Be Made To Work*. New York: Simon & Schuster, 1987.

Blacker, C. D., and Duffy, Gloria, eds. *International Arms Control: Issues and Agreements*. Stanford, Calif.: Stanford University Press, 1984.

Blechman, Barry. "Do Negotiated Arms Limitations Have a Future?" *Foreign Affairs* (Fall 1980).

Brennan, Donald G., ed. *Arms Control, Disarmament, and National Security*. New York: Braziller, 1961.

Brodie, Bernard. *Strategy in the Missile Age*. Princeton, N.J.: Princeton University Press, 1959.

Davis, Lynn E. "Lessons of the INF Treaty." *Foreign Affairs* 66 (Spring 1988).

Dunn, Lewis. *Containing Nuclear Proliferation*. London: Brassey's for IISS, 1992.

Hedley Bull on Arms Control. Selected and introduced by Robert O'Neill and David N. Schwartz. New York: St. Martin's Press, 1987.

Frank, Jerome D. *Sanity and Survival: Psychological Aspects of War and Peace*. New York: Random House, 1967.

Halperin, Morton H. "War Termination as a Problem in Civil–Military Relations." *Annals* (November 1970): 86–95.

Kemp, Geoffrey, and Shelley A. Stahl, eds. *Arms Control and Weapons Proliferation in the Middle East and South Asia*. New York: St. Martin's Press, 1992.

Lenin, V. I. *Imperialism*. New York: International Publishers, 1939.

Lorenz, Konrad. *On Aggression*. New York: Harcourt Brace, 1966.

Malthus, Thomas. *An Essay on the Principle of Population*. New York: Macmillan, 1895.

May, Mark A. *A Social Psychology of War and Peace*. New Haven, Conn.: Yale University Press, 1943.

Moodie, Michael. "Transparency in Armaments: A New Item for the New Security Agenda." *The Washington Quarterly* 15 (Summer 1992).

Myrdal, Alva. *The Game of Disarmament*. New York: Pantheon Books, 1976.

Roberts, Brad. *Chemical Disarmament and International Security*. London: Brassey's for IISS, 1992.

Smith, Gerard. *Doubletalk: The Story of SALT I*. Garden City, N.Y.: Doubleday, 1980.

Talbott, Strobe. *Deadly Gambits: The Reagan Administration and the Stalemate in Arms Control*. New York: Knopf, 1984.

Talbott, Strobe. *Endgame: The Inside Story of SALT II*. New York: Harper & Row, 1979.

Tourtellot, Arthur, ed. *Selections for Today*. New York: Cuell, Sloan & Pearce, 1945.

Waltz, Kenneth N. *Man, the State, and War*. New York: Columbia University Press, 1959.

24

National Security Perspectives for the 1990s

Perhaps the best way in which to conclude this book is to summarize the environmental factors, present and emerging, that are broadly apparent to policymakers and that are strongly influencing U.S. national security policy. These factors are transitional guideposts to policy formulation. They do not determine national security policy's content, but policymakers seeking effective policies must consider how these factors, both foreign and domestic, are now shaping and will further shape the security environment. We will also frame for analysis the evident challenges U.S. national security policy must address as the nation moves through the 1990s, and conclude by sketching some of the likely main themes in the emerging policy.

Even the current guideposts, however, are rapidly changing from those previously used. In the recent past one common, crucial guidepost for national security policy considerations was the "threat," in all its different manifestations and dynamics. Now, as the Director of Central Intelligence testified in early 1992, that overwhelming threat has receded, and in its place are myriad "destabilizing, dangerous, and, in many cases, unexpected challenges, such as the appearance of fifteen new countries in the place of a single, familiar [Soviet] empire."[1] This fading threat has caused decision-makers within the National Security Council to reformulate national security policy, particularly its defense component, with very little certainty as to what challenges or opportunities lay ahead. As JCS Chairman General Powell has noted:

> The decline of the Soviet threat has fundamentally changed the concept of threat analysis as a basis for force structure planning. We can still plausibly identify some specific threats—North Korea, a weakened Iraq, perhaps even a hostile Iran. But the real threat is the unknown, the uncertain. In a very real sense, the primary threat to our

security is instability and being unprepared to handle a crisis or war that no one expected or predicted.[2]

Policymakers must, however, continue with their analysis and decision-making, regardless of how many guideposts are changing or how uncertain and murky the environments are, both external and internal. American interests and our political system demand no less. What follows, therefore, is our best estimate of the factors now guiding and likely in the future to guide the development of U.S. national security policy.

Scanning the Foreign Environment: Three Major Influences. Without doubt, the current and future security environment of the United States is radically altered from that of the past forty-plus years. Many have found it difficult to acknowledge the extent of change and its implications, particularly because U.S. foreign policy has been so successful in bringing the cold war to a successful close without a catastrophic nuclear exchange. As former Secretary of Defense James R. Schlesinger noted, "We are tempted to rest on our laurels; rather than seriously to reconstruct our foreign policy, we are tempted to believe that a few modest adjustments will suffice."[3] So what are these influences in the external environment that must serve as guideposts to the future? At a minimum, three stand out:

1. Replacement of the cold war and its bipolar, competitive superpower relationship by a complex multipolar international system. Most fundamentally, the demise of the Soviet Union and its Eastern European empire means that our nation's security now needs redefinition; and the role of the United States in world affairs to provide for that security, however redefined, needs complete rethinking. Gone for the foreseeable future is the need for the United States to lead Western democracies in a global effort to protect the Eurasian land mass from hostile domination. Not only is there no longer a political threat to our values, but there is no immediate military threat to our physical security—beyond, that is, the highly unlikely prospects of a nuclear attack from one of the former Soviet states still holding such weapons.[4]

The immediate implications of this change are striking, to say the least. The vast military capabilities of the United States, particularly the nuclear components, seem remarkably in excess. In 1991 President Bush moved well ahead of the laborious arms control processes of the cold war and unilaterally eliminated all tactical nuclear weapons from the U.S. army and the surface forces of the U.S. navy. Our foreign policy toward Europe can now expect the Europeans, confronting lesser threats, to establish more of their own security identity, and to bear fully the economic burden for it. And our relations with the Third World need not be seen any longer through the prism of the cold war, wherein the two superpowers competed for influence and prestige, often being played off one another by the developing nations.

Thus, the demise of the Soviet Union means that the well-understood organizing principles of U.S. foreign and defense policy and the resulting patterns of relationships are gone. The world is now a much less dangerous place, but not necessarily a more stable community. How we will define our interests in this new international order, and seek to pursue them in relation to other members of the community of nations, is the central challenge.

The disappearance of one superpower, and hence bipolarity, does not mean unipolarity. Although there has been some sentiment in the United States (and some concern elsewhere) that the United States should ensure that no rival superpower emerges—that is, ensure unipolarity—that aspiration is debatable, in terms of both practicality and wisdom. The argument over the concept of a "one-superpower international system" surfaced in the media in early 1992 when a Pentagon planning document was leaked: It advocated an American focus "on precluding the emergence of any potential future global competitor." Although the document made plain that this aim was to be accomplished through the exercise of benign and effective American leadership, it also stated clearly that American defenses should be so strong that potential competitors, from Western Europe or Asia as well as the former Soviet Union, would be deterred "from even aspiring to a larger regional or global role."[5] The leaked document created such a storm of criticism that it was disavowed by the administration, including the Pentagon, as a mere draft.

But many believers in *realpolitik* and skeptics about world politics find merit in unipolarity and pour scorn on one widely cited alternative to it, namely, "collective internationalism," as exercised through the United Nations; they warn that the real alternative to unipolarity is not an ineffective United Nations but superpower multipolarity—that if the United States

> gives up its worldwide predominance, Germany and Japan, military midgets today, will quite reasonably seek to assure their own security by turning themselves into military giants. . . . The alternative is Japanese carriers patrolling the Straits of Malacca and a nuclear Germany dominating Europe.[6]

Remembering the dependence of the United States on its friends and allies for forces, bases, fuel, and finances during the Gulf war (when its own forces and flexibility were far greater than will be the case in the future), it seems clear that full unipolarity is impractical. Yet, taking into account all the elements of power and not just military forces or economic strength, it is equally clear that American power far outdistances that of any other state. The extent to which the United States uses that power wisely will greatly influence the degree to which others follow its leadership. In some cases that leadership can best be exercised through the U.N.'s "collective internationalism," in others, through bilateral treaty relationships, in still others, through regional organizations. Although the emphasis and mix of relations will vary over time and with specific issues, it seems likely that America's policy approach (and the overall pattern of the international system as a whole) can best be described as "complex multipolarity."

2. *A focal shift from global to regional strategy for U.S. national security policy.* From the end of World War II in 1945 to the end of the 1980s, U.S. national security policy was global in character, an inherent derivative of

Kennan's formulation of the strategy of containment.[7] While the main line of defense was across a divided Europe, countervailing pressure to Soviet expansionism was to be applied around the periphery of that empire wherever it attempted to extend its influence.

In contrast, the end of that bipolar confrontation now allows U.S. foreign policy to be focused on each individual region of the world in which we have threatened interests. This focus also responds, as it must, to trends in international economic relationships, particularly the creation of regional economic arrangements to foster free trade on a regional basis and to enhance various regions' competitive stature in global markets, for example, the North American Free Trade Area, and the European Economic Community.

Other factors also have influenced the move toward a regional policy focus, factors such as the rise of aspiring regional hegemons with extensive military power that could threaten U.S. allies or interests, hegemons such as Iran and Iraq in the Middle East. In fact, just as President Bush was announcing in the now famous Aspen speech of August 2, 1990, that the demise of the Soviet Union and the reunification of Germany—the end of the cold war—would allow a 25 percent reduction in U.S. military forces, Saddam Hussein's forces were invading Kuwait.[8]

Thus began the first major war of the post–cold war era, a limited, regional war fought by a remarkable coalition of Western nations and their Arab allies under U.N. auspices against a rival Arab power. At stake were both vital U.S. economic interests (access to oil) and important political interests (the rule of law and the peaceful settlement of disputes). Also at stake was U.S. leadership, as President Bush attempted, successfully, to create the unique ad hoc coalition that successfully prosecuted the war under the auspices of the United Nations. The successes of the war will be debated for years, though most observers agree on several very clear lessons for future U.S. foreign policy.

First, the world is still a very dangerous place, replete with animosities and awash in a vast pool of armaments left over from decades of production rivalry during the cold war. Second, the United States has a unique leadership role to play in world affairs as the residual superpower of the cold war. For example, there was widespread agreement after the Gulf war that only the United States had had the political legitimacy and influence necessary to lead a multilateral response to Iraq's aggression.

Third, it was also clear that, although American leadership was essential, the contributions of the allied coalition—including the financial ones—were also crucial; ad hoc coalitions may be the only feasible way to meet most regional challenges in the future.

Fourth, the conduct and cost of the war were reflections of the new technology of conventional warfare, a form of war so lethal that it holds the potential to change the way policymakers will view the military instrument of power in the future. And, fifth, it was agreed that, notwithstanding their lethality, U.S. military forces were dependent on the logistical support of our allies to execute the war successfully, particularly for airlift, sealift, and in-theater transportation.[9] This created some very real constraints on the yet-undefined leadership role the United States could assume in the future.

Thus, several of the guideposts for future national security policy established by the Gulf war were unambiguous. A focus at the regional level was clear, as was the necessity for U.S. political leadership.[10] Also clear were the real limitations to that leadership, and therein resided the dilemma of just what role in the world the United States should pursue, a dilemma that will take some years to resolve.

Taken together, these first two changes mean that the central paradigm of cold war foreign policy is hopelessly outdated. Stated simply, it had three elements: (1) contain Soviet expansion, defeating it if the cold war became hot; (2) promote an open, global economic system; and (3) provide the U.S. leadership requisite to moving the free world to accomplish the first two elements. That paradigm embodied ideological conflict, was global and heavily focused on defense (and arms control) issues, and employed the theoretical, abstract, often arcane approach of nuclear deterrence theory and related fields. While no new paradigm had emerged by the early 1990s, it was at least clear that the new model would have a regional focus.

3. *The changing elements of national power.* This third major change in the external security environment is found in the evolving structure of the post–cold war international political system. It is not only much more fragmented, but at the same time more interdependent. The fragmentation comes from the demise of the major bipolar blocs of the cold war, as well as the corresponding alignments of Third World nations within that structure. Nation after nation, and even some subnational groups, are now relatively free to pursue independently their interests among the community of nations. Obviously, this means a high degree of instability and potential for conflict in many regions of the world.

But at the same time the ability of these nations, as well as that of the United States, to pursue their interests will be channeled and constrained by growing patterns of interdependence. These patterns are caused by the continued growth in global trading and financial systems; development of nonstate actors, such as transnational corporations and international interest groups for "transnational" issues such as the global environment; and by the pervasive flow of ideas and information via global communications systems.

In the emerging structure, national power is much more diffuse, making the exertion of influence by any nation over any other nation much more difficult. With global diffusion of power, national security policy becomes harder to define and pursue. "Soft" forms of power, such as the ability to manipulate interdependencies, become more important, as does the long-term economic strength of the nation, which is the base for both hard and soft forms of power.[11]

The obvious question this raises for U.S. foreign policy is whether America has, or is developing for the future, the right mix among the elements of national power. Specifically, is U.S. economic power, eroded by massive internal and external debts and negative international financial flows, too weak relative to the military? And, in terms of implementing U.S. policies, are the policy instruments available to pursue U.S. foreign policy interests—informational, diplomatic, economic, and military—sufficient to the tasks ahead? Since we can no longer exert power and influence by exporting national security in the form of extended nuclear deterrence, does America have other instruments of effective influence and persuasion? Some observers are doubtful, one noting that Washington "must now strive for multiple channels of influence without in many cases the assurance either of a continuing commanding role or of easy policy coordination—to do this with grace will be hard, to do it effectively, still harder."[12]

Scanning the Domestic Environment: Three Major Influences. As earlier chapters in this book have made clear, the making of U.S. national security policy is a shared responsibility between the Executive and the Congress, thus ensuring that the domestic influence on U.S. policy is large indeed. Even the judiciary has a valid, if lesser, role. Traditionally, these shared roles have left the Executive in the position of "proposing" the policy initiatives, such as treaties or agreements, and the Congress, particularly the Senate, in the role of "disposing," such as ratifying treaties or approving foreign aid budgets and the appointment of ambassadors.[13] A reversal of these roles has occurred on occasion, such as the unilateral Nicaraguan peace initiative by House Speaker Jim Wright in 1987, which sparked intensely heated controversy on the American political scene.

As that instance demonstrated, there have been, and doubtless will continue to be, deep differences over both *policy* and *process* between these two institutions, which share the responsibility for making U.S. foreign policy.[14] Largely, this is due to the fact that the members of these institutions represent different constituencies and thus tend to see the same issue from different perspectives. The President can view a matter of foreign trade policy, such as the North American Free Trade Agreement, from the perspective of the nation as a whole, and how that policy will influence overall macroeconomic performance. Individual members of Congress, however, tend to view the same issue from the perspective of its impact on their particular constituents, seemingly regardless of the overall impact.[15]

By mid 1992, a number of major changes in the U.S. domestic environment served to heighten these institutional differences and to make more difficult the coordination and cooperation necessary for the formulation of a coherent, consensus-based foreign policy for the United States. As we view U.S. national security policy for the rest of the 1990s, these domestic changes and their influences on both policy and process need to be highlighted, because they also serve as guideposts to future policy formulation.

1. Increasing primacy of the domestic agenda. There are many explanations why the U.S. government has not made choices in the recent past on domestic issues of acknowledged strategic importance to the nation. Part of the reason is obviously economic, a federal government spending about one billion dollars each day in excess of its revenues (the U.S. federal deficit for 1992 alone exceeded 380 billion dollars) has no easy choices to make. Therefore, it does not

"I don't see why all this should be our problem."

Reprinted with permission of Renan R. Lurie.

address the difficult choices. Part of the reason is also lack of domestic consensus, with deep, but roughly equal, divisions within the electorate on many value-laden domestic issues. Thus, in the early 1990s our society continued to drift in several major areas: energy policy, social and health care policies, federal deficits, entitlements, and education policy, to mention but a few.[16]

Now, after four decades of the cold war and with no clear military threat, many feel that these areas of drift are really issues of national security. The failure to invest in productive capacity, research and development, and infrastructure; the crisis in American education; the exploding underclass; the pervasive drug culture, and other domestic problems may well have a greater direct impact on our future security than any foreign military threat.[17] As expressed in the foreword of the October 1992 "Strengthening of America Commission Report," sponsored by the Center for Strategic and International Studies,

> We are most vulnerable not on the Russian steppes or in the Persian Gulf, but in our factories, our classrooms and our halls of government. It is in these places that we will either maintain or lose the strength to influence world affairs for the foreseeable future.[18]

What this means for future U.S. foreign policy is straightforward, at least in some areas. In the near term it means the primacy of the domestic agenda over the foreign policy agenda. This does not necessarily mean a more isolationist foreign policy, but it does mean that the nation's traditional foreign policy and national security focus will necessarily be broadened considerably to consider much more fully the domestic dimensions of national security. For the institutions of our government this means, given expected resource constraints, more frequent and visible tradeoffs between pursuit of foreign versus domestic policy goals. Just such a choice was faced in mid 1992 between U.S. foreign aid for Russia (the Freedom Support Act of 1992) and assistance to U.S. cities in crisis.

In contrast and at a more specific level, it is not clear what it means for future U.S. foreign policy when these "more visible and frequent" tradeoffs have to be made. The implications for foreign policy of focusing on strengthening America in the 1990s need urgent clarification. World events and relationships simply do not wait for any particular nation to decide whether it is interested in emerging issues, particularly a nation aspiring to a leadership role.

2. *The impact of "divided government" on foreign policymaking*. Since the early 1980s, political science literature has increasingly documented the impacts of "divided government"—the fact that the major institutions of the U.S. government, the Congress and the Presidency, each have been dominated by a different party. In twenty of the past twenty-four years, the Republican party, occupying the White House, did not have a majority in Congress, and usually not even in one house of Congress. Whether the "ticket-splitting" voting was a deliberate choice or not, the electorate during the 1970s and 1980s chose not to give one party "the chance to govern."[19]

However, when combined with the congressional reforms of the 1970s, which weakened the role of parties and decentralized decision-making within the Congress, the result of "divided government" has been a form of "gridlock" in which many issues of critical concern to the nation, both domestic and foreign, cannot be resolved for lack of an effective political consensus.[20] Along with the lack of consensus was the evident lack of trust and comity with which the two parties, and institutions, viewed each other—as first one institution and then the other attempted to assert primacy over foreign policy-making during the late 1970s and 1980s. One participant of the process noted in 1989:

> We are witnessing government by procedural improvisation: crucial foreign policy decisions are being shaped in Washington today by awkward parliamentary gimmicks. Controversies are resolved on the basis of last-minute presidential letters, nongermane legislative amendments, and executive orders waiving statutory requirements. Whether the issue is aiding the Nicaraguan rebels or arming Middle East belligerents, prosecuting war or concluding a peace, process has become almost as important as policy. Many of the toughest issues are ducked again and again. . . . In the midst of such parliamentary confusion it is virtually impossible to build a governing consensus.[21]

As this institutional struggle continues into the 1990s, it is necessary to understand the evolving implications. As the conflict from the late 1970s continues unabated over which branch should dominate in the *formulation* of foreign policy, that is, the setting of national objectives, it has also spread in the 1980s to policy *implementation*. This has occurred, under the auspices of legislative oversight, in the form of "congressional micromanagement." While many in the executive branch lament the often counterproductive burden caused by such "intrusions" into executive department administration, there are instances of improved implementation when Congress imposes effective oversight.[22]

In sum, there is little likelihood that this costly interbranch conflict will decrease, causing the executive to maneuver the gauntlet of legislative procedures which allow Congress to influence strongly both the direction and implementation of future U.S. national security policy. Such issues as foreign economic and developmental assistance, the sale of U.S. arms abroad, the control of security-related technology and investment, and particularly the stationing and use of U.S. military forces, will remain contentious, often impeding the design and effective execution of policy.

3. *The reduction and restructuring of U.S. military capabilities after the cold war.* In August 1990, President Bush announced to the American people a gradual 25 percent reduction in U.S. military forces, thereby creating a small "peace dividend" at the end of the cold war. This was the first announcement of a detailed plan to reduce and restructure U.S. military capabilities for the post–cold war era—a plan that was not fully presented to Congress until early 1991.

When fully presented, the plan had two major components—a new military strategy and a military "base force," which the administration believed to be the minimum necessary to execute the new strategy in the uncertain future. This post–cold war military strategy contained four central concepts:

- Strategic nuclear deterrence and defense
- Forward-presence
- Response to regional crises
- Reconstitution (of more military capabilities, if needed)

The last two elements, new to this strategy, were designed in response to the changes in the foreign environment already discussed, with a focus at the regional level as well as the recognition that smaller threats could be countered with fewer standing forces because longer warning time allowed a "reconstitution" period should greater forces be needed.[23] (Ironically, this new "reconstitution" dimension of the post–cold war era is a partial move back to the mobilization dimension of pre–cold war strategy.)

Accompanying the new strategy was a "base force" that the administration intended to reach as result of a planned scale-down during FY 1991 through FY 1997. Measured in active duty forces, it would contain about one-half million fewer military personnel, twelve Army divisions as opposed to sixteen, fifteen tactical fighter wings instead of twenty-two, and eighty-two fewer battle force ships than in 1991.[24] In terms of dollar resources, the administration requested budgets for the Department of Defense for FY 1992 through FY 1997 that represented a real reduction in defense outlays of 20 percent between 1991 and 1997. By 1997 outlays were to be reduced to a level of about 3.6 percent of gross national product, as compared with 5.5 percent in 1990 and 6.4 percent in 1987. Further, with military procurement overall sharply reduced, and over one hundred programs cancelled outright, about 1.1 million defense-related jobs were expected to be eliminated by 1995.[25]

That was the Bush plan. But Bill Clinton ran on a campaign platform calling for a savings of 100 billion dollars in defense spending over 5 years, or 60 billion more than the Bush administration proposed. President Clinton's new Secretary of Defense, Les Aspin, called early on for rapid progress toward these cuts, directing the military on February 2, 1993 to find, over a period of four days, ways to save at least 10.8 billion dollars for the next fiscal year.

The failure of the August 1991 coup in the Soviet Union and the subsequent dissolution of the Soviet Union, as well as pressing needs in the United States, led many in Congress and the larger policy community to believe that even larger reductions could be made.[26] And ultimately that will probably happen, but the lingering recession throughout 1991 and 1992 led Congress to reduce at roughly the schedule preferred by the White House, at least through FY 1993. But even if that pace continues, by 1997 the proportion of resources allocated to defense will be at the lowest level since the attack on Pearl Harbor.

The importance of the defense scale-down for future U.S. foreign policy derives from the fact that dollars do strongly influence future defense capabilities and, hence, policies. As one authority has noted elsewhere, "The defense budget is the linchpin of U.S. defense policy. Planning is irrelevant and operations impossible if the budget process does not result in the correct mix of manpower and materiel."[27]

Not only is the right mix important, but so are the locations of the forces. Under the new military strategy of the early 1990s, the role of "forward-presence" forces is particularly important if U.S. military capabilities are to leverage our diplomatic and economic relationships, as will likely be needed in order to foster stability in regions of U.S. national interest. However, given planned force reductions, particularly in forces stationed overseas, that leveraging capability is problematic. Before the Persian Gulf war, America had no "forward-presence" forces in or near Kuwait. As one former diplomat put it, "If we had an effective forward presence, we could have brilliantly deterred the Gulf War, rather than having to fight to brilliantly win it."[28] The point is, future U.S. military power, as one of the major instruments of our national security policy, is also undergoing a very turbulent transition, the outcome of which will be highly consequential to our ability to implement future policies.

Specific Challenges for U.S. National Security Policy. U.S. policymakers during the 1990s will have to focus on several key aspects of our national security policy as it is redefined to fit the changing environment and strategic imperatives just described. Since not all aspects can fit the category of "key" (even such important aspects as immigration policy), we indicate here only the few we could judge in 1992 to fit that category.

1. Adapting and bolstering the U.S. relationships with Germany and Japan. In many ways U.S. relations with its former World War II adversaries will now, some five decades later, be pivotal to the formulation and execution of our new policies. These are key democratic and economic powers, whose influence in their respective regions is immense, both for good and, in the eyes of some, potentially for bad. The challenge will be to manage these relationships to reassure all nations that the economic power centers of the free world are like-minded and cooperative on the central issues. The United States, Germany, and Japan will be redefining their roles in the world during this uncertain period, heightening the importance of their relationships and of the formulation of a collective approach to national security policy that respects the interests of each nation.

2. *Fostering a ''democratic peace'' with states of the former Soviet Union and Eastern Europe*. Simply stated, the ''crown jewels'' of the cold war will not be secured until the experiments in democratic and economic freedom under way throughout Eastern Europe and the former Soviet Union are successfully completed. Speaking on behalf of the Freedom Support Act of 1992, President Bush stated the challenge concisely:

> Today I want to talk to you all about the most important foreign policy opportunity of our time—an opportunity that will affect the security and the future of every American, young and old, throughout this entire decade. The democratic revolutions underway in Russia, in Armenia, Ukraine, and the other new nations of the old Soviet empire represent the best hope for real peace in my lifetime. . . . The Cold War is over. The specter of nuclear Armageddon has receded, and Soviet communism has collapsed. In its wake, we find ourselves on the threshold of a new world of opportunity of peace. But with the passing of the Cold War, a new order has yet to take its place. The opportunities are tremendous, but so, too, are the dangers. So we stand at history's hinge point—a new world beckons, while the ghost of history stands in the shadows.[29]

The outcome of the experiments in political democratization and economic marketization is very much in doubt. The needed changes throughout the region are encountering strong resistance as well as confusion and inertia on a major scale. A great deal of help of all kinds is needed if the required transitions are to occur. Whether the industrial democracies, including the United States, will provide that assistance in sufficient amounts and kinds and in a timely enough manner remains to be seen. Even if they do, the grand experiment could collapse.

3. *Strengthening an open economic order, and U.S. competitiveness within that emerging order*. The fruits of economic integration, the wave of the future, can best be captured in an open international economy. The global marketplace is already upon us; it ''had surely arrived when villagers in the Middle East followed the Gulf War on The Cable News Network (CNN), via Soviet government satellite and through a private subsidiary of a local government enterprise.''[30] Unproductive General Agreement on Tariffs and Trade (GATT) negotiations, still sputtering in late 1992, are but one major indication of a global economic order struggling to preserve and strengthen openness.

The rise of regional trade cooperation arrangements, North America included, is a healthy sign, but only if those arrangements do not cause trade divisiveness and protectionism that lowers world trade openness. The primary challenge to the United States is to get its own economic house in order, particularly its federal deficits, so that it can lead credibly and effectively, influencing others toward more and wider economic freedom. The United States will inevitably have to play a major role in building the needed international cooperation in trade, investment, and currency flow in such a way that both the developed and developing nations' interests are served.

4. Containing the proliferation of weapons of mass destruction. Everyone, from the Director of Central Intelligence to leading members of Congress and the Executive branch, agreed in the early 1990s that one of the largest U.S. security challenges ahead, global or regional, will be the proliferation of weapons of mass destruction and their potential impacts on regional instabilities. But consensus on a challenge does not necessarily make it more tractable. In this case, different solutions must be pursued within each region, while strengthening global safeguards under a number of regimes, most notably the Nuclear Non-Proliferation Treaty (NPT), the Missile Technology Control Regime, the chemical and biological arms control treaties and the various suppliers' cartel arrangements that have developed in recent years.[31] Obviously, pursuing control arrangements will cause difficult trade-offs for U.S. policymakers. One example is our continued testing of nuclear weapons versus our efforts to exert antiproliferation leadership through the NPT. Another is the future direction of U.S.–Chinese bilateral relations, given that China has become a major exporter of intermediate-range missiles and their production technology to the developing world. Despite the difficulty of tradeoffs, it is hard to overemphasize the importance of checking—or at least drastically slowing and containing—proliferation.

5. Building a force projection capability for unilateral or coalition use in promoting regional stability. Although the United States clearly cannot be the world's policeman, its own interests and the prospects for a viable international order depend on American power. History is littered with the wreckage of nations and empires that attempted to ignore the ancient lessons of power in world politics. No other nation or international institution will defend American interests or act in concert with this country if there is doubt about America's power, political will, and sense of direction.

Diplomacy and economic strength may resolve most challenges, particularly if the "last argument of kings" is in the background. The threat of force or mere military presence may suffice for other challenges; but in some cases it will be necessary to apply appropriate military power. Whether the application will be unilateral, as part of an ad hoc coalition, or in the context of regional or global organizations, the American force must be sufficiently strong and technologically advanced and flexible enough to meet a variety of threats and environments. Most importantly, it must be sustainable in terms of the American public's willingness to finance it and back its use. Building such intervention forces and developing the doctrinal and political bases for its use are major challenges.

Heading for the 21st Century. The foregoing discussion should have made clear the four tasks we believe minimally necessary to accomplish in order to have a successful national security policy for the United States in the 1990s:

- Deciding to what extent and how the U.S. should play a leadership role in the world.
- Coalition building for "collective engagement" as the norm for conflict management and resolution.
- Restructuring U.S. security policy instruments and institutions.
- Renewing the American economy at home and ensuring that it competes in an open world economy.

Easy to say, yet the tasks ahead are daunting. However, even in our increasingly interdependent world, the vast majority of the tasks are at home and within our power to achieve. Given a bipartisan national consensus on a vision for the future, which must be built as a first priority, Americans have proven repeatedly that they can rise to almost any challenge. As this volume has tried to suggest, the challenges to American national security are many and varied, and many tough choices must be made. But with leadership at home, the United States can not only put its own house in order, but also provide the leadership the world expects and requires.

Discussion Questions

1. What are the principal characteristics of the emerging international security environment? Which is the most important? Why?

2. What is the utility of collective security today? What role does a collective security organization play in the affairs of a major power? What can be done to increase its relevance to American national security concerns?

3. What are the principal lessons that can be derived from a study of the U.S. conduct of its national security policy since the end of World War II? What do those lessons suggest about the ability of the United States to manage its security affairs in the next decade?

4. What would you single out as the greatest national security need of the United States today? Why is it important for the future conduct of U.S. national security policy?

5. Can you define an optimal political role of the United States in the emerging world order? What are the principal alternatives to this role?

6. What is the current role of military power in world politics? How has that role changed since 1945? Is military power likely to have greater, less, or the same political utility in the 1990s as at present? Why?

7. What are the differences between "hard power" and "soft power"? Will one or the other be more important in the years ahead? Why?

8. Chapter 1 discussed a trend of convergence between the realms of foreign policy and national security policy? Will this trend continue? Why or why not?

9. Why should the United States bear any responsibilities for the economic recovery and political reform of its former adversaries in the old Warsaw Pact?

10. If you were inaugurated as President of the United States today, what would be your highest national security priority? How would you turn your priority into policy and programs? What hurdles would you have to overcome?

Recommended Reading

Beyond Distrust: Building Bridges Between Congress and the Executive. Washington, D.C.: National Academy of Public Administration, January 1992.

Crabb, Cecil V., and Pat M. Holt. *Invitation to Struggle: Congress, the President, and Foreign Policy*. Washington, D.C.: CQ Press, 1989.

Facing the Future: American Strategy in the 1990s. Aspen, Colo.: The Aspen Institute, 1991.

Huntington, Samuel. "America's Changing Strategic Interests." *Survival* 33 (January–February 1991).

Kapstein, Ethan B. *The Political Economy of National Security: A Global Perspective*. New York: McGraw-Hill, 1992.

Kaufman, Daniel J., Clark, David S., and Sheehan, Kevin P., eds. *U.S. National Security Strategy for the 1990s*. Baltimore: Johns Hopkins University Press, 1991.

Kaufmann, William, and Steinbrunner, John. *Decisions for Defense: Prospects for a New World Order*. Washington, D.C.: Brookings Institution, 1991.

Kruzel, Joseph, ed. *American Defense Annual: 1991–1992*. New York: Lexington Books, 1992.

National Military Strategy. Washington, D.C.: U.S. Government Printing Office, January 1992.

Nunn, Senator Sam. *Nunn 1990: A New Military Strategy*. Washington, D.C.: Center for Strategic and International Studies, 1991.

Peterson, Peter G., and James K. Sebenius. "The Primacy of the American Agenda." In *Rethinking America's Security: Beyond the Cold War to New World Order*, ed. Graham Allison and Gregory Treverton. New York: American Assembly of Columbia University, 1992.

Schick, Allen. *The Capacity to Budget*. Washington, D.C.: The Urban Institute, 1990.

Notes

Chapter 1: National Security: The International Setting

1. Helmut Schmidt. "The 1977 Alastair Buchan Memorial lecture," October 28, 1977, reprinted in *Survival* (London: International Institute for Strategic Studies, January–February, 1978).

2. For a more thorough expression of Professor Hoffmann's categorization, see his *State of War* (New York: Praeger, 1965), pp. 3–21.

3. Hans J. Morgenthau, *Politics among Nations,* 5th ed. (New York: Knopf, 1973).

4. Morton A. Kaplan, "Variants on Six Models of the International System," in *International Politics and Foreign Policy,* ed. James N. Rosenau (New York: Free Press, 1969), pp. 291–303.

5. Still one of the best surveys of the field is James E. Dougherty and Robert L. Pfaltzgraff, Jr., *Contending Theories of International Relations,* 3rd ed. (New York: Harper & Row, 1990).

6. J. David Singer, "The Level of Analysis Problem in International Relations," in *International Politics,* ed. Rosenau, pp. 21–22.

7. John Foster Dulles, *War or Peace* (New York: Macmillan, 1950), pp. 72–73.

8. See Henry A. Kissinger, *American Foreign Policy,* 3d ed. (New York: Norton, 1977), pp . 416–17.

9. Wolfram F. Hanrieder, "The International System: Bipolar or Multibloc?" in *The International Political System: Introduction & Readings,* ed. Romano Romani (New York: Wiley, 1972), pp. 188–89.

10. Charles Krauthammer, "The Unipolar Moment," in *Rethinking America's Security: Beyond Cold War to New World Order,* eds. Allison and Treverton (New York: Norton, 1992), pp. 295–306.

11. Joseph Nye, "What New World Order?" *Foreign Affairs,* 70 (Spring 1992): 83.

12. K. J. Holsti, *International Politics: A Framework for Analysis,* 2d ed. (Englewood Cliffs, N.J.: Prentice-Hall, 1972), pp. 155–56.

13. Harold Sprout and Margaret Sprout, *Foundations of National Power,* 2d ed. (New York: Van Nostrand, 1951), pp. 108–11.

14. Clifford German, "A Tentative Evaluation of World Power," *Journal of Conflict Resolution* 4 no. 1 (1960):138–44.

15. Ray S. Cline, *World Power Assessment,* 1977 (Boulder, Colo.: Westview Press, 1977).

16. Klaus Knorr, *Military Power and Potential* (Lexington, Mass.: Heath, 1970), p. 143.

17. Holsti, *International Politics,* pp. 160–61.

18. These assumptions on power politics are variations of and suggested by those expressed in Charles O. Lerche, Jr., and Abdul A. Said, *Concepts of International Politics,* 2d ed. (Englewood Cliffs, N.J.: Prentice-Hall, 1970), pp. 109–10.

19. Hans Kelsen, "The Essence of International Law," in *The Relevance of International Law,* ed. Karl Deutsch and Stanley Hoffman (Garden City, N.Y.: Doubleday, 1971), p. 118.

20. George F. Kennan, *The Cloud of Danger: Current Realities of American Foreign Policy* (Boston: Little, Brown, 1977), p. 29.

21. Klaus Knorr, *On the Uses of Military Power in the Nuclear Age* (Princeton, N.J.: Princeton University Press, 1966), p. 33.

22. Helga Haftendorn, "The Proliferation of Conventional Arms," Adelphi Papers, no. 133 (London: Institute for International and Strategic Studies, Spring 1977), p. 34.

23. Daniel Bell, "The Future World Disorder," *Foreign Policy* 27 (Summer 1977): 132–33.

24. Arthur S. Banks, ed., *Political Handbook of the World: 1977* (New York: McGraw-Hill, 1977), p. 497.

25. Joseph S. Nye, "What New World Order?" *Foreign Affairs* 70 (Spring 1992): 91.

26. Lord Ritchie Calder, "The Doctor's Dilemma," *Center Magazine* 4, no. 5 (1971): 72.

27. Daniel J. Boorstin, *The Americans: The Democratic Experience* (New York: Random House, 1973), p. 598.

28. Lerche and Said, *Concepts of International Politics,* p. 137.

29. Samuel P. Huntington, "Transnational Organizations in World Politics," *World Politics* 25, no. 3 (1973): 338–39.

30. Compare here "The Fortune 500," *Fortune Magazine,* April 28, 1986, p. 182, and statistics on national GNP in *World Development Report, 1985* (New York: Oxford University Press for the World Bank, July 1985), pp. 178–79.

Chapter 2: Military Power and the Role of Force in the Post–Cold War Era

1. K. J. Holsti, *International Politics: A Framework for Analysis,* 2d ed. (Englewood Cliffs, N.J.: Prentice-Hall, 1972), p. 77.

2. Henry Bienen, *The Military and Modernization* (New York: Aldine Atherton, 1971), pp. 11–14.

3. See Bernard Brodie, *Strategy in the Missile Age* (Princeton, N.J.: Princeton University Press, 1959), pp. 319–21.

4. Holsti, *International Politics,* p. 305.

5. See Thomas C. Schelling, *Arms and Influence* (New Haven, Conn.: Yale University Press, 1966), pp. 69–86.

6. See J. I. Coffey, *Strategic Power and National Security* (Pittsburgh: University of Pittsburgh Press, 1971), pp. 72–73.

7. See David C. Gompert et al., *Nuclear Weapons and World Politics: Alternatives for the Future* (New York: McGraw-Hill, 1977), pp. 83–88.

8. Klaus Knorr, *On the Uses of Military Power in the Nuclear Age* (Princeton, N.J.: Princeton University Press, 1966), pp. 67–68.

9. See Stanley Hoffman, *Gulliver's Troubles, or the Setting of American Foreign Policy* (New York: McGraw-Hill, 1968), pp. 418–21, and Hanson W. Baldwin, *Strategy for Tomorrow* (New York: Harper & Row, 1970), pp. 237–46. However, rearmament was again an issue of political debate in Japan in 1978.

10. See Hans J. Morgenthau, *Politics among Nations: The Struggle for Power and Peace,* 5th ed. (New York: Knopf, 1973), pp. 532–40.

11. See Chapter 14.

12. Knorr, *Military Power in the Nuclear Age,* p. 49.

13. Morgenthau, *Politics among Nations,* p. 181.

14. Norman J. Padelford and George A. Lincoln, *The Dynamics of International Politics,* 2d ed. (New York: Macmillan, 1967), p. 5.

15. This discussion of alliance motives is adapted from Raymond F. Hopkins and Richard W. Mansbach, *Structure and Process in International Politics* (New York: Harper & Row, 1973), pp. 306–8.

16. See *The Atlantic Partnership: An Industrial Perspective in Transatlantic Defense Cooperation* (Washington, D.C.: The Center for Strategic and International Studies, May 1991), pp. ix–x.

17. Robert F. Randle, *The Origins of Peace* (New York: Free Press, 1973), p. 117.

18. Robert Endicott Osgood, *Alliances and American Foreign Policy* (Baltimore: Johns Hopkins University Press, 1968), pp. 21–22.

19. *Webster's Third New International Dictionary of the English Language,* 2d ed., unabridged, p. 711.

20. Jerome D. Frank, *Sanity and Survival: Psychological Aspects of War and Peace* (New York: Random House, 1967), p. 139.

21. See Morton H. Halperin, *Defense Strategies for the Seventies* (Boston: Little, Brown, 1971), pp. 104–7.

22. See André Beaufre, *Introduction to Strategy* (New York: Praeger, 1965), pp. 85–86.

23. For detailed presentation and analysis of "firebreaks," see Herman Kahn, *On Escalation: Metaphores and Scenarios* (New York: Praeger, 1965), and Klaus Knorr and Thornton Read, eds., *Limited Strategic War* (New York: Praeger, 1962), especially Chapters 1, 2, 3, and 8.

24. Adapted from Edward L. Warner III, "Escalation and Limitation in Warfare," in *American Defense Policy,* eds. Richard G. Head and Ervin J. Rokke, 3d ed. (Baltimore: Johns Hopkins University Press, 1973), p. 185.

25. See Robert McNamara, "The Military Role of Nuclear Weapons," *Foreign Affairs,* no. 1 (1983): 59–80.

26. For the United States, even the world wars were "limited" in the sense that not all material resources were mobilized. See Henry A. Kissinger, "The Problems of Limited War," in *The Use of Force,* eds. Robert J. Art and Kenneth N. Waltz (Boston: Little, Brown, 1971), p. 102.

27. See Beaufre, *Introduction to Strategy,* p. 85.

28. Kissinger, *Limited War,* p. 104.

29. See Samuel P. Huntington, *The Common Defense* (New York: Columbia University Press, 1961), pp. 342–43.

30. For the quotation on Vietnam, see W. Scott Thompson and Donaldson D. Frizzel, eds., *The Lessons of Vietnam* (New York: Crane, Russak, 1977), p. 279. For a discussion of limited war, see Robert E. Osgood, "The Reappraisal of Limited War," in Head and Rokke, *American Defense Policy,* pp. 168–69.

31. From Luke 14: 31–32.

32. See Philip D. Zelikow, "Force without War," *Journal of Strategic Studies* 1 (March 1984): 35.

33. Ibid., p. 37.

34. Ibid., p. 46.

35. Casper W. Weinberger, "The Uses of Military Power," *Defense '85* (Arlington, Va.: American Forces Information Service, January 1985), pp. 2–11.

36. See *Survival* (May/June 1991).

37. See *The Gulf War: Military Lessons Learned* (Washington, D.C.: The Center for Strategic and International Studies, July 1991), pp. v, vi.

38. Hans J. Morgenthau, *Politics among Nations,* 5th ed. (New York: Knopf, 1973), p. 80.

39. See Barry M. Blechman and Stephen S. Kaplan, "The Use of Armed Forces as a Political Instrument" (Washington, D.C.: Defense Advanced Research Projects Agency, 1976), p. 18.

40. Leonard S. Spector, "Nuclear Proliferation in the 1990's: The Storm After the Lull." Appendix in *New Threats; Responding to the Proliferation of Nuclear, Chemical, and Delivery Capabilities in the Third World.* Aspen, Colo.: An Aspen Strategy Group Report, 1990.

Chapter 3: Traditional American Approaches to National Security

1. Gabriel A. Almond, *The American People and Foreign Policy,* 2d ed. (New York: Praeger, 1977), p. 54.

2. Alexis de Tocqueville, *Democracy in America* (New York: Knopf, 1945), 1:234–35.

3. Walter Lippmann, quoted in Melvin Small, "Public Opinion," in *Encyclopedia of American Foreign Policy,* ed. Alexander DeConde (New York: 1978), 3:844–45.

4. See Charles O. Lerche, Jr., *Foreign Policy of the American People,* 3d ed. (Englewood Cliffs, N.J.: Prentice-Hall, 1967), pp. 120–22; Daniel Yankelovich, "Farewell to 'President Knows Best,' " in *America and the World,* ed. Council on Foreign Relations (New York: Pergamon Press, 1978), pp. 670–93; Bruce Russett, *Controlling the Sword: The Democratic Governance of National Security* (Cambridge, Mass.: Harvard University Press, 1990), pp. 87–118.

5. See, for instance, Gene E. Rainey, *Patterns of American Foreign Policy* (Boston: Allyn & Bacon, 1975), pp. 81–82.

6. Charles O. Lerche, Jr., and Abdul A. Said, *Concepts of International Politics,* 3d ed. (Englewood Cliffs, N.J.: Prentice-Hall, 1979), pp. 23–24.

7. See Ralph B. Levering, *The Public and American Foreign Policy, 1918–1978* (New York: Morrow, 1978), p. 94.

8. Lyndon Johnson, reported in "An Interview with Eric Sevareid," *TV Guide,* March 14, 1970, pp. 6–7.

9. Arthur M. Schlesinger, Jr., *The Crisis of Confidence* (Boston: Houghton Mifflin, 1969), p. 135.

10. Ralph B. Levering, *The Public and American Foreign Policy*, pp. 134–37.

11. Ibid.

12. For details on one example of erosion—foreign aid—see the *Congressional Quarterly Weekly Report* 24 (May 15, 1976): 1163–54.

13. Lewis Burwell, quoted in R. W. Van Alstyne, *The Rising American Empire* (New York: Oxford University Press, 1960), p. 15.

14. Louis L. Snyder, ed., *The Imperialism Reader* (Princeton, N.J.: Van Nostrand, 1962), p. 20.

15. Thomas Jefferson, quoted in R. W. Van Alystne, *Rising American Empire*, p. 87.

16. See Frederick H. Hartmann, *The New Age of American Foreign Policy* (New York: Macmillan, 1970), p. 30.

17. Selig Adler, *The Uncertain Giant: American Foreign Policy between the Wars* (New York: Macmillan, 1965), pp. 87–92.

18. See Carl Becker, *The Declaration of Independence: A Study in the History of Political Ideas* (New York: Knopf, 1942), pp. 76–78.

19. Thomas Hobbs, *Leviathan* (New York: Collier Books, 1962), p. 100.

20. Ibid., p. 101.

21. See Robert E. Osgood, *Limited War: The Challenge to American Strategy* (Chicago: University of Chicago Press, 1957), p. 38.

22. See Hans J. Morganthau, *Politics among Nations*, 5th ed. (New York: Knopf, 1973), pp. 33–34.

23. Frederick H. Hartmann, *The Relations of Nations*, 4th ed. (New York: Macmillan, 1973), pp. 101–2; and Kenneth W. Thompson, *American Dipomacy and Emergent Patterns* (New York: New York University Press, 1962), pp. 45–46.

24. See Hartmann, *The Relations of Nations*, p. 102.

25. See Harry R. Davis and Robert C. Good, *Reinhold Niebuhr on Politics* (New York: Scribner, 1960), pp. 308–13.

26. See Frederick Merk, *Manifest Destiny and Mission in American History* (New York: Knopf, 1963), p. 261.

27. Albert Gallatin, quoted in ibid., pp. 262–63.

28. See Lerche, *Foreign Policy*, pp. 110–11.

29. See Davis and Good, *Reinhold Niebuhr*, p. 140.

30. Karl von Clausewitz, *On War* (Princeton, N.J.: Princeton University Press, 1976), p. 87.

31. Lerche, *Foreign Policy*, p. 117.

32. See Osgood, *Limited War*, p. 31.

33. Robert W. Tucker, *The Just War: A Study in Contemporary American Doctrine*, 2d ed. (Baltimore: Johns Hopkins University Press, 1979), p. 11.

34. See also Michael Walzer, *Just and Unjust Wars* (New York: Basic Books, 1977), pp. 76–78.

35. Harry S. Truman, quoted in ibid., p. 15.

36. Daniel J. Boorstin, *The Americans: The Colonial Experience* (New York: Random House, 1958), p. 356.

37. George Washington, quoted in ibid., p. 368.

38. James Gerhardt, *The Draft and Public Policy* (Columbus: Ohio State University Press, 1971), pp.83–122.

39. Resolution, Continental Congress, quoted in Samual P. Huntington, *The Soldier and the State* (Cambridge, Mass.: Harvard University Press, Belknap Press, 1957), p. 144.

40. George F. Kennan, *American Diplomacy, 1900–1950* (Chicago: University of Chicago Press, 1951), pp. 65–66.

41. President McKinley, quoted in Samuel Flagg Bemis, *A Diplomatic History of the United States* (New York: Holt, 1955), p. 472.

42. Stanley Hoffmann, *Gulliver's Troubles, or the Setting of American Foreign Policy* (New York: McGraw-Hill, 1968), pp. 236–37.

43. See Almond, *American People and Foreign Policy*, pp. 30–31, 48–50.

44. See ibid., p. 51.

45. The phrase, as well as the analysis that folows, is Rob Paarlberg's. See his "Forgetting about the Unthinkable," *Foreign Policy*, no. 10 (1973): 132–40.

46. Office of Civil Defense, Office of the Secretary of the Army, *Civil Defense and the Public: An Overview of Public Attitude Studies*, Research Report no. 17 (October 1971), pp. 31–32.

47. Ibid.

48. See Thomas W. Graham, *American Public Opinion on NATO, Extended Deterrence, and the Use of Nuclear Weapons* (Lanham, Md.: University Press of America, 1989).

49. For a discussion of American public opinion and the Reagan administration, see Daniel Yankelovich and Sidney Harman, *Starting with the People* (Boston: Houghton Mifflin, 1988), pp. 31–38, 90–101. See also Graham, *American Public Opinion on NATO, Extended Deterrence, and the Use of Nuclear Weapons*.

50. See *Americans Talk Security Issues: Serial National Surveys of Americans on Public Policy Issues*, Survey #17 (Field Dates: Nov. 25–Dec. 2, 1991), pp. 27–28.

Chapter 4: The Evolution of American National Security Policy

1. Walter Lippmann, *U.S. Foreign Policy: Shield of the Republic* (Boston: Little, Brown, 1943), p. 51.

2. Henry Kissinger, *American Foreign Policy* (New York: Norton, 1974), p. 13.

3. *Report of the President's Commission on Strategic Forces* (Washington, D.C.: U.S. Government Printing Office, April 1983), passim.

4. Samuel P. Huntington, *The Common Defense* (New York: Columbia University Press, 1961), pp. 3–4.

5. Henry T. Nash, *American Foreign Policy: Response to a Sense of Threat* (Homewood, Ill.: Dorsey Press, 1973), p. 19.

6. Huntington, *Common Defense*, p. 35.

7. Nash, *American Foreign Policy*, p. 19.

8. George Kennan, "The Sources of Soviet Conduct," *Foreign Affairs* 25, no. 4 (1947): 575–76.

9. Walter Millis, ed., *The Forrestal Diaries* (New York: Viking Press, 1951), p. 350.

10. Huntington, *Common Defense*, p. 41.

11. Ibid, p. 42.

12. Ibid, p. 43.

13. Chief of Staff, *Final Report*, United States Army, February 7, 1948, pp. 11–12.

14. G. A. Lincoln, *Military Establishment Appropriations*, 1948, pp. 11–12.

15. Huntington, *Common Defense*, p. 45.

16. Ibid., p. 47.

17. President Harry S. Truman, Address delivered to a joint session of Congress, March 12, 1947, reprinted in Joseph M. Jones, *The Fifteen Weeks* (New York: Harcourt, Brace & World, 1955), p. 272.

18. Nash, *American Foreign Policy,* p. 25.

19. Ibid., p. 29.

20. Warner Schilling, Paul Hammond, and Glenn Snyder, *Strategy, Politics, and the Defense Budget* (New York: Columbia University Press, 1962), p. 292.

21. Paul H. Nitze, "The Need for a National Strategy," Address delivered at Army War College, Carlisle Barracks, Pa., August 27, 1958.

22. Huntington, *Common Defense,* p. 54.

23. For a discussion of U.S. perceptions of Communist intentions, see Morton Halperin, *Limited War in the Nuclear Age* (New York: Wiley, 1963), chap. 3.

24. Huntington, *Common Defense,* p. 54.

25. Ibid., p. 56.

26. Ibid., pp. 73–74.

27. Jerome Kahan, *Security in the Nuclear Age* (Washington, D.C.: Brookings Institution, 1975), p. 28.

28. *New York Times,* January 13, 1954, p. 2.

29. John Foster Dulles, "The Evolution of Foreign Policy," *Department of State Bulletin* 30 (January 25, 1954): 108.

30. Huntington, *Common Defense,* p. 88.

31. Ibid., p. 92.

32. Ibid., pp. 96–97.

33. Morton Halperin, *Defense Strategies for the Seventies* (Boston: Little, Brown, 1971), p. 46.

34. Huntington, *Common Defense,* p. 105.

35. John Foster Dulles, "Challenge and Response in U.S. Foreign Policy," *Foreign Affairs* 36, no. 1 (October 1951): 31.

36. Maxwell D. Taylor, *The Uncertain Trumpet* (New York: Harper 1959), pp. 82–83.

37. William W. Kaufmann, *The McNamara Strategy* (New York: Harper & Row, 1964), p. 29.

38. Alain C. Enthoven and K. Wayne Smith, *How Much Is Enough?* (New York: Harper & Row, 1971), p. 21.

39. U.S. Congress, House, Committee on Armed Services, *Hearings on Military Posture,* 85th Cong., 2d sess., 1962, p. 3162.

40. Kaufmann, *McNamara Strategy,* pp. 53–54.

41. Ibid., p. 71.

42. Edward R. Fried, Alice M. Rivlin, Charles L. Schultze, and Nancy H. Teeters, *Setting National Priorities: The 1974 Budget* (Washington, D.C.: Brookings Institution, 1973), p. 292.

43. *U.S. Department of Defense Annual Report, Fiscal Year 1975* (Washington, D.C.: U.S. Government Printing Office), p. 22.

44. Halperin, *Defense Strategies for the Seventies,* p. 52.

45. Alton H. Quanback and Barry M. Blechman, *Strategic Forces: Issues for the Mid-Seventies* (Washington, D.C.: Brookings Institution, 1973), pp. 6–7.

46. Ibid., p. 9.

47. Halperin, *Defense Strategies for the Seventies,* p. 126.

48. Ibid.

49. Ibid., p. 127.

50. Bernard Brodie, "Technology, Politics, and Strategy," *Adelphi Papers*, no. 55 (London: International Institute for Strategic Studies, March 1969), p. 22.

51. See John Lewis Gaddis, *How Relevant was U.S. Strategy in Winning the Cold War?* (Carlisle Barracks, Pa.: The Strategic Studies Institute, 1992), p. 14.

52. See Don M. Snider, *The National Security Strategy: Documenting Strategic Vision* (Carlisle Barracks, Pa.: The Strategic Studies Institute, 1992), pp. 8–9.

53. See "Statement of the Secretary of Defense Dick Cheney Before the Senate Budget Committee, 3 February 1992," p. 1.

54. See *National Military Strategy of the United States* (Washington, D.C.: U.S. Government Printing Office, January 1992), pp. 6–10.

Chapter 5: Presidential Leadership and the Executive Branch in National Security

1. Alexander Hamilton, *The Federalist No. 74*, Great Books of the Western World, ed. Robert M. Hutchins, vol. 43 (Chicago: Encyclopedia Britannica, 1952), p. 21.

2. Arthur M. Schlesinger, Jr., *The Imperial Presidency* (Boston: Houghton Mifflin, 1973), p. 3.

3. Edwin S. Corwin, *The President: Office and Powers, 1787–1957* (New York: New York University Press, 1957), p. 171.

4. Schlesinger, *Imperial Presidency*, p. 291.

5. Robert A. Diamond and Patricia Ann O'Conner, eds., *Guide to Congress* (Washington, D.C.: Congressional Quarterly, 1976), p. 279.

6. Richard Lacayo, "A Reluctant Go Ahead," *Time*, January 21, 1991, p. 32.

7. Clinton Rossiter, *The American Presidency* (New York: New American Library, 1960), pp. 14–40.

8. Keith C. Clark and Laurence J. Legere, eds., *The President and the Management of National Security* (New York: Praeger, 1969), p. 19.

9. George Reedy, quoted in Doris Kearns, *Lyndon Johnson and the American Dream* (New York: New American Library, 1977), p. 339.

10. Richard E. Neustadt, "Approaches to Staffing the Presidency," in *The Presidential Advisory System*, ed. Thomas E. Cronin and Sanford D. Greenberg (New York: Harper & Row, 1969), p. 15.

11. Ibid., p. 19.

12. Discussion of the Hoover staffing arrangements is from Henry T. Nash, *American Foreign Policy: Response to a Sense of Threat* (Homewood, Ill.: Dorsey Press, 1973), p. 113. Comments on the proliferation of presidential assistants are derived from Harold Seidman, *Politics, Position, and Power: The Dynamics of Federal Organization* (New York: Oxford University Press, 1970), p. 213.

13. Seidman, *Politics, Position, and Power*, p. 165.

14. Ibid., p. 91.

15. For a discussion of presidential *modus operandi*, see Andrew J. Goodpaster, "Four Presidents and the Conduct of National Security Affairs: Impressions and Highlights," *Journal of International Relations* 2 (1977): 27–29.

16. Dwight D. Eisenhower, "The Central Role of the President in the Conduct of Security Affairs," in *Issues of National Security in the 1970s*, ed. Amos Jordan (New York: Praeger, 1967), p. 214.

17. John F. Kennedy, quoted in Clark and Legere, *President and Management of National Security,* p. 70.

18. For detailed views of the Johnson presidency, see Kearns, *Lyndon Johnson.*

19. Ibid., p. 294.

20. Henry A. Kissinger, *The White House Years* (Boston: Little, Brown, 1979), p. 30.

21. *Report of the President's Special Review Board* (Washington, D.C.: U.S. Government Printing Office, 1987), p. II-5.

22. Bob Woodward, *The Commanders* (New York: Simon & Schuster, 1991), p. 41.

23. For a detailed discussion of the functions and organizational culture of the Department of State, see Nash, *American Foreign Policy,* pp. 65–99.

24. Kissinger, *White House Years,* pp. 26–31.

25. Woodward, *The Commanders,* and *U.S. News and World Report, Triumph Without Victory* (New York: Warner Books, 1992) provide the best descriptions of Bush's decision-making style.

26. Nash, *American Foreign Policy,* pp. 71–72. See also Roger Hilsman, *The Politics of Policy Making in Defense and Foreign Affairs* (New York: Harper & Row, 1971), pp. 47–48.

27. J. M. Destler, *Presidents, Bureaucrats, and Foreign Policy* (Princeton, N.J.: Princeton University Press, 1972), pp. 156–60.

28. Nash, *American Foreign Policy,* p. 91.

29. Ibid., p. 74.

30. Alain C. Enthoven and K. Wayne Smith, *How Much Is Enough?* (New York: Harper & Row, 1971), p. 3.

31. For example, see *Defense Organization. The Need for Change.* Staff Report to the Committee on Armed Services, United States Senate, 99th Congress, 1st Session, 1985, Senate Report 99–86, pp. 422–23.

32. The flavor of this criticism is captured in Ronald Reagan's remarks contained in "Yes or No on the Panama Treaties," *National Review,* February 17, 1978, pp. 210–17.

33. Matthew B. Ridgway, "My Battles in War and Peace," *Saturday Evening Post,* January 21, 1956, p. 46.

34. Samuel P. Huntington, *The Common Defense* (New York: Columbia University Press, 1961), p. 146.

35. Henry Stimson, quoted in Miles Copeland, *Without Cloak or Dagger* (New York: Simon & Schuster, 1974), p. 36.

36. Nash, *American Foreign Policy,* pp. 146–49. See also Marjorie Hunter, "Carter Won't Oppose CIA Cost Disclosure," *New York Times,* April 28, 1977, p. 17.

37. Theodore C. Sorensen, *Decision Making in the White House* (New York: Columbia University Press, 1963), pp. 29–30.

38. For a detailed discussion of the origins of legislative central clearance, see Richard E. Neustadt, "Presidency and Legislation: The Growth of Central Clearance," *American Political Science Review* 48, no. 1 (1954): 641–71.

39. Richard E. Neustadt, *Presidential Power* (New York: New American Library, 1960), p. 42.

40. Ibid., pp. 53, 47.

41. Kearns, *Lyndon Johnson,* pp. 258–59.

42. *Triumph Without Victory,* p. 188, 206, 207.

43. Sorensen, *Kennedy,* pp. 296–97.

44. Jimmy Carter, "Middle East Peace: New Opportunities," *Washington Quarterly* (Summer 1987).

45. Graham Allison, *Essence of Decision: Explaining the Cuban Missile Crisis* (Boston: Little, Brown, 1971), pp. 141–42.

46. Patrick Tyler, "Pentagon Imagines New Enemies to Fight in Post-Cold War Era," *New York Times,* February 17, 1992, p. 1.

Chapter 6: The Impact of Congress on National Security Policy

1. Richard Haass, "Congressional Power: Implications for American Security Policy," *Adelphi Papers,* no. 153 (London: International Institute for Strategic Studies, Summer 1979), p. 2.

2. David Abshire, *Foreign Policy Matters: Presidents vs. Congress,* Sage Policy Papers, no. 66 (Washington, D.C.: Center for Strategic and International Studies, 1979), p. 10.

3. Charles B. Brownson, ed., *Congressional Staff Directory* (Mount Vernon, Va.: Congressional Staff Directory, 1980).

4. Haass, "Congressional Power," p. 3.

5. Abshire, *Foreign Policy Matters,* p. 11.

6. Theodore Roosevelt, *An Autobiography: Theodore Roosevelt* (New York: Scribner, 1923), p. 552–53.

7. Haass, "Congressional Power," p. 32.

8. President's Blue Ribbon Commission Defense Management, *An Interim Report to the President* (Washington, D.C.: U.S. Government Printing Office, February 28, 1986), p. 5.

9. Ibid., p. 5–6.

10. Tim Weiner, *Blank Check: The Pentagon's Black Budget* (New York: Warner Books, 1990), p. 5.

11. Ernest W. Lefever, *TV and National Defense* (Boston: Institute for American Strategy Press, 1974).

12. Abshire, *Foreign Policy Matters,* p. 47.

13. Lee D. Hamilton and Michael H. Van Dusen, "Making the Separation of Powers Work," *Foreign Affairs* 57, no. 1 (1978): 22.

14. Haass, "Congressional Power," p. 6.

15. Ibid., p. 14.

16. Abshire, *Foreign Policy Matters,* p. 53.

17. "Crises on Cyprus: 1975," *U.S. Congress, Senate, Staff Report to the Committee on the Judiciary,* 94th Cong., 1st sess. (Washington, D.C.: U.S. Government Printing Office, July 20, 1975), p. 57.

18. Public Law 93–448, p. 2.

19. *Immigration and Naturalization Service v. Chadha,* 426 U.S. 919, 972, 973 (1983).

20. *Congressional Record,* speech by Senator Joseph Biden, September 18, 1986, p. 5.

21. Ibid.

22. Ernest Graves and Steven A. Hildreth, eds., *U.S. Security Assistance: The Political Process* (Lexington, Mass.: Lexington Books, 1985), p. 176.

23. Public Law 93–148, pp. 1–4.

24. Haass, "Congressional Power," p. 21.

25. "Helping to Hold the Line," *Time,* October 3, 1983, p. 31.

26. Francis D. Wormuth and Edwin B. Firmage, *To Chain the Dog of War: The War Power of Congress in History and Law* (Dallas: Southern Methodist University Press, 1986), p. 265.

27. U.S. News and World Report, *Triumph Without Victory* (New York: Warner Books, 1992), pp. 173–214.

28. Haass, "Congressional Power," p. 8.

29. Dennis Farney, "A Bureaucracy Grows in Congress as Panels and Staffs Mushroom," *Wall Street Journal,* December 18, 1979, p. 1.

30. Abshire, *Foreign Policy Matters,* p. 63.

31. Quoted in *Dallas Morning News,* May 22, 1985, p. 1A.

32. Abshire, *Foreign Policy Matters,* p. 68.

Chapter 7: Intelligence and National Security

1. Tyrus G. Fain, ed., *The Intelligence Community,* Public Document Series (New York: Bowker, 1977), p. 973. This volume encompasses the body of official reports, hearings, and studies released by the government from 1970 to 1976 concerning the U.S. foreign intelligence establishment.

2. Bob Woodward, *The Commanders* (New York: Simon & Schuster, 1991), pp. 205–17.

3. Ibid., p. 248.

4. See Alexander Hamilton, *The Federalist No. 75, Great Books of the Western World,* ed. Robert M. Hutchins, vol. 43 (Chicago: Encyclopedia Britannica, 1952).

5. See John Jay, *The Federalist No. 64, Great Books of the Western World,* ed. Robert M. Hutchins, vol. 43 (Chicago: Encyclopedia Britannica, 1952).

6. See the remarks of Gerald R. Ford, "Statement by the President," in *Report to the President by the Commission on CIA Activities within the United States* (Washington, D.C.: U.S. Government Printing Office, 1975), p. 273. President Carter's concern for preservation of the information-reporting capability is reflected in remarks quoted in James T. Wooten, "Carter Says Foreign Sources Are Questioning Their Safety in Providing Secrets after CIA Reports," *New York Times,* February 25, 1977, p. A-9. President Reagan's views appear in the *Weekly Compilation of Presidential Documents* 17, no. 49 (December 7, 1981): I335–36. See also the remarks of Senator Frank Church, former chairman of the Senate Foreign Relations Committee, in U.S. Congress, Senate, Select Committee to Study Governmental Operations with Respect to Intelligence Activities, *Final Report,* 94th Cong., 2d sess., 1976, S. Rept. 94–755, bk. 1, *Foreign and Military Intelligence,* p. 563. (Hereafter cited as the Church Committee's *Final Report.*)

7. Robin Wright, "Efforts to Halt Arms Race Called Limited," *Los Angeles Times,* June 21, 1992, p. 2.

8. The applicable directives are described in U.S. Congress, Senate, Select Committee to Study Governmental Operations with Respect to Intelligence Activities, *Alleged Assassination Plots Involving Foreign Leaders,* 94th Cong., 1st sess., 1975, S. Rept. 94–465. (Hereafter cited as the Church Committee's *Interim Report.*)

9. George Lardner, "Restrictions Approved on Covert Action," *Washington Post,* August 16, 1991, p. 22.

10. R. Jeffrey Smith, "U.S. Tolerated Arms Sales to Iraq After Iran War," *Washington Post,* June 11, 1992, p. 19.

11. Roy Godson, ed., *Intelligence Requirements for the 1980s: Elements of Intelligence* (Washington, D.C.: National Strategy Information Center, 1983), p. 50.

12. A similar intelligence production model, and real-world deviations from it, are also described in the Church Committee's *Final Report,* p. 18.

13. Fain, *Intelligence Community,* p. 319.

14. Ibid., p. 347.

15. Robert Gates, "Statements on Change in CIA" (Washington, D.C.: Office of the DCI, April 1, 1992).

16. Prominent examples are Victor Marchetti and John D. Marks, *The CIA and the Cult of Intelligence* (New York: Knopf, 1974); Philip Agee, *Inside the Company: CIA Diary* (New York: Stonehill, 1975); and L. Fletcher Prouty, *The Secret Team* (Englewood Cliffs, N.J.: Prentice-Hall, 1973).

17. An excellent example is Nelson Blackstock, *COINTELPRO: The FBI's Secret War on Political Freedom* (New York: Random House, 1975).

18. Ray S. Cline, for instance, has provided insightful and knowledgeable commentary in "Policy without Intelligence," *Foreign Policy,* no. 17 (1974/75): 121–35, and in *Secrets, Spies, and Scholars: Blueprint of the Essential CIA* (Washington, D.C.: Acropolis, 1976)

19. Fain, *Intelligence Community,* p. 409.

20. Marchetti and Marks, *CIA and the Cult of Intelligence,* pp. 229-37.

21. "Brutal Intelligence," *New Republic,* December 6, 1975, p. 5.

22. Agee, *Inside the Company,* pp. 561–92.

23. See, for example, Harry Rositzke, "America's Secret Operations: A Perspective," *Foreign Affairs* 53, no. 2 (1975): 334; William J. Barnds, "Intelligence and Foreign Policy: Dilemmas of Democracy," *Foreign Affairs* 47, no. 2 (1969): 285; Nicholas DeB. Katzenbach, "Foreign Policy, Public Opinion, and Secrecy," *Foreign Affairs* 52, no. 1 (1973): 15.

24. See, for example, Morton Halperin, "CIA, Denying What's Not in Writing," *New Republic,* October 4, 1975, pp. 11–12.

25. Mark M. Lowenthal, *U.S. Intelligence* (New York: Praeger, 1984).

26. Church Committee's *Final Report,* pp. 423–74.

27. U.S. Congress, Senate, Select Committee on Intelligence, 95th Cong., 1st sess., 1977, S. Rept. 95–217.

28. Ibid., p. 1.

29. Text of the proposed charter was printed in full in the *Congressional Record,* February 10, 1978, p. E-533.

30. S. Rept. 95–217, pp. 6–7.

31. Godson, *Intelligence Requirements,* p. 95.

32. Elaine Sciolino, "Conferees Agree to Curb President on Covert Action," *New York Times,* July 27, 1991, p. 1.

33. The citation for the act is Foreign Intelligence Surveillance Act of 1978 (50 U.S.C.). Carter's remarks are printed in the *Weekly Compilation of the Presidential Documents* 14, no. 43 (October 30, 1978): 1853–54. For a rare discussion of how the act has been implemented, see Leslie Maitland, "A Closed Court's One-Issue Caseload," *New York Times,* October 14, 1982.

34. White House press release, January 24, 1978, "Remarks of the President upon Signing of the Intelligence Executive Order," referring to Executive Order 12036, "United States Intelligence Activities," January 24, 1978.

35. 277 U.S. 438 (1928).

36. *Katz v. United States,* 389 U.S. 347 (1967), and *Berger v. New York,* 388 U.S. 41 (1967). See also Justice Stewart's opinion in *Giordano v. United States,* 395 U.S. 314 (1967).

37. See *United States v. United States District Court,* 407 U.S. 297 (1972), and *United States v. Butenko,* 494 F.2d 3 (3d Cir., en banc, 1974), cert. den. 419 U.S. 881 (1974).

38. *Berlin Democratic Club v. Brown,* 410 F. Supp. 144 (1976). Description of this case can also be found in bk. 3 of the Church Committee's *Final Report,* pp. 818–21.

39. U.S. President, Executive Order 11905, "United States Foreign Intelligence Activities," *Federal Register* 41, no. 34 (February 19, 1976): 7701.

40. David Boren, "The Intelligence Community: How Crucial." *Foreign Affairs,* Summer 1992, p. 54.

41. Fain, *Intelligence Community,* p. 87.

42. Ibid., p. 92.

43. R. Jeffrey Smith and John Goshko, "Ill-Fated Iraq Policy Originated Shortly After Bush Took Office," *Washington Post,* June 27, 1992, p. 7.

44. Molly Moore, "Schwarzkopf: War Intelligence Flawed," *Washington Post,* June 13, 1991, p. 1.

45. This excerpt from the report of the commission is reprinted in Fain, *Intelligence Community,* p. 96.

46. Ibid., p. 46.

47. Church Committee's *Final Report,* Book I, pp. 268–69

48. Elaine Sciolino, "CIA Chief Rejects Push for Change," *New York Times,* April 2, 1992, p. D22.

Chapter 8: The Role of the Military in the National Security Policy Process

1. Forrest Pogue, *Command Decisions,* p. 381, cited in Urs Schwarz, *American Strategy: A New Perspective* (New York: Doubleday, 1966), p. 48.

2. Walter Millis, *Arms and the State* (New York: Twentieth Century Fund, 1958), pp. 124–32.

3. John C. Ries, *The Management of Defense* (Baltimore: Johns Hopkins University Press, 1964), pp. 26–30.

4. Gerhard Loewenberg, "The Remaking of the Germany Party System," in *European Politics: A Reader,* ed. Mattei Dugan and Richard Rose (Boston: Little, Brown, 1971), pp. 259–80.

5. See Cordell Hull, *The Memoirs of Cordell Hull,* vol. 2 (New York: Macmillan, 1948), pp. 1625–1713.

6. Public Law 243, 80th Cong., 1st sess., approved July 26, 1947, 61 *Stat.* 495. This section draws largely on Lawrence J. Korb, *The Joint Chiefs of Staff: The First Twenty-five Years* (Bloomington: Indiana University Press, 1976), pp. 15–21.

7. Public Law 253, 61 Stat. 44.

8. Millis, *Arms and the State,* p. 214.

9. Samuel P. Huntington, *The Common Defense* (New York: Columbia University Press, 1961), p. 35.

10. See Burton M. Sapin and Richard C. Snyder, *The Role of the Military in American Foreign Policy* (New York: Doubleday, 1954).

11. Lawrence M. Martin, "The American Decision to Rearm Germany," in *American Civil Military Decisions,* ed. Harold Stein (Birmingham: University of Alabama Press, 1963), pp. 652–60.

12. Huntington, *Common Defense*, p. 54.

13. A good discussion of the many issues involved in the MacArthur case can be found in Millis, *Arms and the State*, pp. 259–332.

14. Message JCS95977, JCS to UNCFE, July 10, 1951.

15. See Huntington, *Common Defense*, pp. 282–83, and *U.S. Department of Defense Annual Report, Fiscal Year 1979* (Washington, D.C.: U.S. Government Printing Office 1978), p. 366. (Hereafter cited as *DOD Report, FY 79*.)

16. Huntington, *Common Defense*, p. 380.

17. For a good discussion of the many postwar problems of interservice rivalry, see Ries, *Management of Defense*, pp. 129–92. For a discussion of why defense issues frequently are resolved by political bargaining, see Huntington, *Common Defense*, pp. 123–96.

18. An illuminating discussion of the intricacies of the joint staffing process may be found in Lawrence B. Tatum, "The Joint Chiefs of Staff and Defense Policy Formulation," *Air University Review*, May–June 1966, pp. 40–45; July–August 1966, pp. 11–20; reprinted in Mark D. Smith III and Claude J. Johns, eds., *American Defense Policy* (Baltimore: Johns Hopkins University Press, 1968), pp. 377–92.

19. Quoted in Millis, *Arms and the State*, p. 348.

20. Adam Yarmolinsky, *The Military Establishment* (New York: Perennial Library, 1973), pp. 175–76.

21. Ibid., pp. 138–40.

22. See, for example, Maxwell Taylor, *Swords and Plowshares* (New York: Norton, 1972), p. 249; or Yarmolinsky, *Military Establishment*, pp. 37–40.

23. Lannon Walker, "Our Foreign Affairs Machinery: Time for an Overhaul," *Foreign Affairs* 27, no. 2 (1969): 311–15.

24. See, for example, David Halberstam, *The Best and the Brightest* (New York: Random House, 1972).

25. For the best analysis of the army's management of its civil disturbance control mission during the period 1962–1973, see James R. Gardner, "The Regular Army and Domestic Disorder, 1963–1973: An Analysis of Role Perceptions, Restraint, and Policy," Ph.D. diss., Princeton University, 1977.

26. U.S. Congress, Senate, Subcommittee on Constitutional Rights, Committee on the Judiciary, *Hearings*, 88th Cong., 1st sess., February 23, 1971.

27. See, for example, Bruce Russett, *What Price Vigilance?* (New Haven, Conn.: Yale University Press, 1970), pp. 56–90.

28. See Yarmolinsky, *Military Establishment*, Chapter 4.

29. U.S. Congress, Senate, Department of Defense Appropriations, *Hearings*, 1974, pt. I, p. 17.

30. Korb, *Joint Chiefs of Staff*, pp. 103–11.

31. Ibid., pp. 111–21; Arnold Kanter, *Defense Politics: A Budgetary Perspective* (Chicago: University of Chicago Press, 1975), pp. 55ff.

32. Korb, *Joint Chiefs of Staff*, p. 121.

33. Ibid., pp. 121–38; Lawrence J. Korb, "The Budget Process in the Department of Defense, 1947–1977," *Public Administration Review* 37, no. 4 (1977): 334–46. For a discussion of the difference in style between McNamara and Laird, see James M. Roherty, "The Office of the Secretary of Defense: The Laird and McNamara Styles," in *The New Civil-Military Relations*, ed. John P. Lovell and Phillip S. Kronenberg (New Brunswick, N.J.: Transaction Books, 1974), pp. 299–54.

34. Lawrence J. Korb, "The Civil-Military Balance at the Policymaking Level in the

Carter Administration: An Assessment,'' in *Final Report,* Senior Conference, United States Military Academy, June 14–16, 1979, pp. 147–56.

35. George C. Wilson, ''Joint Chiefs of Staff Break with Carter on Budget Planning for Defense Needs,'' *Washington Post,* May 30, 1980, p. A-1.

36. For the B-1 bomber, see ''Senate Panel Approves Aircraft Carrier Funds,'' *New York Times,* May 11, 1978, p. A-18; and Brooks Jackson, *New York Times Supplementary Material,* August 28, 1978, pp. 1–4; for the neutron bomb, see Richard Burt, ''Pressure from Congress Mounts to Reverse Ban on Neutron Bomb,'' *New York Times,* April 6, 1978, p. 1; for increases in defense spending, see Charles Mohr, ''Nunn Links His Support for Pact to Arms Budget Rise,'' *New York Times,* July 26, 1979, p. A-5.

37. For a description of Powell's role in the Bush administration, see Bob Woodward, *The Commanders* (New York: Simon & Schuster, 1991) and *U.S. News and World Report, Triumph Without Victory* (New York: Warner Books, 1992).

38. Data on active force and dependents are from *Selected Manpower Statistics,* Department of Defense, OASD (Comptroller), May 1977, and *U.S. Department of Defense Annual Report, Fiscal Year 1981*; data on defense contractors are from U.S. Department of Commerce, Bureau of the Census, *Statistical Abstract of the United States,* 1979.

39. For a balanced perspective on the ''military-industrial complex,'' see Benjamin Franklin Cooling, ''The Military-Industrial Complex: Update on an Old American Issue,'' in *The Military in America: From the Colonial Era to the Present,* ed. Peter Karsten (New York: Free Press, 1980), pp. 317–29.

40. Douglas MacArthur, Address delivered at West Point, May 12, 1962.

41. Matthew Ridgway's ''Farewell Letter'' to Secretary of Defense Charles E. Wilson, June 27, 1955.

42. Millis makes one of the most comprehensive analyses of these changes in the second part of his book with Harvey C. Mansfield and Harold Stein, *Arms and the State.* See also William Fox, ''Representativeness and Efficiency: Dual Problem of Civil-Military Relations,'' *Political Science Quarterly* 76 (September 1961): 354–66. For a short summary and critique of the fusionist theory, see Huntington, *Common Defense,* pp. 350–54.

43. John F. Kennedy, Commencement address, delivered at West Point, June 1962.

44. Robert Lovett, Address delivered at West Point, May 1964. For an elaboration of this point, see William J. Taylor, Jr., ''Military Professionals in Changing Times,'' *Public Administration Review* 37, no. 6 (November–December 1977): 633–41.

45. Maxwell D. Taylor, Address delivered at West Point, February 18, 1969.

46. See Amos A. Jordan and William J. Taylor, Jr., ''The Military Man in Academia,'' *Annals* 406 (March 1973): 129–45.

47. See Samuel P. Huntington, *The Soldier and the State* (Cambridge, Mass.: Harvard University Press, Belknap Press, 1957). In the literature on American civil-military politics, this book is a landmark. Written from a conservative perspective, Huntington's book is one of the most comprehensive analytical critiques of the fusionist doctrine. Its polar opposite is Morris Janowitz's *The Professional Soldier* (New York: Free Press, 1960), an important book that advanced the thesis that external sociological and political forces made fusionism inevitable in the American military. See also Arthur D. Larson, ''Military Professionalism and Civil Control: A Comparative Analysis of Two Interpretations,'' *Journal of Military and Political Sociology* 2, no. 1 (1974): 57–72, for an incisive critique of Huntington's and Janowitz's analyses.

48. Huntington, *Soldier and the State,* p. 163.

49. For evidence that the military's administrative functions are beginning to dominate the instrumental-operational priorities, see William J. Gregor, "The Leader as Subordinate: The Politics and Performance of Unit Commanders in the U.S. Army," Ph.D. diss., Yale University, 1980; and Richard A. Gabriel and Paul C. Savage, *Crisis in Command: Mismanagement in the Army* (New York: Hill & Wang, 1978).

50. For a discussion of the military's evolving ethics, see Sam C. Sarkesian, "Professional Problems and Adaptations," in *The Limits of Military Intervention,* ed. Ellen P. Stern (Beverly Hills, Calif.: Sage, 1977), pp. 301–23; William L. Hauser, *America's Army in Crisis* (Baltimore: Johns Hopkins University Press, 1973); and Charles C. Moskos, Jr., "The All-Volunteer Military: Calling, Profession, or Occupation?" *Parameters* 7, no. 1 (1977):2–10.

51. Edward N. Luttwak, "A Critical View of the U.S Military Establishment," *Forbes,* May 26, 1980, p. 38.

52. See for example the testimony of Admiral David Jermiah, the Vice Chairman of the JCS, before the House Armed Services Committee, March 12, 1991.

53. John G. Kester, "The Future of the Joint Chiefs of Staff," *AEI Foreign Policy and Defense Review* 2, no. 1 (1980): 11.

Chapter 9: Defense Planning, Budgeting, and Management

1. Charles L. Schultze et al., *Setting National Priorities: The 1972 Budget* (Washington, D.C.: Brookings Institution, 1971), pp. 12–13.

2. "National Security Amendments of 1949," *United States Statutes at Large,* 81st Cong., 1st sess., vol. 63, I, p. 81.

3. Lawrence J. Korb, "The Secretary of Defense and the Joint Chiefs of Staff in the Nixon Administration: The Method and the Men," in *The New Civil-Military Relations,* ed. John P. Lovell and Philip S. Kronenberg (New Brunswick, N.J.: Transaction Books, 1974), p. 258.

4. Lawrence J. Korb, *The Joint Chiefs of Staff: The First Twenty-five Years* (Bloomington: Indiana University Press, 1976), p. 129.

5. Alain C. Enthoven and K. Wayne Smith, *How Much Is Enough?* (New York: Harper & Row, 1971), p. 14.

6. Among the most important of these were Arthur Smithies, *The Budgetary Process of the United States* (New York: McGraw-Hill, 1955); Maxwell Taylor, *The Uncertain Trumpet* (New York: Harper, 1960); and a series of articles for the Rand Corp. by David Novick, Charles Hitch, and Roland McKean.

7. Enthoven and Smith, *How Much Is Enough?* p. 66.

8. William J. Broad, "Pentagon Analyst Questions Plan For Early Star Wars Deployment," *New York Times,* June 2, 1992, p. 1.

9. Harvey Sapolsky, *The Polaris System Development* (Cambridge, Mass.: Harvard University Press, 1973), pp. 53–54.

10. Aaron Wildavsky, *The Politics of the Budgetary Process* (Boston: Little, Brown, 1964), pp. 147–67.

11. U.S. Senate, Subcommittee on National Security and International Operations, *Hearings on Planning-Programming-Budgeting,* 91st Cong., 1st sess., pt. 1 (Washington, D.C.: U.S. Government Printing Office, 1969), p. 16.

12. Dick Cheney, *Defense Management Report to the President,* July 1989, pp. 2–7, and Business Executives for National Security, *Report of the Bens Commission on Fundamental Defense Management Reform,* February 1992.

13. For an excellent analysis of the Goldwater–Nichols Act, see Vincent Davis, "Organization and Management" in Joseph Kruzel, ed., *American Defense Annual, 1987–1988* (Lexington, Mass.: Heath, 1987), pp. 171–200.

14. Graham T. Allison, "Military Capabilities and American Foreign Policy," *Annals* 407 (March 1973): 32.

Chapter 10: The National Security Decision-making Process: Putting the Pieces Together

1. Samuel P. Huntington, *The Common Defense* (New York: Columbia University Press, 1961), p. 1.

2. Roger Hilsman, *The Politics of Policy Making in Defense and Foreign Affairs* (New York: Harper & Row, 1971), pp. 118–22. Hilsman uses three circles; the concept has been modified to five here.

3. The best sources on the national security decision-making process during the Gulf war are Bob Woodward, *The Commanders* (New York: Simon & Schuster, 1991) and U.S. News and World Report, *Triumph Without Victory* (New York: Warner Books, 1992).

4. *Report of the President's Special Review Board* (Washington, D.C.: U.S. Government Printing Office, 1987). (Hereafter called the *Tower Commission.*)

5. James Bamford, "Carlucci and the NSC," *New York Times Magazine,* January 18, 1987, pp. 16–19, 26, 38, 76, 79, 92; and "NSC Change," *The Economist,* February 11, 1989.

6. National Security Directive 1 (NSD-1), January 1989.

7. *Triumph Without Victory,* pp. 65–66.

8. Russell Watson, "A Talk with Zbig," *Newsweek,* May 9, 1977, p. 58.

9. *Tower Commission,* pp. 11–15; and NSD-1.

10. Graham T. Allison et al., *Adequacy of Current Organization: Defense and Arms Control,* Commission on the Organization of the Government for the Conduct of Foreign Policy, vol. 4 (Washington, D.C.: U.S. Government Printing Office, 1975), p. 3.

11. Alain C. Enthoven and K. Wayne Smith, *How Much Is Enough?* (New York: Harper & Row, 1971), p. 5.

12. Morton H. Halperin, *Bureaucratic Politics and Foreign Policy* (Washington, D.C.: Brookings Institution, 1974), p. 51.

13. Patrick Tyler, "Pentagon Imagines New Enemies to Fight in Post–Cold War Era," *New York Times,* February 17, 1992, p. 1; Barton Gellman, "Pentagon Abandons Goal of Thwarting U.S. Rivals," *Washington Post,* May 24, 1992, p. 1; and Robin Wright, "U.S. Quietly Redefining World Role," *Los Angeles Times,* June 15, 1992, p. 1.

14. For a complete description of the analytic model, see Graham Allison, *The Essence of Decision: Explaining the Cuban Missile Crisis* (Boston: Little, Brown, 1971). The quote is on p. 162.

15. See Allison, *Essence of Decision,* pp. 164–77, and Halperin, *Bureaucratic Politics and Foreign Policy,* pp. 16–25, for further explanation of this concept.

16. *Triumph without Victory,* p. 48.

17. Henry T. Nash, *American Foreign Policy: Response to a Sense of Threat* (Homewood, Ill.: Dorsey Press, 1973), p. 126.

18. R. Jeffrey Smith and John Goshko, "Ill-Fated Policy Originated Shortly After Bush Took Office," *Washington Post,* June 27, 1992, p. 7.

19. Robin Wright, "Efforts to Halt Arms Race Called Limited," *Los Angeles Times,* June 21, 1992, p. 3.

20. Hilsman, *Politics of Policy Making,* pp. 123–24.

21. Marriner S. Eccles, *Beckoning Frontiers* (New York: Knopf, 1951), p. 336.

22. Thomas E. Cronin, *The State of the Presidency,* 2d ed. (Boston: Little, Brown, 1980), p. 274.

23. Richard E. Neustadt, "White House and White Hall," *Public Interest* (winter 1966): 64.

24. Henry A. Kissinger, *The White House Years* (Boston: Little, Brown, 1979), pp. 18–19.

25. Halperin, *Bureaucratic Politics and Foreign Policy,* p. 279.

26. For a detailed analysis of the Cuban Missile Crisis, see Allison, *Essence of Decision.*

27. Bamford, "Carlucci and the NSC," p. 19.

Chapter 11: Nuclear Strategy

1. Michael Nacht, *The Age of Vulnerability* (Washington, D.C.: Brookings Institution, 1985), p. 85; Robert Jervis, *The Illogic of American Nuclear Strategy* (Ithaca, N.Y.: Cornell University Press, 1984), p. 24; and Morton Halperin, *Nuclear Fallacy: Dispelling the Myth of Nuclear Strategy* (Cambridge, Mass.: Ballinger, 1987).

2. Janne E. Nolan, *Guardians of the Arsenal: The Politics of Nuclear Strategy* (New York: Basic Books, 1989), pp. 35–38.

3. Desmond Ball, "Targeting for Strategic Deterrence," *Adelphi Papers* No. 185 (London: International Institute for Strategic Studies, Summer 1983), pp. 2–6; and Lawrence Freedman, *The Evolution of Nuclear Strategy* (New York: St. Martin's Press, 1981), pp. 1–224.

4. Ball, "Targeting for Strategic Deterrence," p. 6.

5. Nacht, *The Age of Vulnerability,* p. 86. See also, David Alan Rosenberg, " 'A Smoking Radiating Ruin At the End of Two Hours': Documents on American Plans for Nuclear War with the Soviet Union, 1954–1955," *International Security* 6 (Winter 1981–1982).

6. Quoted in Ball, "Targeting for Strategic Deterrence," pp. 9–10.

7. Michael Intrilligator, "The Debate Over Missile Strategy: Targets and Rates of Fire," *Orbis* 11 (Winter 1968): 1140.

8. Scott D. Sagan, *Moving Targets: Nuclear Strategy and National Security* (Princeton, N.J.: Princeton University Press, 1989), p. 74. See also, Earl Ravenal, "Counterforce and Alliance: The Ultimate Connection," *International Security* 6 (Spring 1982).

9. Philip Bobbitt, *Democracy and Deterrence: The History and Future of Nuclear Strategy* (New York: St. Martin's Press, 1988), p. 8.

10. William C. Martel and Paul L. Savage, *Strategic Nuclear War: What the Superpowers Target and Why* (New York: Greenwood Press, 1986), p. 175.

11. Ball, "Targeting for Strategic Deterrence," pp. 12–15; Freedman, *Evolution of Nuclear Strategy,* pp. 331–71; Nolan, *Guardians of the Arsenal,* pp. 89–117.

12. Robert Scheer, *With Enough Shovels: Reagan, Bush and Nuclear War* (New York: Random House, 1982), pp. 261–262.

13. Thomas C. Reed and Michael O. Wheeler, "The Role of Nuclear Weapons in the New World Order." Washington, D.C.: Department of Defense, December 1991, pp. 4, 15 (mimeograph).

14. Carl Kaysen, Robert S. McNamara, and George W. Rathjens, "Nuclear Weapons After the Cold War." *Foreign Affairs* 70 (Fall 1991), pp. 95–96.

15. William Daugherty, Barbara Levi, and Frank von Hippel, "The Consequences of 'Limited' Nuclear Attacks on the United States." *International Security* 10 (Spring 1986).

16. Robert Jervis, *The Illogic of American Nuclear Strategy* (Ithaca, N.Y.: Cornell University Press, 1984).

17. Robert McNamara, *Blundering Into Disaster: Surviving the First Century of the Nuclear Age* (New York: Pantheon Books, 1986), p. 139.

18. James G. Blight, *The Shattered Crystal Ball: Fear and Learning in the Cuban Missile Crisis* (Savage, Md.: Rowman & Littlefield, 1990), pp. 162–63.

19. Scott D. Sagan, *Moving Targets: Nuclear Strategy and National Security* (Princeton, N.J.: Princeton University Press, 1989), pp. 58–97.

20. McGeorge Bundy, "To Cap the Volcano," *Foreign Affairs* 48 (October 1969), pp. 9–10.

21. Kaysen, McNamara, and Rathjens, p. 107.

22. National Academy of Sciences, *The Future of the U.S.–Soviet Nuclear Relationship* (Washington, D.C.: National Academy of Sciences Press, 1991), p. 30.

23. Harold A. Feiveson and Frank N. von Hippel, "Beyond START: How to Make Much Deeper Cuts," *International Security* 15 (Summer 1990), p. 155.

24. Cited in W. Thomas Wander et al., *Science and Security: Technology and Arms Control for the 1990s* (Washington, D.C.: American Association for the Advancement of Science, 1989).

25. Charles Glaser, *Analyzing Strategic Nuclear Policy* (Princeton, N.J.: Princeton University Press, 1990), pp. 200–201.

26. Sagan, *Moving Targets,* pp. 91–93.

27. Glenn A. Kent and David E. Thaler, *First-Strike Stability and Strategic Defenses* (Santa Monica, Calif.: Rand Corporation, October 1990), p. 37.

Chapter 12: Limited War

1. See Martin Van Creveld, *Supplying War: Logistics from Wallenstein to Patton* (New York: Cambridge University Press, 1977).

2. See James A. Blackwell, *Thunder in the Desert: The Strategy and Tactics of the Persian Gulf War* (New York: Bantam Books, 1991).

3. Geoffrey Blainey, *The Causes of War* (New York: Free Press, 1973), pp. 196–97.

4. Ibid., pp. 193–94.

5. Alan Morehead, *The Russian Revolution* (New York: Harper, 1958), p. 51.

6. See Fred C. Iklé, *Every War Must End* (New York: Columbia University Press, 1991), pp. 84–105.

7. Quoted in Samuel P. Huntington, *The Common Defense* (New York: Columbia University Press, 1961), p. 80.

8. Bernard Brodie, *Strategy in the Missile Age* (Princeton, N.J.: Princeton University Press, 1959), pp. 316–21. See also Morton Halperin, "The Korean War," in *American Defense Policy,* ed. John E. Endicott and Roy W. Stafford, Jr., 4th ed. (Baltimore: Johns Hopkins University Press, 1977), pp. 191–200.

9. Thomas Schelling, *Arms and Influence* (New Haven, Conn.: Yale University Press, 1966), pp. 18–24.

10. See Gregg Herken, *The Winning Weapon: The Atomic Bomb in the Cold War 1945–1950* (Princeton, N.J.: Princeton University Press, 1981).

11. See Interim Report of the CSIS Study Group on Lessons Learned from the Gulf War, *The Gulf War: Military Lessons Learned* (Washington, D.C.: Center for Strategic and International Studies, July 1991).

12. At this writing (March 1992), the basic official document of U.S. strategy is Colin Powell, *National Military Strategy of the United States* (Washington, D.C.: Government Printing Office, January 1992). See also Dick Cheney, *Report of the Secretary of Defense to the President and the Congress* (Washington, D.C.: Government Printing Office, February 1992).

13. See Don Oberdorfer, "Strategy for a Solo Superpower: Pentagon Looks to 'Regional Contingencies,' " *The Washington Post,* May 19, 1991, pA1.

14. Final Report of the CSIS Conventional Arms Control Project, *A New Military Strategy for the 1990s: Implications for Capabilities and Acquisition* (Washington, D.C.: Center for Strategic and International Studies, January 1991), p. 29.

15. Ibid.

16. See William J. Taylor, Jr. and James Blackwell, "The Ground War in the Gulf," *Survival* 33, no. 3 (1991): 230–245.

17. The vote in the Senate supported the President by a margin of only 52 to 47. In the House, the margin was slightly larger—250 to 183, with 86 Democrats voting in the majority. See U.S. News and World Report Staff, *Triumph Without Victory: The Unreported History of the Persian Gulf War* (New York: Times Books, 1992), p. 207. By most accounts, the congressional debate was a detailed and important discussion of the use of force and a president's powers in that area.

18. See Major General Perry M. Smith, *How CNN Fought the War: A View From the Inside* (New York: Carol Publishing Group, 1991).

Chapter 13: From Low Intensity Conflict to Forward-Presence Operations

1. Michael McClintock, *Instruments of Statecraft: U.S. Guerrilla Warfare, Counterinsurgency, and Counter-terrorism, 1940–1990* (New York: Pantheon Books, 1992), p. 334.

2. Secretary of State Alexander Haig is credited with first using the phrase "drawing the line" in reference to El Salvador in a briefing to the congressional leadership on the State Department's White Paper, *Communist Interference in El Salvador*.

3. Eugene N. Russell, "Low Intensity Conflict in a Changed and Changing World," *National Security: Papers Prepared for GAO Conference on Worldwide Threats,* General Accounting Office/National Security and International Affairs Division, 92-104S, April 1992, p. 125.

4. Seth Cropsey, "Barking Up a Fallen Tree: The Death of Low Intensity Conflict," *The National Interest,* Spring 1992, p. 58.

5. Russell, "Low Intensity Conflict in a Changed and Changing World," p. 126.

6. See *U.S. Department of Defense Annual Report to the President and the Congress,* Fiscal Year 1992 (Washington, D.C.: U.S. Government Printing Office, 1992).

7. James Schlesinger, "New Instabilities, New Priorities," in *Foreign Policy* 85 (Winter 1991–92), p. 5.

8. For an exhaustive treatment of one aspect of political violence, see Robert B. Asprey, *War in the Shadows,* 2 vols. (Garden City, N.Y.: Doubleday, 1975); see also Walter Laqueur, *Guerilla* (Boston: Little, Brown, 1976).

9. Nikita Khrushchev, Speech delivered January 6, 1961, quoted in *Documents on International Affairs,* 1961 (London: Oxford University Press, 1965), pp. 259–73.

10. Mao Tse-tung, ''Why Is It that Red Political Power Can Exist in China?'' and, ''The Struggle in the Chingkand Mountains,'' in *Selected Military Writings of Mao Tse-tung* (Peking: Foreign Language Press, 1963), pp. 9–18, 19–50.

11. Mao Tse-tung, ''Problems of Strategy in China's Revolutionary War,'' in ibid., pp. 75–150.

12. Karl von Clausewitz, *On War,* ed. and trans. Michael Howard and Peter Paret (Princeton, N.J.: Princeton University Press, 1976), p. 596.

13. Originally *Hukbo ng bayan Laban sa Hapon* (People's Army to fight the Japanese), it changed in 1948 to *Hukbo ng Magpalayang Bayan* (People's Liberation Army).

14. Chalmers Johnson, *Peasant Nationalism and Communist Power* (Stanford, Calif.: Stanford University Press, 1962).

15. Examples of revolutions that have withered through lack of endurance are legion, but for a few, conveniently treated, see Geoffrey Fairbairn, *Revolutionary Guerilla Warfare* (Baltimore: Penguin, 1974).

16. J. Bowyer Bell, ''Unconventional War: The Army in the Year 2000,'' in Robert H. Kupperman and William J. Taylor, Sr. ed. *Strategic Requirements for the Army to the Year 2000.* (Washington, D.C.: Center for Strategic and International Studies, 1984), p. 179.

17. Ibid., p. 180.

18. Michael D. Shafer, *Deadly Paradigms: The Failure of U.S. Counterinsurgency Policy* (Princeton, N.J.: Princeton University Press, 1988), p. 24.

19. Andrew Krepinevich, *The Army in Vietnam* (Baltimore: Johns Hopkins University Press, 1986), p. 29.

20. Ibid., pp. 3–26.

21. Bruce Palmer, *The 25-Year War: America's Military Role in Vietnam* (New York: Simon & Schuster, 1984), pp. 40–41.

22. Krepinevich, *The Army in Vietnam,* pp. 100–127.

23. Michael McClintock, *Instruments of Statecraft: U.S. Guerrilla Warfare, Counterinsurgency, and Counterterrorism, 1940–1990,* p. 348.

24. Sam C. Sarkesian, ''Commentary on Low Intensity Warfare: Threat and Military Response,'' in *Proceedings of the Low Intensity Warfare Conference,* January 14–15, 1986, Fort McNair, Washington, D.C., p. 38.

25. Benjamin C. Schwarz, *American Counterinsurgency Doctrine and El Salvador* (Santa Monica, Calif.: Rand, 1992), p. 1.

26. William E. Odom, *On Internal War: American and Soviet Approaches to Third World Clients and Insurgents* (Durham, N.C.: Duke University Press, 1992), p. 107.

27. Schwarz, *American Counterinsurgency Doctrine and El Salvador,* p. x.

28. Ibid., p. xi.

29. See Stephen Flynn and Gregory Grant, *The Transnational Drug Challenge* (Washington, D.C.: Center for Strategic and International Studies, 1992).

30. Indar Jit Rikhe, *Strengthening UN Peacekeeping: New Challenges and Proposals,* (United States Institute for Peace, 1992), p. 28.

31. *Public Report of the Vice President's Task Force on Combatting Terrorism* (Washington, D.C.: U.S. Government Printing Office, February 1986), p. 4.

32. U.S. Department of State, *Patterns of Global Terrorism: 1990* (Washington, D.C.: U.S. Government Printing Office, April 1991), p. 25.

33. Ibid., p. 18.

34. Seth Cropsey, ''Barking Up a Fallen Tree: The Death of Low Intensity Conflict,'' p. 58.

35. Seth Cropsey, "Barking Up a Fallen Tree," p. 55.

36. Bernard F. McMahon, "Low Intensity Conflict: The Pentagon's Foible," *ORBIS*, Winter 1990, p. 15.

37. Shafer, p. 282.

38. Steven David, "Why the Third World Matters," *International Security* 14, 1989, p. 58.

39. Shafer, p. 281.

Chapter 14: Economic Challenges to National Security

1. International Trade Administration, Department of Commerce, *Business America*, March 2, 1987, p. 20.

2. Harold Bullis and James Mielke, *Strategic and Critical Minerals* (Boulder, Colo.: Westview Press, 1985), p. 12.

3. Franklin R. Root, *International Trade and Investment* (Cincinnati: South-Western, 1978), pp. 17–21.

4. Graham Bannock, R. E. Baxter, and Ray Rees, eds., *The Penguin Dictionary of Economics* (London: Penguin Books, 1978).

5. Robert W. Tucker, *The Inequality of Nations* (New York: Basic Books, 1977), pp. 47–51.

6. See, for example, Felix Kessler, "West Germany Resists U.S. Plans to Increase Outlays and Aid Growth," *Wall Street Journal*, February 9, 1977, p. 1; and R. Jansen and R. Levine, "London Summit Strengthens Willingness of West to Continue Fighting Inflation," *Wall Street Journal*, May 9, 1977, p. 2.

7. Klaus Knorr and Frank N. Trager, eds., *Economic Issues and National Security* (Lawrence, Kans.: Regents Press of Kansas, 1966), pp. 246–50.

8. Mordechai E. Kreinin, *International Economics: A Policy Approach* (New York: Harcourt, Brace, Jovanovich, 1979), p. 3.

9. "EMS Lives: Europe's Antidote to the Dollar Makes Fine Debut," *Financial Times World Business Weekly*, March 19, 1979.

10. A. Bryan, A. A. Jordan, and M. Moodie, *Facing the International Energy Problem* (New York: Praeger, 1979).

11. Knorr and Trager, *Economic Issues*, p. 13.

12. Knorr and Trager, *Economic Issues*, pp. 1–14.

13. Daniel Bell, "The Future World Disorder," *Foreign Policy*, no. 22 (1977), p. 115.

14. Department of Defense Annual Report to the Congress: Fiscal Year 1990 (Washington, D.C.: U.S. Government Printing Office, 1989), p. 221.

15. John Yemma, "International Debt Crisis," *Christian Science Monitor*, March 19, 1987, pp. 18–19.

16. Bill Orr, "After a Decade, Bankers Say 'Adios' to Latin Debt Crisis." *ABA Banking Journal*, July 1992, pp. 36–44.

17. Henry Nau, "The American Competitiveness Renaissance," typescript to be published in *CEO Strategies International*, 1992, pp. 1–6.

18. U.S. Central Intelligence Agency, *Handbook of Economic Statistics, 1985* (Springfield, Va.: National Technical Information Service, 1985), p. 125.

19. Irving Louis Horowitz, *Three Worlds of Development: The Theory and Practice of International Stratification* (New York: Oxford University Press, 1966), p. 24.

20. Ibid., pp. 44–46.

21. See Klaus Knorr, ''International Economic Leverage and Its Uses,'' in Knorr and Trager, *Economic Issues,* pp. 99–126.

22. Hirsh Goodman, ''Pretoria Connection,'' *New Republic,* April 20, 1987, p. 20.

23. ''Soviet Invasion of Afghanistan,'' Department of State Bulletin Current Policy no. 123 (Washington, D.C.: Bureau of Public Affairs, U.S. Department of State, January 4, 1980).

24. ''U.S. Sanctions against Russia: A Flop,'' *U.S. News and World Report,* June 16, 1980, pp. 33–34.

25. Paula Stern, ''Economic Leverage on the U.S.S.R.,'' in *Executive* (Ithaca, N.Y.: Cornell University Press, 1979), pp. 35–37.

Chapter 15: Research and Development

1. Richard G. Head, ''Technology and the Military Balance,'' *Foreign Affairs* 56, no. 3 (1978): 553.

2. *Random House Dictionary of the English Language,* unabridged, s.v. ''science.''

3. Charles J. Hitch and Roland N. McKean, *The Economics of Defense in the Nuclear Age* (Santa Monica, Calif.: Rand, 1960), p. 246.

4. Ibid., pp. 245–46.

5. Ibid., p. 243.

6. Stefan J. Possony and J. E. Pournelle, *The Strategy of Technology* (Cambridge, Mass.: Dunellen Press, 1970), p. xxvi.

7. Office of Management and Budget, *Budget of the United States Government, Fiscal Year 1993* (Washington, D.C.: U.S. Government Printing Office, 1987), p. I-87.

8. Possony and Pournelle, *Strategy of Technology,* p. 62.

9. Keith Berner and Stephen Daggett, *CRS Report for Congress: Defense Budget for FY 1993,* February 10, 1992, p. 14.

10. Organization for Economic Cooperation and Development, *Science and Technology Policy Outlook: 1985* (Paris: OECD, 1985), p. 42.

11. Aerospace Industries Association of America, *The National Technology Program* (Washington, D.C.: AIAA, December 1972), p. 6.

12. *Budget of the United States Government for Fiscal Year 1993,* pp. 1–131.

13. U.S. Congress, Senate, Committee on Armed Services, *Hearings, Department of Defense Authorization for Appropriations for Fiscal Year 1979, Statement of Undersecretary of Defense for Research and Engineering William J. Perry,* 95th Cong., 2d sess., February 28, 1978, p. 5509.

14. For a theoretical treatment of this point, see Klaus Knorr, *Military Power and Potential* (Lexington, Mass.: Heath, 1970), pp. 73–90.

15. For details of this campaign, see Arnold L. Horelick and Myron Rush, *Strategic Power and Soviet Foreign Policy* (Chicago: University of Chicago Press, 1965), pp. 58–70, passim.

16. AIAA, *International R&D Trends and Policies,* p. 9.

17. *Budget of the United States Government for Fiscal Year 1993,* pp. 1–87.

18. Possony and Pournelle, *Strategy of Technology,* p. 2.

19. *United States Government Manual, 1976–1977* (Washington, D.C.: Office of the Federal Register, National Archives and Records Service, General Services Administration, 1976), pp. 98–99.

20. U.S. Congress, Senate, Committee on Armed Services, *National Defense Authorization Act for Fiscal Years 1992 and 1993, Report 102–113*, 102d Cong., 1st sess. (Washington, D.C.: U.S. Government Printing Office, 1991), pp. 233–34.

21. Jack N. Merritt and Pierre M. Sprey, "Negative Marginal Returns in Weapons Acquisition," in *American Defense Policy*, ed. Richard G. Head and Ervin J. Rokke, 3d ed. (Baltimore: Johns Hopkins University Press, 1973), p. 494.

22. Possony and Pournelle, *Strategy of Technology*, p. 4.

23. Adam Yarmolinsky, "The President, the Congress, and Arms Control," in *The Military-Industrial Complex: A Reassessment*, ed. Sam C. Sarkesian (Beverly Hills, Calif.: Sage, 1972), pp. 278–79.

24. Ibid., p. 293. For a thorough treatment of the problem of congressional self-interest, see Bruce M. Russett, *What Price Vigilance?* (New Haven, Conn.: Yale University Press, 1970), pp. 72–90; and Kenneth Mayer, *The Political Economy of Defense Contracting* (New Haven, Conn.: Yale University Press, 1991).

25. Arthur F. Burns, "The Defense Sector: Its Economic and Social Impact," in *The Military and American Society*, ed. Martin B. Hickman (Beverly Hills, Calif.: Glencoe Press, 1971), p. 60.

26. See, for example, Martin Binkin, *Military Technology and Defense Manpower* (Washington, D.C.: Brookings Institution, 1986).

27. Merritt and Sprey, "Negative Marginal Returns," p. 494.

28. For examples, see both William Proxmire, *Report from Wasteland* (New York: Praeger, 1970), Chapter 10, and Sidney Lens, *The Military-Industrial Complex* (Philadelphia: Pilgrim Press, 1970), pp. 79–99.

Chapter 16: The Former Soviet Union

1. A selected bibliography of works on the cold war can be found in Toby Trister, "Traditionalists, Revisionists, and the Cold War," in *Caging the Bear: Containment and the Cold War*, ed. Charles Gati (New York: Bobbs-Merrill, 1974), pp. 211–22.

2. George Kennan, "The Sources of Soviet Conduct," *Foreign Affairs* 25, no. 4 (1947), reprinted in Gati, *Caging the Bear*.

3. Walter Lippmann, *U.S. Foreign Policy: Shield of the Republic* (Boston: Little, Brown, 1943), pp. 1–10.

4. Samuel Huntington, *The Common Defense* (New York: Columbia University Press, 1961), pp. 35–37.

5. Harry S. Truman, Address delivered to joint session of Congress, *Congressional Record*, 80th Cong., 1st sess., 1947, 93, pt. 2, p. 1981; and Kennan, "Sources of Soviet Conduct."

6. Adam Ulam, *Expansion and Coexistence: Soviet Foreign Policy, 1917–1973*, rev. ed. (New York: Praeger, 1974), pp. 543–44.

7. Urs Schwarz, *Confrontation and Intervention in the Modern World* (Dobbs Ferry, N.Y.: Oceana Press, 1970), p. 59.

8. For a complete record of the crisis, see Theodore C. Sorensen, *Kennedy* (New York: Harper & Row, 1965), pp. 667–719.

9. V. V. Kuznetsov, quoted in Schwartz, *Foreign Policy of the U.S.S.R.*, p. 60, and John Newhouse, *Cold Dawn: The Story of SALT* (New York: Holt, Rinehart, & Winston, 1973), p. 68.

10. Herbert Dinerstein, "The Soviet Outlook," in *America and the World*, ed. Robert Osgood et al. (Baltimore: Johns Hopkins University Press, 1970), pp. 82–83.

11. The conceptual framework behind détente (on the U.S. side) can be found in Henry Kissinger, ''Détente with the Soviet Union: The Reality of Competition and the Imperative of Cooperation,'' *Department of State Bulletin* (Washington, D.C.: U.S. Government Printing Office, October 14, 1974), pp. 505–19. Cf. Theodore Draper, ''Appeasement and Détente,'' *Commentary* (February 1976); Pierre Hassner, ''Western European Perceptions of the U.S.S.R.'' *Daedalus* (Winter 1979): 115.

12. Kissinger, ''Détente with the Soviet Union,'' p. 509.

13. Leonid Brezhnev, quoted in *Current Soviet Policies VII: The Documentary Record of the Twenty-fifth Congress of the Communist Party of the Soviet Union* (Columbus, Ohio: American Association for the Advancement of Slavic Studies, 1975), pp. 13–14.

14. Dimitri Simes, ''Détente, Russian-Style,'' *Foreign Policy,* no. 32 (Fall 1978): 51.

15. For a concise account of this crisis, see Scott Sagan, ''Lessons of the Yom Kippur Alert,'' *Foreign Policy,* no. 36 (Fall 1979).

16. See Donald S. Zagoria, ''Into the Breach: New Soviet Alliances in the Third World,'' *Foreign Affairs* 57, no. 4 (1979): 733–35. Cf. Robert Legvold, ''The Super Rivals: Conflict in the Third World,'' in the same issue.

17. These tactics are described in Kenneth Adelman, ''Fear, Seduction, and Growing Soviet Strength,'' *Orbis* (Winter 1978).

18. Edward Luttwak, ''After Afghanistan, What?'' *Commentary* 69, no. 4 (1980): 40–48.

19. The material on the Afghan invasion is adapted from Joseph Collins, ''The Soviet Invasion of Afghanistan: Methods, Motives, and Ramifications,'' *Naval War College Review* 33, no. 6 (1980). For a penetrating analysis of the fear and bluster behind the Soviet view of the correlation of forces, see Vernon Aspaturian, ''Soviet Global Power and the Correlation of Forces,'' *Problems of Communism* (May 1980): 1–18.

20. Richard Pipes, ''Why the Soviet Union Thinks It Could Fight and Win a Nuclear War,'' *Commentary* 64, no. 1 (July 1977). Cf. Raymond Garthoff, ''Mutual Deterence and Strategic Arms Limitation in Soviet Policy,'' *International Security* (Summer 1978).

21. For an explanation of Minuteman vulnerability and its alleged political consequences, see interview with Henry Kissinger, ''Kissinger's Critique,'' pt. I, *Economist* (February 1979): 17–22. A balanced examination of this and other Soviet threats can be found in Grayson Kirk and Nils Wessell, eds., *The Soviet Threat: Myths and Realities* (New York: Academy of Political Science, 1978).

22. Adelman, ''Fear, Seduction, and Growing Soviet Strength.'' For Soviet economic relations with Europe, see Fritz Stern, ''Germany in a Semi-Gaullist Europe,'' *Foreign Affairs* 58, no. 4 (1980): 877–86, which contains a description of European problems related to East–West détente. See also Hassner, ''Western European Perceptions.''

23. See *NATO and the Warsaw Pact Force Comparison* (Brussels: NATO Information Service, 1984), pp. 8–13.

24. For a description of NATO efforts to redress the imbalances, see *U.S. Department of Defense Annual Report, Fiscal Year 1981* (Washington, D.C.: U.S. Government Printing Office, 1980).

25. Manfred Hamm, *Chemical Warfare: The Growing Threat to Europe,* Occasional Paper no. 8 for the Institute for European Defense and Strategic Studies, September 1984.

26. For an analysis of this metaphor, see Adam Garfinkel, ''Finlandization'': A Map to a Metaphor, Foreign Policy Research Institute Monograph 24 (Philadelphia: FPRI, 1978), pp. 1–56. For an analysis of other structural options that might develop if Western Europe were separated from the United States, see Warner Schilling et al., *American Arms*

and a Changing Europe: Dilemmas of Deterrence and Disarmament (New York: Columbia University Press, 1973), pp. 123–95.

27. David Ottaway, ''Angola Gets Infusion of Soviet Arms,'' *Washington Post,* May 12, 1987.

28. Paul Mann, ''Soviet Defense Crumbling, U.S. Intelligence Says,'' *Aviation Week and Space Technology,* June 15, 1992, pp. 35–36.

29. Ibid., p. 36.

Chapter 17: East Asia

1. Stephen W. Bosworth, ''The United States and Asia,'' *Foreign Affairs,* Volume 71, No. 1, 1992, p. 113.

2. ''U.S. Strategy Plan Calls For Insuring No Rivals Develop.'' *New York Times,* March 8, 1992, p.14.

3. Ibid.

4. James A. Baker, ''America in Asia: Emerging Architecture for a Pacific Community,'' *Foreign Affairs* 70, no. 5 (1991/92), p. 5.

5. Leslie H. Brown, ''American Security Policy in Asia,'' Adelphi Papers, no. 132 (London: International Institute for Strategic Studies, Spring 1977).

6. Richard H. Solomon, ''American Defense Planning and Asian Security: Policy Choices for a Time of Transition,'' in Solomon, ed., *Asian Security in the 1980s: Problems and Policies for a Time of Transition* (Santa Monica, Calif.: Rand Corp., November 1979), pp. 9–11.

7. Ibid., p. 2.

8. William G. Hyland, ''The Sino-Soviet Conflict: A Search for New Security Strategies,'' in Solomon, ed., *Asian Security,* pp. 39–53.

9. Goh Keng Swee, ''Vietnam and Big Power Rivalry,'' Solomon, ed., *Asian Security,* pp. 148–52.

10. Yuan-li Wu. *U.S. Policy and Strategic Interests in the Western Pacific* (New York: Crane, Russak, 1975), pp. 1–16.

11. Solomon, ''American Defense Planning,'' pp. 27–28.

12. ''Gorbachev's Speech at Vladivostok,'' *New York Times,* July 29, 1986, p. A1.

13. Department of Defense. *A Strategic Framework for the Pacific Rim: Report to Congress,* 1992, p. 21.

14. International Monetary Fund, Direction of Trade Statistics (Washington, D.C.: IMF, 1990).

15. Address by Prime Minister Miyazawa, National Press Club, Washington, D.C., July 2, 1992.

16. Ibid.

17. From authors' personal interview with Deng Xiaoping, July, 1988.

18. Harry Harding, *China's Second Revolution, Reform After Mao* (Washington, D.C.: Brookings Institution, 1987), pp. 172–201.

19. Edwin K. Snyder, A. James Gregir, and Maria Hsia Chang, ''The Taiwan Relations Act and the Defense of the Republic of China'' (Berkeley: Institute of International Studies, University of California, 1980), p. 102.

20. Reuters Wire Service, July 13, 1992, dispatch from Taipei.

21. ''Proposed E16 Sale Draws Strong Protest,'' *Beijing Review,* September 14, 1992, p. 7.

22. Cheng, Tuan. *Economic Diplomacy in the Pacific Basin of the Republic of China on Taiwan* (Policy Report Series, Honolulu: Pacific Forum/CSIS, July 1992), pp. 1–4.

23. Huntington, Samuel P. *The Third Wave* (Norman: University of Oklahoma Press, 1991), pp. 302–4.

24. Swee, ''Vietnam and Big Power Rivalry,'' pp. 148–168.

25. Bosworth, p. 128.

26. Secretary of Defense Cheney's speech in Tokyo, November 22, 1991.

27. Department of Defense. *A Strategic Framework,* pp. 27–33.

Chapter 18: The Middle East

1. For comprehensive discussion of U.S. interests in the Middle East before the 1967 war, see George Lenczowski, ed., *United States Interests in the Middle East* (Washington, D.C.: American Enterprise Institute for Public Policy Research, 1968), pp. 14–76.

2. James Schlesinger, ''The Strategic Vortex,'' *Washington Quarterly* (Winter 1980): 177–84.

3. Lenczowski, *United States Interests,* pp. 39–40.

4. British Petroleum Co., *BP Statistical Review of the World Oil Industry,* 1974 (London: BP, 1974), p. 21.

5. James A. Bill and Robert W. Stookey, *Politics and Petroleum: The Middle East and the United States* (Brunswick, Ohio: King's Court Communications, 1975), pp. 123–24.

6. ''Latest Saudi Borrowing Develops Kingdoms Debt Strategy, but Some Bankers Unhappy,'' *Middle East Economic Survey,* vol. XXXV, no. 29, April 20, 1992, p. B2.

7. R. J. Sontag and J. S. Beddie, eds., *Nazi–Soviet Relations, 1939–1941* (Washington, D.C.: U.S. Government Printing Office, 1948), p. 259.

8. Tareq Y. Ismael, *The Middle East in World Politics* (Syracuse, N.Y.: Syracuse University Press, 1974), pp. 124–27.

9. Perhaps the best treatment of the conflict between competition and détente in the Middle East is Lawrence L. Whetten, *The Canal War: Four-Power Conflict in the Middle East* (Cambridge, Mass.: MIT Press, 1974), pp. 331–40.

10. For a detailed discussion of the issue, see William B. Quandt, *Decade of Decisions: American Policy toward the Arab–Israeli Conflict, 1967–1976* (Berkeley and Los Angeles: University of California Press, 1977), pp. 9–12.

11. Ibid., pp. 15–24.

12. Whetten, *Canal War,* pp. 137, 165, 203–5, 289.

13. Letter to Gerald Ford, May 1975, quoted in *The Middle East: U.S. Policy, Israel, Oil, and the Arabs* (Washington, D.C.: Congressional Quarterly, 1977), p. 96.

14. W. Seth Carus, ''The Military Balance of Power in the Middle East,'' *Current History,* no. 74 (January 1978): 29–30.

15. A comprehensive treatment of such problems can be found in Majid Khadduri, *Political Trends in the Arab World* (Baltimore: Johns Hopkins University Press, 1970). Iran and Turkey faced the same difficulties but to a lesser extent.

16. The classic treatment of this subject is Malcolm Kerr, *The Arab Cold War,* 3d ed. (London: Oxford University Press, 1971).

17. Sidney H. Zebel, *Balfour: A Political Biography* (Cambridge: University Press, 1973), p. 238.

18. Janet L. Abu-Lughod, ''The Democratic Transformation of Palestine,'' in *The Transformation of Palestine,* ed. Ebr Abu-Lughod (Evanston, Ill.: Northwestern University Press, 1971), pp. 141–53.

19. Ann Mosely Lesch, ''The Palestine Arab Nationalist Movement under the Mandate,'' in *The Politics of Palestinian Nationalism,* ed. William B. Quandt (Berkeley and

Los Angeles: University of California Press, 1973), pp. 33–40. See also, David Hirst, *The Gun and the Olive Branch: The Roots of Violence in the Middle East* (New York: Harcourt Brace Jovanovich, 1977), pp. 97–106.

20. For a detailed discussion of the U.N. partition plan and the role of the United States in getting it passed, see Fred J. Khouri, *The Arab Israeli Dilemma,* 2d ed. (Syracuse, N.Y.: Syracuse University Press, 1976), pp. 43–67. For its immediate effects in Palestine, see Quandt, *Politics of Palestinian Nationalism,* pp. 45–48.

21. Khouri, *Dilemma,* pp. 72, 77.

22. Ibid., pp. 187–89.

23. David A. Deese and Joseph S. Nye, eds. *Energy and Security* (Cambridge, Mass.: Ballinger, 1981), pp. 88–91.

24. Sharham Chubin and Sepehr Zabih, *The Foreign Relations of Iran* (Berkeley and Los Angeles: University of California Press, 1974), pp. 178–81. See also, McLaurin et al., *Foreign Policy Making in the Middle East* (New York, Praeger, 1977), pp. 130–39, and Rouhollah K. Ramazani, *The Persian Gulf: Iran's Role* (Charlottesville: University Press of Virginia, 1972), pp. 45–68.

25. See Amos A. Jordan, "Saudi Pillar on Firmer Soil," *Washington Star,* February 18, 1979, p. D-1.

26. Craig R. Whitney, "Soviet Union and Turkey Sign Nonaggression, Trade and Cultural Pacts," *New York Times,* June 24, 1978, p. 3.

27. Robin Wright, "Islam and Democracy," *Foreign Affairs,* 71, no. 3 (1992), pp. 132–33.

28. McLaurin et al., *Foreign Policy Making,* pp. 20–25.

29. Alef A. Gawad, "Moscow's Arms-for-Oil Diplomacy," *Foreign Policy,* no. 63 (Summer 1986): 147–68.

30. Whetten, *Canal War,* pp. 59–60.

31. Robert O. Friedman, *Soviet Policy toward the Middle East since 1970* (New York: Praeger, 1975), pp. 172–79.

32. See John Kifner, "Soviet Acts to Win Back Influence in Mideast," *New York Times,* May 11, 1987, p. 1; Jim Muir, "Soviets, Saudis Aim to Unite Arab World in Bid for Mideast Meeting," *Christian Science Monitor,* May 11, 1987, p. 11; John Walcott, "Soviet Road to Heightened Influence in Middle East Runs through Syria," *Wall Street Journal,* May 11, 1987, p. 22; and Robert S. Luttwak and S. Neil MacFarlane, "Soviet Activism in the Third World," *Survival* 29, no. 1 (1987): 21–39.

33. Bill and Stookey, *Politics and Petroleum,* p. 123.

34. The discussion in the following section on Iraq is taken primarily from James Blackwell, *Thunder in the Desert: The Strategy and Tactics of the Persian Gulf War* (New York: Bantam Books), 1991, pp. 1–28.

35. For details on the operational aspects of Operation Desert Storm, see R. A. Mason, "The Air War in the Gulf," and William J. Taylor, Jr., and James A. Blackwell, Jr., "The Ground War in the Gulf," in *Survival,* 33, no. 3 (1991), pp. 211–245.

36. For further discussion of these possibilities, see *The United States and the New Middle East: Strategic Perspectives after the Persian Gulf War* (Washington, D.C.: Center for Strategic and International Studies, March 1992).

Chapter 19: Sub-Saharan Africa

1. For an elaboration of the U.S. interests in Africa discussed in this chapter, see U.S. Congress, House, Committee on Foreign Affairs, Subcommittee on Africa, *Hearings,*

U.S. Interests in Africa, Prepared Statement of Hon. Joseph J. Sisco, President, American University, 96th Cong., 1st sess. (Washington, D.C.: U.S. Government Printing Office, 1980), pp. 7–10.

2. Anthony Lake, Director of Policy Planning Staff, U.S. Department of State, in a speech for the Christian A. Herter Lectures, Johns Hopkins University, October 27, 1977 (Washington, D.C.: Bureau of Public Affairs, Department of State, 1977).

3. *The World Almanac and Book of Facts, 1987* (New York: Newspaper Enterprises Assoc., 1986), p. 148.

4. Philip L. Christenson, "Some Economic Facts of Life," *AEI Foreign Policy and Defense Review* 1, no. 1 (*Options for U.S. Policy toward Africa*), ed. Helen Kitchen (1979). (Hereafter cited as *AEI FPDR*.)

5. For an excellent discussion of the military coup as an African political institution, see Aristide Zolberg, "The Structure of Political Conflict in the New States of Tropical Africa," *American Political Science Review* 62, no. 1 (March 1968): 70–87; Claude E. Welch, Jr., ed., *The Soldier and the State in Africa* (Evanston, Ill.: Northwestern University Press, 1970); and Henry Bienen, *Armies and Parties in Africa* (New York: Africana, 1978).

6. Abdul A. Said, *The African Phenomenon* (Boston: Allyn & Bacon, 1968), pp. 120–22.

7. On Zaire's massive internal problem, see Crawford Young, "Zaire: The Unending Crisis," *Foreign Affairs* 57, no. 1 (1978): 169–85; idem, "Optimism on Zaire: Illusion or Reality?" *CSIS Africa Notes,* no. 50 (November 22, 1985).

8. For a review of the 1974–1975 crisis in southern Africa, see John A. Marcum's chapter, "Southern Africa after the Collapse of Portuguese Rule," in *Africa: From Mystery to Maze,* ed. Helen Kitchen (Lexington, Mass.: Heath, 1976).

9. See Gerald A. Funk, "Some Observations on Strategic Realities and Ideological Red Herrings on the Horn of Africa," *CSIS Africa Notes,* no. 1 (July 1, 1982); idem, "Can Ethiopia Survive Both Communism and Drought?" *CSIS Africa Notes,* no. 40 (March 15, 1985).

10. Michael Clough, "Africa in the 1990s," *CSIS Africa Notes,* no. 107 (January 29, 1990).

11. Martin Lowenkopf, "If the Cold War is Over in Africa, Will the United States Still Care?," *CSIS Africa Notes,* no. 98 (May 30, 1989).

12. Leonid Fituni, "New Soviet Priorities in Africa," *CSIS Africa Notes,* no. 123 (April 29, 1991).

13. Text of the U.S.–Soviet Joint Statement on Cooperation on Conflict Resolution in Africa, released at the signing of the Angolan peace accords in Lisbon, Portugal on May 31, 1991. See U.S. Department of State, *Dispatch,* vol. 2, no. 23, (1991): 409.

14. Leonid Fituni, "Russia's Third Discovery of Africa," *CSIS Africa Notes,* no. 134 (March 1992).

15. For a discussion of the French military in Africa, see John Chipman, *French Power in Africa* (Cambridge: Oxford University Press, 1989).

16. See "Mounting Challenges," *West Africa,* 27 May–2 June 1991, p. 833.

17. Carol Lancaster, "The New Politics of U.S. Aid to Africa," *CSIS Africa Notes,* no. 120 (January 1991).

18. Adebayo Adedeji, "Sustaining Democracy," *Africa Report,* (January–February 1992), p. 36.

19. In December 1986, Kaunda tried to raise the price of maize meal (a dietary staple of Zambia). Food riots ensued, resulting in twenty-three deaths. See Carol Graham,

"Zambia's Democratic Transition: The Beginning of the End of the End of the One-Party State in Africa?" *The Brookings Review* (Spring 1992): 41.

20. Marina Ottoway, "South Africa After the Referendum," *CSIS Africa Notes,* no. 135 (April 1992).

21. Herbert M. Howe, "The SADF Revisited," *CSIS Africa Notes,* no. 126 (July 16, 1991).

22. World Bank, *World Debt Tables, 1990–91: External Debt of Developing Countries,* vols. 1 and 2 (Washington, D.C.: World Bank, 1990).

Chapter 20: Latin America

1. James Monroe, Annual message delivered to the Congress, December 2, 1833.

2. Article 5f, Charter of the Organization of American States.

3. Donald M. Dozer, "The Contemporary Significance of the Monroe Doctrine," in *Latin America Politics, Economics, and Hemispheric Security,* ed. Norman A. Bailey (New York: Praeger, 1965).

4. For example, see Anibal Quijano Obregon, "Imperialism and International Relations," in *Latin America and the United States,* ed. Julio Cotler and Richard R. Fagen (Stanford, Calif.: Stanford University Press, 1974), pp. 67–91; and C. Wright Mills, *Listen Yankee* (New York: Ballantine Books, 1960).

5. An excellent account is Bryce Wood, *The Making of the Good Neighbor Policy* (New York: Columbia University Press, 1961).

6. John M. Hunter and James W. Foley, *Economic Problems of Latin America* (Boston: Houghton Mifflin, 1975), p. 204. U.S. Department of Commerce, *Survey of Current Business* (Washington, D.C.: Bureau of Economic Analysis, June 1991), p. 29.

7. See Frank D. McCann, *The Brazilian–American Alliance, 1937–1945* (Princeton, N.J.: Princeton University Press, 1974).

8. In 1991, just prior to the collapse of the Soviet Union, Cuba received an annual Soviet subsidy of approximately $4 billion. That same year the Soviet Union supplied 71 percent of Cuba's imports. Figures for subsequent years were not available as of the time this edition went to press. See the *World Fact Book 1991*

9. David Ronfeldt, Richard Nehring, and Arturo Gandara, *Mexico's Petroleum and U.S. Policy Implications for the 1980s* (Santa Monica, Calif.: Rand, June 1980), p. 78.

10. See U.S. Department of State Dispatch, March 23, 1992: Statement of Bernard W. Aronson, Assistant Secretary for Inter-American Affairs, before the Subcommittee on Western Hemisphere Affairs of the House Foreign Affairs Committee, March 12, 1992.

11. For a fuller discussion of the measures taken by the two countries, see Wayne Selcher, "Brazil and the Southern Cone Subsystem," in *South America into the 1990s: Evolving International Relationships in a New Era,* ed. G. Pope Atkins (Boulder, Colo.: Westview Press, 1990), pp. 87–120, and especially pp. 93–110.

12. The debt service ratio, a measure of annual payments of principle and interest against export revenue, was estimated at 32.3 percent for 1992. See the *World Economic Outlook,* October 1991 (Washington, D.C.: International Monetary Fund, 1991).

13. Norman J. Padelford, George A. Lincoln, and Lee D. Olvey, *The Dynamics of International Politics,* 3d ed. (New York: Macmillan, 1976), pp. 477–78.

14. Norman D. Arbaiza, *Mars Moves South* (Jericho, N.Y.: Exposition Press, 1974), pp. 17–19.

15. This is confirmed by taking inventory of the weapons possessed by the Latin

American states. International Institute for Strategic Studies, *The Military Balance, 1991–1992* (London: IISS, 1979), pp. 70–77.

16. Robert D. Bond, ''Venezuela's Role in International Affairs,'' in *Contemporary Venezuela and Its Role in International Relations,* ed. Robert D. Bond (New York: New York University Press, 1977), pp. 248–56. Cf. *Veja* (Sao Paolo, Editora Abril), January 14, 1976.

17. U.S. Arms Control and Disarmament Agency, *World Military Expenditures and Arms Trade, 1963–1973* (Washington, D.C.: U.S. ACDA, 1975). Cf. John Samuel Fitch, ''The Political Consequences of U.S. Military Assistance to Latin America,'' paper, University of Florida, January 1977.

18. Larry Rohter, ''Brazil Stepping Up Arms Output,'' *New York Times,* December 18, 1977.

19. C. H. Waisman, ''Incentives for Nuclear Proliferation: The Case of Argentina,'' in *Nuclear Proliferation and the Near Nuclear Countries,* ed. Onkar Marivah and Ann Schuby (Cambridge, Mass.: Ballinger, 1975), Chapter 12.

20. See Wayne Selcher, ''Brazil and the Southern Cone Subsystem,'' in *South America into the 1990s*, vide supra note 11, pp. 93–110.

Chapter 21: Europe

1. Interview with the Bureau of European and Canadian Affairs, U.S. Department of State, June 1992.

2. For elucidation of this point, see James Blackwell, Michael J. Mazarr, and Don M. Snider, project directors, *The Gulf War: Military Lessons Learned* (Washington, D.C.: Center for Strategic and International Studies, 1991), pp. 5–8.

3. David M. Abshire, Richard B. Burt, and R. James Woolsey, *The Atlantic Alliance Transformed* (Washington, D.C.: Center for Strategic & International Studies, June 1992), p. 41.

4. Henry A. Kissinger, ''The Future of NATO,'' *The Washington Quarterly* 2, no. 4 (1979): 7.

5. For a brief but useful discussion of the military doctrine of flexible response, see Richard Hart Sinnreich, ''NATO's Doctrinal Dilemma,'' *Orbis,* 19 (Summer 1975): 461–77; see also, Robert Kennedy, ''NATO Defense Posture in an Environment of Strategic Parity and Precision Weaponry,'' in *Strategies, Alliances and Military Power: Changing Roles,* ed. James A. Kuhlman (Leiden, the Netherlands: A. W. Sijthoff, 1977), pp. 297–317.

6. For a discussion of the problems inherent in collective systems, see Mancur Olson, Jr., *The Logic of Collective Action: Public Goods and the Theory of Groups* (Cambridge, Mass.: Harvard University Press, 1965).

7. ''Partnership with the Countries of Central and Eastern Europe,'' Statement issued by the North Atlantic Council meeting in Ministerial Session in Copenhagen, June 6 and 7, 1991, Press Communique M-1(91)42 (Brussels: NATO, June 6, 1991).

8. ''The Alliance's New Strategic Concept,'' Press Communique S-1(91)85 (Brussels: NATO, November 7, 1991).

9. Much of the ensuing discussion is based on Stanley Hoffmann, ''Away from the Past: European Politics and Security 1990,'' in *Facing the Future: American Strategy in the 1990s*, Aspen Strategy Group Report (Lanham, Md.: University Press of America, 1991).

10. Josef Joffe, "One and a Half Cheers for German Unification," *Commentary,* 89, no. 6 (1990): 32; and Pierre Lellouche's articles in *Le Point,* as cited in Hoffmann, "Away from the Past."

11. Mary Battista, "Conference on Balkan Refugee Crisis Pledges Aid but Not Havens," *Washington Post,* (July 30, 1992): A22.

12. James E. Goodby, "Peacekeeping in the New Europe," *The Washington Quarterly,* 15, no. 2 (1992): 154.

13. Stephen J. Flanagan, "NATO and Central and Eastern Europe: From Liaison to Security Partnership," *The Washington Quarterly* 15, no. 2 (1992): 143.

14. This is a point made by Blaine Harden, "Can the West Stop the Rape of Bosnia? Should It?" *The Washington Post* (July 24, 1992): A30.

15. For a discussion on why a collective security system is unlikely to materialize in Europe, see: Josef Joffe, "Collective Security and the Future of Europe: Failed Dreams and Dead Ends," *Survival* (Spring 1992).

16. Text of Maastricht Treaty, cited in Robert Mauthner, "Common Policy Relies on WEU," *Financial Times* (December 12, 1991): 2.

17. During the June 1992 Lisbon summit of the EC, discussion of the crisis unfolding in Bosnia-Herzegovina dominated the proceedings. It is telling that, although at the beginning of the summit the member states were considering endorsing WEU action to protect U.N. peacekeepers in Sarajevo, by the conclusion of the talks the EC released a statement merely endorsing the continued efforts of the U.N.

18. James E. Goodby, "Peacekeeping in the New Europe," p. 164.

19. "Final Communique," Press Communique M-NAC-1(92)51 (Brussels: NATO, June 4, 1991).

20. U.S. Department of Defense, *National Military Strategy of the United States* (Washington, D.C.: U.S. Government Printing Office, 1992), p. 7.

21. Don M. Snider, "Residual U.S. Military Forces in Europe," appendix A to David M. Abshire, Richard B. Burt, and R. James Woolsey, *The Atlantic Alliance Transformed* (Washington, D.C.: Center for Strategic and International Studies, June 1992), p. 46.

22. See Snider, "Residual U.S. Military Forces in Europe."

23. Alice M. Rivlin, David C. Jones, and Edward C. Meyer, "Beyond Alliances: Global Security Through Focused Partnerships," in *Facing the Future: American Strategy in the 1990s,* The Aspen Strategy Group (Lanham, Md.: University Press of America, 1991), p. 292.

Chapter 22: International Forces and Peacekeeping

1. Brian Urquhart, "International Peace and Security: Thoughts on the Twentieth Anniversary of Dag Hammarskjold's Death," *Foreign Affairs* (Fall 1981): 6.

2. Brian Urquhart, *A Life in Peace and War* (New York: Harper & Row, 1987).

3. The Russian Federation officially assumed the Soviet seat in January 1992.

4. Paul Lewis, "World Leaders, at the U.N., Pledge to Expand Its Role to Achieve a Lasting Peace," *New York Times* (February 1, 1992), p. 1.

5. Indar Jit Rikhye, *Strengthening UN Peacekeeping: New Challenges and Proposals* (Washington, D.C. United States Institute for Peace, 1992), p. 10.

6. *Charter of the United Nations,* Chapter VII.

7. H. G. Nicholas, *The UN as a Political Institution,* 5th ed. (New York: Oxford University Press, 1975), pp. 51–54.

8. Brian Urquhart, *A Life in Peace and War,* pp. 131–39.

9. Brian Urquhart, ''Beyond the Sheriff's Posse,'' *Survival* 32 (May–June 1991): 198.

10. At the end of 1992, more than 850 peacekeeping personnel had been killed in action.

11. Javier Perez de Cuellar, *Report of the Secretary-General on the Work of the Organization 1991* (New York: United Nations), p. 10.

12. Rikhe, *Strengthening UN Peacekeeping,* pp. 15–17.

13. Boutros Boutros-Ghali, *From Peacekeeping to Peace-Building,* The Ninth David M. Abshire Endowed Lecture (Washington, D.C.: Center for Strategic and International Studies, 1992), pp. 6 and 16.

14. See, for example, Robert C. Johansen, ''UN Peacekeeping: the Changing Utility of Military Force,'' *Third World Quarterly* 12 (April 1990): 53–70.

15. ''Yugoslavia: Price of Peace,'' *The Economist* (February 29, 1992): 56; ''Cambodia: Short of Men and Money,'' *The Economist* (April 25, 1992): 38–40.

Chapter 23: Conflict and Arms Control

1. Kenneth N. Waltz, *Man, The State, and War* (New York: Columbia University Press, 1959), p. 12.

2. Thomas Malthus, *An Essay on the Principle of Population* (New York: Macmillan, 1895), pp. 47–48; Benedict de Spinoza, ''Political Treatise,'' chap. 1, sec. 5, in *The Chief Worlds of Benedict de Spinoza,* trans. R. H. M. Elwes, 2 vols. (New York: Dover, 1951); Sigmund Freud, in his 1932 letter to Albert Einstein, see Freud, ''On War,'' reprinted in *War: Studies from Psychology, Sociology, and Anthropology,* ed. Leon Bramson and George W. Goethals (New York: Basic Books, 1964), p. 72; Konrad Lorenz, *On Aggression* (New York: Harcourt Brace, 1966), esp. Chapters. 7 and 13.

3. Mark A. May, *A Social Psychology of War and Peace* (New Haven, Conn.: Yale University Press, 1943).

4. V. I. Lenin, *Imperialism: The Highest State of Capitalism* (New York: International Publishers, 1939). See also, John Hobson, *Imperialism* (London: Allen & Unwin, 1916).

5. See Arthur Tourtellot, ed., *Woodrow Wilson: Selections for Today* (New York: Duell, Sloan & Pearce, 1945), p. 131.

6. Jerome D. Frank, *Sanity and Survival: Psychological Aspects of War and Peace* (New York: Random House, 1967), p. 109.

7. Chapter II, Article 9, Constitution of Japan, promulgated November 3, 1946.

8. U.S. Arms Control and Disarmament Agency, *Arms Control Report* (Washington, D.C.: U.S. ACDA, 1976), p. 3. See also, Bernard Brodie, ''On the Objectives of Arms Control,'' *International Security* (Summer 1976).

9. See, for example, Thomas Schelling, *Arms and Influence* (New Haven, Conn.: Yale University Press, 1966).

10. Michael Moodie, ''Transparency in Armaments: A New Item for the New Security Agenda,'' *The Washington Quarterly* 15 (Summer 1992).

11. For a discussion of the possibly stabilizing effects of nuclear weapons proliferation, see Kenneth Waltz, *The Spread of Nuclear Weapons: More May Be Better* (London: International Institute for Strategic Studies, 1981).

12. Alan Platt, ed., *Arms Control in the Middle East* (Washington, D.C.: United States Institute for Peace, 1992).

Chapter 24: National Security Perspectives for the 1990s

1. Robert Gates, Statement of the Director of Central Intelligence before the Senate Armed Services Committee, January 22, 1992 (mimeograph copy): 1.

2. General Colin Powell, testimony before the House Committee on Foreign Affairs, March 4, 1992 (mimeograph): 3.

3. James R. Schlesinger, statement before the House Committee on Foreign Affairs, May 6, 1992 (mimeograph): 2.

4. Robert Gates, "Statement of the Director of Central Intelligence before the Senate Armed Services Committee," January 22, 1992 (mimeograph): 4.

5. Patrick Tyler, "U.S. Strategy Plan Calls For Insuring No Rivals Develop," *New York Times* (March 8, 1992): 1.

6. Charles Krauthammer, "U.S. Must Stay Predominant," *Honolulu Advertiser* (March 16, 1992): 7.

7. See Chapters 2 and 3 of John Lewis Gaddis, *Strategies of Containment: a Critical Appraisal of Postwar American National Security Policy* (New York: Oxford University Press, 1982).

8. President George Bush, "Address to the Aspen Institute Symposium," August 2, 1990 (White House Press Release, mimeograph): 2.

9. See Chapter II of *The Gulf War: Military Lessons Learned* (Washington, D.C.: Center for Strategic and International Studies, July 1991): 5–10.

10. *National Security Strategy Report* (Washington, D.C.: U.S. Government Printing Office, August 1991): v.

11. Joseph S. Nye, Jr., "American Power and a Post-Cold War World," in *Facing the Future: American Strategy in the 1990s* (Aspen, Colo.: Aspen Institute, 1991), pp. 36, 40–54.

12. Catherine McArdle Kelleher, "US Foreign Policy and Europe, 1990–2000" *Brookings Review* (Fall 1990): 9.

13. See, for example, Edward S. Corwin, *The President: Office and Powers, 1787–1957* (New York: New York University Press, 1957); or Cecil V. Crabb and Pat M. Holt, *Invitation to Struggle: Congress, the President, and Foreign Policy* (Washington, D.C.: CQ Press, 1989).

14. Roger H. Davidson and Walter J. Oleszek, *Congress and Its Members,* 3d ed. (Washington, D.C.: CQ Press, 1990): 394.

15. See Chapters 4 and 5 of I. M. Destler, *American Trade Politics: System Under Stress* (Washington, D.C.: Institute for International Economics, 1986).

16. Peter G. Peterson and James K. Sebenius, "The Primacy of the Domestic Agenda" in *Rethinking America's Security: Beyond the Cold War to New World Order,* ed. Peter G. Peterson and Gregory Treverton (New York: The American Assembly of Columbia University and the Council on Foreign Relations, 1992), pp. 85–93.

17. For examples, see Samuel Huntington, "America's Changing Strategic Interests," *Survival* 33 (January/February 1991): 3–17; and Robert Hormats, "The Roots of American Power," *Foreign Affairs* 70 (Summer 1991): 132–149.

18. Senators Sam Nunn and Pete Domenici, Cochairmen, *The Strengthening of America Commission: First Report* (Washington, D.C.: Center for Strategic and International Studies, 1992), p. i.

19. David Broder, "Bob Michel's Challenge: The only real way to ensure accountability is to end divided government," *Washington Post* (May 27, 1992): A12.

20. For a compelling review of the impact of "gridlock" on federal budgeting,

including foreign aid assistance, see Allen Schick, *The Capacity to Budget* (Washington, D.C.: Urban Institute, 1990).

21. Gerald Warburg, *Conflict and Consensus: The Struggle between Congress and the President over Foreign Policymaking* (New York: Harper & Row, 1989), pp. xviii–xix.

22. National Academy of Public Administration, *Beyond Distrust: Building Bridges Between Congress and the Executive* (Washington, D.C.: National Academy of Public Administration, January 1992), pp. 8–9.

23. General Colin L. Powell, *National Military Strategy* (Washington, D.C.: U.S. Government Printing Office, January 1992), pp. 6–8.

24. General Colin Powell, "The Base Force: A Total Force," presentation to the House Appropriations Committee, Subcommittee on Defense, September 25, 1991, pp. 1–17.

25. Congressional Budget Office, "The Economic Effects of Reduced Defense Spending" (Washington, D.C.: U.S. Government Printing Office, February 1992), pp. ix, 22.

26. See William Kaufmann and John Steinbrunner, *Decisions for Defense: Prospects for a New World Order* (Washington, D.C.: Brookings Institution, 1991); and Representative Les Aspin, House Armed Services Committee, "An Approach to Sizing American Conventional Forces for the Post-Soviet Era" (Washington, D.C.: mimeograph, January 24, 1992 and February 25, 1992).

27. Lawrence Korb, "The 1991 Defense Budget and the 1991–1995 Defense Program," in *Facing the Future: American Strategy in the 1990s* (Aspen, Colo.: Aspen Institute, 1991), p. 317.

28. Former U.S. Ambassador to NATO, David Abshire, testimony before the House Armed Services Committee, Defense Policy Panel, December 11, 1991 (mimeograph): 3.

29. President George Bush, "Aid to the New Independent States: A Peace We Must Not Lose," *Dispatch* 3, no. 15 (1992): 1.

30. Murray Weidenbaum, "The Future of Business," *The Washington Quarterly* (Winter 1992): 173.

31. For more detailed discussion of this challenge, see Steve Fetter, "Ballistic Missiles and Weapons of Mass Destruction: What is the Threat? What Should be Done?" *International Security* 16, no. 1 (Summer 1991): 5–41; and Lewis A. Dunn, "Containing Nuclear Proliferation" (London: International Institute for Strategic Studies, Adelphi Papers no. 236, Winter 1991).

Index